Coaching Education Essentials

Kristen Dieffenbach, PhD

Melissa Thompson, PhD
EDITORS

HUMAN KINETICS

Library of Congress Cataloging-in-Publication Data

Names: Dieffenbach, Kristen, editor. | Thompson, Melissa, 1979- editor.

Title: Coach education essentials / [Edited by] Kristen Dieffenbach and
   Melissa Thompson.

Description: Champaign, IL : Human Kinetics, [2020] | Includes
   bibliographical references and index.

Identifiers: LCCN 2018049657 (print) | LCCN 2018055170 (ebook) | ISBN
   9781492558620 (epub) | ISBN 9781492558606 (PDF) | ISBN 9781492521075
   (print)

Subjects: LCSH: Coaching (Athletics)--Training of. | Coaching
   (Athletics)--Study and teaching. | Physical education and training--Study
   and teaching. | Mentoring in education.

Classification: LCC GV711 (ebook) | LCC GV711 .C577 2020 (print) | DDC
   796.07/7--dc23

LC record available at https://lccn.loc.gov/2018049657

ISBN: 978-1-4925-2107-5 (print)

Copyright © 2020 by Kristen Dieffenbach and Melissa Thompson

The web addresses cited in this text were current as of December 2018, unless otherwise noted.

Managing Editor: Dominique J. Moore; **Copyeditor:** Pamela S. Johnson; **Indexer:** Rebecca L.
McCorkle; **Permissions Manager:** Martha Gullo; **Senior Graphic Designer:** Nancy Rasmus; **Cover
Designer:** Keri Evans; **Cover Design Associate:** Susan Rothermel Allen; **Photographs (interior):**
© Human Kinetics, unless otherwise noted; **Photo Asset Manager:** Laura Fitch; **Photo Production
Manager:** Jason Allen; **Senior Art Manager:** Kelly Hendren; **Illustrations:** © Human Kinetics;
Printer: Sheridan Books

Human Kinetics books are available at special discounts for bulk purchase. Special editions or book
excerpts can also be created to specification. For details, contact the Special Sales Manager at Human
Kinetics.

Printed in the United States of America   10 9 8 7 6 5 4 3 2 1

The paper in this book is certified under a sustainable forestry program

Human Kinetics

P.O. Box 5076
Champaign, IL 61825-5076
Website: www.HumanKinetics.com

In the United States, email info@hkusa.com or call 800-747-4457.
In Canada, email info@hkcanada.com.
In the United Kingdom/Europe, email hk@hkeurope.com.

For information about Human Kinetics' coverage in other areas of the world, please visit our website:
www.HumanKinetics.com

E6687

Tell us what you think!
Human Kinetics would love to hear what we
can do to improve the customer experience.
Use this QR code to take our brief survey.

Coach Education Essentials

HUMAN KINETICS

Contents

PART I
ESTABLISHING A STRONG EDUCATIONAL BASE TO COACH

PART II
TEACHING COACHES TO EXCEL WITHIN THEIR CONTEXT

PART III
DEVELOPING THE BEST COACHES

PART IV
EVALUATING THE IMPACT OF COACH EDUCATION

CHAPTER 18 **Coach Behavior
and Performance Analysis   349**
Stephen Harvey, Edward Cope,
and Luke Jones

Preface

Kristen Dieffenbach and Melissa Thompson

This book is intended for anyone within sport and physical activity who is directly or indirectly responsible for or a part of the coach education system. The availability of both formal and informal qualified mentors, content developers, facilitators, and educators with an understanding of the current standards and guidelines as well as the emerging trends and research is essential for the continued growth of quality sport experiences. Top professionals, representing a wide range of expertise, explore the essential elements of coach development and how to best understand, develop, and evaluate quality coaching.

Part I: Establishing a Strong Educational Base to Coach

The first part of this book focuses on the importance of a strong educational base for coaches within the sport coach education model. As educators and leaders who are expected to both teach and tease out winning performances and who are also expected to be role models and serve as culture keepers, coach education programs need to be designed to adequately prepare coaches with a wide variety of skills as well as a self-awareness and understanding of their own values, particularly as they relate to the context in which they coach.

Specifically, chapter 2, Ethical and Philosophical Grounding of Coaches, explores the importance of professionalism as it relates to ethics and philosophy in coaching. While the concept of having a coaching philosophy is a common foundation for most coach education programs, the emphasis is commonly on the beliefs related to running a practice and athlete behavior expectations. This chapter focuses instead on the importance of personal values clarification and one's philosophy of what it means to be a coach as the foundation of an individual's professional ethics and moral decision-making.

Chapter 3, Holistic, Athlete-Centered Coaching Orientation, provides the reader with an overview of the holistic athlete development process as a coaching orientation. In defining the term "athlete-centered coaching approach" and discussing its application in coaching, the role of the coach–athlete relationship and the coach-created motivation climate are explored. This chapter also brings together the best coaching practices for using a holistic, athlete-centered approach.

Leading models of athlete development that blend research and best practices to provide guidance for building environments designed to enrich athlete impact are presented in chapter 4, Athlete Development Process and Coaching. The models represent different approaches to understanding how athleticism is developed as well as how sport and physical activity can also influence personal development based on the stage and readiness of the individual. The similarities, differences, and application of these models are explored, with an emphasis on the education and skills a coach needs to be successful working across different developmental contexts in sport.

The final chapter in part I, chapter 5, Coach Instruction for Effective Athlete Instruction, provides an overview of the pedagogy and learning environment knowledge and skills a coach needs to be successful in order to be the right coach for the specific needs of athletes within a specific context. Key concepts such as learning styles, skill acquisition, and feedback are explored, as are the changes in the needs of athletes at different stages of maturity and cognitive development in children and adolescents in particular.

Part II: Teaching Coaches to Excel Within Their Context

Part II examines the different coaching contexts as they relate to the stage of the athlete's developmental participation and the organizational systems the participation opportunities occur within. These chapters contextualize the roles and responsibilities of the coach from five different perspectives across the continuum—from recreational settings to highly competitive sports.

Chapter 6, Educating Youth Sports Coaches: An Empirically Supported Training Program, focuses on the coach within the youth sports culture comprised of young, usually prepubescent, participants. Chapter 7, Coaching Club and Scholastic Sports, explores the role of the coach in terms of the leadership and coaching needs of the typical teenage athlete competing at the level of sport organization or community club and high school. Chapters 8, 9, and 10—College and High-Level Amateur Sports, Coach Education of Professional- and Olympic-Level Coaches, and Paralympic Sport Coaching, respectively—provide similar overviews of the coach's responsibilities for end-of-puberty and postpuberty athletes competing at high levels within college and high-development sport and at professional and Olympic levels, as well as for Paralympic sport coaching.

Part III: Developing the Best Coaches

In the third part of the book, the focus shifts from the coaches to the systems and practices of preparing coaches. Research and best practices for educating, preparing, and developing coaches across all levels will be examined to explore how coach preparation is changing over time.

Chapter 11, Current Models of Coach Education, Training, and Certification, examines the current models that are designed to prepare coaches as part of a systematic development plan aligned with an athlete development model.

The prevailing international model of coaching as a profession and the educational needs of the profession are shared in chapter 12, International Coach Education and Development: A Case Study. The utility, application, and needs-based adoption modification of the materials will be explored.

Professionalism as a career-learning plan is explored in chapter 13, Professional Development Opportunities for Coaches. Multiple modality and environments for coach learning are discussed, as are applications of different development approach strategies.

In an evolution of the traditional athlete-to-apprentice-coach pathway, chapter 14, Career Guidance and Mentorships for Coaches, examines the best practices of mentoring from both a formal and an informal coach education perspective.

The final chapter in part 3—chapter 15, Long-Term Coach Development Process—considers the essential elements of a systematic coach development process and the educational leadership necessary within this process to provide meaningful learning opportunities with the abilities to facilitate learning through curriculum and program design. The leadership role, responsibilities, knowledge level, and skill level necessary to ensure that coach education and development opportunities are designed and delivered effectively are explored.

Part IV: Evaluating the Impact of Coach Education

Within any profession, there is a need for consistent and appropriate training that considers the needs of the audience. The final part of this book focuses on the quality assurance of coach education and coach development programs. Following best practice guidelines and seeking quality program recognition or accreditation will elevate the standards and expectations of coach professionalism within sport. These measures, coupled with coach behavior and practice evaluations to assess the application of knowledge, create a system focused on improvement that benefits not only the coach but also the athletes within the system.

Chapter 16, Reflection on Accreditation and Endorsement of Coach Education and Development Programs, addresses accreditation recommendations and concerns. The strengths and limitations of competency- versus standards-based models are discussed and current accreditation models are explored.

Chapter 17, Standards for Coaching Effectiveness, explores the literature regarding coaching effectiveness and efficacy to highlight the elements central to fostering coaching efficacy. The impact of coaching efficacy on the athlete experience and outcomes is explored, and recommendations are made for coaching efficacy enhancement within coach development programs.

In addition to a well-designed coach development curriculum, it is also essential to evaluate what learning has taken place. This can be done in a number of ways, but perhaps the most meaningful way is to assess how coach learning influences their coaching. The final chapter in the book, chapter 18, Coach Behavior and Performance Analysis, will examine the literature related to in-the-field coach behavior evaluations for the purposes of understanding, supporting, and facilitating behavior change and growth, particularly when considering how to enrich coach learning.

Acknowledgments

While play is timeless, how we play is ever evolving. Sport has an amazing power to enrich lives and bring people together. We have both been fortunate to have had opportunities to play and compete across many levels of sport, to coach, and to build professional lives dedicated to the science of sport. This book represents our shared passion and drive to contribute to the future of quality sport.

This book would not have been possible without the support of our families. Kristen thanks Chris and Ryder and Melissa thanks Brian, Aubrey, and Eliza for their patience through the many late nights and extra-busy weekends.

We are grateful to those who have shaped and guided our thinking, encouraged our questions, and challenged us to follow new paths. We would like to thank Pat Duffy, Dan Gould, Cathy Sellers, Jodi Yambor, and the many colleagues with whom we have collaborated. We hope this text can help inspire and educate future colleagues as we have been inspired.

We would like to thank the editorial team at HK for their support throughout this process.

PART I

Establishing a Strong Educational Base to Coach

Chapter 1

Frameworks for Coach Education and Development

Kristen Dieffenbach

Sport has long been a part of the human experience and has created an indelible footprint worldwide. Historians, archeologists, and anthropologists have contributed to our understanding of humanity through their descriptions of past civilizations' competitive games such as the Ancient Greeks' Olympic Games, *tlachtli* as played by both the Incas and Aztecs, and the Native North American game of lacrosse. Today, in over 200 countries, the tradition of engagement in competitive sport continues with millions of people of all ages across the globe participating in, competing in, and consuming a myriad of sports from the recreational level to elite competition.

The modern passion for sport is at the core of the over $145 billion world industry (Statistica 2016), with top-level athletes and coaches earning rock star salaries (Strauss 2016). Every culture has its revered and iconic coaches who are studied and whom others seek to emulate. Books by and about current and past coaches' philosophies and coaching styles, such as those of Vince Lombardi, John Wooden, Phil Jackson, Eddie O'Sullivan, and Pat Summitt, reach best-seller status, and their words and ideals are shared as inspirational social media memes and as platitudes on locker room walls.

In modern sport, the winning expectations of and pressures on athletes are high, and for coaches they are even higher across almost every level. While the firing of collegiate and professional coaches following losing seasons is nothing new, over the past few years the trend to fire coaches before any real opportunity for growth to occur has been noted across several high-level sports, including the Premiere League (Klomhaus 2015), American collegiate football (Poliquin 2014), and the NFL (Reimer 2016). Little to no patience is granted to allow the development and growth of the coach within a new system.

Despite the high demands and expectations of the job of coach, there is no universal standard within the profession, no clear job title, and often little to no formal training requirements. Professional development networks and opportunities are not among sporting industry norms. At the youth level, the pay is much lower (and is often nonexistent), and hair-trigger firings are less common. However, the pressures and expectations on youth coaches can be just as high, if not higher, and are embedded in systems that often have minimal, if any, credential requirements that would provide a foundation for professional competency and support for development. Despite evidence of the value of quality training in the development of effective teachers and leaders, supplanting the old adage that suggests the skills of leadership are inherent traits (e.g., Nohria and Khurana 2010; Northhouse 2018), the notion that the most effective coaches are those with both experience and high-quality educational support has been slow to gain widespread acceptance.

Building upon the emerging recognition of the profession of sport coaching as a discipline of study (see the *Routledge Handbook of Sports Coaching* [Potrac, Gilbert, and Dennison 2015] for a detailed review of this emerging field) and the identification of sport coaches as educators (Jones 2007), this chapter will introduce the research and conceptual foundations of coaching as a profession requiring specialized training and development beyond supporting prescriptive guidelines, sport mechanics, and game-specific details. Additionally, this chapter will explore the role of sport leaders, coach educators, and sport administrators as coach developers in creating quality materials and facilitating learning and application of skills within coaching.

The Intersection of Sport Culture and Coaching

Among and within countries, sport team loyalties have the power to bring people together as well as drive them apart. Events such as the opening ceremonies of the modern Olympics inspire national pride as well as foster a sense of global family. A loss or perceived injustice on the field can spark turmoil leading to physical violence and political disharmony. The long history of sport as both a recreational and competitive outlet and the impact on us collectively and individually has been documented and discussed by those who study sport philosophy, sociology, and psychology, with these academic disciplines having emerged and grown since the start of the twentieth century. See Guttmann (2007), Mechlikoff (2013), or Stoddart (2013) for excellent reviews of sport history and the historical interaction between sport and culture. From this foundation, a holistic understanding of the sport environment and its essential elements emerges. To better understand the current conversation around coach professionalism and the need for developmental, supportive coach education, it is helpful to further understand this context in which the conversation is grounded.

Coach as Community Icon

Winning athletic performances are celebrated and valued across all levels of sport. Top scorers and medal winners gain international fame, often on par with a Hollywood celebrity. Even in the smallest communities, the athletic prowess of their sons and daughters is praised and commemorated in high school gymnasiums and on local sports pages in a way that few other achievements are honored. Perhaps even more notable than the ethos of sport is the cultural pedestal reserved for the "Coach" at all levels of play.

Regardless of sport level, "Coach" is a revered position within sport and the broader community of sport fans, as sport is embraced by many as a rite of passage, an inherently beneficial experience, and a source of pride, social affiliation and identity, and entertainment. Despite the fact that the honorific "Coach," like "Doctor," imparts a high level of influence and power and grants an individual a level of trust and respect based on the title alone, the designation also carries with it implied professional responsibilities toward those being coached. Unfortunately, the qualifications for earning the title have typically been remarkably low. They have also gone unquestioned and unexamined, even as ethical concerns and issues related to athlete well-being continue to emerge.

The Lost Continuum of Physical Education and Sport

In the past, in many countries, sport coaching training had connections with physical education teacher training. Currently, these bonds are often tenuous at best. And in many places the connections between the two areas of professional preparation seem all but forgotten, disregarded by both sides (Dieffenbach and Wayda 2010).

As noted, outside the physical education classroom and away from individuals trained in youth development, youth sport experiences have increasingly adopted many of the characteristics of professional sport entertainment. Globally, matching uniforms, youth scouts, manicured fields, and intensive practice and travel schedules have turned what was once a youth pastime into a booming global industry. We now see international youth competitions such as the Youth World Series and Youth Olympics, web-based high school sport channels, and youth sport scouting reports. While these are not in and of themselves negative, the outcome-oriented emphasis inherent in them overshadows the greater values of developing physical literacy, sport participation skills, and lifetime athleticism. Further, the emphasis has been placed on the development of perceived "elite talent" at a young age rather than on a system that seeks to develop athleticism in order to facilitate talent development with age. This has led to a system that encourages and rewards early specialization, a reduction of recreational sport participation opportunities, and an increase in youth athlete injuries, all at the expense of the athlete (e.g., Brenner 2007; Caine, DiFiori, and Maffulli 2006; DiFiori et al. 2014). This influence can also be seen in the approach youth sport coaches take, running youth practices and employing training and competition strategies more appropriate for far more advanced players.

As sport participation models evolved in many parts of the world, an early uncoupling of sport coaching from formal physical education teacher preparation began. As Lyle (2005) noted, sport coaching has overwhelmingly been viewed through a one-dimensional lens rooted in a tradition of coaching based on one's own sport experiences. This coach preparation approach has been perpetuated by the athlete-turned-coach formula used to fill coaching roles at the youth through elite levels of sport. This myopic approach has led to an "I played therefore I am sufficiently prepared to coach" myth similar to but less well documented than the "subjective warrant" often seen in pre- and early-career physical educators. The concept of subjective warrant in teaching is concerned with "individual's perceptions of skills and abilities necessary" (Dewar and Lawson 1984). In the physical education setting, that warrant is often influenced by early experiences as a student or participant rather than by formal, evidence-based education.

The "personal experience as adequate preparation to coach" bias skews away from a perceived need for or valuation of formal coaching education and training, deferring instead to hands-on experiences and apprenticeships. This is not to say that hands on learning is not valuable, as both can be potentially valid approaches. However, when unregulated, concerns arise regarding the consistency and quality of these experiences, whether athlete learning will occur (depending on the individuals involved), and whether quality and depth of knowledge of a profession can be developed properly without a learning framework (Kuhn 2008; Young and Baker 2004).

Unfortunately, the mentality that unmediated, informal, self-selected learning experiences are sufficient to prepare someone to be an effective coach has been noted not only in coaches and spectators, and at the sport organizational level, but in research as well (Sheehy, Dieffenbach, and Reed 2018). Such research has documented coach "learning preferences" without significantly challenging whether an individual's preference is sufficient preparation for such a complex task. While this lack of informed preparation approach has not always been the case (see Dieffenbach and Wayda 2010 for a review of the 1960s separation of physical education teacher education and coach education in academia in the United States), a similar bias can be seen in current academic physical activity teaching training programs as well (Schoenstedt, Vickers, and Carr 2016).

Interestingly, in discussing the development of expertise in coaching, Schempp, McCullick, and Mason (2014) note that the "I played" mindset is a hallmark of the novice, with higher-order professional development being distinguished by a quest for new ideas and knowledge from multiple sources outside one's self and one's own experiences. It could, by extension, be argued that a similar lack of sophistication or maturity in thinking related to coach professional development can be found in many sport programs and organizations.

Coach Education: Time for an Upgrade

Across all levels of sport, the responsibility for the best possible outcomes has always been placed on the shoulders of the coach. Ironically, the requirements and job qualifications to coach in most countries and across most sport contexts rarely formally call for more than a minimum level of specialized knowledge or training, if any has been required at all. While factors such as where a person played and whom they know have typically been placed at a premium over formal, professional-model preparation, that placement is often driven by the limited knowledge of self-selected experiences rather than being informed by a broader knowledge base, leading to less innovation and more conformist thinking. In response to the paradox of high-outcome expectations being attached to low-level requisites for formal qualifications, the professionalization of coaching movement is designed to empower and enrich coaches across sport contexts by developing better systems and pathways to promote and provide better learning and development opportunities (ICCE 2016; see also chapter 12).

In any discussion about coaches and their preparation to fulfill their role effectively, it is essential to understand the context within which they will operate. Central to sport is, of course, the participation of the athlete. Without players, there can be no play and there would be no need for coaches. Organized sport, the focus of this text, exists within a structured environment or system that provides standardization for the competitive rules and resources, as well as other necessary parameters of participation, including the coach role. It is through the better understanding of what athletes need and at what point in their development they need it that we can begin to reimagine how to better provide coaches with quality coaching education that will improve their effectiveness.

Developing the Athlete and Athleticism

Leading the movement to better structure sport to ensure healthier environments for both the development of the individual and his or her athleticism is the renewed interest in and contemporary take on long-term athletic development as a systematic design. This approach is grounded in the value of providing opportunities for all individuals to develop their athleticism and a right of everyone to be an "athlete," where athlete is defined as "a person who is trained in or good at sports, games, or exercises that require physical skill and strength" (Merriam-Webster, n.d.).

While the long-term athletic development approach has value across the life span of an individual, it can be argued that the most important contribution is the guidance it provides for the development of a quality physical literacy and sport foundation essential for athleticism, long-term health, and the opportunity to maximize personal potential in sport. The movement to realign youth and developmental sport with the age and developmentally appropriate needs of the athlete is in response to growing concerns about the lack of the youth experience and true opportunities to grow in an environment that has become more focused on outcome and following an adult model (e.g., Fraser-Thomas, Côté, and Deakin 2005; Hedstrom and Gould 2004).

Beyond poor skill development, lack of fun, and dropout, the potential risks of a poorly designed training/learning environment have been associated with overuse injuries, burnout, overtraining, and acute injury (e.g., Brenner 2007; Caine, DiFiori, and Maffulli 2006; DiFiori et al. 2014). Because the coach has been identified as an essential figure (e.g., Conroy and Coatsworth 2006; Hill 2007; Smith, Smoll, and Cumming 2007; Smoll and Smith 2002), these concerns have led to numerous movements to improve the youth sport experience around the world. One such effort is the Aspen Institute's Project Play, which identified quality coach education and the need to "Train All Coaches" as an essential play in their summary report on key changes needed within the American sport culture (Aspen Institute 2015).

The efforts to align coach education with age- and stage-appropriate athlete developmental needs is also supported in the work of the International Council for Coaching Excellence (ICCE), the United States Center for Coaching Excellence (USCCE), and a growing number of sport ministries, national governing bodies/organizations (NGBs or NGOs depending on the country), and private sport organizations. A selection of the models and the implications for coaching will be explored in chapter 4.

Finally, coach education needs to return to its roots—education—to revisit and integrate essential elements of preparing educators with the skills and content knowledge necessary to affect learning. The role of coach as teacher (Jones 2007) needs to be reinforced throughout all coach education with an emphasis on learned application beyond content understanding. The alignment of teacher skills and knowledge to learner needs is the foundation for academic teacher preparation in subject matter and physical education preparation programs (e.g., Shape America's CAEP, Council for the Accreditation of Education Preparation). The importance of age-appropriate preparation can also be brought from education into coach education. Formal academic preparation pathways for teachers are commonly differentiated along the lines of development such as early childhood education, primary or elementary school, secondary school/middle and high school, college or university, and adult learning. The pathways are based on understanding the value of respecting learning abilities and using age-appropriate teaching strategies for key development stages. These educational frameworks present an approach that supports the development of one's professional expertise and can be effectively used to enhance the current coach education approach, mirroring the recommendations by the ICCE and others.

Complexities and Concerns

In recent years, the acknowledgement of coaching as a complex, multifaceted profession has been noted across the literature (e.g., Bowes and Jones 2006; Cushion 2007; Jones 2007; Potrac et al. 2000). As noted, the term "coach" does little to encapsulate the vast range of roles and responsibilities that an individual might perform and be responsible for, particularly across age and life-stage development models. Gaining a better understanding of both the complexity of coaching and the differing requirements associated with different contexts is essential for developing meaningful and appropriate coach education and coach development systems.

Coaches are expected to be moral leaders as well as teachers, motivators, strategists, disciplinarians, and so on. The title "Coach" puts the individual in a position of power over the individuals on his or her team. This power can be used positively or negatively to reward, coerce, inform, and lead (Respect in Sport 2008). Without proper training, there is an increased potential for misuse of power and lack of recognition of misuse by others.

Scandals involving crimes, unethical decisions, and questionable actions in which a coach has abused or misused his or her positional power can be found in every sport organization. Paradoxically, despite the role model expectations inherent in coaching, while coaching mistakes, fails, and blunders with regard to the scoreboard and stopwatch are quickly and often loudly noted, the response to failings by a coach related to legal and or ethical violations (e.g., DUIs, sexual misconduct) may or may not be noted. Research and sports commentators have noted that the sins of the coach are much more likely to be overlooked, forgiven, and forgotten based on the most recent win–loss tally. It is especially disturbing to note that research has documented a willingness across the spectrum to overlook abuse by a coach when winning and access to top opportunities in sport are involved (e.g., Fasting 2015; Kirby, Greaves, and Hankivsky 2000).

Developing the Profession of Coaching

According to Merriam-Webster's online dictionary, a profession is defined as the "type of job that requires special education, training or skill" (n.d.). The professional position need not be paid, nor does it confine itself to working with only a single population. It allows for the concept of professionalism to be applied across the pay range, from volunteering to highly paid elite positions. It also recognizes that specialized knowledge might be needed across a wide range of contexts, not just the context of professional sport. The special training or skill of professionalism is imparted through prepared education and often requires formal qualifications with the necessary education delivered in such a way that it facilitates both metacognition as it relates to one's professional roles and responsibilities and innovation in coaching. The concept of professionalism also does not specify that training has to be provided in an academic setting. Finally, a profession has an ethical code of practice as well as a means of regulation. Developing a professional identity sets a standard both for protecting the consumer and providing quality control and for protecting the integrity of the profession itself. These standards benefit the professional by raising the standard of care and offering protection of expertise.

Despite the fact that there have been coaches for as long as there has been organized sport, coaching can be best described as an emerging profession. Professional education standards are in existence, such as the *National Standards for Sport Coaches* (NASPE 2006) and the *ICCE Standards for Higher Education: Sport Coaching Bachelor Degree* (2016). Requirements for having appropriate credentials to work within the sport profession are being set by different countries and governing bodies. Organizations such as the Football Association (FA) in the United Kingdom and US Soccer have detailed sport coach education programs with sequential levels of credentials. These have become well-respected industry standards in their respective countries and have qualified coach developers who facilitate learning within their system. On a national scale, Brazil currently stands alone in its requirement that all sport professionals (coaches, fitness instructors, etc.) must complete an appropriate, approved bachelor's degree in either sport coaching or physical education with a sport coaching extension. These professionals must also register with the Brazilian sports authority prior to being allowed to work with athletes or the public in a sport or physical activity setting. In 2015, EuropeActive created the European Standards, requirements for training and education for thirteen different sport and fitness professions, including youth fitness instructor and active aging trainer (EuropeActive 2016). Most recently, Canada, which already has the Canadian Coaches Association and a detailed model for coach preparation that includes workshop through university-based training, has passed legislation to make kinesiology, the study of principles of mechanics and anatomy in relation to human movement (Merriam-Webster n.d.), a regulated health profession.

The ICCE's International Sport Coaching Framework (2013) utilizes Côté and Gilbert's 2009 definition of coaching effectiveness that is being used to provide a foundation for the professionalism of coaching and support the movement for improving the quality of coach preparation globally. Centered around clarity of one's personal values, philosophy, and goals, the model calls for interpersonal and intrapersonal skills and content knowledge, all specific to and appropriate for the context. While standards of preparation, and in some cases qualifications, to coach are not standardized around professional core, many organizations and NGB/NGOs do provide structure to their coaching system. However, the majority of programs emphasize the technical, tactical, and physical development aspects of content knowledge with little to no attention paid to other content areas such as motor learning, pedagogy, and sport psychology. From a safe environment perspective, background checks for criminal and sexually based violations are relatively standard, though not yet universal, for volunteer and paid coaches. However, little is done to clarify core values and develop and reinforce the moral decision-making skills.

In further evidence of the move toward professionalization of sport coaching, many major sport organizations have ethical codes that coaches are expected and often required by contract to adhere to as a part of their coaching obligation. While for many these codes of conduct are more guidance than regulatory, numerous organizations do have clear policies and guidelines regarding their ethical codes whereby being found in violation can result in the loss of earned credentials or certifications and, by extension, employment opportunities (e.g., National Strength and Conditioning Association, Coaching Association of Canada).

As noted, the "I played, I coach" model is a common career path across sport contexts. Even at the elite and professional levels, where the financial stakes are the highest and the expectation of the need for a highly qualified and prepared coach would seem paramount (although the human stakes are certainly higher at the other end of the continuum), it is still common to see former elite athletes named to coach leadership roles with no qualifications beyond their playing experiences. This is despite the fact that successful transitions appear to be at best challenging (as evidenced by the less than successful transition efforts of Wayne Gretzky, Isiah Thomas, Pete Rose, Diego Maradona, Magic Johnson, and Sheryl Swoops). These examples serve as a cautionary reminder that the skills and knowledge necessary to be successful in one context are not an automatic guarantee for success in a different context. Recognition of former elite athletes' specialized knowledge, coupled with an understanding of the complexities of effective coaching, led some organizations to develop resources and training programs specifically designed to support the transition from elite performers into qualified professional coaches Where little to no formal learning had taken place, the programs provided the means to supplement and accelerate this formal learning. Notable programs that have emerged in recent years include Cricket Australia's High Performance Coaching Program (Portch 2018), USA Volleyball's Coaching Acceleration Program (CAP), and the USOC's National Team Coach Leadership Education Program (NTCLEP; Ferrar et al. 2018).

Finally, the concept of professionalization of sport coaching is probably most challenging when considering volunteer youth and near-volunteer development-based coaching. Despite the potentially positive importance of the youth sport coach's role and impact on the quality of athletes' physical activity experiences and development, becoming a sport coach within these contexts typically requires the least amount of preparation. As volunteers are, in most cases, essential to sustaining participation and play opportunities at the youth and developmental levels, the collective approach has always been to be cautious about adding requirements or hurdles to coach in fear of creating insurmountable hurdles to entry.

However, it is essential to acknowledge that poorly behaved, poorly trained, or poorly supported volunteers do not provide quality sport experiences and can actually contribute to negative and potentially dangerous situations for our most vulnerable athletes. Since increasing training demands on volunteers is not practical in most situations, the responsibility falls on the people within the organizational structures to coordinate and organize the volunteers to develop systems that can help identify the more important core knowledge. Furthermore, they should develop systems to support volunteer coaches in understanding how to apply the core knowledge through mechanisms such as volunteer supervision, volunteer on-field training, and support from a qualified coach developer, with ongoing support resources that help transfer knowledge to application. The American Alliance for Health, Physical Education, Recreation and Dance's (now SHAPE America) position statement, *Recommended Requisites for Sport Coaches* (AAHPERD 2013) provides an excellent foundation document when considering the base entry requirements across a range of coaching contexts. Also, the coach development concepts within this text will begin to discuss the emerging field of coach development support roles.

Re-Envisioning the Coach Educator as Coach Developer

The early 1990s saw the foundation of a National Coaching Foundation in Great Britain, an organization that laid the foundation for the international sport coaching leadership organization the ICCE, established in 1997. Despite the popularity of sport, and particularly youth sports programming (exemplified by the passing of the Ted Stevens Olympic and Amateur Sports Act in 1978), in the United States, the efforts to provide coaching education guidance did not crystalize until the mid-1990s when the first edition of the National Standards for Athletic Coaches (NSAC) was published in 1995 by the National Association of Sport and Physical Education along with the founding of the Coaching Congress. The publication of the standards allowed for the creation of the National Council for Athletic Coaching Education (NCACE) in 2000, an organization dedicated to certifying coach education programs, which evolved into the United States Council for Coaching Excellence (USCCE) in 2017.

The efforts to develop and provide leadership in coach education has been a multidisciplinary effort that brings together sport practitioners and sport science researchers from a wide variety of fields. The original US NSAC standards, revised in 2006 and renamed the National Standards for Sport Coaches, were produced through a large collaboration of organizations and were endorsed by over 100 sport organizations in the United States, representing academic programs, NGBs, and private sport groups. The 2016

ICCE international task force effort that included individuals from seventeen countries and included NGB/NGO, academic, and sport ministry leaders produced the *ICCE Standards for Higher Education: Sport Coaching Bachelor Degree*, an important document outlining the multidisciplinary expertise of the profession (Lara-Bercial et al. 2016).

Unfortunately, despite the early and ongoing efforts to recognize the importance of preparation to coach that is driven by best-practice research and an understanding of the related sport science and pedagogy fields, as recently as 2006, Nelson and Cushion noted that coach learning had not been prioritized as an area of importance within the sport learning and sport development research. The introduction of the International Sport Coaching Framework (ICCE 2013) and the parallel document, the International Sport Coach Developer Framework (ICCE 2015), provides a foundation for developing better-quality preparation models and approaches for coach education and professional development support.

In addition to helping evolve the cultural expectation regarding coach learning needs, in 2003 Peter Davis, the then-director of the US Olympic Committee's coach education division, challenged coaches in an Olympic Coach article entitled "Why Coaches Education?" He asked them to examine their own commitment to excellence as coaches by asking what they were actively doing to improve their skills across all aspects of leadership. Positive culture change to a development-focused professional paradigm in which active multimodal learning is the expectation and the norm, moving away from a mandated or promotion-related credential seeking, will also require the buy-in and support of the coaches themselves. Designing coach education systems that invite in current coaches while also continuing to raise the professionalism opportunities for new and prospective coaches is a necessary, ongoing challenge and essential discussion point.

Acknowledging the need for an evolution from the current limited coach preparation practices to a model of development that delivers quality, contextually appropriate educational content, the conversation needs to expand to include the importance of moving beyond content presentation to the development of actual learning environments that facilitate knowledge application. This paradigm shift requires the input of professionals who have the skills and knowledge to go beyond content presentation and summary and who are able to facilitate and assess learning as well as foster key skills necessary for knowledge-to-application transfer. This trainer who will "train the coaches" (or, the teacher of teachers) will have an understanding of the professional demands and expectations of coaching contextually. The trainer also needs to have an understanding of the relevant emerging sport science literature to ensure coaches are prepared to provide high-quality, safe, and contextually appropriate sport experiences. Finally, the trainer will have an understanding of curriculum design, knowledge development, and teacher training. Filling these requirements necessitates a re-examination and evolution in how coach education has been done and supported by sport organizations and leadership positions such as coach educators, athletic directors, and program administrators who work with and oversee coaches. And it becomes necessary to examine the roles, responsibilities, and skills of those who are the teachers and supporters of those who coach.

While this may be a new concept in the broad picture of sport coach education, the preparation of coaches as qualified teachers with depth of content knowledge and depth of application skills is not. The German Sport University in Cologne, founded in 1947, was developed to prepare and train sport coaches, while Canada's National Coaching Certification Program (NCCP), founded in 1974, provided models that allowed for credentialing that did not require formal school. These and other programs like them were created and run by individuals dedicated to creating learning environments within the context of coach education. However, it wasn't until the early 1990s that there began to emerge a peer professional network for the purpose of sharing collective concerns and challenges related to quality coach education and development.

The lack of preparation to be contextually prepared to coach is not the sole responsibly of the coach. Sport leadership programs and systems are necessary to structure, validate, and provide opportunities for the necessary training. As previously mentioned, to date, only Brazil has law requiring that coaches, at any level—youth through high-level sport, as well as those working in recreational settings (e.g., fitness trainer, strength and conditioning specialist)—must have the appropriate academic degree and be properly registered within the coaching system. Other countries and organizations may have internal requirements based on their coach education materials and structures, but these requirements are, more often than not, minimal. The requirements are presented in a linear fashion, with the least amount of training being required for what is seen as the lowest level of coaching ("youth sport") and subsequent training being provided that goes up the chain to elite-level performance. The UK Sport Coach model provides an exciting paradigm shift by changing the language of their coach education from "performance coaching," which emphasizes the top gains being related to outcome alone, to a model that emphasizes "performing coaches," which emphasizes the complexity of becoming a highly qualified coach within a given context.

In their analysis of effectiveness and expertise in coaching, Côté and Gilbert identified that coaches need preparation in not only context-specific knowledge and skill areas but that expertise also requires inter- and intrapersonal knowledge and skills (2009). This emphasis on the "how to" as well as the values-based "why to," beyond the foundation of "what to," highlights the importance of building learner-centered coach education systems that are curricular in nature and that emphasize participant learning and knowledge acquisition skills, as well as developing the ability to apply those skills. Without intrapersonal skills such as self-awareness, reflection, and critical thinking, coaches' ability to examine, understand, and process the personal "why to's" that are an essential element to quality leadership, as well as their potential professional development and effective coaching, will stagnate.

Another core tenet of the professionalization of coaching that requires a skilled coaching education facilitator or coach developer involves developing a sense of professional responsibility, a "duty of care," as the leader. Developing and fostering this professional awareness of core ethical issues and duty of care responsibilities, and gaining clarity in ones' own values to facilitate moral decision-making, is a standard part of professional preparation across a wide range of careers from accounting to teaching to medicine. Similarly, the profession of coaching would benefit from this addition as an essential element in professional development. Unfortunately, current practices often reduce the expected moral leadership to share platitudes or codes of conduct without providing the guidance and ongoing support necessary to both understand and develop the skills necessary to develop professional moral leadership and decision-making skills.

Future Directions

The rich history of sport and sport coaching is entering an exciting new era led by the continued growth of sport science knowledge and a growing understanding of the potential benefits to be gained individually and culturally, if the systems are well designed and individuals within those systems are appropriately prepared. Across the past several decades, facilitated by leading sport and research groups, organizations and individuals from a wide range of disciplines and backgrounds have joined the growing conversations and efforts to work together in evolving the quality and level of the coach education opportunities for all levels of sport coaches, from volunteers at the youth sport–level through elite-level sport. Conferences such as the ICCE Global Coach Conference, the ICCE Global Coaching House, the North American Sport Coach Development Summit, and the Petro-Canada Sport Leadership Sportif Conference bring together sport leaders and academics to allow for continued facilitation of quality growth and progressive guidelines for the further professionalism of coaching.

If the understanding of the value that a well-prepared and well-supported coach brings to an athlete's development potential and quality experience is to grow beyond the sport research and leadership circles, broader cultural education is necessary for sport parents, administrators, and even athletes. Many of those involved in sport continue to view sport coaching as an "I played, I know" endeavor, where prowess on the field is mistaken as the sole valuable prerequisite for the ability to coach.

Sport leaders and coaches are reminded that going beyond today and beyond what is working "fine" is the very essence of the drive to achieve in sport. As leaders and future leaders within the discipline of coach education and development, we need to embrace, reflect upon, and frequently revisit the five essential questions raised by John Crawly in a keynote address entitled "Better: Cultivating an Environment of Sporting Excellence" at the 2016 National Coaching Conference (now the North American Sport Coach Development Summit) in Seattle, Washington:

1. Are we good at what we do?
2. Are we getting any better?
3. What must we do to get better?
4. How long do we have to get better?
5. Is our performance sustainable and consistent?

Summary

Ideally, given the growing understanding that quality, well-trained sport leadership is necessary for quality sport experiences and outcomes, along with the continued growth of coach education and coach development as fields of study, this book will provide an overview of the core ideas and foundational research guiding this important emerging specialized discipline of coach education and coach development. The chapters have been designed to provide clear definitions and contexts within coach education and coach development, as well as to raise questions and inspire programs, researchers, and educators to build on what is currently understood about the professionalization of coaching to help further enrich the sport experience for the next generation.

As the profession of coaching, the field of coach education, and the roles and responsibilities of the sport coach developer continue to evolve, we encourage the reader to explore how the concepts, ideas, and research outlined in this book apply within their context of sport. Key considerations for the future should include the following:

- What is the model or foundation for your current coach education program?
- What is needed to enhance your system for coach education and development?
- What resources are needed to develop a program that aligns with the current best practices in coach education and development?
- What challenges need to be considered and planned for in developing such a program?
- What new skills must you (your organization) develop, and what mind sets need to be challenged?
- What will culture change look like within this context?
- How can you develop a coach education and development model where growth, for both the program and for the individuals within the program, is an expectation, sustainable, and consistent?
- How will you assess the progress and impact of your coach education program?

Chapter 2

Ethical and Philosophical Grounding of Coaches

Melissa Thompson

An exploration of one's ethics and coaching philosophy is not easy, but it is a beneficial task for new and veteran coaches alike. While it is not uncommon to hear stories of poor ethical decisions made by coaches, the reality is that most coaches are making a positive impact with athletes. But how do coaches make decisions about who gets playing time, the consequences of breaking rules, and what to do when confronted with ethical dilemmas? The purpose of this chapter is not to prescribe a list of right and wrong but rather to gain a better understanding of why and how coaches make decisions that will affect those involved in the sport environment.

Ethics in Sport Coaching

As sport coaching emerges as a profession (see chapter 1), the question of ethics and ethical behavior becomes a central point of discussion. In previous writings about what makes an occupation a profession, Barber describes four requisite attributes:

> A high degree of generalized and systematic knowledge; primary orientation to the community interest rather than to individual self-interest; a high degree of self-control of behavior through codes of ethics internalized in the process of work socialization and through voluntary associations organized and operated by the work specialists themselves; and a system of rewards that is primarily a set of symbols of work achievement and thus ends in themselves, not a means to some end of individual self-interest. (Barber 1963, 672)

As discussed in subsequent chapters, the knowledge base in sport coaching is rapidly expanding, a definitive early marker of an emerging profession. Further, coaching has long been an occupation of social prestige, which offers some reward in itself. Evidence of a strong reward system, although much more grounded in self-interest and contradictory to the requisites above, is the recent growth in compensation in the competitive setting. However, the remaining two elements of professions are somewhat scarce in coaching. For example, evidence suggests that coaching education can lead to positive outcomes for athletes (see chapter 6). Therefore, a community-oriented approach would support some minimal level of required coach education, which coaches support (Vargas-Tonsing 2007). However, many organizations argue formal coach education would reduce the already small number of volunteer coaches, reflecting a more self-interested approach. Despite these concerns, research regarding the potential impact (both positive and negative) of sport on moral development makes the issue of a stronger moral foundation in sport an important one. The focus of this chapter, therefore, is on a system of ethics and ethical behavior in the coaching profession.

Perhaps the most logical place to start in a discussion of ethics is with a definition. While some variability exists in defining ethics, there are some consistent elements across definitions. Therefore, for the purpose of this chapter, ethics can be defined as a system of personal values, morals, and beliefs that influence one's perceptions of right and wrong action, decision-making, and behavior. Because coaching is a position riddled with decisions that influence others and have lasting effects, it's imperative that a text on coaching address coaching ethics.

Approaches to Understanding Ethics

A number of approaches to understanding ethics and ethical behavior exist in the literature. While four considerably influential approaches to understanding ethics and ethical behavior in sport will be discussed in this chapter, further reading can be found on others (e.g., Kant's Categorical Imperative, Mill's Utilitarianism, etc.). In this section, Kohlberg's Theory of Moral Reasoning (Kohlberg 1973), Rest's Four Component Model of Morality (Rest, Narvaez, Bebeau, and Thoma 1999), and Forsyth's Theory of Ethical Relativism (Forsyth 1980) will be discussed. Following a description of the approach and relevant literature, a summary of how that approach applies to sport coaching will be provided.

Kohlberg's Theory of Moral Reasoning

One of the most prominent theories in understanding moral reasoning was proposed by Lawrence Kohlberg (Kohlberg 1973, 1976) as an extension of the work done by Piaget (1965). Kohlberg's theory is organized into six stages of moral development within three levels. The first level, Pre-Conventional Thinking, is exhibited with labels of right and wrong or good and bad. Children learn these labels through interactions with others and associated consequences of actions. This level houses the first two stages. Stage one, *punishment and obedience*, reflects an orientation to avoid punishment. In this stage, there is no consideration of why an action is right or wrong, but simply an effort to avoid negative consequences. Stage two, *instrumental-relativism*, is an orientation toward meeting one's own needs. At this stage, individuals see interpersonal relationships as a way to secure personal needs in the form of reciprocity. In other words, when people function in this stage, they see the value of relationships in what they can get from others: "I will do this for you if you can do this for me."

The second level of moral reasoning in Kohlberg's theory is Conventional Thinking. When individuals enter this level of reasoning, their cognitive approach revolves around maintaining the expectations of one's family, social group, and larger nation. This type of thinking results in loyalty to the group one belongs to and, therefore, behaviors that maintain expectations. The third stage of moral development, *interpersonal concordance*, is housed in this level and reflects one's understanding that good behaviors are those that help others and receive approval. In society, boys and girls earn such approval by being "nice." The fourth stage is also housed in this level and is termed *law and order*. In this stage one's thinking and decision-making reflect the need to obey authority and rules in order to maintain order in society.

The progression into adopting one's own morals and values happens in the final level, termed Postconventional Thinking. In this level, less emphasis is placed on what the social norms are for rule-governed behavior and more on the utility and validity of those values within one's own life. The fifth stage of moral reasoning, *social contract and individual rights*, reflects an awareness and understanding that there is importance in what is legally right in a situation, but that some flexibility in changing law must be present for special circumstances and individual rights. The sixth and final stage of Kohlberg's theory, *universal ethical principle*, reflects an orientation toward decision-making where right actions are determined by one's own ethical principles. Kohlberg suggested that these principles would be somewhat abstract and reflect justice, universality, and consistency.

Kohlberg's theory has received much criticism since inception. Krebs and Denton (2005) provide a concise argument about some of the issues, most notably the lack of connection between stage of moral reasoning and moral behaviors. In essence, one's moral stage did not always determine one's moral judgment or behavior. In fact, Krebs and Denton argue that moral reasoning is not always used when making moral choices but rather, at times, people make a decision and then use moral reasoning to justify that decision. Regardless of some of the criticisms of the theory, a considerable amount of research exists related to Kohlberg's theory.

Kohlberg and Sport

Much of the research related to sport ethics reflects Kohlberg's theory of moral development. The most extensive body of literature related to ethics in sport revolves around the athlete. In their seminal work examining moral reasoning of high school athletes, Beller and Stoll found that athletes "reason from a less consistent, impartial, and reflective moral reasoning than do non-athletes" (1995, 352). Several subsequent studies have supported Beller and Stoll's findings of lower moral reasoning among various athletic populations (Bredemeier and Shields 1995; Rudd and Stoll 2004) along with a downward trend in moral reasoning the longer one participates in athletics (Bredemeier and Shields 1995; Rudd and Stoll 2004). Beller and Stoll concluded that something in the sport environment was shaping athletes' inability to reason on moral issues and dilemmas. Yet studies on other factors, such as age and sport type, have mixed results. In some instances, findings indicate females have higher moral reasoning than males (Beller and Stoll 1995), and in other instances no differences are found (Bredemeier and Shields 1986). Studies examining differences between individual and team sport athletes and contact versus noncontact sports are inconclusive Beller and Stoll 1995; Bredemeier and Shields 1986; Bredemeier et al. 1987; Tucker and Parks 2001). While these results are somewhat alarming, intervention research does show attenuation of the effects of sport participation with an intense moral reasoning intervention (Beller and Stoll 1992). Limited research exists, however, examining moral reasoning and ethical behavior in coaching.

The literature examining moral reasoning in the sport setting is vital. It does not, however, provide an adequate foundation for understanding behavior. In fact, previous literature shows no connection between moral judgment and one's actual moral behaviors (Forsyth and Berger 1982). These findings would suggest a more holistic understanding of morality is necessary.

Rest's Four Component Model of Morality

Rest and colleagues (1999) have proposed a four component model of morality, accounting for four separate psychological processes that influence one's moral behavior. The first process, *moral sensitivity*, accounts for one's ability to recognize a situation as being a moral dilemma and to incorporate perspective-taking about the possible outcomes for all involved based on each potential behavior. The second process, *moral judgment*, accounts for one's decisions about the rightness or wrongness of a behavior and one's decisions about the most morally justifiable option. The third process, *moral motivation*, involves one's commitment to choosing the morally justifiable behavior as well as valuing moral values over other values (such as fame or security). The fourth process, *moral character*, reflects one's ability to be courageous in moral decisions and overcome societal pressures to behave in less morally acceptable ways. It is important to emphasize that Rest

(1983) considers the four processes as interactional with one another and with a number of influencing factors. Therefore, while one might correctly identify a moral dilemma and an appropriate course of action, the actual behavior may be influenced by a number of variables (including context and potential outcomes). Understanding the entire four-stage process can be quite challenging.

In terms of research, Rest's model has not been heavily examined with sport populations. In fact, due to complexity, most of the research around this model is subdivided into the four processes. Research on moral sensitivity would reflect the ability of individuals in the sport context to recognize moral dilemmas. Previous research in this area suggests that moral sensitivity is somewhat variable (Bebeau 1994a) and can be influenced through educational intervention (Duckett and Ryden 1994). Research on moral judgment is actually reflective of Kohlberg's theory, suggesting that much of the work presented earlier would fall into this category and was discussed at the beginning of this chapter. Finally, very little work exists on moral motivation and moral character in general, let alone in the sport context. However, researchers have suggested that the context in which sport occurs, the motivational climate, might have an effect on the third and fourth processes in the model (Bredemeier and Shields 1994; Kavussanu and Roberts 2001).

Bredemeier and Shields (1994) actually argue that each of the four processes proposed by Rest is actually influenced by context, one's personal competencies, and the situationally evoked ego processing. Ultimately, this approach demonstrates the complexity of the decision to act morally. While the sport context and moral development are discussed in other areas of the chapter, the role of ego processing is not. Therefore, literature on motivational climate will be discussed here.

Motivational Climate

While not specifically a framework to examine ethics and ethical behavior, the body of literature related to motivational climate is important to include here. Much of this research has examined goal orientation to explain how people perceive achievement as it relates to their respective context (Bandura 1997). Two primary approaches to the environment exist: task and ego. A task orientation exists when one assesses success through an evaluation of one's own improvement or learning (Nicholls). An ego orientation exists when individuals perceive their success to be determined by comparisons to others (i.e., winning or losing).

The literature on motivational climate in sport offers great insight into how one's values might be put into action. In fact, Kavussanu and Ntoumanis (2003) studied the effects of ego orientation and moral functioning in sport and found that ego orientation predicted low levels of moral functioning in contact sport athletes. Further, multiple studies have connected ego orientation to intentionally injurious acts in sport (Duda, Olson, and Templin 1991;

Dunn and Dunn 1999; Kavussanu and Roberts 2001). Finally, research in goal orientation with athletes suggests that those with higher ego orientation perceive the purpose of sport to be related to increasing one's social status, enhancing career mobility, and building competitive spirit, while those high in task orientation believe sport should provide avenues for engaging in cooperative experiences and improving one's skills (Duda 1989; White, Duda, and Keller 1998). However, as argued by Shields and Bredemeier (1995), sport participation in itself is neither moral nor immoral.

Achievement Goal Theory (Nicholls 1989) would support the notion that individuals develop their goal orientation through a socialization process. Therefore, the unique context of the sport environment must be considered. As evidence has grown for the important role leaders (e.g., coaches) play in the sport environment, researchers have turned their focus to the psychological environment created by those leaders (Ntoumanis and Biddle 1999). In general, researchers suggest that a more task-involved climate would support more adaptive responses from athletes, positive attitudes, and well-adjusted emotional responses than would an ego-involved climate (Duda and Balaguer 2007). Further, athletes report that the coach is incredibly important in creating the climate within elite sport (Pensgaard and Roberts 2002). Balaguer, Duda, and Crespo (1999) have provided support for this notion with findings that competitive tennis players who reported a more task-involved climate perceived their improvements to be greater, were more satisfied with their coach, and had a more positive experience with tennis overall. In the youth sport setting, Cumming and colleagues (2007) report similar findings. Athletes in their study reported positive relationships between their attitudes toward their coach and a task-involved climate. In summary, the motivational climate created by the coach is likely a reflection of her or his values (such as self-improvement and mastery versus winning and competition) and plays an important role in the athlete sport experience.

Forsyth's Theory of Ethical Relativism

A third way of looking at coaching ethics is to examine Forsyth's (1980) Theory of Ethical Relativism. His theory suggests that one's moral philosophy is governed by two primary constructs. The first, *idealism*, is reflective of the extent to which a person believes harm should always be avoided. Individuals who are high in idealism would support this notion while individuals who are low in idealism might believe that harm is sometimes necessary for the greater good. *Relativism*, as the second construct, reflects the degree to which individuals believe in universal moral rules. Individuals who are high in relativism would argue against such rules, believing that the complexity of the environment is too great to have universal rules. On the other hand, those who are low in relativism believe that such guiding principles (e.g., thou shalt not steal) are important rules that individuals should use to guide behavior.

Idealism and relativism constructs have been examined in relation to a number of variables outside the sport context but still related to coaching. For example, Forsyth, Nye, and Kelley (1988) found that individuals who reported a high ethic of caring also tended to be more idealistic and less relativistic. Caring has been highlighted as an important element in coaching in recent literature (Côté and Gilbert 2009; Fry and Gano-Overway 2010) but is beyond the scope of this chapter. Ethical ideology has also been connected to feelings about cheating (Forsyth and Berger 1982) and moral judgments about psychological research (Forsyth and Pope 1984). Researchers note, however, that differences exist among individuals based on their interpretation of potential harm to others and the relationship between the benefits and risks. It's easy to see how these same considerations would apply to a sport setting.

Forsyth and Sport

Literature examining idealism and relativism in the sport context is somewhat limited. In a previous study, Caswell and Gould (2008) examined idealism and relativism of athletic training educators and students. Overall, the sample reported higher idealism scores than relativism scores. Further, educators had lower idealism and relativism scores than students. They concluded that educators should be mindful about the differences in how students perceive situations when instructing about ethical dilemmas in the profession. Thompson and Dieffenbach (2016) examined ethics positions in a sample of coach education students. Slightly higher levels of idealism were reported by females in the sample, which supports previously reported gender differences (McHoskey 1996). Lower levels of idealism and relativism were reported by the graduate students in the sample. Coupled with the Caswell and Gould (2008) findings, there seems to be a reduction in idealism and relativism as a function of either age or professional experience. This relationship should be explored further as there are likely factors specific to the sport setting that would decrease both idealism (such as in some situations where harm to an athlete may be necessary, e.g., intense training) and relativism (such as when to abide the letter of rules that govern the game). Further exploration of the connection of idealism and relativism to behavior in the sport setting is also of importance.

Although not termed relativism, there is a considerable amount of literature in sport surrounding the idea of "bracketed morality" (Bredemeier and Shields 1986). Bredemeier and Shields suggest that a shift occurs to a more assimilative style of moral reasoning in the sport setting. In these instances, athletes temporarily use a less mature style of moral reasoning. In one study, researchers asked athletes to consider four ethical situations, two that were sport related and two that were life related (Bredemeier and Shields 1984). Their findings showed that athlete responses to the sport situations used lower levels of moral reasoning than their responses to the life situations, suggesting an effect of the sport environment on the level of reasoning. The notion of the setting influencing decision-making is somewhat reflective of the concept of relativism in that those high in relativism would argue that the context doesn't allow one to follow a set of universal moral rules. But, although there is overlap with the construct of relativism, the effects of bracketed morality are often discussed as an effect of the established motivational climate.

Each of the approaches to understanding ethics and ethical behavior described above offer insight into the function of ethics within the sport context. From a coaching education perspective, however, it is important to discuss the development of one's system of ethics. The remainder of the chapter will focus on research related to the development of ethics and the implementation of one's ethics into a functional coaching philosophy.

Developing Ethics

As noted previously, ethics can be considered a personal system of beliefs and values that directs how right or wrong one sees an action and how one chooses to behave. While it's widely acknowledged that all of us function with a set of personal rules that have developed as a result of cultural context, family influence, religious beliefs, and life experiences, often times these belief sets go unexamined. When this occurs, decision-making and behavior is often influenced subconsciously. Within the coaching context, researchers argue that the complex nature of sport requires coaches to be able to continually adjust to their environment through ongoing decision-making (Jones, Armour, and Potrac 2003; Saury and Durand 1998). The ability to carry out such high-level functioning, including ethical decision-making, is a skill many believe only comes with experience (Cushion, Armour, and Jones 2003; Jones, Armour, and Potrac 2003). Of course, one's belief systems develop over time and with life experiences, but research also supports the ability to influence the development of ethics through education (Bebeau 1994b; Bredemeier et al. 1986; Duckett and Ryden 1994; Romance, Weiss, and Bockoven 1986). It is for this reason that many professions (e.g., medicine, science, psychology, etc.) have embraced including ethics education as part of professional development.

Ethics Education

Referring back to the discussion of Rest's Four Component Model of Morality (Rest, Narvaez, Bebeau, and Thoma 1999), ethical decision-making is a complex process that is not easily taught. However, considerable strides have been made in understanding how to design programs around teaching professional ethics (Rest and Narvaez 1994).

Duckett and Ryden (1994) have established a body of knowledge surrounding professional ethics in nursing. In their research on developing ethics, they concluded that embedding training in ethics into the educational curriculum demonstrates change in students' moral reasoning over time. Further, evidence suggests that level of moral reasoning can be used as a predictor of clinical performance for nursing students (Krichbaum et al. 1994; Sheehan et al. 1980). Bebeau (1994b) has demonstrated similar results with dental students, suggesting the effectiveness of ethics curriculum at developing students' ethical processing over the course of their professional preparation.

As a result of their work, Duckett and Ryden (1994) suggest four elements of ethics that can be learned. First, some level of ethical knowledge (i.e., some understanding of moral theory) is required to develop the skills necessary for making ethical decisions and to enhance the capability to discuss ethical issues in the profession. Second, critical thinking must be fostered so students can question the critical elements of the decision and the nature of the profession. Third, an awareness of one's personal system of beliefs and the ability to recognize when those beliefs might be in conflict with one's responsibilities or position is necessary for ethical behavior. Finally, and potentially the most challenging, is knowing how to implement an ethical decision once it's been made. Support for a number of strategies in formal ethics education also exists (Rest and Narvaez 1994). Case studies, role play and perspective taking, and reflection are some of the strategies suggested that could easily be implemented into the coach education curriculum.

Codes of Conduct

A common approach to dealing with ethics in the professions is to create codes of conduct to reflect the ideals of those in the profession and to help guide behavior. Codes of conduct have become quite common (and in some cases required) in a number of professional contexts including business (FAR 2015), healthcare (NAHQ 2015), and higher education (CAS 2015). Further, several exist in the domain of sport. For example, the British Institute for Sport Coaches established a code of conduct for coaches that addresses the multiple areas (e.g., integrity, confidentiality, abuse of privilege, safety) in which coaches should maintain ethical behavior (Mackenzie 2001). The National Youth Sport Coaches Association asks member coaches to sign their code of ethics, reflecting the commitment to create a safe environment for athletes including promotion of emotional and social well-being, a drug-free environment, and adherence to league rules (NAYS 2015). The Coaching Association of Canada has established a core course on making ethical decisions, which they offer for their professional coach training (CAC 2016). And, finally, the United States Olympic Committee (2016) has created a Coaching Ethics Code based on previous codes established though the American Psychological Association as well as other organizations in Canada and the United Kingdom.

While it's important for organizations to express their position about what conduct is expected of coaches, there are multiple challenges with organizations developing codes of conduct or codes of ethics. First, the nature of the sport environment, in its complexity, makes it almost impossible for an organization to have a statement of ethics that would encompass all the possible choices a coach will have to make. Second, the utility of a code of ethics is somewhat questionable because most organizations simply publish the code but offer no further training or parameters related to implementing the code. Third, regulating compliance with the code is somewhat difficult and would require a system of governance larger than most sport organizations could manage. This is not to suggest that codes of conduct are unimportant, but rather they provide support for the importance of coach education that focuses on strategies for exploring one's personal ethics and how those guiding principles are applied to one's coaching. The development of a coaching philosophy grounded in one's own values and beliefs that also accounts for the goals and ideals of the organization in which one is coaching is just one example of a potential strategy. The development of such a philosophy is explored in the next section.

The Coaching Philosophy

As noted in the previous section, one's behaviors are a reflection of one's underlying values and belief systems. However, in some contexts such as sport, individuals may behave in more egocentric ways that are incongruent with how they would behave in everyday circumstances. This phenomenon was discussed earlier in this chapter and is often termed "bracketed morality" (Bredemeier and Shields 1986). One potential reason this lapse in moral behavior occurs is the coalescing of forces within the sport context. The unique combination of competition, performance, physical exertion, and sometimes high-stakes outcomes can result in flawed decision-making. This is why a values-based foundation to developing one's philosophy is a potentially beneficial approach and is, arguably, the most useful direction for coaching programs. Rather than attempt to construct a statement of what choices coaches should make, coach development programs can focus on facilitating awareness of one's values as the foundation for exploring ethics.

A solid philosophy can act as a guide for a coach when he or she is confronted with a tough decision and can perhaps create more consistency in coach behavior. Further, if the philosophy is grounded in one's values system, it's possible the coach will feel a greater sense of commitment to said decisions. The remainder of this chapter will focus on how coach development programs might facilitate the development and implementation of a values-based philosophy.

Developing a Values-Based Philosophy

The construction of a values-based philosophy takes considerable reflection, time, and energy. At the heart, of course, is a deep understanding of the values one holds. Once a firm grasp of one's values is in place, exploring the effects of the context can take place. Finally, connecting those values to specific behaviors is of critical importance. Coach development programs must, therefore, dedicate sufficient time to the process of exploring the coaching philosophy. A three-phase process is suggested below but should be adapted to the unique needs of each organization and coach.

Phase I: Exploring Values

There are a number of methods for exploring one's values (Stringer and Cassiday 2003), so just a few options for this process will be discussed here. When working with individuals who have done little exploration or reflection of values, it may be helpful to have a worksheet with many values listed. The Rokeach Values Survey (1988) is a great option for this. Rokeach provides a list of 18 instrumental (reflecting how you live your life) and 18 terminal (reflecting outcomes of existence) values with short descriptions of what each means. The survey instructions ask an individual to rank order the values, considering the degree to which the value is a guiding principle in life. Once the task is complete, the higher-ranked values should provide an accurate representation of what is most important to the individual. While more reflective individuals might find this task impersonal and a surface approach to understanding values, it's actually a very challenging but beneficial task for those who are just starting to explore their value system.

A values exploration option for individuals who consider themselves a bit more self-aware might be to construct the list of values with the simple prompt: "What do I think is the most important thing to me?" Each time something new comes to mind, the coach writes it down. Once a good list has been generated, the coach attempts to sort the values into those that are most important to least important. A facilitator encourages coaches to improve the list by finding some values that can be combined or that overlap. Once the coach is confident in the list, the coach moves on to a subsequent task in the learning program. In roughly 24-48 hours, ask the coach to revisit the list, then ask again two weeks later. Encourage the coach to reflect on the values viewed as the most important, because these will likely influence behavior. Also encourage the coach to consider if there are values that are missing. Remind the coach that this should be an ongoing process and that reflection and self-awareness are critical aspects of one's coaching practice.

To this point, you have been encouraging coaches to reflect on values in general. However, in the construction of the coaching philosophy, it becomes important to also examine the values system each coach holds. In order to encourage this kind of thinking with coaches, you can opt to complete the aforementioned tasks again, asking coaches to think specifically of the sport setting. Or you can suggest a review of the list of most important values the coach constructed and ask him or her to consider if and how those values are exhibited in the sport setting. Regardless, coach developers can't ignore the influence of the sport context, which will be explored further in the next phase, with the previously discussed tasks serving as a nice transition.

Phase II: Exploring the Influence of the Sport Context

In order to effectively prompt the coach to explore how she or he interprets the sport context, there are a number of questions you might pose. For convenience, a sample list is included in worksheet form in figure 2.1. Just as with the exploration of values, encourage coaches to take time in responding to these questions and to ask the questions more than once over a period of days or weeks. This will aid in the depth of information generated and will account for changes in mood and timing.

By simply looking at the questions, coach developers might predict, and rightly so, that generating responses is a challenging task that requires a considerable amount of reflection and willingness to be honest on the part of the coach. However, asking coaches to consider these concepts will provide a great deal of insight to their approach to coaching. The first two phases of the process have provided the coach a foundational understanding of what is most important to his or her personal approach to coaching contexts. This allows the coach developer to stretch the coach to consider how to connect the two phases to everyday practice.

Phase III: Connections to Coaching Behaviors

Determining which coaching behaviors are congruent with one's stated values can be an eye-opening task. Typically, when discussing how values are put into action, a distinction between espoused (or stated) values and enacted (or carried out) values is necessary. While tasks like those previously described can provide information about stated values, coach developers should also provide coaches an opportunity to examine the connection between values and behaviors. Two suggested approaches can be used in this phase, either reflective or proactive.

As noted in a recent study conducted by the ICCE (2016), serial winning coaches at the highest level discuss the importance of self-awareness. Coaches with high levels of self-awareness and several years in coaching likely benefit from the reflective approach. In this approach, coaches think about their typical behaviors in the sport setting. How do they typically interact with athletes? How do they communicate with other coaches? How do athletes approach them? How do they use the power that comes with their role as coach? What strategies do they use to communicate their philosophy? Once the coaches think about their typical behaviors, they can

[handwritten margin note: All of this being covertly influenced by our individual cultural narratives]

Global Context Questions

What is the purpose of sport?

_____

_____

_____

What is the purpose of competition?

_____

_____

_____

What are the ways sport can have a positive impact? Negative?

_____

_____

_____

Coaching Context Questions

Why do you coach?

_____

_____

_____

What do you believe is your role as a coach?

_____

_____

_____

How do you define your success as a coach?

_____

_____

_____

Whom do you coach and why?

_____

_____

_____

What do you coach (skills, character, strategy, etc.) and how (behaviors) do you coach it? *How might your Behaviors Be influenced By the cultural narratives you were raised w/?*

_____

_____

FIGURE 2.1 The sport context worksheet.

take those behaviors and compare them to the list of values established in previous exercises. Coaches should identify how their behaviors align with stated values.

Some reflection regarding the distribution of behaviors might also be of importance. For example, a coach may have identified family as one of the most important values, but only a small number of the identified coaching behaviors were reflective of that value. In this case, the coach developer would encourage the coach to determine the importance of increasing the coaching behaviors that align with the values rated as most important. While the frequency of behaviors isn't necessarily what is important, it does help coaches think about how clearly their messages about what they value are conveyed through their role as coach. As mentioned, this is a good strategy for coaches who have been coaching for some time and who have the ability to be reflective. That doesn't mean that, following that activity, they wouldn't still benefit from a more proactive approach.

In the proactive approach, coaches are simply asked to reflect on the list of values they generated and to create corresponding coaching behaviors that would be in alignment with those values. A sample completed worksheet for this task can be seen in figure 2.2. New coaches, or those with little coaching experience to draw from, might find the proactive approach challenging because they can't think of modifications to their coaching behaviors that might fit their values. Coach developers can facilitate this exploration in the learning program or might suggest discussions with a mentor or other coaches as a helpful approach to generating a list of practical applications of values in the sport setting.

The purpose of the third phase of this process is to directly connect the coach's values to coaching actions. Although this is helpful for the coach as an individual, the congruence between espoused and enacted values is incredibly important in interpersonal relationships. Simons (2002) terms the congruence of espoused and enacted values *behavioral integrity*. Coaches with high behavioral integrity have high congruence between espoused and enacted values and can expect greater levels of athlete satisfaction. Coaches who are espousing values that are vastly different from their behaviors can expect to have less trust and credibility with athletes. One option you might suggest to coaches for checking congruence of values and behaviors is to ask athletes to list, based on typical coaching behaviors, what they believe are the top three values the coach holds. Of course, urging coaches to make the responses anonymous will likely result in better feedback. The trick for coach developers is setting up this task with enough foundation in reflection that the coach is open to the feedback received from the athletes.

Helpful Hints

While coaches may find it a challenge to write out their coaching philosophy, it should also be an enjoyable experience. Here are a few other hints that might help a coach in constructing her or his philosophy.

Stated value	Example coaching behaviors
Honesty/being genuine	• Keep an open-door policy with athletes • Listen to athletes about experiences (sport or otherwise) • Provide honest feedback about skills
Independence	• Keep up with workload without asking others to help • Be reflective about my coaching • Be self-directed in learning about coaching (books, etc.)
Family	• Include all members in decisions • Hold weekly team gatherings outside of sport • Share my sense of values and goals • Give unconditional love
Loyalty	• Give the benefit of the doubt • Create a solid practice plan each day
Faith	• Express my faith through caring • Get to know athletes and their families on a personal level • Maintain perspective about the importance of winning
Wisdom	• Take time and seek council in making important decisions • Maintain perspective about why we compete • Reflect on previous experiences to pave the road for the future
Ambition	• Use language about constant improvement • Set daily goals for improvement • Ask athletes about their goals and help them set milestones for achieving them • Encourage visionary and creative thinking for improvement

FIGURE 2.2 Sample values in practice worksheet.

- *Write over time.* Trying to construct the coaching philosophy in a single sitting might prove to be mentally exhausting. Encourage coaches to use plenty of time to construct the document. Also, prompt coaches to consider what time of day they would be most successful with this type of cognitive task to ensure the best possible product. For example, coach development programs may create a system of long-term reflection on the coaching philosophy that asks the coach to revisit the philosophy at each phase of training. This not only models the importance of reflection, but it also allows coaches to adapt their philosophy to exposure to new ideas that come with training.

- *Reflect.* Encourage coaches to conceptualize the coaching philosophy as a living document that changes as they change. This results in a more enjoyable process. Saving the older documents separately can provide the coach with concrete evidence of how he or she is changing and developing as a coach over time.

- *Write vividly.* Stress to coaches the importance of providing a considerable amount of detail in descriptions and words chosen for the philosophy so it comes to life when read by the coach and others.

- *Incorporate quotes.* Once the coach has a solid foundation for the philosophy, encourage him or her to add some favorite quotes that match his or her sentiments. Better yet, ask the coach to create a quote that summarizes the philosophy.

- *Include personal growth.* Encourage the coach to add personal goals or elements of how continued development as a coach will occur. Suggest that the coach embed these in the philosophy as a means to communicate commitment to continued improvement.

- *Consider athlete goals.* Coaches may also construct parts of the philosophy to include objectives or outcomes for athletes who participate in the program as a result of their interactions with the coach.

Implementing a Coaching Philosophy

Many coaches will spend the time developing their coaching philosophy but lose the connection between the development stage and implementation. This can happen for a number of reasons, including taking on the role of assistant coach, being comfortable with current coaching behaviors, lacking planning, and dealing with a challenging administration. While some implementation strategies are offered here (see table 2.1), this is by no means an exhaustive list or a prescription. Each coach will determine which implementation strategies are effective within her or his own context. Having said that, reflection is a key skill, universal to everyone, that becomes necessary in this transition (for more, see chapter 15). As you will note, it is a component of each of the strategies provided.

TABLE 2.1 Strategies for Implementing the Coaching Philosophy

Strategy	Outcome
Review the philosophy frequently	This will create salience of the philosophy for the coach and will likely prompt reflection
Choose one element to focus on at a time	Deeper reflection on the implementation of that element of the philosophy in practice
Accountability	Sharing the philosophy with a mentor or other stakeholders creates accountability in the implementation
Consider all facets of coaching	Allows the coach to broadly implement the philosophy in all responsibilities and decision-making

Decision-Making

Regardless of the approach the coach takes to implementing the philosophy, it can become one of the most powerful tools available for decision-making. Sport is an environment littered with ethical pitfalls and tough decisions, and having a well-constructed, values-based philosophy can be the first line of defense. Working with coaches to create one or two prompts, such as "considering my values, what is the best decision here?" or "would this decision be representative of my philosophy?", is one quick strategy. Of course, for situations where coaches have more time to contemplate their decision, a more detailed look at the elements of the philosophy should be encouraged. Providing opportunities to role play or practice this kind of decision-making in coach development programs is encouraged.

Communication

While many coaches say they have a philosophy, few have constructed it in a format that can be distributed to athletes and parents. A well-constructed philosophy that is consistently implemented can help coaches communicate expectations to athletes while simultaneously giving them a blueprint for what can be expected from the coach. It is for this reason that coach developers might encourage coaches to share their coaching philosophy. Descriptions of why and how a coach coaches can immediately set the tone for the type of team climate. It can also create a shared language among the coach and the team.

Motivation

A values-based philosophy can also help a coach maintain motivation. The long and trying hours coaches put in can be challenging, but philosophies that reflect on the true reason a coach has committed to the role and responsibilities can offer support during tough times. It can also direct the motivation and behaviors of athletes if properly communicated.

Summary

The ethical and philosophical grounding of coaches is a critically important topic for any coaching text. In the first half of the chapter, a number of concepts related to ethical decision-making were covered. Several theoretical perspectives for moral behavior were reviewed and relevant research was noted. A more practical approach was taken for the second half of the chapter, which focused on the development and implementation of a values-based coaching philosophy. The content of this chapter should provide a lens through which the rest of the text can be examined.

Chapter 3

Holistic, Athlete-Centered Coaching Orientation

Charles H. Wilson Jr. and Trey Burdette

Read almost any coaching book and it will open with a chapter or section on the importance of a sound coaching philosophy. A coaching philosophy sets coaches' understanding of what they are trying to accomplish and how they intend to do it. In fact, Vealey (2005) calls coaching philosophy the foundation to reaching an "inner edge." However, as it is well established that coaching is a complex, social activity, there simply is no one, correct way to coach all athletes in all contexts; no recipe steps to blindly follow; no cure-all method to motivate every athlete to peak performance. There are many different ways to coach, but the chief purpose of this chapter is to provide an orientation that will juxtapose two extremes of the coaching continuum: traditional Conquest Coaching, which is primarily focused on outcomes such as wins and losses or event times, and modern Holistic, Athlete-Centered Coaching (HACC), which incorporates a comprehensive perspective beyond the scoreboard or stopwatch.

Though some of the components of HACC may appear to be relatively new terms or labels in coaching, in reality they are well-established concepts that many coaches have implemented for years. We define HACC as the intentional consideration of all aspects of athletes' personal development, including cognitive, physical, mental, emotional, social, and spiritual, while leading the athletes to strive to reach their potential. Often, one or more of these areas gets either intentionally or unintentionally ignored. For example, contrary to common practice at many public universities, Huffman's (2014) research into college athletes found that coaches and administrators should intentionally and explicitly consider their athletes' spiritual health within their athlete well-being model. It is important to note that coaches cannot be all things to all people, but they should make an honest attempt to thoughtfully consider the context of the athlete and the situation before rushing to a decision that is solely scoreboard, or outcome, motivated.

Many will question if a coach can be a holistic, athlete-centered coach and still win. The answer is absolutely! There are many examples of holistic coaches who win, including John Wooden, Eddie Robinson, Dean Smith, Pat Summitt, and Jose Mourinho. Another current example is high school American football coach Joe Ehrmann. He has been featured on *HBO's Real Sports with Bryant Gumbel*, wrote the book *InSideOut Coaching* (2011), and was the subject of Jeffrey Marx's (2003) work *Season of Life*. Ehrmann became an assistant American football coach for Gilman High School in Maryland, one of the most successful teams in the country by traditional definitions. He and the other Gilman coaches behave very differently from the stereotypical American high school football coaches. Instead of yelling, screaming, and berating to elicit high performance from their athletes, Ehrmann and company "love 'em to death." Their explicit focus is not on winning, which they do plenty of, but on building young boys into men that will make the world a better place. This message is the essence of holistic coaching. It is not to say that Gilman High School and Coach Ehrmann don't strive to win, because they certainly do. It means they pay as much, if not more, attention to the development of their young people—physically, emotionally, spiritually. They develop the entire athlete and they happen to win a lot, too.

Coaching in the Real World

Sandra worked for years to position herself to reach her goal of becoming a high school, head varsity basketball coach. She had studied the game's tactics and strategies, worked with successful coaches, attended countless coaching clinics, and viewed numerous coaching videos. She had worked her way up the coaching ladder, starting out coaching youth and working her way up to the junior varsity. Now, Sandra had earned her first head coaching position at the varsity level, and her team was in a battle for first place in the league. This was only her first season at the helm, but she had coached the team to a drastic improvement in their won–loss record by mid-season.

However, everything was not going as she had planned. In the past few weeks she had faced several tough situations: (a) the mom of Sandra's best eighth grader called and said she was going to pull her daughter from the program unless Sandra called her up to the varsity immediately; (b) her principal called her into his office and said her coaching contract would not be renewed for the next season unless she made the state playoffs; (c) a travel team coach bought her best players' mom a house so the player could go to another school; (d) one player's dad told Sandra that his daughter had a hairline fracture in her wrist from a softball injury in the fall and the doctors wanted to go ahead with surgery, but he wanted his daughter to finish out the season and would like Sandra to convince the girl to play; (e) a junior player felt that she was being played out of position for the "next level" and that her college recruiting would suffer if it was not changed; (f) yet another player confided to Sandra that she felt like her parents only loved her when she played sports but she wanted to quit; (g) a starter skipped practice twice; and (h) a role player was caught with drugs in the school parking lot. Does this sound too far-fetched, like this could never all happen in the real world? In reality, all of these are based on true life situations. It is no wonder that some veteran coaches commonly claim that coaching is becoming more crisis management than strategy or tactics.

The question, then, is how does Sandra's coaching philosophy help her handle these eight, and other, unexpected situations? Should Sandra simply do what she thinks will help her team win more games? Or, should Sandra take into account the individual background, needs, and circumstances of the people involved in each situation? Despite increasing calls for coaching to become more compassionate and considerate of athletes as individuals (Burton and Peachey 2013; Rieke, Hammermeister, and Chase 2008; Vella, Oades, and Crowe 2010), coaches are still often evaluated by their results on the scoreboard. Even more worrisome is that it is no longer enough to win, but coaches must win immediately, win consistently, and win in a way that is pleasing to stakeholders (Wilson 2014). In addition, the higher the level of the sport, the greater that pressure to win becomes. Managing this pressure is a key component of elite coaching (Frey 2007; Kelley and Gill 1993; Olusoga et al. 2009; Richman 1992; Wang and Ramsey 1998), but it is also evident at lower levels of competition.

How do coaches, such as Sandra in our example, navigate the pressure-filled world of coaching while not viewing their players as disposable commodities that are to be exploited for short-term success, regardless of long-term consequences or considerations? On what framework or foundation does she base her decisions? Perhaps she had created a team handbook with rules and punishments that she could rely on, but what if all of these situations weren't covered in her handbook? These eight situational examples include handling the influence or interference of parents, administrators, and community members, along with ethical issues of injury recovery, collegiate recruiting, and player discipline. This is a broad range of issues that requires a broad perspective, which is exactly what HACC provides.

Foundations of HACC

Before beginning a discussion of HACC, we must break down and operationalize the definitions of its components, "holistic" and "athlete-centered," to avoid the ambiguity in definition that some argue have slowed its adoption

(Cassidy 2010b; Kretchmar 2010). Holistic coaching and athlete-centered coaching are relatively new terms, but they are age-old concepts. In fact, many coaches who read the descriptions of HACC will find much overlap with aspects of their own coaching, even though they did not describe it with those terms (Cassidy 2010a). However, we should heed Kretchmar's warning to not use terms like holistic coaching to create a false sense of importance because they are new and impressive sounding. Furthermore, we aim to explain these terms in language that "bears some resemblance to real life" (Lyle 2010, 449) and give specific examples of HACC in action. But first, we will briefly set the context by discussing coaching in general.

Over the years, coaching has been described, defined, and analyzed with a myriad of definitions, models, and theories. Much as with the definition of leadership, a precise definition of coaching has proven difficult to form due to complex and overlapping responsibilities and roles (Abraham and Collins 2011; Abraham, Collins, and Martindale 2006). Still, there remains a clear historical understanding of the general nature of coaching. As far back as 1917, Bancroft and Pulvermacher wrote that "the skill or wisdom of a trainer consists largely in getting his team to its highest point of efficiency at just the right time for a competitive event" (2). This understanding of coaching has not changed much in nearly 100 years, as evidenced by Abraham and Collins' (2011) summation that a coach simply helps athletes achieve their potential. While the definition of coaching has remained relatively consistent over at least the last century, what has varied significantly is the terminology surrounding the manner in which a coach seeks to help his or her athletes reach their potential by intentionally nurturing the athlete physically, mentally, emotionally, socially, and spiritually. For example, Burton and Raedeke (2008) defined coaching as "creating and utilizing relationships to foster an athlete's development" (4). This definition supports the argument that has emerged in recent years recognizing coaching as a complex social process that goes far beyond physical training for peak performance (Jones, Edwards, and Viotto Filho 2014). Athletes are not like emotionless video game characters that can be consistently controlled with a joystick, but are real people with real lives, problems, fears, and joys.

Holism

HACC is, of course, based on the concept of holism, which can be traced back to the ancient Greeks (Mallett and Rynne 2010). Holism views the entire entity or whole as greater than the sum of its parts. Lyle (2010) goes a step further by stating that the whole may not even be divisible into its parts. In this case, athletes are individuals who are more than just their athletic performance and cannot be divided into parts such as their physical conditioning, mental preparation, or emotional hardiness (although we may train those separate areas). A holistic coach considers the interrelatedness of every athlete's whole. Athletes are more than just their speed, power, technical

Should consider their own interrelatedness & how those interact to influence their coach behaviors.

skills, mental toughness, or agility. Similarly, in medical fields, professionals seek to treat the entire person and not just that person's specific symptoms. Kamphoff (2010) noted that in the field of sport psychology, developing the athlete beyond the physical is often stressed even though the term "holistic coaching" is rarely used. However, as Cassidy (2010a) pointed out, our understanding of holism is dependent on the culture, academic discipline, and philosophy or belief system.

Transpersonal Theory

Holism is often linked to transpersonal theory, which acknowledges that there is more to life than what is easily observable or measurable. Transpersonal theory also places a great emphasis on the spiritual side of life that transcends personal experience (Rominger and Friedman 2013). Transpersonal theory emerged from humanism, which is often called the fourth influential wave or force in psychology. Mallett and Rynne (2010) argued that if a coach includes spiritual growth in their athletes' development, then transpersonal psychology clearly fits. *What about into their own development? So they model spiritual growth.*

Humanistic Psychology

Likewise, humanism or humanistic psychology are also closely linked to holistic coaching. Humanistic psychology considers the importance and uniqueness of each individual. The main difference is that humanistic psychology does not typically delve into the spiritual dimension (Lombardo 2010), but defines life as a positive growth experience (Lombardo 1987). Huber (2013) summarizes the coach's role in this positive growth experience with the question, "what good does it do for coaches to develop individuals as athletes and not as human beings?" (258). A coach's positive influence should last far beyond the immediate playing season and go beyond solely athletic skills. *What good does it for coaches to only develop themselves as coaches & not as human beings?"*

Athlete-Centered Coaching

Athlete-centered coaching is a concept that has received much more attention than holistic or humanistic coaching. However, Kidman (2010) contended that humanistic and athlete-centered are interchangeable terms because both are holistic terms. Others have used the term player-centered, but Hamel and Gilbert (2010) agreed that coaches shouldn't get bogged down in terminology. Returning to our previous discussion of humanistic psychology, Van Nieuwerburgh (2010) noted that an athlete-centered approach is based on Carl Rogers' humanistic, person-centered psychological approach.

There are many definitions of athlete-centered coaching, but here are a few to consider. Its importance is highlighted by the fact that the very first standard of the National Association for Sport and Physical Education's coaching standards (2006) is to develop and implement such a philosophy.

The fact that this is the first standard is not coincidental. However, this is not just an American phenomenon, as the International Council for Coaching Excellence and Association of Summer Olympic International Federations (2012) explained that "the premise of an athlete-centered approach is the protection and respect for the integrity and individuality of those with whom coaches work" (13). Again, we see the individual emphasized in this example, and the wording is intentionally broad enough to include both athletes and others with whom a coach may come in contact. For a definition with more specific details embedded, read Nelson, Potrac, and Marshall's (2010) definition of athlete-centered coaching: "application of a questions-based pedagogy with the intention of identifying and working toward shared goals . . . associated with the need to maintain a positive, cheerful, caring, coaching front at all times" (467). This definition incorporates the specific method of asking questions, the specific task of goal setting, and the importance of establishing the motivational climate through positive energy.

Becoming a Holistic, Athlete-Centered Coach

Becoming a holistic, athlete-centered coach is a process that leaders should be striving for throughout their coaching careers. But how do coaches go about adapting their coaching styles, particularly ones that might be ingrained over many years of practice? The first step to becoming a holistic, athlete-centered coach is to develop an athlete-centered coaching philosophy. The following are suggestions from Martens (2012) and McGladrey and colleagues (2010) in creating a coaching philosophy that is holistic, athlete-centered, and aligns with SHAPE America's *National Standard for Sport Coaches* Domain 1 (2006):

[handwritten: understand who you are & how that influences/has influenced]

1. Identify why you want to coach. *[handwritten: you]*
   [handwritten: How might your answer to #1 effect your why?]
2. Develop your coaching goals and objectives. *[handwritten: How " " " effect what kind of goals / how you make them?]*
3. Develop the values and principles on which your program will be based. *[handwritten: How " " " influence the values you choose.]*
4. Assess what you prefer your athletes learn from playing on your team. *[handwritten: Then ask them what they'd like to learn.]*

Developing, constructing, and writing your philosophy is the first, and arguably the easiest, step in becoming a holistic, athlete-centered coach. The next step is to implement it. Your coaching philosophy will be communicated less by what you say but more by your actions. This means your coaching philosophy should guide you in your day-to-day behaviors and decisions. McGladrey and colleagues (2010) provide some guidelines for implementing a holistic coaching philosophy. To begin, coaches must recognize the various groups in their program, because each have a part in the process. Three groups emerge:

Coaches

- Create an environment that is developmentally *& culturally* appropriate for your athletes
- Focus on performance process rather than outcomes (i.e., winning)
- Remain positive when athletes make mistakes

Athletes

- Include athletes in the goal-setting process
- Identify objectives

understand them as cultural beings.

Important Others

- Communicate the holistic approach to parents

Create the Right Motivational Climate and Culture

How can coaches improve the motivational climate of their teams? Nichols' (1984) Achievement Goal Theory (AGT) provides a blueprint. AGT focused on two terms, task involvement and ego involvement. Task involvement refers to individuals seeking mastery by improvement. Ego-involved individuals interpret ability by how it compares to others. In a sport context, a task-involved coach or athlete would be concerned with learning new skills independent of winning or placing ahead of other athletes. Ego involvement in sport would be reflected in an athlete or coach seeking validation about performance only if winning or placing ahead of a competitor occurs. For our purpose, ego-involved coaches would utilize the win-at-all-cost mentality, whereas the task-involved coach would display a more athlete-centered and holistic view. Let's dispel the notion that holistic, athlete-centered coaches do not want to win. They want to win just as much as every other coach or athlete. The difference is the holistic coach's primary focus is the development of the athlete.

Possibly the single best expression of a holistic, athlete-centered coaching philosophy, and arguably the most crucial part of the process, is developing an appropriate motivational climate or culture. Many benefits, including intrinsic motivation, self-confidence, and moral sport behavior seem to be connected to a supportive climate (see chapter 2). If coaches can cultivate the appropriate motivational climate, athletes will benefit more from sport participation. The holistic coach uses task orientation, thereby increasing intrinsic motivation, self-confidence, and self-esteem, and athletes feel competent because self-improvement is the goal rather than winning or high rankings. The question for coach developers: How do I help coaches create the right motivational climate?

• *Redefine success.* Success should not be defined by whether one wins or loses. It should be evaluated on self-improvement. Self-improvement, mastery, and competence, all tenets of task orientation, motivate athletes for the long term and increase confidence. Self-referenced improvement also allows the athlete to feel a sense of autonomy; they have control over their development. Smoll and colleagues (1993) examined youth athletes' self-esteem using a social support training intervention for youth sport coaches. The training intervention aimed to teach coaches to redefine success to maximum effort (holistic approach), use positive approaches, and increase relationships within the team. They found that players rated trained coaches as better teachers, had more fun playing the sport, and were attracted to the relationships on the team. For more on this research, see chapter 6.

• *Set proper goals.* Focus on performance and process goals rather than outcome goals. Performance goals are associated with achieving a performance objective such as running a certain time or making a certain free throw percentage in basketball. Process goals are ones that focus on execution of a skill or performance such as keeping the elbow high when throwing a ball or rotating the hips when swinging a golf club. Kingston and Hardy (1997) and Pierce and Burton (1998) both found in their respective experiments that focusing on performance and process goals improved the performance of the competitive athletes. Outcome goals, or goals associated with winning, are valid and should be in your program. However, conquest coaches only value outcome goals. Winning and losing is a function of many factors: your performance, your opponents' performance, luck, etc. Performing well and not winning a game or contest should not be deemed a failure. Therefore, the focus should remain on goals that you can control. Performance and process goals are the focus of holistic coaches.

• *Include democratic processes.* Holistic coaches will allow athletes to have some decision-making responsibilities. Self-Determination Theory (SDT) was developed by Ryan and colleagues (1997) and examined self-regulation and autonomy as a piece of intrinsic motivation. They developed three psychological needs, Relatedness, Competency, and (relative to this section, most important) Autonomy. Autonomy can be simply described as an individual having some ownership over their course of action. Ryan and Deci (2000) state that this ownership or autonomy enhances intrinsic motivation. Enter the democratic process: the ownership element can be manifested in numerous ways. For example, athletes may have a say in the rules and consequences of a program. Athletes might choose the uniform for a given game or lead warm ups. Using a democratic process gives the athlete autonomy, teaches responsibility, and reinforces accountability. Mallett (2005) concurred, concluding a paper on enhancing quality coaching by stating coaches should create an autonomy-supportive environment because of the resulting increased sport performance.

Democratic Processes → Increased Autonomy → Enhanced and Sustained
Intrinsic Motivation

- *Provide proper feedback.* Coaches are teachers. This means that coaches must provide appropriate feedback in order for athletes to grow to their potential.

  - *Use a positive approach.* Utilize a positive approach with your athletes. All too often, coaches only recognize athletes when they make a mistake. A positive coach makes an effort to reinforce the good things athletes do and by default, encourage athletes. An example is, "Virginia, excellent throw. This time, open your hips to have more velocity on the throw. Keep up the great work!" In this example, not only is the coach correcting points of performance, but also reinforcing the great effort being shown by the athlete. Negative coaches affect motivation, confidence, and performance. Positive coaches not only increase these, but athletes like playing for positive coaches.

  - *Focus on informational feedback.* The feedback holistic coaches provide is high in information. They do not ignore mistakes and they sparingly give only general praise such as "good job" or "nice." Great teachers give informational feedback such as, "Way to shuffle your feet, Mia" or "Lila, excellent job keeping your elbow tucked." Smith and colleagues (2005) found that perceived encouragement and positive feedback from coaches were interpreted by athletes as creating a task-oriented culture, and Weiss and colleagues (2009) found that positive and informational feedback increased athletes' competence, enjoyment, and intrinsic motivation. Therefore, provide informational cues to create a task-oriented environment and increase the quality of feedback.

Challenges to Holistic, Athlete-Centered Coaching

How difficult is it to be a holistic, athlete-centered coach? To be clear and frank, *being a holistic, athlete-centered coach is not easy.* It is, no doubt, a challenge. It is crucial when becoming a holistic, athlete-centered coach to have an open mind and critically evaluate what sport has become. Consumers of sport are bombarded with information that reinforces the idea that sport is about winning, and only winning. In order to break this cycle, the holistic, athlete-centered coaches must change their mentality. They must operate under a different system, one that places athlete well-being first. This is challenging not only because you must re-think your coaching but you must also sell this notion to others, including your boss.

After you have solidified your position as a holistic, athlete-centered coach, you must have people around you who share your philosophy and passion, specifically, your club, school, or league administrators. If they believe winning is paramount and you believe athlete well-being should be the predominant focus, it will be a frustrating and potentially devastating partnership. The parents in your program also must know that you are a holistic, athlete-centered coach and you must persuade them that it is the best way to coach because it means the decisions and actions of the coach are based on their child's best interest. Having a transparent coaching philosophy and being consistent with this philosophy will help sway those who think sports are only about winning.

The day-to-day implementation and approach of holistic coaching requires great effort on the part of the coaching staff, primarily because it goes beyond the standard job description of X's and O's. The technical and tactical aspects of sport are major pieces of a coach's job. Teaching how to set a screen, correctly execute a tennis serve, set up a free kick, and so on, is a primary responsibility. But athlete-centered coaches know their responsibility does not end here. The best coaches not only are excellent teachers of the technical and tactical aspects of sport, but they are also superb at developing other dimensions in athletes such as academic achievement, social development, and decision-making.

John Wooden, one of the greatest coaches ever, is known by many as the coach who won 88 consecutive games and seven NCAA championships in a row as the Men's Basketball coach at UCLA. Naturally, many associate his success with winning. However, Coach Wooden defined his own success as "peace of mind attained only through self-satisfaction in knowing you made the effort to do the best of which you're capable" (Wooden 2009). This definition of success is not widespread in sport. Unfortunately, some people adopt a definition of success that simply measures wins and losses, or the conquest of sport.

Conquest Coaching

A middle school football team is practicing during the middle of its season. They have not won many games and the coaches, athletes, and parents are experiencing anger and frustration as a result of the poor record. During practice, the coaches berate players that make even an easily correctable mistake; they routinely cuss at, scream at, and humiliate the players. Because of how the coaches interact with the players, the players develop a mentality that breeds fear of failure. They fear making mistakes because of the emotional abuse the coaches will deliver. Coaches call them names, belittle their self-worth, constantly scream and yell at them, and express disappointment.

Game day arrives and the pre-game speeches from the coaches emphasize winning above all else. The same fear of failure that the athletes experienced in practice begins to manifest in the game. They become timid and play poorly. Meanwhile, the coaches' frustrations elevate further. They not only criticize the players but they also admonish the officials. This behavior models for others in the program. The players begin to mouth off, and the parents begin to scream and chastise the officials. The football team loses another game. In the post-game speech, the head coach discusses his disappointment in the team because they lost again. The kids see their value and self-worth not based on their effort or performance, but only on the outcome of the game. As a result, the athletes have a poor experience and lose the enjoyment of playing the sport. The experience of playing for such coaches is so unsatisfying that it has long-term effects. Down the road, some of these athletes might themselves develop this warped view of sport, outcomes, and self-worth, while others will quit playing entirely. The domino effect all stems from an attitude that winning is the most important aspect of sport.

This is not an uncommon cycle in present-day sport. Evidence of this attitude is prevalent in such television shows as *Coaching Bad* (Irwin 2015) and *Friday Night Tykes* (Maranz 2014), news stories such as the Mike Rice abuse scandal and subsequent firing at Rutgers University, countless coaches being fired for not winning enough games, and fans calling for the removal of coaches after successful years. University of Kentucky Head Men's Basketball Coach John Calipari stated in interviews that after his first year, several fans discussed the "tough" year his team had despite finishing 35-3 and reaching the Elite 8 of the NCAA basketball tournament, a great season by most reasonable standards. Not for Kentucky fans, however, as success was defined by a championship or the season was deemed a failure. Present-day sport is too often focused on one outcome: winning and *only winning*. This approach, the focus on the conquest, has warped the purpose and positive impact that sport participation can have for young people.

Conquest Coaching in Action

The definition of Conquest Coaching is the approach to leading sport teams whereby the sole measure of success is winning and losing. Sport is entirely about the conquest, or triumph, over an opponent rather than the development of the athlete. This approach is one that focuses exclusively on winning many times at the expense of all other objectives. Coaches might tell players, parents, and administrators that they believe in development of athletes, but their actions speak to their focus on winning. They ignore the physical, psychological, emotional, and spiritual growth of athletes, all of which can be enhanced by participating in sport. By ignoring the development of the entire athlete, coaches devalue sport participation and miss the enormous impact that it can have.

Negative Consequences of Conquest Coaching

Research has found that coaching behaviors contribute to many poor outcomes from sport participation (Gearity and Murray 2011). Remember that Conquest Coaching is solely focused on the outcome of winning, often in spite of all other objectives. When examining the effects of this type of approach, a host of negative consequences arise, including decreased athlete motivation, lack of self-confidence, athlete burnout, and possible decreased morality and ethical behavior in athletes.

Decreased Motivation

Motivation has been operationally defined many times. Anshel (2003) defines it as the direction of selection of activity, and the tendency of that behavior continues until a goal is met. Burton and Raedeke (2008) describe motivation by three behaviors: choice (to participate), effort, and persistence. All definitions indicate that motivation is demonstrated by direction and effort toward a goal. Some coaches believe that athletes have motivation or not and nothing can be done about it. However, the coaches create an environment that can enhance athlete motivation or diminish it. Black and Weiss (1992) examined coaching behaviors and self-confidence and motivation in competitive swimmers ages 10–18. They concluded that young athletes' motivation was related to the quantity and quality of the feedback from coaches. Hollembeak and Amorose (2005) investigated coaching behaviors and athlete motivation across a variety of ages and sports. They found that training and instruction, democratic behavior, social support, and positive feedback were positively correlated with intrinsic motivation of athletes. Studying the negative psychosocial outcomes of poor coaching, Gearity and Murray (2011) found, among many other negative outcomes, that athletes viewed poor coaches as only concerned with winning (conquest coaches) and were perceived to demotivate the athletes, thus inhibiting performance: "Poor coaches were significant contributors to a poor athletic experience because they undermined the athletes' intrinsic motivation" (Gearity and Murray 2011, 216).

Coaches who tend to focus only on outcomes and ignore the day-to-day improvements that athletes may experience are likely decreasing athlete effort and persistence. These daily improvements are important steps for athletes and are discredited by conquest coaches.

To continue to increase intrinsic motivation, athletes must feel like they are getting better. They must believe they are competent, or becoming competent, in the task they are performing. By focusing on outcome goals, competence can only be achieved by winning. Athletes will feel success when they win and feel like a failure when they lose. If the only measure of competence is the win–loss record, motivation can be fleeting. Consider the following example of an outcome-oriented coach, and, by the transitive property, an outcome-oriented athlete:

A golf coach is teaching a player a new skill, how to hit a draw (or a shot that curves right to left for a right-handed player). While teaching the draw, the coach bases success on whether the shot hit the green (outcome goal) instead of basing it on whether the ball actually curved. Because this is a new skill combined with the warped definition of success, the athlete fails far more than he succeeds. In other words, he doesn't hit the green very often. Because the failure is linked to competency, the player begins to fear playing a draw. As such, his motivation for practicing that shot decreases.

If the coach in the above example had focused on goals other than hitting the green, the definition of success might have changed. For example, success should have been defined as whether or not the ball curved to the left. It shouldn't have mattered if it landed on the green, as this was a new skill and should have been practiced with a broad goal. Once the player became more comfortable hitting the draw, then the goal of hitting a specific target may have been introduced.

Outcomes should not be completely ignored when setting goals. But they shouldn't be the only types of goals, nor the most important. Coaches and athletes should focus on performance and process goals that will increase intrinsic motivation over time.

Decreased Self-Confidence

Winning is not easy to accomplish. There are many factors that influence whether a team or athlete wins or loses. The skill level of the athlete or team, the other athlete or team, bad calls, and even luck all play a role in the outcome of competition. The only factor that an athlete can control is his or her own performance. Consider an Olympic lifter who successfully lifts her personal best, yet she finishes in fourth place. Was this a successful or unsuccessful outcome for her? Conquest coaching might say that she didn't win so it is unsuccessful. Yet, she lifted more weight than she ever has! That is the definition of a successful meet.

With conquest coaching, improvement is discounted unless the outcome is a win. This is problematic because athletes begin to associate competence and self-confidence with winning. When winning doesn't occur (and remember, winning is based on many things outside the control of the athlete), self-confidence is likely to decrease. Athletes begin to directly relate winning with confidence, which can be a dangerous association.

Dropout and Burnout

Scanlan and colleagues (1993) developed the Sport Commitment Model and they found the biggest factor by far for sport commitment was enjoyment. Bailey and colleagues (2013) concurred, stating that positive sport experiences lead to greater commitment to playing. However, an alarming number of youth sports participants cease playing, citing poor coaching, abuse, and other negative experiences (Coakley 2015). Goodger and colleagues (2007) also found sport enjoyment negatively correlated with burnout. Youth athletes who experienced burnout and subsequently quit participating stated that the stresses became so great that the fun was reduced to the point that participation "wasn't worth the effort" (cited in Coakley 2015, 60). Anshel (2003), citing previous sources (Roberts 1984, 1993), states that upwards of 80% of youth who participate in sport cease to continue playing, citing reasons such as poor experience and poor coaching, but the prime reason for dropping out of sport was too much emphasis on winning (Gould 1984, 1987)—or the conquest. When coaches overemphasize winning, the positive reasons, such as having fun by learning new skills, improving, trying hard, and so on (Visek et al. 2015), for participation among youth are deemphasized. Although coaches often wrongly assume it is, winning simply isn't the top priority for young athletes. Clearly, coaching behaviors have some relation to athlete burnout and dropout, at varying levels of competition. Specifically, behaviors that exhibit conquest coaching seem to contribute to the negative consequence of athletes leaving sport.

Compromised Morality and Unethical Behavior

The pressure to win in modern-day sport is enormous. Coaches being fired for not winning enough, coaching salaries at the college and professional levels rising to staggering levels, media coverage of youth sports, and parents pushing for winning are all realities that coaches face routinely. This crushing pressure can be so immense that coaches sometimes lose sight of their values and principles in order to win.

Hodge and Lonsdale (2011) found that coaching styles that used a mastery climate as motivation for athletes was positively correlated to prosocial behavior and negatively associated with antisocial behavior. Simply stated, coaches that used a self-evaluative means of motivation had athletes who exhibited higher levels of moral behavior.

Most coaches would say (whether their actions corroborate it or not) that they want their kids to learn ethical behavior though sport participation. This doesn't happen simply by playing. Research has suggested that athletes are more likely to cheat in other contexts, academics for example, than are nonathletes. However, research also has found that athletes are more ethical in decision-making in areas outside of sport. Both strands are cited in Kavussanu and Ntoumanis (2003). They examined whether participation in medium- to high-contact sports influenced moral reasoning. They hypothesized that participation in sports such as basketball, hockey, rugby, and football would have higher levels of ego orientation and thus lower levels of moral reasoning. This hypothesis was supported, but, more important, it was not the inherent participation in these types of sports but the goal orientation that was the major factor in lower moral reasoning. This means that coaches who use winning as the primary definition of success may have athletes with lower moral and ethical behavior.

It is easy to argue that athletes don't learn moral reasoning simply by participating in sport. It takes leaders explicitly teaching right from wrong for the athletes to gain life lessons from sport participation. If neglected, ethics suffer. Consider the following case:

> A high school baseball team is playing in their first-ever State Championship game. It is late in the game and they have runners on first base and third base with one out. A ground ball is hit to the shortstop and the runner on first must try to break up the double play so that the tying run can score. The runner at first base knows he must break up the double play any way he can. He chooses to slide late and spike the second baseman, effectively trying to hurt his opponent. He made a decision to injure his opponent so his team could score a run in the State Championship game.

Regardless of the outcome of the game, win or lose, this athlete displayed poor moral reasoning. Coaches, players, or parents might say,

> *You don't get a chance to win titles very often. When you get the chance, you must do whatever it takes to secure the win.*

What if, several years later, that second baseman developed loss of function in his knee or ankle based on the decision to slide late and spike him? Does possibly winning the title game justify the opponent's long-term health issues? Conquest coaching says yes because the ultimate goal is to win. Holistic coaching says absolutely not. Placing the health of the athlete below the chance to win, even a state title, is not justifiable because the athletes' well-being, health, and development are the main objectives. This approach allows coaches to justify decisions because they are made in the best interest of the athlete, whether it be physical, mental, emotional, or spiritual. Holistic decision-making does not acquiesce to outside pressure. See table 3.1 for a summary comparison of conquest and holistic coaching.

TABLE 3.1 Comparison of Conquest Approach and Holistic Approach

	Conquest coaching	Holistic coaching
Focus	Winning	Athlete *& Coach*
Achievement	Ego-involved	Task-involved *& Self reflection*
Goals	Outcome-focused	Performance and process: outcomes are a by-product of both
Views on winning	Winning is primary focus; other objectives are deferred to winning	Striving to win and effort is highly important; will not sacrifice athlete well-being for wins
View of athletes	Commodity to be exploited to achieve a desired outcome or win	Individuals have unique goals, motivations, and needs; coach adjusts style and approach accordingly
Development	Short-term oriented	Long-term oriented

Summary

This chapter has presented the continuum of modern coaching philosophies ranging from Conquest Coaching, in which athletes are viewed only as elements of the game and outcome is the focus, to HACC, which is based on the complexity of human experience and extends the roles and responsibilities of the coach to athlete growth and well-being, both on and off the playing field. As with many professions, individuals in coaching have the autonomy to determine their own professional philosophy based on their own personal beliefs. Ideally, a coach's guiding philosophy will be developed based on an understanding of the elements of this continuum.

Chapter 4

Athlete Development Process and Coaching

Matt Robinson

The purpose of this chapter is to present the relationship between the various roles of the coach within the existing athlete development model. While a great deal of research has been done in developing the models, more needs to be done to educate coaches about their roles and responsibilities and to provide stage-specific, coach development opportunities within each of the individual stages of the holistic athlete development model. Specifically, education and resources are needed to inform coaches coach education program developers, sport system personnel, and key stakeholders about the critical value of having the right coach with the right training specific for each age and stage of development as part of an essential long-term system for both quality lifetime physical activity engagement and to maximize sport potential. It is essential for coaches to recognize that there is a logical and sequenced process associated with developing athletes and to understand these stages and know the appropriate role, skills, and knowledge of the coach for each one. Athlete development should be an essential topic or specific course in all coach education programs offered within an academic setting or in the licensing courses offered by national governing bodies. The concept of coaches becoming specialists in a particular developmental stage will be presented within a theoretical framework.

Athlete Development

At its most basic level, athlete development can be described as the activities experienced and the pathways followed by athletes during their careers.

Current athlete development models and pathways are based on the belief that athletes should progress through clearly defined developmental stages as they advance chronologically, physically, psychologically, technically, and tactically. In addition to being planned, systematic, and progressive, current talent development pathways are also holistic in nature so that when effectively implemented they lead to an athlete achieving a desired positive outcome. Depending on the model stage, these outcomes range from an enjoyable experience, the development of physical literacy, competitive success, and laying the groundwork for being active for life. The significance of athlete development is such that DeBosscher, Bingham, Shibli, von Bottenburg, and De Knop (2008) identified it is as an essential variable associated with a nation achieving international sport success, the argument being that an athlete not developed correctly will not achieve his or her true potential. It is not an accident that coach education and provision is also one of the variables the researchers presented. Although achieving international sport success is important, the reality is that the majority of the participants in a development pathway will not reach elite status. Therefore, emphasis is placed on the development of physical literacy so that an individual will develop the abilities to remain active throughout his or her life. This is best demonstrated by the fact that in Canada, the goal is for every child to be physically literate by age 12, which increases the likelihood that child will stay active for life (www.ltad.ca, n.d.).

In recent years there has been significant research conducted and numerous models conceptualized across multiple sports that have incorporated a variety of theoretical bases related to the athlete development process. Bailey and colleagues (2010) sought to identify the main findings or principles associated with athlete development and focused on three broad areas of inquiry: the biological, psychological, and social domains. Increased interest in research and inquiry has also led to increased debate. At the core of the debate has been the conflict between the views of nature versus nurture in relation to sport performance (Vaeyens et al. 2008). The nature side focuses on the belief that great athletes are born with innate talents and gifts that enable them to achieve their success. The nurture side argues that those talents are a base, and if not developed in the right manner, they may go untapped or be underutilized. In turn an athlete may not achieve his or her true potential. Those who adhere to the nurture view refer to the multiple theoretical bases from the areas of talent development. Although the theoretical base may differ and the number of stages varies, the consensus is that talent is made and not born, and the coach plays a significant role in the process. It is most likely that peak athletic performance comes from a combination of both views, requiring both nature and nurture. However, the complexity of the model (and the many variables beyond the control of any coach, individual, or sport system) and the well-documented potential benefits from engagement in physical activity support an emphasis on nurturing and developing individual athletes' talents and skills over a physical skills model, which seeks to cherry-pick and exploit innate physical skills, overlooking lower skill levels that may actually flourish when properly nurtured. Coaches who are equipped to both understand and recognize skills and talents and, more important, are prepared to teach and educate (nurture) their athletes serve as the keys to effective holistic athlete development plans.

The nurture mindset reinforces the importance of the role of the coach in athlete development. Ericsson and colleagues (1993) found no support for fixed innate characteristics that would correspond to general or specific natural ability. Bloom (1985) believed that regardless of the initial characteristics of an individual, unless there was a long and intensive process of encouragement, nurturance, education, and training, an individual will not attain extreme levels of capability in any particular field. With this in mind, a coach's duty is to be that guidance as their athletes progress through zones that were defined by Vygotsky (1978) as zones of proximal development. This is done through an idea labeled by Wood and colleagues (1976) as scaffolding. Scaffolding is defined as "those elements of the task that are initially beyond the learner's capacity, thus permitting him [or her] to concentrate upon and complete only those elements that are within his [or her] range of competence" (Wood et al. 1976, 90). The role of the coach is to guide each of their athletes through one zone and then pass them into another zone where again there will be tasks beyond the learners' capacity and potentially a new coach with an expertise in that zone to guide them.

While De Bosscher and colleagues (2008) do recognize coach development and opportunity as separate essential variables related to elite athlete success, one of the significant outcomes desired in athlete development, the two variables are co-dependent. If athletes are made, then someone must be doing the making. Many athletes have benefitted from great coaches in their development. However, many have not reached their true potential because of poor coaching or inappropriate coaching at a particular developmental stage. Gulbin and colleagues (2010) reported that elite athletes found coaching was critical and highly influential to their talent development at every level.

Athlete Development Defined

In trying to define the process, Ford and colleagues (2011) recognized that talent development is holistic in nature due to the complex interaction of interdisciplinary issues that directly impact on athletic opportunity and progression. Bailey and colleagues (2010) identified four prominent models worthy of review: Balyi and Hamilton's (2004) Long-Term Athlete Development (LTAD); Côté's (1999) Developmental Model for Sport Participation (DMSP); Abbott and Collins' (2004) Psychological Characteristics of Developing Excellence (PCDE); and Bailey and Morley's (2006) Model for Talent Development in Physical Education.

Bailey and colleagues (2010) examined each of the models in terms of their aims, primary disciplinary background, research method, key sources, main theoretical frameworks, core constructs, and practical applications. There were distinct differences between the models: for example, the primary disciplinary background for Balyi's is exercise physiology; this contrasts with Abbott and Collins (2004), who used performance psychology, and Bailey and Morley (2006), who utilized education and philosophy. There were, however, consistencies across the models.

Each of the models accepts the fact that athlete development is a process extended over multiple years, ten years often being the standard (Simon and Chase 1973). Recently, the 10-year, 10,000 hours of deliberate practice has become a standard concept in discussing what is necessary for achieving excellence. While Ericsson, the original study author himself, and others have noted that the number itself is not a valid benchmark necessary for achievement, the concept of necessary deliberate practice accrued over time is essential. Further, Bailey and colleagues (2010) noted that these models have evolved away from the traditional models that were linear in nature and present developmental pathways that are nonlinear and that athletes pass through several discrete stages as they develop from novice to expert (Abbott and Collins 2004; Côté and Hay 2002; Vaeyens et al. 2008).

Bloom (1985) was one of the first to offer a model for overall talent development, and it included sport as one of the environments. The model consists of three stages or what can be considered a pathway. In Bloom's model, in the Early Years the athlete shows characteristics of joyfulness, playfulness, and excitement. The Middle Years are where the athlete becomes more committed to her or his sport and her or his identity is linked to the support received. In these years the athlete is consumed, responsible, and obsessed but may participate in more than one sport. The Later Years, which begin around age 15, are marked by the athlete's move toward specialization. The model addresses the role of the coach and parents in each of the stages. Although it seems basic compared to the more recent interdisciplinary models, it introduces the concept of stages and a pathway.

Côté's (1999) DMSP expanded upon Bloom (1985) by proposing a similar model in terms of three stages, but introduced Ericsson and colleagues' (1993) deep practice into the model. In Côté's model, the sampling years occur from ages 6–13, when the goal of the athlete is to participate in as many sports as possible. The specializing years happen from ages 13–15. Sport still remains fun for the athlete, but a focus develops on one or two sports and practice becomes more important, focused, and demanding. Finally, the perfection years begin at 18, when the athlete is concerned with the maintenance and mastery of the skill. Côté relied upon social and developmental psychology as the theoretical base in developing the model.

Balyi and colleagues' LTAD model (2013) has been widely accepted as a theory and has been implemented in several countries and across multiple sports. It has also served as a foundation for the physical literacy programs in several countries. In developing the LTAD Model, Balyi and colleagues referred to several criticisms of existing athlete development practices that LTAD addresses. Those criticisms included young athletes over-competing and undertraining; adult training and competition programs being superimposed on developing athletes; training methods designed for males being superimposed on females; focus on short-terms outcomes (winning) instead of long-term development; and chronological rather than developmental age being used for classifying athletes and competition planning.

The LTAD model has six stages and proposes appropriate focus and activities for each stage as well as competition-to-training ratios. The model is appropriate for replication across multiple sports and it has served as the theoretical foundation for the current coach education and talent development frameworks for several countries, including England, Ireland, and South Africa. Current iterations of the model include USA Hockey's American Development Model and the USOC's version, which differs slightly but is also called the American Development Model. To differentiate here, the USA Hockey model will be referred to as the ADM and the USOC model will be referred to as the five-stage ADM, because a key difference between the two is the number of stages of development they define.

Ford and colleagues (2011), however, are critical of the LTAD model in that it is one dimensional. As stated earlier, the prevailing view is that talent development is a holistic interdisciplinary process that relies upon not only the biological domain but also the psychological and social domains. While Balyi's model aim was to present an all-embracing coaching philosophy, Ford and colleagues (2011) warn against accepting LTAD as fact until longitudinal empirical studies are conducted to test some of the premises of the model. A major area that needs to be investigated is whether the windows of opportunity discussed in LTAD actually do exist. Balyi and colleagues' (2013) windows of opportunity can be defined as periods in an athlete's development where skill acquisition occurs more easily than at other times during the development process. Balyi stressed the importance of coaches and athletes recognizing these windows and capitalizing on them.

A more recent model, developed by Lloyd, Jon, and Oliver (2012), addressed windows of opportunity, developmental ages, and which components of fitness should be addressed at what ages. The Youth Physical Development Model (YPD) presents a comprehensive model for boys and girls and proposes all components—fundamental movement skills (FMS), sport-specific skills (SSS), strength, power, speed, agility, and hypertrophy—should be trained, but some can be emphasized more than others at specific developmental ages.

In the Psychological Characteristics of Developing Excellence (PCDE) model, Abbott and Collins (2004) emphasized the importance of psycho-behaviors, which are psychomotor and physical factors that facilitate transitions between stages. While Balyi, Côté, and Bloom all focused on stages that participants move through in their development, Abbott's work emphasizes the psychological domain as being integral to athletes' success while in a particular stage as well as while transitioning between stages. Abbott and colleagues' PCDE model includes goal setting; realistic performance evaluation; imagery; planning and organizational skills; commitment; focus and distraction control; coping with pressure; and self-awareness. Abbott and colleagues (2007) again promote the significance of psychology but present a multidimensional model that includes additional psycho-behaviors. The psycho-behaviors were slightly modified to include goal setting and self-reinforcement, planning and organization, effective and controllable imagery, performance evaluation, and attributions. The psychomotor variables include hand–eye coordination and balance, and the physical factors include variables such as height and muscle composition.

In the case of Bailey and Morley's Model for Talent Development in Physical Education (2006), the focus is on multidimensional abilities that are associated with achieving a desired outcome of elite success. Rather than a progression through stages, the model focuses on an individual's abilities and dispositions that include physical, cognitive, interpersonal, intrapersonal, and creativity aspects. The individual should have access and opportunity for practice, identification, and provision. Personal traits (genetics, resilience and commitment, task orientation, motivation, and self-efficacy and belief systems) along with environmental factors (teachers and coaches, peer socialization, family support, and social values) will determine whether or not one of the desired outcomes is attained.

Each of the before-mentioned models should be recognized for their strengths. Vaeyens and colleagues (2008) suggest that to further the growth of research related to talent development, steps should be made to develop a singular holistic model that includes the primary disciplinary backgrounds as well as the main theoretical frameworks of the four models.

The creation and practical implementation of an athlete development plan is viewed as critical in promoting sport participation and in developing elite athletes. Olympic committees and national sport federations recognize the development and identification process as one of the key pillars in achieving international sport success and thus have become more involved in developing athlete or talent development plans based upon the different conceptual models.

Robinson, Dorrance, DiCicco, and Steinbrecher (2011) found in their study of the top ten FIFA women's soccer nations that eight of the ten countries have an established and publicized player development plan in place. The stages in those plans range from three to seven. The athlete development plans are communicated through coaching schools and seminars hosted by the federation, which encourage regional and local coaches to observe training sessions. Athlete development systems in Germany, Japan, and Australia have strong regional representation throughout the country to emphasize the plan.

The Football Association (FA) in England and the Canadian Soccer Association (CSA) proposed an athlete development model based on the LTAD. In both cases, the model is used to structure appropriate drills and activities for each of the stages as well as determine competition to training ratios, so that an athlete can successfully progress through each of the stages.

Even though research indicates that talent is not innate but created, the general population at times is skeptical and often buys into the notion of the natural athlete. Along with this, there is often resistance based on the fact that in the early stages of athlete development the models emphasize skill acquisition over winning and competition, and that goes against cultural norms of many countries who view winning competitions as the definition of success at all levels. Thus a greater awareness and understanding is still needed by parents and the general public.

The role of the coach in implementing the plan is critical. Athlete development should be at the core of coach education. As much as it is important to understand the various aspects of the sport, it is critical that coaches understand the developmental process of the athlete and their critical role in working with the athlete to achieve a desired outcome at the different stages of development.

Status of Athlete Development in the United States

While the United States has benefited from macro variables such as population and Gross Domestic Product (GDP), it can be argued it has been less than efficient in developing athletes. Smaller countries in terms of population are more efficient per capita in their development of athletes. While the United States won the overall medal count at the 2016 Rio Summer Olympic games, it ranked only 43 when the medal count per population size was considered. One of the variables that can contribute to that efficiency is coach training and provision. In many countries, certification for coaching is required and coaches often have a sound sport science base before they enter into sport-specific coaching. In some of these countries, athlete development platforms are more common than in the United States, and coaches move the athletes through defined stages. Kuper and Szymanski (2009) pointed out three countries, Norway, Sweden, and New Zealand, that are more efficient than the Unites States in athlete development. In the case of Norway, there is ample opportunity for athletes to participate in an environment where the coaches who train them are usually required to have some form of training or a diploma. Along with this requirement, these countries promote physical activity for all through the promotion and funding of physical literacy programs.

While there are timeless lessons, values, and principles that drive success, the environment and methods that produced the athletes for the Miracle on

Ice in 1980; the Dream Team of 1992; or individual athletes such as speed skater Dan Janson, swimmer Janet Events, or sprinter Michael Johnson may not achieve the same desired result today. To replicate the outcomes of the past, the United States needs to look at how athletes at the lower or younger stages are being developed.

The mistakes that are made at the younger stages by potentially well-intentioned coaches may lead to the production of athletes who don't achieve their full potential at the higher stages of development. When winning is emphasized, it may lead to individuals dropping out of sport and not leading an active lifestyle. Balyi and colleagues (2013) noted that past athlete development that focused on specialization and competition early on has led to dropout and increased injuries, which has led to those athletes becoming physically inactive. Malina (2014) reported that more than one-third of youth are overweight or obese, and obese youth have less coordination and poorer performances in tasks requiring movement.

In response to this concern, the USOC in partnership with National Governing Bodies has developed and implemented the five-stage Athlete Development Model (ADM) that was mentioned earlier in the chapter. Inspired by and modeled after the work of Balyi and the LTAD model, the five-stage ADM is modified to fit within the context of the US sporting environment and coaching context and addresses the goals of physical activity, sport participation, and sustained achievement of Olympic and Paralympic success.

The USOC five-stage ADM consists of these stages: Stage I, Discover, Learn, and Play; Stage II, Develop and Challenge; Stage III, Train and Compete; Stage IV, with two substages: Excel for High Performance, Participate and Succeed; Stage V, Mentor and Thrive. In the implementation of the five-stage ADM, the USOC and individual National Governing Bodies advocate five principles: universal access; developmentally appropriate activities that emphasize motor and foundational skills; multisport participation; a fun, engaging, and progressively challenging atmosphere; and quality coaching at all levels (USOC 2017).

The Role of the Coach in the Developmental Stages

Along with understanding the stages of athlete development, it is essential that the role of the coach in each of the stages be defined. Côté and Gilbert (2009, 316) described effective coaching as "the consistent application of integrated professional, interpersonal and intrapersonal knowledge to improve athletes' competence, confidence, connection and character in specific coaching contexts." While this definition is comprehensive and thorough, it should be noted that how it is achieved at the different developmental levels may vary based on the nature of the participants in the different developmental stages. Athlete development should be an integral part of coach development curriculums because coaches need to understand their roles in the developmental stages. They also need to understand their athletes' needs and where the athletes are physically, emotionally, mentally, and socially so that they can communicate with their athletes to ensure positive outcomes from a particular developmental stage as well as the overall process.

If one adheres to the concept of developmental stages, whether for performance or for long-term well-being, it can be argued that coaches need to become specialists in a particular developmental stage. In the case of the United States, this goes against the existing culture, where it is common for a coach to move through the developmental stages along with a group of athletes, taking them from the participation level to the elite level. However, the skill set required of an effective coach changes from stage to stage. A coach of a ten-year-old group in the Learning to Train stage of Balyi and colleagues' model (2013) would train and behave quite differently from a coach who is training athletes in the Training to Win stage. In the later stage, success in an international event is one metric that would be used for measuring success based on the athlete as well as the expectations of a particular stage. This assertion would be applicable to all developmental models.

With this in mind, coaches as well as those who supervise coaches and coach developers must not only teach the developmental stages but also address the role of the coach in each of those stages. Lehrer and Smith (2015) observed that coach education programs offered by National Governing Bodies exist to improve the specific skill set of coaches at any given point in time, but they do not provide the systematic, immersive, and sport-specific education curriculum necessary to bring coaches along the developmental pathway from novice to expert. National Governing Bodies should consider offering courses and or licensing for coaches at the various stages to ensure that coaches understand their role at a given stage and are supplied with stage development training plans and competition-to-training ratios. Further, it would be beneficial for coaches to focus on a particular developmental stage and rise to the level of a master coach in that particular stage, rather than progressing through the developmental process along with an athlete or group of athletes. This practice of progression is common in the United States based on the volunteer coach model. This is not to say that a successful progression cannot be done, for there are those coaches who can adapt both their training design and inter- and intrapersonal knowledge to the athletes and their various needs in the different developmental stages. However, the idea that there is one way to coach regardless of the stage is not an effective mindset. Gulbin and colleagues (2010) confirmed this, finding that athletes indicated that coaching was critical and highly influential to their talent development at every competition level and the most important qualities of the coach varied by developmental stage.

The Role of the Coach in Athlete Development

Although it is not the intent of the chapter to endorse one athlete development model over another, the five-stage Athlete Development Model (ADM) developed by the USOC and accepted by multiple National Governing Bodies within the United States will serve as an example. The USOC's five-stage ADM was selected because it is based on Balyi's LTAD and is an example of a sport entity utilizing a theoretical framework to develop an athlete development model that fits its purpose and environment. Using the five-stage ADM will demonstrate how the focus, the athlete experience, and the role of the coach differ across stages.

The five stages of ADM will serve as the framework to introduce the focus, the athlete experience, and the role of the coach for each stage. In Stage IV there are two sub-stages. Each sub-stage, (1) Excel for High Performance and (2) Participate and Succeed, will be examined. Gilbert and Côté's (2013) knowledge areas will be used to demonstrate the role of the coach in the different developmental stages by addressing the recommended professional or content knowledge, interpersonal knowledge, and intrapersonal knowledge coaches should have learned. Additionally, the coaching competencies put forth in the International Sport Coaching Framework developed by the International Council for Coaching Excellence (ICCE 2013) will help define the role of the coach in each stage. These competencies include setting a vision and strategy; shaping the environment; building relationships; conducting practices and preparing for competitions; reading and reacting to the field; and learning and reflecting. In all of the stages, the needs of the athlete (from physical, psychological, mental, technical, and tactical skills perspectives) should be the focus of the coach to ensure a positive experience for the athlete.

Stage I: Discover, Learn, and Play (ages 0–12)

- *The focus of this stage:* The Discover, Learn, and Play stage entails a participant's first step toward involvement with sports or when he or she is first introduced to a new sport. In this stage, the participant discovers the key concepts and motor skills and learns how to play. Many skills are transferable across sports in this stage and athletes should be encouraged to try different sports and programs should accommodate the athletes desire to explore and discover. Bloom (1985) referred to this stage as the "Romance Stage," for it is where an individual begins to fall in love with sports or a particular sport. Sports are introduced in such environments as physical education class, open gym, and free or spontaneous play.

- *The athlete experience:* The Discover, Learn, and Play stage focuses on athletes learning the basic rules and sport techniques. The athlete should be encouraged to play multiple sports both for the experience and to accelerate motor skill development. The emphasis is on skill development, where age-appropriate training and play is prioritized over competition. However, skill development should not come at the expense of fun for the athlete. The athlete should be developing the ABCS of sport—Agility, Balance, Coordination, and Speed—which are transferable across all sports. The ABCS and sport skills can be taught through fun games. It is hoped that the athlete will develop a love for sport participation in general and for a particular sport. In this stage there should be equal chance of play for all athletes. Participants should be grouped on skill level so no participant gets a feeling of incompetence, which could lead an athlete to stop participating in sports.

- *The role of the coach in this stage:* The role of the coach in this stage is to be very focused on setting a vision, shaping the environment, and building relationships with the participants. The professional knowledge required at this level is to know the basics and have the ability to demonstrate and teach the basic skills associated with the sport. Additionally, coaches should be familiar with practice design and age-appropriate drills, and recognize the athletes' attention span in designing a training session. This is a great stage to get athletes involved in coaching. They know the basic skills themselves from playing. Some sport clubs require athletes in the advanced stage of development to either serve as volunteer coaches at this stage, or offer the opportunity as a part-time job. This is an opportunity to educate potential coaches about all aspects of coaching and not just the technical and tactical aspects of the role.

Stage II: Develop and Challenge (ages 10–16)

- *The focus of this stage:* The athlete enters the second stage of the development process for the purpose of engaging in a more organized training environment. The athlete's focus is on refining those skills needed to succeed in a particular sport by training and competing in recreational and organized sport programs. An athlete's readiness and motivation determine the selection of a sport at this stage, and entrance into the stage varies based on the physical and mental maturation of each athlete. Fun and socialization are still important in this stage to encourage continued participation and to prevent athletes from burning out.

- *The athlete experience:* In this stage, athletes understand the rules and techniques of each sport they participate in. Athletes should be encouraged to participate in multiple sports for continued motor and physical development, but some will opt to specialize. Athletes will see increased requirements for the ABCS, and will begin to develop and use interpersonal and communication skills to adapt to challenges in their sport development. Along with this, they will continue to develop technical skills and begin to incorporate the skills into tactical decisions associated with competition. The athletes will participate in more structured sport environments and will begin to compete beyond his or her training level against competition that is commensurate with athlete or team abilities. Even with the introduction to competition, the emphasis should still be on skill development. Among all athletes, there will be noticeable differences in maturation rates and some athletes will be more advanced than others.

- *The role of the coach in this stage:* Professional knowledge takes on increased importance at this stage. The coach will introduce more advanced technical skills while beginning to include tactics. Competition becomes an important part of this stage. The coach will be required to prepare individuals and teams for competitions through appropriate practice and training design, while also identifying appropriate competition environments. Practices become more demanding at this stage and coaches must recognize the physical differences between athletes based on maturation. During competitions, the coach must be engaged and be prepared to read and react to the situations in those competitions.

Stage III: Train and Compete (ages 13–19)

- *The focus of this stage:* At stage three, athletes begin to train and compete in a program that matches their personal interests, goals, and developmental needs. Competition is more clearly defined and team selection is based on ability. The commitment necessary for certain sports and the skill sets needed to excel at the next competitive level are more clearly defined in this stage. Now the technical, tactical, physical, and psycho-social development are all-important to the athlete experience. In this stage, sport-specific training is introduced and, while multisport play may continue, there is a greater emphasis on single sport participation.

- *The athlete experience:* At this stage, athletes begin to focus on particular sports and may use them for cross-sport development. They will be competing in situations that will challenge them technically, tactically, and psychologically. The athletes will also seek opportunities to further develop their skills through a focused and consistent training schedule. Athletes will be exposed to sport-science related variables such as nutrition, strength and conditioning, and sport psychology to enhance training and performance. It is also at this stage where an athlete will be identified for an elite performance environment such as national teams or intercollegiate athletics.

- *The role of the coach in this stage:* Starting at this stage, professional knowledge is crucial. The coach should be acquiring advanced coaching certificates in sports and have a strong understanding and appreciation of the sport sciences. Athletes will look for this knowledge and gravitate toward coaches who were trained to develop that knowledge. Athletes will benefit in competitions from the coach's experiences in competitive situations. A good portion of a coach's credibility is based on this professional knowledge, and it leads to performance success.

Stage IV: Excel for High Performance
or Participate and Succeed (ages 15+)

- *The focus of this stage:* At stage four, there comes a fork in the road where athletes will have to choose between focusing on sport for high performance and increased competition or competing for fun, health, and social aspects. Athletes will be able to choose the pathway that best represents their interests and abilities (however, in some cases the pathway will choose them). Physical characteristics, experience, and commitment to training may determine which path an athlete takes, but there remains the opportunity to compete or participate to the degree the athlete desires. Fun and socialization remain key elements of this stage, although the definition of fun may differ. For the elite athlete, fun may be defined by the joy of succeeding in a very high-pressure competition, where for another athlete it may be defined by a friendly game where not much is at stake in terms of the outcome.

- *The athlete experience in Excel for High Performance*: In this option, the athlete is dedicated to maximizing athletic potential and is committed to a single sport and an ongoing annual or other long-term training program aimed at maximizing performance. The training is guided by an elite-level coach. The athlete will compete at a level commensurate with his or her skill level, which will lead to performance development. This may mean competing at elite national and potentially international level competitions.

- *The role of the coach in Excel for High Performance:* The coach at this level should be experienced and accomplished in all facets of professional knowledge. The focus here is on training an athlete and or a team to peak for important competitions. The focus is much more on tactics and chemistry than on teaching techniques. As with the previous stage, a coach's credibility is based on professional knowledge and the ability to use that knowledge to prepare athletes and teams for success in competition and to provide the right direction and tactics during the competition.

- *The athlete experience in Participate and Succeed*: The athletes' experience in this stage is focused on participation. Athletes may pursue multiple sport opportunities and prioritize enjoying the time playing as well as reaping the health benefits of sport participation. Athletes remain active and strive for personal achievement. They compete in environments that are commensurate with their motivations and ability.

- *The role of the coach in Participate and Succeed:* While coaches should have a strong command of the elements of coaching knowledge, the context in which they coach is different from that of the "excel and elite" performance path at stage four. Athletes will seek out that knowledge to enhance the experience as they define it. Relating to the athlete at this level is important, for although the athlete is still interested in competing, a lack of ability or desire to be elite often causes an athlete's commitment to be lower than at the "excel and elite" level. Coaches need to relate to that mindset and tailor the relationship to the athlete as such. Finally, at this stage, coaches can reflect upon their interactions with the athletes and determine if they are providing the appropriate experience for the athletes. For some athletes the competitive drive may be there but the physical abilities do not match the drive to pursue the elite path. On the other hand, there will be those who consciously choose this course because they do not want to make the commitment to be elite. Coaches should reflect on whether they are meeting those varied interests and on how best to improve in the future.

Stage V: Mentor and Thrive

- *The focus of this stage:* The focus of this stage is on life after competing. It is in this stage that a participant can give back to his or her sport as a coach, administrator, or official. The participant can also remain active through participating in age-group or master-level training or competition.

- *The athlete experience:* In this stage there is varying degrees of emphasis. There will be those who take master- and age-group competition seriously and will train accordingly. For others it is about transitioning from athlete to mentor and taking on the role of the coach. This stage is about giving back to a sport for which they have developed a competence and love.

- *The role of the coach in this stage:* For those coaching athletes at this stage, there needs to be an understanding and agreement in terms of the expected commitment. Athletes at this stage are balancing other aspects of their lives, and their participation is often fit into their disposable time. Coaches need to understand and work within the framework. The coach role would focus on providing training plans and competition schedules because the athletes will be self-directed in their training. This is also a stage where athletes take on the role of coach while still competing. The challenge here for the athlete-turned-coach is being responsible for their own training as well as their teammates'.

Coaching in an Athlete Development Model

Balyi and colleagues (2013, 8) were critical of the structure of athlete development programs in terms of the role of the coach when they commented, "the most knowledgeable and experienced coaches work at the elite level where less trained coaches are assigned to the developmental levels; the competition schedule interferes with an athlete development program; unstructured talent identification programs are ineffective in identifying talent and increased pressure for athletes to specialize."

These criticisms can be directed at coaches and programs that do not have an appreciation for the importance of athlete development. The role of the coach in the athlete's achieving success is well documented. While coach development and athlete development are separate variables, they are very much interrelated. Whether success is defined at a local, regional, state, national, or international level really does not matter. The quality of the coach is an integral part of an athlete attaining success at every level of their sport development.

The roles in each stage need to be clearly defined, and sport-specific and age-appropriate training needs to be developed and implemented. While athlete development models provide the theoretical base, actual training plans have to be developed that are consistent with the theory. Thus, the involvement of national governing bodies has been essential because they know their sport and know what training methods are best for the stages of development.

The Five-by-Four Coaching Model

The Five-by-Four Coaching Model can be used as a means to develop coaches in the stages of development. The model is based on the coaching roles as defined in the International Sport Coaching Framework and incorporate the defined roles from the USOC five-stage ADM Model. The Five-by-Four ADM Coaching Model is based on the ultimate goal of developing coaches in each of the stages so that eventually the best coaches can be classified as master coaches in a particular stage. For instance, in educational settings teachers are assigned to a particular grade They stay in that grade and eventually can become mentors for the younger teachers. This model presents the same concept. It is not to say that a coach cannot develop expertise in multiple areas, but rather to say that coaches can focus on an area in which they are comfortable and capable and they understand the athletes and expectations of each of the stages in the model.

The ICCE's International Sport Coaching Framework (2013) defined the coaching roles as follows:

- *Coaching Assistant.* A coaching assistant's responsibilities are to assist in the delivery of sessions; plan, deliver, and review basic coaching sessions, sometimes under supervision; have a basic level of knowledge, competence, and decision-making to deliver the primary functions with guidance; and support the engagement of pre-coaches.

- *Coach:* A coach's responsibilities are to plan, deliver, and review coaching sessions over a season, and sometimes as part of a wider program; extend their level of knowledge, competence, and decision-making independently to deliver the primary functions; and support the engagement and development of pre-coaches and coaching assistants.

- *Advanced Senior Coach:* An advanced senior coach's responsibilities are to plan, deliver, lead, and evaluate coaching sessions and seasons; extend their integrated knowledge, competence, and decision-making to deliver the primary functions and to mentor others; work independently and play a leading role in the structure of the program; and manage the development of coaches, coaching assistants, and pre-coaches.

• *Master Head Coach:* A master head coach's responsibilities are to oversee and contribute to the delivery, review, and evaluation of programs over seasons in medium- to large-scale contexts, underpinned by innovation and research; possess an integrated level of knowledge and competence, leading to them being recognized as an expert with highly developed decision-making skills; and often be involved in designing and overseeing management structures and development programs for other coaches.

The combination of these two theoretical bases leads to a framework for developing coaches with an expertise in a given development stage. The athlete development model spells out what should be accomplished in a particular stage, and the coach roles provide a progression for an individual to develop expertise and potentially master a developmental stage as a coach.

Summary

Athlete development is at the heart of the sport experience for an athlete. While there are multiple theories seeking to explain the process, there remain two main concepts that are present in all of the discussions: the idea of stages and the importance of the coach. Trained coaches are invaluable for working with athletes to acquire skills and attain the desired outcome, whether that be elite status or the fun of participating. Modern athlete development provides a holistic view of talent development, emphasizing the importance of the right approach at the right age and stage to maximize the potential personal and performance gains. The goal of better athleticism for participants provides both long-term health and well-being benefits as well as the potential to elevate performance. Further, this foundation provides the base for a change in how sport experiences can be valued, structured, and supported both culturally and within sport systems.

Chapter 5

Coach Instruction for Effective Athlete Instruction

Matthew A. Grant

The ability of a coach to effectively instruct athletes is critical to successful skill acquisition and motor learning. If a coach applies pedagogical methods that lead to greater learning, individual and team athletes will be more successful during competition. Therefore, it is incumbent on the coach to understand sound teaching practices and implement them when instructing athletes. Within sport coach education, Trudel and Gilbert (2006) proposed a bifurcated paradigm for understanding the demands placed upon a coach education program. In essence, any coach education program, whether formal, informal, or nonformal, must teach coaches what they should know and what they should do. This simplistic approach provided a rigorous platform upon which the goals and expectations of coach education could build sound curriculum, authentic learning experiences, and valid assessment of coaches. It is from this same approach that this chapter has been divided. First, expertise and skill acquisition theories and forms of feedback will be presented in the context of what a coach should know. Second, the application of this learning will be presented in order to help coach developers train coaches on what to do when instructing athletes.

What Coaches Should Know

The International Sport Coaching Framework provides sport organizations, coaches, and educational institutions with considerations and issues surrounding sport coaching (ICCE 2013). Of particular note was the treatment of coaches' professional knowledge (i.e., knowledge of sport, athletes, sport science, coaching theory, and fundamental skills) and how that allows coaches to understand the content and teaching methods to effectively instruct athletes. By learning effective instructional practices through the use of content knowledge (the ways coaches effectively educate athletes within particular contexts, such as sport), coaches can plan practices that promote athlete learning. To accomplish this task, it is essential that coaches understand how people gain knowledge and learn skills. The scope of coaches' knowledge must go beyond how athletes learn a new motor skill, such as throwing a baseball or swimming the freestyle stroke, to include a strong understanding of how athletes develop expertise within their chosen sport. Several theories offer insight into how athletes gain expertise and acquire skills. The remainder of this section will present three dominant theories—expertise theory, Fitts and Posner's three-phase model of skill acquisition, and Gentile's two-stage model for learning—along with deeper discussions of those aspects of effective coaching practices.

Expertise Theory

Expertise theory attempts to define how a person, athlete or coach, learns to consistently outperform colleagues and nonexperts within a specific domain such as a sport (Ericsson 2006; Ericsson, Krampe, and Tesch-Romer 1993; Feltovich, Prietula, and Ericsson 2006). Extensive research since the 1970s provides a rigorous foundation for understanding the characteristics, experiences, skills, and knowledge required for attaining expert status. Although a time approximation has been emphasized, scrutinized, and questioned within elite sports in recent years (Johnson, Tenenbaum, and Edmonds 2006), the traditional, quintessential benchmark for becoming an expert is the accumulation of 10,000 hours or 10 years of deliberate practice—the strategically planned, repetitive, and inherently boring exercises for enhancing performance (Ericsson and Smith 1991; Simon and Chase 1973a, 1973b). Coach developers can make two important points for coaches here. First, consistent, high-level performance will not happen overnight. Second, the quality of practice design will greatly affect athlete development.

According to expertise theory, traditional practice—reiterations of exercises to acquire or maintain proficiencies—does not necessarily lead to better performance nor will it lead to becoming an expert within a domain (Feltovich et al. 2006); the use of deliberate practice does. For instance, let's take the scenario of a golfer who practices a fade shot. Assuming the technique was being correctly practiced, the essential question was whether the practicing of the fade shot was targeted by the golfer and coach as a weakness that was a key to better scores on the course or just part of the repetition of skills that are always practiced over and over as part of a routine or "what is always done." Deliberate practice, as compared to traditional practice, essentially focuses on only those critical, salient qualities of performance—characteristics, experiences, skills, or knowledge used by top performers—that have been selected for enhanced performance. As the targeted, repetitive training of those critical qualities leads to improved results, the athlete or coach develops consistently greater performance, knowledge, and skills or expertise within the sport. This could be accomplished through the deliberate practice of a specific shot of golf as a single, performed skill or as part of course management, depending on the needs of the golfer. For the purposes of this chapter on effective practices, it is important to note that the creation of deliberate practice is normally accomplished through an outside source (i.e., instructor, coach, or mentor) for an athlete or a coach (see more detail on augmented feedback later in this chapter). Further, coaches are also on a journey of developing expertise in coaching. Therefore, coach developers can address these concepts with coaches as related to both personal and athlete development.

As a coach or athlete participates in deliberate practice, the individual progresses along a developmental continuum (Ericsson 2006) [1]. Each distinctive stage represents general characteristics and learning preferences of the coaches or athletes (see table 5.1). Of particular importance for this chapter are the learning preferences for each of the stages. The beginner learns almost exclusively from experience. A person must encounter various situations, conditions, or skills in order to learn the rudimentary elements of the sport. The competent athlete or coach still relies heavily on experience, but begins to make connections to past education such as formal programs, informal discussion, or nonformal seminars or camps that provide greater insight into the skills, tactics, and strategies within the sport. For a coach, this could be attending courses or seminars; athletes could attend camps, take lessons, or join a developmental or elite performance club. In the proficient stage, the athlete or coach becomes more autonomous and begins seeking out various sources of information such as media and publications both within and outside the specific sport context. Finally, an expert expands self-education by leaning heavily on peer relationships and resources outside of the specific sport context. As an athlete or coach gains expertise and moves from one stage to the next, the learning preferences change. This does not mean, for example, that a proficient player no longer learns from new experiences, but the learning preference shifts from almost complete reliance on practical experiences to other sources of information such as learning from educational programs.

The Fitts and Posner Three-Phase Model of Skill Acquisition

One traditional model for understanding motor skill acquisition was postulated by Fitts and Posner (1967). This model provided three distinct, but not discrete, phases [2] of progression through which a person advances to gain

TABLE 5.1 Characteristics and Learning Preferences Within Stages of Expertise

Stages	Characteristics	Learning Preferences
Beginner	Learns established rules and procedures. Follows the rules and rituals. Does not get the overall picture, but is lost in accomplishing tasks, such as taking attendance. Does not feel control over the environment and lacks a sense of responsibility for actions. Teacher abdicates responsibilities to learner for lack of achievement, misbehavior, etc. Finds trial and error important for learning, not reading and listening to others. Does not lean on professional training to problem solve.	Learns almost exclusively from experience. Must encounter various situations, conditions, or skills in order to learn the rudimentary elements of the sport.
Competent	Begins to see commonalities between situations and can use those to choose the correct course of action. Is content to help determine when rules apply, but is still rule dependent. Bases in-class decisions on a combination of experience and formal training. Even with more experience, competent teachers do not recognize cues from the environment.	Still relies heavily on experience, but begins to make connections to past education (formal programs, informal discussion, nonformal seminars, or camps) that provide greater insight into the skills, tactics, and strategies within the sport.
Proficient	Demonstrates the ability to distinguish the important from the unimportant in the learning. Due to experience, teachers can create contingency plans. Creates goals due to control over curriculum, and makes plans to reach these goals. Is not rules-dependent and thus takes control of the environment. Tends to hold himself or herself accountable for the actions and success or failure of students. Becomes more intuitive in teaching; not thinking about overreacting. Can predict possible outcomes.	Becomes more autonomous and begins seeking out various sources of information such as media and publications both within and outside the specific sport context.
Expert	Has extensive knowledge base and domain specificity. Uses hierarchical organization of knowledge. Has acute perceptual capacities Engages in problem representation and solving Displays automaticity of behavior Uses long- and short-term memory Self-monitors own skills Consistently outperform their peers over time. Uses intuition in life and learning environments rather than logic, analysis, and deliberate decision-making. Performance seems fast, fluid, and natural Displays automaticity in action (knowing-in-action) Attends more to atypical situations	Continues self-education and expands to lean heavily on peer relationships and resources outside of the specific sport context.

Adapted from Simon and Chase (1973a, 1973b), Ericsson and Smith (1991), Berliner (1994), Ericsson and Lehmann (1996), Bell (1997), Tan (1997), Schempp (1985, 1997), Carter et al. (1987), Bloom (1986), and Housner and Griffey (1985).

the declarative (intellectual) and procedural (physical) knowledge of a motor skill (Abernethy et al. 2007). Using vintage computer calculation procedures (subroutines and executive programs) as the backdrop, Fitts and Posner evoke an informational-processing theory that attempts to understand the manner in which a person's mind works when enacting a motor skill. In this analogy, subroutines are the previously learned, discrete units of movement that are sequentially and hierarchically organized in order to complete a motor skill or an executive program (Fitts and Posner 1967). As an athlete is learning a new skill, the subroutines, to use another analogy from these scholars, are stitched together, or transferred, to create the pattern of movement or motor skill. In order for this to happen, the athlete must first understand the nature of the movement intellectually in the cognitive phase.

The *cognitive phase* [3], the first phase, occurs when an athlete is introduced to a new motor skill. The athlete must learn the restrictions of the movement (Coker 2009), which include the defining of the action, the procedures/cues therein, and the common errors associated with the new motor skill (Fitts 1965). This learning allows athletes to gain a mental or cognitive representation of the motor skill and how to react when performing the skill in order to avoid errors (Feltovich, Prietula, and Ericsson 2006). To accomplish this task, athletes verbalize the steps of a motor skill. This verbalization helps with the processing of the information learned through demonstrations, enactments, explorations, and instruction and creates the representation of the steps (cues) needed for success.

During this phase, coaches and athletes should focus on those kinesthetic and visual aspects of the skill that will get overlooked or uncorrected as the athlete continues to the next phases (Fitts and Posner 1967). In particular, Lindor (2004) recommends that the athletes are taught more than the mechanics of the skill, such as how to create a plan that helps overcome errors, increase self-feedback (i.e., task-intrinsic feedback), assist in transfer of information, and process information for decision-making demands. The length of time that an athlete will remain in the cognitive phase depends on the nature and complexity of the motor skill (McMorris 2004). Open skills, those that occur within an environment that is ever changing (dribbling a soccer ball in a game), will take more time to learn than closed skills, those occurring within a strictly controlled environment (i.e., free-throw shot), due to the necessity of better perception and decision-making. The complexity of the skill, the number of cues or prompts, and the amount of transfer of subroutines can also affect the time needed to cognitively understand the skill. Once the athlete understands the motion, the rules, and errors connected with the motor skill, he or she moves into the associative phase.

Athletes in the intermediate or *associative phase* (Fitts and Posner 1965) practice the various subroutines (skills learned from past athletic experiences) and begin to test the most effective manner for successful completion of the motor skill. As referenced above, this combining or stitching together of old habits or skills creates a new representation of the motor skill. This means that various strategies are used, evaluated, and selected in terms of sequence and prominence as gross errors are eliminated during performance. For instance, when learning a free-throw shot in basketball, an athlete might attempt to add a height or flatten out the arch of the shot by changing the arm motion and release of the basketball in order to be more successful in this closed-skill performance. Tweaks, or technique changes, occur during this phase and provide opportunities for refinement. Task-intrinsic and augmented feedback (see more detail on feedback later in this chapter) in the forms of success of the performance (knowledge of results), technique corrections from a coach (knowledge of performance, augmented feedback), or the feeling of the body during the performance (task-intrinsic feedback) are some of the sources of information that help to evaluate the actions of the athlete in this process. During this phase, coaches should create constructive practice experiences, such as practicing components of the skill or alternating between part and whole practices, to allow better perception of the environment, situations, and conditions in which this skill is performed (Coker 2009; Fitts and Posner 1967). As with the cognitive phase, the amount of time that an athlete remains in the associative phase depends of the complexity of the skill and capabilities of the athlete; that said, this phase takes more time than the cognitive phase. Once the motor skill can be performed consistently, accurately, and with little overt cognitive demands, the athlete is considered to enter the final phase—the autonomous phase (McMorris 2004).

Athletes in the *autonomous phase* can correctly, automatically perform the skill (Fitts and Posner 1967). The performance would have little or no error and need little cognition. This allows the athlete to concentrate on perceiving other factors within the sport environment that need split-second reactions during performance. These cues can dictate a change in the angle of a soccer shot, the release point of a football pass, or the running speed within a race. In the associative phase, the athlete is focused on practicing and perfecting the motion of the skill. The athlete in this final stage has infused the movement pattern into her or his performance and can adapt that pattern to fit a context-specific situation based on the variables occurring prior to or during the execution of the motor skill. Further, the athlete is now autonomous in his or her correction of the performance based on the task-intrinsic feedback (feel of the performance) and knowledge of results (the comparison of the outcome of the performance based on past success). The coach continues to provide constructive practice experiences that enhance the skill level of the athlete. This phase of learning, as might be gathered from the description, is rare because most athletes do not reach this level of skill acquisition. For most coaches, the athletes instructed will be at either the cognitive or associative phases of motor learning. This is an important point because most coaches will be working with athletes who are continually using cognitive effort and control to execute skills.

Gentile's Two-Stage Model for Learning

Gentile's model for learning is another traditional view of skill acquisition (Gentile 1972, 2001). Instead of three phases that start with cognition and end with automaticity, Gentile groups the learning into the "getting the idea of the movement" and "fixation/diversification" stages. In the first stage, athletes learn the nature of the new skill and what it involves. Beginning with a problem that needs to be solved through movement, the athlete perceives stimuli (selective attention) within the given environment (momentarily effective stimulus population) to dictate the possible, effective solutions to the problem (motor plan). The key is the ability of the athlete to recognize "the events to which his movement must conform . . . [and] selectively attend to the stable or variable regulatory conditions . . . [in order] to consistently organize a movement that matches the environmental demands" (Gentile 1972, 7). For example, when learning to spike a ball in volleyball, a player must track the pass or set and understand the movement patterns of jumping and contacting the ball within the context of a volleyball game. The necessary skills are learned through feedback (in various forms) from different attempts—trial and error—based on whether the goal was accomplished (knowledge of results) and if the movement was performed as planned (knowledge of performance). In the decision process, the evaluation of a successful attempt is where the motion was planned and if it accomplished a goal (Gentile 1972, 2001). Once the learner consistently performs a planned skill that achieves the goal, the skill is considered learned and the athlete progresses to stage two.

The second stage, fixation/diversification, relates to either refinement of the movement within a stable environment (fixation) or adaptation to the demands of a dynamic environment (diversification). This stage relates quite closely with Fitts and Posner's cognitive phase [4] because the athlete continues to practice and reach a particular level of proficiency using the skill. In closed skills, the environment is stable and the athlete can more quickly attain a consistent level of accomplishment as the movement becomes habitual and the pattern is firmly established. Within unstable environments (open-skill sports), the regulatory conditions continually change and, unless the athlete encounters a similar situation or subset, the athlete will not be effective in the motor skill. Additionally, an ever-changing environment adds cognitive function and mental demands that can impede perception and, consequently, performance. Whether through fixation or diversification, the athlete remains in this stage and continues to refine and improve her or his skill. Conceptually, then, the coach has a responsibility to help every athlete with this ongoing refinement of skill.

Theory Comparison

Ericsson (2006) on the one hand, and Fitts and Posner (1967) and Gentile (1972, 2001) on the other, provided similar but distinct views of expertise development and skill acquisition, respectively. Expertise theory [5] and the skill acquisition models seem divergent based primarily on scope; the former being a grand theory of development within any domain and the latter investigating singular motor skill development. However, all three contain essential concepts that can help coaches and athletes improve specific skills that lead to greater performance. A comparison of these paradigms in light of expertise development and skill acquisition will illuminate these keys to learning within sport. The starting point for this comparison is the foundational, theoretical perspective of all three paradigms: cognitive theory [6].

Expertise theory emanated from the work of DeGroot (1966) and Simon and Chase (1973a, 1973b), which are studies that tested the cognitive function (i.e., memory, performance, automaticity, hierarchical knowledge, pattern recognition, and problem solving) of experts and nonexperts within the world-class chess domain. Fitts and Posner and Gentile grounded their models within informational-processing theory, a subdiscipline of cognitive theory, which uses a computer program analogy to understand the effect on memory, particularly the building of long-term memory, through the use of perception, decision-making, action, and feedback (McMorris 2004; Moe 2004) [7]. Although expertise theory (Ericsson 2006) uses a phenomenological approach and the skill acquisition models (Fitts and Posner 1967; Gentile 1972, 2001) use a more mechanized, calculated approach of inputs and outputs, the broader perspectives emanated from cognitive theory. Indeed, the seemingly divergent foundations and, consequently, the methods that impact the scope and results of these studies (i.e., acquisition of a single motor skill or development of skills essential for expert status) do not necessitate a methodological misalignment that makes comparisons unfeasible, but, instead, draw similarities that seem to show complementary aspects of these theories of learning. Whereas significant differences based on scope and methods exist, there are several critical elements within all three paradigms that directly relate to coaching athletes and professional development for coaches.

First, individuals begin learning a new skill by gaining declarative knowledge. Declarative knowledge is the understanding of what to do to perform the skill. This knowledge is stored in one's memory and can affect the development and performance of a skill (Wall 1985). Dreyfus and Dreyfus (1986) made the use of declarative knowledge clear within expertise theory by stating that novices start with noticing different features, facts, rules, and objects accompanying skills within a domain. Using guidance from more experienced colleagues, teachers, or coaches, the novice uses general rules to understand what tasks need to be completed and the rudimentary steps for completion (Berliner 1994; Schempp, McCullick, and Grant 2012). These reference points and instructions allow the novice athlete or coach to learn the new skills within specific contexts and recognize different situations in which to respond effectively with these skills during various circumstances such as competition or during general coaching sessions. Due to the larger scope of expertise theory, the starting point of declarative knowledge is focused on gaining skills, knowledge, experience, or characteristics within a domain such as a sport (athlete) or sport career (coach). In comparison, skill acquisition models begin with declarative knowledge with the individual learning the rudimentary movements and restrictions connected with a singular motor plan or skill within a sport during the cognitive phase and "getting to know the movement" stage. Although the focus of the skill acquisition models is much smaller in scope than that of expertise theory, the use of declarative knowledge is the same; it allows the learner a reference point for putting together the necessary knowledge of the skill, whether for better performance in a game or for skill acquisition. In addition to learning what to do to complete a motor skill, the athlete or coach needs the knowledge of how to perform the skill [8].

Procedural knowledge [9] allows the athlete to understand how the action is performed and control how the skill is performed. Fitts and Posner's (1967) associative or intermediate phase contains this shift because a learner knows the restrictions and features of a movement and now practices the skill to create a motor plan that reduces error. Gentile's fixation/diversification parallels these phases as individuals perform the movement within both practice and authentic settings. Both models end, whether explicitly or implicitly, with automaticity of the skill being performed. At this point, procedural knowledge seems to supplant or become more important for the learner than declarative knowledge. Expertise theory also uses procedural knowledge to increase skill and improve performance. An athlete within a sport targets specific skills that need learning or maintaining to improve performance through the repetitive nature of deliberate practice and elimination of error until reaching the automatic use of skills in the expert stage. This aligns with the learning derived from the motor skill acquisition models.

Second, the modes of learning for these theories include instruction, experience, and self-educational sources. Expertise theory gives the clearest delineation of preferred modes of learning within each of its stages (see table 5.1). Notice that experience is connected with the earliest stages of expertise development, followed by instruction with programs, and ending with self-instruction and leaning on colleagues as the individual reaches the proficient or expert stage. Another way to look at this progression is from explicit learning (being taught by another person) to implicit learning (teaching oneself). As an individual gains more expertise, self-reflection and review of practices point an expert toward self-education in those areas of weakness or in need of correction. The skill acquisition models present the first two learning preferences of expertise theory (instruction and experience) when acquiring a singular skill. An athlete begins with explicit learning through instruction from a coach in the cognitive and associative stages or "getting to know the movement" stage. As the athlete reduces performance error and becomes more automatic in the skill, implicit knowledge of learning allows greater knowledge of the movement pattern and, more important, the application within performance experiences. For example, a basketball player adds knowledge of how to dribble around an opponent after several times down the court or because of cues learned through experiences in games or practices. These do not need to be taught to the athlete, but are learned individually through experience. As can be derived from these theories, there is no single mode of education that is perfect or more effective for all learners. There are only preferred learning modalities depending on the development of the athlete or coach within a sport. A key insight from the types of knowledge used to understand a sport or singular skill, whether declarative or procedural, implicit or explicit, is that athletes need both instruction and experience in order to gain a more holistic understanding of the skill being learned. Whereas the theories suggest learning preferences based on expertise or stage/phase of learning, athletes learn in many different ways that can be utilized by coaches depending on what is working for that individual athlete at that moment.

Finally, feedback from a multitude of sources is key to learning and progressing. As described above, athletes develop both explicitly and implicitly depending on their stage. The same pattern seems to occur when learning an individual skill. The key elements of these theories are the various types of feedback that can be leveraged for more effective learning. Understanding the multiple types of feedback and how they can be used in practice enhances knowledge, learning, and performance by an athlete. In short, the importance of feedback cannot be overstated. The next section of this chapter will examine the multiple types of feedback that can be used for effective instruction. Coach developers should help coaches differentiate what these types of feedback look like in practice.

Feedback

Within motor skill acquisition or learning, feedback is performance-related information received by an athlete during or following the completion of a motor skill. Feedback has been divided into two major categories: intrinsic/task-intrinsic and extrinsic/augmented [10] (Huber 2013; Magill 2001; Schmidt 1988). Based upon these broader categories of feedback, an athlete can examine and correct performance inherently through the use of her or his senses (task-intrinsic feedback) or extrinsically through the words of a coach or watching of a video (augmented feedback). After a brief overview of the task-intrinsic feedback, the majority of this section will examine augmented feedback due to its utility for coaches. More specifically, the two roles of augmented feedback (i.e., information and motivation) as well as the two types of augmented feedback (knowledge of performance and knowledge of results) [11] are reviewed. The ability of a coach to understand and effectively implement the various types of feedback is critical for teaching and refining motor skills within practices and competition.

Task-Intrinsic Feedback

Task-intrinsic feedback uses the internal feeling of how the body moved throughout the motor skill (perception of the body's movement within space using the body's senses, such as sight and sound) to inform the athlete as to the correct performance of a movement plan or skill (Huber 2013; Magill 2001; Newell 1991; Schmidt 1988). A major theory surrounding task-intrinsic feedback is the closed-loop system (Adams 1971; Adams et al. 1972). In this theory, the ability of the athlete to detect errors during or following a motor skill performance is based upon perceptual trace, which locates specific positions of the body during motor performance as a result of concurrent informational feedback (Adams et al. 1972). This learned movement pattern acts as a reference of correctness for instantaneous comparison against a motor skill performance and leads to subjective reinforcement through the athlete's evaluation of the action (Adams 1971; Adams et al. 1972). For instance, a professional golfer hits a drive far right of the intended target-landing area. Immediately following the drive and prior to the next drive, the golfer makes practice swings and stops at specific points to check alignment, swing plan, hand position, body rotation, and timing in order to correct the mistake from the drive. The information comes from the learned motor pattern (perceptual trace), comparison with the feeling of the swing (instantaneous comparison), and the possible error found within the swing of the missed shot (subjective reinforcement). The athlete's ability to trust what he or she is feeling and knowledge of the technique are major keys to using task-intrinsic feedback or teaching an athlete how to use it (Huber 2013; Schmidt 1988). Further, task-intrinsic feedback helps to keep athletes from solely relying on feedback from a coach in order to make corrections. The key place to teach athletes to use this feedback is during practices. One of the easiest ways coaches can embed more task-intrinsic feedback in athlete performance is to prompt self-reflection. Coaches prompting athletes with "how did that swing feel?" or similar questions can direct athlete attention to the task-intrinsic feedback.

Augmented Feedback

The majority of research on feedback examines augmented feedback. Augmented feedback is motor-related information from a source outside the athlete that informs her or him about performance of a motor skill (Huber 2013; Magill 2001; Magill and Anderson 2012). Sources can be any person or object that provides information, such as coaches, trainers, stopwatches, buzzers, scores, performance statistics, or videos. This is the most common type of feedback used by coaches to help athletes improve performance by giving athletes either information about performance or motivation to continue performance (Magill 2001). This occurs through at least three functions (Magill 2001; Magill and Anderson 2012): teaching the athlete a new skill through performance-based information by which the athlete learns what to do and what not to do when performing a motor skill; helping a more experienced athlete determine how to be more effective within a sport-specific circumstance or context based on the information given by an outside source; and motivating the athlete to continue to refine skills or perform within a sport. These functions point to the two roles of feedback—providing information and motivation.

Information   The first role of augmented feedback is informational in nature (Magill 2001; Magill and Anderson 2012). This "informational feedback" presents general or specific instruction or evidence that descriptively or prescriptively aids in error correction or points to more successful ways of performing a skill (Huber 2013). A less experienced athlete might need to understand the total motion of shooting a basketball while a more expert player works on a singular part of that same motion, such as the release, in order to refine the shot. The coach could provide this information through several means such as specific, corrective instructions or showing a video of the shot so that the athlete can see exactly what is happening when shooting the basketball.

Motivation   The second role of augmented feedback is motivation (Magill 2001; Magill and Anderson 2012). The key for effective use of this role of feedback rests in the ability of the coach to select the pertinent corrections needed by the athlete, which is based on the expertise of the coach. When a coach provides feedback within practices, research has shown that athletes try harder, practice longer, and enjoy the practices more, in part because of improvement of skills (Duda and Treasure 2006; Schmidt and Wrisberg 2000, as cited by Huber 2013). In short, as coaches help athletes refine skills and become more effective within a sport, the athletes, in turn, want to remain within the sport and achieve greater performance. Effective use of motivational feedback is to convince the athlete that the training and corrections will lead to more success once the new or improved motor skill is fully learned and can be implemented in competition. For example, when a swimmer learns a new technique, the motion in the water feels strange, foreign, and slow. It is uncomfortable and only begins to feel normal after continuous practice with the new technique. The coach might encourage the athlete that although the stroke feels strange and she or he feels slower in the water, the change will, in time, result in improved performance. Once the improvement occurs, the swimmer will be more motivated to make changes, trust in the new techniques taught by the coach, and want to learn more because it results in faster times in the water. Underlying these roles of augmented feedback are two types of feedback: knowledge of performance and knowledge of results.

Gentile (1972) originally used the terms knowledge of performance and knowledge of results to discern between two types of information used by coaches and athletes for evaluation of a motor skill. Knowledge of performance (KP) refers to the kinematic information about the movement characteristics during the execution of a skill (Gentile 1972; Magill 2001; Magill and Anderson 2012; Wallace and Hagler 1979; Weeks and Kordus 1998). Knowledge of results (KR) is feedback that provides verbalized, post-response information about the outcome of the motor skill within a specific environment (Anderson, Magill, and Sekiya 2001; Magill 2010; Weeks and Sherwood 1994). Both KP and KR can be given to athletes concurrently (during) and terminally (following) the enactment of the skill(s) (Magill 2001). Additionally, KP is viewed as more effective (Gentile 1972; Wallace and Hagler 1979) and used by more coaches than KR (Fishman and Tobey 1978). Few studies have compared KP and KR to see which is more effective; however, results from such studies support the view that KP is more effective. They suggest that when KP and KR are used in concert, KR is an important factor and is used for interpreting KP (see Magill 2001 for discussion). Due to the importance placed on KP and KR through research within augmented feedback, each of these types of augmented feedback will be discussed next as well as research investigating effective ways to use them within skill acquisition.

Knowledge of Performance

Research surrounding KP provides critical insights that can enhance its use when coaching. As stated before, early research examining KP showed that it is more effective than KR (Wallace and Hagler 1979). In their seminal study, Wallace and Hagler asked 24 right-handed male collegiate students to shoot basketballs using their nondominant hand. Two randomly selected groups were formed in which one group received KP and the other social reinforcement (SR). This two-phased experiment initially provided the participants with both KR and KP or SR, followed by the removal of the KP or SR verbal feedback. Results showed significant change in both phases of the experiment for the KP and KR group. Researchers reported that providing KP for athletes would be highly beneficial in the acquisition phase if it were specific to the cues and learning of the correct form. In short, this experiment showed that telling athletes "'Too bad,' 'Good going,' 'Fantastic,' 'Try a little harder next time,' 'Concentrate,' and 'You can do it,'" is not effective KP for athletes' learning (Wallace and Hagler 1979, 267). Coaches need to prioritize feedback, such as commenting on stance prior to motion, with specific directions for improvement based on learning cues.

Another point of interest is the quality of the KP that should be shared with athletes for successful and optimal skill acquisition. Schmidt and Young (1991) and Young and Schmidt (1992) suggested a new methodology for the study of kinematic feedback (KP) and used this protocol to investigate the impact and schedule of both KP and KR. Young and Schmidt (1992) provided 60 college students both KP and KR when acquiring and retaining a new coincident-timing skill in which the participants had to hit a ball with a bat positioned in their right hand. The type of feedback was based on how well the optimal motor pattern, as determined over trial and error, matched that of real-world coaches, who know optimal technique of various motor patterns within their sports. Results showed that KP is effective for skill acquisition in the short term, which confirmed previous research (Salmoni, Schmidt, and Walter 1984; Schmidt 1988); however, the simple fact that a coach uses KP in practice does not equate to retention (long-term learning). In fact, only one of four KP variables was shown to outperform KR in retention. This suggests that there are types of KP that are effective as well as ineffective. In an extension of this study, Brisson and Alain (1996) used a similar task as Young and Schmidt (1992), but allowed the 36 university participants to use the kinematic characteristics of the experiment in order to produce their own pattern of movement for successful performance (i.e., highest score). Results supported the findings of Young and Schmidt (1992) and expanded the findings by showing that providing athletes with optimal KP was not necessary for effective learning, which might have confounded past research (Brisson and Alain 1996). For coaches, especially on teams or within sport levels where athletes have a diverse set of abilities due to genetic dispositions and changes due to physical growth, researchers suggested that a broader teaching of KP, in which the athletes find their own optimal motion pattern, results in acquisition and retention of the motor skill.

A final study of interest dealt with the frequency of KP when teaching. Weeks and Kordus (1998) divided 34 boys at a basketball camp into two experimental groups. One group would receive KP after each attempt at a soccer throw-in; the other group received KP after 33% of the attempts. Results revealed that reduced KP increased learning of form and encouraged the development of task-intrinsic feedback, enhanced the ability of learners to detect errors inherently, and could reduce dependency on KP during performance. These results aligned with past research that found the reduction of feedback did not degrade performance and, in essence, outperforms KP provided following every trial (Young and Schmidt 1992). Interestingly, both Weeks and Kordus (1998) and Young and Schmidt (1992) thought that KP might fundamentally function in a similar manner to KR, which is the next type of augmented feedback to be discussed.

Knowledge of Results

Research examining KR seems to center on two lines of inquiry: specificity and frequency of KR. Wright, Smith-Munyon, and Sidaway (1997) examined the use of less specific qualitative and more specific quantitative KR during practices. Based on the guidance hypothesis that augmented feedback (i.e., KR) scaffolds learning for the athlete by providing a temporary support for skill acquisition, KR has a positive effect on learning if the changes to technique fit within the targeted movement bandwidth or the predetermined range of correctness. In this study, each group received either qualitative KR (i.e., "correct" or "incorrect") or quantitative KR (direction and magnitude of performance) as to performance within the expected bandwidth—the parameters within a range of acceptable or expected performance—of the motor skill. In this sense, when an action is outside of these parameters, then feedback is provided to the participant as either qualitative KR or quantitative KR. Results found that the less precise qualitative KR was beneficial for short-term retention when the movement was well outside the bandwidth—large errors were occurring. The more precise quantitative KR was effective in both short-term and long-term retention for both large and small errors, which supports the guidance hypothesis and past literature in precision of KR (i.e., Magill and Wood 1986).

Researchers examined the effect of qualitative and quantitative KR on bandwidth (error-based) and reverse-bandwidth (correction-based). Procedures tested the use of specific qualitative and quantitative KR in the learning of a skill (Cauraugh, Chen, and Radio 1993). Unlike Wright, Smith-Munyon, and Sidaway (1997), both the qualitative and quantitative KR gave participants specific information for learning. All groups of graduate students received qualitative KR for their attempts and quantitative KR for when they were outside the bandwidth (traditional bandwidth procedure) or inside the bandwidth (reverse bandwidth procedure), respectively. Researchers suggested that quantitative KR aided only in the traditional bandwidth procedure that focused on when the participant made errors, whereas specific qualitative KR helped both bandwidth and reverse-bandwidth procedures. In summary, past research shows that more precise KR leads to better skill acquisition. As the body of knowledge grew about KR, researchers began to question the effects of frequency of feedback.

Winstein, Pohl, and Lewthwaite (1994) tested the frequency and specificity of augmented feedback (i.e., guiding presentation/practice versus KR) with a sample of 40 graduate student volunteers. Results indicated that less frequent guiding augmented feedback (the use of an apparatus to help physically hone skills such as stopping motion at the desired point for optimum technique) resulted in performance at the same level as infrequent KR in acquisition and retention. Researchers suggested that this reduction in feedback allowed for information-processing functions based on the success or failure of the performance. The amount of KR provided, ranging from 33% to 83%, did not diminish learning; only giving KR after each trial (100%) reduced learning. These results reflected earlier studies that suggested that athletes needed to use context-specific cues to figure out motor problems in the absence of KR, which led to improved performance (Lee and Magill 1983; Schmidt 1982). Interestingly, this same review of literature on KR suggested that if KR was readily given, it acted as a prop and would be a detriment to performance once removed, as compared to delayed or reduced KR.

Weeks and Sherwood (1994) investigated the issue of the schedule of KR when performing trials as well as the type of KR when instructing athletes.

In this study, 45 right-handed participants engaged in 75 static force trials in which she or he received KR immediately after each trial, KR of each trial after every fifth trial, or a summary of the average output of five trials. Results showed that the latter two groups—the summary groups—promoted consistent skill acquisition and retention. KR after every trial (100%) seemed to lead to overcompensation, a change to technique leading to reduction in consistent long-term performance, or the blocking of informational-processing of the skill (Weeks and Sherwood 1994; Winstein, Pohl, and Lewthwaite 1994). There seems to be an optimum amount of augmented feedback and KR needed for reduced variability and heightened long-term retention. One hypothesis might be enough delay to allow for subjective estimation or task-intrinsic feedback.

Research of KR suggested that delaying the time from the completion of the skill for the delivery of KR allows athletes to use task-intrinsic evaluation, which leads to subjective estimation of performance outcomes and better retention of the skills (Schmidt and Shapiro 1986; Swinnen et al. 1990). Lui and Wrisberg (1997) tested these findings to better understand if delayed KR intervals helped or hindered acquisition and retention in skill learning. Results showed that immediate KR did not help with retention of the skills in either immediate or delayed retention tests and supported past findings and showed the importance of subjective estimation. Anderson, Magill, and Sekiya (1994) found similar results when testing immediate versus delayed KR, concluding that learners were forced to pay closer attention to task-intrinsic feedback instead of KR, which could be detrimental to performance, especially if KR were removed from the learner.

Summary of What Coaches Should Know About Feedback

Task-intrinsic and augmented feedbacks work together to aid in skill acquisition. The use of task-intrinsic feedback should be taught to athletes by coaches. This is a critical source of information for athletes that can reduce reliability on augmented, coach-provided feedback and build the confidence of athletes. Research also showed that less-frequent exposure of KP and KR produced greater learning and retention when specificity was appropriate. This could be due to the athletes' need to access task-intrinsic feedback and the subjective estimation of needed corrections for enhanced performance.

What Coaches Should Do

To this point, this chapter introduced and discussed what coaches should know about the development of expertise and skill acquisition in theory and through the use of feedback as part of effective pedagogical practices that relate specifically to sport coaching. The ability of coaches to take this knowledge base and apply it to current coaching practices is critical for more effective instruction of athletes. This section will apply this understanding through practical suggestions that a coach can use to enhance motor skill acquisition. This section is divided into similar divisions found in what coaches should know, mainly theory and feedback. Each of these two sections will begin with a practical example followed by specific examples of how coaches can apply theory.

Skill Acquisition Theory

Expertise theory, Fitts and Posner's skill acquisition model, and Gentile's model for learning are theories specifically related to development and skill acquisition. For the purposes of this chapter, the application of these theories to the learning of both coaches and athletes is highly profitable. Therefore, this part of the application section will relate these theories to both coaches and athletes.

Coach Learning

As stated earlier, expertise theory relates to the development of knowledge, skills, experiences, and characteristics through the application of deliberate practice over a considerable amount of time. From beginner through expert, individuals progress through discrete stages in which researchers have found generalized hallmarks and learning preferences (see table 5.1). This theory has been applied to coach education through several studies regarding the acquisition of knowledge (Ericsson, 1998; Ericsson and Charness 1994; Glaser and Chi 1988; Siedentop and Eldar 1989; Simon and Chase 1973a, 1973b), teaching practices (Berliner 1994; DeMarco and McCullick 1997; Housner and Griffey 1985), and sources of learning (Ericsson and Charness 1994; Fincher and Schempp 1994; Schempp, Manross, Tan, and Fincher 1998), to name only a few. More generally, coaches need to honestly assess their level of expertise based on their level of knowledge, skills, and learning preferences. The best example of development of expertise would be the example of John Wooden, arguably one of the most successful collegiate basketball coaches in the history of the game [12]. At the end of each basketball year, including those in which he won a national championship, Coach Wooden would pick one area of coaching that he felt needed improvement (Nater and Gallimore 2006). Over each offseason, he would research that topic, talk with other coaches, and, in a real sense, write a small thesis on the subject and how he could apply his learning to his coaching practices. Through this continual practice of learning, Coach Wooden would expand his knowledge of a particular area of coaching and his skills therein. This skill acquisition helped his teams win ten consecutive national championships between 1964 and 1975 [13].

Any coach can learn new skills in the same manner. This is not to advocate for writing of a yearly thesis on a topic related to coaching, but is a call to learning the craft of coaching based on self-reflection on individual and staff weaknesses and strengths. As charted in table 5.1, coaches should avail themselves of various sources of knowledge, both published and in person, for development through inherently repetitive, or even boring, practices that are targeted for enhanced performance as a coach—or deliberate practice. This is not to assert that development of expertise occurs through rigorous study alone. In fact, talking with colleagues, attending seminars, going to coaching conferences, attending formal educational programs, or learning from athletes are some of the sources of knowledge that have been shown to aid in coach education and heightened expertise (see chapter 14). Further, the application of the skill acquisition models points to specific learning as well.

According to the two models presented above, there are two or three stages or phases that learners use in the acquisition of new skills, respectively. Although the application of these models might seem only pertinent to the development of athletes, these models, like expertise theory, are reflective of the general ways that people learn. Expertise theory is related through cognitive learning of knowledge, skills, and experiences. The models of skill acquisition seems more suited for applied skills that coaches carry onto the playing fields. The first step is to understand the pattern of behavior that is desired for improved coaching. This begins with getting the idea of the skill being learned (Gentile 1972, 2001). For instance, when I began coaching, I reflected the emotional temperament of the coach I had growing up. He was passionate to a fault of outbursts, and, in some cases, tirades. A mentor coach took me aside and pointed out the obvious—I needed to relax and change the way I coached. Through modeling and education, the mentor coach showed me what it means to coach with passion that mutes the negative behaviors that he, parents, and athletes were witnessing during practices and meets. In short, I needed to understand what the idea of this new-to-me style of coaching meant in practical application. Through my mentor's continual correction and scaffolding, I progressed through and remain in the associative or practice phase as I continue to refine behaviors and automaticity with regard to this skill. The major application is finding a mentor or someone who can teach the declarative knowledge and help lead you to the procedural knowledge, which is enactment of the skill among the athletes, coaching staff, administrators, and parents. (For more information on long-term coach development, see chapter 15).

Athlete Learning

Too often coaches move through a progression of drills during practice without paying close attention to athlete learning. The focus is more on completing rote movements within an allotted time during a practice for the repetition of the movement or the maintaining of specific drills rather than the learning of skills. This type of repetition can be beneficial if the athletes are already in the automaticity phase (Fitts and Posner 1967), which is hallmarked by extremely low rates of errors and high proficiency, if used as warm-up before performance, or if used as reminders of form corrections or benefits for their fitness. The downside to this type of practice is the possibility of uncorrected form leading to degrading skills.

Expertise theory and the models of skill acquisition provided areas of application that enhance pedagogical methods for sport coaches. First, coaches need to start with teaching the skills through instruction, demonstration, and modeling. There should be clear pre-practice instructions about goals for the day, demonstrations of cues or stringing together of those cues for each part of the motor skill, differentiation for the various skill levels of the athletes (i.e., beginner, competent, proficient, or expert/elite), and progression of skills throughout a practice that aligns with the goals of the practice (Hodges and Franks 2002). The instruction and demonstrations should show both the optimum technique as well as the expected outcomes based on the ability level of the athletes; coaches should not expect young athletes to have perfect form. This conforms to the cognitive phase or "getting the idea of the movement" stage for beginners.

Second, coaches should train the sub-routines of skills, not just the whole skill (Glaser 1965). There are benefits to dividing complex skills into parts and teaching from the partial to the whole movement. For instance, the body position of a swimmer is more important than the kicking or arm movements. A coach teaching such skills should focus on this aspect first and then build the stroke from this fundamental position. If the coach is assessing a more advanced swimmer, this should be the starting point of the evaluation and, possibly, retooling the stroke. A swim stroke is quite complex, but, by dividing the technique into learnable parts, the stroke can be developed over time through prioritized, small components.

Finally, athletes should be allowed to "over practice" the skills (Glaser 1965). This occurs when a coach provides room within a practice session for individual practice in order for the athlete to figure out how to perform a skill successfully. For instance, a fellow swim coach teaches competitive swim camps every summer consisting of four-hour days in which one stroke is taught per day. Even with breaks for eating, drinking water, and restroom use, for most coaches this much attention would be too long for any one stroke; in fact, other coaches wonder why he would teach one stroke for such a long duration. The reason for the length of the sessions is to give the athletes time to understand the movement's proper technique and to have individual practice time to learn to perform the strokes correctly. This falls in line with the skill acquisition models that underscore the need for enough time to learn the skill during the association phase or fixation/diversification stage. This more extreme approach to "over practice" might not work for every sport or each skill within a sport. Issues such as type of performance (i.e., individual versus team), physical demands, athlete attention, and overall fatigue must be taken into account by a coach or risk decreased learning, loss of motivation, or possible injury.

Feedback

Coaches and athletes provide augmented and task-intrinsic feedback surrounding performances, respectively. As described above, the division of these categories of feedback is artificial for the benefit of study; in real-life situations these feedbacks work seamlessly because the athlete can both feel and sense the movement and evaluate success and necessary corrections based on KP from the coach and KR from the attempt. Based on the characteristics of task-intrinsic and augmented feedback and their interworking, there are several applications that can assist coaches in effective instruction.

First, coaches need to reduce the complexity of the skills by limiting the number of cues (three to five) and the focus of the practice. For instance, an American football coach teaches blocking to offensive linemen. Too often coaches approach this skill by demonstration and then correcting errors without first creating the expected level of proficiency. The athletes are only provided with several basic steps or learning cues and are then expected to successfully perform the skill. Each time the athlete takes a turn performing, the coach corrects a different error. By the fifth attempt, the athlete could be thinking about five or more corrections, which is confusing to adults, no less beginners. Instead, coaches need to write down the skills to be taught or reviewed and the goal for the level of proficiency, and then provide augmented feedback only for those communicated goals for the skill and associated drills.

Second, change the practice plan to meet the day's goals. Past research examined different types of practices. Schmidt and Wrisberg (2000) defined a block practice as one in which an athlete practices the same skill through repetition and order; a random practice allows athletes to practice a wider variety of skills in an undefined order. Research suggests that a block practice is more effective for skill acquisition and random practice for retention of skills (Fitts and Posner 1967; Gentile 1972; Schmidt and Wrisberg 2000; Shea, Kohl, and Indermill 1990). Coaches can use these practice structures to create a learning environment that is conducive to the type of learning needed by the athletes. If coaches introduce a new skill, they should create a practice plan that allows for instruction, demonstrations, and individual or group practices in a highly structured manner that asks athletes to focus on three to five cues within the same motor skill. Once a skill is learned, coaches can review the skill using a random practice in which there are several different drills that focus on complementary skills or build toward a team tactic. This switching of practices to meet the needs of the athletes allows for variation and contextual interference that is beneficial to athlete learning and keeps them motivated (Magill, Porter, and Wu 2005).

Third, coaches can allow athletes to choose when they receive feedback. Self-controlled feedback occurs when the athletes are allowed to request when they would like augmented feedback, such as that from coaches or other informational sources. Research has shown that when given the choice of when to receive feedback, learners clearly demonstrate greater learning than those who do not have a choice (Chiviacowsky and Wulf 2002; Janelle, Kim, and Singer 1995; Wulf and Tool, 1999). One suggestion was that the self-controlled feedback allowed the athletes to schedule feedback when it would benefit the needs or preferences of the athletes. Taking this concept a step further, Wu and Magill (2011) allowed self-control participants to choose the schedule of feedback, frequency of demonstrations, and the practice tasks. Results found that self-control participants switched tasks after experiencing a successful trial, reduced mindless repetition through the use of task-intrinsic feedback, and used self-evaluation to eliminate repetition through changes in problem solving (i.e., changing technique to be more successful). This is not to suggest giving the athletes complete control of practices, but that some autonomy during practices improves self-regulation, teaches use of task-intrinsic feedback, and provides appropriate feedback when most needed, all of which could lead to greater learning.

Summary

This chapter focused on the effective instructional practices of coaches within the context of sport. Starting with what coaches should know, we considered the implications of expertise theory (Ericsson 2006) and two skill acquisition models (Fitts and Posner 1967; Gentile 1972, 2001). These theories state that athletes learn new skills through a combination of instruction and experience, through the uses of declarative knowledge and procedural knowledge, explicit learning, and task-implicit learning. Within these types of knowledge and interactions, whether between the coach and athlete or between the athlete and himself or herself, the importance of augmented feedback cannot be overstated. Through the use of information feedback, motivational feedback, knowledge of performance, and knowledge of results, the athlete compares the intended action with the result of the performance to correct, learn, and refine skills. To effectively apply this approach to what a coach should do, there are several key instructional practices that will allow for increased learning. First, coaches should instruct athletes through the use of demonstrations, modeling, and augmented feedback. These practices provide athletes with the declarative knowledge, examples of how the movement should look, and consistent pointers or advice for increased performance. Second, coaches should allow enough time so that the athlete can learn the skills. Too often coaches march through a practice with more concern for time management than increased athlete learning of the skills. By allowing athletes the time to combine the cognitive or declarative learning with experience or procedural knowledge, greater learning can occur through "over practicing" (Glaser 1965). Third, coaches can increase learning through the breaking the skills down into subroutines. This allows the athletes to increase proficiency of the smaller skills that lead to better performance in the larger movement pattern. Finally, a coach should strive to increase his or her expertise within the sport. Through the example of John Wooden, who applied deliberate practice to his coaching in each offseason, a coach should examine his or her skill level, identify a weakness, learn how to improve, and then practice those skills that will improve coaching performance. This will lead to better coaching and increased learning by athletes through the use of some or all these effective practices. The application of these practices might be overwhelming to novice or competent coaches, who are still learning how to be a coach. Additionally, adopting these effective practices might take time for planning and testing the best type of implementation. But, by applying these principles and actions into coaching practice, athlete learning will increase.

---

[1] The specific amount of stages along this continuum has varied through the ages (Ericsson 2006, chapter 1). A more traditional view of five stages—novice, beginner or advanced beginner, competent, proficient, and expert—has been used when investigating skill acquisition and teacher development (Berliner 1994; Dreyfus and Dreyfus 1986). More recent publications have used four- and three-stage approaches when discussing the learning preferences of sport and strength and conditioning coaches (Grant and Dorgo 2014; Schempp, McCullick, and Grant 2012; Schempp, McCullick, and Mason 2006). For this discussion, a four-stage approach will be used due to the limit of space and the distinctiveness of learning preferences at various stages.

[2] Fitts and Posner originally use the term "phases" to understand the progression through which a person must move to learn a new motor skill. Later authors use the term "stages." I have chosen to return to the original language of Fitts and Posner and will refer to the phases of this model.

[3] Different authors have called this phase by various names, such as the mental stage (Martens 2012) or understanding step (Schempp 2003).

[4] Interestingly, in an early version of Fitts and Posner's model (Fitts 1965), the associative phase is titled the fixation phase.

[5] Expertise theory is a grand theory that encompasses the holistic learning, whether through skill acquisition, knowledge building, or authentic experiences, toward becoming an expert. For the purposes of this comparison, the focus will rest upon those aspects of the greater theory that pertain to motor skill acquisition, which will include deliberate practice, knowledge modalities, learning preferences, and theoretic perspective (i.e., cognitive theory).

[6] Cognitive theory is used generally to denote investigations in the cognitive functions.

[7] McMorris (2004) argues that Fitts and Posner (1967) is a more "general cognitive theory," (175) while Gentile (1972) is an informational-process theory. Moe (2004) firmly places Fitts and Posner's model within informational-processing. I agree with Moe (2004) considering in the earliest works, their model contains all the hallmarks of informational-processing theory, including the analogy to computer programming.

[8] McMorris (2004) states unequivocally that there is "no proof that we move from declarative to procedural knowledge" (169), which is in agreement with Masters (2000), whom McMorris cites. Interestingly, Masters (2000) focused on implicit learning as compared with explicit learning. It can be argued that implicit learning would be instances in which procedural knowledge is emphasized over declarative knowledge in explicit learning, such as a classroom or gymnasium. Based on the descriptions of phases and stages within the skill acquisition models, there seems to be an implication that the learning of a new skill within an educational context begins with declarative knowledge being taught by an instructor. The statements by McMorris (2004) are recognized, but, in following the stages and phases of skill acquisition, declarative knowledge is presented in earlier stages or phases than procedural knowledge.

[9] Wall (1985) uses schema theory to explain the use of procedural knowledge. For many, schema theory and informational-processing stand opposed based on characteristics of memory storage and recall. At the same time, scholars such as Wall (1985) connect the notion of procedural knowledge with Fitts and Posner and Gentile based on the larger context of cognition and tractable progression from declarative to procedural knowledge. This possible dichotomous position is recognized, but not discussed within the scope of this chapter.

[10] For the remainder of this chapter, the terms task-intrinsic and augmented feedback will be used to represent these major categories. As Magill and Anderson (2012) state, "the advantage of the term task-intrinsic feedback is its acknowledgement of the skill-specific nature of sensory feedback sources associated with performing sport skills" (4). Additionally, augmented feedback was chosen as the term being used based on the definition of augment being to add or enhance something, which more closely aligns with its use by coaches (Magill and Anderson 2012).

[11] The major focus of feedback within this chapter will be on augmented feedback. This is not to suggest that the listed types of feedback do not apply to task-intrinsic feedback. For example, knowledge of performance and knowledge of results occur within task-intrinsic feedback (Gentile 2001). That said, many scholars (i.e., Magill 2010; Magill and Anderson 2012; Schmidt 1988) examine these types of knowledge largely within augmented feedback. Magill (2010) states that using KP and KR within task-intrinsic discussion leads to "confusion of an area of study already beset by lack of understanding of the roles of various sources and types of information and skill acquisition" 87). Therefore, KP and KR will be described within augmented feedback alone.

[12] After winning his first national championship in 1964 until his retirement in 1975, Coach Wooden won 10 NCAA national championships, won 38-straight NCAA tournament victories, completed an 88-game winning streak over a three-year span, earned six national Coach of the Year awards, and was named the coach of the century by sports writers (Miller 2004).

[13] *ibid*

PART II

TEACHING COACHES TO EXCEL WITHIN THEIR CONTEXT

Chapter 6

Educating Youth Sports Coaches: An Empirically Supported Training Program

Frank L. Smoll and Ronald E. Smith

Youth sports refers to "adult-organized and controlled athletic programs for young people in the age range 6 to 18 years. The participants are formally organized into teams and leagues, and they attend practices and scheduled competitions under the supervision of an adult leader" (Smoll and Smith 2002, xi). The programs are complex psychosocial systems that are firmly established parts of societies around the world, and they directly touch the lives of millions of children, adolescents, and adults (De Knop, Engstrom, Skirstad, and Weiss 1996). Based on a report of US trends, more than 45 million youngsters participate in team sports (Sports & Fitness Industry Association 2015). Millions more likely participate in individual sports, such as swimming and tennis. That represents over half of the population in the 6-to-18-year age range. (US Census Bureau 2013).

Despite their success in attracting participants, the desirability of youth sports continues to be a topic of controversy. Those who favor youth sports see them as providing miniature life situations in which children and adolescents can learn to relate more effectively to other people and to cope with realities they will face in later life. *Physically*, athletes can learn sport skills and increase their health and fitness. *Psychologically*, they can develop leadership skills, self-discipline, respect for authority, competitiveness, cooperativeness, sportsmanship, and self-confidence. Moreover, sports can be just plain fun!

Socially, sports provide an opportunity to become part of an ever-expanding network of friends and acquaintances (Smoll and Smith 2012).

Youth sports do, however, have more than their share of critics, who claim that these programs place excessive physical and/or psychological stress on young athletes, rob youngsters of the creative benefits of spontaneous play, and develop antisocial attitudes and behaviors by encouraging cheating and aggression. They also say that youth sports are conducted primarily to satisfy self-serving interests of parents and coaches, who try to achieve glory through young athletes.

A realistic appraisal of youth sports indicates that participation does not automatically result in either beneficial or detrimental effects for all children. Indeed, any of the positive or negative outcomes described can occur. The real issue is how the programs can be effectively structured and operated in ways that ensure attainment of favorable outcomes. Concerning this, it is generally held that the relationship between coaches and athletes has a profound impact on the effects of participation. We have therefore devoted most of our careers to developing and conducting scientifically validated programs that positively affect coach behaviors and consequently the personal and social well-being of young athletes who play for them.

In this chapter, we describe the evolution of our research on coach behaviors and interventions that has resulted in an empirically supported coach training program. *Empirically supported* means that the program is founded on firm empirical evidence, and it has demonstrated efficacy derived from experimental outcome research in which the intervention is formally compared with control conditions (American Psychological Association Task Force on Psychological Intervention Guidelines 1995; Chambless and Hollon 1998). We explain the manner in which a theoretical model has helped guide our basic and applied research. Consideration is also given to the cognitive-behavioral principles constituting the core of our training program.

Theoretical Model and Research Paradigm

Beginning in the early 1970s, our coaching-behaviors project was guided by a mediational model of coach-athlete interactions, the basic elements of that are represented as follows:

Coach Behaviors → Athlete Perception and Recall → Athletes' Evaluative Reactions

This model was inspired by the "cognitive revolution" that was occurring at the time and the contributions of social cognitive theory (Bandura 1969; Mischel 1973). It stipulates that the ultimate effects of coach behaviors are mediated by the meaning that athletes confer on them. We assumed that how athletes perceive their coach's behaviors and what they remember about them affects the way that athletes feel about the coach and evaluate their sport experiences. Furthermore, a complex interaction of cognitive and affective processes is involved at this mediational level. Athletes' perceptions and reactions are likely to be affected not only by the coach's behaviors but also by other factors. These factors include the athlete's age, what the athlete expects of coaches (normative beliefs and expectations), and certain athlete personality variables such as self-esteem and anxiety. Eventually, the basic three-element model was expanded to reflect these factors (Smoll and Smith 1989). The elaborated model (figure 6.1) specifies a number of situational factors as well as coach and athlete characteristics that could influence coach behaviors and the perceptions and reactions of athletes to them. Using this model as a starting point, we have sought to determine how observed coach behaviors, athletes' perception and recall of the coach's behaviors, and athlete attitudes are related to one another. We

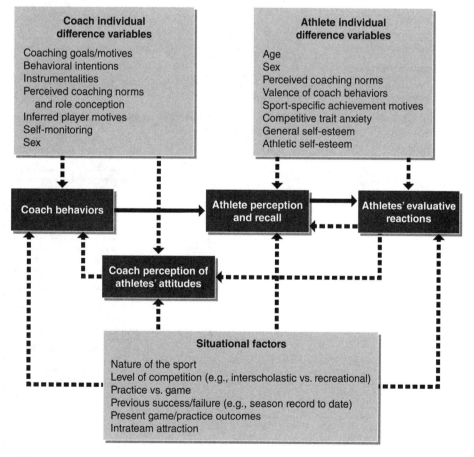

FIGURE 6.1   A model of adult leadership behaviors in sport, showing hypothesized relations among situational, cognitive, behavioral, and individual difference variables.

Adapted by permission from F.L. Smoll and R.E. Smith, "Leadership Behaviors in Sport: A Theoretical Model and Research Paradigm," *Journal of Applied Social Psychology* 19, no. 18 (1989): 1522-1551.

have also explored the manner in which athlete and situational characteristics might serve to affect these relations.

Measurement of Coach Behaviors

In order to measure coach behaviors, the Coach Behavior Assessment System (CBAS) was developed to permit the direct observation and coding of coaches' actions during practices and games (Smith, Smoll, and Hunt 1977). The behavioral categories, which are shown in table 6.1, were derived

TABLE 6.1 Response Categories of the Coach Behavior Assessment System

Response category	Behavioral description
CLASS I: REACTIVE BEHAVIORS	
Responses to desirable performance	
Reinforcement	A positive, rewarding reaction (verbal or nonverbal) to a good play or good effort
Nonreinforcement	Failure to respond to a good performance
Responses to mistakes	
Mistake-contingent encouragement	Encouragement given to an athlete following a mistake
Mistake-contingent technical instruction	Instructing or demonstrating to an athlete how to correct a mistake
Punishment	A negative reaction (verbal or nonverbal) following a mistake
Punitive technical instruction	Technical instruction following a mistake given in a punitive or hostile manner
Ignoring mistakes	Failure to respond to an athlete's mistakes
Responses to misbehavior	
Keeping control	Reactions intended to restore or maintain order among team members
CLASS II: SPONTANEOUS BEHAVIORS	
Game related	
General technical instruction	Spontaneous instruction in the techniques and strategies of the sport (not following a mistake)
General encouragement	Spontaneous encouragement that does not follow a mistake
Organization	Administrative behavior that sets the state for play by assigning, for example, duties, responsibilities, and positions
Game irrelevant	
General communication	Interactions with athletes unrelated to the game/practice

from content analyses of observers' verbal descriptions of coach behavior-situation units using a time-sampling procedure.

The 12 CBAS categories are divided into two major classes of behaviors. *Reactive* (elicited) behaviors are responses to the immediately preceding athlete or team behaviors, while *spontaneous* (emitted) behaviors are initiated by the coach and are not a response to a discernible preceding event. Use of the CBAS in observing and coding coach behaviors in a variety of sports by us and by other research teams has shown that the scoring system is sufficiently comprehensive to incorporate the vast majority of overt leader behaviors, that high interrater reliability can be obtained, and that individual differences in behavioral patterns can be discerned (see Smith, Smoll, and Christensen 1996).

Coach Behaviors and Children's Evaluative Reactions

Following development of the CBAS, a systematic program of basic research was carried out over a period of several years (Curtis, Smith, and Smoll 1979; Smith and Smoll 1990; Smith, Smoll, and Curtis 1978; Smith et al. 1983; Smoll, Smith, Curtis, and Hunt 1978). This involved pursuing several questions concerning the potential impact of youth coaches on athletes' psychological welfare. For example, how frequently do coaches engage in behaviors such as encouragement, punishment, instruction, and organization, and how are observable coach behaviors related to children's reactions to their organized athletic experiences?

The results indicated that the typical baseball or basketball coach engages in more than 200 codable actions during an average game. We were thus able to generate behavioral profiles of up to several thousand responses over the course of a season. In large-scale observational studies, we coded more than 80,000 behaviors of some 70 male youth coaches, then interviewed and administered questionnaires after the season to nearly 1,000 children in their homes to measure their recall of their coaches' behaviors and their evaluative reactions to the coach, their sport experiences, and themselves. We also obtained coaches' postseason ratings of how frequently they engaged in each of the observed behaviors. These data provided clear evidence for the crucial role of the coach.

Relations between coaches' scores on the behavioral dimensions and player measures indicated that players responded most favorably to coaches who engaged in higher percentages of supportive and instructional behaviors and low rates of punitive behaviors. These relations were significantly enhanced when the game situation (e.g., winning or losing) was taken into account; supportive behaviors had comparatively greater impact while winning and punitive behaviors while losing (Smith et al. 2009).

Players on teams whose coaches created a supportive environment also liked their teammates more. A somewhat surprising finding was that the team's won-lost record was essentially unrelated to how well the players liked the coach and how much they wanted to play for the coach in the future. This finding that coach behaviors were far more important predictors of liking for the coach than the won–lost record was replicated in another study involving 268 male and female youth basketball players (Cumming et al. 2007). It is worth noting, however, that winning assumed greater importance beyond age 12, although it continued to be a less important attitudinal determinant than coach behaviors.

Another important finding concerns how accurately coaches perceive their own behaviors. Correlations between CBAS observed behaviors and coaches' own ratings of how frequently they performed the behaviors were generally low and nonsignificant. The only significant correlation occurred for punishment. Children's ratings on the same perceived behavior scales correlated much more highly with CBAS measures than did the coaches' ratings! It thus appears that coaches have limited awareness of how frequently they engage in particular forms of behavior, and that athletes are more accurate perceivers of actual coach behaviors. This finding suggested that any effective intervention would need to increase coaches' self-awareness of their behavior.

Of particular interest within our research program was the notion that how people feel about themselves influences how they respond to the behaviors of other people (Brown 2007). We therefore hypothesized that level of self-esteem would moderate relations between coach behaviors and children's attitudes toward themselves, the coach, and other aspects of their sport experience. In one study, analysis of the children's attraction responses toward the coaches revealed a significant interaction between coach supportiveness (the tendency to reinforce desirable performance and effort and to respond to mistakes with encouragement) and athletes' level of self-esteem (Smith and Smoll 1990). Specifically, the children with low self-esteem were especially responsive to variations in supportiveness in a manner consistent with a self-enhancement model of self-esteem (Swann 1990). We therefore concluded that children who are low in self-esteem are especially in need of a positive sport experience, and that coaches can help provide that experience.

Achievement Goal Theory and Coaching

The sport environment is inherently a competence and achievement context. Consequently, motivational factors play an important role in the ultimate effects of participation on psychosocial development. As a theoretical framework, achievement goal theory (AGT) provides an appropriate vantage point to explore factors (e.g., coach behaviors) that might affect motivated behavior in youth sports. AGT (Ames 1992a; Dweck 1999; Nicholls 1989) focuses on understanding the function and the meaning of goal directed actions, based on how participants define ability and how they judge whether or not they have demonstrated competence. Although a variety of variables are incorporated into AGT (e.g., goal states, attributions, fear of failure, self-perceived competence, incremental and entity implicit theories of competence), two of the central constructs have received particular attention in the sport literature—namely, individual *goal orientations* that guide achievement perceptions and behavior, and the *motivational climate* created within achievement settings. An overview of these constructs as related to coach–athlete interactions follows. Comprehensive discussions of AGT and its implications for coaching appear elsewhere (e.g., Duda and Balaguer 2007; Duda and Ntoumanis 2005; Roberts, Treasure, and Conroy 2007).

Achievement Goal Orientation

In essence, goal orientation involves the criteria individuals use to define success. This dispositional variable is a product of and contributes to (along with situational factors) goal involvement states in achievement situations. AGT focuses on mastery and ego orientations and states. When an individual is in a mastery state, success is defined in a self-referenced manner and is focused on skill development, task mastery, and exerting maximum effort.

In an ego state, social comparison plays a major role in self-perceived success, and the emphasis is on outperforming others in order to attain recognition and status. Thus, ego-oriented people define success as winning or being better than others. They are always comparing themselves with others and don't feel successful unless they view themselves as performing better than others. Anything short of victory is failure and indicates to them that they are inferior.

Historically, several different labels have been attached to the two major classes of achievement goal orientations. *Mastery* and *task* have been used interchangeably by various theorists and researchers, as have *ego* and *performance* (e.g., Ames 1992a, 1992b; Duda and Whitehead 1998; Dweck 1986; Midgely et al. 2000; Nicholls 1989; Roberts, Treasure, and Kavussanu 1997). We find the terms *mastery* and *ego* to be more semantically meaningful in relation to the underlying constructs, as well as the characteristics of the measures developed to assess them (Cumming et al. 2008; Smith, Cumming, and Smoll 2008). Thus, we have chosen these labels in our work.

Motivational Climate

Achievement behavior is influenced by interacting personal and situational factors. Motivational climate is an important situational construct in AGT. Situational factors can predispose individuals to enter particular goal states and, over time, to acquire a disposition toward experiencing mastery or ego goal states. This is influenced, however, by the way in which the situation is structured and success is defined by relevant adults. Ames (1992a, 1992b) described a mastery climate as one in which teachers, coaches, or parents define success in terms of self-improvement, task mastery, and exhibiting maximum effort and dedication. In such a climate, students and athletes tend to adopt adaptive achievement strategies such as selecting challenging tasks, giving maximum effort, persisting in the face of setbacks, and taking pride in personal improvement.

In contrast, an ego-involving climate promotes social comparison as a basis for success judgments and tends to foster an ego achievement orientation. When coaches create an ego climate, they tend to give differential attention to and concentrate positive reinforcement on athletes who are most competent and instrumental to winning, the importance of which is emphasized. Skill development is in the service of winning rather than personal improvement (Duda and Hall 2001).

In both academic and sport settings, a wide range of salutary outcomes have been linked to a mastery-involving motivational climate, including a stronger mastery orientation on the part of participants, greater feelings of enjoyment and satisfaction, stronger intrinsic and self-determination motivation, group cohesion, and lower levels of performance anxiety (Ames and Archer 1988; Carpenter and Morgan 1999; Chi 2004; Walling, Duda, and Chi 1993). Several studies also indicate that creating a mastery climate in academic and physical education settings produces similar effects (e.g., Ames and Archer 1988; Goudas et al. 1995; Papaioannou and Kouli 1999).

Translating Basic Research Findings Into a Coach Intervention

Data from our basic research indicated clear relations between coach behaviors and the reactions of youngsters to their athletic experience. Along with findings from research inspired by AGT, these relations provided a foundation for developing a set of coaching guidelines that formed the basis for an intervention that was initially called Coach Effectiveness Training (Smith, Smoll, and Curtis 1979). Although the intervention we developed in the mid-1970s preceded the development of AGT in the mid-80s (Nicholls 1989), its principles and guidelines were clearly aligned with the promotion of a mastery motivational climate. With the later emergence of AGT and the wealth of research it inspired, we incorporated its principles into an evolved program called the Mastery Approach to Coaching (MAC) that explicitly focuses on the development of a mastery motivational climate. An overview of MAC content and procedures for its implementation is now presented. A more comprehensive discussion of cognitive-behavioral principles and techniques used in conducting psychologically oriented coach training programs appears elsewhere (Smoll and Smith 2015).

Mastery-Oriented Coaching Guidelines and Philosophy of Winning

The MAC program incorporates two major themes. First, it strongly emphasizes the distinction between positive versus aversive control of behavior (Smith 2015). In a series of coaching *dos* and *don'ts* derived from the foundational research on coach behaviors and their effects, coaches are encouraged to increase four specific behaviors—positive reinforcement, mistake-contingent encouragement, corrective instruction given in a positive and encouraging fashion, and sound technical instruction. Coaches are urged to avoid nonreinforcement of positive behaviors, punishment for mistakes, and punitive technical instruction following mistakes. They are also instructed on how to establish team rules and reinforce compliance with them to avoid discipline problems, and to reinforce socially supportive behaviors among team members. These guidelines, which are summarized in table 6.2, are designed to increase positive coach–athlete interactions, enhance team solidarity, reduce fear of failure, and promote a positive atmosphere for skill development.

TABLE 6.2 Summary of Mastery Approach to Coaching Guidelines

I. REACTING TO ATHLETE BEHAVIORS AND GAME SITUATIONS
A. Good plays
Do provide *reinforcement!* Do so immediately. Let the athletes know that you appreciate and value their efforts. Reinforce effort as much as you do results. Look for positive things, reinforce them, and you will see them increase. Remember, whether athletes show it or not, the positive things you say and do remain with them.
Don't take their efforts for granted.
B. Mistakes
Do give *encouragement* immediately after mistakes. That's when the youngster needs your support the most. If you are sure the athlete knows how to correct the mistake, then encouragement alone is sufficient. When appropriate, give *corrective instruction,* but always do so in an encouraging manner. Do this by emphasizing not the bad things that just happened but the good things that will happen if the athlete follows your instruction (the "why" of it). This will make the athlete positively self-motivated to correct the mistakes rather than negatively motivated to avoid failure and your disapproval.
Don't punish when things are going wrong! Punishment isn't just yelling. It can be tone of voice, action, or any indication of disapproval. Athletes respond much better to a positive approach. Fear of failure is reduced if you work to reduce fear of punishment. Indications of displeasure should be limited to clear cases of lack of effort; but, even here, criticize the lack of effort rather than the athlete as a person.
Don't give corrective instruction in a hostile, demeaning, or harsh manner. That is, avoid *punitive instruction.* This is more likely to increase frustration and create resentment than to improve performance. Don't let your good intentions in giving instruction be self-defeating.
C. Misbehaviors, lack of attention
Do maintain order by establishing clear expectations. Emphasize that during a game all members of the team are part of the activity, even those on the bench. Use reinforcement to strengthen team participation. In other words, try to prevent misbehaviors by using the positive approach to strengthen their opposites.

> *continued*

TABLE 6.2 *> continued*

*Don't g*et into the position of having to constantly nag or threaten athletes to prevent chaos. Don't be a drill sergeant. If an athlete refuses to cooperate, deprive him or her of something valued. Don't use physical measures, such as running laps. The idea here is that if you establish clear behavioral guidelines early and work to build team spirit in achieving them, you can avoid having to repeatedly *keep control.* Youngsters want clear guidelines and expectations, but they don't want to be regimented. Try to achieve a healthy balance.
II. GETTING POSITIVE THINGS TO HAPPEN AND CREATING A GOOD LEARNING ATMOSPHERE
Do give technical instruction. Establish your role as a caring and competent teacher. Try to structure participation as a learning experience in which you are going to help the athletes become the best they can be. Always give instruction in a positive way. Satisfy your athletes' desire to improve their skills. Give instruction in a clear, concise manner and, if possible, demonstrate how to do skills correctly.
Do give encouragement. Encourage effort, don't demand results. Use encouragement selectively so that it is meaningful. Be supportive without acting like a cheerleader.
Do concentrate on the activity. Be "in the game" with the athletes. Set a good example for team unity.
Don't give either instruction or encouragement in a sarcastic or degrading manner. Make a point, then leave it. Don't let encouragement become irritating to the athletes.

Reprinted by permission from F.L. Smoll and R.E. Smith, *Mastery Approach to Coaching: A Leadership Guide for Youth Sports* (Seattle: Youth Enrichment in Sports, 2009).

The second important MAC theme is a conception of success as giving maximum effort and becoming the best one can be, rather than an emphasis on winning or outperforming others. MAC coaches are thus encouraged to adopt a four-part philosophy of winning (Smith and Smoll 2012, 27–28):

1. *Winning isn't everything, nor is it the only thing.* Young athletes cannot get the most out of sports if they think that the only objective is to beat their opponents. Although winning is an important goal, it is not the most important objective.

2. *Failure is not the same thing as losing.* It is important that athletes do not view losing as a sign of failure or as a threat to their personal value.

3. *Success is not equivalent to winning.* Neither success nor failure need depend on the outcome of a contest or on a win-loss record. Winning and losing pertain to the outcome of a contest, whereas success and failure do not.

4. *Athletes should be taught that success is found in striving for victory (that is, success is related to commitment and effort).* Athletes should be taught that they are never "losers" if they give maximum effort.

This philosophy is designed to maximize young athletes' enjoyment of sport and their chances of deriving the benefits of participation, partly as a result of combating competitive anxiety (Smith, Smoll, and Passer 2002). Although seeking victory is encouraged, the ultimate importance of winning is reduced relative to other participation motives. In recognition of the inverse relation between enjoyment and post-competition stress, *fun* is highlighted as the paramount objective. The philosophy also promotes separation of the athlete's feelings of self-worth from the game's outcome, which serves to help overcome fear of failure. The mastery-oriented coaching guidelines and philosophy of winning are thus consistent with the procedures designed by Ames (1992a, 1992b) and Epstein (1988, 1989) to create a mastery learning climate in the classroom.

We should note that the principles and techniques cited above that form the core underpinnings of our coach intervention are not restricted to youth sports. Instead, they find applicability in the practices of elite coaches at all levels of competition, including the collegiate level (e.g., Wooden 2003) and professional sports (Carroll, Roth, and Garin 2001). Similar guidelines are appropriately emphasized for coaches at all levels of expertise and competition in the International Sport Coaching Framework (Duffy, Harrington, and Bercial 2013).

MAC Workshop Conduct

During a 75-minute MAC workshop, behavioral guidelines are presented verbally with the aid of animated PowerPoint slides and cartoons illustrating important points. Additionally, a mastery climate is explicitly described, its creation is strongly recommended, and a list of beneficial effects derived from our research is presented. The didactic presentation of MAC principles is augmented by modeling both desirable and undesirable methods of responding to specific situations (e.g., athlete mistakes, performance and effort). Coaches are also invited to role play desired responses.

To reinforce the didactic portions of the workshop, coaches are given a 32-page booklet that highlights the advantages of a mastery motivational climate and provides behavioral guidelines for creating one (Smoll and Smith 2009a). It also supplements the guidelines with concrete suggestions for communicating effectively with young athletes, gaining their respect, and relating effectively to their parents.

A notable finding from our basic research was that coaches had very limited awareness of how often they displayed coach behavior, as indicated by low correlations between observed and coach-rated behaviors (Smith, Smoll, and Curtis 1978). Similar findings occurred in another youth sport observational study (Burton and Tannehill 1987). Thus, an important goal of MAC is to increase coaches' awareness of what they are doing, for no change is likely to occur without it. MAC coaches are taught the use of two proven behavioral-change techniques; namely, behavioral feedback (Edelstein and Eisler 1976; Huberman and O'Brien 1999) and self-monitoring (Crews, Lochbaum, and Karoly 2001; Kanfer and Gaelick-Buys 1991). To obtain feedback, coaches are encouraged to work with their assistants as a team and share descriptions of each other's behaviors. Another feedback procedure involves coaches soliciting input directly from their athletes.

With respect to self-monitoring (observing and recording one's own behavior), the workshop manual contains a brief Coach Self-Report Form (figure 6.2). MAC coaches are instructed to complete the form immediately after practices and games, and they are encouraged to engage in self-monitoring on a regular basis in order to achieve optimal results.

MAC also includes discussion of coach–parent relationships and provides instructions on how to organize and conduct a sport orientation meeting with

---

Figure 6.2   Coach Self-Report Form

Complete this form as soon as possible after a practice or game. Think about what you did, but also about the kinds of situations in which the actions occurred and the kinds of athletes who were involved.

1. When athletes made good plays, approximately what percent of the time did you respond with REINFORCEMENT? _____%

2. When athletes gave good effort (regardless of the outcome), what percent of the time did you respond with REINFORCEMENT? _____%

3. About how many times did you reinforce athletes for displaying good sportsmanship, supporting teammates, and complying with team rules? _____

4. When athletes made mistakes, approximately what percent of the time did you respond with:

   a. A. Encouragement only _____%
   b. B. Corrective instruction given in an encouraging manner _____%

   (Sum of A and B should not exceed 100%)

5. When mistakes were made, did you stress the importance of learning from them? _____Yes _____No

6. Did you emphasize the importance of having fun while practicing or competing? _____Yes _____No

7. Did you tell your athletes that doing their best is all you expect of them? _____Yes _____No

8. Did you communicate that winning is important, but working to improve skills is even more important? _____Yes _____No

9. Did you do or say anything to help your athletes apply what they learned today to other parts of their life (for example, doing the right thing in school, family, or social life)? _____Yes _____No

10. Something to think about: Is there anything you might do differently if you had a chance to coach this practice or game again?

Reprinted by permission from F.L. Smoll and R.E. Smith, *Mastery Approach to Coaching: A Leadership Guide for Youth Sports* (Seattle: Youth Enrichment in Sports, 2009).

parents. Some purposes of the meeting are to inform parents about their responsibilities for contributing to the success of the sport program and to guide them toward working cooperatively and productively with the coach (see Smoll, Cumming, and Smith 2011).

Outcome Research

Sweeping conclusions are often drawn about the efficacy of intervention programs in the absence of anything approximating acceptable scientific evidence. We therefore felt it was important not only to develop an empirical foundation for a coach-training program, but also to measure its effects on coaches and the athletes who play for them. This phase of our research is in accord with the criteria established by the American Psychological Association's Task Force on Psychological Interventions for empirically supported interventions, which requires controlled outcome studies and replication by independent investigators. Randomized control trials (RCTs) involving comparisons between intervention and control groups were regarded as the gold standard for efficacy studies, although replicated single-subject studies were also considered acceptable (Chambless and Hollon 1998).

There is a paucity of controlled RCTs in the Langan, Blake, and Lonsdale (2013) review of 51 scientific articles describing the effectiveness of educational coach interventions that addressed psychosocial outcomes. They found only eight articles that met acceptable standards for RCTs, all of which involved the CET/MAC intervention or a derivative. We now summarize the results of CET and MAC field experiments conducted by our research group in the sports of baseball and basketball, and by other investigators in basketball, soccer, and swimming. For a more comprehensive discussion of the research, see the review by Langan and his colleagues.

Effects on Coach Behaviors

The CET/MAC intervention is designed to positively influence coach behaviors, and these changes, in turn, are thought to mediate other effects of the training on young athletes. A major goal of the intervention is to increase supportive behaviors and reduce aversive coach behaviors so as to create a more positive and enjoyable sport experience for young athletes (see table 6.2). The coach training intervention resulted in observed (CBAS) and athlete-perceived behavioral differences between trained and untrained coaches that were consistent with the CET/MAC principles and behavioral guidelines. Thus, the training program was successful in promoting a more desirable pattern of coach behaviors (Cruz et al. 2016; Lewis, Groom, and Roberts 2014; Smith, Smoll, and Curtis 1979; Smoll, Smith, and Cumming 2007; Sousa et al. 2006; Sousa, Smith, and Cruz 2008).

Motivational Climate

Both the MAC and its historical CET predecessor are explicitly designed to produce a coach-initiated mastery climate and to discourage a "win at all costs" ego climate. Athletes' reports of their team's coach-initiated motivational climate clearly supported the efficacy of the intervention (Smoll, Smith, and Cumming 2007). More exactly, compared with untrained coaches, trained coaches received significantly higher mastery-climate scores and lower ego-climate scores on the Motivational Climate Scale for Youth Sports (Smith, Cumming, and Smoll 2008).

Athlete Attitudes and Perceptions

The positive behaviors encouraged by the CET/MAC research-derived guidelines would be expected to be reflected in more positive dispositions on the part of athletes to their coaches and other aspects of their sport experience. In regard to this, behavioral differences resulting from the training program were accompanied by athlete evaluative responses that favored the trained coaches. They were better liked and rated as better teachers, and their athletes reported more fun playing the sport and a higher level of attraction among teammates (Smith, Smoll, and Curtis 1979). Increases in athletes' perceptions of both task-related and social group cohesion have also been reported for youngsters who played for trained versus untrained coaches (McLaren, Eys, and Murray 2015).

Achievement Goal Orientation in Sports

A major effect of a coach-initiated mastery climate is to promote the development of a mastery achievement goal orientation in young athletes. Research substantiated that differential patterns of change occurred in achievement goal orientations over the course of the season. Male and female athletes who played for trained coaches exhibited increases in mastery goal orientation scores and significant decreases in ego orientation scores. In contrast, athletes who played for control group coaches did not change in their goal orientations from preseason to late season (Smoll, Smith, and Cumming 2007).

Achievement Goal Orientation in School

Paralleling a significant difference between intervention and control groups in sport-related mastery scores, a significant group difference was found on the mastery score of an academic achievement goal scale (Smoll, Smith, and Cumming 2007). This result suggests the importance of assessing generalization effects of sport-related interventions on athletes' functioning in other life domains.

Self-Esteem

We have been interested in self-esteem as both a moderator of athletes' responses to their coaches and to the effects of the intervention on athletes' feelings of self-worth. Our expectation (based in part on the moderator effect shown in our basic research) was that the supportive and instructive behaviors engaged in by CET/MAC coaches would be especially well-received by low-self-esteem athletes. Consistent with a self-esteem enhancement model, children low in self-esteem who played for trained coaches showed significant increases in feelings of self-worth. Youngsters with low self-esteem in the control group did not change (Coatsworth and Conroy 2006; Smith, Smoll, and Curtis 1979; Smoll et al. 1993).

Performance Anxiety

Our initial interest in developing a coach intervention was partly stimulated by concerns that youth sports can place inappropriate pressures on children, thereby causing excessive anxiety. The CET/MAC intervention is designed to create a positive athletic environment that serves to combat competitive anxiety. Research substantiated that young athletes who played for trained coaches showed significant decreases in sport performance anxiety over the course of the season (Conroy and Coatsworth 2004; Smith, Smoll, and Barnett 1995; Smith, Smoll, and Cumming 2007.

Dropout

Sport attrition research shows that a major reason why children say they drop out of programs is aversive coach behaviors and pressures to win. It follows that athletes who play for CET/MAC coaches should be more likely to continue their sport participation. Season-to-season attrition was assessed for youngsters who had played for two groups of coaches. With won–lost records of the groups controlled, the results showed a 26% dropout rate among the control group. In contrast, only 5% of the children who had played for the trained coaches failed to return to the sport program in the next season (Barnett, Smoll, and Smith 1992). In line with this, young athletes who played for trained coaches were more likely to stay engaged on a daily basis in the program (Smoll, Smith, and Cumming 2007).

Summary of Outcome Research

Evidence for the efficacy of the brief CET/MAC intervention has been provided by five different research groups and in both RCTs and single-subject analyses of coaches exposed to the principles. Based on the outcome studies, it appears that coaches can readily apply the empirically derived behavioral principles, and that their application has salutary effects on a range of psychosocial outcome variables in young male and female athletes.

Dissemination

As youth sports continue to grow in scope and popularity, the need for effective coach-training programs is obvious. Likewise, the large coach turnover from year to year creates an ongoing demand for coach education. Our experience in offering more than 500 CET and MAC workshops has shown that coaches are willing to spend time to acquire information that will enhance their ability to provide positive sport experiences for youngsters. Indeed, more than 26,000 coaches have participated in our workshops sponsored by a variety of sport-specific organizations (e.g., US Soccer Federation, Minnesota Hockey) and multi-sport organizations (e.g., YMCA, community recreation departments). Workshops have also been offered as in-service training for physical education teachers and coaches in public school districts.

The need for effective dissemination of empirically supported treatments has been recognized within the fields of medicine (US Institute of Medicine 2001) and clinical psychology (McHugh and Barlow 2010). But the impact of an intervention, no matter how promising, is limited if a means cannot be found to make it accessible to its target population. In order to maximize the distribution of MAC, we have transformed the workshop into a self-instructional format, consisting of a video and an accompanying manual (Smoll and Smith 2009a, 2009b). The 66-minute video presents recorded segments of a live workshop and incorporates several educational procedures (lecture, dynamic interaction, modeling, and role-playing). It is specifically designed to teach the mastery-oriented principles with the aid of animated graphics, photos, and embedded videos. The fully integrated instructional package (video plus manual) is available online at www.y-e-sports.org.

In collaboration with colleagues in the United Kingdom and Europe, we are currently developing another dissemination mechanism that entails teaching coach developers how to present MAC workshops. The approach will involve a workshop leader (a coach developer) playing a MAC DVD to a group of coaches and stopping it at various points for discussion. In addition to the DVD, the developer's module will include a booklet with (a) instructions on how to deliver the program, (b) group-discussion questions geared to the DVD content, (c) supplementary information on the coaching guidelines, and (d) answers to questions that coaches typically ask. In essence, the "train the developer" program will be a manualized coach developer package.

Summary

In concluding this chapter, we wish to affirm our belief that coach-training programs *must* be empirically supported. Indeed, from a social accountability/responsibility perspective, improvement of coach education is best achieved via well-conceived and properly conducted evaluation research (see Lipsey and Cordray 2000).

Several promising programs with reasonable content have attained wide circulation in the United States and abroad (e.g., National Alliance for Youth Sports [www.nays.org], Positive Coaching Alliance [www.positivecoach.org], Positive Coaching Scotland [www.winningscotlandfoundation.org]). The proprietors of the programs have good intentions and deserve credit for increasing awareness of the importance of coach education. To this point, however, these programs have not been subjected to formal evaluations with control conditions. Therefore, despite *claims* of beneficial effects based on sound theoretical underpinnings and empirical findings in other contexts, the needed scientific data that would tell what effects the programs have on coaches and athletes and how well they achieve their objectives do not exist. Now it is entirely possible that systematic outcome research would provide empirical support for the programs, but at this point we do not know which coach behaviors and athlete outcomes they affect (and do not affect) and which characteristics of athletes influence outcomes. For example, in our own research involving baseball players, we found that CET had a strong positive effect on liking for the coach and desire to play for the coach in the future (more so for children who were initially low in self-esteem than those high in self-esteem) but did not increase athletes' liking for the sport of baseball (Smith, Smoll, and Curtis 1979). In a more recent example, a comprehensive and conceptually oriented 6-hour intervention based on AGT and self-determination theory was tested in a massive RCT involving 854 soccer teams and nearly 8,000 10- to 14-year-old athletes in five countries. Results showed that the Empowering Coaching training program reduced observed coach behaviors that produce "disempowering" motivational climates and increased empowering behaviors (Duda 2013; Project PAPA 2016). Athletes rated their coaches as less disempowering and expressed a stronger desire to remain in soccer. Unexpectedly, however, significant differences were not found between intervention and control groups on other targeted outcome variables, including athletes' autonomy, competence, and relatedness; need satisfaction; participation enjoyment; self-esteem; performance anxiety; athlete burnout; and general physical activity. While disappointing, null results such as these provide information needed to make alterations in an intervention that can ultimately enhance its effects, and they should discourage unwarranted claims about a program's efficacy.

Interventions that are labeled "evidence based" by their promoters based merely on "established scientific principles" (for example, AGT or self-determination theory) or on other empirically supported interventions cannot be said to meet the more rigorous requirements of being termed "empirically supported" until they are themselves subjected to controlled experimental tests and shown to be efficacious (American Psychological Association, 1995). Moreover, the scientific quality of any empirical study requires that the intervention procedures be highly standardized across administrators (coach developers) and administrations. Loosely structured intervention protocols that permit variability in administration may produce uneven results. In the end, specific behavioral guidelines that are conveyed and demonstrated in a consistent fashion may yield more positive effects than more general or abstract conceptual principles that are not as readily translated into explicit coach behaviors (Baldwin and Baldwin, 2001).

The principle of empirical validation applies to our work as well. More exactly, the video version of the MAC intervention (Smoll and Smith 2009a, 2009b), though based on (and actually showing) the trainer-administered and empirically supported "live" version, remains to be tested in this manner. To do so in an RCT design, similar groups of coaches would be randomly assigned to either an intervention condition that is led through the digitized workshop presentation or to a control group (ideally one that controlled for attentional effects by being exposed to an alternative presentation on delivering technical instruction of athlete development principles). Relevant outcome variable measures used in our previous studies would be administered at the end of the season and, where appropriate, also at the beginning so that changes could be tested. We are happy to provide the materials needed for such research upon request so that studies can be conducted by different groups of investigators and with differing athlete populations.

Systematic evaluation research is greatly needed to provide scientifically credible information about the efficacy of existing programs. Such efforts will ultimately serve to enhance the quality and value of coach education by enabling delivery of empirically supported training programs.

Chapter 7

Coaching Club and Scholastic Sports

Daniel Gould and Jenny Nalepa

Outside of those who coach sports for children under the age of 12, the vast majority of coaches in the United States and around the world coach athletes 13 to 18 years of age who participate on a wide variety of scholastic or club teams, ranging from highly popular sports such as soccer, basketball, and baseball/softball to more regionally focused sports such as rodeo and skiing. For instance, in the 2014–15 school year over 7,800,000 participants took part in US high school sports (National Federation of State High School Associations, 2015). Whether it be school or club programs, participating in sports has also been found to be the most popular extracurricular activity for youth in this age group (Mahoney, Larson. Eccles, and Lord 2005).

It is not just in North America that youth sports are so popular. Youth sports participation is a worldwide phenomenon. For example, 22 million youth (18.7 males, 2.9 females) are playing soccer worldwide with the greatest number of youth players in Europe, followed by North America, Central America and the Caribbean, South America, Asia, and Africa (FIFA 2007).

Not only do millions of teens take part in scholastic and club sports, but they do so at an important time in their development, both as athletes and as young people. For example, after the age of 12, young people are more capable of understanding competition as adults view it. Most youth in this age group have entered or are going through puberty, so they have greater performance potential. It is in this time period that winning and performance also become more important not only to young people but to many adults in their communities. Finally, participation often becomes more competitive with athletes having to try out for teams and with more attention focused on athletic talent development. At the same time, keeping large numbers of youth involved in sports is beneficial for their health and well-being. With a growing epidemic of obesity and lack of physical activity among youth, scholastic and club sports are seen as critical vehicles for combatting these problems. Therefore, it is imperative that coaches and coach educators understand the opportunities and demands involved in coaching club and scholastic sports.

In this chapter, we discuss coaching athletes in club and scholastic sports. While these two contexts involve athletes of similar ages or even the same athletes at times, it is important to recognize they differ in some important ways. First, scholastic sports are sponsored by schools and for this reason needs to be educationally focused. In addition to developing athletic talent and successful teams, school sports are designed to supplement the school curriculum by providing educational experiences that cannot be achieved in the classroom and by helping keep young people connected to school. The club sports context is different. Although some club sports may have a similar focus on education, many do not. Instead, their primary goal may be athletic talent development. They are also often private businesses that need to make a profit to function, and therefore winning becomes a primary objective to attract more athletes to participate in the club. Typically, however, club sports also have mission statements that speak to holistic athlete development, claiming to develop participants physically, athletically, psychologically, and socially. In the end, long-term athlete development focuses on developing the entire person so scholastic and club coaches have much to learn from the literature focusing on coaching in either context.

We will begin by first describing the physical, social, and emotional characteristics of young athletes in this age group. The research on the effects of scholastic and club sports participation on young people will then be summarized for the purpose of identifying ways to maximize beneficial effects and minimize detrimental ones. Third, the research on best coaching practices for club and scholastic sports will be identified and discussed. Challenges and key issues facing coaches such as managing multiple and potentially conflicting objectives (for example, winning versus fun and personal development, talent development versus mass participation, sports diversification versus specialization, and dealing with sport parents) will be examined. Finally, what coaches need to know to maximize their effectiveness and best coaching practices will be identified.

Characteristics of Scholastic and Club Athletes

One of the most important distinctions of working within the scholastic and club-level contexts is recognizing that this time period is second only to infancy in rate and scope of growth. These changes must be considered when training athletes safely and appropriately.

Physical Characteristics

Young athletes experience many physical changes between the ages of 13 to 18. Most teens have entered puberty by the age of 13, but for significant portions of this time will still be going through the later stages of this critical development process because puberty can span a five-year period. In addition, some young athletes will be late physical maturers and will only be entering puberty at the start of this stage in their lives. Finally, what complicates coaching in this period is that young athletes will often look like their adult counterparts in terms of their physical stature and musculature and respond to some aspects of training in similar ways. However, exercise physiologists and motor development researchers have discovered that while in many ways young athletes in this age range are more similar to adults than to children, they are not adults and often respond to training loads in dissimilar ways. Hence, it is important to keep the old adage that "kids are not miniature adults" in mind even when coaching players who may look and act more like adults. Coaches must use developmentally appropriate training practices and competitive regiments.

A detailed review of the physical development and training capacity of young athletes (ages 13 to 18) is beyond the scope and purpose of this chapter. However, because this information is so important for scholastic and club coaches to know, we have summarized much of this information in the following list (based on Haywood and Getchell [2014], Kenny, Wilmore, and Costill [2012], and Naughton et al. [2000]).

Females

- The greatest increase in height occurs in earlier stages of puberty for girls.
- The average of peak height in girls is achieved at age 16.
- Muscle mass peaks between ages 18 and 20.
- Girls show an increase in body fat after puberty.
- At physical maturity, body fat averages 25% in females.
- Late maturation for girls is associated with shorter height and less weight, a more linear physique, less fat, and generally better performances.
- Early maturing girls have slightly higher maximum oxygen uptake than late maturing girls.
- Girls' peak height velocity is reached, on average, at 12 years.
- Girls tend to stop growing at age 16.

Males

- Early maturers have performance advantages in the early phases of this period. However, late maturers have longer to grow and may have advantages at the end of the period.
- Boys who mature earlier are associated with larger height, weight, fat-free mass, strength, and power.
- The greatest increase in height occurs in later stages of puberty for boys.
- The average of peak height in boys is achieved at age 18.
- The rate of muscle mass increase peaks at puberty.
- Muscle mass peaks between ages 18 and 25.
- Boys show a decrease in body fat after puberty.
- At physical maturity, body fat averages 15% in young males.
- Fat percentage reaches its lowest point at about 16 to 17 years in boys and then gradually rises into young adulthood.
- There is a marked increase in aerobic trainability following puberty.
- Males' peak high velocity is reached on average at age 14.

Both Males and Females

- Just prior to puberty is the greatest rate of height increase, averaging age 12.5 for girls and 14.5 for boys with height continuing to increase at a steady rate until age of full height reached.
- Growth in weight follows the same pattern as height.
- Bones begin to fuse in puberty and become completely fused by the early 20s.
- When compared to adults, the power generated during high intensity exercise is lower in adolescents.
- Higher maximum lactate levels are expected in adolescence.
- Adolescents are somewhat less efficient relative to energy expenditure than are adults.
- While improvements occur in weight-bearing activities, adolescents do not demonstrate adult levels of movement economy.
- Normal levels of physical activity are not associated with bone injuries.
- There is an increase in aerobic trainability.
- Ligaments are stronger than bone, which results in increased risk of epiphyseal fractures.

Recognizing the physical characteristics of high school and club athletes, ages 13 to 18, has a number of coaching role implications. First, the potential for aerobic, anaerobic, and muscular strength trainability is increased during this time period. However, careful monitoring of training volume and intensity is essential because teens are not equivalent to adults on many parameters and may be especially susceptible to overuse injuries. What complicates this matter even more is that the post-puberty athlete is at an optimal time to begin to specialize in one sport. This holds true for the vast majority of sports with the exception of gymnastics and figure skating, where peak performance is often associated with younger years, especially for females. However, adolescents engaging in high volumes of training may be at greater risks of injury than at other stages of development because musculature may be stronger than bones and ligaments, which have not fully fused. Finally, many benefits can be achieved via weight training. However, especially at the early stages (ages 13 to 14), the focus should be on correct technique and lower weights. Careful planning and supervision is absolutely essential, regardless of the young person's age. Lastly, while there are clear patterns of growth and physical development in young people ages 13 to 18, there is tremendous variability. A key role of the coach, then, is to try to plan and monitor training for his or her athletes while at the same time considering individual differences between athletes.

Social–Emotional Characteristics

High school and club athletes do not differ from their child and adult counterparts just physically, they also differ from them socially and emotionally. Writing about youth in this age group in general, leading youth development expert Reed Larson (2012) indicates that recent scientific advances in the study of the brain reveal that adolescents' brain development allow them to have new reasoning and thinking capabilities. This development enables them to engage in higher forms of abstract reasoning, have an increased capacity to think about hypotheticals, take on the perspectives of others, understand systems, develop their decision-making skills, and understand and manage emotions. He goes on to argue that these capacities are biologically driven but these biological changes only signal potential. Youth need opportunities to ignite and develop these capacities, and structured youth activities such as sports, which are intrinsically motivating and allow youth to be fully engaged and challenged, are excellent vehicles for doing so. This has led researchers in youth development and sport psychology to examine what psychological, social, and emotional benefits youth derive from sport participation, detailed in the following list (from Gould and Nalepa [2015]).

Ages 13 to 15

- Can differentiate effort and ability and task difficulty and luck
- Are better able to understand feelings of others and empathize
- Develop community/awareness of others and the common good
- Are concerned about feelings and being liked

- Use multiple sources of information to define self
- Experience greater fluctuations in self-esteem/can have shaky self-esteem
- Work to establish self-identity
- Find self-esteem is vulnerable to peer pressure
- Has friendships predominately based on shared interests and common characteristics
- Can hurt others to feel superior
- May develop body dissatisfaction
- Find peers becoming very important and near peers serving as a source of competence
- Depend on group status and conformity to group norms for social status
- Psychologically distance selves from parents
- See coaches as more important authority figures and parents as less important
- Are able to critically think
- Uses more adult-like coping strategies
- Show increased emotional management

Ages 16 to 17

- Have friendships based on trust and loyalty
- Can better delay gratification
- Become self-directed
- Shift toward use of internal sources of competence information
- Use personal effort to judge competence
- Can better tolerate frustration
- Challenge rules and become less accepting
- Develop greater understanding of multiple domains of self
- Are more capable of expressing feelings
- Are able to think abstractly so can ponder moral dilemmas
- Want leadership roles
- Want autonomy and to engage in decision-making
- Show an increase in peer and social relationships
- Are less influenced by peers
- Are more likely to engage in risky behavior

Reprinted by permission of Springer from D. Gould and J. Nalepa, "Mental Development in the Youth Athlete," in *The Young Tennis Player: Injury Prevention and Treatment*, edited by A.C. Colvin and J.N. Gladstone (New York: Springer, 2015), 37-53.

Participation Effects or Outcomes

Most coaches of scholastic and club athletes and teams feel that sport participation leads to a number of desirable outcomes for the young people who participate. They report outcomes such as enhanced health and well-being, teamwork, competitiveness, and leadership. Critics of the current structure and functioning of scholastic and club sports, however, question these outcomes. Sport sociologist Jay Coakley (2011), for instance, suggests that coaches have been socialized to believe in the great evangelistic myth of American youth sports participation. This myth claims that participants develop a range of highly desirable psychological and social outcomes from mere participation. He argues that youth sports are too adult dominated and controlled, where children become pawns in programs structured to meet adult needs and desires. The result is lost motivation, heightened anxiety, and high levels of burnout.

However, it is not just social scientists who have been critical of the benefits of youth sports participation. The medical community has become increasingly concerned with the physical well-being of scholastic and club athletes, with reports of increasing numbers of overuse injuries, overtraining, and concussive outcomes associated with participation (Powell and Barber-Foss 1999; Rechel, Yard, and Comstock 2008). Luckily, youth development and sport science researchers have been studying these issues and a database is being developed relative to the outcomes of youth sports participation. For example, a recent think tank on youth sports specialization brought experts from a variety of sport science and medicine fields together. Based on their review of the scientific evidence, this panel suggested as a practical guideline that youth should not train and compete for more hours a week than their age (LaPrade et al. 2016).

Psychosocial Outcomes of Participation

Researchers from both youth development and sport psychology have been studying the psychosocial outcomes of sport participation. These studies have typically taken four forms. First, in-depth interviews have been conducted with sport participants and their coaches to determine the perceived effects of participation on young athletes (e.g., Kendellen and Camire 2015). Second, self-report surveys assessing potential outcomes of participation such as learning to give effort, control emotions, or develop teamwork have been administered to large groups of young athletes and sometimes nonparticipants, and comparisons were made between sport participants and nonparticipants (e.g., Larson, Hansen, and Moneta 2006). At other times, outcomes of the athlete surveys have been correlated with variables such as perceptions of coach behavior, how welcoming or caring the sport climate is or intensity of activity involvement (e.g., Gould, Flett, and Lauer 2012; Hansen and Larson 2007). Third, assessments of sport and other extracurricular activity outcomes have been administered longitudinally and comparisons made across time (e.g., across the years of high school involvement [e.g., Eccles and Barber 1999; Eccles, Barber, Stone, and Hunt 2003]). Finally, in a few cases interventions have been conducted where coaches are trained to use specific psychosocial strategies, and then qualitative and quantitative effects of these strategies on athlete development are examined (e.g., Weiss, Bolter, and Kipp 2016).

Several recent reviews of this literature have been completed (Eime et al. 2013; Gould, Cowburn, and Shields 2014) showing that sport participation is associated with a number of positive psychosocial outcomes. Eime and colleagues, for example, concluded,

> there is substantive evidence of many different psychological and social health benefits of participation in sport by children and adolescents. Furthermore, there is a general consensus that participation in sport for children and adolescence is associated with improved psychological and social health. (2013, 19)

They also indicated that because of their social context, team (versus individual) sports are more often associated with beneficial effects and that any beneficial effects are dependent on positive interactions with peers and adults involved in these programs.

Based on their review of the research, Gould and Nalepa (2015) came to the same conclusion as Eime and colleagues (2013) but identified additional factors influencing the relationship. Specifically, Gould and Nalepa (2015) indicated that the results

> clearly show that sports involvement is linked to a number of important benefits like enhanced confidence, academic involvement and success, teamwork, and social skills. These effects are more likely to occur when sports programs identify and target these outcomes, utilize trained coaches who place priority on the development of these attributes, and when task-oriented and caring motivational climates are created by the parents and coaches involved. (10)

The specific beneficial and detrimental psychosocial outcomes of participation are summarized in the following list (Gould, Cowburn and Shields 2014). It should also be noted that more research supports the beneficial versus negative psychosocial outcomes of participation. However, in many ways arguing over the beneficial versus detrimental outcomes of scholastic and club sports participation is a moot question. The real question for coaches in these programs is how they can structure their programs and coach in ways to enhance the beneficial effects of participation and minimize the detriments. As noted sport psychologist and coach educator Rainer Martens (1978) said so many years ago, youth sports participation can be viewed as a double-edged sword that can cut two ways. Participation may have either positive (even very positive) or negative (even very negative) effects. Most important, these effects are dependent on those who wield the sword—chief among them is the coach.

Positive Outcomes and Benefits

- Enhanced academic performance (e.g., school grades, homework completion), especially for school sports
- Higher academic aspirations (e.g., number of university applications), especially for school sports
- Increased feelings of confidence and competence
- Greater initiative (effort, identity, and goal-setting)
- The learning of teamwork and social skills
- Enhanced moral functioning

Negative Outcomes and Benefits

- Increased stress and burnout
- A shift from intrinsic to extrinsic motivation
- Increased alcohol consumption, especially for boys' team sports
- Greater rates of negative peer interactions
- Inappropriate adult behaviors
- Lower levels of moral thinking and greater bracketed morality (where one adopts lower moral standards in sport compared to general life)

Physical Outcomes of Participation

There are any number of physical benefits of sport participation. Many of these are summarized in the following list (Pate et al. 2000; Strong et al. 2005 and range from enhanced movement skills and lower body fat to increased fruit and vegetable consumption. However, not all the outcomes are positive. Negative outcomes of scholastic and club sports participation include an increased risk of acute and chronic injuries. As was the case with psychosocial outcomes, physical outcomes are dependent on the quality of coaching and the context in which the young athletes participate. Other things being equal, the positive physical benefits outweigh any negative outcomes.

Physical Outcomes and Benefits

- Higher levels of physical activity
- Enhanced movement skills
- Lower body fat
- Better cardiac health (e.g., lipids, proteins)
- Beneficial effects on skeletal/bone health
- Increased muscular strength and endurance
- Increased aerobic capacity
- Increased fruit and vegetable consumption

- Decreased use of cigarettes, cocaine, and other illegal drugs
- Decreased rates of sexual intercourse

Physical Detriments

- Increased risk of acute injuries (e.g., ACL tear, concussions)
- Increased risk of chronic overtraining injuries (e.g., stress fractures, growth plate injuries)

Best Coaching Practice

It is our experience that the quality of coaching is one of, if not the single most, important factor insuring the benefits of a scholastic or club sports experience. Caring, competent coaches who embrace a philosophy of educational athletics that places emphasis on holistic athlete development and education, versus a singular focus on performance success, are needed (Roberts 2008).

There is also a strong research base supporting best coaching practices for scholastic and club coaches. For example, research shows that coaches whose athletes receive the most desirable psychosocial benefits from their participation create caring and welcoming climates for their athletes (Fry 2010) and are positive in their orientation (Smoll and Smith 2001). On a daily basis they greet all their athletes by name, create psychologically safe environments for participation, and focus on catching them doing things correctly versus constantly criticizing them for errors. They also engage in autonomous supportive coaching that involves focusing on individual self-improvement (not just beating others), allowing their athletes to have input into their training and to make meaningful decisions (Amorose and Anderson-Butcher 2007). Effective coaches also have philosophies that place prime importance on personal and social development, develop strong relationships with their athletes, have strategies for intentionally teaching life skills, and customize their coaching to the life contexts of their athletes (Gould et al. 2007). Finally, these coaches model the psychosocial skills and attributes they want their athletes to develop (Gould, Cowburn, and Pierce 2012).

Other coaching science research has shown that coaches who create task-oriented motivation climates where the focus is on self-improvement, and not merely on comparing players to each other, have teams that are more cohesive (Horn et al. 2012). Vella, Oades, and Crowe (2013), studying adolescents between ages 11 and 18, found that coaches who practiced transformational leadership behaviors had athletes who experienced more positive development outcomes from their sport experience. Specifically, the most influential leadership behaviors of coaches were individual consideration (the coach shows genuine concern for their athletes and gives individual attention), intellectual stimulation (challenges their athletes to be innovative), and appropriate role modeling. Thus, positive development outcomes can occur both in team success and failure when coaches capitalize on teachable moments through individual consideration, intellectual stimulation, and appropriate role modeling.

The research is clear. Club or scholastic coaches have a great influence on the psychological and social outcomes of participation that your athletes develop, especially when intentionally targeting and coaching these skills.

Challenges, Barriers, and Key Issues

While coaching scholastic and club athletes can be very rewarding, there are also numerous challenges that those who coach at this level face. Some of these are discussed next.

Potential Conflicting Motives

Scholastic and club coaches are asked to do much today. These tasks may include fielding winning teams, managing their programs, keeping their athletes safe, developing talented players, providing opportunity for youth of varying ability levels by maintaining large roster sizes, teaching life skills to their athletes, helping athletes develop educationally, fundraising, advancing one's own coaching career, and doing all these things in a fun and enjoyable atmosphere. Balancing these varying objectives is no easy task. For example, a star player breaks a team rule that requires he or she sit out a game. However, the next game is a very important one and sitting the player most likely will result in a loss. What does one do as a coach? The most experienced and effective coaches would sit the player because they understand that while allowing the athlete to play will likely result in a win, doing so also signals to the player that breaking the rules is excusable behavior if you are talented and sends a message to your team that you play favorites.

Another potentially conflicting motive for coaches is balancing concern for one's current athletes and program with one's own upward coaching mobility motives for career advancement. For a coach wanting to move up the ranks to the next level, having a winning program and garnering individual attention is often seen as very important. This can result in a coach using his or her athletes (e.g., pushing them to play when injured, sacrificing long-term athlete development for short-term success on the field or in the gym) or not showing loyalty to his or her head coach or program (e.g., upstaging the head coach). While there are certainly isolated cases where this has been a successful strategy, most experienced coaches who have made it to the top recommend not doing so because such behaviors can damage your reputation. You can be viewed as someone who uses athletes instead of developing players (remember, it is much easier to damage a reputation than build and or repair it), or this strategy backfires because highly regarded established coaches will not recommend you for other positions because you are not seen as a team player. The best way to advance your career is to assume you will coach in your current position for the long term and do the best job possible to build a successful program and develop your athletes. If you do a great coaching job in your current position, people will notice and you will have opportunities to advance. And, if you are an assistant coach, focus on doing your job well and doing whatever you can to help your head coach succeed. By doing so the head coach will become your biggest advocate.

Club sport coaches may also need to balance their coaching duties with running a business or making a living. An elite figure skating coach may coach just four or five junior skaters (all paying for private lessons and ice time). When one skater wants to quit midseason, the coach needs to wrestle with what is in the skater's best interest (e.g., discontinuing) with losing 20 to 25 percent of his or her income for a few months. Similarly, a club soccer program that owns its own facility pays rent or a mortgage all year, so giving athletes an off-season to allow them to rest and recover means the facility will not be used and income will not be generated. Planning is therefore needed to balance what is in the best interest of the athlete while sustaining one's business.

Finally, nothing will eliminate the tough calls associated with contemporary coaching challenges, but if coaches have a well thought-out coaching philosophy that aligns well with their school or club's objectives they will be better prepared to make good decisions. It is also important to educate stakeholders such as players' parents or booster club members about one's coaching philosophy and subsequent rules emanating from it. It is easier to enforce coaching rules that are well known and circulated versus trying to convey one's philosophy in the midst of a controversial coaching situation.

Sport Specialization Versus Diversification

Historically, scholastic athletics in the United States, Canada, and Britain were built on the philosophy of providing opportunities for multisport participation. Sport clubs around the world also encouraged youth to participate in multiple sports, especially in childhood. In recent years, however, there has been a sharp rise in athletes specializing in single sports at the exclusion of other sports, often at early ages. In addition, sports specialization is often associated with higher levels of competition and training intensity. There are many reasons for the increase in sport specialization. Some of these include (1) the perception that to develop expertise, athletes have to amass thousands of hours of deliberate practice; (2) modeling effects with young athletes and their parents emulating the career path stories of elite athletes who started early; (3) the fact that one often obtains better early coaching if one specializes because more experienced coaches often work with the more talented players; (4) the feeling on the part of parents that if their child is going to keep up with the competition and not fall behind, their child needs to specialize early; (5) myths associated with athletic talent development such as if one starts early she or he will have an advantage; (6) scholastic coaches feeling that their athletes need to train year round in one sport if they are to keep up with the competition who are doing so; (7) the economics of youth sports with for-profit sports clubs, private coaching, and personalized private trainers needing year-round customers to keep their businesses viable; (8) parents judging their parenting self-worth on their child's achievements; (9) the increased emphasis of playing scholastic or club sports with the goal of earning a college scholarship; and (10) parents' commitments to allowing children to become all they are capable of being.

Those in the field have both made arguments for and outlined the detriments associated with youth sports specialization (Donnelly 1993; Ewing, Laskey, and Munk 2008; Gould 2010; Hill and Simons 1989; Strachan, Cote, and Dekin 2009). Proponents of sports specialization argue that specializing at an early age allows the child to have better coaching and skill instruction as well as enhanced skill acquisition with deliberate practice accumulation. It helps them develop better time management, structures the use of young person's time in a productive way, and allows the young person to enjoy sports and talent development. Critics contend that these programs make the costs of youth sports soar and places considerable time and travel demands on the child. It is also felt that early intense sport specialization places increased stress and pressure on the young person; often socially isolates them from peers; results in a lost childhood; and may lead to premature identity foreclosure, an increase in physical injuries, lost motivation, and burnout.

Positive Consequences of Sport Specialization

- Better coaching and skill instruction
- Enhanced skill acquisition with deliberate practice accumulation
- Better time management
- Structured use of time in a productive way
- Enjoyment of sports and talent development
- More diverse peer group experiences
- Greater linkages with local community
- Greater integration of sport and family

Negative Consequences of Sport Specialization

- Financially expensive
- Increased time demands
- Greater social isolation
- Loss of childhood
- Increased risk of overuse injuries
- Potential for lost motivation due to demands of training and competition

- Increased stress and burnout
- Premature identity foreclosure

So what does the scientific evidence say about sport specialization? First, additional research in this area is badly needed, but there is enough evidence to draw recommendations. Most sports medicine and science professionals who have reviewed the literature suggest the early sport specialization and year-round training is inappropriate for young athletes under the ages of 13 to 16 because of the risks of overuse injuries, the potential for lost motivation because of demands of training and competition, and chances of increased stress and burnout (Côté, Lidor, and Hackfort 2009; DiFiori et al. 2014; Jayanthi et al. 2013). Instead, these professionals suggest child athletes play a range of sports until late adolescence, when specializing is appropriate for those youth who chose to excel. It is argued that diversifying early sports experiences results in a number of benefits, including allowing the young athlete to develop a range of movement and athletic skill competencies, exposure to different coaches, reduced threat of overuse injuries because different muscle groups are used in the different sports, and facilitating positive youth development because more contexts are experienced. Finally, it is argued that by the age of 16 youth have the cognitive, physical, social, emotional, and motor skills needed to invest their effort and effectively cope with highly specialized training in one sport (Côté, Lidor, and Hackfort 2009).

It must also be remembered that the probability that young athletes will move on to play at the college or professional levels of sport is extremely small. In the United States, for example, NCAA (2016) statistics show that the probability that high school athletes will make it to professional athletics is less than 1% for almost all sports. Judging one's coaching success on taking athletes to the highest levels of sport, then, is a very poor bet. However, scholastic and club coaches can have a huge impact for that vast majority of participants who will not play at the highest levels of competitive sport. Coaches can help these thousands of young people develop movement skills and competencies and set the stage for healthy bodies that can equip a young person for an active, healthy lifestyle.

The message is simple if a coach is interested in scholastic or club coaching. Prior to high school, emphasize sport diversification and use multiple sports experiences to shape children's basic movement competencies and general athletic abilities while keeping their motivation high and helping protect them from athletic injuries and burnout. Once in high school they may choose to play fewer sports then they did when younger, but still play multiple sports. In fact, this is the path taken by most college and professional athletes. If they choose to specialize in one sport, map out definitive seasons so they get down time for rest and recovery. A good rule of thumb is to remember that the athlete should not be training or competing for more hours a week than his or her age (e.g., a 16-year-old should not train and compete for more than 16 hours per week). Do not let them train or compete year round with no time off. Finally, a major responsibility of club and youth coaches is to provide positive youth sports experiences that leave players with healthy bodies and the motivation to stay healthy and physically active for a lifetime.

Sport Parents

Sport parents play an integral but also paradoxical role in scholastic and club sports. Researchers have shown that sport parents play critical functions as role models (e.g., active parents tend to have active children), providers (e.g., sign their children up for programs, transport them), and interpreters (e.g., help their child define success and failure) of their child's youth sports experience (Fredericks and Eccles 2005). At the same time, there seem to be constant media reports of sport parents behaving badly, whether that involves yelling at young players, officials, and coaches or even attacking officials and fighting with one another. Because of bad experiences with a few sport parents, many club and scholastic coaches avoid their players' parents and react by wanting little to do with any of them.

Sport parents have been extensively studied over the last several decades and there have been several reviews of the research (e.g., Holt and Knight 2014; Gould, Cowburn and Pierce, 2012) on the topic. This research shows that sport parenting matters and the parent–athlete–coach relationship is critical to youth sports success. Athletes function best when athlete, coach, and parent attitudes, values, and expectations align. Both developmentally appropriate and inappropriate sport parenting have been linked to athletic success. However, developmentally inappropriate sport parenting often results in parent–child relationship issues, lost motivation, and burnout. In terms of coaching, it is suggested that coaches inform and communicate with their sport parents by setting expectations, providing information, and providing sport education using varied methods of delivery. Coaches should convey to parents that they should also create task-oriented motivational climates and supportive environments for their athletes. Finally, parents should be encouraged to exhibit what have been found to be positive sport parenting behaviors and actions, including providing financial and logistical support and socio-emotional support, exhibiting unconditional love, making sacrifices for their children, holding their children to moral and sportspersonship standards, emphasizing hard work, and maintaining a positive attitude. At the same time, coaches should understand, and through education and policy, work to minimize negative sport parenting behaviors and actions such as focusing on outcome goals, criticizing the children, pressuring the children for results, modeling poor sportspersonship, over-protecting their children, and acting as a coach when not trained as a coach.

As a coach, avoiding athletes' parents is a grave mistake. First, the majority of sport parents, as supported by the literature, do not cause problems and do provide logistical and social–emotional support to their children as well as support program goals. A coach does not want a few problem parents to prevent him or her from utilizing the vast majority of parents to support athlete and program goals. Second, coaches can also use players' parents to assist them in other ways. For example, in getting to know their athletes' parents, a coach may discover that parents have expertise in fundraising or connections that can help secure needed equipment and supplies. Third, parents can provide helpful information to facilitate a better understanding of one's players. Finally, sport parents with whom coaches have cultivated good relationships will often support them directly and indirectly if problems arise with other parents.

While most sport parents are well meaning and have the best interest of their children at heart, they do not always understand the best way to support their children. Therefore, parent education is absolutely necessary to open lines of communication and provide some form of sport education for parents. This can be done in a number of ways. Some coaches, for instance, have found it useful to send letters to all their players' parents welcoming them to the program, thanking them for allowing their child to play, and outlining expectations, rules, and when it is appropriate to contact them.

A successful high school basketball coach used another approach in educating parents. When players made the team the players could only receive their uniforms by having the player and their parents meet with the coach. At this meeting, the coach would not only distribute the uniform but discuss rules, playing time, and expectations with the player and parents together. It also provided an excellent way to get to know the parents and develop a relationship with them.

Still other coaches have found that having parents sign a code of parent conduct useful. These contracts discuss expectations for parent behavior. This is especially useful if the players and coaches also agree to sign such a code.

Finally, other coaches have found conducting a parent orientation program at the start of the season is a good way to educate and open communication channels with athletes' parents. Often this can be combined with a social event where the parents have the opportunity to get to know one another and the coaches. This meeting should be mandatory and occur as soon as possible after the team is chosen, with parents invited individually. It is up to the coach whether players should attend the meeting along with the parents; however, including them may help to further open communication between coaches, parents, and players. Providing a handbook that outlines the coaching philosophy, team objective, and program vision should be given out to parents and used throughout the meeting (Martens 2004).

An agenda for such a meeting might involve a welcome and introductions of the coach and his or her staff as well as the parents, along with logistical information (e.g., practice times and schedules) and basic rules of the sport if the parents have little background with it. An explanation of the coach's philosophy and objectives for the season should include the benefits the athletes should gain from their participation on the team, the coach's methodology for teaching skills, and the belief in the importance of long-term athlete development. Additional information provided during this meeting should include player rules and expectations, playing time expectations, and explanations of when and how to best communicate with the coaches. Parent policies of what is expected of them and guidelines for behavior during practices and competitions should also be included. A question and answer period should also be included, and questions should be invited at any time during the meeting (Martens 2004).

No discussion of the role of parents in scholastic and club sports would be complete without addressing parents who coach their own children. This is a very common practice at the entry level of sports with as many as 90 percent of coaches having children in the programs they coach in. Sport parents who coach their children have not been studied extensively. In one of the few studies conducted to date, Weiss and Fretwell (2005) interviewed father coaches and their sons who participated in U12 soccer. The sons reported both pros and cons to having their fathers coach. Specifically, the boys indicated receiving perks, praise, and technical instruction were all benefits of having their fathers coach, as well as their dad's understanding their ability, providing insider information, involving them in decision-making, and providing them with special attention, quality time, and motivation. Costs perceived by the players included pressure from higher expectations, negative emotional responses, lack of understanding or empathy, conflict, criticism for mistakes, and unfair behavior resulting from their dad not wanting to show favoritism. It was concluded that being coached by one's own father can be cordial or contentious, and father coaches must work hard to define their roles in an effort to avoid role conflict.

So, what does this mean if a coach is also a parent of a young athlete on his or her team? First, it is important for the parent to talk to the child about being his or her coach and how one's behavior might differ in the two roles (e.g., while he loves the child unconditionally as a parent he or she needs to treat all the players on the team equally when coaching). Second, if an assistant coach is available have him or her do more individual coaching with the coach's child. This helps avoid parent–child role conflict. Third, before the season give permission to and ask some other adult close to the team (an assistant coach or a trusted parent of another player) to observe practices and games and identify if the parent coach is unknowingly treating his or her child differently from the other players (e.g., showing favoritism or being harder on him or her).

Implications for Guiding Practice

Millions of teenagers play in scholastic and club sports programs each year. Research has shown that sport can have both positive and negative effects on young people, and competent, knowledgeable coaches with the right philosophy are needed to maximize the benefits of participation. Coaches must be aware of the physical and social–emotional characteristics of the young athletes they coach. Additionally, the physical, psychological, and social effects that their coaching has on young people must be understood. Lastly, coaches must take steps to intentionally employ coaching strategies and approaches that maximize the beneficial and minimize the detrimental effects of sport participation on the young people they coach.

It is essential that scholastic and club coaches receive initial coach education as well as continuing coach education to stay current with developments in the field. Benefits of youth sports are not guaranteed from mere participation. Quality, well-informed coaches are needed to maximize the benefits of and minimize the potential detriments from sport participation. Coaches must understand and continue to learn about adolescent needs and development. The best way to achieve this is through coach education—education focused not only on the technical aspects of the sport but also on adolescent learning and development, health and safety, psychological and social issues, and best administrative and legal practices.

Key best coaching practices that all scholastic and club coaches should be prepared for and be able to do include the following:

• Develop your coaching philosophy and understand why you coach. A coaching philosophy is based on personal values and beliefs about the role of a coach and behaviors toward athletes. A coaching philosophy is created through self-reflection where you determine your core values and the best style for conveying those core values to your players. The most sound coaching philosophies balance the importance you place on optimal performance, development, and experience and helps you maintain perspective when dealing with different challenges throughout your coaching career (Vealey 2005).

• Create a vision for your program and make sure that vision aligns with the values and priorities of the club or school you coach within. As a coach, you should have a vision of what you want to accomplish and how you are going to accomplish it. Gathering information and seeking out others' perspectives help you match your vision to that of the organization you work with. To develop a plan to achieve the vision, you need to write out the specific objectives, implement a goal-mapping program, and create a sense of commitment to vision among coaches, athletes, and parents.

• Embrace clear coaching goals that focus on the technical, physical, social, and emotional development and align with your overall vision for the program. Although the context of scholastic and club sports may differ in the importance of these objectives, both visions should have a long-term goal of assisting with the athletes' long-term development. Short-term goals such as winning and performing should be made compatible with the overall vision of the program.

- Develop and incorporate deliberate strategies for meeting coaching goals. Be intentional in your coaching directly by employing specific coaching strategies and indirectly by creating task-oriented caring climates for your athletes to train and compete in. Task-oriented caring climates can encourage intrinsic motivation and self-confidence and are characterized by a focus on individual improvement, effort, learning, and mastery of tasks (Treasure and Roberts 1995). To create a task-oriented caring climate, coaches should give athletes a role in decision-making, reward athletes for improvement rather than social comparison, and have multiple methods for evaluating personal improvement.

- Build effective relationships with your athletes by creating a caring climate that is characterized by autonomy and supportive coaching. This type of coaching is characterized by giving athletes a sense of control, acknowledging their perspective, offering information, and allowing athletes to be involved in making decisions. Using this approach to coaching gives athletes a sense of self-determination over their actions, which helps to increase intrinsic motivation.

- Ask effective questions versus focusing only on talking at and directing others. Asking effective questions of athletes can help build self-awareness, generate self-responsibility, and create self-beliefs (Whitmore 2009). However, not all questions are effective. Closed-ended questions do not require the athletes to think beyond just "yes" or "no" answers, while open-ended questions require the responders to give more in-depth answers because they must elaborate, clarify, or illustrate. As a coach, you can use open-ended question to challenge their answers while learning more about them and their thoughts and feelings.

- Provide clear rationales for your coaching decisions. Sharing your thoughts and rationale for making decisions will strengthen the athletes' trust in you and will help them understand how your decisions are helping them improve their skills.

- Provide feedback to your athletes. Provide higher ratios of positive versus negative feedback; coaches who provide mostly positive feedback have athletes who like their coaches more, enjoy their athletic experience, and have great team cohesion. Make sure the feedback you give is high in information, succinct, appropriate, and sincere. Providing feedback with high amounts of information tells athletes about the accuracy and success of their performance and gives them specific information for corrections. Information should include specific behaviors that should be performed, the level of proficiency, and the athlete's current level of performance. Feedback should be sincere and appropriate by linking it to a specific behavior or performance. Additionally, feedback should not be focused entirely on outcome, but rather effort, performance, emotional and social skills, and improvement should all be reinforced with positive feedback.

- Educate sport parents and hold them accountable for supporting program goals. This can be done through a parent orientation program at the start of the season as a way to open communication channels with athletes' parents. At this orientation, you can help the parents understand your philosophy and objectives of the program, explain the rules and policies of the team, let parents express their concerns, and foster appropriate parent involvement.

- Anticipate potential challenges and barriers to your coaching such as managing potentially conflicting motives, premature sport specialization, and dealing with sport parents. By anticipating these challenges, you can create a plan for navigating them successfully. Use your coaching philosophy and program vision to assist you in dealing with challenges and barriers.

- Engage in transformational leadership to help your athletes pursue excellence by facilitating their attributes and creating situations that support goals and promote a motivational climate. Transformational leadership consists of modeling desirable behaviors you hope to instill in the athletes, inspiring your athletes, and providing and finding an optimal mixture of athlete support and challenge. You can achieve this by individualizing attention and providing personal recognition, promoting self-efficacy and esteem, instilling a task-oriented climate, and incorporating cognitive, emotional, and technical training.

Summary

Scholastic and club sports provide a wonderful opportunity for millions of young people to not only enjoy participation, but to develop physically, psychologically, and socially. When done right, youth sports can lead to any number of positive outcomes. It is therefore imperative that those who desire to coach scholastic and club athletes understand the physical and psychosocial development of youth in this age group, recognize and be prepared to deal with the challenges that may derail educational athletics, use best coaching practices, and make intentional efforts to both structure the scholastic and club sports environment and to use specific coaching strategies to maximize the likelihood that the benefits of sport participation will outweigh the detriments.

Chapter 8

College and High-Level Amateur Sports

Cecile Reynaud

Coaching at any level is an important role and an exciting task. Whether someone is coaching at the youth level or professionally it is important to understand the expectations for that particular level. At the college and high-level amateur programs there are numerous responsibilities and concepts coaches need to be aware of and, as professionals, it is necessary for them to have a level of expertise in many areas in order to be successful. This chapter will provide an overview of the coaching culture and demands of working with performance-level athletes, namely those at the amateur and collegiate levels of sport, who are striving to become high-performance athletes. The key task-related, context-specific competencies associated with the six primary functional areas as described in the International Sport Coaching Framework (International Council for Coaching Excellence [ICCE] 2013) will be examined in depth to help coaches and coach developers gain a better understanding of the educational and support needs of the amateur and collegiate coaching populations.

Amateur sport programs are typically those in which athletes' sport performance is still developing and where athletes receive little to no compensation for their sport engagement. In some amateur settings, athletes might receive small stipends or school tuition waivers or no compensation at all for participating and playing depending on the nature of the program. In contrast, some but not all coaches at these levels may make very lucrative professional salaries while others will work for stipend or token salaries. Regardless of the compensation level, the roles and responsibilities of the amateur and collegiate coach center on performance skill refinement, athlete development (in and out of sport), and on competitive outcomes.

Beyond the basic demands of amateur coaching, being a collegiate-level coach adds tasks such as recruiting student-athletes into programs, helping the athletes develop as young people while they are living independently for the first time, juggling practice times with academic classes, and monitoring academic progress and eligibility, all while overseeing the details of the athletic program. At this level of sport, not only are coaches working on strategies and tactics for their team, they are also responsible for making sure the total program is on track for success with staff members in other departments who may be working on marketing, promotions, strength training, event management, fundraising, speaking engagements, community involvement, and more (depending on their program and professional goals). Trying to manage a program that operates in a very "complex and ever-changing environment" can be overwhelming (Fletcher and Scott 2009, 127). The challenges and stress of being a collegiate coach can have serious implications for stress and burnout.

> You work so hard it's like your life becomes this program and this team, so I guess I might feel stress in the sense that I don't have a big social network outside of my job and the people I work with. . . . [laughing] I mean, we're supposed to be problem solvers, not people with problems. (Frey 2007, 38)

This quote illustrates one coach's sentiments regarding the demands and expectations of college coaching. Although it is understood that athletics is a domain that is highly conducive to feelings of stress and anxiety, coaches' experiences with stress in this environment have not received significant attention, perhaps because of the misconception that coaches should be solving the problems rather than succumbing to them (Frey 2007, 38). Coaches at the college and amateur level will constantly be interacting with a variety of people—individual athletes, parents, coaches of other teams, athletic trainers, game officials, strength training coaches, administrators, event managers, and game officials—and thus experience high levels of occupational stress. Moreover, coaches might find themselves in the uncomfortable position of having to satisfy various, and possibly conflicting, requests of other people in addition to fulfilling their coaching duties (Frey 2007; Belias et al. 2013; Cushion 2007).

High-Level Amateur Sports

Every sport has an upper level of amateur competition where talented developmental and emerging elite athletes play. Depending on the sport and the setting, these athletes may receive little to no pay and they may even have to pay to participate. At this level, coaches may receive a coaching fee or be able to make a living, depending on the sport and the nature of the coaching situation.

The fact that there is no singular sports ministry or guiding body in the United States has created a unique entrepreneurial system of opportunities for competitive participation in high-level amateur sport. The largest organization that offers highly competitive opportunities for athletes on the elite development pathway is the Amateur Athletic Union (AAU). This nonprofit, multisport organization offers sports for all ages at local, regional, and national levels. There are many other organizations with sport teams and leagues organized for elite amateurs such as USA Swimming and USA Volleyball.

In countries with a sport performance system centralized by a government-based sport ministry, opportunities to participate and coach at the developmental elite level are more likely to be associated with sophisticated club systems. Many amateur sport opportunities can be found with a quick Internet search in a particular city or country.

Collegiate Coaching

Collegiate sports participation is a unique category of high-level amateur competition. The collegiate setting provides a wide range of sport engagement opportunities for students from the fan, recreational, and intramural levels through to high-level and highly selective amateur competition. The scope of this chapter covers coaching at the amateur level, so the collegiate focus will be on the collegiate-sports level that emphasizes competition. Within these types of collegiate programs, coaching staff size varies depending on the sport and program size. Similar to nonscholastic amateur programs, these programs will include a head coach and an assortment of assistant coaches and volunteer coaches.

Dating back to 1852 and the Yale Harvard regatta (Smith 2000), sport in the United States has been intertwined with the collegiate experience. Outside the United States, college- and university-based athletic program opportunities may be less prevalent and much lower profile, while in the United States, collegiate sports rival professional sports, with the most recognized collegiate coaches of high-profile sports earning salaries that make them some of the highest paid professionals in the US university system. Program funding is provided by affiliated universities and they are organized through various sport governing bodies such as the NCAA, NAIA, NJCAA, and others. These teams are administered by an athletic department and compete against other universities organized in numerous conference affiliations. While collegiate sports program models exist in other countries such as Canada and Scotland, the degree of emphasis on collegiate sports within each countries' performance structure varies.

While the National Collegiate Athletic Association (NCAA) is the most recognizable and highly regulated collegiate sport governing body in the United States, there are other collegiate multisport athletic organizations of note. One such program is the National Junior College Athletic Association

(NJCAA), comprised of institutions that offer two-year academic programs. These institutions allow student-athletes to study and compete for two years and earn an associate's degree before moving on, usually to a larger program at a different level. Here they continue to study and compete with two more years of eligibility while pursuing a bachelor's degree. Additional US collegiate sports organizations include the National Association of Intercollegiate Athletics (NAIA) and the National Christian Collegiate Athletic Association (NCCAA). Both provide specific and unique guidelines and rules that collegiate sports programs follow related to student-athlete recruitment, competition schedules, and other related organization structural and philosophical concerns.

EXAMPLES OF US COLLEGIATE-BASED SPORTS ORGANIZATIONS

National Collegiate Athletic Association (NCAA): http://ncaa.org

National Association of Intercollegiate Athletics (NAIA): www.naia.org

National Christian Collegiate Athletic Association (NCCAA): www.thenccaa.org

National Junior Collegiate Athletic Association (NJCAA): www.njcaa.org

California Community College Athletic Association (CCCAA): http://cccaasports.org

As noted, the largest and arguably most complex US collegiate sport system for amateur athletics falls under the umbrella of the NCAA, the National Collegiate Athletic Association. Universities that want to compete for NCAA Championships must adhere to certain sport programming requirements in order to be eligible to participate at each of the three levels. For example, a university competing at the NCAA Division I level must offer a minimum of seven teams for men and seven teams for women and adhere to numerous rules concerning the initial eligibility of prospective student-athletes along with extensive rules and regulations regarding recruiting, practice, and competition regulations as well as financial aid limitations. Divisions II and III also have rules and regulations covering a variety of areas such as the minimum number of teams required along with the recruiting, financial aid, and competition regulations, but they are not quite as extensive. The competitive pressure varies at each of these levels based on the amount of funding provided, so coaches must be aware of the expectations for winning at their particular university.

While not as extensive as the American system, intercollegiate performance sports can also be found in other countries. The level of formal structure varies by country and by sport. In Canada, colleges and universities with intercollegiate-based sports programs may, depending on the sport, belong to one or both of the governing organizations, the Canadian Collegiate Athletic Association and Canadian Interuniversity Sport. Further, men's university-based elite development soccer programs in Mexico are often affiliated with parent professional clubs. Within Southeast Asia, the Philippines has both the National Collegiate Athletic Association (Philippines), which has no relationship with the US-based NCAA, and the University Athletic Association of the Philippines. The former, established in 1924, is composed of 10 colleges and universities. The latter is slightly younger, established in 1938, and is home to eight universities. The British collegiate sports system is based around BUCS, British Universities and Colleges Sport, and is estimated to support over 5,000 teams in 16 different sports across 162 universities. In countries where no formal intercollegiate governing body exists, such as Australia, New Zealand, Japan, and China, intercollegiate sport competition still occurs. In many of these countries where colleges and universities focus on specialized areas of study, sport competition can be found within the specialized government and private universities. Examples include the Nippon Sport Science University in Tokyo, Japan, and GIH, The Swedish School of Sport and Health Sciences, in Stockholm.

Regardless of the system, just as with coaching at other levels, the professional expertise required for effective collegiate and high-level amateur coaching consists of "the consistent application of integrated professional, interpersonal, and intrapersonal knowledge to improve athletes' competence, confidence, connection and character in specific coaching contexts" (Côté and Gilbert 2009, 316). This chapter will focus on examining the key elements for effective coaching within the collegiate and high-level amateur contexts.

Set the Vision and Strategy

While the core elements of the profession are the same regardless of the level of coaching, understanding contextual differences is essential for being successful. Collegiate and high-level amateur sports present a complex mix of motivations and expectations. The following steps will help a coach develop a vision and strategy for success at this level.

Appreciate the Big Picture

Coaches must understand the context and expectations for the particular team they are coaching, whether it is an NCAA Division I team or a high-level amateur or semiprofessional team. The amount of work will usually depend on the funding level, desire of the administration or governing body to prioritize winning, and emphasis placed on development (both personal and sport performance). Before accepting a position within any organization, the expected outcomes need to be clear so the coach can make an informed decision about whether her or his professional coaching philosophy and style are a good fit with the organization. If the organization's commitment is too low or the core philosophies are not aligned, the coach could become frustrated with the lack of financial support and personnel. Likewise, if the expectations are extremely high, the coach will need to understand and be ready to make the commitment of time and effort necessary for developing a successful program.

Grasp the Coaching Position's Alignment and Governance

The move from recreational or youth developmental sports settings into a competitive amateur sport includes many changes, including context-specific written and unwritten rules that govern all facets of the sport. These rules include such things as who can participate, how the sport is played, compensation rules, and sportsmanship guidelines. Knowing and following the rules and regulations of the sport governing body is an essential responsibility of any coach at this level. Some organizations may require coaches to study and pass an exam as a way to ensure a level of competence regarding key rules and regulations. One example of this approach is the mandatory NCAA Division I compliance test that coaches must pass regarding specific conference regulations and rules before being allowed to recruit off-campus.

Conduct a Needs Analysis

A needs analysis can be an important strategy to use when first starting a position with a team and as an annual process to determine what is going well and what the next directions might be. This type of complex process requires time, critical thinking, and reflection. Thus, this is an ideal area for a coach developer to support a coach who is transitioning into a new role. As part of a needs analysis, a coach must make an effort to study the history of the program or team and know the success or lack of success behind it. This type of historical analysis would provide a new coach with information about program resources, sources of support, and areas of weakness. Next, the coach should organize the needs into short- and long-term categories. For each need, also identify the necessary resources as well as the change strategy that will be implemented to meet the need. Short-term needs can typically be addressed first, depending on the required resources. The new coach can also select one or two long-term needs and begin to initiate change in those areas.

Establish a Vision

Based on the experience level of the coach, his or her knowledge of the past, and the expectations of the current administration, the coach should be able to establish a credible vision for the direction of the program. The vision is an aspirational description of what the program will look like in the future and should elicit an emotional response from the reader. A clear vision will also provide the basis for many of the decisions that the coach will need to make (Vallee and Bloom 2005). The vision should be shared with athletes,

137

other coaches in the program, parents, fans, and those who support the program financially. This is another area in which a coach developer can guide a coach. Effective vision statements aren't easily created and often will undergo many revisions. The coach developer can provide feedback and support in this process.

Devise a Strategy

When stepping into a coaching position, it will be important to develop a three- to five-year master plan for the program. Although this could be developed and shared during an interview process to show a vision for the program, it should then be updated annually as a road map for where the program has been and where the coach is working to take it. The plan will also help provide clarity and specifics for the entire scope of the program moving forward.

A master plan should be divided into various areas of the program (budget, staffing, competition goals, recruitment, facilities, etc.), and should include where the program currently stands and the annual incremental improvements the coach is working toward each year. Basic competitive goals for the team or athlete might include "finish in the top three in the conference," "have a 70% win–loss record," "make it to the national championship tournament," and so on. The coach developer can work with the coach to establish goals that are reasonably, progressively higher each year.

The master plan should include staffing needs and ideas for expanding the staff by adding full-time assistants, volunteer assistants, a strength and conditioning coach, a full-time athletic trainer, a sports information specialist, marketing personnel, and others. A coach developer can aid the coach in determining the specific knowledge and competencies necessary for team success (ICCE 2013). Further, as part of a master plan, continued development of the staff should be systematically approached to maximize continued improvement. Coach developers can conduct assessments of coaches and provide feedback for continued development to aid in reflection.

The budget is another area to include in the master plan because expectations for success may be tied to budgetary constraints. A well thought-out and specific master plan is an excellent way to show administrators the reasoning behind certain budget items and why increases in various areas of the budget may be necessary. This could include an increase in travel expenses to enable the team to get better national exposure or in the recruiting budget to be able to do a more thorough job of evaluating recruits by maximizing opportunities to observe them (within the restrictions of the recruiting rules).

Facility and equipment needs are an important part of a long-term plan because many of those areas will be expensive and need to be phased in over time. By breaking down requests for improvements in a facility and upgrading equipment over several years, administrators can plan for the increases ahead of time.

Other areas to consider for inclusion in the master plan may be the predicted number of athletes to be recruited each year, scheduling ideas, fundraising ideas, and much more. Coaches should study every part of the program and each part's strengths and weaknesses as the plan is built. This will also provide a sense of accomplishment as the coach looks back over the years to see what has been done, and will provide direction for the future as the work continues. Table 8.1 provides an example of a planning chart that can be used by a head coach to design a long-term approach to coaching athletes at this level.

TABLE 8.1   Example of a Five-Year Professional Program Development Plan for Coaches

		Year 1	Year 2	Year 3	Year 4	Year 5
Coaching staff	• Paid assistant(s) • Volunteers • G.A.s • Interns • Fifth-year athletes • Past athletes • Future coaches to watch					
Support staff	• Director of operations • Administrative assistant • Secretary • Statistician • Videographer • Athletic trainer • Strength coach • Academic advisor • Nutritionist • Sport psychologist					
Facility (practice and competition)	• Availability • Maintenance needs • Seating • Concessions • Ticket office • Flooring • Lighting					
Facility (ancillary areas)	• Weight room • Locker room • Training room • Academic area • Equipment area • Laundry • Equipment storage					
Office space	• Furniture • Conference room • Whiteboard • Technology • Computers, laptops, tablets					

		Year 1	Year 2	Year 3	Year 4	Year 5
Equipment	• Apparel contract • Sport equipment contract					
Team roster and recruiting	• Current athletes by position and year • Needs by upcoming years • Recruiting services					
Recruiting travel	• Calendar of recruit competition • High school visits • Practices to attend • Budget					
Budget	• Current budget by line item • Ideal budget to be successful					
Schedule	• Conference schedule • Out-of-conference schedule • RPI considerations • Off season					
Team travel	• Mode of travel • Travel party size • International trip					
Camp	• Objectives • Facility • Equipment • Staff • Recruits • Schedule • Housing and meals • Safety					
Home events	• Event staff • Promotions • Marketing • Set up • Match management • Officials • Volunteers					
Employment contract	• Annual or multiyear • Salary • Benefits • Courtesy car • Country club membership • Bonus • Camp • Apparel • Other benefits					
Technology	• Software • Statistical programs • Video review • Recruiting					

> *continued*

TABLE 8.1 *> continued*

		Year 1	Year 2	Year 3	Year 4	Year 5
Consultants	• Sport psychologist • Team-building expert • Nutritionist					
Annual training plan	• Current plan • Next-year plan • Five-year plan					
Booster support group	• Fan support • Education • Travel party • Fundraising					
Fundraising	• Program needs • Plans for raising funds • Endowed scholarships • Naming opportunities					
Community service involvement	• Athletes volunteering • Coaches volunteering • Annual charity support					
Communication	• Newsletters • Websites • Blogs • Twitter • Facebook • Instagram • Other social media • Speaking engagements					

Shape the Environment

Once a clear professional vision and strategy within the collegiate or high-level amateur setting has been determined, it is necessary to create the environment. The most essential element of any successful environment will be the people, both the staff (or colleagues) and the athletes. Careful consideration should be given to both who is bringing recruited to join a program and how. Having a clear philosophy and strategy, as well as understanding one's own strengths will allow a coach to clarify what resources or skills are needed in another. Being able to articulate these things will be an important part of clarifying team member expectations to colleagues and athletes. Consider the following steps when building an environment to support your vision and strategy.

Develop an Action Plan

Once the five-year plan has been developed, the coach should map out the specific steps to take during the next few years. Coach developers can provide assistance in this area by helping coaches create an annual evaluation tool. At the end of each year, every area of the program can be assessed to determine the progress that has been made and what it will take to continue moving forward in terms of success for the athletes and the organization (Vallee and Bloom 2005).

Identify and Recruit Personnel

To be successful, leaders must surround themselves with great people, starting with the coaching staff. Various levels of coaching staff could include the master/head coach, the advanced/senior coach, the coach, and the coaching assistant (ICCE 2013). The leader should search for people who can complement the entire coaching staff with diverse skills and thinking. Regardless of each staff member's strengths, all coaches must present a united stance on the approach to the program as initiated by the head coach. Managing a staff can be one of the more challenging parts of coaching and can certainly be an area where a mentor coach's advice would benefit a developing coach. While a large staff seems like an ideal objective, it could create a situation where a lack of communication can lead to an unpleasant work environment. When applying for a coaching position or hiring someone, coaches should take time to find the best fit for the program. Coach developers can help coaches create tools for checking references and asking good questions during an interview. Above all, staff should know the professional expectations of their positions. If someone understands the philosophy and expectations of the coach and the program, he or she can make an informed decision whether to work there. If for some reason a staff member isn't working out, a coach developer might aid the coach in constructing a plan to improve the staff member's performance. If that is unsuccessful, help the staff member find another job; addition by subtraction is a possibility. A coach developer may also assist the coach in developing a set of staff guidelines such as the following one:

Sample Staff Guidelines to Be Given to Potential Employees:

- Dress and behave professionally
- Keep your office and desk neatly organized
- Give support in front of the team and discuss problems later in private
- Do not socialize with the team
- Do not use profanity with the team
- Maintain regular office hours
- Provide athletes with positive feedback
- Provide head coach with feedback and input
- Make lack of communication an exception
- When in doubt . . . ask

- Refer athletes to the head coach if there is a disagreement
- Keep the head coach informed . . . no surprises
- Instill pride in the athlete, program, and university
- Voice opinion . . . then support the decision

Organize the Setting and Personnel Around a Strong Philosophy

One of the most basic but important concepts a coach must understand and develop is her or his individual coaching philosophy. That philosophy should be the basis for how he or she makes decisions in many areas such as hiring other coaches, recruiting and disciplining athletes, communicating with parents, setting up the training plan, and much more.

The pressures of coaching high-level amateur athletes can be intense, with livelihoods and potential professional playing opportunities on the line. It is easy for development opportunities and responsibilities to get overshadowed by a myopic focus on outcome. Having a clear and personal coaching philosophy that outlines the coach's ideals, values, and beliefs about being a coaching professional and implementing the coach's vision is an essential tool for mindful coaching. This coaching philosophy should be written down and widely distributed. It should be shared during a job interview, with a recruit and her or his parents, and with athletes so they can make an informed decision to play for that coach. The coaching philosophy demonstrates how decisions will be made and what the priorities and ethics are for that particular coach or program. As noted in chapter 2, the coach developer can guide the coach in the development and implementation of this philosophy.

Many young coaches tend to use a coaching style or coaching philosophy similar to the way they were coached. While that may be successful, it will be important for coaches to discover their own style and know the reasons why they are making certain decisions about their program and the direction they want it to go. The individual coaching philosophy becomes apparent when a major decision needs to be made, usually at a critical time in the season, such as whether to suspend an athlete for a disciplinary problem, find another form of discipline, or let them play and go for the win.

The coaching philosophy will most likely change slightly as the coach becomes more experienced and comfortable as the leader of the program. If a coach is struggling with identifying a philosophy, the coach developer might suggest that the coach ask the athletes to write down the coach's philosophy. These perceptions will be an immediate and accurate reflection from the athlete or team of how the coach approaches the game (Bloom, Crumpton, and Anderson 1999; Bloom, Durand-Bush, and Salmela 1997; Côté and Sedgwick 2003).

Athlete Recruitment

At the collegiate and elite amateur level, it is common knowledge that recruiting is the name of the game. Athletes are preparing for high-level performance and are seeking the guidance and opportunities to hone their sport skills. The recruitment of good athletic talent is key for a collegiate program to be successful. Athletic recruitment is a complicated process and is ongoing for any college coaching staff. Not to mention that once an athlete has finally signed a letter of intent to attend a college, she or he is committed to that university, whether or not the coach who recruited the athlete is still there (Hersch 2012).

Developing a solid recruiting philosophy will help a coach narrow down an unlimited number of prospective student-athletes who are available world-wide. After considering the current student-athletes in the program based on positions played, year of eligibility, and future potential, the coaching staff will decide how to best complement that group to make the program stronger each year. Questions that need to be considered in the recruiting process include the following:

- What types of athletes (e.g., tall, quick, great jumper, good ball handler, 3-point shooter, shot maker, having great endurance) do we need to fit into our current group of student-athletes?
- How many scholarships are available in the next few years?
- What are the scholarship or financial-support needs of each athlete being recruited?
- What does the team or squad currently look like? Who is currently injured but scheduled to return?
- Does the incoming player need time to further develop or would he or she be ready to play immediately?
- If recruiting athletes into an academic setting such as a university, what is the academic status of returning student-athletes and prospective student-athletes? Have they maintained their academic eligibility? Are the prospects going to be able to fit into the university academically?

Once some of these questions have been answered, the coaching staff can begin evaluating athletes with the idea of thinking about how they would fit into the program.

Coaches are often aware of and constantly evaluating potential prospects for their program. However, it is important to note that within many of the sport systems, recruiting athletes may be governed by rules and regulations. For example, the NCAA requires every head and assistant coach to take an open-book recruiting certification test each summer that consists of 30 multiple-choice or true–false questions related to NCAA amateurism and recruiting rules. Coaches who don't get at least 80 percent of the questions correct must wait 30 days to take the exam again in order to earn the right to recruit off-campus. The recruiting rules are different for each level in NCAA Division I, II, or III and for the other governing bodies. Example practice exams for the NCAA Division I are available online at http://web1.ncaa.org/coachesTest/exec/practiceexam?division=1.

Another major focus of recruiting is the efficient use of resources—time and money. The amount of the budget available for recruitment purposes will determine how much time a coach will spend on the road evaluating athletes in their practice sessions with their high school or club teams. The budget will also control how many times an athlete can be evaluated (based on rules), how much a coach can spend on official visits for athletes coming to campus, whether there will be trips made internationally, and how many scholarships are available for in-state versus out-of-state athletes. Decisions will need to be made about which venues are the best for recruiting. Would it be better to watch athletes in their practice sessions or watch them in a large tournament or meet with numerous other prospects? Is it important to a particular athlete that someone is always at her or his competition, even though there are, potentially, limits to the number of times a coaching staff can evaluate or watch an athlete during a competitive season?

Once the coach has determined the basics of his or her recruiting needs—type of student-athlete, in-state, international, and other criteria—it is time to put together the recruiting strategy. This is a well thought-out plan to convince the prospects the staff has identified to attend that particular school. This requires a certain amount of marketing and sales experience. How can you sell the university and athletic program to student-athletes every other program is recruiting? What makes a program unique and why should they want to be a part of it? Why is it a good fit for them? How will they fit into the team culture? What is student life like on the campus? Who is the most influencing person in each of the athletes' lives and how does a coach get to know that person? What is the most important factor to each particular athlete in making a decision on which college to attend for the next four years? How can this university and athletic program prepare the recruits for the next phase of their life? Do they want to play professionally after college? How can the coaching staff help them achieve that goal? What do they think of the coaching staff and the coaching in general (Kamphoff and Gill 2008)?

Safeguard and Protect Athletes

Probably the most important part of coaching is to take care of the athletes and staff. Coaches must ensure the program has policies and procedures in place that reduce risks by developing a plan that creates a safe environment for athletes and coaches. This can be done through training and education, establishing boundaries, and responding to any policy violations. While safety in practice and competition is a key, there must also be an awareness of misconduct or inappropriate behavior away from the practice and competition arena.

Coaches and administrators must not only prevent but also recognize, misconduct in sports such as sexual abuse, bullying, hazing, harassment, and any other emotional, physical, and sexual misconduct. There should be ongoing educational programs set up for the athletes so they understand these terms and can assist in assuring the safety of everyone. Athletes should know how and where to ask for help if they are having a problem or see an issue with another athlete or coach, particularly since coaches have sometimes been known to bully athletes (Swigonski, Enneking, and Hendrix 2014). Research has shown that nearly one quarter of collegiate student-athletes show signs of clinical depression, which is comparable to the general college student population (Wolanin et al. 2016). Thus, coaches must be aware of changes in the behavior of their athletes that might indicate mental health issues. This type of emotional intelligence is a skill developed over time and is yet another area in which a coach developer can offer assistance. Further, athletes and staff should report any misconduct or violations to the proper authorities such as the athletic department administration as well as campus or local law enforcement officials. Coaches should report suspicions or allegations to the appropriate law enforcement authorities, cooperate fully with inquiries and investigations, and encourage disclosure among athletes.

Several high-profile programs exist to protect athletes at all levels and to provide training and resources for sport leaders. Programs such as the Canadian Red Cross' Respect in Sport program and Safe Sport International have led the way in expanding the dialogue about athlete abuse in sport and in providing better training and support for the sport community. These efforts have led to programs such as the US Center for SafeSport training, which is mandated for any coach within the US Olympic sport system and who holds a national governing body (NGB) certification or license. Further, this organization compiles a list of those who have been banned from coaching within an NGB for some sort of offense. While this type of training and monitoring is not yet part of all coach education programs or required for being hired, more and more organizations are recognizing the value and importance of such education and monitoring for their professional coaches.

Develop Progress Markers

It is the responsibility of the coach to establish expectations for the team and for each individual athlete on and off the field of play. These expectations should cover a variety of areas such as physical training (e.g., speed, jump height, weight training, etc.), sport-specific measurements (e.g., shooting percentage, rebounds, yards per down, batting percentage, kill percentage, etc.), academic performance (when applicable), and personal conduct. It is critical that statistics and measurements are recorded in practice sessions as well as in competition. This gives a clear view of how all the athletes are progressing, not just those who achieve playing time.

Build Relationships

Not every team that looks good on paper will function well, and over time the challenges and strains of high-level competition can cause stress even among the most cohesive groups. One of the most important things a coach can do toward building a solid program foundation and proactively in planning for inevitable tough patches, is to build and tend to quality relationships with all the individuals on the team.

Manage Personnel Positively

Ask coaches what they do, and most will say they "coach volleyball" or "coach basketball." In reality, coaches don't get a volleyball to do anything. Coaches coach people. While coaches spend a great deal of time learning the X's and O's, techniques, tactics, and game strategy, they should really be devoting more time to learning how to coach people. The first step in this process is for coaches to explore who they are as individuals. Part of this is identifying why they coach and what they hope to achieve. Second, coaches should engage in self-analysis of coaching strengths and weaknesses. Although difficult, coach developers can help coaches engage in this type of critical self-reflection. At this stage, coaches should consider their plan for development and self-care. Once coaches feel like they have a good handle on how they approach life and coaching, they can then turn to the team.

There are a number of strategies coaches can use to positively engage the members of the team. Developing an annual team mission with a group of athletes and staff will go a long way toward helping everyone understand where they want to go athletically and what it will take to get there. The team mission can be posted in the locker room, training facility, at home, in the office, and anywhere the group can be reminded of why they are working so hard at getting better. This will also help establish a healthy team culture of commitment and responsible behavior by everyone. *How to Build and Sustain a Championship Culture: Your Ten-Step Blueprint to Build a Winning Culture of Commitment, Accountability, and Ownership* (Janssen 2014) is an excellent resource for shaping the culture of the overall program.

Team building activities can also be part of a proactive approach and are essential to fostering a well-functioning team. These should be done on a regular basis to build camaraderie and respect for one another. Having a strong sense of togetherness can help bring the team to another level when the going gets tough on the field. There are a number of outstanding books and resources available on this topic.

Nurture Individual Relationships

No matter the sport, a respectful relationship between a coach and an athlete is critical. Coaches should take the time to get to know each of their athletes individually, no matter how large the team, so they can relate to them more positively. Previous research in this area suggests the coach–athlete relationship is related to athlete satisfaction with performance (Jowett and Don Carolis 2003) and team cohesion (Jowett and Chaundy 2004). A critical aspect of this line of research, however, is that this relationship is bi-directional. Both the coach and athlete have a role in the relationship and, thus, the relationship must be developed and fostered over time.

Many coaches don't think they have time to meet with their athletes individually, or they only meet with them at the beginning of the season, at the end of the season, or when things go horribly wrong. A best practice would be to develop a regular meeting time, possibly every two weeks, even if for just a few minutes to talk about classes, family, playing time, watching film, training ideas, or whatever the athlete wants to talk about. The athletes are the biggest asset of the program and coaches must spend time with them. Meetings should be held in an open setting such as outdoors at a picnic table, in an open office, or anywhere the athlete would feel safe meeting and talking with the coach. Coaching staffs might even rotate the athletes they meet with so they have a chance to connect with everyone. It's important, however, that during the meeting athletes feel a sense of genuine interest from the coach, rather than it being just another thing on the coach's to-do list.

Coaching staffs should meet regularly as a group as well. The more the entire staff understands the daily direction of the program, the better it is for everyone. If a coach identifies a lack of direction as an area of weakness, seeking development on management styles, effectively leading small groups, and communication might be of benefit. It is important that the staff meetings include two-way communication, with the assistants being encouraged to share their thoughts. This will not only establish a clear direction, but also serve as an area of growth for all coaches. In this setting, the head coach might take on a mentorship role with the assistants, guiding and directing their self-reflection. Once a plan has been determined and agreed to, the entire staff should emerge from the meeting on the same page with the same message for the team.

Be an Educator

All members of the program should have a good understanding of the basics of the sport and what is needed for the specific outcomes that have been determined by the staff and administration. However, to actually attain those outcomes, the coaches must be educators. A critical element of this role requires educators to put learners first. In other words, to be a coach who is an educator means to put the athlete first. This athlete-centered approach allows coaches to focus on nuances and experiences from the athletes' perspective (Penney 2006). Beyond that, coaches must understand the elements of effective teaching practice. While coaches might be experts in the game, they must also be expert teachers. And to accomplish that, they must also be committed to lifelong learning themselves (Penney 2006).

Lead and Influence

A head coach must be the public face of the team and should work to promote the athletes and program in a large setting such as the athletic department, the university, and the community. It takes a village of individuals to make a program successful. Coaches must educate and fully engage all who have a part in their program. The marketing and promotional staff must understand the vision and mission of the program and how to present them to the community and to fans. The athletic trainer and the strength coach must be included in all phases of the planning to ensure athletes can reach their maximum potential. However, the trainer and strength coach also must give special attention to preventing injuries as much as possible, and minimize overtraining tendencies by the coaching staff or individual athletes.

Conduct Practices and Structure Competitions

The day-to-day nature of practice can make it feel routine and thus simple; however, quality leadership in coaching is based on careful planning. Practice needs to be purpose-based planning in alignment with the program vision and strategy, needs to be flexible, and needs to be frequently evaluated and adjusted. One area that is often overlooked in planning is competition. While day-of strategy against the competition plans are routine, expert coaches plan for and use competition to build and develop their athletes' skills.

Guide Practice

Fun is such an important concept in sport, but it is usually the first thing that coaches forget about. Every level of athlete competes because it is fun. This may be a challenge for collegiate coaches to grasp, but perhaps considering a different conceptualization of fun could be helpful. In previous literature, the term fun as used by athletes has been connected to positive affect (Wankel and Sefton 1989). Positive affect can come from successful experiences, quality interpersonal interactions, and self-improvement. It is imperative that coaches keep this in mind as they prepare training sessions and plan for a competitive schedule. This concept should be included in every aspect of the program to attempt to maintain a positive environment. If the process is not fun, the outcome will usually not be good or be as enjoyable as it could have been. Unfortunately, if the season is not going as planned, the last thing a coach thinks about is keeping the process fun. Even though there may have been some losses or injuries, if coaches can remember to keep the practice environment fun, while keeping it competitive and upholding the standards of performance, athletes will work harder and continue to enjoy the daily process. This, of course, requires continual reflection and planning by the coach.

While the primary objective of every college athletic department or competitive amateur team is winning, the daily process is what drives that outcome. Successful coaches should concentrate on making every day as productive and enjoyable as possible. It shouldn't only be about winning or losing the last competition of the year, but enjoying the daily journey or the process. This type of mastery focus has been connected to athlete persistence and effort through adversity (Duda 1989) and can certainly be adopted by the coach as an approach to setting the environment. Coach developers can support coaches in this role by providing strategies around developing a mastery-oriented motivational climate (Ntoumanis and Biddle 1999).

From a physical training perspective, understanding the principles of periodization and the importance of setting up an annual training plan, known as a Bompa chart (figure 8.1), will give athletes and coaches the edge to achieving peak performances and the right time of the year. Coaches must also be cognizant of preparing athletes for the next level, whether that is for a transition to a national team, a professional team, or a nonplaying career. In order to prepare the athletes and team for the highest level of success, coaches must have a good understanding of exercise physiology. They should know the principles of training, the body's energy systems and how they work, proper nutrition and hydration for athletes, the scientific need for recovery, and the negatives of overtraining. This knowledge will provide coaches with the background needed to run a high-level program. Coach

The annual plan					
Phases of training	Preparatory			Competitive		Transition
Sub-phases	General preparation	Specific preparation	Pre-competitive	Competitive	Transition
Macro-cycles					
Micro-cycles					

FIGURE 8.1   A sample periodization planning template.

Reprinted by permission from T. Bompa and C.A. Buzzichelli, *Periodization Training for Sports*, 3rd ed. (Champaign, IL: Human Kinetics, 2015), 90.

developers can consolidate some of this information to make it easier for coaches to consume, but coaches are responsible for integrating this knowledge into the overall training environment.

Structure Competitive Experiences

There is a science to scheduling with the goal of having a team or athlete peak at the right time of the year. If coaches are responsible for creating their own schedule, they will need to consider a variety of issues such as the experience level of their team (freshmen or seniors, rookies or all-stars), balancing home and away events, marketing opportunities to promote key opponents, availability of the facility, and other activities taking place in the community during that time. Does the team need to build confidence by winning early or do they need to play the toughest competition they can find and learn from it early? Coaches will likely be planning schedules in advance, so considering the overall budget and team dynamics will require communication with the administration and many others in the athletic department.

Read and React to the Field

Coaching is a hands on profession with many in-the-moment opportunities in practice and competition that require fast and accurate assessment and decision-making. A fundamental understanding of sport psychology, quality record keeping. and studying opponents creates a foundation from which a coach can appropriately read and react to the field when making essential preparation decisions.

Mental Skills

Having a basic knowledge of sport psychology concepts can contribute greatly to a coach's ability to run a successful program. Some of these concepts include, but are not limited to, goal setting for an athlete or team, concentration skills and how to maintain focus, athlete motivation for training and competition, managing stress and relaxation techniques, the use of imagery, building confidence and positive self-talk for athletes, as well as the importance of team cohesion through team-building activities. Knowledge of these various areas would enable a coach to teach mental skills necessary for their athletes to perform consistently in training and competition and to help each person realize their potential as athletes.

Sport psychology is a complex field, so it would be ideal if a program could hire a trained professional to work with the group of athletes throughout the year. Many colleges have academic programs in sport psychology and could be approached for assistance with providing services to athletes. Doctoral and master's students are always looking for opportunities to observe teams and coaches. It is still, however, the role of the coach to develop relationships with graduate students who become involved with the team, and monitor the activities the students are initiating with the team. A first step could be to have the mental performance consultant work with the coach by observing training sessions and competition from the beginning of the season. The coach would need to be receptive to the observations and suggestions being made by the consultant on a daily or weekly basis. This would serve as an incredible opportunity for growth for a coach who intends to be in coaching for a long time. Individual athletes may want or need to work with the consultant on an individual basis with the approval of the coach. Coaches at this level are interested in providing whatever resources necessary for the athletes to reach their potential, and sometimes this involves seeking others with a greater expertise to support the athletes.

Record and Evaluate

Collegiate coaches are also aware of how beneficial technology can be in the training environment. Be aware of the best software programs for keeping statistics and video review for your particular sport. The use of video and statistics in practice sessions are some of the best tools for learning. They can also be used in preparing for competition, in the area of scouting, and in the development of game plans for opponents. Knowledge of motor learning concepts will assist a coach in creating sound practice opportunities that challenge athletes to improve in a positive setting. Providing appropriate and effective feedback, properly setting up a structured training environment, knowing whether a skill is open or closed, paying attention to the environment, and controlling the specificity of training are all areas that are key to running a successful program. The use of video can aid in this type of evaluation. Using video in practice also allows nonstarters the opportunity to study themselves in drills and scrimmages. If they are expected to improve, they will need this feedback as much as any of the other athletes.

The use of a "competitive cauldron" in training is an excellent tool for athlete development. It is a method of ranking players in various fitness categories and drills. The rankings are primarily used to motivate players to get better. Secondarily, they allow the players to evaluate their strengths and weaknesses and, along with the coach, decide on a course of action to improve parts of their game that need it. See more on this tool at http://competitive-cauldron.com.

Make Decisions and Adjustments

Coaches want to be able to make sound decisions using data to adjust training schedules and intensity. Keeping records of all training sessions and competition data each year can provide a history to help guide coaches in the future. If the annual training plan was a success the past year, it should be adjusted for the next season with attention to the level of the athletes in the program. Strong coaches will be ready to make decisions and adjustments in their plans to always have their team at their best. Chapter 18 will further address ways in which coaches can use technology to better inform their coaching decisions and practices.

Respond With Sensitivity to Wider Events

Be aware of what is happening around the team and in the community. As athletes of this age are developing a sense of community and their contribution to a larger society, it's part of a coach's role to ensure athletes are developing a sensitivity to the needs of others. A coach can support this type of civic engagement by committing to taking time to give back to the community and support a local or national charity. Athletes can be great role models for children and should be encouraged to promote their program and sport while helping others.

Learn and Reflect

In addition to quality planning and in-the-moment coaching, being a professional coach requires the skills to assess, evaluate, and refine plans. Unfortunately, while these skills are often applied to the training and preparation of athletes' elements of coaching, many professionals overlook applying these same principles to their own actions, skills, and knowledge development. Coaches who are unable to reflect on their own professional coaching and who are not dedicated to enhancing and learning as leaders and teachers are doomed to repeat the same mistakes or worse, be unable to grow and evolve. Self-awareness, active reflection habits, and a dedication to innovation are essential elements of quality professional development.

Develop Professionally

An important part of being a professional coach in the elite sport setting is belonging to a national or international coaches' association for the coach's particular sport. Examples include the American Volleyball Coaches Association (AVCA), National Soccer Coaches Association of America (NSCAA), US Track & Field and Cross Country Coaches Association (USTFCCCA), Canadian Coaches Association (CAC), Sports Coach UK, or a regional chapter of the Deutscher Fussball-Bund. Members of these professional organizations will have access to extensive educational materials, annual conventions, coaches' clinics, webinars, and a large resource of videos, books, DVDs, and more. Attending an annual convention is a great way for coaches to network, learn, observe, and grow professionally from coaches in their sport ranging from young amateur levels to high school, college, international, and professional leagues. This type of mediated development is critically important for professional coaches.

Innovate

It is also necessary for professional coaches to attend to other aspects outside the particular sport being coached. For example, soccer coaches should study basketball, football, and hockey for different ways of training and playing the game. Watch other coaches and how they manage personnel and game situations. Read books on sales and learn how to better promote a program. Learn motivational techniques and leadership styles to keep coaching fresh. Observe others in a variety of leadership roles. Take what you can from their success and apply it to the particular situation in a program. This type of continued development can certainly be aided through a mentor coach or personal coach developer. These individuals can help facilitate meaning-making of various situations and provide the appropriate reflective tools for optimal growth. Don't be afraid to try something new in training or competition. Become an expert in the sport and change the game.

Evaluate the Program

At the end of every season it is important to evaluate the program. This evaluation should be comprehensive and include the training methods, the training and competition schedule, as well as the entire coaching staff, the athletes, and the support staff. Getting feedback from a variety of sources such as the administrators, parents, athletes, and others will make the program stronger if the coach is willing to listen to the comments and make needed changes.

The evaluation methods can vary from written surveys to individual meetings and much more. While the evaluation of the overall program is important, another key component is the effectiveness of the coach. The United States Olympic Committee (USOC) has an extensive coach effectiveness tool that contains several forms: one for the athlete to evaluate the coach, one for the national governing body to evaluate the coach, and one for a self-assessment of the coach. The self-assessment portion contains eight items under task effectiveness, thirteen items under interpersonal assessment, and four items under performance analysis. This entire tool can be found in appendix A.

Work–Life Balance

Coaching is a labor- and time-intensive profession. It will be important to develop a time-management plan so coaches can do everything they need to do with coaching and still take time for themselves, family, and friends. They will need to schedule their days to get office work done at the best time for them, which may be early morning or after team practice. They should make sure to allow drop-in time for athletes and other issues as they arise. Scheduling short, regular meetings every two weeks with individual athletes will help manage time more predictably. The NCAA has published an excellent resource on work–life balance (www.ncaa.org/sites/default/files/aMatterOfBalanceHandbook.pdf) to help coaches understand the importance of and to practice a healthy work–life balance. This balance has even more importance if they plan to stay in coaching for a long time.

Summary

Coaching high-performance athletes within the collegiate and amateur settings presents the professional coach with a unique blend of developmental and competitive-based challenges. Striving to create a training plan to maximize both player growth and elicit peak performance requires a professional with a clear understanding of the foundation needed for success and an understanding of what it takes to be successful at the next level. Developing a clear understanding of the demands of high-level amateur and collegiate coaching environments and ensuring that coaches have both the necessary preparation and resources for success are essential elements for creating a system that allows athletes to excel in both the short- and long-term sport context.

Chapter 9

Coach Education of Professional- and Olympic-Level Coaches

Cameron Kiosoglous

The Olympic and professional coach settings are highly complex and unique in their own right. Thus, this chapter attempts to establish a better understanding of the professional and Olympic coach settings so coach educators and developers can better support professionals at these levels. The chapter focuses on evaluating coaching success at the professional and Olympic level of sport while accounting for the number of external factors that severely affect a coach's ability to be successful. This chapter attempts to highlight the challenges and complexities of coaching at the professional and Olympic level and offer suggestions for the coach to be successful and explore how and where coach educators can support and provide better resources for these coaches' success. Further, this chapter will explore what coaches need to know to excel in coaching at the professional and Olympic level of sport and what makes coaching at this level unique. Understanding the coaching context is not unique to the Olympic and professional levels of coaching. However, defining the context of sport at this level is differentiated by the level of complexity that comes with professionalization. Coaching is often described as an endless process of problem solving. Included here are examples from coaches, coach educators, and coach developers that provide insight into dynamics of working as a coach at the professional and Olympic level of competition in sport.

The following key terms as used in this chapter are defined next:

- The *professional level* is considered a level at which athletes are being paid full-time to compete at the highest level in their sport such as basketball,

Premiere League Soccer, international-level cricket, and rugby and sports in the United States such as American football, baseball, and ice hockey.

• The *Olympic level* encompasses a context in which athletes are in pursuit of competition at the Olympic Games.

• *Elite coaching* is used in this chapter as a reference to sport that includes the professional and Olympic levels. The highest level of sport competition is a fundamental component of the elite sport coaching context (Trudel and Gilbert 2006). This level includes some college athletics in many countries, national and Olympic teams, and professional sport.

• *Context* is defined as the factors outside of the control of the athlete or coach. These factors include everything from resources to the environment, such as policies, procedures, and funding.

• *Coaching success* at the Olympic and professional level of sport, specifically in this chapter, is more broadly referencing the multitude of factors that affect the evaluation of a coach, rather than just wins and losses.

• *Deliberate practice* is planned, highly structured, and effortful activity with an expressed desire for improvement.

Defining and Understanding the Context of Professional and Olympic Sports

The highest level of sport competition is a fundamental component of the elite sport coaching context (Trudel and Gilbert 2006). This level includes some college athletics in many countries, national and Olympic teams, and professional sport. One distinction in the context of elite sport is defining participation versus performance. Participation coaching is distinctive because competition performance is not emphasized, and participants are less intensively engaged with the sport, goals are short term, activities are fun, and outcomes are health-related. Performance coaching is a more intensive commitment to a program preparing for competition and requires influencing variables to produce peak performance. For coaches at the professional and Olympic level, success is linked to future financial support relative to other nations' or programs' budgets and performance targets (Green and Houlihan 2005).

The elite coaching context is an environment with many complex interrelated factors acting simultaneously (Côté, Salmela, and Russell 1995; Jones, Armour, and Potrac 2002; Mallett and Côté 2006; Martens, Vealey, and Burton 1990; Nash, Sproule, and Horton 2011; Partington 1988; Potrac, Jones, and Armour 2002; Saury and Durand 1998; Schinke, Bloom, and Salmela 1995; Woodman 1993). Côté, Salmela, and Russell (1995) identified organization, competition, and training as three components of elite coaching and highlighted that working conditions are a vital dimension of the elite-coaching context. Elite-level coaches require a competence and confidence in applying their coaching knowledge that needs to be constantly advancing to stay competitive and to address the ongoing challenges that are required to pursue Olympic success (Partington 1988). Interpersonal expertise is also a requirement for the elite coach to manage, guide, and develop aspiring and elite athletes (Bloom and Salmela 1998; Bowes and Jones 2006; Cushion, Armour, and Jones 2006; Gould, Giannini, Krane, and Hodge 1990; Jones and Wallace 2005; Poczwardowski, Barott, and Henschen 2002). In addition to the communications needed to share the appropriate coaching knowledge to manage athlete logistics, elite coaches have an administrative and political responsibility that is far reaching and a significant aspect of producing international and Olympic success (Martens, Vealey, and Burton 1990).

Understanding context in a sport environment such as the National Football League (NFL) can help explain the performance of different teams. A successful franchise such as the New England Patriots, who have won multiple NFL championships since 2000 (through the Tom Brady, Bill Belichick, and Robert Kraft eras) represents a model of consistency, perseverance, and winning. The Dallas Cowboys football team may still maintain the most recognizable brand in the NFL, sharing the top rankings with other teams like Manchester United, the New York Yankees, and the Olympic Rings. Perhaps one of the most profitable franchises in the NFL is the Washington Redskins. Despite having high turnover of coaches and key players (including at the quarterback position), limited success on the field, and one of the largest NFL stadiums, it continues to be a profitable business venture for owner Dan Snyder.

Coaching at the professional and Olympic level inherently comes with added pressure. One cause of this pressure is the intense rivalries that accompany this level. It's not that there aren't rivalries at other levels of sport, but professional and Olympic events tend to bring greater media attention. Examples of rivalries at the highest level of sport include the Major League Baseball rivalry between the New York Yankees and the Boston Red Sox, the NFL rivalry between the Washington Redskins and the Dallas Cowboys, the international rugby rivalry between the Australian Wallabies and the New Zealand All Blacks, or even more historic rivalries like the English and French in sports such as soccer.

Being under the constant microscope of the media is another added pressure at the professional and Olympic level of sport. Coaches not only have to manage their profile through media attention, but they must also be aware of how the media may affect athletes and, in turn, their performance. There are examples of athletes at this level getting into trouble with the law (yet another factor that is more prevalent for athletes at the highest level), which ultimately results in media attention. Athletes such as Michael Phelps, Marion Jones, Tiger Woods, Lance Armstrong, Michael Vick, Ben Johnson, OJ Simpson, and Alex Rodriguez are all examples of great athletes who have made decisions that became media firestorms, which will ultimately cloud their legacy as athletes. Understanding the context, however, is only one component of the picture. Coaches must also consider the lifetime of learning that has occurred at the individual athlete level.

Understanding Deliberate Practice in the Context of High-Performance Coaching

Understanding factors that predict performance dates back to the first social scientific study on genius and greatness (Simonton 1994). Galton (1869) explored how excellence in diverse fields and domains has a common set of causes and found exceptional performance is virtually an inevitable consequence of natural ability, but training and practice are a requirement to reach maximal levels of performance in any domain. Mendel (1865) should be credited as the first to write about the mechanism of heredity in biology and thus gave birth to the study of genetics. Understanding the genetic basis of expert performance in sport is in relative infancy, but it is acknowledged that genetic contribution to performance is enormously influential in an athlete's sporting experience (Côté, Baker, and Abernethy 2007; Howe, Davidson, and Sloboda 1998; Johnson and Tenenbaum 2006; Singer and Janelle 1999).

From ancient times, the understanding of the value of heredity for exceptional athletic performance was evident with the successes of the Diagoras family, who were winners of nine ancient Olympic boxing crowns (Christopher 2008; Findling and Peele 2004; Green 1918). Yet, even with genetics, deliberate practice is required to produce maximal performance in the ideal environment (Ericsson et al. 1993). The expertise literature in sport views the following as complementary rather than competing factors in the development of athletic success; knowledge (French and Thomas 1987; Mann et al. 2007; McPherson and Thomas 1989; Starkes 1987; Thomas and Thomas 1998), perceptual ability (Abernethy 1989; B. Abernethy 1990; Abernethy 1991), biological and physiological characteristics (Thomas and Thomas 1998; Thomas and Thomas 1994), psychological characteristics (Thomas and Thomas 1998), maturation (Baxter-Jones et al. 1995; Boucher and Mutimer 1994; Brewer et al. 1992), self-efficacy beliefs (Bandura 1977, 1986, 1990, 1997; Feltz and Lirgg 1998), and practice (Ericsson and Charness 1994; Starkes et al. 1996; Starkes and Helsen 1998; Thomas and Thomas 1994).

The expertise literature is extensive and relevant to the discussion of high-performance coaching because it focuses on optimal human performance, measurable improvement, and getting the best out of oneself and others (Allen 2007; Anderson 1981; Baker, Horton, Robertson-Wilson, and Wall 2003; Bloom 1985; Bryan and Harter 1897, 1899; Chase 1973; Chi et al. 1988; Clancey and Shortliffe 1984; Cornford and Athanasou 1995; De

Groot 1965; Duncker and Lee 1945; Ericsson 1996; Ericsson and Smith 1991; Feltovich, Ford, and Hoffman 1997; Galton 1869; Germain 2011; Hoffman 1992; Klissouras 2001; McPherson and Thomas 1989; Starkes 2000; Starkes and Allard 1993; Starkes and Ericsson 2003). The expertise literature dates back to Münsterberg (1892), a protégé of William Wundt, who developed more efficient workplace processes leading to the foundations of task analysis. Binet (1894) identified that knowledge was a key part of expertise. Bryan and Harter (1897, 1899) found that skill acquisition plateaus, but with suitable incentives and rewards, maximal performance is produced. Taylor (1911) conducted a scientific workplace management time and motion study involving designing more efficient shovels. Thorndike (1921) observed that adults can perform far lower than their maximum even when tasks are frequently carried out.

Claparède (1917) is credited for the thinking-out-loud method of problem solving. De Groot (1946, 1965) extended Binet's work on knowledge and Claparède's problem solving by determining expert performers make better decisions despite having no difference in thought speed, basic memory capacity, and solutions considered by weaker performers. Thinking out loud during the completion of tasks in one's domain of expertise remains a key to mediating superior performance (Chi et al. 1988; Ericsson and Smith 1991; Starkes and Allard 1993). Duncker and Lee (1945) was responsible for the foundations of the core concepts of modern reasoning. Miller (1956, 1994) wrote about chunking large amounts of information into between five and nine smaller chunks. French, Raven, and Cartwright (1959) and Collins and Raven (1969) described the notion of expert power, or influence due to the perception of superior knowledge or experiences. Tichomirov and Poznyanskaza (1966) established the concept of investigating the importance of the visual search in experience-based problem solving. Simon and Barenfeld (1969) analyzed expert behaviors through eye movement to understand the importance of their perceptions in successful decision-making. Chase and Simon (1973) extended Miller's (1956, 1994) findings on expert memory, suggesting that expert perception is superior to that of other performers in that it creates larger chunks (or ways of organizing relevant information) to recode information in order to make effective decisions. Chi (1978) found that the expert performer has metacognitive skill superior to the novice performer when executing effective behaviors. Ericsson and Charness (1994) defined expert performance as an acquisition of complex skills and physiological adaptations. Expert performance is viewed as an extreme case of skill acquisition (Proctor and Dutta 1995; Richman, Gobet, Staszewski, and Simon 1996; Van Lehn 1996). This map of the emergence of the study of expertise in the sport setting leads to the current, widely accepted views on expert performance.

Ericsson and Lehmann (1996) identified three characteristics of expert performance. First, the general capacities of an expert may provide no evidence to predict success in a domain. Second, the superior performance of experts is often very domain specific and transfer outside their narrow area of expertise is surprisingly limited (Djakow, Petrowski, and Rudik 1927; Ericsson 2006; Ericsson and Lehmann 1996; Glaser and Chi 1988). Last, systematic differences between experts and less-proficient individuals nearly always reflect attributes acquired by the experts during their lengthy training and deliberate practice.

Deliberate practice is planned, highly structured, and effortful activity with an expressed desire for improvement (Ericsson et al. 1993). In sport coaching, the pursuit of mastery is an ongoing journey, requiring a commitment to constant improvement and lifelong learning (Gallimore, Gilbert, and Nater 2014). Deliberate practice differentiates itself from other activities such as free play according to four criteria: Deliberate practice

1. includes critical reflection of the activity;
2. focuses on the weaknesses of the performance;
3. looks at specifics when difficulty is encountered or when there are unexpected problems; and
4. is driven by the goal of improvement (Mamede and Schmidt 2004).

Developing Expertise

In general, the amount of deliberate practice has been linked to the performance level of experts of different fields such as music, mathematics, and several sports (Ericsson 1996). Coaching effectiveness is fostered by coaching experience; the development of expertise through deliberate practice is estimated at about 10 years, or 10,000 hours (Erickson et al. 2007; Ericsson et al. 1993). Simon and Chase (1973) found that the 10-year rule is supported by data from a wide range of domains. These sports form a benchmark of optimal performance:

- Archery (DeWeese 2012)
- Biathlon (DeWeese 2012)
- Bobsled (DeWeese 2012)
- Canoe and kayak (DeWeese 2012)
- Field hockey (Helsen et al. 1998)
- Figure skating (Starkes et al. 1996)
- Karate (Hodge and Deakin 1998)
- Long-distance running (Wallingford 1975)
- Mathematics (Gustin 1985)
- Music (Hayes 1981; Sosniak 1985)
- Ski jumping (DeWeese 2012)
- Soccer (Helsen et al. 1998)

- Sport coaching (Baker, Côté, and Abernethy 2003; Côté, Salmela, and Russell 1995; Erickson et al. 2007; Sari and Soyer 2010; Sedgwick et al. 1997; Wiman 2010)
- Swimming (Kalinowski 1985)
- Tennis (Monsaas 1985)
- Weightlifting (DeWeese 2012)
- Wrestling (Hodges and Starkes 1996)

Interestingly, little transfer exists from high-level proficiency in one domain to proficiency in other domains even when the domains seem, intuitively, very similar (Djakow et al. 1927; Ericsson 2006). Reaching an elite level in more than a single domain of activity is very rare (Ericsson and Lehmann 1996). An expert with extensive training in only one domain may reach a similar level in another domain only after undergoing extensive training in the new domain, and this has proven to be one of the most enduring findings in the study of expertise (Glaser and Chi 1988).

The difference between expert and less-skilled subjects is that knowledge is stored differently, not only in terms of quality or quantity of accumulated knowledge but the organization of the knowledge and its representation, which allows for rapid and reliable retrieval (Chi et al. 1988). Novice performance improves until an acceptable level of performance is attained and further improvements are unpredictable. The number of years of experience in a domain is a poor predictor of attained performance (Ericsson and Lehmann 1996). Continued improvement only occurs with deliberate practice activities designed, typically by a teacher, for the sole purpose of effectively improving specific aspects of an individual's performance (Ericsson et al. 1993). The accumulated amount of deliberate practice is closely related to the attained level of performance of many types of experts, such as musicians (Ericsson et al. 1993; Sloboda, Davidson, Howe, and Moore 1996), chess players (Charness, Krampe, and Mayr 1996), and athletes (Starkes et al. 1996).

Human Limitations

Three limits to expert performance are limit of attention, working memory, and long-term working access (Ericsson 2006). A nonexpert performer is able to work on and make decisions about only one unfamiliar task at a time. Nonexpert performers may rapidly move from task to task, but still are only working one task at a time. Nonexpert performers, limited by their environment and access to long-term memory, need more data and knowledge to perform a task than do expert performers. For example, access to long-term memory for nonexpert performers is typically called the "tip of your tongue" phenomenon, in which you know something but you cannot retrieve it (Brown 1991; Brown and MacNeil 1966).

Experts as well appear to derive more from their experiences than do nonexperts (Berliner 1994; Selinger and Crease 2003). In fact, a desire for improvement must exist on the part of the expert (Bloom and Salmela 1998). The construction of professional knowledge is the responsibility of the individual (Jones et al. 2003). Self-reflection is essential for expert performers to monitor and evaluate their own performances and they must design their own training and assimilate new knowledge in order to continue improving (Ericsson 1996; Flavell 1979; Glaser 1996; Wiman 2010). This process of identifying areas for improvement and then planning and implementing strategies for improvement is a cornerstone of deliberate practice.

Expert Coaching

In the sport coaching context, expertise is developed by learning from past coaching experiences and by receiving mentoring from expert coaches (De Marco and McCullick 1997; Sari and Soyer 2010). While no universally agreed measures test expertise, variables such as performance record, world rankings, experience, and some behaviors are evidence of expertise in the sport coaching context (Horton and Deakin 2008). An antecedent of expertise in the sport coaching context is valuing education, and expert coaches are highly educated (Schempp, You, and Clark 1999). De Marco and McCullick (1997) extended the sources of developing expertise of coaches to include making coaching automatic by being more perceptive, recognizing problems more quickly and resolving them immediately, identifying the important issues, gaining more knowledge, engaging in regular self-evaluation, and improving short-term and long-term memory. The following list highlights activities that coaches can use to develop expertise in the high-performance sport coaching context (according to Sari and Soyer [2010]).

Activities to Develop Expertise for Sport Coaches

- Partake in mentoring
- Use self-evaluation
- Deliver clear and proper instructions
- Focus pre-event talks to prioritize strategies
- Set desired goals
- Conduct thorough postevent analysis before drawing concrete conclusions
- Observe masterfully and analyze with completeness
- Believe in your athletes' ability to achieve
- Consider the diversity of your athletes in your training program design
- Set enjoyable and learner-friendly training sessions
- Continue to develop your own coaching style
- Understand your athletes' feelings
- Ask for feedback

- Make plans and control them
- Develop your athletes' leadership skills
- Seek your own coaching learning opportunities such as seminars and resources that cover the latest research and best practices
- See similarities and links in opportunities and make decisions quickly and effectively
- Develop expertise through experience

Despite the growth of the expertise literature, some criticisms have been highlighted. Epstein (2014) extended our understanding of the nature versus nurture argument as it relates to what elevates a person to the elite status in sport. Almost all elite athletes have a genetic advantage that contributes to their elite sporting abilities. He highlighted that research indicates that some experts may take less than 10,000 hours to reach expert status and others will take longer. Ericsson and Pool (2016) also contributed to the research on expertise by minimizing the 10,000-hour rule of developing expertise. They refocus attention toward the concept of building mental representation through deliberate practice. Regardless of one's adoption of a specific theory of expertise, conceptualizing athletes at this level as expert performers does afford the coach a chance to communicate knowledge about the sport at a greater depth than might be possible in other sport contexts. Coaching elite athletes does not, however, ensure winning. In fact, because the skills and capabilities of athletes at this level are so close, it is necessary for coaches at this level to consider how they might define their own coaching success.

Defining Sport Coaching Success

According to the Online Etymology Dictionary, "success" comes from the Latin *successus;* from the 1530s, defined as "a desired result, advance succession, or a happy outcome." Stogdill (1950) discussed success in the context of leadership by making the distinction between an organization and a group. An organization consists of two or more people, at least one of whom is the leader and exerts influence in the pursuit of a specific goal. The organization has a common goal and purpose, and each member has clear roles and responsibilities in pursuit of its outcomes.

Sport coaching success is not covered in the literature like career success, which has a comprehensive range of issues that have been examined relevant to this discussion. Career success is defined as the positive psychological or work-related outcomes or achievements one accumulates (Seibert, Crant, and Kraimer 1999). Upward mobility is a function of contest-mobility (getting ahead by performance and adding value) or sponsor-mobility (getting ahead by whom you know) (Turner 1960). The conceptualization of career success includes the objective measures of success (such as responsibilities, salary, and promotion) and the subjective criteria, starting with satisfaction. Other important elements of judging career achievement (Stebbins 1970) include

- knowing why one is successful (Ng et al. 2005);
- knowing how one is successful (Gunz, Evans, and Jalland 2000); and
- knowing with whom one is successful, including network, mentors, and contacts (Arthur, Inkson, and Pringle 1999).

Defining success in a boundary-less career is more complex than the traditional assumptions. Career success is more than accomplishments within a single organization or in a single position; it transcends organizational membership and consists of a sequence of experiences across organizations and jobs (Arthur, Khapova, and Wilderom 2005; Arthur and Rousseau 1996; Eby, Butts, and Lockwood 2003; Ng et al. 2005).

Grusky (1963) offered an important perspective on sport coaching success in terms of winning percentage of games played in research of Major League Baseball managers, which looked at the cost and disruption from management turnover on organizational effectiveness. The foundation literature on succession planning originates from Gouldner (1954), who documented scenarios when changes in management disrupt operations and organizational efficiency.

The origins of the theories that exist in the literature relating to managing sport coaches' evaluation, succession planning, and management of sporting organizations in times of changing leadership stem back to Grusky (1963). The "common sense" theory states that the decision to change is normally taken following a series of negative sporting results and a change in leadership will result in an improvement in the sporting performance of the team (Kesner and Sebora 1994). The "vicious-cycle" theory upholds that a change of management disrupts the team and has a negative impact on performance, and if a change in leadership is made, it is in order to change strategy, which requires time for the team to learn and adapt to (Rowe et al. 2005). The "ritual scapegoating" theory contends that the role of the manager is not as relevant as the quality of athletes when it comes to explaining sport performance of teams. In this case, removing the coach is more to appease stakeholders and the wider community (Gamson and Scotch 1964). The literature on professional sport performance evaluations is extensive in sports such as American football (Hadley et al. 2000; Mondello and Maxcy 2009; Smart and Wolfe 2003), baseball (Fabianic 1993; Kahn 1993; Porter and Scully 1982; Singell 1993; Smart, Winfree, and Wolfe 2008; Smart and Wolfe 2003), basketball (Fizel and D'itri 1996; Giambatista 2004), ice hockey (Audas, Goddard, and Rowe 2006) and soccer (Dawson and Dobson 2002; Dawson, Dobson, and Gerrard 2000; Picazo-Tadeo and Gonzalez-Gomez 2010; Tena and Forrest 2007).

When a coach's performance is evaluated by his or her athletes' achievement in terms of win and loss records, the coach in the coaching context will be assessed personally and publicly by the relevant individual(s) for rehiring purposes (Mallett and Côté 2006). Coaching success is a function of many factors in the coaching context that include the athletes' and the coach's knowledge, but ultimately wins in competitions is the underlying evaluation (Potrac and Jones 2009). At the Olympic level, medals won is even more important than the number of athletes selected onto the national team and is often used to evaluate the elite coach's performance (Mallett and Côté 2006).

At the professional and Olympic level, coaches and athletes share some qualities that reflect those who are masters of their craft or represent a high level of expertise in their field. These athletes and coaches

- have little time and patience for mediocrity;
- have a competitive edge and unrelenting desire to win;
- have a determination to constantly improve;
- have an incredible capacity to be focused and not be distracted;
- experience large amounts of internal and external pressure to perform; and
- are exposed to unusual levels of activity that can cause distractions.

Côté and Gilbert (2009) stated that "coaching success as measured by team or athlete success is highly dependent on a multitude of unstable variables (athlete skill level, injury rates, competition schedules, officiating, etc.)" (428). Coaching at the highest level is characterized by higher levels of time and emotional commitment, and a greater focus on planning, monitoring, decision-making, and management skills to facilitate control of performance variables in the short, medium, and long-term (Lyle 2002). Mallett and Côté (2006) stated coaches are often held completely responsible for competition results; however, sometimes the coach cannot control some external factors (e.g., inexperienced players, injury, or illness) that can adversely impact competition and or performance. Mallett and Côté (2006) continued by saying

> The evaluation is result driven and clearly focuses on the expected return (medals) on the amount of investment. The evaluation of that investment is understandable in light of the context of high performance sport and its accountability to publicly funded organizations. (214)

Excelling Within This Context

Coaching at the highest level in any sport requires a level of execution of the key elements of coaching effectiveness that is constrained by the smallest degree for error. Coaches need a capacity to create a learning environment for their athletes, and need assistant coaches who are able to perform at their best. The application of coaching knowledge may be more results-oriented at the highest level than at any other level of sport. Underlying the highest level of coaching is a coach's capacity to understand and work within the context of a given coaching environment. Basically, what works at one organization may not always work at another. At the Olympic and professional level, coaches are always seeking some edge over the competition, but even at the top level, the fundamentals are still key. Furthermore, refraining from unethical practices in coaching at this level of sport is an underlying theme that is associated with success.

Team Dynamics

One element of coaching at the highest level that is sometimes overlooked is the interpersonal relationships on a team. For a coach, the question is, Are you coaching a team of champions or a champion team? Different personalities are important to make up a successful group of talented people. As a result, chemistry in the team setting is critical and how athletes come together to be successful is almost always a function of how they respond to adverse situations. After examining thousands of successful sporting teams, Walker (2017) determined that the top sixteen successful sporting dynasties in all of sport were unified in one critical element in each case. It was not team harmony or coaching superiority, nor was it technology or even the best facilities. The critical element was the leadership from within the group of athletes. Thus, coach developers should consider elements of training around team dynamics, leadership, and related concepts.

At the elite level, teamwork is more critical to achieve success as compared to lower levels of competition. This is due to the equality of athlete ability and skills. At lower levels, skilled athletes can dominate a team game more easily than at higher levels, where coaches can negate them through game plans and strategies to expose their limitations. One of the biggest issues we see with Generation Y athletes is the lack of team-member skills. Basic interpersonal skills such as communication, understanding others, and putting the team's values above your own are often not taught at a young age anymore. Younger athletes have experienced skills-focused coaching and this focus has neglected key skills that go beyond how to kick or pass a football.

Career Transition

Another challenge of coaching athletes at the professional and Olympic level is the pressure that accompanies the end of a career. For most professional- and Olympic-level athletes, the daunting question of what is next hangs over their head as they approach the end of their competitive sporting life. For only a small portion is there the prospect of staying in sport as a coach, administrator, or member of the media. The finality of the end of an athlete's sporting career is a problem that is not talked about and often creates pressures not just on the athlete but also on their family, coaches, and other members of the athlete entourage. As a high-profile example, Michael Jordan's decisions at the end of his career is a demonstration of how difficult it can be for an elite athlete to decide to end his or her career. Thus, professional- and Olympic-level coaches must be equipped with tools to support athletes in this time of transition.

Many newcomers to coaching at the professional and Olympic level bring significant expertise as athletes to this context of coaching. Developing a circle of trust, reaching out to mentors, understanding the complexity of the coaching context and lessons from the past are all recommendations from more experienced coaches at the highest level. Coach developers can help coaches who are new to this level through a systematic reflection on what expertise they bring to the professional level and how to leverage that knowledge in their new role. This may include qualities such as understanding what it is like to be an athlete at that level, managing people, or understanding human motivation. Mastering the basics and fundamentals of quality coaching is a critical way of staying grounded for new coaches.

International Context

Coaching across different countries is more or less evolved. Some countries are still chasing physiological advantages through sport science while others have realized that physical ability is only a piece of the puzzle. Within every country, the coaching used has to reflect that country's culture. This is why it is hard for coaches to connect and engage with athletes if they do not understand their cultures.

Mature Athletes

Elite athletes are usually older and, with this life experience, generally have more awareness of what winning or not winning means. This presents challenges around staying focused on what creates best performances and not being distracted by results or other people's opinions. These athletes really do need to know themselves well and what works for them. Then the challenge is to stick to what works and not be distracted by the many social commentators whose view is not accurate. So, elite-level athletes need more support in managing these challenges. Also, these athletes tend to have more opinions on what they need or ideas around how to play and perform in their sport. The coach has to be able to collaborate with them but not be pushed into doing everything the athlete wants. Ultimately, the coach must remain the leader of the program and team.

Mentoring

It is best for new coaches to find mentors whom they trust and who know their coaching philosophy and can help them stay true to their philosophy. Coaches should be conscious about continually developing as a person and practicing what they preach. Coaches should always look outside their sport for new ideas and ways to improve themselves. Coaches can create a coaching group with coaches they respect; technology allows this to easily be done online. The best coaches never think they already have all the answers because coaching is often not about what is right or wrong but how can it be done differently to suit a different situation and athlete.

Continued Development

The fundamental challenge to elite-level coaching is the need to look for every possible 0.1% improvement gain. This can be found in so many areas, but unless coaches are aware of all the factors that create success, they simply do not know where to look or what to look for. Elite coaches must have an in-depth working knowledge of mental capacities and an understanding of how people function. A fairly extensive list of knowledge areas includes biomechanics, physiology, technical skill applied to their unique sport, nutrition, strategies and tactics for their sport, leadership of staff, culture creation, resolving conflict, and problem-solving skills. The best coaches are experienced across all these areas, and even if they appoint chosen experts to manage an area, head coaches still know what they are looking at and for. They are never blind to an issue and should be educated on each of these key areas.

Application in Practice

In order to provide the reader with real-world feedback about coaching at this level, this section of the chapter provides quotes from professional- and Olympic-level coaches about what they believe to be the most important elements to coaching at their level. Of course these comments are nested within their experiences and unique settings, but nevertheless they provide insight into high-performance settings.

Darren Smith: International Triathlon Coach

Some of the best characteristics to get right for the Olympic-level coach are simplicity and to keep confidence in themselves. The variety and shear amount of external input facing coaches is enormous, but the ability to decide on what needs to happen long-term, and be happy to adjust short-term according to their gut feel given the feedback from the athlete, what the coach sees directly, and objective measures such as times/science input and so forth, is a crucial attribute. Coaches need the confidence and strength of character to go on their own path at times when short-term issues arise, or to resist knee-jerk reactions when other programs challenge them. Finally, coaches need to hold the athletes accountable when standards start to slip is another. Leadership is a pretty lonely place to exist at times.

For coaches reaching this level for the first time, be very aware that more is not always better, and "sexy" almost never beats good, consistent work.

Just like the elite athletes who aspire to a world or Olympic medal, there is also not much room to move for the coach from a slightly unbalanced keel for most of the previous years before a major game, so get used to working uncomfortable hours, because if you aren't, then someone else will be. Get a mentor who has been there before, has real engagement with you and, crucially, has an objective view of the world.

Eric Lawson: Professional Ice Hockey, Professional American Football, and Strength and Conditioning Coach

When dealing with elite athletes and other elite coaches, I think that a coach has to have a pedigree. In other words, the athlete has to be aware that the coach has had demonstrable successful experience at the highest level (e.g., has won an Olympic medal, been successful as a pro athlete or coach, etc.). Then, and this is the tricky part, the coach must develop a relationship built upon trust. The athletes begin to sense that the coach is helping them achieve their lofty goals. This can be done in a million different ways. Our defensive coach in Tampa was Craig Ramsay. He has about 40 years of experience as a coach, player, and manager in the NHL. One of his favorite expressions is; "There are no 100%ers." I love that expression because to me it says that you better have a very good intuitive sense of what the athlete or team needs in order to be successful and that the situation is fluid and constantly changing. The pro level is quite a bit different from the Olympic level in many respects. I can't go into that here because I could write a book about the differences.

Bo Hanson: International Sporting Consultant and Olympic Medal–Winning Athlete

This is what I philosophically believe and have now seen to be some patterns of the highest performing coaches in the United States and here in Australia. A lot of our clients have won NCAA championships across many different sports now. In Australia, most clients are head coaches of NRL, AFL, basketball, netball, swimming, cycling, rowing, and other professional sports including the best cricket umpires and NRL officials.

Fundamentally, coaches must know themselves. Self-awareness is the cornerstone of personal effectiveness in any leadership role. Self-awareness for coaches means understanding how they lead, communication style, knowledge of their strengths and limitations, and the ability to structure an environment that plays to their strengths and mitigates their limitations. This includes knowing whom to recruit to support them as assistant coaches and administrative staff. Coaches are leaders and teachers at the core of their roles. High-level coaches must understand their systems they purposefully create to deliver high-performing athletes. The system includes all the necessary pieces of the jigsaw puzzle that fit together. If coaches do not know what their system is, they usually take parts of other successful coach's systems and "bolt" them onto their system, but often bolted on pieces do not fit correctly with the other pieces, and it ends up doing more harm than good. Most of all, coaches *must* understand that they are in the people industry. Sport is played by people, coached by people, and managed by people; if coaches do not understand how to work incredibly well with people who are similar to and different from themselves, they are destined to fail.

An excellent free educational resource is the *Olympic Coach Magazine*, an online journal published three times a year: www.teamusa.org/About-the-USOC/Athlete-Development/Coaching-Education/Coach-E-Magazine.

Summary

This chapter has attempted to examine the complexities of coaching at the professional and Olympic level of sport while accounting for the various external factors that affect the ability for a coach to be successful at that level. Successful coaches are able to identify the complexity and challenges for working at this level. Included here are examples from coaches, coach educators, and coach developers to use in their environments to aid in coach success at the elite level.

Chapter 10

Paralympic Sport Coaching

Gordon A. Bloom

The World Health Organization recently estimated that over one billion individuals have reported some kind of mental or physical disability or impairment (United Nations 2016). In the United States, over 5 million youth live with a disability, with nearly 1 million having a physical disability (Brault 2011). In Canada, it was reported that less than 1% of individuals with a physical disability (age 16+) are involved in organized sport or physical activity programs compared to approximately 31% of Canadians without a disability in the same age group (Sport Canada 2006). There are numerous physical and psychosocial benefits of regular physical activity involvement for all individuals, including a reduced risk of cardiovascular disease, diabetes, osteoporosis, anxiety, and depression (Biddle and Mutrie 2001; Shapiro and Martin 2014; Warburton, Nicol, and Bredin 2006). Physical activity also helps individuals with a disability shift their focus from impairment to accomplishment by highlighting their physical well-being, perceptions of health and independence, pain control, and the maintenance of function (Carvalho and Farkas 2005; Goodwin and Compton 2004).

An important initiative in disability sport was the creation of the Committee on Sport for the Disabled by the United States Olympic Committee in 1986 (DePauw and Gavron 2005; Reid and Prupas 1998). This committee recommended seven key priority areas, including one on coaching athletes with a disability. They concluded that advancing disability sport would require empirical coaching research specific to this domain, as well as attention to the selection and training programs of these coaches (DePauw and Gavron 2005; Reid and Prupas 1998). However, since 1986 when the priority of coaching was identified, little growth in this field has been achieved. For example, Reid and Prupas (1998) conducted a documentary analysis of research in disability sport at which time they reviewed articles from 1986–1996 to assess the progress on the seven key research areas. Among their findings, only 5% of empirical publications pertained to coaching, which led them to conclude: "The coaching area is in dire need of data-based research to assess the effectiveness of coaches' training programs" (Reid and Prupas 1998, 172). More recently, Lee and Porretta (2013) conducted a similar analysis for 2001–2011. Their results indicated that the majority of publications focused on the physiological and biomechanical aspects of disability sport. Compared to the first time period analyzed by Reid and Prupas, it appears that the frequency, percentage, and number of data-based publications on the selection and training of coaches of athletes with a disability decreased from 2001–2011.

Just as there are few empirical articles on coaching in disability sport, there are few practical resources specifically designed for coaches of athletes with a disability. The Coaching Association of Canada (CAC) is a national organization that endeavors to improve the effectiveness of coaching at all levels and types of sport. In fact, coach development programs in the disability sport field offered by the CAC were almost nonexistent prior to 2005. At that time, the CAC published a manual entitled *Coaching Athletes with a Disability*, which was written by a task force composed of administrators and coaches who had extensive involvement in disability sport (Abbott et al. 2005). The purpose of the manual was to provide inexperienced disability sport coaches with basic information, guidelines, and tips to help them coach in this domain. Furthermore, the authors noted that the document was a generic resource that "focuses primarily on aspects that are likely to be encountered by all coaches, regardless of the sport, or the disability" (Abbott et al. 2005, 5). Consequently, this manual did not attend to the various challenges associated with different disabilities or different levels of coaching, including those at an elite level.

The purpose of this chapter is to provide information on coaching elite athletes with physical disabilities. Advancing disability sport requires empirical research specific to the selection and training of coaches, the effectiveness of training programs, and coaches' backgrounds (DePauw and Gavron 2005; Reid and Prupas 1998). Information in this chapter will address the developmental pathways for acquiring knowledge and becoming an elite-level coach for athletes with a physical disability, as well as strategies and behaviors specific to coaching in this context. This includes information designed to develop the athlete as an individual as well as ways to develop the team context. Information in this chapter will not address other specialized coaching contexts, such as individuals with intellectual disabilities (cf. MacDonald, Beck, Erickson, and Côté 2016) or youth sport athletes with physical disabilities (cf. Goodwin 2016) because of their own unique contextual elements. The information contained within this chapter should help both current and aspiring coaches for athletes with physical disabilities acquire the information they need to serve the best interests of their athletes.

History of Paralympic Sport

At the end of World War II, many rehabilitative hospitals throughout Europe and North America were created as a result of individuals who accumulated war-related injuries (Steadward and Foster 2003). One hospital in England, Stoke Mandeville, along with neurosurgeon Ludwig Guttmann, played an instrumental role in the rehabilitation process of World War II veterans. Dr. Guttmann believed that work and rehabilitative sport would improve the physical and mental well-being of those with spinal cord injuries. As a result, Guttmann founded the Stoke Mandeville Games in 1948, and competitive disability sport was born. The initial games included 14 male and 2 female wheelchair participants, and the Mandeville Games continued on a yearly basis. In 1960 the International Stoke Mandeville Games left British ground for Rome, where they held the first Paralympic Games, focusing strictly on athletes with a spinal cord injury (Steadward and Foster 2003). The 1976 Paralympics were the first games to include athletes from multiple disability backgrounds.

Today, the Paralympic Games are just like the Olympic games, in that they alternate between summer and winter sports. In addition, the country hosting the Olympic Games also hosts the Paralympic Games. The word *paralympic* has had different connotations attached to it, the first being "para" signifying paraplegic. However, the second view was that "para" reflected a movement in parallel to the Olympic Games, and that is the one that exists today (DePauw and Gavron 1995). The Paralympics have embraced new sports and encompassed a wider range of disabilities that includes athletes with mobility impairments, amputations, blindness, and Cerebral Palsy. The Paralympic movement has greatly expanded over the past fifty years and is currently the largest multisport event in the world for athletes with a physical disability, and second in size only to the Olympic Games (International Paralympic Committee 2007). The Summer Paralympic Games consist of approximately 4,000 athletes from 150 different countries competing in 20 sports, while the Winter Games include approximately 600 athletes from 40 different countries competing in five sports. The Paralympic Games have played a major role in changing community perceptions of persons with disabilities, and they continue to portray the remarkable capabilities and success of these athletes. In fact, it may have helped shape the common view shared by many experts that there are more similarities than differences between elite able-bodied athletes and elite athletes with a disability (Cregan, Bloom, and Reid 2007; Dieffenbach and Statler 2012).

Career Progression and Learning of Paralympic Coaches

Researchers in the 1990s identified self-coaching in disability sport as one of the major impediments facing its growth and development (Bradbury

1999; DePauw and Gavron 1995; Liow and Hopkins 1996). In fact, Bradbury (1999) reported that approximately 50% of the 1996 Paralympians said they self-coached. Today, things seem to be changing where access to trained coaches in disability sport is becoming more common. As a result, a small number of empirical studies have identified some of the career pathways for becoming a disability sport coach (e.g., Douglas, Falcão, and Bloom 2018; Cregan, Bloom, and Reid 2007; Duarte and Culver 2014; Fairhurst, Bloom, and Harvey 2017; McMaster, Culver, and Werthner 2012; Tawse et al. 2012; Taylor, Werthner, and Culver 2014). Many of the commonalities that emerged from these studies will be discussed, including personal sporting experiences, learning from others, personal self-reflection, as well as formal (e.g., national certification) and informal (e.g., hands-on experience, observing coaches, and mentoring) learning opportunities.

Previous Sporting Experiences and Desire to Coach Disability Sport

To bridge the gap in coaching research and to develop an understanding of coaches in disability sport, Cregan, Bloom, and Reid (2007) offered one of the first examinations of the career evolution and knowledge of elite coaches in disability sport. A total of six swimming coaches (one with a disability) were interviewed and all six of them began by coaching able-bodied swimmers. None of the coaches intended to coach swimmers with a disability and only began doing so when an athlete with a disability arrived at one of their training sessions and asked to participate along with their able-bodied swimmers. Furthermore, the six participants had very diverse experiences in aquatics that ranged from one former Paralympian, to two who competed nationally in able-bodied swimming, to three who had little to no competitive able-bodied swimming experiences.

Falcão, Bloom, and Loughead (2015) recently interviewed seven current Paralympic coaches across four individual and three team sports. The coaches were able-bodied individuals who had extensive competitive sport experiences ranging from varsity to regional and national levels. They had not been Olympic athletes. The participants described different pathways to becoming a Paralympic coach. Some migrated from nondisability sports while others accepted job opportunities based on their interest in coaching athletes with a disability. Another study, from Fairhurst, Bloom, and Harvey (2017), interviewed six male Paralympic coaches from various individual, team, and co-acting sports who averaged 12 years of coaching experience and who were identified by a panel of experts as being among the best in Canada. The coaches were all born able-bodied, played a variety of sports throughout their youth, and reached varying levels of competition. One participant began his athletic career as an able-bodied athlete but sustained a life-changing injury as a teenager, and subsequently competed as a Paralympian. Five of the participants began coaching in able-bodied sport contexts. They were exposed to disability sport through postsecondary adaptive physical activity courses or by having an athlete with a disability approach them about their coaching services. One able-bodied participant began his coaching career in disability sport. He had intended to become a physical education teacher, but was exposed to disability populations during his postsecondary education, which led him to pursue coaching in the disability sport context.

Tawse and colleagues (2012) completed one of the few studies of Paralympic coaches where the majority of the sample had a physical disability. They interviewed four male participants (three with a disability) who were identified as the top wheelchair rugby coaches in Canada. Because wheelchair rugby had only recently emerged as a high-performance sport at the time of the study, previous elite athletic experience in wheelchair rugby for these participants was not possible. However, all of the coaches were involved in elite sport at various times in their lives. Interestingly, one participant in this study had a congenital disability and participated in both able-bodied and disability sports growing up, which included two appearances at the Paralympics. Two participants were classifiable in wheelchair rugby after they acquired a spinal cord injury in their twenties. The one able-bodied participant competed at the University level in basketball. Tawse and colleagues also found that three of the four participants did not initially intend to coach wheelchair rugby. They fell into the coaching role either out of obligation when their current coaches resigned or to fulfill a job requirement at a provincial wheelchair sports association.

An even more unique sample of participants came from a recently published study by Douglas and colleagues (2018) who purposefully selected and interviewed five Paralympic head coaches who had all previously competed as United States Paralympic athletes. All the participants won numerous World Championship and Paralympic medals, ranged in age from 36 to 58, coached both individual and team sports, and had head coaching experience at the Paralympic level ranging from 2 to 12 years, with an average of just under six years. The participants were first asked to coach by their current or former head coaches. Interestingly, three of them were still training and competing as Paralympians when they were asked to be assistant coaches on their national team. While some were hesitant about their knowledge and preparation to become coaches, they all accepted the invitation and they all commented on the positive impact their athletic careers had on their evolution as coaches—both in their understanding of the Paralympic sport context and in the personal connections they had accumulated as athletes that would open more doors for them and help them rapidly progress up the coaching ladder. More precisely, the results found that parasport coaches with a disability who were Paralympians were fast-tracked directly into national team coaching opportunities. Consequently, aspiring parasport coaches with a disability who never competed as Paralympians may need to invest considerably more time and effort toward their coaching evolution and development.

In conclusion, the results from research in this area appear to differ from research on elite able-bodied coaches, where the majority personally sought out coaching careers in their desired sport and that elite athletic experiences were important to their career development and success (i.e., Gilbert, Côté, and Mallett 2006; Schinke, Bloom, and Salmela 1995). It appears that many Paralympic coaches do not initially seek out coaching roles in disability sport. These coaches initially worked with able-bodied athletes and became involved in disability sport as a result of chance (e.g., an athlete with a disability asked to be coached by them), or from personal exposure to disability sport, or due to other connections to the sport, and subsequently became motivated to become successful disability sport coaches, despite not having previous athletic experience in disability sport. The results also suggest that elite athletic experiences in disability sport are not a pre-cursor for coaching success, which may not be surprising since few of them (i.e., 5 of the 23 coaches in the four studies cited in this section—Cregan et al. 2007; Fairhurst et al. 2017; Falcão, Bloom, and Loughead 2015; Tawse et al. 2012) had a disability and/or competed in disability sport. The one difference came from the Douglas et al. (2018) sample, which found that previous sporting experiences as a Paralympian gave those individuals quicker access to a high-performance coaching position in the parasport context. Given the small sample of individuals who are coaching elite disability sport and who have a disability, it would be interesting to continue studying their career paths and to see if changes occur as more people with disabilities begin to purposefully enter this coaching field

Learning from Shared Relationships

Research in disability sport coaching has found that coaches acquired a great deal of knowledge from their athletes themselves, athletes' family members, and the athletes' caregivers (Cregan et al. 2007; Duarte and Culver 2014; Fairhurst, Bloom, and Harvey 2017; Falcão, Bloom, and Loughead 2015; Tawse et al. 2012). For example, Cregan and colleagues (2007) noted how the participants' journey into disability sport coaching involved a constant quest for more knowledge of their athletes' disabilities. They felt that regularly communicating with their athletes' caregivers and support caretakers were important steps in their acquisition of coaching knowledge. Similarly, Tawse and colleagues (2012) said that the integrative support team (physiotherapists, sport psychologists, etc.) were valuable sources of knowledge acquisition Along the same line, the Paralympic coaches in Falcão et al.'s (2015) study also highlighted the role of athlete support personnel as an integral part of the team, given that they often shared hotel rooms during trips and engaged in social activities with the athletes off the playing field. As such, coaches highlighted their importance in their acquisition of knowledge, as well as in team dynamics.

The coaches in Cregan, Bloom, and Reid's (2007) study also highlighted the importance of using the athlete as a source of knowledge, particularly as a result of the limited coaching resources such as manuals, clinics, and seminars for athletes with a disability. In a similar manner, Fairhurst and colleagues (2017) noted that the Paralympic coaches in their sample developed a personal relationship with their athletes that characterized a shared-learning environment where both the coach and athlete had equal input into the coaching process. Fairhurst and colleagues also found that the parents of athletes with a disability as well as the athletes' caregivers provided the coaches with information about their athletes' emotional and physical states and how these affected their daily training plans. In the same vein, Taylor, Werthner, Culver, and Callary (2015) found that the coaches in their study all highlighted the importance of learning from their athletes as well as other experts in their field in order to improve their coaching knowledge and behaviors. Finally, Duarte and Culver (2014) explored the process of becoming an adaptive sailing coach. Using a life-story methodology, the authors revealed that the coach utilized collaborative networks of individuals that included colleagues, athletes, and mentors to acquire disability coaching knowledge and progress in her career.

In summary, the results of the studies cited in this section reveal that that the coaches constantly pursued learning opportunities to hone their skill sets, including building trusting relationships with the athlete and the athletes' caregivers. Learning appeared to be a lifelong process for these coaches, and they were not afraid to use whatever resources were available to them to help them acquire knowledge.

Formal Learning: Coach Education

Although coaches require a specialized skill set when working with athletes with a disability, there is a lack of available coaching resources and educational learning opportunities to acquire this knowledge (Cregan, Bloom, and Reid 2007; Douglas et al., 2018; McMaster, Culver, and Werthner 2012; Tawse et al, 2012; Taylor et al. 2015). Many Paralympic coaches are not trained in the specific circumstances that define disability sport because many have completed coach education programs designed for able-bodied sport contexts (Cregan, Bloom, and Reid 2007; Tawse et al. 2012; Taylor et al. 2015). For example, Tawse and colleagues (2012) noted that the wheelchair rugby coaches in their sample desired formal coach education specific to wheelchair rugby when they began coaching in this field, but at that time specific training was not available. As a result, they acquired their knowledge from other sports and through general coaching theory courses. This finding is consistent with Cregan, Bloom, and Reid (2007), who also found there was a lack of disability-specific coach education available to coaches of swimmers with a physical disability, and coaches instead had to utilize formal coach training for able-bodied athletes.

In order to determine how Paralympic coaches acquired disability-specific knowledge, McMaster, Culver, and Werthner (2012) observed and interviewed five Paralympic coaches from different sports. Two of the coaches in their sample had access to formal education with disability-specific information. Not surprisingly, they found these courses to be extremely advantageous. The other three coaches did not have access to disability-sport coach education and thus felt their coach training courses were decontextualized (cf. Cushion, Armour, and Jones 2003; Mallett et al. 2009) because they primarily focused on able-bodied coach settings. These coaches desired more hands-on experience. For example, technical issues with disability apparatus, athlete differences in mobility, and information about disability classification were recommended. Because the coaches felt that their formal education was lacking, they relied heavily on informal learning experiences (e.g., the Internet, books, DVDs, observing other coaches, having a mentor).

In sum, while disability sport coaches in North America support the value of coach education, they often criticized the lack of disability sport–specific knowledge in coach education programs (McMaster et al. 2012; Taylor et al. 2014), leaving many of them with a lack of available formal coach education programs specific to their context (Cregan et al. 2007; Douglas et al. 2018; McMaster et al. 2012; Taylor et al. 2014). This differs from able-bodied coaches in North America who have access to coach education training in their sport. This lack of formal education has resulted in a lack of confidence required to effectively coach an athlete with a disability (Duarte and Culver 2014; Martin and Whalen 2014), and it furthers the need for formal coach education worldwide to enhance the skills and confidence of those working in this specific domain.

Informal Coach Learning

Coaches in all sports often acquire knowledge through informal learning situations such as hands-on experience, observing other coaches, and mentoring (Bloom et al. 1998; Cushion, Armour, and Jones 2003). Possibly as a result of a lack of formal coach education for disability sport, informal education methods such as mentorships or coach observation, learning through reflection, postsecondary adaptive physical education courses, trial-and-error practices, their athletes, athletes' caregivers, disability specialists, and accessing available resources such as the Internet, DVDs, and books seem to have been most used by individuals in this domain (Cregan et al. 2007; Fairhurst et al. 2017; McMaster et al. 2012; Tawse et al. 2012).

In another study, Fairhurst and colleagues (2017) carried out perhaps the most direct examination of coaching and mentoring in Paralympic sport. Although the coaches sought mentoring relationships when they first entered the field, only four of the six participants reported working with a mentor coach during the early stages of their development. They all described this relationship as their most significant learning experience. The two participants who did not work with a mentor coach at any point in their careers were still able to become successful Paralympic coaches, but they relied more heavily on their creativity and other informal learning situations. All six of the coaches in the study have given back to their sport by making mentoring opportunities available for aspiring coaches once they had become expert coaches. Given the increased participation rates in disability sport, future research may investigate the evolution in training and mentorship opportunities with the next generation of Paralympic coaches who may have more opportunities available to them. Finally, it would be interesting to research the small number of female Paralympic coaches to see if they have similar or different responses to their male counterparts.

In a related manner, interactions between the coach and athlete was a valuable source of information, particularly if the coach was able-bodied and trying to learn about accessibility or equipment matters (Cregan et al. 2007; Dieffenbach and Statler 2012; Fairhurst et al. 2017; McMaster et al. 2012). While learning from others was a valuable source of information, coaches have reported that there was also merit to learning through introspection or reflection of personal experiences (Duarte and Culver 2014; Taylor et al. 2014; Taylor et al. 2015).

For example, Taylor and colleagues interviewed four experienced disability sport coaches to determine how they used reflective practices to learn and further their careers. All four of the coaches spent a significant amount of time thinking and reflecting on their daily coaching tasks, which may have been partly attributable to the fact that most of their coach training occurred in non-disability sport contexts. As a result, they all spent considerable time thinking about ways to adapt their information to the disability sport context. The results of this study have shed light on the value and importance of coach reflection in this context. Furthermore, Duarte and Culver (2014) discussed reflection in a broader sense, including the value of disability sport coaches working together and sharing their knowledge about disability sport with one another. Evidently, research findings suggested that coaches relied on informal methods of learning to access coaching resources, to build a strong network of like-minded coaches, and used their own reflection or introspection skills to develop innovative and effective coaching practices in disability sport.

To compensate for the lack of formal coach education in wheelchair rugby, the coaches in Tawse and colleague's (2012) sample sought informal learning opportunities through observing other successful wheelchair rugby coaches. This finding was in accordance with previous research with elite able-bodied coaches in able-bodied sport (e.g., Carter and Bloom 2009; Werthner and Trudel 2006). For example, Werthner and Trudel (2006) suggested that an important source of learning came during informal learning situations, such as watching other teams practice or having discussions with other coaches on training techniques and strategies. All four coaches in Tawse and colleagues' study discussed the importance of practical learning experiences and described how these were important to both experienced and inexperienced wheelchair rugby coaches. For example, the able-bodied coach in their study who had no previous knowledge about the sport of wheelchair rugby described the importance of experiential and practical learning from experienced coaches (e.g., learning about the athletes' injuries, how to transfer them, and how to work with them in their daily lives). Therefore, it can be suggested that new coaches entering wheelchair rugby, and perhaps other disability sports, may require informal practical training in addition to formalized coach training for them to both improve their coaching skills and to better facilitate their coaching responsibilities in the sport. Additionally, sustained practical training is important for all disability sport coaches in order for them to stay up to date with the best practices in the sport and for the continued success of their athletes.

Finally, given the lack of coaching books, manuals, and education programs, some coaching researchers have supported the use of trial and error techniques for disability sport coaches (Hanrahan 2007; Taylor et al. 2014). For instance, Hanrahan (2007) encouraged coaches to brainstorm new or innovative strategies together with their athletes and to try them out in practice. One disability sport coach in Taylor et al.'s study noted that "what works today may not work tomorrow" (132). Moreover, technology and sport science are changing rapidly and coming up with new and innovative strategies all the time, which reinforces the notion of coaches being proactive in adopting strategies that have the potential to maximize their athletes' strengths.

Conclusions

Most Paralympic coaches are able-bodied and have a wide range of competitive sport experiences ranging from novice to varsity to national levels. Few of the Paralympic coaches in the reported studies intended to coach athletes with a disability and few of them took coach education courses designed for athletes with a disability. As a result, they gathered information informally from others and through personal reflection and self-learning. As this field continues to grow, evolve, and prosper, there is a need for more research on the career development patterns of Paralympic coaches.

Paralympic Coach Leadership

Sport leaders have many different roles, including teacher, mentor, and community leader. Within sport teams, there are two important sources of leadership, which emanate from coaches and athletes. These leadership roles affect the development of athletes, both on and off the field of play. In contrast to the well-developed body of literature examining coaching able-bodied athletes, there is limited research specifically examining the coaching skills and behaviors of coaches of athletes with a physical disability. This is disconcerting since there are many unique aspects to coaching athletes with a disability, such as awareness and understanding of disability, aspects of accessibility, and various socialization factors (Banack, Sabiston, and Bloom 2011; Cregan, Bloom, and Reid 2007; Falcão, Bloom, and Loughead 2015; Tawse et al. 2012). Thus, exploring the leadership skills and behaviors of Paralympic coaches will serve to further enhance the understanding of coach leadership in different domains.

Fostering Athlete Independence

Cregan, Bloom, and Reid (2007) alluded to the importance of coaches' fostering autonomy in athletes with a disability as a way to improve both their athletic and personal skills. As stated by one of the coaches in their study,

> If you can get a person [to] go from not swimming at all to swimming a mile, you've given them that ability, then you've successfully done what you said you were going to do—empowered them, taught them how to be autonomous, and given them an improved lifestyle, because what they are doing is only going to help in the end. (Cregan, Bloom, and Reid 2007, 343)

A similar finding emerged from Banack and colleagues' (2011) study, although their data came from the Paralympic athletes themselves. Central to their finding, the Paralympic athletes preferred an autonomy-supportive coaching style (cf. Mageau and Vallerand 2003), which is one that provides athletes with choices, opportunities for initiative taking, and constructive feedback. Research in able-bodied sport has consistently demonstrated that athletes who perceived their coaches' behaviors to be autonomy supportive experienced increased motivation, enjoyment, and connectedness to others (Amorose and Horn 2000; Hollembeak and Amorose 2005). According to Banack and colleagues, the Paralympic athletes in their study preferred that their coaches adopt an athlete-centered approach that fostered feelings of independence and helped to create a positive coach–athlete relationship and team environment.

Tawse et al. (2012) also revealed information about the benefits of Paralympic wheelchair rugby coaches' adopting an autonomy-supportive coaching leadership style. More specifically, they found that these coaches viewed their players as elite athletes (as opposed to a person with a disability), promoted independence, and developed well-rounded athletes and community leaders. Moreover, the coaches considered the personal development of their players as a fundamental role in their coaching responsibilities and perceived the players' independence as having a great impact on the team and their athletic performances. To accomplish these goals, the coaches pushed their athletes to increase their independence by learning to manually use a wheelchair, to self-transfer, and to work on bowel/bladder management skills that enabled them to improve their functioning in both wheelchair rugby and in their daily living. This finding is consistent with research that found that participation in wheelchair rugby promoted independence for its athletes (e.g., Goodwin et al. 2009). For example, elite wheelchair rugby athletes in the Goodwin and colleagues study noted that participation in their sport helped them to function independently after their injury. One athlete from their study said, "I get way more independence by playing rugby than I ever did from any doctor . . . that's an absolute truth" (Goodwin et al. 2009, 10).

Additionally, research has also found how team travel reinforced athlete independence by providing inexperienced players new opportunities to gain experience in nonaccessible settings (e.g., Goodwin et al. 2009; Tawse et al. 2012). The four coaches in Tawse and colleagues' (2012) study described how they assisted their athletes while traveling on the road. For example, the two participants with spinal cord injuries and the one participant with a congenital disability provided experiential knowledge and practical support to their athletes. The one able-bodied coach described his limitations in helping facilitate independence with his athletes. He created a shared learning environment where he asked veteran athletes to provide guidance to new athletes when they had to perform tasks such as transferring into a nonaccessible vehicle or into a bathtub in a hotel room for the first time.

In summary, Paralympic coaches' leadership style requires an emphasis on both the personal and the athletic development of their players, which appears to be a common element in coaching both elite able-bodied athletes (cf. Vallée and Bloom 2005) and elite athletes with a disability. When coaches care about their players at the personal and athletic level, players feel a greater connection and commitment to their coaches and athletic goals. Some of the unique aspects of Paralympic coaching relate to the coaches' knowledge and their ability to adjust to their athletes' distinct needs where their leadership strategies often encourage athletes to overcome challenges experienced in and out of sport. Taken together, these findings can inform practitioners of coaching strategies used to satisfy the psychological needs of elite athletes with a disability.

Fostering Team Cohesion

On a given team for athletes with a disability, a coach may have to simultaneously develop training plans for an athlete who is an upper-limb amputee, one with a visual impairment, and an athlete with paraplegia. Aside from affecting individual athlete growth and development, their knowledge and behaviors could also have an impact on team cohesion and success.

In Canada, attention to recommended coaching behaviors is central to various coach development programs, including those conducted by the National Coach Certification Program (NCCP). One of the mandates of the NCCP is to establish effective coaching programs, usually in the form of workshops. While the importance of these workshops cannot be underestimated, most of the knowledge coaches receive focuses on factors that influence individual outcomes in athletes, such as skill analysis, injuries, and tactical components of the sport. Little information is presented that explains how coaches can influence the team environment, and even less information is focused on coaching disability sport teams (Lefebvre et al. 2016). This is surprising given that research has shown that coaches who were trained at improving team cohesion for able-bodied athletes created a more positive team environment that was linked to improvements in team performance and success (Bloom, Stevens, and Wickwire 2003; Carron, Bray, and Eys 2002). In addition to the psychosocial and team outcome benefits that enhanced social relationships provides, physical activity for individuals with a disability also has the ability to profoundly influence their development, behavior patterns, and attitudes (Berndt 2002), as well as their perceptions of health and independence, pain control, and the maintenance of function (Goodwin and Compton 2004; Tawse et al. 2012).

Sport psychology practitioners working with the United States Paralympic program have suggested that sessions devoted to the development of team cohesion would be most helpful and effective for their athletes (Moffett, Dieffenbach, and Statler 2009). Recently, Falcão, Bloom, and Loughead (2015) provided strategies used by Paralympic coaches to foster cohesion with their teams. Many of the techniques and strategies for enhancing cohesion that were presented by the coaches were similar to those in nondisability sport settings, such as task-related activities, goal setting, and regularly communicating with their athletes. However, the researchers also identified some unique aspects specific to a disability sport context.

Among their results, Falcão, Bloom, and Loughead (2015) found the Paralympic coaches described how teammates helped each other with several daily tasks that might impact team cohesion, such as those related to transportation and personal care. Additionally, the Paralympic coaches created many interpersonal activities (e.g., team dinners and going to the movies) that were designed to foster social cohesion among their teams. These activities were more challenging for Paralympic teams since some individuals needed to rely on their team leaders for help related to transportation and to arrange wheelchair access. Similarly, Caron, Bloom, Loughead, and Hoffmann (2016) also found that Paralympic athlete leaders said they made decisions and designed activities to enhance their team's cohesiveness. Not only did the leaders value and organize social team gatherings, they also spoke about the importance of enhanced task cohesion. For example, one participant described how doing activities with a teammate gave him information about whether to pass to the teammates strong or weak hand in various aspects of competition. Evidently, coaches and athlete leaders shared the perception that team cohesion was an important strategy to implement when coaching athletes with a disability for both the emotional growth of the individual person and the performance of the team (Caron et al. 2016; Falcão et al. 2015).

Conclusions

Although the individual makeup of a Paralympic athlete is more similar to than different from an Olympic athlete (Banack et al. 2011; Cregan et al. 2007; Dieffenbach and Statler 2012), the leadership skills of a Paralympic coach require adaptations to some of the individual and team differences that are part of this unique context. Individually, coaches in disability sport should adopt autonomy-supportive coaching strategies that facilitate the individual growth and development of the athlete both inside and outside of sport. Additionally, these coaches need to work more closely with their athletes to understand their level of functioning. From a team perspective, Paralympic coaches must take into consideration how various levels of functioning might affect team play on the field of play and team togetherness off the field of play. As a result, developing team cohesion would be an important attribute in this domain that could improve both individual and team success.

Summary

The pioneer of the Paralympic movement, Sir Ludwig Guttmann, introduced sport as a form of recreation to aid in the rehabilitation process of persons with a spinal cord injury. Since then, the Paralympic movement has continued to grow. However, the same growth has not occurred in the academic community, and more specifically, in coaching research. This chapter has relied on the small body of empirical research to provide some information for becoming a Paralympic coach for those individuals who are interested in coaching in this domain.

The content of this chapter would encourage coach development agencies around the world to adopt formal coach certification training programs specific to disability sport, in addition to the informal and experiential learning that these coaches require to fully develop. Most countries have yet to create coach development courses for athletes with disabilities or are in their early stages. As well, it is important to note that this chapter did not delve into the specifics of classification and disabilities, even though disability provides opportunities for athletes with a visual impairment, a spinal cord injury, amputations, cerebral palsy, spinal bifida, multiple sclerosis, or other disabilities to participate. The content of this chapter has summarized some of the preliminary findings in this domain and has identified gaps in the literature for further inquiry, ideally from a global perspective.

PART III

DEVELOPING THE BEST COACHES

Chapter 11

Current Models of Coach Education, Training, and Certification

Sarah McQuade

We know that coaches play a central role in sport participation and athlete development. We also know, that "coaching is in its most dynamic era in history" (International Council for Coaching Excellence [ICCE] 2012, 4). Today's coaches wear many hats—surrogate parent, scientist, technician, psychologist, and business manager, among others. The expectations from athletes, parents, and sport organizations for not just winning, but also for overall child and athlete development is far higher than before. In this new climate of sport, the coaching game has changed significantly across the globe. In order to meet these additional, transparent requirements, organizations that employ coaches are responsible for providing quality-assured education and ongoing professional development. The coaches are responsible for accessing these resources in order to meet the needs of the athletes they serve. International federations, national organizations, governing bodies, and private for-profit and not-for-profit organizations also play a lead role in providing coach education and coach development.

It is important to make the distinction between coach education and coach development, as follows:

- *Coach education* typically refers to those opportunities, such as coaching awards and degrees, that are presented through mediated formal learning. This learning "takes place in an institutionalized, chronologically graded, and hierarchical educational system" (Coombs and Ahmed 1974).

- *Coach development* refers to the wider opportunities for learning that are presented through the informal learning environment; that is, through self-directed study, coaching practice, and reflection (ICCE 2015).

Programs at the forefront of this modern approach to coaching and coach preparation are developing a coaching system that follows a logical development flow. The coaching framework effectively becomes the blueprint for coaching, coach education, and coach development and the foundation upon which the organization's coaching "house" is constructed. The Player Development Model is the first layer to be constructed and laid down. This identifies the pathways (participation and performance) and the populations being coached. In order to establish the capabilities required to coach effectively within each age and stage, the development milestones; performance markers (technical, tactical, physical, mental, and personal/social); and the implications for training, practice, and competitions have to be identified. At this point it is then possible to identify the coaching knowledge and skills (capabilities) required to operate effectively. Typically these too are housed within a model or pathway structured across various coaching domains or populations and constructed from beginner to master coach.

The distinction between beginner and master coach is important. To follow the coaching house analogy, developing expertise along this continuum will require coach education providers to add extensions or additional floors. This chapter will provide a series of case studies, exploring how various countries, and in turn coach education providers (governing bodies and private for-profit and not-for-profit organizations), have constructed their modern coaching houses. It will identify how they prepare coaches to work effectively within and across participant and performance pathways and with various coaching populations. It will provide examples of how coach development has been prioritized to support positive action initiatives across the globe, including in developing nations with underserved populations. It will also show how the advent of national and international coaching frameworks has streamlined the global drive for consistency and standardization in coach education.

Many coaching houses are still in the process of being built because design, development, construction, and inevitably re-build always take time. The research underpinning the effectiveness of specific coach development programs is also in the making.

The United Kingdom

Coaching frameworks are relatively new concepts, but are already referred to as blueprints. They are the starting point for the development of coaching systems that place the right coach in the right place at the right time. In 2008, the National Coaching Foundation (the UK government's lead agency for coaching), published the UK Coaching Framework: A 3-7-11 Year Action Plan (North 2009). The ambition was to create a world-leading ethical, valued, inclusive, and cohesive coaching system by 2016 that could "provide skilled, active, and qualified coaches to support and guide the improvement of children, players, and athletes at all stages of their development [and] enhance the quality and quantity of coaching delivered by volunteer, part-time, and full-time coaches" (North 2009, foreword). The phased development plan was structured across 11 years, with each phase designed to run concurrently and focus upon the following milestones:

- Building the foundations (2006–2008)
- Delivering the goals (2006–2012)
- Transforming the system (2006–2016)

In the UK, national governing bodies (NGBs) are recognized as the lead agencies in sport-specific coaching. They typically work in close partnership with clubs, schools, communities, local authorities, and further education and higher education sectors. The policy document was designed to act as a reference point for the development and implementation of sport-specific coaching systems by these stakeholders. Specifically, it was hoped the framework would enable partners to create coaching systems with excellent coaching practice embedded, resulting in the provision of skilled coaches who support children, players, and athletes at all stages of their development, contributing to sustained and increased participation and improved performances in sport.

This ambition predated the beginning of the timeline for the UK Coaching Framework, and time has moved on. Supported by sports coach UK, sport-specific coaching systems have advanced steadily in recent years through the work of governing bodies of sport, local delivery partners, home county sports councils, and UK Sport. Headline achievements suggest that individual sports are focusing on the creation and delivery of inclusive coaching systems as opposed to offering ad-hoc coach education opportunities. There is now a greater recognition that needs-led education and development is a priority for coaches and coaching. More developed local networks of partners are playing a key role in the recruitment, development, and retention of coaches. Critically, the call for robust and informed evidence to influence decision-making, determine priorities, and allocate resources to support development work is stronger than ever.

The UK Coaching Framework has since been updated and continues to provide the coaching industry with a common vision, reference point, and practice guide to drive the development of excellent coaching practice. It is guided by various assumptions, perhaps the most obvious, yet worth reiterating, being that "great sports need active, skilled, and qualified coaches to work at each developmental stage of the participant pathway" (National Coaching Foundation 2012). The revised framework guides the development of coaching across the UK through eight components, which are best depicted visually (figure 11.1). This illustrates how the eight components work together using the plan, do, review, coaching process to model and achieve excellent coaching practice. Each component plays a vital part in the development of an excellent coaching system. Effective coaching systems

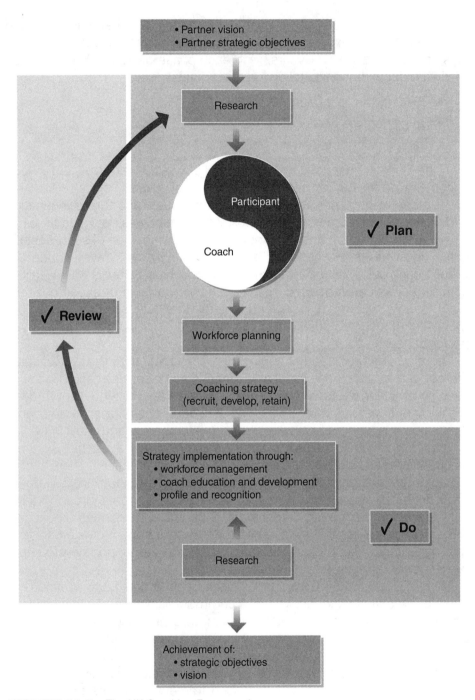

FIGURE 11.1   The UK Coaching Framework.

Reprinted by permission from the National Coaching Foundation, *The UK Coaching Framework: Embedding Excellent Coaching Practice* (Leeds, UK: Coachwise, 2012), 17. For the latest strategic information relating to coaching frameworks and standards, please visit ukcoaching.org/about.

assume that the eight components are fully addressed and integrated and interact in a coherent way.

A critical feature of the development of the UK Coaching Framework is the Coach Development Model (CDM; figure 11.2). Again, it serves as a reference point, not a mandate, and maps the development of coaches as they progress from novice to master, as related to the four key participant populations identified in the Participant Development Model (PDM; figure 11.3).

Coaches operate across varied environments with different populations and at different levels with experienced, capable coaches assuming more complex roles and greater levels of responsibility. The development of coaching expertise from novice to master is universally acknowledged although the levels across which expertise develops can vary in number. The ICCE's International Sport Coaching Framework, consistent with the UK's Coaching Framework, identifies four coaching roles, as outlined in table 11.1.

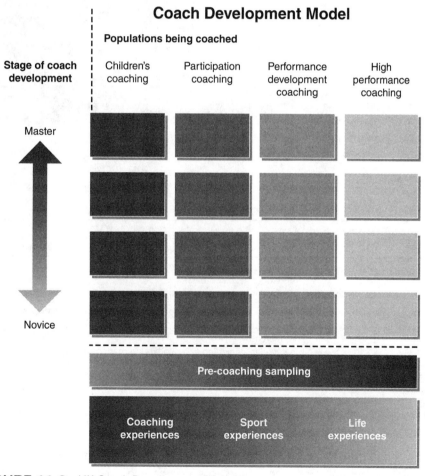

FIGURE 11.2 UK Coach Development Model.

Reprinted by permission from the National Coaching Foundation, *The UK Coaching Framework: Embedding Excellent Coaching Practice* (Leeds, UK: Coachwise, 2012), 29. For the latest strategic information relating to coaching frameworks and standards, please visit ukcoaching.org/about.

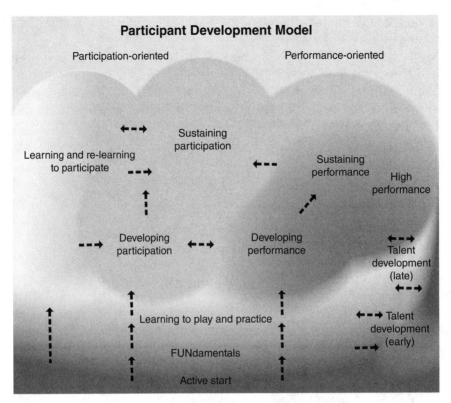

FIGURE 11.3 UK Participant Development Model.

Reprinted by permission from the National Coaching Foundation, *The UK Coaching Framework: Embedding Excellent Coaching Practice* (Leeds, UK: Coachwise, 2012), 27. For the latest strategic information relating to coaching frameworks and standards, please visit ukcoaching.org/about.

TABLE 11.1 ICCE Coach Roles

Coaching Assistant	Assists in the delivery of sessions*
Coach	Delivers sessions over a season, often as part of a wider program
Advanced/Senior Coach	Oversees and contributes to the delivery of programs over seasons and in specific contexts Involved in the management and development of other coaches
Master/Head Coach	Oversees and contributes to the delivery of programs over seasons, in medium- to large-scale contexts, underpinned by innovation and research Involved in designing and overseeing management structures and development programs for other coaches.

*Sessions include both practices and competitions

Adapted by permission from International Council for Coaching Excellence, Association of Summer Olympic International Federations, and Leeds Beckett University, *International Sport Coaching Framework (Version 1.2)* (Champaign, IL: Human Kinetics, 2013), 26.

Clarifying the key roles that coaches may be asked to play across all domains is critical. Each coaching role consists of core functions, which inevitably will vary according to the sport, country, and context in which the coach is engaged. The detail underpinning each role refers to the core capabilities and competences required to undertake the coach role effectively. In coach education speak, it allows education providers to determine the learning outcomes and need-to-know content that serve as the foundation for the qualification, certification, or accreditation; curriculum; learning program; and associated coach resources. It is also the basis against which coaching knowledge and performance is assessed. This detail is essential to create the route map for coach employment and will help employers determine the most appropriate candidate and potential training needs for coach development.

The UK CDM, a generic model, has been used mostly by UK NGBs to determine whom their coaches are, where the coaches are operating, whom the coaches are working with, and what tools need to be created to support the recruitment, development, and retention of coaches within the system. The England and Wales Cricket Board (ECB) support the development of coaches and coach developers at all levels of the game. They are keen to ensure players have access to the best possible experience of playing cricket and the necessary skills, knowledge, and understanding of the game to help them fulfill their potential. Much like other NGBs, they created a CDM, based on the player development model. Although this model is no longer in use, the ECB CDM (figure 11.4) highlights the intricacies of creating a coach development model, operating across four levels, that supports coaches operating across various environments and levels of the game including the community (primary and secondary schools, clubs), performance (working with the most talented young players in ECB's performance pathway) and at the elite end.

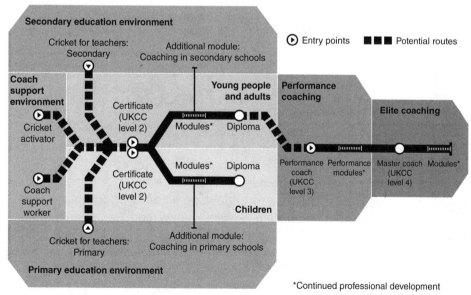

FIGURE 11.4 ECB Coach Development Model.
Reprinted courtesy of The England and Wales Cricket Board.

The Professional Golf Association of Great Britain and Ireland (PGA of GB & I), using the UK Coaching Framework as a reference point, created a Golf Coaching Vision (2008–2016), adopting the mantra "Right Coach, Right Place, Right Time." The association's philosophy underscores the belief that individual sport organizations need to ensure that they have coaches with technical knowledge (what to coach) combined with the ability to use that knowledge to help improve the performer (how to coach). Historically, the how-to-coach skills were not taught to coaches. They now feature overtly in modern coach education programs. They combine traditional models of skill acquisition with more recent developments in motor learning, coaching behaviors, and instruction. Show and tell (or demonstration and explanation), sitting at the "push" end of the spectrum of learning techniques, remain an important element of the coaching process. But show-and-tell techniques are also supplemented at the opposite end of the spectrum (or on the other side of the coaching dance) with "pull" concepts such as experiential learning, problem solving, task-oriented learning, and facilitation.

Using the PGA of GB & I's distinction between what to coach and how to coach, the former sits under the professional knowledge banner and refers to the sport (technical and tactical or X's and O's, rules, equipment and facilities), the athletes, and the sport science. The latter, (or as Côté and Gilbert refer to it, the coaching methodology) is housed under interpersonal knowledge. It sits here because it relates directly to the quality of the relationship between the coach and athlete and emphasizes that coaching, learning, and development all happen within the coach–athlete relationship and wider social context, which is influenced by the coaching environment, the coaching provider or employing organization, parents and the athlete entourage, fellow coaches, officials, and the media. The coach's philosophy, mindset, and commitment to lifelong learning are key elements of intrapersonal knowledge.

South Africa

The UK is not the only the country to have adopted a systematic approach to long-term coach development. In 2009, the South African Sports Confederation and Olympic Committee, alongside the Department of Sport and Recreation and other key stakeholders, created the South African Coaching Framework. To the question of why to develop a framework, the answer for South Africa was relatively simple: "develop new coaching pathways and standards for all the South African sporting codes that will support the different stages of development, participation, and excellence" (South African Sports Confederation and Olympic Committee [SASCOC]: Coaches Commission 2009; 2010). Specifically, the ultimate goal was the transformation of the South African coaching system into one with a skilled professional workforce (volunteer and paid) to meet mass participation and high performance and education goals.

The South African Coaching Framework proposed a new model of Long-Term Coach Development, which includes the following:

- Defined coaching roles (Assistant Coach, Coach, Senior Coach, Master Coach)
- Recognition of "pre-coaching roles" played by the parents, athletes, and others
- Recognition of volunteer, part-time paid, and full-time paid roles
- Recognition of four coaching domains: Children, Participation, Performer Development (Talent), and High Performance
- Training of coach developers who will support the education and the ongoing development of coaches
- Establishment of systems of prior learning
- Linkage to the National Qualifications Framework
- A Code of Ethics and Good Practice for Coaches
- Minimum standards licensing and registration on a phased system

Much like the UK Coaching Framework, South Africa proposed a phased development for adoption and implementation:

1. *Laying the base 2010–2012.* Priorities for this phase of development were to establish structures, sign-off the framework, and harness resources to ensure that there is full alignment of available resources in coaching to the goals of the South African Coaching Framework.

2. *Making an impact 2010–2014.* This phase was committed to the concerted implementation of an inclusive framework with an emphasis on recruiting and training coaches to reflect the social and demographic makeup of the country. To support the translation of concept to practice, this phase saw the delivery of a tutor-training program for a number of sports. With a focus on school sport, this cascade approach was designed to train large numbers of coach educators and assessors, who in turn would then educate large numbers of school coaches in these sports.

3. *Transforming the system 2014–2018.* In order to affect the work of coaches on the front lines, this phase is contingent upon the framework being adapted and implemented by national federations and associated delivery partners. National federations are critical to the success of the framework. A prerequisite for participation in the first-wave roll-out was that the national federation needed to have either launched its LTPD (long-term player development) model or be in the process of developing their model. At the end of 2011, national federations were requested to complete an honest *Willing, Ready, and Able* (WRA) assessment in order to determine which sports should participate in the first roll-out wave. The WRA assessment tool served to assist federations to identify gaps and prioritize efforts. However, many national federations face significant capacity issues, which has limited the number of sports currently able to make an impact.

There are a number of consistencies with the UK model. First is the time investment required to create the system, implement key action areas, and drive change within the sport; it requires a visionary approach and a long-term, perhaps generational commitment before the return on investment may be realized. Second, the building blocks of participant development and coach development are overt in order to strengthen and transform the sporting system. Third, positioning coaching knowledge and expertise to support age/ stage appropriate development is critical to support the delivery of effective front-line coaching. Fourth, the responsibility for translating concept to practice lies with the national federations working at district, provincial, and national levels. Fifth, access to government funding for sport is contingent on being aligned with the South African Coaching Framework.

It is perhaps too soon to comment on the effectiveness of the implementation of the South Africa Coaching Framework. This is undoubtedly where the heavy emphasis on research will come into its own as it seeks to determine the long-term impact of key elements of the framework.

New Zealand

The New Zealand Coaching Framework derives from the New Zealand Coaching Strategy and outlines the structures, policies, and procedures to improve coach education requirements and qualifications.

The strategy provides the blueprint for coaching in New Zealand. It sets out how New Zealand and key partners will develop a world-class coaching environment. While the strategy sets out the broad vision and philosophical basis for coaching in New Zealand, it also identifies the need to have two separate, but connected, coaching plans sitting beneath the strategy: community sport (2012–2020) and high performance (2011–2020). Two plans have been driven by the increasingly specialized requirements for coaching high-performance athletes in the modern era of professional sport.

What connects the strategy and the two coaching plans is the central philosophy that good coaching is all about the participants or athletes and the process to deliver the support they need to enjoy their sport and fulfill their potential at whatever level that may be. To be able to deliver on this philosophy, New Zealand needs capable coaches at all stages of the participant and athlete pathway. The development stages and coaching populations are identified in figure 11.5, which presents the New Zealand Coaching Strategy: Aligned Community Sport and High Performance Coaching plans.

There is a fundamental difference between how the High Performance and the Community Sport Coaching Plans will operate. In the High Performance area, the focus is on a small number of identified coaches and the High Performance Sport New Zealand (HPSNZ) coaching consultants work directly with these coaches. By way of contrast, in the Community Sport area there are literally hundreds of thousands of coaches, so the plan must

FIGURE 11.5 New Zealand Coaching Strategy: Aligned Community Sport and High Performance Coaching Plans.

Reprinted by permission from Sport New Zealand, *New Zealand Community Sport Coaching Plan 2016-2020.* Accessed December 10, 2018, https://sportnz.org.nz/assets/Uploads/Community-Sport-Coaching-Plan-2016-2020.pdf.

instead focus on leading, enabling, and investing in national sports organizations so that they can establish and deliver quality coach development programs within their sports.

The New Zealand Coaching Framework provides a vision, establishes consistent national parameters, and aligns the roles of the key players for coach development in New Zealand. This vision is simple and mirrors the aspirations of other frameworks, which is to create a world-class coaching environment. Philosophically, it assumes that coach development is based on continuous improvement through the increasingly effective integration of coaching skills, knowledge, and understandings in coaching practice.

New Zealand advocates athlete-centered coach development based on athlete stage of development needs. This is reflected in the image (figure 11.6). Coach development will equip the coach to apply, in a practical context, requisite knowledge, skills, and understanding to meet the collective and individual needs of athletes in the coaching communities in which they coach. This includes athletes with disabilities and athletes from all ethnic backgrounds and cultures.

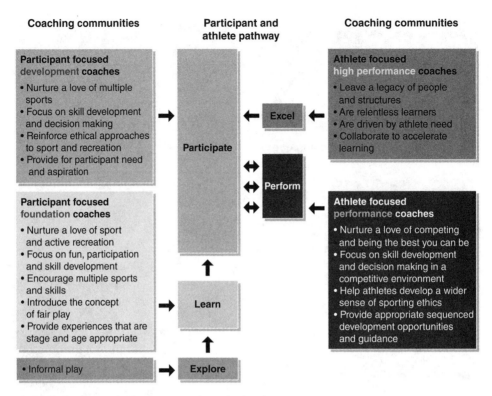

FIGURE 11.6   Athlete-centered coach development.

The New Zealand Framework also provides the structure for supporting the ongoing development of the coach. It presents sufficient information to enable national sport organizations to create coach development programs and accreditation systems, but at the same time is sufficiently flexible to meet the varying needs of different sports. National sport organizations are encouraged to provide coaches with access to formal and informal development opportunities. Learning opportunities for formal coach development programs are grouped under general and sport-specific principles and are broken down into knowledge and skills packages (modules). This enables flexible delivery and the potential to progressively accumulate learning, according to the needs and priorities of individual athletes, coaches, and sports. Examples of informal coach development include trial-and-error learning in conducting coaching practice, attendance at seminars and conferences, mentoring, informal networking opportunities with coaches from their own and other sports, and access to individual research opportunities (through both written and electronic media).

Assessment is a key feature of the coach accreditation process, which is the responsibility of the national sport organizations. Competency-based assessment is advocated, and a mix of tools are recommended to test knowledge and performance; that is, the application of effectiveness of the coach in applying their learning in a practical context. Tools include observation of work-based and simulated practice, professional discussions, and written evidence such as coaching logs, reflective journals, and quizzes. The assumption is that assessment is fair, valid, and reliable.

Much as with UK governing bodies and the challenge that has been laid down to South African federations, New Zealand's governing bodies of sport have created sport-specific coaching frameworks. New Zealand Squash are one such governing body. Their approach is aligned with the New Zealand Coaching Strategy, and is constructed on pathways and across various domains. It is player-centered, needs-led, aligned to a player's stage of development, and promotes ongoing context specific coach development.

The NZ Squash Coach Development Framework (figure 11.7) has been developed to cater to the needs of coaches in the squash community working across performance and participation domains. It allows coaches to personally develop themselves to a high standard in their chosen coaching community. What makes this framework unique when compared to others created across the globe is the referencing of specific modules targeted within the various domains areas that are linked to the needs of athletes on the athlete pathway. The framework is modular, with one, two, or three modules required to qualify in the specific coaching communities. In addition, the framework encourages vertical and lateral professional development through the acquisition of Extension Modules that coaches can add to their specific community qualifications, allowing them to improve their coaching and meet the needs of their athletes, much like the example offered earlier from the

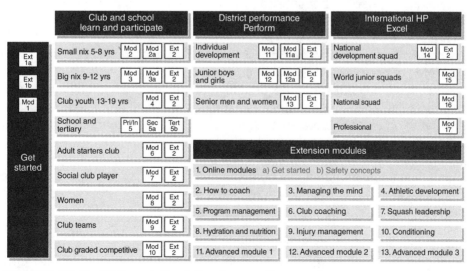

FIGURE 11.7 NZ Squash Coach Development Framework.

Used with permission of Squash New Zealand.

PGA of GBI and the "How to Coach" Extension Module is a prerequisite for many of the communities. However, supporting the transferability of learning agenda, it will not need to be repeated if a coach is gaining qualifications in a number of communities.

Canada

Canada has an extensive system for coaching education and certification. Coaching and coach education is the responsibility of the National Coaching Certification Program (NCCP). Launched in 1974, it is the Coaching Association of Canada's (CAC) flagship program. It is currently the largest adult continuing education program in Canada. The NCCP is designed and delivered in partnership with the government of Canada, provincial/territorial governments, and national/ provincial/ territorial sport organizations.

The UK and South African frameworks presented earlier focus on the strategy that sits behind the delivery of coaching education. By contrast, the NCCP presents coach education from a more pragmatic perspective. Figure 11.8 highlights the fact that coaches operate in various domains (community, competition, and instruction) and coaches work with different types of athletes with various needs and at different levels of ability. Recognizing its responsibility to support the development of coaching expertise, coach education is offered at different levels of mastery from beginner to master coach.

The NCCP model distinguishes between training and certification. Coaches participate in training opportunities to acquire or refine the skills and knowledge required for a particular coaching context (see Competition: Introduction in figure 11.8) as defined by the sport. At this point, they are considered *trained*. To become *certified* in a coaching context, coaches must be evaluated on their demonstrated ability to perform within that context in areas such as program design, practice planning, performance analysis, program management, ethical coaching, support to participants during training, and support to participants in competition.

Certified coaches enjoy the credibility of the sporting community and of the athletes they coach because they have been observed doing and evaluated on what is required of them as a competent coach in their sport. Being certified is directly aligned to vocational competence, a key quality assurance metric that recognizes that coaches have met or exceeded the high standards embraced by more than 60 national sport organizations in Canada. Fostering confidence at all levels of sport, certification is a benefit shared by parents, athletes, sport organizations, and our communities.

The PGA of Canada is one of 67 sport organizations participating in the NCCP. The PGA of Canada's coaching program is developed in partnership with Golf Canada and the Coaching Association of Canada (CAC) with the goal of providing coaches with the best practical experience in an optimal

Coach Certification

The National Coaching Certification Program certifies coaches who have demonstrated their ability to apply critically important competencies to coaching situations relevant to the stage of athletes they coach. This means that coaches must not only know about coaching but be able to demonstrate their ability to apply this knowledge in the coaching situation.

Coaches can be trained in any of the following eight coaching contexts, which are specific to the type of athlete they are working with, and can progress through to a "Master Coach" level in any context.

Community sport

The **Community Sport – Initiation** context focuses on participants who are being introduced to a sport. In many sports this is very young children participating in the sport for the first time. In a few sports, initiation into the sport can occur with youth or adults. Participants get involved to meet new friends, have fun, and to learn a new activity. The role of the coach is to ensure a fun and safe environment and to teach the development of some of the "FUNdamentals" stage skills and abilities for participants.

The **Community Sport – Ongoing participation** context is typically for either youth participating in a recreational environment, or masters participants participating for recreation, fitness, and socialization reasons. The participants are in the Active for Life stage of long-term athlete development. The role of the coach is to encourage participants to continue their involvement in the sport.

Competition

The **Competition – Introduction** context is designed for coaches of athletes moving from the FUNdamentals to the Learn to Train and Train to Train stages of long-term athlete development.

The **Competition – Development** context is designed for coaches of athletes ranging from the Train to Train to the Train to Compete stages of long-term athlete development.

The **Competition – High performance** context is typically reserved for coaches of athletes in the Train to Win stage of long-term athlete development although there is the possibility of some phasing in of a Train to Compete athlete into the High Performance level because of the fluidity of the stages of long-term athlete development. Coaches in this context require specific skills and abilities in order to meet the needs of their athletes.

Instruction

Instructors in the **Instruction – Beginners** context are usually working with participants who are experiencing the sport for the first time through a series of lessons. Typically there's no formalized competition at this level — it's strictly about skill development and there is a short timeframe of interaction between the instructor and the participant.

Instructors in the **Instruction – Intermediate performers** and **Instruction – Advanced performers** contexts are very specialized and are specifically there to assist athletes crossing over from competitive sport to gain enhanced skills, and in some cases, tactical development specific to their sport.

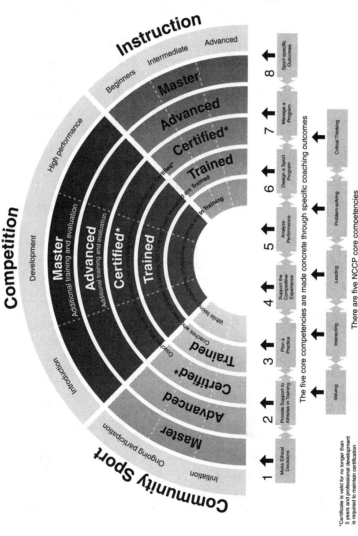

FIGURE 11.8 National Coaching Certification Program.

learning environment. Cognizant of the fact that great golf ability does not guarantee great coaching ability, the PGA of Canada's certification requires that a coach's teaching, technical, and coaching skills meet an internationally recognized standard for coaching practice. Assessment and evaluation are key features of the program. Consistent with the pathways advocated by the NCCP, the PGA of Canada's coaching program is broken into three streams:

1. *Community stream.*
    o Community golf coach. The Community Sport–Initiation pathway has been designed for the community golf coach working with children or youth to introduce the basic skills of the game.
    o Special Olympics golf coach. The PGA of Canada remains the only sport in Canada to have sport-specific coach training for Special Olympics athletes.

2. *Competition stream.* Coaches in the Competition stream (Coach of New Competitors and Coach of Developing Competitors) usually have previous coaching experience or are former athletes in the sport. They tend to work with athletes over the long term to improve performance, often in preparation for provincial, national, and international competitions.

3. *Instruction stream.* The Instruction stream (Instructor of Beginner Golfers, Instructor of Intermediate Golfers, and Instructor of Advanced Golfers) is designed as part of the mandatory requirements for candidates for membership in the PGA of Canada on their pathway to become a Class "A" member.

All coaches interested in Golf's NCCP are required to complete the pathway highlighted in figure 11.9. The pathway emphasizes a systematic, progressive approach that assesses skills to ensure that coaches' technical skills meet the required standards. Portfolio and video evaluations are also key features of the assessment process, and successful completion of these is required to progress to the next level.

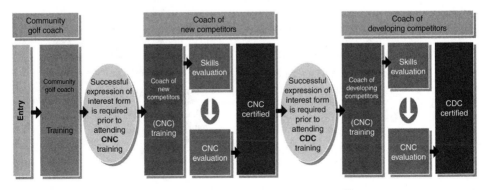

FIGURE 11.9   PGA of Canada's NCCP Pathway for Non-PGA Members.
Used with permission of Professional Golfers' Association of Canada.

Of course, not all coach education and coach development efforts are led by or fall under the umbrella of a national sport system or authority. In many cases, the drive for better quality coach education and development has emerged from within various for-profit and not-for-profit sport organizations. A few of these programs will be highlighted here.

Coach Development in Developing Nations and Underserved Populations

An estimated 67 million children around the world do not attend school regularly. Sport can be used to promote social inclusion through participation and positive action initiatives.

Right to Play

Right to Play, founded in 2000 by four-time Olympic gold medalist and social entrepreneur Johann Olav Koss (a Norwegian speed skater) is now a global organization, using play as a transformative vehicle to educate and empower children and youth. Right to Play uses sport and games to teach children essential life skills that will help them overcome the effects of poverty, conflict, and disease so that they can create better futures and drive lasting social change in their communities and beyond. Right to Play programs are facilitated by more than 16,400 local volunteer coaches and more than 600 international staff. Local teachers and community leaders are trained to become coaches to deliver their play-based educational programs before, during, and after school classes on a weekly basis. The programs' impact, while by no means complete, is tangible. With play as an incentive, school attendance rates are improving and children are more actively engaged in their lessons, which leads to better learning. In Rwanda, the programs' activities are approved for use in primary schools across the country, and they have helped develop a national physical education and health curriculum.

UP2US

UP2US, a US-based nationwide leader in sport-based youth development, harnesses the power of sports to reduce youth violence, promote health, and inspire academic success for kids in every community. In partnership with Coach Across America (CAA), coaches are trained and placed in sport-based youth development settings such as non-profits, schools, and faith-based and recreational organizations to ensure every program session, practice, or game positively affects a child's future. CAA offers all coaches extensive training and other professional development opportunities, a modest stipend, and an education award that can be used to pay off student loans or be put toward future tuition. The 40 hours of coach training in youth development and mentoring strategies focus on a trauma-sensitive approach to coaching. This training prepares coaches to promote physical activity, healthy living, and good decision-making, while cultivating caring, trust-based relationships with the youth they serve. To date, 1,800 coaches across 33 states working within numerous communities have positively affected 300,000 children and young people, inspiring them to be leaders and contributing members of their communities.

Run England

Such is the popularity of charitable running and walking initiatives such as Race for Life (the UK-based Cancer Research's women-only fundraising program) that England Athletics (the national governing body for athletics) established Run England as their recreational running project. Run England's responsibility is to support participants in achieving their goals through running communities led by educated and trained leaders. Leaders can access a one-day leadership Training course, which qualifies them to deliver safe and fun running sessions. UK Athletics (UKA), the UK governing body, offers qualified lowercase leaders the opportunity to extend their skills and expertise through the next level Coach in Running Fitness Award. This initial training and qualification and the Athletics Coach Award are positioned overtly in UKA's Coach Development Pathway (figure 11.10).

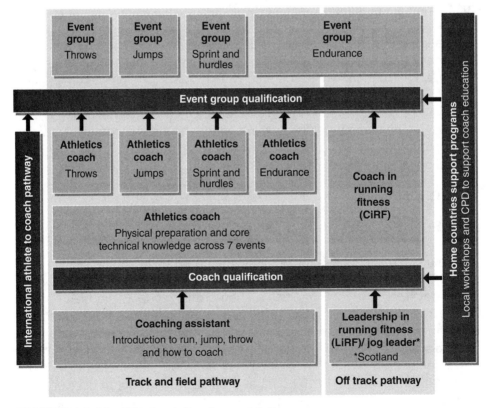

FIGURE 11.10 UKA Coach Development Pathway.

Used with permission of United Kingdom Athletics.

UP2US, Right to Play, and UKA coach education and training programs are designed to ensure that skilled coaches are operating within discrete environments. All are responsible for the education and training of coaches, although UKA's authority stretches across a range of track-and-field disciplines. This broad educational offering is reflected within their coach development pathway. UKA offers participation and performance pathways structured across four levels designed to guide the initial education, training, qualification, and career development of athletics coaches. This example of a coach development pathway is not unique. As highlighted in this chapter, it is one of a number of UK Coach Development Pathways that have been developed using the UK Coaching Framework as a reference point.

What are positively highlighted with the UKA, Run England, and Cancer Research examples are the inextricable links forged between strategy, operations, and implementation when those functions are built on a solid foundation. It highlights how strategy can positively inform and affect practice to drive change and support personal development at the participation end of the development spectrum.

International Sport Coaching Framework

Many of the examples offered here have influenced the global coach development and coach education landscape. On behalf of the international community the International Council for Coaching Excellence (ICCE) recognized the challenges that accompany the coaching role and acknowledged the need for a common set of criteria to inform the development and qualification of coaches. In 2012 at the Global Coaches House during the Olympic and Paralympic Games, they released the International Sport Coaching Framework, version 1.1. This framework was created to provide a reference point for the education, development, and recognition of coaches. The framework articulates the different coaching environments: participant and performance pathways; the various coaching roles; the knowledge, skills and expertise required; and how to educate, train, and accredit coaches.

The International Sport Coaching Framework is not a mandate to be parachuted into an existing or nonexisting system; rather, it is a reference point to be dutifully considered in the context within which the organization is operating. Variables such as the type of sport; its popularity; the number, demographics, and geography of participants; the type and quality of existing education programs; the infrastructure and resources of the organization; and, critically, the vision all have to be carefully weighed. The International Sport Coaching Framework has presented the international coaching industry with a shared vision informed by robust evidence and practice, a common and universal language, and shared resources. It is a standardized practical reference point to drive the development of excellent coaching practice and a catalyst for the development of sport-specific coaching systems.

Summary

Sport has a global appeal. It is underpinned by similar values, philosophies, and practices and, critically, the desire to establish coaching as a profession is high on many agendas. The questions now are, How do we share best practices? How can we learn from the global trailblazers?

The aim of this chapter was to examine how various countries and their coach education providers (governing bodies and private for-profit and not-for-profit organizations) have constructed their modern coaching houses to prepare coaches to work effectively within and across participant and performance pathways and with various coaching populations. There is a range of practices evident. Some international federations, governing bodies, and sport training providers are more mature in this space. This is inevitably a function of time, resources, creative thinking, persistence, critical reflection, learning, and re-thinking. We believe the practices are beneficial, but the research base testifying to this is embryonic. Linear studies are required to effectively show that planning is being translated into practice.

Key learning drawn from the research presented in this chapter may be best presented as a series of reflective questions that the organization or practitioner should seek to answer before committing to constructing any form of coaching framework, model, or system. The following questions are not a prescriptive or exhaustive list but offer some opportunities for critical reflection and development before a commitment to action:

- Is there a central lead agency for coaching in your country? How can that agency support your work?

- What sport-specific reference points exist to inform and guide your development work?

- What is your role within the coach education and coach development landscape? How significantly can you influence political and national and local agendas?

- Where are you now relative to current best practices in coach education and coach development? Think about your own coaching house:
  - Do you have a player development strategy, pathway, or model?
  - Do you know what coach capabilities (skills, knowledge, and expertise) are required to work within the participation and performance pathways and with the different populations?
  - Are you building from the ground up, or do you have an existing infrastructure for coach education? How stable is this infrastructure?

- Any change agenda requires significant investment in terms of time and human, physical, and financial resources:
  - What resources do you have to drive the change you want to create? Where will you source these?

- What expertise can you tap into? What evidence bases already exist?

- What is the anticipated cost? What funding sources are available?

• What will success look like? How will you know your program is working? How will you monitor and evaluate the development journey and the impact agenda?

Chapter 12

International Coach Education and Development: A Case Study

Sergio Lara-Bercial and John Bales

As emphasized in previous chapters, sport plays a central role in twenty-first-century society. What for the most part started as games played during local festivities to entertain villagers and visitors (traditional games) has given rise to a whole host of professional leagues and events (organized games) (Parlebas 2011). Moreover, sport has also become a leisure activity of choice for an ever-growing number of individuals across the lifespan. It has also been assigned a major role to play in the development of healthy lifestyles and positive attitudes and adaptive behaviors beyond sport for both youth and adults and in both developed and developing countries (Weiss and Wiese-Bjornstal 2008). Sport is a major driving force.

Against this background, the figure of the coach has emerged as a fundamental player in this new game. Millions of coaches engage in delivering sport to millions of people every day (North 2009; North et al. 2016). Be it in a community setting or in a performance environment, coaches are expected to deliver a return on investment (Lyle 2002). For a youth community coach, this may mean that young children are having an engaging and motivating first experience of organized sport that may set them on a path to lifelong participation. For a coach in a performance environment, this may look more like gold medals, major trophies, or dealing with the intricacies of the transfer market every season. Coaches are at the heart of the sporting experience and outcomes of the participant and the athlete.

Owing to this rise in organized and leisurely sport participation and the subsequent investment by sport organizations and governments over the last couple of decades, coaches, and the ways in which they are educated and developed, have come under scrutiny. A coach at any level is no longer expected to open the gym and roll the ball in or let athletes run around the track mindlessly and without purpose. Coaching has become athlete-centered, and thus coaches are expected to effectively and repeatedly maximize participants' outcomes, wants, and needs, whatever these may be. For coaches to do this, they must somehow have gained the relevant knowledge, skills, and attitudes to produce such outcomes.

A major realization of coaching stakeholders over the last decade is that coaches do not develop their practice in isolation (ICCE, ASOIF, and LBU 2013). While coaches may be at the forefront of sport, they form part of a very intricate and interconnected coaching system. This system contains a large number of stakeholders and moving pieces, and for the system to be effective, all those pieces must be aligned and work in unison or the promise of coaching and sport will not be realized. Coaching and coach education, development, and employment happen within these complex systems. Figure 12.1 below depicts the main elements of a coaching system.

As a result of the situation described above, in many parts of the world and in varying sporting environments, coaching has evolved toward becoming a professionally regulated occupation regardless of whether a coach is

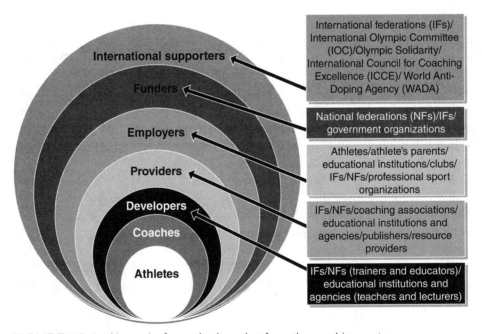

FIGURE 12.1   Network of organizations that form the coaching system.

Reprinted by permission from International Council for Coaching Excellence, Association of Summer Olympic International Federations, and Leeds Beckett University, *International Sport Coaching Framework (Version 1.2)* (Champaign, IL: Human Kinetics, 2013), 8.

remunerated or not. Until recently, however, "there has neither been the sustained discourse nor the vehicle to advance the position of coaching as a professionally regulated vocation" (Duffy 2010, vii). Today, international agencies such as the International Olympic Committee (IOC), the International Paralympic Committee (IPC), the World Anti-Doping Agency (WADA), the European Commission, individual governments, national lead agencies, federations, educational institutions, leagues, and coaches' associations around the world have started to mobilize around coaching. However, without clear reference points, a common language, and a sense of overarching guidance and direction, these efforts could lead to a mosaic of initiatives and outcomes that run the risk of having a relatively low impact compared to what a more concerted approach could achieve. The International Council for Coaching Excellence (ICCE) has attempted to provide a platform and a vehicle to galvanize this existing interest and facilitate the creation of a suitable, common discourse for international cooperation and development in coaching.

The International Council for Coaching Excellence

The International Council for Coaching Excellence (ICCE) is a not-for-profit organization established on 24 September 1997 by delegates representing 15 countries during the second International Coach Education Summit at the Wingate Institute in Israel. The guidelines and aims for this new organization had been first established back in 1994 at a meeting marking the 20th anniversary of the Trainerakademie Köln, Germany, and refined at the inaugural International Coach Education Summit in 1995 in Leeds, England, organized by the National Coaching Foundation (now sports coach UK), the national lead agency for coaching in the United Kingdom of Great Britain and Northern Ireland. The ICCE has since grown to represent over 30 countries spread over five continents.

The ICCE's mission is "to lead and support the development of sport coaching globally" (ICCE 2015, 1) toward the fulfillment of a vision of "quality coaching systems which support and develop excellent coaches" (ICCE 2015, 1). The organization was founded on the premise that international collaboration and exchange can accelerate positive change in the realm of coaching development. ICCE members thus seek to enhance the quality of coaching at every level of sport and therefore support the millions of coaches around the world striving daily to give athletes and participants a chance to fulfill their goals and ambitions.

As part of this global mission and vision, the ICCE specifically aims to

- promote sport coaching as a profession;
- promote international relationships, social and cultural, with those who are engaged in coach education;

- promote sport and sport values;
- promote and utilize research in the field of training and competition;
- exchange knowledge in the field of coaching;
- disseminate information about curricula, qualifying standards, etc. among members;
- co-ordinate coach education courses and resources across member countries;
- promote a moral code in coaching;
- improve relationships among the coach, management, and athletes;
- publish a professional publication in the field of coach education; and
- encourage and assist countries in the field of coach education.

The expected net outcomes of the ICCE initiative are

- a network of national and international organizations that actively play a part in the development of coaching in their respective nations or sport;
- international accords on coaching issues such as ethics, safety, and knowledge/competency;
- an international coaching culture that supports the values of Olympism: integrity, honesty, fairness, inclusion, tolerance, and commitment to excellence; and
- a global community of coaches.

The ICCE's membership and organizational and governance structure is designed to facilitate the achievement of the vision and mission. The membership structure includes four categories of members:

- *Category A:*. This category is for national representative bodies and international federations; that is, national organizations with a direct public mandate to lead the development of coaching in a country, or an international federation responsible for a specific sport globally. Currently, over 40 countries are represented at this level, including the United States, the United Kingdom, Australia, China, India, Germany, France, South Africa, and Japan to mention a few.
- *Category B:* Other organizations that play an active role in the development of coaching (e.g., coaches associations, national federations, educational institutions, etc.).
- *Category C:* Individuals with a keen interest in coaching.
- *Category D:* Honorary members.

In addition, in 2011 ICCE created the Innovation Group of Lead Agencies (IGLA). The IGLA brings together a select group of national organizations with a proven track record in the development of coaching and coach education. The purpose of the IGLA is to advance coaching in a number of priority areas such as coach developers, quality assurance, high-performance coaching, or higher education. Currently, this group contains the following organizations: Trainerakademie Köln (DOSB, Germany); NOC*NSF (Netherlands); Coaching Association of Canada; BASPO Switzerland; The Norwegian Olympic and Paralympic Committee and Confederation of Sports; Leeds Beckett University; UK Sport (United Kingdom); SASCOC (South Africa); INSEP (France); Israel Sport Authority; Australian Sports Commission; and High Performance Sport New Zealand.

ICCE has also forged very close working relationships with key international sport organizations such as the IOC (Entourage Commission and Olympic Solidarity), the IPC, the associations of summer and winter Olympic federations (ASOIF and AWOIF), the European Commission, and the World Anti-Doping Agency (WADA). The ICCE is therefore uniquely qualified to address its mission because its members and partners comprise the world's leaders in coaching development. There exists no other international sport body with such a makeup.

The ICCE organizational structure includes a General Assembly, Executive Board, and Inspection Committee. For the purposes of this chapter, it is important to briefly explain the composition of the Executive Board because it gives the organization its true cooperative and international flavor. The Board consists of fifteen members, elected by the General Assembly to a four-year term of office: President; Vice President; Past President; General Secretary; Treasurer; five continental vice-presidents (one each representing Africa, the Americas, Asia, Oceania, and Europe); and five additional members recruited from "A" member organizations or key international stakeholders [1]. The Board is responsible for establishing the programs, policies, and procedures of the ICCE.

Furthermore, the ICCE has a Research Committee chaired by leading figures from the academic coaching world [2]. The committee has global representation and its mission is two-fold: on the one hand, it ensures that any ICCE initiatives and programs have a sound evidence base; on the other, the committee is tasked with bringing the coaching research community together and promote the sharing and exchange of ideas between academics from across the globe. An example of the latter is the hosting of a biennial Coaching Research Fair alongside the ICCE's Global Coach Conference where researchers from all over the world come together to share the latest advances in coaching research and to set the research agenda for the future.

The ICCE has developed a broad portfolio of activities and services to support the fulfillment of its mission of leading and developing coaching globally:

- *Advocacy, policy, and guidance documents:* A fundamental part of what ICCE does is bring together coaching stakeholders to develop evidence-based policy and system development guidelines and support documents. Two key examples of this work are the International Sport Coaching Framework Version 1.2. (ISCF) and the International

Coach Developer Framework (ICDF). For more information on the former, please see later in this chapter. For the latter, please refer to chapter 15.

- *Global Coach Conference:* Now in its 11th edition, the biennial Global Coach Conference brings together coaches, coach developers, system builders, administrators, technical directors, sport scientists, and researchers from across the globe to share in best practice examples and the latest research.

- *Global Coaches House (GCH):* The GCH is both a physical and virtual space for the coaching community around the world to meet, interact, share, and learn from each other cooperatively and from experts in the field. Successful editions ran during the London 2012 and Rio 2016 Olympiads and the Glasgow 2014 Commonwealth Games.

- *Advice and consultancy:* ICCE also provides support to its members directly on the ground through advice and consultancy services. This may take the shape of short-term consultations or fully fledged, longer development projects. The latter part of this chapter provides a sample of the variety of projects ICCE is or has been involved with recently.

Now that we have a clearer understanding of what coach education and development consists of in the twenty-first century and of the role of the ICCE, let us turn our attention to the foundational text guiding these advances, the International Sport Coaching Framework.

The International Sport Coaching Framework

With growing appreciation of the role of coaches in society and the challenges that accompany the job, the global sport community and its partners recognized the need for a common, worldwide set of criteria to inform, guide, and support the development and qualification of coaches globally. Previous efforts at national (e.g., the UK Coaching Framework [Sports Coach UK 2008] and the South African Coaching Framework [SASCOC 2011]) and international levels (e.g., the European Framework for the Recognition of Coaching Competences and Qualifications [European Coaching Council 2007]) had shown the benefits of this approach.

To this effect, the ICCE, in conjunction with ASOIF and with the support of Leeds Beckett University, brought together in 2011 a thirty-strong project group containing a wide representation of international sport coaching stakeholders, organizations, coaching experts, and researchers to develop the International Sport Coaching Framework (ISCF; ICCE, ASOIF, and LBU; Duffy and Lara-Bercial 2012, 2013). Meetings of the working group and consultation events took place in France, Spain, England, China, Bulgaria, and South Africa, leading to the publication of version 1.1 of the ISCF in

London in August 2012 during the XXX Olympiad. The publication of version 1.1 stimulated a high level of interest and support and fueled further debate about the benefits of such a document and the key issues it should address. Following a 12-month consultation period, version 1.2 of the ISCF was launched at ICCE's Global Coach Conference in Durban, South Africa, in September 2013. Both versions have been published by ICCE's partner, Human Kinetics.

The Framework's Purpose

Given the above, the purpose of the ISCF is therefore

> to provide an internationally recognized reference point for the development of coaches that is flexible and responsive to the needs of different sports; countries; organizations and institutions and which provides benchmarks for the recognition and certification of coaches. (ICCE, ASOIF, and LBU 2013, 10)

The ISCF recognizes that the context for implementation of coaching systems will vary significantly between sports, countries, and continents. Thus, the principles and elements outlined by the ISCF need to be informed by and adapted to the specific situations and objectives of the organization using it. Nevertheless, a globally accepted reference point provides all members of the coaching family with a common language and a powerful tool to evaluate, plan, develop, and compare their systems and processes around coach education, development, deployment, and employment. Moreover, the ISCF supports coaches' employment and mobility through the provision of a tool to compare qualifications obtained in different countries and systems. Likewise, the ISCF supports the creation of a clear research and evaluation agenda for coaching, stimulates and facilitates global exchange, and helps organizations and countries consider and gain traction for specific political decisions related to coaching.

The Framework's Key Features

The ISCF provides a common language for understanding and facilitating quality coaching educational needs that are addressing both the foundational roles and responsibilities of the profession as well as acknowledging the essential contextual uniqueness created when considering motivational, developmental, and performance-based differences of sport participants.

Coaching Defined

The ISCF defines coaching as "a process of guided improvement and development in a single sport at identifiable stages of athlete development" (ICCE, ASOIF, and LBU 2013, 14).

Such definition implies a number of fundamental concepts. First, it proposes that coaching should be athlete centered. A person's engagement in sport throughout the lifespan follows varying trajectories underpinned by different motives, goals, and aspirations. If we accept this tenet, it follows that from an athlete-centered perspective, a coach should therefore strive to fulfill the motives, goals, and aspirations of athletes and participants at all times and at different stages of their lives in an appropriate manner. Coaches must be aware of how these motives, goals, and aspirations may change over time and act accordingly.

Second, the definition moves beyond improvement, which can be construed as short term and specific to sport performance, to include the idea of development. Development signals a focus on the long-term nature of what the participant is trying to achieve over time, as well as the need for coaches to concern themselves with the person as well as the athlete. From the perspective of the ICCE and the ISCF, there is no plausible justification for coaches to act against this developmental principle and to put short-term gain in sporting terms above long-term benefit for the person behind the athlete.

Participant Pathways and Coaching Categories and Domains

In order to facilitate this athlete-centered thinking process for organizations developing coaching systems, the ISCF proposes two main categories of sport engagement, namely participation and performance, and six associated domains. This classification, based on the work of Côté (1999), Balyi and Hamilton (1995), and Lyle (2002), is represented in figure 12.2.

Participants and athletes in the various domains will have different motivations to take part in sport as well as diverse goals, needs, and requirements. The obvious consequence for coaches is that in order to meet their needs, they will require distinct capabilities according to whom and where they coach. Therefore, two discrete coaching categories are defined: Participation coaching and Performance coaching (figure 12.3).

The ICCE and the ISCF propose that the overall aim is to achieve coaching excellence at all levels of the participation spectrum.

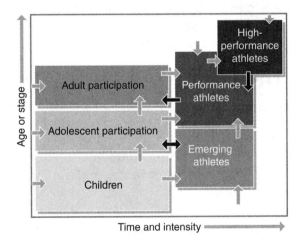

FIGURE 12.2 Sport participation spectrum and pathway.

Organizations must strive to improve the quality of their coaches not only at the performance level but also across the board. Coaches, along with the organizations that employ or deploy them, therefore are responsible for developing their capabilities and competencies to do the job in relation to the domain in which the coach practices. This has some major implications.

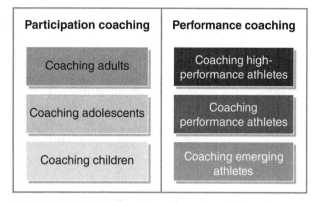

Participation coaching	Performance coaching
Coaching adults	Coaching high-performance athletes
Coaching adolescents	Coaching performance athletes
Coaching children	Coaching emerging athletes

FIGURE 12.3   Coaching categories and domains.

Reprinted by permission from International Council for Coaching Excellence, Association of Summer Olympic International Federations, and Leeds Beckett University, *International Sport Coaching Framework (Version 1.2)* (Champaign, IL: Human Kinetics, 2013), 23.

Sport organizations need to gain an in-depth understanding of their current participation spectrum and pathways. In other words, they need to understand who plays their sport and why. This has been referred to as participant development modelling and the resulting map as a Participant Development Model, or PDM (Sports Coach UK 2008). Once an organization has built this image of what their current PDM looks like, it needs to decide if this picture works for them or if there are any gaps or new additions that need to be put into place. An organization should ask questions such as the following: Are there enough adults playing the sport? Is there enough and adequate provision for female participation? Are the entry points into the sport and the transitions between the segments of the spectrum fit for purpose? Is provision at each level stage-appropriate? If the answer to any of these questions is *no,* the organization needs to consider if any changes have to be made at the structural level in the short-, mid-, or long-term. Practical examples of this process will be provided in the final section of the chapter. In addition, a fully developed tool for this process is available at www.coachlearn.eu.

Moreover though, once a given organization has clarity about what their PDM looks like, or needs to look like in the future, there is a very important job that needs to be done: a coaching workforce audit. Put simply, organizations need to understand who is coaching their sport, with what participants, where the coaching is done, and how well prepared the coaches are to do their job. Sport organizations also have to look at the future picture and decide what kind of coaches and how many they are going to need to meet the future demand of the sport for the benefits of its participants and the very growth and sustainability of the sport itself.

Only once clarity around the participation spectrum, the pathways, and the coaching workforce has been achieved can a sport organization set out to develop coaching qualifications and development opportunities that will equip coaches to fulfill their roles within the system.

Coaching Roles

As well as differentiating between the capabilities of coaches working in different categories and domains (e.g., performance versus participation; children versus adults), the ISCF proposes that the role of the coach varies as a function of the levels of expertise, knowledge, responsibility, and autonomy required to fulfill it. The ISCF offers four generic roles that aim to describe the four most common roles played by coaches (table 12.1).

These generic roles need to be customized to reflect the reality of a country or a sport and, most important, qualification curricula must be able to show

TABLE 12.1 Coaching Roles

Role Descriptor	Knowledge and Competence
Coaching Assistant (*Note*: the term *Assistant Coach*, as opposed to the role of Coaching Assistant, may be applied at a number of levels. For example, an Assistant Coach in High Performance might be operating to the level of the Advanced/Senior Coach role descriptor)	Assists in the delivery of sessions* Plans, delivers and reviews basic coaching sessions, sometimes under supervision Basic level of knowledge, competence and decision making to deliver the primary functions, with guidance Supports the engagement of pre-coaches
Coach	Plans, delivers and reviews coaching sessions over a season, sometimes part of a wider program Extended level of knowledge, competence and decision making to independently deliver the primary functions Supports the engagement and development of pre-coaches and Coaching Assistants
Advanced/Senior Coach	Plans, delivers, leads and evaluates coaching sessions and seasons Extended and integrated knowledge, competence and decision making to deliver the primary functions and mentor other coaches Works independently and plays a leading role within the structure of the program Manages the development of Coaches; Coaching Assistants and pre-coaches
Master/Head Coach	Oversees and contributes to the delivery, review and evaluation of programs over seasons, in medium- to largescale contexts, underpinned by innovation and research Specialist and integrated level of knowledge and competence, recognized as an expert with highly developed decision making skills Often involved in designing and overseeing management structures and development programs for other coaches

*Sessions include both practices and competitions.

a link between their content and delivery format and the role the coach is expected to fulfill once the qualification has been achieved.

Coaching in Action: The Primary Functions and Competences

The ISCF then proceeds to offer an evidence-based blueprint of the primary functions of the coach and the required competences underlying each function. Based on the work of Côté and Gilbert (2009) and Gilbert and Côté (2013), the ISCF also proposes that the functions and competencies are underpinned by the integrated application of three types of knowledge basis:

- Professional knowledge: content knowledge and how to teach it
- Interpersonal knowledge: the ability to connect with people
- Intrapersonal knowledge: of the self

Figure 12.4 summarizes the above.

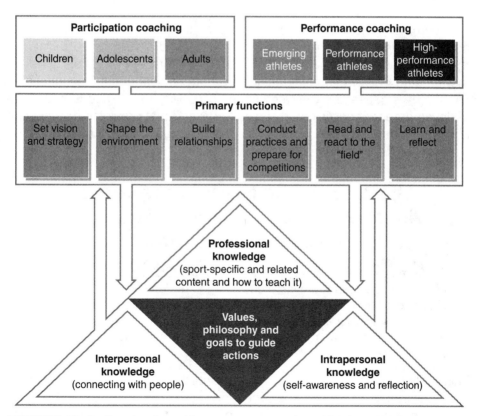

FIGURE 12.4 Functional coaching competence and coaching knowledge.

Reprinted by permission from International Council for Coaching Excellence, Association of Summer Olympic International Federations, and Leeds Beckett University, *International Sport Coaching Framework (Version 1.2)* (Champaign, IL: Human Kinetics, 2013), 31.

Clarity in determining the amount of expertise, knowledge, responsibility, and autonomy required of each coaching role in relation to the primary functions, competencies, and knowledge basis is at the heart of developing coaching qualifications that meet the needs of the coaches, the athletes, and the coaching system in general.

Coach Learning and Development

Finally, the ISCF states that coach education and development must take into account the existing evidence regarding how coaches learn in order to design programs that are effective not only in the transfer and acquisition of new knowledge but also in the development of applied and integrated coaching skills. Moving beyond the traditional episodic nature of coach education into a much more continuous and guided form of coach development is vital for success. The development of a highly trained Coach Developer workforce is paramount to support the design and delivery of such suitable and effective programs. The ICCE has recently published the International Coach Developer Framework (ICDF), outlining the key elements of this process (please refer to chapter 15 for detailed coverage of this topic).

In summary, the ISCF proposes that coaching should concern itself with both the development of lifelong participation and enhanced performance; that in doing so it can and should produce a wide array of multiple developmental outcomes beyond the acquisition of physical skills; that for this to happen, it is necessary to match coach capability to the needs and stage of development of participants and athletes; and that providing relevant and continuous development and learning opportunities for coaches should be a major goal of coaching organizations.

Examples of a Framework Approach to Coach Education and Development

Far from being constraining and restrictive, the ISCF aims to be a flexible tool that supports organizations trying to evaluate or develop their coaching systems. In that sense, the ISCF does not claim to have all the answers, but rather attempts to ask the right questions. The answers will be invariably dependent upon the context, resources, and objectives of the organization.

This section thus tries to provide mini-case studies of how different countries and organizations have used the concepts proposed by the ISCF, and in some cases the services provided by ICCE, to solve the coaching challenges they were presented with. The mini-case studies will be labelled according to the layer of the coaching system (see figure 12.1) the intervention was aimed at. The examples will be presented from the center of the diagram out.

Coaches and Athletes: The Philippines Academy of Sport

In December 2012, ICCE and LBU were commissioned by the Republic of the Philippines Department of Education (DepEd) to lead an overhaul of their High School Special Program in Sport (SPS) under the new banner of the Philippines Academy of Sport (PHAS). The project is funded by the British Council and coordinated by Magna Anima Education Systems Inc. The SPS program is a government initiative run in over 30 high schools across the Philippines. SPS schools recruit talented student-athletes out of elementary schools and offer them the opportunity to study and train for four years between grades 7 and 10. The initial aims of the program were to increase the performance of Filipino athletes at the South East Asia and Olympic Games. In operation since 2001, the program had yielded a relatively low return.

The project team traveled to the Philippines where it met with DepEd to discuss the aims of the project and to visit three SPS schools in order to conduct a scoping exercise looking to identify areas that were working well and areas that perhaps could be improved. At the schools, the team was able to conduct in depth interviews and focus groups with the school principals, the SPS coordinators, the coaches, and the athletes. The ISCF was at all times used as a reference point to analyze the picture emerging in front of the researchers.

For instance, the participation spectrum was used to determine and explain to the DepEd and SPS staff where the student-athletes sat. Once the implications of working with "emerging athletes" were understood, the goodness of fit between their current practice and internationally accepted best practice within this domain was evaluated. A collaborative dialogue ensued to map the way forward. The use of the ISCF as an analysis tool allowed for a number of key issues to come to the fore:

- The talent identification system was inefficient and potentially allowing talent to slip through the net or go unrealized.
- In the main, coaches were not qualified and lacked knowledge and experience of coaching methodology and pedagogy specifically pertaining to the coaching of emerging athletes.
- Student-athletes were mentally and physically unequipped to successfully meet the demands of their academic courses and a performance development environment at the same time.

The project team agreed on two main interventions, namely the Coach Advancement Program and the Enhancement Program for Student-Athletes.

The Coach Advancement Program

Guided by the core functions, competencies, knowledge basis, and principles of coach learning described in the ISCF, a ten-month Coach Advancement

Program was designed and implemented. The program included a six-day Introductory Course, on-the-job supported learning over the course of one academic year, and a five-day Consolidation Course at the end of the year. Twenty-eight coaches from two schools attended the program.

The Introductory Course focused on supporting the coaches to integrate and apply new professional, interpersonal, and intrapersonal knowledge into their current practice and context. For the duration of the course, coaches spent a lot of time, individually or in groups, working out what their new knowledge base meant in their context and for their programs and how to apply it. They were supported by a team of international and local coach developers.

On the last two days of the course, coaches were asked to consolidate their learning by developing mission, vision, and values statements for their schools. They were also asked to start to sketch out a new talent-identification strategy, an age- and stage-appropriate sport-specific curriculum, a fully fledged season plan, and a personal development plan taking into account their personal reflections over the course.

The coaches then returned to their schools tasked with completing these documents and with keeping a reflective journal. Coaches were encouraged to run coach meetings and development activities at their schools and support was provided by the coach developers through a number of site visits and online webinars.

At the end of the academic year, the coaches gathered again for the five-day Consolidation Course. Here they spent most of their time reviewing how their year had played out and what new competencies they felt they had developed. They also had an opportunity to share their working documents and consult with other coaches and with the coach developers in order to refine their plans.

Enhancement Program for Student-Athletes

As mentioned earlier, it became clear from the scoping study that one of the greatest challenges faced by the coaches and the student-athletes was the lack of preparation of some of the athletes to adjust to life as performance student-athletes. Taking into account the themes coming from interviews with coaches and athletes and research in this area, the project team set out to develop an awareness-raising and skill-development program to help student-athletes better navigate the choppy waters of life as a student-athlete. The program, titled "Learning 2 Be," contains nine modules tackling different areas but in the main is aimed at raising the student-athletes' levels of self-awareness of what it means to be a student-athlete, including the perks, the challenges, and some key knowledge and skills so they can help themselves increase their chance of succeeding both academically and in the sport arena, and, most important, beyond their sporting careers. To date, there has not been a study of the outcomes of the "Learning 2 Be" program, but it will be evaluated in due course.

Over time, the PHAS project is expected to encourage country-wide change in the way coaches are educated and in the way sport is delivered to young people. For now, it provides a clear example of how the ISCF can be used to develop activities on the ground for very specific contexts and purposes.

Coaches: Project CoachNet, "The Voice of the Coach"

The ISCF stresses that the development of sport coaching globally is not only about qualifications and continuous learning. Coaches need to learn their trade in the best possible way, but attention must also be paid to the structures surrounding them and the environments in which they carry out their craft. Creating effective channels to enhance coaches' representation and give coaches a voice that can be heard by all relevant stakeholders is paramount to ensure coaching gains recognition as a professional area and that coaches are supported appropriately once they are qualified and employed to fulfill a coaching role.

The European arm of the ICCE, the European Coaching Council (ECC), in partnership with Leeds Beckett University, was successful in a bid to the European Commission under the Preparatory Action in the Field of Sport (EAC/18/2011). In addition to ECC and LBU, another twelve European organizations representing sport federations, sport universities, national coaching agencies, and coaches' associations were recruited into the project group. The overall project was designed to develop an innovative approach that would contribute to the strengthening of the organization of sport in Europe as part of the "good governance" strand of the EU Preparatory Action in the Field of Sport (Duffy, North, and Curado 2013). The primary objective was to examine ways in which the organization of coaching could be enhanced in Europe, with a particular focus on the greater involvement of coaches in decision-making.

A research design was put into place, and primary and secondary data was collected in the form of questionnaires, best practice examples, and partner interviews. Varying arrangements for the development and management of coaching were observed through a review of practices across different European countries. Within this varied landscape, the representation of coaches was sporadic, ranging from no representative mechanism to a number of good practice examples that made provision for the tiered engagement of coaches depending on their role, sport, and coaching status category. These examples included confederated models across sports, blended models across coaching status categories, and single and multisport models for the engagement and representation of coaches.

The CoachNet final project report concluded that there is a need for a more considered approach to the involvement of coaches in decision-making, with a number of recommendations developed for consideration by member states and the European divisions of the International Federations:

- The principle of coaches' representation and involvement should be enshrined in the activities of all sporting organizations.
- ICCE and its European branch, ECC, should continue to deepen the structure to lead on the promotion of sport coaching as a blended professional area. This structure should continue to embed coaches and coaches' associations as an integral element of the organization.
- ICCE and ECC should establish a concerted program of advocacy and action on the voice of the coach. This should include engagement with IOC, ASOIF, IPC, WADA, and other international organizations.
- Each sport should consider the establishment of sport-specific structures for the engagement and representation of coaches.
- There is a continued need to listen to the needs and voice of the coach, as part of ongoing research and development activity within the sport sector.

All these approaches need to be tempered, the CoachNet final report warns, with the realization that coaches are individual decision-makers, operating in a wide variety of contexts. Many coaches do not show a propensity for involvement in formal "representative" structures. The need for alternative methods to more closely and effectively connect with and engage coaches is identified as a major priority.

The CoachNet project exemplifies the more systemic nature of the ICCE's mission to lead and develop coaching globally. ICCE and ECC are now working on the implementation of the CoachNet recommendations.

Coach Developers: The Nippon Sport University International Coach Developer Academy

The ISCF and the ICDF (see chapter 15) stress the importance of developing a world-class coach developer workforce for the success of any coaching system. The ICDF states

> Coach developers are not simply experienced coaches or transmitters of coaching knowledge. They are trained to develop, support and challenge coaches to go on honing and improving their knowledge and skills to provide positive and effective sport experiences for all participants. . . . Coach developers play a crucial role not just in the initial formal training of coaches but also in the way coaches are educated, supported and nurtured "on the job." (ICCE, ASOIF, and LBU 2014, 8)

The Nippon Sport Science University (NSSU) Coach Developer Academy (https://www.ncda.tokyo/) has been established to support the development of future international coach developers and to construct a global network of coach developers. The academy is part of the broader "Sport for Tomorrow" program of Japan's Ministry of Education, Culture, Sports, Science and Technology (MEXT) linked to the 2020 Tokyo Olympic and Paralympic Games. NSSU and ICCE have collaborated on this project to apply the principles of the ISCF and the ICDF to the development and delivery of a blended learning training program for coach developers.

The NSSU Coach Developer Academy is led by ICCE Research Committee member Dr. Masa Ito, and internationally renowned Master Coach Developer Mrs. Penny Crisfield (author of chapter 15) has served as the Trainer. Mrs. Crisfield has helped coach developers in a wide variety of sports and in over 25 countries to develop the skills they need to help coaches at all levels of the coaches' pathway. As chair of the ICCE Coach Developer Workgroup, she is leading the development of this essential workforce.

The NSSU Coach Developer Academy aims to develop coach developers who are competent in the critical skills of facilitation, coach assessment, mentoring, and coach education program design and evaluation; all the skills that will help them and their organizations develop better coaches. The Academy offers a blended online and residential program, including two mandatory one-week courses at NSSU in Tokyo, and online support and e-modules to help with preparation and assessment pre- and post-course. The Academy will also organize international events such as the annual International Coach Developer Symposium and the Coaching System Leaders' Think Tank, which will bring together global leaders in coach development to share their experiences and progress the field. The Coach Developer Academy undoubtedly presents a best-practice example in the area of coach developer preparation and support.

Providers: The International Sailing Federation Coaching Framework

The International Sailing Federation (ISAF) was one of the original members of the ISCF working group between 2011 and 2013. Represented by its Training and Development Manager at the time, Mr. Dan Jaspers, it was clear from the inception of the project that ISAF believed in a systems approach to coach development. It is for this reason that, while continuing to make an invaluable contribution to the development of the ISCF in that period, ISAF worked in parallel to review their current coaching system and programs looking for ways to improve them. As a result of this process the ISACF Coaching Framework was developed (ISAF 2013).

In applying the principles of the ISCF, the ISAF Coaching Framework

> aims to provide all ISAF Member National Authorities (MNAs) a common ground for developing and evaluating coaching qualifications, encouraging coach education and training, working across international boundaries, and establishing ethical guidelines and models or standards of international best practice. (ISAF 2013, 2)

International sport federations such as ISAF face a significant challenge in that they support nearly one hundred and fifty MNAs all over the world.

These federations come in all sizes and shapes. The level of staffing, the financial resources, and the number of participants varies greatly between MNAs. Some of them have large coach education departments and are able to design, develop, and deliver their own coach education and development programs. Others rely on the programs produced by ISAF. The ISAF Coaching Framework aims to be able to support all MNAs regardless of their nature.

Following the principles of the ISCF, the ISAF Coaching Framework pathway distinguishes between the participation and the performance domains. Within each of those domains, it goes on to define the various coaching roles and the competencies required for each role, and provides a mapping tool for MNAs to compare their own qualifications and roles to those described in both the ISCF and the ISAF Coaching Framework (figure 12.5).

By doing all of the above, the ISAF Coaching Framework supports MNAs to achieve the following (ISAF 2013):

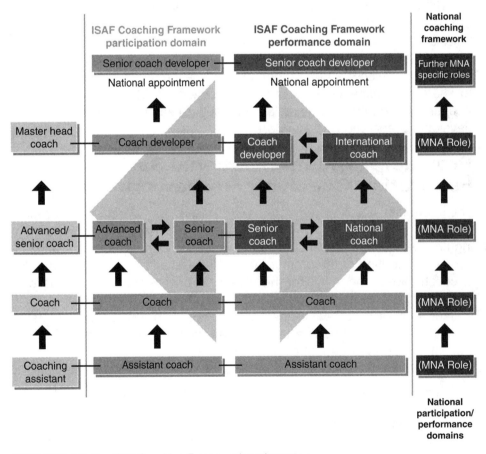

FIGURE 12.5 ISAF Coaching Framework pathways.

- Map existing qualifications to a recognized international reference point
- Assess and recognize coaching competencies of coaches coming into their country holding qualifications from a different MNA, thus improving coach mobility and employment prospects
- Develop new qualifications based on the domain, role, and competencies blueprint provided
- Identify gaps in the knowledge and skills of their coaches and develop further development opportunities
- Align their coach development efforts to the needs of the participants and athletes.

In addition, the ISAF Coaching Framework presents a comprehensive flowchart depicting the necessary steps for those MNAs looking to develop their own qualifications and coaching systems (figure 12.6).

In summary, the ISAF Coaching Framework demonstrates the flexibility and adaptability of the ISCF and how it can be used by an international federation to guide the development of its own qualifications and those of

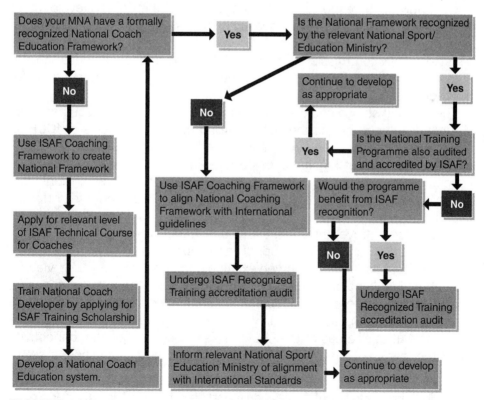

FIGURE 12.6 Process for development of National Training Program.

its national members, providing a common reference point without taking away a federation's own individuality and context specificity.

Funders and Providers: Redeveloping the Malaysian Coach Development System

Since hosting the Commonwealth Games in 1998, Malaysia has put in place the key components of a successful performance sport system: state-of-the-art national sport facilities in Kuala-Lumpur; national team programs that employ full-time coaches; developmental programs through state and national sport schools; sport science and medicine support; a coach development program; and funding programs for national sport federations. The foundation has been built for Malaysia to become a power in South East Asian sport and a significant player on the global stage in selected sports. With all the pieces in place, there is a belief that there are potential significant improvements that could make a difference in the delivery of all these programs, including coaching, to develop a culture of excellence that better supports athletes, coaches, and organizations to achieve their performance goals.

On 1 July 2015, responsibility for the running of the Coach Development Academy (CDA), the coaching qualification system in Malaysia, switched from the National Sport Council (NSC) to the National Sport Institute (ISN). As a first step, ISN commissioned a panel of ICCE experts to conduct a scoping study of the current CDA in order to propose a set of recommendations for the redevelopment of the system.

The scoping study used the Quality in Coaching Model Assessment Tool (QiCM) developed by the Innovation Group of Lead Agencies of ICCE as a research framework. In short, this evidence-based best-practice model revolves around four key areas of performance (i.e., coaching leadership, coaching system strategic plan, coach education and development, and coaching system evaluation), which when considered together offer an overview of how well a particular coaching system is doing and highlights key areas for improvement. The QiCM uses other fundamental ICCE texts such as the ISCF and ICDF to support and substantiate the analysis.

The ICCE expert panel reviewed existing documentation and interviewed a number of stakeholders including ISN staff, national federations, coaches, and coach developers. This process of iterative inquiry unearthed a large variety of findings relative not only to coach education and development systems, but to all areas of the QiCM. This highlights the interconnectivity of all the pieces of the coaching system. Based on the findings, a set of recommendations was put forward:

- The key leaders of Malaysian sport, led by the Minister for Sport, should commit to a common set of practices and objectives in order to further enable and drive sport performance for Team Malaysia.

- The National Coaching Academy program should be updated to reflect current research and practice related to coaching development, specifically to develop domain-specific programs for youth, developmental, and high-performance coaches. Working groups for the development of the qualifications in each domain should be assembled.

- A national coach accreditation database to collect and maintain records of coaching courses and qualifications should be established.

- The development of a modern and cohesive coach developer workforce should be a priority

- Each of the national federations should develop and be held accountable for a four-year coaching plan that documents their current status, goals and objectives, gaps, planned activities, and evaluation processes.

The scoping exercise provides a clear "state of affairs" statement informed by international best practice and research evidence. The relevant Malaysian stakeholders will now have to consider these recommendations and agree on which ones to implement and in which order. The redevelopment of the Malaysian Coaching System offers a significant example of the value of looking at coach education and development from a systems perspective and showcases the tools that have been recently developed by ICCE and its partners to support the global coaching community at this level.

International Supporters: The International Olympic Committee and the World Anti-Doping Agency

The significance of the coach in the life of athletes has been recognized by the highest levels of the sport administration. More and more, international organizations, which play a very important part in the running of sport, are taking steps to guarantee that coaches are sufficiently prepared to have a positive impact on the lives and careers of athletes.

The Athlete's Entourage Commission

The International Olympic Committee (IOC) created the Athlete's Entourage Commission in the realization that today's athletes do not work in isolation. The Entourage (see figure 12.7) is defined as

> all the people associated with the athletes, including, without limitation, managers, agents, coaches, physical trainers, medical staff, scientists, sports organizations, sponsors, lawyers and any person promoting the athlete's sporting career, including family members. (International Olympic Committee 2011, 1)

FIGURE 12.7   The Athlete's Entourage.

The Athlete's Entourage Commission, chaired by former pole vault world-record holder Mr. Sergey Bubka, has developed guidance principles relating to the appropriate conduct of the Entourage (International Olympic Committee 2011). These general principles state that all members of the Entourage must promote ethical principles, including those contained in the Olympic Charter, the IOC Code of Ethics, and the WADA Code, and to always act in the best interest of the athlete. Integrity, transparency, confidentiality, and accountability are highlighted as fundamental to the conduct of the Entourage.

Within this context, the coach is seen as "a central figure in the day-to-day life of the athlete" (Sergey Bubka, ISCF, back page). The coach–athlete relationship, the Commission adds, bears a significant impact on the athlete's satisfaction, motivation, and performance, and coaches play the role of "teacher, counsellor, innovator, leader and protector of the athlete's health and integrity" (International Olympic Committee n.d.). In relation to this, the Commission proposes that "members of the Entourage, including coaches, should be adequately qualified to work in their area of expertise, through licenses, certificates or diplomas, particularly when such are proposed by the IF and any national sport organization" (International Olympic Committee 2011, 1). Thus, a representative of the commission (Sir Clive Woodward, Great Britain) joined the working group for the development of the ISCF and ensured that the principles outlined by the Commission were upheld and given the necessary relevance and visibility in the final document. The ISCF, in return, informs the work of the Commission in relation to the competence and qualifications expected of coaches working with emerging, performance, and elite athletes.

IOC/Olympic Solidarity

Formed in 1981, the Olympic Solidarity Commission (OS) aims to support all the National Olympic Committees (NOCs), but especially those with the greatest needs, through multifaceted programs focused primarily around athlete development, the training of coaches and sports administrators, and the promotion of the Olympic values (International Olympic Committee 2006). Through the programs offered to the NOCs, OS recognizes that coaches are extremely important for athletes at all levels of participation and they should have access to high-quality training (International Olympic Committee 2013).

OS was therefore an ideal partner to contribute to the development of the ISCF as a member of the working group. As a result of this cooperation, OS also encourages the NOCs and IFs to have a common language and to refer to training standards, such as those proposed by the ISCF, while developing proposals for projects related to coach education and development (International Olympic Committee 2013).

In this way, the ISCF serves as a translating device and a quality assurance tool to ensure that coaches are trained to the highest possible standards, while adapting the tools to the specificities of the sport and country concerned.

The World Anti-Doping Agency

The World Anti-Doping Agency (WADA) was established in 1999 to promote, coordinate, and monitor at the international level the fight against doping in sport in all its forms. The Agency is composed and funded equally by the sports movement and governments of the world (WADA 2009).

One of the most important achievements to date in the fight against doping in sport has been the drafting, acceptance, and adoption of a uniform set of anti-doping rules, the World Anti-Doping Code (WADA 2015). The purpose of the Code and the programs that support it is

- to protect athletes' fundamental right to participate in doping-free sport and thus promote health, fairness, and equality for athletes worldwide, and
- to ensure harmonized, coordinated, and effective anti-doping programs at the international and national levels with regard to detection, deterrence, and prevention of doping (WADA 2015, 11).

In promoting acceptance and adhering to the Code, WADA's education programs are designed to ensure athletes and their entourage have all the information they need to comply with the requirements of the Code. Within this context, WADA considers coaches as a fundamental part of the anti-doping effort. This is true not only from the compliance perspective but also in the acceptance that coaches are best placed to impart a values-based education to their athletes, which could buffer against the threat of doping (Backhouse, Patterson, and McKenna 2015; Patterson, Duffy, and Backhouse 2014; WADA 2015, article 21.2).

WADA's Education Manager at the time of the development of the ISCF, Mrs. Lea Cléret, became a member of the working group to ensure the ISCF supported WADA's mission and that anti-doping education became a fundamental component of any coach education and development program globally. Likewise, the principles of the ISCF have informed WADA's thinking and new development particularly around the understanding of the special characteristics and features of the different segments of the participation pathway and the impact this has for the promotion of clean sport in each of them.

Since then, WADA has worked with ICCE and Leeds Beckett University to develop a research project around the role that high-performance training centers may play in the education of high-performance coaches to maximize their role as guardians of athletes' safety and integrity. Over ninety high-performance centers from around the world have taken part in this ground-breaking research (Patterson, Backhouse, and Lara-Bercial 2017).

The relationship between the Entourage Commission, Olympic Solidarity, WADA, and the ICCE is a perfect example of the symbiotic relationships that can be forged between international organizations that share common objectives through the development of international accords such as the ISCF. Although work at this upper level of policy may seem far removed from the day to day of coaches working with children or in recreational environments, its impact tends to filter down to these areas over time. Likewise, coaches working at any level of the participation spectrum should be aware of the support structures and systems in place they can rely on nationally, regionally, and locally. For instance, UK Coaching provides support both to governing bodies of sport and to individual coaches through the continuous professional development programs. The United States Center for Coaching Excellence provides support to coach education and development providers throughout the country to ensure quality training and development and access to the most up-to-date research in coach development.

Implementation Challenges

Using a framework approach to build a coaching system is not an easy task. Lara-Bercial and colleagues (2017, 15) identify some common stumbling blocks:

- *Lack of leadership and an official mandate.* It is problematic to galvanize the whole of the coaching system when no single organization or consortium of organizations has the official mandate and leadership to drive its development. It is also difficult to mobilize stakeholders when the leader organization does not have the backing of the relevant government department or ministry or lacks any kind of leverage.

- *Sport and coaching have low priority on the national agenda.* Similar to the problem described in the point above, it is a very tall order to create the necessary conditions for system development or change if sport and coaching take a low priority. It may be necessary to raise the profile of coaching through lobbying and campaigns to raise awareness before embarking on system development.

- *Conflict of interest between stakeholders.* Sometimes, stakeholders within the system, while sharing the common interests of sport and coaching, find themselves in stern competition for a piece of the pie or holding competing views. Following are examples of this:
  - Federations competing to keep their standing in the overall sport picture
  - Education providers wishing to maintain their share of the market
  - Those holding divergent views of different segments of the sport/education sector (e.g., physical educators and coaches, sport for all versus high-performance sport)

Reprinted by permission from S. Lara-Bercial, J. North, L. Petrovic, K. Oltmanns, J. Minkhorst, K. Hämäläinen and K. Livingstone, "Enhancing Coaches' Learning, Mobility and Employability in the European Union, Development & Implementation Tool Series, Tool #1: Understanding, Planning and Developing a Coaching System," © CoachLearn. Accessed January 9, 2019, https://www.coachlearn.eu/_assets/files/escf-tool1-coaching-systems-final.pdf.

Summary

Coach education and development is an international growing trend. More and more national and international federations and whole countries are doubling their efforts to develop a highly skilled coaching workforce to meet the demands of participants and athletes. The IOC and WADA have also placed the coach at the forefront of an athlete's life and development. Against this background, the response to the work of ICCE has been overwhelming. Guidance documents such as the ISCF or ICDF have started to be embraced by the global coaching community. These documents affect the way organizations across the world view coaching and how they go about creating new or revamping existing systems. More and more, one of the main goals of the ICCE is being realized: the creation of a global coaching community, a global community driven by the same objectives and goals of developing excellence in coaching at every level for the benefit of participants and athletes. Yet, much more needs to be done in the future.

There is an imperative need to expand the global coaching community to every corner of the globe. The last fifteen years have seen vast developments in Europe, North America, Oceania, and, more recently, Asia. There is now a vital need to engage and activate the coaching community in South America and the African continent. The Rio de Janeiro 2016 Olympic and Paralympic Games have provided a great opportunity to kick-start this process in South America, and ICCE worked with Brazilian stakeholders to hold a Global Coaches House (www.globalcoacheshouse.net) during the Games. With regard to Africa, the outstanding work carried out by SASCOC (South African Sports Confederation and Olympic Committee), which culminated in 2011 with the publication of the South African Coaching Framework (SASCOC 2011), has accelerated developments in other areas of the continent. Led by COSANOC (Confederation of Southern African National Olympic Committees) and African Union Sports Council Region 5 and supported by international organizations such as the Norwegian Olympic Committee and UK Sport International, the prospects of developing an African Coaching Council (ACC) under the ICCE banner is approaching reality.

At a practical level, coaching faces additional challenges. While organizations across the world have realized the importance of coaching and coaches to fulfill the promise of sport as a key social driver, investment in the structures necessary to develop coaching to its full potential is still below optimal levels. Governments and national and international federations must dedicate a higher percentage of their annual budgets to building their coaching systems. International organizations such as the IOC, ASOIF, WADA, and the European Commission must continue their outstanding commitment to elevating the figure of the coach and the value of appropriate and functional coaching systems for participants, athletes, and society at large. Increasing coach representation, as CoachNet demonstrated, is paramount. Only in this way will coaching progress toward being recognized as a professional area.

As the interest in coaching has grown, the coaching research community has also experienced unprecedented growth. Thousands of researchers across the world have started to develop a bulging body of work around coaching in areas such as coach learning and development, participant and athlete development, coaching pedagogy, and coaching effectiveness and expertise. This knowledge is progressively finding its way into mainstream coach education and development and having an impact in the way it is designed and delivered. For instance, domain specific courses, new and innovative ways to deliver blended learning, a greater realization of the value of nonformal and informal activities, and a greater use of technology in coach development have originated from the combined work of coaches, coach developers, and academics. Through its Research Committee and initiatives such as the *International Sport Coaching Journal* (http://journals.humankinetics.com/iscj) or the Research Fair, which brings together academics from all over the world within the activities of the ICCE's Global Coach Conference, ICCE is looking to build the research–practice bridge. Developing a greater understanding of what constitutes best practice in coaching and coach education and understanding that development is everyone's job.

This chapter has offered a review of the current state of affairs in coach education and development from an international perspective. It has described the efforts made by ICCE and its partners to bring coaching to the fore with national and international organizations. A watershed publication such as the ISCF has played a key role in harnessing and legitimizing the work of those in coaching. Key examples of applications of its principles across different contexts and layers of the coaching system have been elaborated on. Finally, the prospective challenges faced by the global coaching community have been outlined, and a call to action to all involved to work collaboratively to overcome them has been made.

Acknowledgments

ICCE would like to thank all its members for their continued support in fulfilling its vision and mission. We would like to specifically acknowledge the work of our board members, continental Vice-Presidents, the Members of the Research Committee, and our key international partners: the IOC, represented by the Entourage Commission and Olympic Solidarity; IPC; ASOIF; WADA; Members of the Innovation Group of Leading Agencies; and Leeds Beckett University. Finally, we would like to recognize the outstanding work of Human Kinetics, our publishing partner, in shaping and spreading our message.

[1] Current President: John Bales (CAN); Secretary General: Dr. Ladislav Petrovic (HUN); Treasurer: Dr. Miguel Crespo, International Tennis Federation (SPA); VP Europe: Kirsi Hämäläinen (Finnish Olympic Committee); VP Africa: Jerry Segwaba (SASCOC); VP Americas: Christine Bolger (USOC); VP Asia: Jiexiu Zhao (Chinese Institute of Sport Science); VP Oceania: Darlene Harrison (ASC).

[2] The Research Committee is currently co-chaired by Professor Jean Côté (Queen's University, CAN) and Associate Professor Cliff Mallet (University of Queensland, AUS).

Chapter 13

Professional Development Opportunities for Coaches

Christine Nash

Sport coaches can and do play a crucial role in the development of sport and in the lives of the performers they coach. Effective coaches ensure participants in sport have positive experiences and are therefore more likely to continue in their sport and achieve their potential (see chapter 17). Currently, coaching systems tend to encourage individuals with more sport experience and greater qualifications to work at the elite level. Within the younger age groups, where the development of physical literacy and general skills is most required, volunteer and novice coaches predominate. This can result in the least experienced coaches operating at the stages most critical to long-term sporting development rather than experienced coaches leading well-organized sessions of age-appropriate activities. This system is perpetuated by the traditional coach education structure where the perceived advantages and recognition are only available at the elite level of coaching. Placing inexperienced coaches at crucial stages of a child's development can result in poor physical literacy and, more important, many children leaving sport as a result of bad experiences. The damage caused by inappropriate coaching practices at the early stages of sport may not be fully repaired over time and can lead to lack of progression to the elite level. This system also implies that coach learning in sport is linear, devaluing the complexities of quality coaching across sport contexts, and it does not support a professional cultural expectation for coaches at all levels of lifelong learning engagement.

Within certain countries the status of coaches is idiosyncratic. For example, within the United Kingdom and in many countries around the world, volunteer coaches play a crucial role in community and youth sport, yet the value, monetary and otherwise, is placed only on coaches working at the top levels of performance-based sport. In these countries, volunteer coaches make sport happen by willingly giving their time to enable others to play the sport they love. Without the time, energy, and commitment of these volunteers, many clubs, team sport sessions, and coaching sessions would not be able to run. Yet, beyond allowing programs to exist, the value of *how* these volunteers coach at the crucial levels of development is often grossly undervalued and unrecognized.

UK Sport presents a vision of the practice of coaching, indicating that it should be "elevated to a profession acknowledged as central to the development of sport and the fulfillment of individual potential."(UK Sport 2001, 5). The International Sport Coaching Framework (ICCE 2013) builds on the concept by presenting a layered approach to coaching that aligns with athlete participation and development models. The ISCF recognizes the importance of coaching context (who is being coached) and the settings in which one coaches (participation coaching versus performance coaching), noting not only the overlap and transition between groups and settings that can occur in multiple directions, but also underscoring the importance of depth of knowledge possible within each area. This concept is presented as the model of coach knowledge and skill within the ISCF, noting that this knowledge and skill is not developed in a linear fashion.

The ISCF provides a useful scaffold for better understanding and valuing the role and importance of qualified and prepared coaches within each stage, phase, and sport setting. Adopting such a model makes it easier to inspire coaches, whether volunteer or paid, and the systems that support them to value and invest in sport coaching as a profession that benefits from an ongoing learning approach. For the purpose of this chapter, the focus will be on the coach as the learner and how he or she might approach learning and ongoing professional development, regardless of the coaching context. The coach educator and developer should make note of the things that can be done within a systems approach to value an ongoing learning approach, provide opportunities for continued development, and support the skills necessary to engage in continued professional development.

A Professionalism Approach

How do individuals stay at the forefront of their sport profession as coaches? Much depends upon their ability to continually update and stay abreast of new developments and practices within their sport as well as stay current on the leading information about the process of coaching. Coaches can extend their capacity for professional development by engaging in learning experiences that promote analysis and critical reflection of their coaching practice. Furthermore, evaluation, continual practice, and ongoing reflection are necessary to develop the essential skills of decision-making, problem-solving, and managing of the coaching process.

Before the learning pathways for professional engagement can be discussed, it is necessary to address, clarify, and make a distinction between numerous key terms. Volunteer coaching status is often associated with novice status or having little to no knowledge when, in fact, it is merely an indication of the unpaid nature of the position. On the opposite end of the spectrum, elite coaching status does not necessarily indicate an expert level of knowledge, because elite designates a level of sport participation such as a professional league or international level competition. More useful to the learning and professional development conversation is an understanding of the differentiation between novice, competent, proficient, and expert practitioner (Schempp, McCullick, and Mason 2006), regardless of context and salary status, as it pertains to the professional knowledge across content, interpersonal skills, and intrapersonal skills, as defined by Côté and Gilbert. (2009). Thus, coach learning will be addressed from an individual growth and development perspective with recommendations for how systems may approach supporting professional development pathways across settings.

Multiple Pathways to Coach Learning

Good coaches never stop learning; development opportunities encompass all types of learning situations including facilitated and nonfacilitated learning (Moon 2004) such as sport-specific provision, academic degrees, formal coursework, conferences, and experiential learning opportunities embedded in practice. Coach learning has been described as intensive and collaborative, ideally incorporating an evaluative stage. The result, therefore, is a variety of approaches to professional development in sport coaching that can be effective, including observation, communities of practice, guided practice, mentoring, reflective supervision, and technical assistance.

Coach learning opportunities do not always lead to a professional qualification, and it is important to appreciate the value of such professional development opportunities that similarly do not lead to formal qualifications but do contribute to enhancing coach effectiveness and practice. A sport culture that emphasizes checking boxes and completing certifications over or instead of an emphasis on learned knowledge and knowledge application will serve to devalue and disincentivize ongoing engagement in learning as a professional standard of practice.

Continuing professional development, professional learning, or lifelong learning are names given to a combination of approaches, ideas, and techniques that help individuals manage their own learning and growth. Within a learning culture, professional learning can include any event, formal or informal, that increases knowledge, experience, and understanding;

improves performance; and contributes to ongoing development and lifelong learning (for more information on long-term coach development, see chapter 15). There are a variety of methods that have been used, and the choice and combination of these methods can be influenced by the following:

- The time available for learning (from both an employer and employee perspective)
- The support available for learning (from an employer perspective)
- The resources required for learning (time, cost, technology)
- The learning needs identified by an individual (perhaps at a 360-degree review)
- Individual learning styles
- Organization and team learning priorities, driven by strategic planning

To ensure that sport coaches can maintain and extend their skills, knowledge, and understanding in relation to their role or roles, many coaching organizations have recommended that coaches, whether paid or volunteer, be entitled to a specified number of professional development activities per year or across the length of the season, depending on the nature of the appointment. This aspirational program goal should encourage sport coaches to continually update using the variety of formats and opportunities that are available today, including distance or online learning.

IOC Gateway – https://doi.org/10.1080/2159676X.2015.1030343

Connected Coaches – https://connectedcoaches.org/

Positive Coaching Alliance – https://www.positivecoach.org/

iCoachKids – https://www.icoachkids.eu/

Canadian Coaches Association – https://www.coach.ca/

True Sport – https://www.usada.org/truesport/

How to Coach Kids – https://howtocoachkids.org/

The process of coach learning has been described as many things: linear, coach driven, experiential, problem based, applied to coach context, etc. For each of the methods ascribed to coach learning practices, there is one thing that is clear—there is no one route, or pathway, that suits every coach, every coaching context, or every sport system. As a result, coach learning is often labeled idiosyncratic and driven by the personal choices, motivations, and level of commitment of the individual coach. As with many other contexts, there are multiple routes to the pinnacle of coaching, the development of coaching expertise. In considering expertise, it is essential to separate the notion of expertise from elite sport. While expertise is defined as having "a high level of knowledge or skill" (Cambridge Dictionary n.d.), the definition does not specify a particular point of context. Thus, expertise can occur within any context or domain in which one can have uniquely defined specialized knowledge or skill.

Within the coaching realm, expertise is often falsely conflated with elite performance. To truly understand and support professional development within coaching, it is essential to separate the coaching expertise, that is, having the knowledge and skills necessary to excel at coaching within a particular context, from the expertise often associated with the athletic performance that is, where expertise is associated with performing the athletic skill at the highest level of competition. Thus it is possible for a coach, when viewed as a professional or "performing other," to be an expert within one or more contexts of coaching. On the other hand, it is possible to be an expert coach within the context of developing youth swimmers but not an expert for the specialized coaching environment for training elite swimmers.

Currently, in most sport organizations coaches come into coaching from a variety of backgrounds and bring a number of existing skills and attributes from their previous experiences, both in and out of sport. Although these experiences determine how their unique coaching styles develop, they also highlight the difficulties in providing useful, effective, and meaningful professional development opportunities for all coaches within the current systems.

Ongoing learning is well established in a number of professions; indeed, for some professions such as the teaching and the legal professions, participating in these learning opportunities is mandatory. Activities can include lectures, seminars, workshops, practical activities, video conferences, online learning, congresses, conventions, in-house company training, and other forms of face-to-face and distance learning programs. The conceptualization of the education of sport coaches has grown organically, through many *ad hoc* routes, often driven by individuals within sport organizations rather than the organizations themselves, and in some countries by regulation. (For more specific details on coach education systems and the evolution of these systems, see chapters 11, 12, and 16.)

Coach learning has, however, received far less attention compared to other vocations such as, medicine, nursing, and teaching. This is perhaps a consequence of the high proportion of volunteer coaches coupled to the entrenched perception that coaching is not a real "profession" and the perpetuation of the myth that experience as an athlete is sufficient preparation for coaching. Consequently, the concept of ongoing coach learning has historically lacked a champion in sport coaching. Therefore, not surprisingly, in the United States and the United Kingdom there is no coherent model of professional development for coaches: some sports have mandatory requirements while others have none. This is not the case in every sport or every country; for example, in Canada, the Coaching Association of Canada recognizes the importance of certified coaches across Canada to be involved in professional development that reinforces the values of continuous improvement and lifelong learning and encourages sharing of learning among coaches.

Case Examples

The four case studies presented below demonstrate the different entry points into coaching, the individual learning, and the development pathways followed by each coach and what each considers to be their successes within systems that did not provide clear vocational direction or professional preparation or development pathways. It was a deliberate choice to highlight both male and female coaches from different countries, coaching different sports, and at different levels within the performance pathway. Each of the coaches provided this information verbally and was asked to verify the resulting case studies to ensure the accuracy of the representations.

When asked to narrate their sport biographies and coach development, the four coaches highlighted in the case studies mentioned a multitude of people who played a significant part in their development. Some of these influences were more powerful than others. While some experiences and personnel were constructive and encouraging, others were de-motivating and considered to be examples of practice that should not be followed. The first case study, Linda, is a highly experienced coach working in a team sport within the NCAA system in the United States.

Linda has been a successful coach for many years in the US collegiate system, a stable system with financial support and well-organized and structured competitive procedures and processes. Jim, another team sport coach but based in the United Kingdom, has had a significantly different development experience. Jim is not a full-time coach and therefore is not able to devote a substantial amount of time to his coaching practice. He has another job to supplement his coaching income, and on some occasions has coached as a volunteer to gain experience.

Case Study 1: Female Field Hockey Coach Based in the United States (Linda)

Major Achievements

- 8 NCAA Championships
- 9 ACC Tournament Championships
- 9-time National Coach of the Year

Background in Sport

- Took part in field hockey, lacrosse, tennis, ice hockey, and figure skating from an early age. I was always competitive, initially excelling in figure skating and competing at the national level. I believe that my initial involvement in skating gave me great balance, which helped my hockey.

Educational Background

- Undergraduate (UG) Physical Education (PE) Degree
- Postgraduate (PG) study in Exercise Physiology and Sport Psychology

Entry into Coaching

- Initially started coaching ice skating at the age of 15 while still competing. After completing my UG degree in PE, I became a Graduate Assistant and assistant field hockey coach. I then became Head Coach at the age of 25 while still playing.

Coach Development

- I acquired my coaching knowledge and skills through a variety of formal and informal learning scenarios. As a player at the highest level, I was able to bring skills, techniques, game-sense, and management into my coaching. My UG PE and subsequent PG study in Exercise Physiology and Sport Psychology provided me with an extensive knowledge base. Working with others gave me the opportunity to analyze coaching practice and see what works. I also use reflective learning to reflect critically and honestly, employ reflections in future practice, and then appraise the effectiveness of any adaptations or modifications to practice.

Most Useful Learning Experience

- Observing and emulating my coach while still at school, I learned that our job as a coaching staff goes far beyond what you see on the field. . . . 80 to 90 percent of our job is what you don't see. We have to be mentors, facilitators, teachers, and parents. A huge part of the job is teaching life lessons.

What to Avoid

- Remember that there are people in the programs and teams. Treat them as individuals, and avoid making the program the most important element. I remember the players who have passed through the program rather than the win–loss record.

Case Study 2: Male Soccer Coach Based in the United Kingdom (Jim)

Major Achievements

- Creating a positive learning environment to allow talent to develop. Won National Cup competitions and National League titles at youth level.

Background in Sport

- Played soccer from age 5. Participated in other sports on an *ad hoc* basis, but soccer was only sport available due to geographic location.

Educational Background

- Went to local college initially. UG Sport Coaching and Development degree. Masters of Research in Tactics in Soccer.

Entry into Coaching

- Went along and helped father coaching at age of 12. Originally ran the demonstrations and took the warm up. Coaching own team of U14 players at the age of 15.

Coach Development

- Completed initial coaching award at age of 16. Due to geography, national governing body was only provider, but I did not take initial coaching awards seriously. I was playing for one team while coaching another so there was a lot of on-the-job development. Differing perspectives of player and coach gave valuable insights.

Most Useful Learning Experience

- University allowed me to develop as I saw the intellectual side of coaching. I feel I was operating at 60% but was then able to release potential. I gained valuable critical-thinking skills and was able to analyze both the art and the science of coaching and, very importantly, relate to coaching soccer.

What to Avoid

- Lot of soccer clubs overemphasized winning at all costs. Clubs sacrificed talented players because they did not conform to club ideals of size and development potential at early ages (12–14). I did not like this approach because it went against my coaching philosophy, so I tended to avoid working in these types of environments.

Unlike the team sports of the highlighted coaches (Linda and Jim), the individual sports of swimming and judo generally involve the coach working with a group of athletes together but developing them as individuals. In the case of swimming, relays are the only opportunity for swimmers to compete as part of a team, but often relays are not practiced extensively, leading to difficulties with changeovers. Coaches of individual sports have been shown to display different behaviors from coaches of team sports (Occhino et al. 2014). For example, Zeng and colleagues (2009) suggested that coaches in individual sports used more questioning techniques and offered more praise than their team sport counterparts. However, little is known about differences in their learning and development activities in preparation to work within their unique professional context.

Kirsten coached within the NCAA system, initially as an assistant coach and later as a head coach, as well as coaching age-groups swimmers (10–18 year olds). Swimming was not a well-financed sport within her university, but she worked with both male and female swimmers aged 18–24 years. She considers herself to be a good planner and reflective, but mentioned that she accepted early in her coaching career that sessions hardly ever go according to plan. This enabled her to become more intuitive within her coaching. Serge's entry into judo coaching followed a distinctly different path from Kirsten's as he progressed to coaching after he finished competing.

Case Study 3: Female Swimming Coach Based in the United States (Kirsten)

Major Achievements

- Worked with world-record holders, national champions, and All-American swimmers.

Background in Sport

- Not a swimmer. International athlete, hockey player, and orienteer.

Educational Background

- UG Physical Education degree, MSc Sport Psychology and Coaching

Entry into Coaching

- Accidental. Sustained career-ending injury as athlete and moved into coaching another sport.

Coach Development

- Coach development was experiential; very steep learning curve while working as assistant with Olympic coach in an age-group swimming club.

Most Useful Learning Experience

- A weekend workshop held in Atlanta, which included a number of top coaches and swimmers. All of the speakers made themselves available and spent a great deal of time interacting with delegates. I remember thinking "Wow, this Olympic coach is talking to me." The real learning happened in the bar after the conference. Similar issues were identified and discussed with lots of input from a wide variety of backgrounds and experiences.

What to Avoid

- Two things: First, I remember as a young coach copying what I saw other more experienced coaches doing and not really knowing why. So try to avoid copying without understanding.
- Second, I never really enjoyed formal coach education courses but I think they are a necessary evil. Avoid the formal learning but really take advantage of the opportunities to mix and interact with other coaches and coach developers.

Case Study 4: Male Judo Coach Based in France (Serge)

Major Achievements

- 4 Olympic Medalists
- 2 National Club Titles
- 7 National Champions

Background in Sport

- Was judo athlete from early age. Did not really take part in other sports as both my parents were judo players too.

Educational Background

- Judo is culturally very important in France and has a long tradition of excellence. Therefore, no educational qualifications are required. Just progress through the system.

Entry into Coaching

- Natural progression from competing to coaching. Made a quick transition to high-performance coaching once I finished competing at international level.

Coach Development

- INSEP (Institute National Du Sport, De L'Expertise Et De La Performance), the French National Institute, runs a comprehensive program of development activities that are suitable for a wide variety of coaches. The French Judo Federation is also very proactive. The system is very rigid, so you have to adhere to the rules or else you will not make it within the system.

Most Useful Learning Experience

- Judo is a very interactive sport, so athlete–coach relationships are very important. I took a course about communicating with athletes and really enjoyed it. There are lots of practice sessions working on different aspects; for example, we expect players to take part in randori (fight practice). The way the training is set up we concentrate on this, so when we communicate with our athletes, we need to motivate them and encourage them as well as giving them technical and tactical information. Communication is very important.

What to Avoid

- Do not try to disagree with the system. Judo is bigger than the individual, so we must all work together for the benefit of French Judo.

Case Studies and Coach Learning and Development: Conclusions

Looking across the four individual journeys into the coaching profession provides insights into how coaching education and professional development can move forward to better prepare and support professionals within sport. The following themes—sport participation, fast tracking, and formal learning—explore how individuals gained access to the professional path within coaching.

Sport Participation

There are a number of immediately obvious similarities and differences when examining these four case studies. For example, all four coaches participated in sport from an early age, although not always the sport they ended up coaching (Linda and Kirsten); however, the two male coaches (Jim and Serge) specialized in their respective sports from a very early age. In a number of sports in many countries around the world, it is common for top coaching positions to be held by former players. Is it the *playing* of a sport that helps develop the skills necessary for *coaching* a sport? Gilbert and colleagues (2006) suggested that successful coaches from a range of sports had accumulated significant time participating as athletes, which they classified as pre-coaching experience. The relevance to coaching of playing a sport, especially at a representative level, was reinforced by Nash and Sproule (2009) in their study of development patterns of elite coaches. However, despite the coaches' perceptions of the relevance of playing to coaching and the apparent natural progression of players to coaches, there is still minimal understanding of how playing may benefit coaching.

Fast Tracking

Three of the four coaches (Linda, Jim, and Serge) found their entry into coaching was facilitated by their playing careers. Due to the perceived value of elite participation experience, sport systems are often designed to value athletic experiences as an important prerequisite to coach; indeed, Linda was a head coach while still competing at a high level. Only Kirsten became a coach in a sport where she had absolutely no experience, a somewhat rare occurrence in sport even at the earliest levels.

There are a number of perceived benefits to coach development if coaches spent significant time as an athlete, including knowledge of the sport culture, familiarity with the written and unwritten rules, ability to demonstrate skills, knowledge of the sport tactics, and a first-hand understanding of the personal investment. Based on this, Rynne (2014) proposed that some ex-players could be fast-tracked into coaching at a high level (Linda and

Serge). Fast tracking can be considered as the affordances given to former elite performers that acknowledge and build upon their athlete-gained sport knowledge. Fast tracking also facilitates the development of the necessary coaching-specific knowledge through a process that either accelerates them through the formal coach accreditation programs or creates a path that addresses their unique knowledge and knowledge gaps, thus providing a specialized path into the formal system. Turner (2008) offers concrete examples in soccer and rugby within the United Kingdom. Also, cricket in Pakistan is fast-tracking coaches where there is a perceived shortage (Pakistan Press International 2011), and the Malawi Football Association aims to fast-track a local coach to take over their national soccer team within a three-month time frame (Kandu 2013). It should be noted that the process of fast tracking is often designed to prepare individuals for the unique demands and high-stress environment of elite-level sport coaching. Unfortunately, little attention with regard to fast tracking is paid to preparing former athletes for the unique and specialized coaching requirements for working within youth or developmental sport where quality teaching skills are essential.

Fast tracking for elite coach positions can take the form of access to courses or entry at a higher level (for example, initial entry point may be at Level 3 rather than the normal entry point of Level 1). These approaches should take into account the skills and knowledge necessary to coach within a given context that can be transferred from playing to coaching, and where there may be skills and knowledge development unique to the role of coach, unexperienced by the athlete. For example, fast-tracking a former collegiate-level athlete to work within developmental sport provides the benefit of an individual who understands the nuances of preparation and competing at higher levels of the sport; however, the ability to perform a skill is not synonymous with the ability to assess or teach the skills within a developmental context. Thus, inappropriately fast-tracking a coach based on participation or competition alone is cause for concern, both for the athlete's development and the coach's professional preparation.

Another important potential problem to consider with fast tracking is a potential pitfall shared by all formal credentialing or certification programs that qualify or prepare coaches for any level or context within sport. Without proper emphasis on learning and application, thinking for innovation, and a developed sense of professionalism that leads to an understanding of the value of engaging as a lifelong learner, these programs can give the impression that clearing the hurdles are sufficient. Creating and defining a professional pathway that emphasizes developing depth of knowledge, professional intuition, and expertise within formal learning will help facilitate a continued engagement beyond the requirements.

Formal Learning

Three of the four coaches in the case studies (Linda, Jim, and Kirsten) had completed undergraduate degrees related to sport as well as some form of postgraduate study. This does not fit the general profile of a number of high-level or elite coaches (Nash and Sproule 2012), and is definitely not a foundational path among volunteer coaches. Most coaches take part in large-scale entry-level coach accreditation or certification programs at some point within their coaching careers (Jim and Serge) depending on the sport system within which they coach; however, this is not always the case (Linda and Kirsten). The provision of these large-scale coach education programs has been promoted by a number of countries, for example, Australia's National Coaching Accreditation Scheme, Canada's National Coaching Certificate Programme, the New Zealand Coaching Strategy, and the United Kingdom Coaching Certificate (Cassidy 2008).

As there is now increasing recognition of sport coaching as a complex learning and development activity and a recognition of the importance of the need for qualified leaders to facilitate athlete development pathways (ICCE 2013), greater attention is paid to the progress of sport coaches through formal certification and accreditation (Nash and Sproule 2011; Rynne, Mallet, and Tinning 2009). However, these formal learning opportunities have not always been welcomed or appreciated by sport coaches (Nash and Sproule 2012). Consider the development and learning pathways of the four coaches discussed here. As all four of these coaches were judged to be both effective and successful in their particular contexts, should the large-scale formal program be the only method of educating sport coaches? A telling point is that none of these coaches considered formal learning opportunities to be a "Most Useful Learning Experience."

Learning experiences recounted by these coaches can be characterized by three elements: (1) emphasis on cognitive elements, (2) relevance to applied coaching environment, and (3) the importance of others within learning and coaching.

A recent study found coaches wanted education experiences that were thought provoking, allowing them to better understand complex coaching issues and, more important, apply them in an improved coaching practice (Nelson, Cushion, and Potrac 2013). Coaches wish to be viewed as the focus of the coach education programs. They want the aim of the program to be to develop their effectiveness as coaches, not, as some felt, to improve their athletes' performances. Once foundation knowledge within a given sport context has been established, creating educational opportunities for professional development that acknowledge the coach as the performing other would encourage a problem-based learning approach to coach education. Progressing beyond the novice phase, the development of expertise in a given profession is predicated on the increasing abilities related to knowledge integration, analysis, and synthesis that facilitates greater depth of understanding, innovation, and creativity—all of which are important for increased effectiveness regardless of the sport context.

Coaching has been recognized as a cognitive activity. Therefore, essential to professional development is the development of critical-thinking abilities. This should replace the more traditional sport-specific program design and presentation that is often presented in recipe format and that does not facilitate application thinking that is necessary to adapt any training plan to the complex environment of sport training. This change requires programs run by skilled facilitators and presentation in a manner that allows for guided skill development and use. This change in formal learning emphasis should allow coaches to develop decision-making skills, reflective abilities, and proficiency in problem solving, in conjunction with learning new as well as more advanced science-based training methods and approaches. This in turn would continue to encourage a sense of automaticity, a key element to the process of developing expertise (discussed later in this chapter).

The significance of the variety of learning opportunities presented to coaches, regardless of context, cannot be overemphasized. As previously mentioned, coaching is multifaceted and, particularly at the elite levels of sport, is constantly changing so coaches must learn quickly in order to maintain the competitive edge and allow their athletes and teams to benefit from the most up-to-date technical, tactical, and developmentally appropriate information communicated in the most suitable manner for the context.

Additional Professional Development: Case Study Insights

Both team sport coaches (Linda and Jim) believe that they are coaching more than athletes on a team—they consider their players as individuals but also people within their own right who need to be developed *through* sport and being part of a team. All of the coaches in the case studies found the continued developmental opportunities that were most relevant to them and were presented in a way that suited their learning styles (Linda, observations on the job; Jim, development of critical-thinking skills; Kirsten, discussions with others; Serge, experiences as athlete).

These case studies have also highlighted some very personal insights into the coaches' entry into coaching as well as ongoing development opportunities. For example, Serge mentioned the cultural significance of Judo in France, where judo is one of the largest participant and spectator sports; this places great expectations on both coaches and athletes to perform. Serge reflected that the system of judo in France transcends individual players and coaches—everyone involved has to agree with the system. This is in contrast with Jim, who deliberately removed himself from the soccer system in the United Kingdom as he found it did not agree with his coaching philosophy. Within the United Kingdom, recent research has highlighted the number of coaches who choose to coach outside the system, perhaps not in the best interests of the coaches or athletes (Nash, Sproule, Hall, and English 2013).

Transitions to Expertise

In their seminal work, Bloom and colleagues (1985) interviewed a number of expert performers in their fields, including world champion swimmers and Grand Slam–winning tennis players. Based on interviews with these athletes and others, they conceived a general framework for the development of expertise, which systematically progressed through a number of stages. There was no definitive evidence on how performers progressed through these stages, although the input of an appropriately informed coach at the vital stages was considered fundamental to the process.

Ericsson carried out a number of subsequent studies into the development of expertise, initially in music, but later in sport (Ericsson, Krampe, and Tesch-Romer 1993). These studies identified the notion of deliberate practice, now more widely known as the 10 year or 10,000 hour rule where "the subjects' motivation to attend to the task and exert effort to improve their performance" is paramount to the development of expertise in any field (Ericsson, Krampe, and Tesch-Romer 1993, 367). However, Ericsson and colleagues suggest that the criteria currently used to identify expertise is not sufficient because "To reach the status of an expert in a domain it is sufficient to master the existing knowledge and techniques. To make an eminent achievement one must first achieve the level of an expert and then in addition surpass the achievements of already recognized eminent people and make innovative contributions to the domain" (1993, 365). This implies that experts in the sport coaching domain need to be leaders in the field, construct creative solutions, and embrace the uncertainty and challenge that sport coaching presents (Nash 2014). Given the apparent lack of learning opportunities available for coaches to develop their expertise as performing others, particularly those coaching at levels other than with elite performers, what would it take to surpass expertise to become creative and innovative?

Recently, the nursing profession has invested heavily in managing transitions through the various stages of nursing proficiency to address the emerging issue of recruitment and retention. (Schoening 2013). Similarly, physiotherapy professionals looked to enhance their clinical practice and demonstrate attributes of clinical expertise (Petty, Scholes, and Ellis 2011). The context for the development of the transitions model in both nursing and physiotherapy is based upon the conceptual framework of learning transition theory devised by Scholes (2006). Both nursing and physiotherapy have a professional domain similar to that of sport coaching, necessitating the application of practical skills based upon theoretical knowledge. The medical professions embedded a three-step process that enabled practitioners with existing domain-specific knowledge to (1) critically question established assumptions and norms of practice; (2) allow practitioners to subsequently adapt their practice for individual diagnosis, becoming more deliberate and creative as a result; (3) enable a reflective cycle involving evaluation of clinical decisions and learning both in and from practice (Petty, Scholes, and Ellis 2011; Scholes 2006). This transitional process has been supported by a variety of professional learning and development opportunities enabled by the medical profession in conjunction with higher education institutions.

The road to coaching expertise is not well understood, particularly because, as has already been discussed, the terms expert and elite are often confused, and because the expertise needed to coach is often not sufficiently separated or valued apart from the expertise of elite performance outcomes. There has been considerable work investigating both the art and science of coaching (see Smoll and Smith, 2010, for a review of coach education; see Nash and Collins, 2006, for a review of expertise). When identifying and examining expertise in sport coaching, the task becomes somewhat problematic. Key studies in this area have observed the specific behaviors demonstrated by the expert coach, the types of knowledge accumulated by the coach over their coaching career, or certain skills, such as decision-making or visual search strategies (Giblin et al. 2013; Koon Teck, Mallett, and Wang 2009; Nash, Sproule, and Horton 2011). These studies have generally characterized expert coaches, regardless of context, as meticulous planners, thorough analysts of practice, and reflective practitioners. However, many have only identified some key aspects, while not discussing the shortcomings associated with coaching and coach learning.

A key issue associated with coaching expertise research is the difficulty in distinguishing truly expert coaches from those who are elite and successful in their practice. A recent meta-analysis of the criteria used by researchers to identify expert coaches revealed 27 differing variations on expert coaching, ranging from no identified criteria to a combination of coaching experience, level of coaching qualifications, development of participants, and level of coaching (Nash et al. 2012). This leads to the obvious question: is research accurately defining and detecting the expert coach? From this, the answer would appear to be a resounding no. The typical research on coach expertise is finding good or very good coaches, often with regard to athlete outcome alone, and qualifying them as experts. Although these coaches possibly have aspects of their practice that are worthy of study and possible dissemination to other coaches, we should bear in mind the caveat delivered by Gilbert and Trudel (2004) after a similar meta-analysis confirming that there were few coaches whose practice was worthy of simulation. Indeed, as has been established both through failed efforts and research that discusses the complexities of coaching, while copying may be the sincerest form of flattery, it is also one of most guaranteed sinking of a competitive season.

Coaches who simulate or copy others may not understand the intent behind each practice or advice offered. Remember, coaching is a cognitive endeavor, so what is appropriate in one situation with a particular individual may reflect the needs analysis in that context based upon certain circumstances. A coach may have thought long and hard, and used problem solving and decision-making, to arrive at a solution; this process cannot be reproduced easily. This acknowledgment serves as an important reminder of the value of a quality base of learning for those coaching, the necessity to understand the "why" behind the "what," and the ability to choose the appropriate "what." It also serves to underscore the importance and value of the development of the skills necessary for quality continued professional development.

The issues described above to the academic study of sport expertise are concerned with identifying and evaluating the factors and processes that distinguish the expert coach, the transition through the stages to expertise, and how these aspects can be integrated into the design and presentation of coach development material and practices. Considering that career progression and development is important to retention in all professions, ambitious coaches may well start their careers as assistant coaches in small organizations and institutions. The International Sport Coaching Framework identifies coaching roles, ranging from coaching assistant to master coach over a number of levels. However, there are evident challenges at all levels and stages of coaching (Dawson and Phillips 2013). The key to managing coaching appointments and transitions effectively is to ensure that coaches are challenged to learn and develop at every stage of their coaching careers in a manner that is engaging and fulfilling. This implies that the management of coaches, from the recruitment stage to their subsequent development throughout their career, is crucial and highlights the important roles that head coaches, coach supervisors, coach educators, and coach developers can and should play in the process. This is all in addition to the need to have coach education systems designed to develop and facilitate ongoing professional development that builds and expands foundational knowledge toward the development of contextual expertise.

It seems reasonable to assume that coaches will not always be able to access the information they need from their sport or governing body. A variety of methods and opportunities for gaining knowledge, both experientially and theoretically, need to be provided as a matter of urgency as part of an ongoing commitment to professional learning. Further, coaches need to be able to access the data they require quickly and easily, given their responsibilities. This requires the recognition and preparation of an appropriate support system for quality ongoing coach development, whether that be within a youth sport setting, with an individual who provides ongoing volunteer coach support throughout a season, or within an elite sport environment where one-on-one professional mentors are provided and communities of practice are developed.

If coaches are considered to be expert as a performing other within their primary context, then the methods by which they achieved this standing need to be scrutinized, evaluated, and, it is hoped, disseminated through coach development opportunities for the benefit of coach development. Currently, large-scale coach education courses tend to present coaches with sport-specific content in a hierarchical process, after which coaches can then be evaluated on a number of predetermined competences that are not aligned with the characteristics of expertise (Nash et al. 2012; Sports Coach UK 2007).

Career Transitions in Coaching: The Importance of Context

The transition process in sport has recently become topical in sport psychology research (Henriksen, Stambulova, and Roessler 2010; Knowles, Tyler, Gilbourne, and Eubank 2006; Storm et al. 2014). As with a number of expertise studies in sport, much of the research concentrates on the development of the athletes and their transition through sport and subsequently into retirement (Lavallee, Kremer, Moran, and Williams 2004; Durand-Bush and Salmela 2002; Kerr and Dacyshyn 2000; Ericsson 1998). This transition appears to place considerable demands on the participants, particularly in terms of adapting behaviors and cognitive strategies.

Career transitions are cyclical and continuous and based on ongoing professional learning and development because professionals must maintain and develop their expertise throughout their career, which involves complex learning processes (Boshuizen, Bromme, and Gruber 2004). Furthermore, research on workplace learning and professional development has indicated that learning from errors is an important way of developing professional competence (Bauer and Mulder 2007). The transition from learner or apprentice to expert professional can be accelerated when a route for change is plotted and made evident to learners. Trajectories or paths toward expertise are domain specific due to the complexities of each domain, and must first be documented and then used within instructional contexts to promote knowledge transitions (Lajoie 2003). The final element of each stage is in fact the beginning of the next transitional cycle, and individuals must renew their relationship with the world in order to control their transitions adequately. Thus, career transitions, whatever their nature may be, are always defined as re-examinations of new modes of relationships to be maintained with the world of work.

Within the context of sport and coaching, as noted by the ISCF (ICCE 2013), coaching roles and responsibilities vary by the context of the athlete (e.g., age, gender, level of sport competition). The ISCF also highlights the importance of considering the responsibilities and knowledge requirements associated with different coaching roles, such as master or head coach, advanced/senior coach, coach, and coaching assistant. Depending on the league and level of play, the depth of roles (and their assigned names, or labels) may vary. Despite the label, while there is some overlap in required skills and knowledge, being good and excelling to expertise at each level will also require specialized knowledge. For example, the master or head coach has the responsibility of being responsible for the large-scale picture, providing a clear vision, and being able to coordinate and lead the team. On the other hand, an apprentice or coaching assistant needs to be able to work effectively within the system and have the skills to effectively execute the vision of the leader. This is an important distinction because it highlights that development is not linear. What allows an individual to be successful and excel at one level will not completely transfer to the next level. Thus, within a coach education and coach development model, learning must be ongoing and contextually based and may require greater emphasis when roles and responsibilities within the profession are modified or changed.

Accelerated expertise is a recent phrase created by Hoffman and colleagues (2014) and examines the training and methods that could enable a faster transition through learning stages. This approach was developed in conjunction with the military to accelerate the accomplishment of high levels of proficiency necessary in this skill sector, but has clear links to sport coaching in areas such as resilience, decision-making, and tactical learning. Many of the methods attributed to the success of this approach could be utilized within a professional learning environment in sport coaching. For example, Spiro and colleagues (2003) suggested that the use of games, simulations, and decision-making exercises are important to compact experience, whereas team expertise could be hastened by introducing "problems" into practice. "Learners will also have the best opportunity to become experts if they have expert mentors" (153). Within the sport world, these concepts should be considered when developing learning support systems to help facilitate the development of the skills that will build personal engagement in meaningful professional development, as well as ensure the coach has the ability to transfer eligible skills and recognize and rebuild areas that require continued investment when faced with a context transition.

Summary

In many countries there is currently no coherent model of professional development and continued learning for coaching personnel. Despite suggestions that lifelong learning should maintain the currency of professional practice as well as enhance knowledge and understanding, this concept has been poorly embraced or supported by the practices of many coach education systems. Studies have shown that professionals, even if they are all in the same profession, are not a homogenous group (Friedman and Phillips 2001), and the variations in terms of "differences in career stage, preferred learning style, [and] individual ambition" (Friedman and Phillips 2001, 6) all provide foundations for barriers, real or imagined, to be constructed by participants. It is thus vital that in the coaching domain, because of the extent of volunteer and part-time coaches, even at the elite level, any professional learning program (in fact, any centralized, compulsory activity) has to be both cost effective and efficiently organized. It should also be designed to both support foundational knowledge gains and cultivate a value and sense of competence for ongoing learning. Professional learning activities must be contextually relevant and meaningful for the individual coaches and should not be seen as a managerial exercise involving merely ticking the boxes every few years. This is only possible when a variety of learning/development activities are available and valued.

The development of expertise in any domain is not an easy task, nor can it be established with any degree of certainty within sport coaching (see the four case studies presented earlier). Coaches take advantage of and learn from a myriad of situations: formal, informal, facilitated, nonfacilitated, and a combination of all available methods. Providing incisive and individual guidance to sport coaches and offering a variety of appropriate and valued professional learning opportunities to supplement existing knowledge and skills is vital to keep sport coaches engaged with lifelong learning.

Chapter 14

Career Guidance and Mentorships for Coaches

Clayton R. Kuklick and Brian T. Gearity

Millions of athletes of various backgrounds, abilities, and aspirations participate in sport at many levels of competition. Sport studies scholars use two terms, engagement and performance, to broadly identify the way coaches and athletes participate in sport (Balyi, Way, and Higgs 2013). In general, a coach's primary mission for athletes in the engagement setting is to teach fundamental sport and life skills. A coach at the performance setting seeks to maximize athletic performance, winning, and often profit (Côté et al. 2007). Regardless of the type of setting, coaches are responsible for enhancing athletes' technical, tactical, physical, and psychological skills to help them and the team achieve the mission (Côté and Vierimaa 2014; Côté et al., 2010). Furthermore, coaches are accountable for enhancing athletes' character, motivation, and enjoyment for sport (Lyle 2002). Coaches at either the participation or performance level who accomplish these goals are considered effective (Côté and Gilbert 2009). To achieve the aforementioned goals, effective coaches draw upon a highly specialized set of professional (i.e., sport science), interpersonal (i.e., understanding others), and intrapersonal (i.e., understanding oneself) knowledge, which is developed over the course of a coaching career (Côté and Gilbert 2009). To understand how coaches acquire this knowledge, sport studies scholars have created ways to identify and measure where learning takes place. Coaches enter the profession and develop knowledge, often described in the literature as passing through developmental stages, through mediated (i.e., learning directed by another person) or unmediated (i.e., self-directed learning) learning situations (Werthner and Trudel 2006). To deepen our understanding of how coaches acquire knowledge, these learning situations can be understood in relation to three learning sources, which are described as formal (i.e., long-term, curriculum-based instruction), nonformal (i.e., short-term, organized conferences or workshops), or informal (i.e., through experience; Nelson, Cushion, and Potrac 2006; Werthner and Potrac 2006; Werthner and Trudel 2006).

In this chapter, we discuss the types of settings where coaches work and explain how professional, interpersonal, and intrapersonal knowledge is acquired through formal, nonformal, and informal learning sources. We focus on how coaches learn informally by collaborating with other coaches. We also discuss the developmental stages coaches pass through on their way to becoming an effective, master coach. Master coaches possess highly specialized knowledge, yet remain flexible and creative (Nash and Collins 2006). This knowledge is used to oversee and contribute to the innovative implementation of a coaching program over multiple seasons (Schempp, McCullick, and Mason 2006). Because we would hope coaches aspire to eventually reach the mark of an effective master coach, we provide suggestions for how coaching knowledge can be acquired by progressing through four developmental stages. In this way, we provide coaches, coach educators, and administrators with ways of facilitating the development of coaching knowledge. Furthermore, throughout this chapter, the first author provides his own reflections on his development as a high-performance baseball coach. The intent of sharing these experiences, which are found in the footnotes, is to bridge the gap between coaching researchers and coach practitioners by providing concise examples of complex topics and language in this chapter.

Types of Sport Participation

In general, coaches engage athletes with different needs and goals at varying ages and levels of competition (Côté and Vierimaa 2014). Researchers have argued there are two distinct types of participation settings (Balyi, Way, and Higgs 2013; Dubois 1986). One type of participation is sport for engagement, which is a setting where the intent for participation is to develop athletes' skills and to achieve an active lifestyle. This type of participation is where athletes are focused on having fun and being involved in the social environment created through sports for interpersonal reasons (i.e., to be with friends; Coakley 1992; Côté , Baker, and Abernethy 2003). Typically, the sport for engagement setting includes, but is not limited to, child, youth, adolescent, or adult sport participants (Visek et al. 2015). Coaches in the sport for engagement setting will use knowledge that is specific to this context (i.e., sport or situation) and athletes' developmental ability to effectively fulfill each athlete's individual needs (Balyi, Way, and Higgs 2013; Côté, Baker, and Abernethy 2003; ICCE, ASOIF, and LMU 2013; North 2009). For example, a youth basketball coach engaging athletes who are participating in a sport for engagement setting would draw upon a different set of coaching knowledge than if they were coaching a team of 25-year-old basketball players also participating in a sport for engagement setting.

The second type of setting, sport for performance, focuses on participation for the purpose of competition and where winning is of great importance (Roberts and Olson 1991). Athletes participating in the sport for performance setting would most likely compete at the interscholastic, club, collegiate, or Olympic level and focus on the development of highly sport-specific physical and psychological skills (i.e., position, or specific skill set; Côté and Vierimaa 2014; Durand-Bush and Salmela 2002). Coaches at this setting will also use a highly specialized set of knowledge that is dependent on the athletes' developmental level and age in order to effectively fulfill their needs (Balyi et al. 2013; ICCE, ASOIF, and LMU 2013; North 2009). For example, the knowledge required for effectively coaching a collegiate women's volleyball team will be different from coaching an interscholastic level women's volleyball team.

We remind the reader that athletes at the engagement or performance setting rarely, if ever, participate simply for either of these purposes alone. Rather, these two types of participation settings tend to place more emphasis on either fun or performance. Yet, athletes and coaches may change across settings throughout their lifetime. For example, researchers exploring the developmental stages of elite high-performance athletes determined that these athletes participated in sport at some point in their athletic career where the emphasis was on having fun and the development of general sports skills, without the focus on winning in competition (Côté , Baker, and Abernethy 2003; Durand-Bush and Salmela 2002). These findings support the idea that effective coaching is of utmost importance despite the type of setting a coach engages because an effective coach has a short- and long-term impact on athletes. Equally important, there are often great variations in athletes' abilities by age and development, which requires a highly knowledgeable coach to adjust to and meet athletes' needs (Côté, Baker, and Abernethy 2003; Côté et al. 2010). In other words, athletes are different and effective coaches can identify their differences in varying settings and use diverse forms of knowledge to enhance their athletes' outcomes.

Types of Knowledge Needed for Effective Coaching

Effective coaching is a dynamic process that draws upon knowledge from a variety of areas to enhance athlete outcomes (Côté and Gilbert 2009). Researchers have argued that all effective coaches, regardless of the athlete they coach, use professional, interpersonal, and intrapersonal knowledge (Côté and Gilbert 2009).

Professional knowledge is the large body of specialized knowledge that a coach possesses related to sport sciences, sport-specific skills, and pedagogical (i.e., teaching) coaching strategies (Abraham, Collins, and Martindale 2006). Professional knowledge is not limited to a sport's technical and tactical skills, but rather includes content related to "what to coach" and "how to coach it" (Cassidy, Jones, and Potrac 2009). Other areas that would be included in professional knowledge are motor learning, biomechanics, exercise science, strength and conditioning, sport psychology, and leadership.

Interpersonal knowledge is the knowledge used by a coach to interact with others (Bowes and Jones 2006). To be effective, coaches obviously interact with athletes, but they also interact with opposing coaches, assistant coaches, parents, officials, community members, and administrators. At the core of this type of knowledge is a coach's ability to learn from others, to read and understand varying personalities, and to communicate an effective response (Cushion, Armour, and Jones 2006; Jones and Wallace 2006).

Intrapersonal knowledge is used by coaches to reflect on and evaluate themselves and their interactions with athletes and others (Gilbert and Trudel 2001). This type of knowledge involves coaches detecting problems while coaching, generating strategies to potentially overcome these problems, and then actively experimenting with those strategies in practice (Gallimore, Gilbert, and Nater 2014). Essentially, the intrapersonal knowledge coaches possess in any given situation is their ability to reflect and develop their coaching practices by creating an appropriate way of responding in that particular situation.

How Coaches Learn to Be Effective

Many researchers study how coaches develop their professional, interpersonal, and intrapersonal knowledge (Abraham, Collins, and Martindale 2006; Erickson, Côté, and Fraser-Thomas 2007). This body of research demonstrates that coaches acquire knowledge from mediated learning sources or unmediated learning situations (Nelson, Cushion, and Potrac 2006; Werthner and Trudel 2006; Wright, Trudel, and Culver 2007). Mediated learning occurs through direct facilitation by another individual who presents information or material in a structured format. In contrast, unmediated learning is initiated by the coach either consciously or unconsciously, where they themselves choose what and how to learn (Werthner and Trudel 2006). Within these two types of learning situations, coaches learn through formal, nonformal, and informal learning sources (Nelson, Cushion, and Potrac 2006; Werthner and Trudel 2006). Mediated learning situations are typically formal and nonformal. Formal learning sources are institutionalized coach education courses that are structured and curriculum based. While formal education is typically long term, nonformal education is short term and includes sources such as clinics, conventions, workshops, camps, or books that present information and knowledge in a standardized format covering a specific topic. The content presented in these formal and nonformal learning sources are typically related to topics such as technical and tactical skills, pedagogy, strength and conditioning programming, sports psychology, biomechanics, and motor learning (Nelson, Cushion, and Potrac 2006; Trudel and Gilbert 2006).

Informal learning sources, which are typical of unmediated learning situations, are where learning occurs within coaching experiences that are considered to be meaningful and insightful to the coach. These meaningful and individualized experiences are where knowledge is constructed within the context or situation where the coach is engaging. Integral to this hands-on or experiential learning is coach collaboration, where coaches acquire knowledge through others such as mentors by strategizing with each other to overcome coaching problems or by simply passing on relevant coaching information to one another (Bloom et al. 1998). In general, informal learning occurs by collaborating with other coaches in three ways: apprenticeships, communities of practice, and dynamic social networks (Jones, Harris, and Miles 2009).

Apprenticeships

The idea of learning through apprenticeship was explained by Lave, Wenger, and Wenger (1991) to understand how novices learn from more skillful practitioners. In essence, apprentices are individuals who learn from a master practitioner or others who possess a greater level of knowledge and expertise. In these interactions, between an apprentice and master practitioner, the apprentice engages in peripheral or noncentral tasks and observes the master practitioner complete more important responsibilities. As an apprentice gains knowledge by watching the master practitioner, she or he gradually becomes more involved and takes on greater responsibilities. In coaching, this mentoring relationship is where a master (i.e., effective and knowledgeable) coach facilitates a less knowledgeable (often an assistant) coach's knowledge development and empowers him or her to take on more challenging and essential responsibilities (Jones, Harris, and Miles 2009).

Communities of Practice

Coaches also learn by interacting and collaborating within communities of practice (CoPs; Wenger 1998). Coaching CoPs are groups of coaches who interact naturally in the sport environment and learn by collaborating on similar coaching problems (Culver and Trudel 2006). However, highly functional (i.e., providing greater and more meaningful learning experiences) CoPs are dependent on the degree to which the coaches in the community maintain three essential aspects: mutual engagement, joint enterprise, and shared repertoire. Mutual engagement means that all coaches within a community or group interact with their own unique background and knowledge. Joint enterprise means all coaches within the community are experiencing similar problems that require resolution. Finally, shared repertoire is the common language and tools used by coaches in the community. In some cases, coaching CoPs contain coaches within a workplace or coaching staff, but could also comprise coaches who have a wide range of experiences and backgrounds coaching different sports (Culver 2004).

Dynamic Social Networks

Another informal learning source in which coaches learn by collaborating is the dynamic social network. Coaches within a dynamic social network know each other well enough to share information that is used to solve or discuss coaching problems, but they are not limited to working in the same environment (Jones, Harris, and Miles 2009). Dynamic social network discussions are haphazard and unplanned, and in many cases they result in stronger relationships over time where more knowledge is shared and discussed (Occhino, Mallett, and Rynne 2013). Dynamic social networks differ from apprenticeships and CoPs because knowledge is passed on rather than worked out, negotiated, or constructed among coaches in person.

In the following sections, we provide a model for coach career development in progressive stages, culminating with the effective, master coach. Within each stage, we describe the role of coaches and how they learn through formal and nonformal learning sources. We also provide highly specific examples of how professional, interpersonal, and intrapersonal knowledge is developed through informal learning sources. We caution readers that the potential learning sources within each stage are not limited to the coaches at that particular stage of development. We understand that our everyday social world results in a wide range of coaches with different needs for professional, interpersonal, and intrapersonal knowledge based on their experiences and current responsibilities. Nonetheless, we provide a sample career development plan to become an effective coach.

Career Development

As previously noted, coaches take on various roles; that is, their responsibilities are dependent on the type of setting they are coaching within and their own level of development (Cushion, Armour, and Jones 2003). Typical coaching categories, or titles, for these roles are volunteer, part-time, graduate assistant, assistant, or head coach, regardless of the type of coaching setting (i.e., engagement or performance). Yet these coaching titles are at times not reflective of the coach's experience or level of knowledge, and therefore may not fully describe a coach's ability to produce effective coaching practices. For example, there may be situations where an assistant coach has a more in-depth knowledge set and produce more effective coaching practices than a head coach. Additionally, in some cases volunteer coaches are head coaches, which makes these titles problematic for indicating a coach's level of knowledge and ability to engage their coaching role. Rather, titles are a reflection of status and what they are responsible for in that particular setting (e.g., head coaches make decisions; assistant coaches take on lesser responsibilities), not what they are capable of based on the knowledge they possess. Therefore, we cannot always assume that the coach's title is congruent with the amount of knowledge he or she possesses.

Research has determined that effective coaches go through a learning progression in a series of stages, which have been described as follows: early sport participant (i.e., variety of sports), competitive sport participant (i.e., high-performance participation), early assistant coach (i.e., coaching immediately after playing), and head coach (i.e., first-time head coach and continued learning; Erickson, Côté, and Fraser-Thomas 2007; Gearity, Callary, and Fulmer 2013). However, it is still unclear specifically how much time and what knowledge is acquired within each stage on the way to developing into an effective coach (Erickson, Côté, and Fraser-Thomas 2007; Gilbert, Côté, and Mallett 2010). Additionally, a majority of effective coaches have spent time as athletes and have played multiple sports. This could upset the model, considering that according to research the preliminary stage of learning and development as a coach is now in the past once a coach enters the profession (Gilbert et al. 2009). The aforementioned issues are problematic for coach educators in developing a clear career development pathway for coaches.

In an attempt to overcome the barriers to career development and because coaches can benefit from progressing through a developmental career plan (Hesse and Lavallee 2010), in the following sections we detail a set of stages for the knowledge that coaches need to acquire as they progress through four developmental stages into an effective master coach. We should note that these stages sequence the development of professional, interpersonal, and intrapersonal knowledge in a progression, and we abandon the use of coaching titles (e.g., head coach) and explain the coaching roles and responsibilities that a coach could engage at each stage. These roles and responsibilities and the stages of coach development outlined in the following sections are derived from the International Sport Coaching Framework (ISCF; ICCE, ASOIF, and LMU 2013). Because coaches are not all the same and may contain knowledge in different areas based on their previous experiences, we provide a framework, informed by existing research on knowledge development, that helps identify gaps or weaknesses in coaches' knowledge at each stage of development. This framework organizes professional, interpersonal, and intrapersonal knowledge and connects what coaches are capable of based on the knowledge they possess in each stage of their development.

Coaching Assistant Stage of Career Development

Coaching assistants typically have not acquired many experiences as a coach. They contain a basic level of knowledge in the respective sport they are coaching, which is typically derived from their previous experiences as an athlete (Gilbert, Côté, and Mallett 2010). Coaching assistants contribute in basic coaching sessions; however, they may be in need of guidance during their practice and game planning or may even require some supervision while coaching. As a result of their lack of a well-rounded understanding of what coaches do and what it takes to be a coach (Kuklick, Gearity, and Thompson 2015), they often search for confidence in their coaching practices (Nash and Sproule 2011). Their most immediate need is the development of a coaching philosophy (Nash and Sproule 2011), which is a set of beliefs and values that will virtually explain everything they will do throughout their career (i.e., behaviors, interactions, coaching practices). Additionally, because we now know more about the negative long-term effects of sport-related injuries, coaching assistants would benefit from knowledge pertaining to injury prevention (Field et al. 2003; Guskiewicz and Mihalik 2011). Other roles and responsibilities for which coaching assistants will generally have a very low level of competency are their ability to set a vision for their athletes or program, create action plans, develop progress markers, manage multiple components of coaching, lead others, and be innovative (ICCE, ASOIF, and LMU 2013). However, coaching assistants do play a role in providing a positive frame of reference as a model coach for other coaching assistants and certainly athletes.

Following are listed specific examples of what would need to be developed and some potential learning sources that could be used in order for coaching assistants to advance to the subsequent stage of development:

Professional Knowledge

- What coaches do
- What coaches need to possess to be effective
- Safety in sport
- Ethical decision-making
- Coaching philosophy

Interpersonal Knowledge

- General understanding of how coaches interact with athletes
- How coaches interact with each other in one-on-one situations
- How coaches interact with parents individually

Intrapersonal Knowledge

- General coaching problems

Potential Formal and Informal Learning Sources

- NASPE (2008) National Coaching Standards
- International Council for Coaching Excellence's International Sport Coaching Framework
- National Federation of State High School Association (NFHS) Safety in Sport Training
- NFHS Concussion Training
- NFHS Heat Illness Prevention Training
- Team USA Safe Sport Training
- Coach Can Reach Higher: Make Ethical Decisions Training
- Ethics and philosophy workshops
- Coaching workshops focused on developing parent–coach relationships
- *The Double-Goal Coach: Positive Coaching Tools for Honoring the Game and Developing Winners in Sports and Life* by J. Thompson
- Positive Coaching Alliance: Double-Goal Coach Workshop

Informal Learning Source of Knowledge Acquisition

Coach Moreski is a volunteer assistant youth ice hockey coach whose athletes are participating in sport for engagement. Coach Moreski is assisting Coach Limpinski, who has been a head coach for four years. Over the first two weeks of practice, Coach Moreski spent most of his time observing Coach Limpinski and taking on small tasks such as working with athletes on passing in small groups while Coach Limpinski worked with the larger group on team offense. While working in small groups, Coach Moreski noticed that two of the athletes seemed very anxious and not very confident in performing a pass. In the previous weeks, Coach Moreski had observed Coach Limpinski immediately build confidence in another athlete by providing verbal, positive encouragement by whispering in the athlete's ear as they were between line changes during a practice session. After practice, Coach Limpinski asked Coach Moreski what he had learned from working with the athletes and what problems he had encountered.

Informal Learning Source Analysis

The preceding example describes how one coach observed the other's use of and implementation of an interpersonal skill. The assistant coach then employed that interpersonal skill in a different situation within the same sport. Although little to no dialogue occurred between the coaches in the midst of coaching, an interpersonal skill was applied into a coaching practice, which was acquired by observing a behavior from another coach. The professional knowledge acquired in this situation was of a pedagogical strategy, where the coach whispered into the athlete's ear to overcome a coaching issue. This identification of a coaching problem in the midst of coaching and the subsequent strategizing to overcome the issue is what would be considered intrapersonal knowledge (i.e., identify problem, strategize, and experiment in the midst of coaching) in the context of coaching pedagogy within youth sport. The above example takes the form of an apprenticeship informal learning situation, in that the assistant coach observed the head coach. The assistant and head coach engage a mentoring relationship as the head coach facilitates other learning experiences by questioning Coach Moreski after practice.

Coaching Associate Stage of Career Development

Coaching associates, which are labeled as being in a "Coach" stage of development in the ISCF, have a fundamental level of knowledge in their respective sport context. They have the ability to plan and implement instructional strategies for their coaching on their own, yet they are in need of acquiring an in-depth understanding of sport-specific content related to technical, tactical, pedagogical, psychological, and motor-learning topics, as well as biomechanics, training methods, and leadership (Abraham, Collins, and Martindale 2006). Coaches in the coaching associate stage are in need of understanding ways of evaluating their own coaching practices and have a moderate to low level of competency in their ability to understand the big picture of coaching, develop strategies for program improvement, organize and manage the athletic setting and personnel, and be an educator (ICCE, ASOIF, and LMU 2013). However, these coaches play an active role in facilitating the development of coaching assistants and may be taking on roles where they are independently planning and developing practice plans and programs for athletes to be successful.

Following are listed specific examples of what would need to be developed and some potential learning sources that could be used in order for coaching associates to advance to the subsequent stage of development:

Professional Knowledge

- Sport-specific technical knowledge
- Sport-specific tactical knowledge
- Pedagogical strategies
- Sport psychology

- Motor learning
- Biomechanics
- Leadership

Interpersonal Knowledge

- How coaches interact with each other
- Differences in body language among individuals
- How coaches interact in one-on-one situations

Intrapersonal Knowledge

- General coaching problems and strategies to overcome the issues
- Issues related to one's own coaching practices

Potential Formal and Nonformal Learning Sources

- University-based bachelor's degree in Athletic Coaching or related field
- NFHS Sport-Specific Technical and Tactical Skills Training
- Sport psychology books
- Sport-specific coaching clinics
- Coaching workshops focused on understanding ways of communicating
- Coaching workshops on building confidence in athletes
- *Understanding Sports Coaching: The Social, Cultural, and Pedagogical Foundations of Coaching Practice* by T. Cassidy, R. Jones, and P. Potrac (2009)
- *Mindset: The New Psychology of Success* by C. Dweck (2008)

Informal Learning Source of Knowledge Acquisition

Coach Templeton is a second-year head volleyball coach at the interscholastic level engaged in the stage of coaching associate. Coach Templeton speaks on the phone weekly with Coach Diffy about each other's past week of practice. Coach Diffy is also at the coaching associate stage. In one of their recent discussions, Coach Templeton discusses her dissatisfaction with one of her athlete's ability to rotate from the read position to the adjust position during practices and games. Coach Templeton says that all of the other athletes were able to grasp the concept except for one, and that she has used hula hoops as landmarks during team drill sets to provide guidance for the rotation. Coach Diffy says she understands the problem and tells Coach Templeton about her most recent sport psychology course, where they discussed many psychological factors, such as anxiety, that inhibit athletes from performing the task in front of others. Coach Templeton realizes that she needs to pay more attention to her athletes' responses to stress and anxiety. Coach Diffy also suggests that it may be a good idea for Coach Templeton to have her athletes report their level of anxiety and stress during different practice situations so that she can gain a better understanding for the individual differences among her athletes. But Coach Templeton explains that in the case of the athlete who is not performing the rotation correctly, it may be better, for the time being, to reduce her anxiety by having her perform it after practice with no other athletes around until she is more comfortable to perform the rotation in front of others. Coach Diffy also explains that strategies such as positive self-talk and pre-set routines maybe beneficial to reduce the anxiety.

Informal Learning Source Analysis

In the preceding example, two coaches engage a dynamic social network. Coach Templeton gained insight on some psychological skills that Coach Diffy learned in her sport psychology course that Coach Templeton implemented into her coaching. However, the new ideas were engaged through collaboration and bouncing ideas off each other until Coach Templeton felt comfortable with how the strategy would fit into her own context. She also develops intrapersonal knowledge by examining and evaluating the individual needs of her athletes. In this way, she is deliberately focusing and searching for problems that interact with anxiety and stress in the practice and competition environment. In the future, upon identifying issues, she will generate strategies and experiment with those strategies, which in turn will further develop the psychological strategies used in her coaching practices to fit different situations.

Advanced Coach Stage of Career Development

Advanced coaches have an extended and integrated level of knowledge in their respective sport context. They have the ability to independently lead and construct an entire program. They also manage the development of coaching associates and coaching assistants. Advanced coaches have a breadth of knowledge and are continuing to develop this knowledge to meet the demands of any given situation. They contain moderate to high levels of competency in their ability to observe, make decisions, evaluate sessions and programming, identify and recruit athletes, and manage multiple components of their coaching (ICCE, ASOIF, and LMU 2013). We know that coaches in this stage are likely to cite informal learning as their most influential learning source (Erickson, Côté, and Fraser-Thomas 2007). However, this could be because their professional knowledge (i.e., biomechanics, motor learning) has been developed exponentially to meet very specific demands in their coaching setting (Abraham, Collins, and Martindale 2006). Yet, these coaches could still benefit from formal and nonformal learning sources that provide new perspectives and ideas in areas that have not been developed or considered (Nash and Collins 2006; Nash and Sproule 2009). These areas could include program evaluation, sport sociology, organizational psychology, technology in sport, and training theory.

Following are listed specific examples of what would need to be developed and some potential learning sources that could be used in order for advanced coaches to advance to the subsequent stage of development:

Professional Knowledge

- Sociology of sport
- Strength and conditioning
- Training theory
- Program evaluation
- Organizational and administrative leadership

Interpersonal knowledge:

- How head coaches interact with assistants
- Individual differences in motivation among athletes
- Anxiety and stress in athletes
- Underlying components of positive coach–athlete relationships
- How to generally create and shape an environment

Intrapersonal knowledge

- Issues related to one's own coaching practices and strategies to overcome issue
- Multiple ways of evaluating one's own coaching practices
- Multiple ways of evaluating athlete's outcomes
- Issues related to differences among athletes and strategies to overcome problems while meeting the needs of individual athletes
- Issues and strategies in specific contexts

Potential Formal and Nonformal Learning Sources

- Master's degree in Athletic Coaching education or related field courses
- Administration and leadership books
- Sport-specific coaching workshops focused on the use of technology
- Coaching workshops focused on reflective practice
- Coaching workshops focused on motivational strategies
- Coaching workshops focused on developing positive coach–athlete relationships
- Formal coaching evaluations

- Self-Reflection and Insight Scale (used to determine intrapersonal knowledge)
- Emotional Intelligence Questionnaire (used to determine interpersonal knowledge)
- Revised Competitive State Anxiety Inventory-2 (used to determine athletes' level of confidence)
- Coach–Athlete Relationship Questionnaire (used to determine relationships between coach and athlete)
- Prosocial and Antisocial Behavior in Sport Scale (used to determine athletes' character and ability to interact with others)
- Perceived Motivational Climate in Sport Questionaire-2 (used to determine athletes' perception of the environment created by the coach)
- *Sociology of Sports Coaching* by R.L. Jones
- *The Fifth Discipline* by P. Senge
- *Eleven Rings: The Soul of Success* by P. Jackson

Informal Learning Sources of Knowledge Acquisition

Coach Harbo is a third-year head tennis coach at the interscholastic level and is engaging in the stage of an advanced coach. Coach Marco is his assistant coach, in the associate stage of development, who has been coaching for two years. The two coaches meet daily to discuss coaching issues and strategize ways to overcome their opponents' weaknesses. Coach Harbo has not made postseason competition in his first two seasons and is in need of an appearance in order to keep his job. Before the final regular-season match, Coach Harbo observes their best player screaming profanities at another teammate during a practice session. Given the excitement of the upcoming match, the practice session was being attended by reporters, members of the community, and youth athletes. The action of the best player was an obvious violation of team policies. If the player does not compete, the team will significantly decrease their chance of winning. Coach Marco suggests that they need to win and the tennis player should be allowed to compete. Coach Harbo initially agrees, but then decides to think about it longer without acting out irrationally. He reflects and asks Coach Marco what other coaches or the community would think about allowing the athlete to compete. Coach Marco also asks what would be the case if the win didn't matter. The coaches engage in collaborative discussions considering varying perspectives. Coach Harbo has challenged his strongly held coaching belief to provide an environment that teaches athletes life lessons. He decides to suspend the tennis player for the last match.

Informal Learning Source Analysis

In the preceding example, two coaches within a community of practice engage in mutual engagement (i.e., the coaches have an understanding of each other and know their individual areas of expertise), joint enterprise (i.e., shared problems with attacking opponents' weakness, problems with athletes), and shared repertoire (i.e., tennis language and content). The coaches within this community encounter a coaching problem that challenges their coaching philosophies. They collaboratively strategize by considering varying perspectives to generate formidable solutions. In this way, we show that despite the stage of development, coaches are constantly challenging their coaching philosophy. This situation also demonstrates how Coach Harbo draws upon interpersonal knowledge by considering how other coaches and the community would perceive his decision to let the athlete compete. This knowledge and thought process would likely be constructed in Coach Marco as well, as a result of collaborating in the CoP. Additionally, we would suggest intrapersonal knowledge being developed in that Coach Harbo allowed time for reflection and to think through the situation. Similarly, Coach Marco could develop this self-awareness as well from engaging in the CoP by learning from Coach Harbo.

Master Coach Stage of Career Development

Master coaches have a highly specialized and integrated level of knowledge, which is highlighted by their superior decision-making abilities (Saury and Durand 1998). They contain high levels of competency in their ability to develop strategies and progress markers, manage relationships, self-reflect, and self-monitor (ICCE, ASOIF, and LMU 2013). Perhaps most important, master coaches are actively engaged in their own professional development and the development of other coaches. However, we should note here that an entire separate system has been proposed by the International Coach Developer Framework (ICDF), which outlines how to develop master coaches into master coach developers (ICCE, ASOIF, and LMU 2014). Regardless, master coaches oversee and contribute innovative insights toward the implementation and review of their evidence-based athletic systems over multiple seasons. Master coaches understand that they will be constantly changing their coaching practices and continuing to develop (Ford, Coughlan, and Williams 2009). In their continuous evolution, they draw upon highly specialized concepts, ideas, and behaviors from areas outside of sport coaching that are then implemented into their own coaching and thus produce creative and innovative coaching practices (Nash and Collins 2006; Nash and Sproule 2009). Master coaches are open to new ideas and are able to quickly determine how, when, and why their new ideas can be implemented into their coaching system (Dorgo 2009; Ford, Coughlan, and Williams 2009). Next we suggest that master coaches draw upon professional knowledge in all areas listed in the earlier stages. However, this knowledge is crafted for any given situation that leads to greater organization and management of their program or system (Nash and Collins 2006; Nash et al. 2009).

Following are listed specific examples of what would be constantly evolving and some potential learning sources that could be used to maintain being an effective master coach:

Professional Knowledge

- Sport-specific technical knowledge
- Sport-specific tactical knowledge
- Pedagogical strategies
- Sport psychology
- Motor learning
- Biomechanics
- Strength and conditioning
- Training theory
- Program evaluation
- Organizational and administrative leadership
- Sociology of sport
- Technology in sport

Interpersonal Knowledge

- Interactions among coaches
- Individual differences in a given situation or context
- Individual differences in developing positive coach–athlete relationships
- Individual differences in motivating others

Intrapersonal Knowledge

- Issues related to one's own coaching practices and strategies to overcome issues
- Multiple ways of evaluating one's own coaching practices
- Issues related to differences among athletes and strategies to overcome problems while meeting the needs of individual athletes
- Issues and strategies in specific contexts
- Issues related to the system and strategies to overcome those issues
- Issues related to the system over multiple years and strategies to overcome those issues

Potential Formal and Informal Learning Sources

- University-based bachelor's or master's degree in Athletic Coaching or related fields
- Coaching workshops focused on technology
- Coaching workshops on latest coaching science research
- Coaching workshops focused on reflective practice
- Coaching workshops focused on motivational strategies
- Coaching workshops on positive coach–athlete relationships
- Formal coaching evaluations
- Self-Reflection and Insight Scale (used to determine intrapersonal knowledge)
- Emotional Intelligence Questionnaire (used to determine interpersonal knowledge)
- Revised Competitive State Anxiety Inventory-2 (used to determine athletes' confidence)
- Coach–Athlete Relationship Questionnaire (used to determine coach-athlete relationships)
- Prosocial and Antisocial Behavior in Sport Scale (used to determine athletes' character)
- Perceived Motivational Climate in Sport Questionaire-2 (used to determine athletes' perception of the environment created by the coach)

Informal Learning Sources of Knowledge Acquisition

Coach Carter is a ninth-year, head master soccer coach at the university level. Coach Blum is an assistant coach engaging in the stage of a coaching assistant and has been part of the program for two years. Coach Carter now feels comfortable with allowing Coach Blum to develop the practices and the yearly plan. Both coaches meet regularly and Coach Carter provides guidance and feedback on the practice plans and how coaching practices are adapted to the subtle differences among their athletes. Part way through the off-season, the coaches agree to purchase a GPS system that tracks each player's path during competition. After a few weeks, Coach Carter notices that Coach Blum has become very familiar with how to use and evaluate athletes' performance using the GPS system. In the regular meetings, Coach Blum trains Coach Carter on the system. Coach Carter then begins learning to evaluate performance using the device as Coach Blum facilitates.

Informal Learning Source Analysis

In this example, we show how a master coach learns by collaborating with a coach who maintains a lesser developmental stage. This idea reflects that learning in a mentoring relationship is not a one-way learning path (Occhino, Mallett, and Rynne 2013). Rather, learning occurs within both coaches participating in the mentoring relationship. The master coach acquired professional knowledge related to a new technological strategy, which will provide new opportunities for developing and utilizing intrapersonal and interpersonal knowledge. Additionally, in the aforementioned example, we also see that the coaching assistant develops professional knowledge related to the use of the technology in soccer. While teaching the master coach, the coaching assistant uses and constructs interpersonal and intrapersonal knowledge.

Up to this point, we have discussed the developmental stages that coaches engage as they progress into an effective master coach. We have also provided what knowledge would likely be acquired and needed at each stage. Subsequently, we have discussed some recommendations for how knowledge could be acquired and developed through formal, nonformal, and informal learning sources. However, research that has focused on how coaches learn has reported there are benefits and barriers to formal, nonformal, and informal learning sources (Cushion, Armour, and Jones 2003; Erickson et al. 2008). In order to provide a better understanding for how to develop knowledge over a career, in the following sections we provide a critique of formal, nonformal, and informal learning sources and provide recommendations for how to highlight the critical components of each type of learning source.

Formal and Informal Learning Sources: Critique and Implications

We know coaches find value in acquiring knowledge in areas of need through formal and nonformal learning sources (Vargas-Tonsing 2007). Additionally, formal and nonformal learning sources have been shown to enhance coaches' confidence in their ability to improve athletes' technical and tactical skills (Campbell and Sullivan 2005; Malete and Feltz 2000) and coaches' interpersonal knowledge (Smith, Smoll, and Curtis 1979). Other research has demonstrated that coaches generally have a positive perception of the sport-specific and pedagogical content presented in formal and nonformal education (Cassidy, Potrac, and McKenzie 2006; Hammond and Perry 2005). Research has shown that additional benefits of formal and nonformal learning sources are that they help coaches in the following ways:

- Improve the ability to motivate athletes (Campbell and Sullivan 2005)
- Improve the ability to build athletes' character (Campbell and Sullivan 2005)

- Improve the ability to engage reflective skills (Knowles et al. 2001; Kuklick, Gearity, and Thompson 2015)
- Improve the ability to create a positive coaching environment (Harwood 2008)
- Improve the ability to provide feedback and communicate with athletes (Smith, Smoll, and Curtis 1979)
- Improve the ability to enhance athletes' self-esteem (Conroy and Coatsworth 2006)
- Improve the ability to reduce athletes' performance anxiety (Smith, Smoll, and Barnett 1995)
- Improve the ability to reduce athlete drop out (Barnett, Smoll, and Smith 1992)
- Construct professional knowledge (Cassidy, Potrac, and McKenzie 2006)

Despite the benefits, the main issues with formal and nonformal approaches to knowledge development are that coaches find difficulty in connecting concepts to their coaching practices out in the field. For example, knowledge acquired through formal and nonformal learning sources needs to be further developed and tweaked to fit the dynamic coaching situations in which coaches are engaged (Abraham and Collins 1998). Likewise, the coaching belief that formal education is not as important as informal learning certainly presents a problem to learning through formal and nonformal approaches (Irwin, Hanton, and Kerwin 2004). The list below shows other possible problems with formal learning sources.

- Power relations between educators and coaches (Cushion et al. 2010)
- A lack of support for their effect on coaching skills (Cushion and Nelson 2013)
- Rarely being a professional development requirement (NASPE 2008)
- May be required and thus coaches lose interest in the content (Cushion, Armour, and Jones 2003)
- Lack of strategies implemented into formal programs that provide coaches with ways to connect content with practice (Knowles, Borrie, and Telfer 2005)
- Coaches already knowing the material presented in formal learning sources (Irwin, Hanton, and Kerwin 2004)
- A lack of learning objectives (Lemyre, Trudel, and Durand-Bush 2007)
- A lack of knowledge retention by coaches (Abraham and Collins 1998; Knowles et al. 2006)

In response to the barriers of formal and nonformal learning sources, research exploring the well-developed and highly specific knowledge set of effective master coaches has traced their knowledge back to foundational professional knowledge that is typically delivered in formal learning sources (i.e., sport specific, pedagogy, sports science; Abraham, Collins, and Martindale 2006). This evidence raises a question as to how this knowledge is further developed as a coach progresses toward being an effective master coach. The following strategies, which have been supported by research, act as ways coach educators can overcome the barriers to formal and nonformal learning:

- Embed problem-based learning strategies (Jones and Turner 2006)
- Embed reflective practice learning strategies (Knowles et al. 2001; Kuklick, Gearity, and Thompson. 2015)
- Embed a clear and specific set of learning objectives (Cushion et al. 2010; Nelson and Cushion 2006)
- Assess measurable outcomes in coaching knowledge and behaviors and in athlete outcomes (Cushion and Nelson 2013)
- Incorporate collaboration among coaches (Sullivan 2009)
- Challenge coaches' pre-existing beliefs (Nelson and Cushion 2006)
- Embed critical-thinking strategies (Cushion et al. 2010)

As you might have noticed, the aforementioned strategies draw upon some of the underlying components of informal learning. In a sense, these strategies "informalize" formal learning sources, which means coach educators use their understanding of how coaches learn informally (i.e., experience, reflection, and collaboration) to better enhance learning within formal and nonformal learning sources. In order to provide a better understanding, we elaborate on a few of the aforementioned strategies to demonstrate how they can be used to overcome the barriers to formal and nonformal learning sources.

When coach educators are developing a workshop, they should first target coaches that would be of interest and then develop measurable learning objectives that meet the needs of that particular group of coaches. Subsequently, when the workshop is being organized and planned, coach educators should incorporate ways of challenging coaches' pre-existing beliefs about the particular topics. Strategies to do this would include incorporating questions that facilitate the development of new ideas, offer varying perspectives on ideas, and present scenarios that engage critical thought. Once material and content has been presented, coach educators could then engage reflective practice by asking coaches to brainstorm potential problems that they may encounter when implementing the content into their coaching. Next, coach educators could ask coaches to brainstorm a set of strategies that could be used to overcome each problem they proposed would occur. To further engage learning within the workshop, coaches could collaborate and interact with other coaches to compare and contrast their potential problems and strategies that would be useful in connecting the content presented in the workshop with practical application.

Informal Learning Through Collaboration With Other Coaches: Critique and Implications

As previously noted, we have discussed informal learning sources where coaches develop professional, interpersonal, and intrapersonal knowledge by collaborating with other coaches. Coaches cite these informal learning situations as being the most preferred career development choice (Irwin, Hanton, and Kerwin 2004; Lemyre, Trudel, and Durand-Bush 2007). Research has further supported these coaching choices as being the most beneficial to the development of coaching knowledge (Jones, Harris, and Miles 2009). Other benefits of informal learning sources through collaboration are that they help coaches do the following:

- Improve the ability to reflect on problems encountered in coaching practices (Gallimore, Gilbert, and Nater 2014)
- Improve the development of positive relationships with other coaches (Occhino, Mallett, and Rynne 2013)
- Construct positive workplace environments (Handcock and Cassidy 2014)
- Enhance coaches' learning outcomes despite developmental stages (Occhino, Mallett, and Rynne 2013)
- Create lifelong and ongoing learning experiences (Bloom et al. 1998)
- Reduce coaching stress (Kuklick et al. 2015)
- Construct well-developed repertoires of professional knowledge (Abraham, Collins, and Martindale 2006)
- Create personalized learning opportunities (Kuklick et al. 2015)
- Develop practical coaching knowledge (Jones, Armour, and Potrac 2003)
- Enhance decision-making abilities (Dorgo 2009)
- Increase the motivation to learn through experience (Erickson et al. 2008)
- Enhance the ability to instruct athletes (Cushion, Armour, and Jones 2003)
- Improve coaches' leadership abilities (Brooks et al. 2000; Magnusen and Petersen 2012)
- Improve the ability to develop athletes (Allen, Eby, and Lentz 2006)
- Improve coaching competence (Gould, Krane, Giannini, and Hodge 1990)
- Improve coaching confidence (Kuklick et al. 2015)

In spite of the benefits of informal learning sources, many barriers exist in developing highly functional collaborations that produce influential learning experiences among coaches (Jones, Harris, and Miles 2009). The most immediate barrier to learning through collaboration is the development of trust among coaches (Bloom et al. 1998; Jones, Harris, and Miles 2009). In essence, if coaches do not trust or value each other, they never engage in collaborative interactions. In this way, many influential learning experiences are left unattended and coaches never gain new perspectives or develop beyond what they already know (Bloom et al. 1998; Cushion, Armour, and Jones 2003). Other barriers to learning through collaboration with others include the following:

- The competitive nature of sport (Culver, Trudel, and Werthner 2009)
- Power and controlling relationships between coaches (Zehntner and McMahon 2014)
- Poor listening and communication skills (Ehrich, Hansford, and Tennent 2004)
- A lack of time (Bloom et al. 1998)
- A lack of willingness to collaborate with others (Culver, Trudel, and Werthner 2009)
- A sole focus on improving athletes' technical skills (Cushion, Armour, and Jones 2003)
- An absence of a facilitator or a mediator to engage collaborations among coaches (Culver, Trudel, and Werthner 2009)
- Too much structure (i.e., tasks for coaches to complete) within collaborative learning situations (Cushion et al. 2010)
- A reproduction of ineffective coaching culture and practices (Cushion and Jones 2001)
- Ineffective and poor coaches engaging in collaborations with others (Bloom et al. 1998; Cushion, Armour, and Jones 2003)

In response to overcoming the barriers of informal learning sources, a variety of strategies have been used to induce the greatest gains in learning. The purpose of these strategies is to provide opportunity for coaches to reap the benefits of experiential learning by collaborating with other coaches. Essentially, these mediated or facilitated strategies are considered, to some degree, to be informal learning sources that bring to the surface the underlying components of learning through experience. The following strategies have been used to overcome the problems associated with informal learning:

- Use trained facilitators that engage and organize learning communities (Culver and Trudel 2006; Gilbert, Gallimore, and Trudel 2009)
- Schedule regular meetings, phone calls, or supervisory observations that are dedicated to improving coaching practices (Farrell and Van de Braam 2014; Gilbert, Gallimore, and Trudel 2009; North 2010)

- Educate mentors and coach collaborators on how to develop care and trust among coaches (Cushion 2015)
- Educate coaches on the process of mentoring and how to collaborate with other coaches (Cushion 2015)
- Use and implement observational feedback among coaches (Griffiths 2015)
- Embed and allow the use of storytelling among coaches (Culver 2004)
- Structure tasks and objectives during coaching collaborations to facilitate learning (Culver 2004)
- Use technology to connect coaches outside of their immediate competitive environment (Kuklick et al. 2015; Stoszkowski and Collins 2014)
- Use athletes' outcomes to provide evidence for coach learning and to identify gaps in knowledge (Gilbert et al. 2009)
- Use a selection process for mentor, mentees, and coach collaborators (Griffiths and Armour 2012)
- Educate mentors, coach collaborators, or facilitators on listening and communication skills (Griffiths 2015)

To provide a better understanding for the reader, we elaborate on a few of the aforementioned strategies to demonstrate how they can be used by coach educators to overcome the problems associated with informal coaching collaborations. A coach educator could first have a community of coaches (e.g., 10 coaches) highlight three of their most essential coaching skills they believe they possess as a coach. Using this information to pair coaches together, the coach educator could present these perceived coaching skills to the group of coaches as an anonymous biography of each coach within the group. The coaches could then select their coach collaborator based on the skills and biography provided by each coach. In this way, each coach has, to some degree, control of whom they are going to be collaborating with. Subsequently, the coach educator could provide structure by organizing the weekly or biweekly coaching meetings, developing a set of questions to facilitate learning, creating tasks such as problems to search for during their week of coaching in between meetings, or set up observation schedules for the coaching groups. If collaboration and sharing is hindered because of coaches' competitiveness, a facilitator could be used to engage the coaching collaboration or CoP. Alternatively, technology could be used to connect coaches from areas outside of the competitive coach environment.

Summary

Coaches begin their careers with varying levels of knowledge and develop this knowledge over the course of their career in a variety of ways. In order to reach the knowledge and abilities of an effective master coach, coaches need to seek out formal and nonformal learning opportunities and develop collaborative coaching networks at the various stages of their development. These coaching collaborations involve sharing and debating authentic coaching situations or collaboratively synthesizing information acquired from formal and nonformal learning sources, which all offer opportunities for meaningful learning situations. When approaching the master coach stage of development, a greater amount of formal and nonformal learning sources are engaged and coaching collaborative networks are expanded rather than shrunk. In this way, we provide in this chapter a useful road map that contains a multitude of strategies for coaches, coach educators, and administrators to help develop effective coaching practices over a career.

Chapter 15

Long-Term Coach Development Process

Penny Crisfield

Continuing development is an important and career-long obligation for all practicing professionals in order to keep up with the relevant knowledge in their field as well as with the newest pedagogical approaches appropriate to the needs of the 21st century. While coaching is often a voluntary occupation, with training and qualification not always being deemed mandatory, coaching fulfills many of the accepted criteria of a profession. This group positions itself as possessing special knowledge and skills in a widely recognized body of learning derived from research, education, and training at a high level, and it is recognized by the public as such. A profession is also prepared to apply this knowledge and exercise these skills in the interest of others (Professional Standards Council of Australia 2016).

Coaching and coach development may also be closely aligned functionally to the well-established teaching profession, not simply due to their focus on skill acquisition but also to their aspiration to contribute to the development of the whole person rather than simply the athlete. In this way, they might also share some alliance with the health professions. Most important within the context of this text, the paralleling of the profession of coaching to other established professions highlights the importance, value, and need for a well-developed professional development system that will support and facilitate appropriate foundational professional knowledge as well as prepare and guide ongoing professional development efforts. This chapter will discuss and explore the concept of the professional coach developer within the coach development system as well as provide relevant real-world examples of existing programs.

The Complexity of Coaching: The Changing Role of Coaches, Coaching, and Coach Development

"Coaching is a tough job, as everyone who has tried it can attest. Goals are inherently challenging, variables within the coaching process are many and dynamic, and intended outcomes can never be a foregone conclusion" (Jones and Wallace 2005, 119). To add to this, coaches are playing an increasingly important and diverse role in sport and the community globally. Whether they are working with novices, children, recreational participants, or elite athletes, coaches are engaging with a broader range of participants who place significantly greater demands on them. They are expected not only to coach the sport technically and tactically but to also coach and develop the person physically, emotionally, socially, and cognitively. Sport coaching is very complex and context dependent (Côté and Gilbert 2009; Lyle and Cushion 2010). As outlined in Côté and Gilbert's definition of professional expertise (2009), to fulfill these expectations, coaches need, in a dynamic and changing situation, to be able to apply a range of professional, interpersonal, and intrapersonal knowledge and develop complex skills such as decision-making, problem solving, critical thinking, and reflection.

Developing Coaching Expertise

Previous chapters discussed the development of sport coaching knowledge and sport coaching expertise, highlighting the roles individual valuation and investment play in the latter and noting the role of a system that provides and supports the necessary ongoing learning opportunities necessary to develop expertise. Given the value and importance of professional expertise, how do coaches develop expertise and, more important within this chapter, what is needed to facilitate the development of professional expertise?

A great deal of work has been done on how people become expert in a range of domains, from physics to poetry and from chess to coaching. Understanding these pathways is essential for those tasked with creating systems in which development can occur. Research has shown that there is no magic bullet, concluding that innate talent plays a less prominent role than previously thought (Peskin 2011). Some of the early work in the development of expertise was carried out by Anders Ericsson, who studied the cognitive structure of expert performers in domains such as medicine, music, chess, and sport in the 1990s (see summary article by Ericsson, Prietula, and Cokely 2007). Ericsson claimed that how people become expert at a skill has more to do with the way they practice and thus learn (deliberate practice) than simply the amount they practice. Experts break down the skills and focus on improving those chunks during practice; they also practice the skill at more challenging levels (at the edge of their ability) with the intention of mastering it. His more recent research (Ericsson and Pool 2016) highlights the difference between purposeful and deliberate practice. Purposeful practice means following this set of principles:

- Training must be done on the edge of one's comfort zone; if it's too easy or automatic, little improvement will take place.
- Training must be focused; that is, there must be a specific goal of improving one aspect of performance.
- Training requires feedback so that the person can figure out what to do to improve performance further.

The Dreyfus and Dreyfus model of skill acquisition (Benner 1984) also throws some light on how people become experts through formal instruction and practice. Their model is based on four binary qualities or mental functions that then lead to five specific roles: novice, advanced beginner, competent, proficient, and expert (see table 15.1).

TABLE 15.1 Dreyfus and Dreyfus Model of Skill Acquisition

Mental functions	Novice	Advanced beginner	Competent	Proficient	Expert
Recollection	Nonsituational	Situational	Situational	Situational	Situational
Recognition	Decomposed	Situational	Holistic	Holistic	Holistic
Decision	Analytical	Analytical	Analytical	Intuitive	Intuitive
Awareness	Monitoring	Monitoring	Monitoring	Monitoring	Absorbed
Description	• Rigid adherence to taught rules or plan • Little situational perception • No discretionary judgment	• Guidelines for action based on attributes or aspects • Situational perception is limited • All attributes and aspects are treated separately and given equal importance	• Coping with crowdedness • Now sees actions as at least partly in terms of longer-term goals • Conscious, deliberate planning • Standardized and routinized procedures	• Sees situations holistically • Sees what is most important in the situation • Perceives deviations from the normal patterns • Decision-making less labored • Uses maxims for guidance, whose meaning varies according to the situation	• No longer relies on rules, guidelines, or maxims • Intuitive grasp based on deep tacit understanding • Analytical approaches used only in novel situations or when problems occur • Vision of what is possible

Adapted from P. Benner, *From Novice to Expert: Excellence and Power in Clinical Nursing Practice* (Menlo Park, CA: Addison-Wesley, 1984) and S.E. Dreyfus and H.L. Dreyfus, "A Five-Stage Model of the Mental Activities Involved in Directed Skill Acquisition," 1980, accessed January 9, 2019, https://apps.dtic.mil/dtic/tr/fulltext/u2/a084551.pdf.

The parallels of the Dreyfus and Dreyfus model with coaches' long-term development from novice to expert are evident. Anecdotal evidence shows that novice coaches tend to have inadequate coaching process skills and technical knowledge and so conform to learned procedures and rules. Gradually, as they move toward competence, their skills and knowledge increase, and they are able to make conscious choices and take more responsibility for the outcome. If they develop as far as the proficient stage, their behavior becomes more intuitive, fluid, and flexible, so they are able to be more athlete-centered and context specific. They have deep coaching and performance knowledge, although their decision-making is more often deliberate and analytical rather than intuitive. Finally, those who achieve the excellent level and become expert coaches have vast knowledge, unconsciously see and know what to do, and make decisions intuitively (Schempp and McCullock 2006).

Nash and colleagues discuss the pivotal question of how to distinguish between effective coaching practice and expert coaching practice. "Coaches who demonstrate high levels of knowledge, enthusiasm and commitment are often labeled experts; however, expertise is more than this" (2006, 313–14). They go on to identify 27 differing explanations or criteria to describe the expert coach (Nash and Collins 2006, 314) and suggest that expert coaches possess expertise in

- "domain specific areas gained over a prolonged period of time,
- recognizing patterns faster than novices,
- structuring knowledge to facilitate recall,
- categorizing problems according to features of their solutions,
- rapid problem solving although they are slower than nonexperts in the initial stages of problem solving,
- adapting to situations in a flexible manner,
- developing routines to focus processing capacity on dynamic environmental factors, and
- assigning meaning to cues."

How then can this information be used to create appropriate professional development opportunities that both facilitate and support ongoing learning? And who are the professionals qualified to develop and guide this learning within the coach education model?

Sport and coaching organizations need to address how best to support coaches and help them develop their coaching expertise in the context in which they wish to coach. They need to devise systems and personnel that can help coaches learn effectively.

How a Professional Learns: Opportunities for Improving the Current Approach

Coaching researchers and practitioners are engaged in considerable and ongoing debate about how coaches learn best and therefore how this expertise can be developed. Much of this is quite critical of traditional formal coach education programs. Cushion and colleagues (2010) go as far as saying that current approaches to coach learning remain largely uninformed explicitly by learning theory. There is evidence that "coach learning tends to be idiosyncratic and that few coaches follow a systematic development route that is standardized for coaches within different sports and stages of development" (Nash 2014, 179), an outcome that can be attributed to a lack of standard recognition of the value of well-designed preparatory and ongoing training within and across sport contexts. There has also been much criticism about the quality and efficacy of coach education programs, with Jones and Wallace (2005) reporting that "few coaches attribute their development to coach education programs," again highlighting an issue around the lack of quality training systems available.

Some of these criticisms of traditional coach education programs may be well founded because some programs have typically focused on developing the technical and tactical knowledge of the coach (the what-to-coach skills and knowledge) rather than developing the ability to coach (the how-to-coach skills). These types of educational programs have tended to adopt a didactic classroom-based approach with limited (if any) opportunities to practice coaching skills and gain high-quality feedback. They are often developed outside of the educational context with limited input from or application of good pedagogy practices. The evaluation of educational programs that focus on prescriptive, what-to skills has been confirmed by Nash (2014) in a study of the perceptions coaches have of their coach education experiences. These programs have a tendency to focus on the "what" of the sport rather than the "how" of coaching and, in addition, have been traditionally delivered using a preset formula (i.e., little if any customization to the actual group or learner) and with little opportunity for interaction between coaches and the coach developer. Coaches also reported their belief that more meaningful learning occurred in informal contexts (e.g., coffee and lunch breaks) than in the formal learning context. This is often misinterpreted as a lack of value in formal coaching, rather than creating a needed call for better-quality design of formal learning opportunities.

A deeper examination of the critiques of the current coach education systems suggests that some of the research protocols or sampling may be flawed. Impact studies are difficult to construct and measure due to the complexity of coaching and the number of variables, and this is especially true in studying the impact of coach education programs on coaches' performance (P. Trudel and P. Werthner, personal communication, 2015). Much of the research has been directed at relatively inexperienced coaches, individuals with both the lowest level of experience and potentially with the least amount of preparation to be engaged learners, and most studies have evaluated the impact immediately after the intervention rather than adopting a longer-term protocol with multiple assessment points as advocated by Kirkpatrick (1994).

With regard to evaluating training programs, Kirkpatrick stresses the importance of the following:

- Evaluating coaches' feelings about the experience
- Assessing whether coaches had achieved the outcomes set out
- Determining whether coaches had put their learning into practice
- Measuring the impact on the environment and the athletes' performance

Outside of the sport-coaching-specific education, Ericsson and Pool (2016) criticize traditional teaching in schools and universities in general, citing that it focused on the assumed transfer of knowledge through lectures, presentations, and reading. They note that many studies have found that this approach to education is not successful in training people to think and reason and that they often fail to be able to apply their knowledge to solve problems in real-world situations. This critique can be appropriately applied to the common professional approaches to coach education as well, compounded by a lack of valuation of the complexities of the profession.

While Ericsson and Pool (2016) accept that a certain amount of knowledge is needed to perform to a high level in areas such as dance, chess, music, and sport, they argue that knowledge comes about as part of the process of developing the skills that are required to excel in that area. They speak of the need to focus on developing mental representations or mental tools that improve people's ability to think and reason about real-world situations and so monitor and evaluate their performance, spotting mistakes and identifying what needs to be done to eradicate such mistakes. They recommend gaining the knowledge first and then using experts to focus on helping them solve problems. This would appear to be an equally effective way of educating coaches, by first building the knowledge base (e.g., by distance learning) and then focusing on applying the knowledge to solve problems in either simulated workshop situations led by expert coach developers or through apprenticeships with expert coaches in the field. Thus it becomes important to critically re-examine the current approach to coach education and coach development and, more specifically, the roles and knowledge areas necessary for the individuals responsible for designing the learning opportunities.

Lara-Bercial and Duffy (n.d.) reported a dearth of either systematic research or longitudinal studies to show the effects of coach learning on improvements in coaching practice or on athlete outcomes. They concluded their literature review by saying

> while coaches acknowledge that a big part of learning happens "on the job" they would like to experience the complementary benefit of perhaps a guiding hand while they are doing so, be it in the shape of formal learning, or via interaction with a mentor or critical friend. . . . If coaching is contingent and at times unpredictable, it follows that a good dose of on-the-job experience, coupled with fair amounts of declarative knowledge and adequate support which can accelerate learning and provide guidance through turbulent waters is paramount to the development of coaching expertise

In line with this assessment, some findings (e.g., Nash 2015; Trudel and Gilbert 2006; Werthner and Trudel 2006) suggest that existing coach education sometimes falls short of current educational best practice. Fortunately, there has been a shift toward a competence-based approach with theory learned through practice whenever possible in some educational domains for other applied professional practices that can serve to provide guidance in the development of appropriate models within coaching education.

Exploring New Models of Learning Within Sport Coach Education

One example of the pioneering work in knowledge-to-application educational design can be found in professional nursing preparation (e.g., Fordham 2005), which has adopted a competence-based approach. There have been similar changes in more progressive coach education programs and many examples of good practice that are often overlooked and under-researched. In the United Kingdom, many sport governing bodies (e.g., England and Wales Cricket Board, British Wrestling, Scottish Swimming) have adopted a competence-based approach to coach education delivery and assessment. Each of these has also focused on developing the how-to-coach as well as the what-to-coach skills and has invested heavily in the training and support of their coach developer workforce.

It should be noted that despite the alignment of these innovative systems with current thinking on quality professional development, there has been criticism about the overly simplistic nature of competence-based systems that fail to cater to the complex decision-making requirements of coaching. Collins and colleagues (2015), for example, recommend that coaching should follow current medical practice and adopt an expertise focus. This more complex methodology may be more suitable for coaching, particularly at the more expert levels where practice is grounded in judgment and not the reproduction of prescribed behaviors.

There is no doubt that coaches develop their skills and knowledge in a range of ways and through different learning situations (Kirkpatrick 1994). Based on the early work by Moon (2004) on generic learning, Werthner and Trudel (2006), who applied the model to coach learning, suggested that a coach's cognitive structure would change under the influence of three complementary types of learning situations: mediated, unmediated, and internal. This model can provide a framework for considering ways in which structured learning can facilitate knowledge-to-application and prepare the learner with the skills necessary to maximize quality learning both within structured settings and in situations beyond those that can be provided. Additionally, it helps support the abilities and self-efficacy necessary for individuals to engage in challenging self-directed learning outside of requirements, an essential element of professionalism.

Within this model, mediated learning situations refer to "learning that is aided directly by another person or through the use of a medium that simplifies the material of teaching" (Moon 2004, 4). Examples of formal mediated learning for coaches would include coach education courses and qualifications, while coaching clinics, seminars, mentoring, and communities of practice would be examples of nonformal mediated learning for coaches.

Unmediated (or informal learning) refers to situations where "the learner is responsible for choosing what to learn about something" (Moon 2004, 74). It refers to learning that occurs when coaches choose what, when, and how to learn (e.g., through consciously initiated self-reflection and through self-directed learning from books, online learning, and DVDs, for example).

Internal learning is when the learner "is not exposed to new material, but rather reconsiders or reflects on existing ideas in his/her cognitive structure" (Werthner and Trudel 2009, 437). This internal learning can happen in both mediated and unmediated contexts and can be subdivided into two categories, incidental learning and unconscious self-reflection. While incidental learning is unplanned and does not occur in a systematic fashion, it can be powerful. The second category of internal learning, unconscious self-reflection, is the result of the introspection that occurs at a subconscious level.

How much time should be spent on each type of learning for effective professional development? Jennings' 70:20:10 model (2016) has gained some credence in the business world and may have useful application within coach education and development. This model describes a framework, not a recipe, that proposes a blended approach of formal and informal learning in the ratio of approximately 70 percent learning through practice in the workplace, 20 percent learning from and with others through conversations and networking, and 10 percent formal learning.

The Jennings' 70:20:10 model is based on three core ideas. The first learning premise, according to Jennings (2016), is that most learning happens as a natural part of work through daily work experiences and interactions with colleagues and others.

> Courses may help with the basics, or to refresh our knowledge, but courses alone won't deliver high performance. Other activities in the workplace—such as challenging experiences; opportunities to practice in "real" situations; support, advice, and guidance from colleagues; and reflection—are all more important than courses in helping do that. (Jennings 2016, para. 3)

The second is that context is critical. Learning is more likely to take place when the learning and work contexts are the same. The third and final core premise highlights the value of providing the learner with real problems to which they need to find real solutions in order to maximize learning.

The recognition of everyday experiences as valuable learning opportunities has gained increased acceptance not just in workplace learning but also in education (Hodkinson and Hodkinson 2005) and sport coaching (e.g., Cushion, Armour, and Jones 2003; Gilbert and Trudel 2001; Mallett et al. 2009; Nelson, Cushion, and Potrac 2006). Mallett and colleagues, in their examination of the relative impact of formal and informal opportunities in coaches' learning, conclude "coaches 'feel' that more learning is taking place in the 'informal' setting (or at the very least that it is valuable)" (Mallett et al. 2009, 332).

The importance and impact of unmediated informal learning for coaches is equally important, and the 70:20:10 framework can be superimposed onto figure 15.1, as shown in figure 15.2. Coaches gain much of their knowledge and skills through unmediated learning and often through hands-on experience,

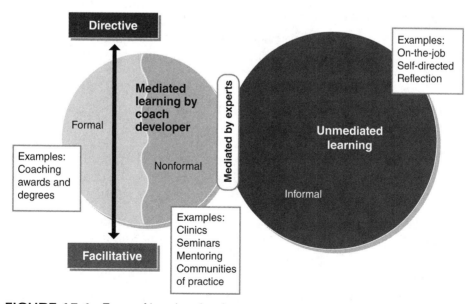

FIGURE 15.1   Types of learning situations.

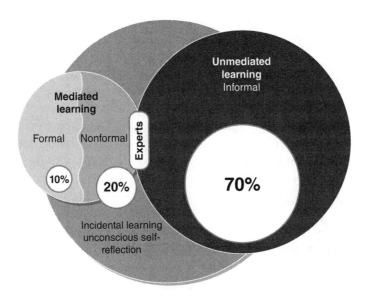

FIGURE 15.2   70:20:10 business model superimposed on types of learning situations.

informally ("the lifelong process by which every person acquires and accumulates knowledge, skills, attitudes and insights from daily experiences and exposure to the environment" [Coombs and Ahmed 1974, 8]).

Hart (2015) explains how a different mindset on the part of the learner and those responsible for the learning environment is needed to capitalize on the informal learning in the workplace. Figure 15.3 details the elements that should be part of modern workplace learning. Hart describes the importance of first building the modern workplace vision, encompassing a range of mediated and unmediated learning opportunities. She next stresses the need to help individuals take responsibility for their own learning, thereby promoting an ethos of learner-centered independent learning. She advocates the need for managers to encourage and support workplace learning in all its forms and highlights the importance of providing modern and innovative training as well as creating opportunities to engage in problem-solving activities. Lessons can be learned from this model and applied to the context of coach education. For example, those organizations or departments responsible for coach education must

- create a clear vision of learning that spans the spectrum of formal, informal, and nonformal opportunities,
- encourage coaches to take responsibility for their own development,
- promote all forms of social learning by encouraging coaches to collaborate and share their knowledge and skills,
- devise much more innovative training regimens including the promotion of mentoring and communities of practice, and

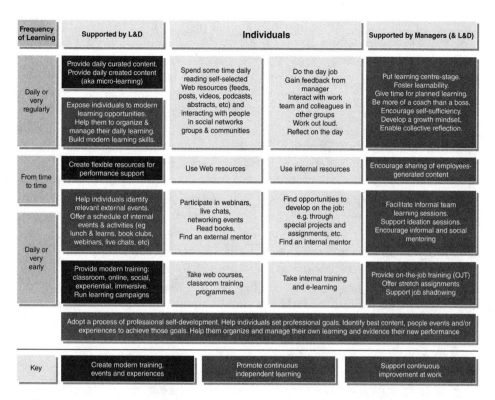

Frequency of Learning	Supported by L&D	Individuals		Supported by Managers (& L&D)
Daily or very regularly	Provide daily curated content. Provide daily created content (aka micro-learning) Expose individuals to modern learning opportunities. Help them to organize & manage their daily learning. Build modern learning skills.	Spend some time daily reading self-selected Web resources (feeds, posts, videos, podcasts, abstracts, etc) and interacting with people in social networks groups & communities	Do the day job Gain feedback from manager Interact with work team and colleagues in other groups Work out loud. Reflect on the day	Put learning centre-stage. Foster learnability. Give time for planned learning. Be more of a coach than a boss. Encourage self-sufficiency. Develop a growth mindset. Enable collective reflection.
From time to time	Create flexible resources for performance support	Use Web resources	Use internal resources	Encourage sharing of employees-generated content
Daily or very early	Help individuals identify relevant external events. Offer a schedule of internal events & activities (eg lunch & learns, book clubs, webinars, live chats, etc)	Participate in webinars, live chats, networking events Read books. Find an external mentor	Find opportunities to develop on the job: e.g. through special projects and assignments, etc. Find an internal mentor	Facilitate informal team learning sessions. Support ideation sessions. Encourage informal and social mentoring
	Provide modern training: classroom, online, social, experiential, immersive. Run learning campaigns	Take web courses, classroom training programmes	Take internal training and e-learning	Provide on-the-job training (OJT) Offer stretch assignments Support job shadowing

Adopt a process of professional self-development. Help individuals set professional goals. Identify best content, people events and/or experiences to achieve those goals. Help them organize and manage their own learning and evidence their new performance

Key	Create modern training, events and experiences	Promote continuous independent learning	Support continuous improvement at work

FIGURE 15.3 Learning and development practices for modern workplace learning.

Adapted by permission from J. Hart, *Modern Workplace Learning 2019: A Framework for Continuous Improvement Learning and Development at Work* (London: Centre for Learning and Performance Technologies, 2019).

- encourage problem-solving behaviors to find innovative solutions to coaching challenges.

While coaches need to be encouraged and properly prepared to meaningfully engage in unmediated learning, mediated learning still has a very important role to play, and so there is a need to consider who is best placed to help coaches learn. The International Council for Coaching Excellence established a working group in 2011 to examine how coaches learn and to develop a framework to "provide sports federations, coaching organizations and educational institutions with good practice guidelines to support the design, benchmarking and refinement of their coach education and development programs" (ICCE 2014, 5). The group quickly recognized the restrictive view of the conventional coach educator concept; it was traditionally focused on mediated, formal education (coaching awards and degree programs), which was often strongly classroom-based, assessment focused, and qualification oriented. To a lesser extent, coach educators structured informal opportunities (for example, through clinics, seminars, mentoring, and communities of practice), but there was little if any cognizance of the importance of stimulating informal, unmediated learning. Yet there is considerable evidence to support the contention that unmediated learning contributes significantly to a coach's learning (Moon et al. 2009), and significant anecdotal evidence that expert coach developers do stimulate unmediated learning.

It is important that a range of delivery strategies is used to meet the diverse needs of the coach learner and to develop the practical expertise required by coaches. Nursing and medical education models have led the way in designing learning strategies that enhance the development of practical knowledge and expertise and the similarities are considerable. "Nurse learners, whether before or after qualification, are by definition adult learners undertaking an academic, professional/vocational programme of studies that includes both theoretical and practical knowledge, behaviors and attitudes and the ability to perform in routine and unpredictable situations" (Hensley n.d.). Nurse training has applied many theories and models, including Bloom's cognitive taxonomy of learning and the Dreyfus and Dreyfus model based on Benner's work (1984), which describes how learners progress from novice to expert and how theory needs to be embedded in practice. In the nursing model just cited, it has been suggested at least half of an appropriate training program be application based with the emphasis placed on providing the learner with opportunities to demonstrate an understanding of evidence-based learning through application and practice.

The nurse-training model has applied four main approaches to learning to their teaching programs that can be useful in examining effective coach development. The first approach, traditional instruction, plays an important role in teaching nursing for novices or at the novice stage of a more complex competence acquisition. Researchers state "craft knowledge is often passed on traditionally and it is appropriate to do so in workplaces where role modelling and coaching develop practices ahead of the evidence base: this applies to both novices and experts." They go on to advocate that the relative amount of time in each approach is dependent on the skill level of the learner. The second, third, and fourth approaches, behavioral, instructional, and constructivist, respectively, are being used more in the early stages where the focus is often on teaching skills (described as first-cycle programs) and where a greater use of constructivist and collaborative models of learning is needed. They argue that "there is often insufficient attention to experiential learning, learning in the workplace" ("Approaches to Teaching, Learning and Assessment and the Subject Area Competences" n.d., 3).

The education of coaches has undergone and is continuing to undergo radical changes to shift away from reliance on traditional didactic instructional regimens that focus on theoretical and technical components of the sport to a greater emphasis on constructivist approach (for example, the coach developer training programs in New Zealand) and experiential learning, where there is a greater emphasis on learning theory through practice. With these shifts comes the recognition for the need for qualified and prepared individuals with multidisciplinary knowledge and skills from sport, sport sciences, educational theory, physical education, leadership development, curriculum design, and other related areas.

Coach Developers

The global shift in thinking toward a more holistic approach to coaching, and thus the need for the growth of coaching education and professionalization of coaching, creates a need for qualified professionals with the knowledge and skills necessary to create and support the professional development of coaches. This is similar to what can be seen in other professions such as teacher education and nursing preparation.

The Concept of Coach Developers

Based on their examination of coach learning, the ICCE's International Coach Developer Framework (ICDF; ICCE 2015) advocates the use of the term "coach developer" to replace terms such as coach educator, tutor, and learning facilitator. Coach developer is the umbrella term used to capture the roles of everyone directly responsible for the development of coaches. Coach developers are not simply experienced coaches or transmitters of coaching knowledge. In the forward for the ICDF, Duffy states "coach developers aren't only subject matter experts, aren't only concerned with delivering courses; they have a key role to play in different learning situations and bring significant expertise in the process of learning." (ICCE 2014, 4)

Coach developers are therefore described as those "trained to develop, support and challenge coaches to go on honing and improving their knowledge and skills in order to provide positive and effective sport experiences for all participants" (Crisfield and Brook 2012). This definition means that the responsibility of coach developers is encapsulated in multiple roles, including those of the coach educator, learning facilitator, presenter, mentor, assessor, learning program designer, and evaluator. This broader responsibility of the coach developer is also congruent with views of Trudel, Culver, and Werthner (2013), who advocate the term coach development over coach education because the former includes mediated, unmediated, and internal learning situations. Coach developers, therefore, should have an impact on encouraging learning through all three types of learning situations, not just mediated situations.

Coach developers should play a crucial role not just in the initial formal training of coaches but also in the way coaches are educated, supported, and nurtured on the job. Coach developers require the capabilities to provide this range of formal and nonformal learning opportunities, to synthesize the input of more experienced coaches and experts, and to assess and support coaches and encourage them to take responsibility for their ongoing development. In this way, coach developers can and should encourage unmediated, informal learning by teaching coaches self-reflective skills, encouraging critical thinking, signposting new learning, and creating a learning environment that encourages and fosters coaches to become "learning coaches" (Armour 2010). Such coaches will be self-motivated with a passion to further and to take responsibility for their own learning and development. The ability to stimulate and trigger unmediated learning may well be an important challenge for coach developers and researchers to establish how this may be most effectively achieved.

Long-Term Coach Developer Model

Coach developers can therefore no longer be perceived as simply experienced coaches. They require an extensive set of additional, although often complementary, skills and need to be experts in learning as well as in coaching their sport. For this reason, the ICCE working group developed a model to help organizations select, train, and grow their coach developers. The model is not a set of mandates but stresses the need for "multiple effective approaches . . . tailored to the sport and country specific circumstances" (ICCE 2013, 5).

The ICCE's Long-Term Coach Development (LTCD) pathway (figure 15.4) provides a suggested progression for coaches to extend their coaching skills from that of a coaching assistant to a coach, senior coach, and, ultimately, to a master coach.

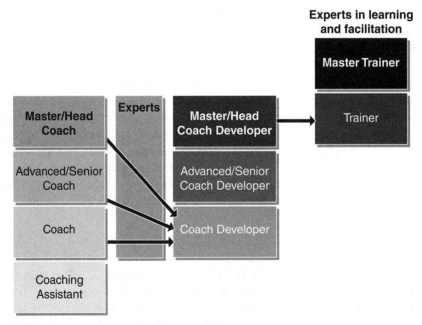

FIGURE 15.4   ICCE's Long-Term Coach Development (LTCD) pathway.

Reprinted by permission from International Council for Coaching Excellence, Association of Summer Olympic International Federations, and Leeds Beckett University, *International Sport Coaching Framework (Version 1.2)* (Champaign, IL: Human Kinetics, 2013), 41.

While every coach has responsibility for developing less-experienced coaches, coaches with appropriate motivation, sufficient experience, and a genuine desire to develop coaches may wish to cross over onto the long-term coach developer pathway. They should undergo training to become coach developers because, while many of the underpinning skills are the same, the context is different. They need to become experts in learning and in facilitation as well as in coaching.

The ICCE's LTCD pathway shows the increasing opportunities and roles available for those who have the interest and mindset to develop coaches. The pathway describes the transition from coach developer to senior coach developer through to master coach developer. An overview of the roles and capabilities is given in table 15.2.

The fourth pathway, the trainer pathway, provides further opportunities for exceptional master coach developers, especially for those working in larger programs or across different sports or organizations. Trainers have additional skills (and typically further and specific training) and they are outstanding

TABLE 15.2 Overview of the ICCE's Coach Developer Roles

	Coach Developers	Senior Coach Developers	Master Coach Developers	Trainers
Descriptor	Have successfully completed initial training and orientation	Are effective and experienced coach developers	Are highly effective and experienced senior coach developers	Are exceptional master coach developers and educationalists
Role	• Facilitate formal learning situations through prescribed coach education programs with minimal customization • Assess coaches, provide leadership, and engage in personal development opportunities	• Customize and facilitate coach education programs and sessions • Co-deliver and support coach developers • Assess coaches, provide leadership, and engage in personal development opportunities	• Provide initial training for coach developers • Support senior coach developers and coach developers through mentoring, co-delivery, and feedback • Design sport-specific coach education programs • Assure quality in their own sport-specific programs and assess coaches and coach developers	• Provide leadership, quality assurance, and verification of coach development and education programs • Design and lead coach developer programs and professional development opportunities • Select, assess, and support senior and master coach developers • Establish, monitor, and evaluate coach developer systems

Reprinted by permission from International Council for Coaching Excellence, Association of Summer Olympic International Federations, and Leeds Metropolitan University, *International Coach Developer Framework (Version 1.1)* (Leeds: Leeds Beckett University, 2014), 18.

experts in learning, learning facilitation, mentoring, and educational program design and evaluation.

Coach Developer Training Philosophy

It is not advocated that the coach developer workforce adopts a train-the-trainer model whereby those trained in the first wave of education become the trainers for the second and so on. This model potentially results in the gradual dilution of training expertise and so ultimately impacts negatively on coach learning. Rather it is recommended that training coach developers should mirror the training of teachers, while recognizing that the majority of coaches in many countries work on a voluntary and part-time basis. Nevertheless, the principles now being adopted in teacher education should be adopted in coach education. In 2010, a report was commissioned by the National Council for Accreditation of Teacher Education (NCATE) entitled *Transforming Teacher Education Through Clinical Practice: A National Strategy to Prepare Effective Teachers*. This report built on the experience of medical education and advocated a number of shifts in the way teachers are educated in the United States. Some key issues are shown in table 15.3, together with the implications for coach education and the work of coach developers. The issues mirror contemporary practice in modern workplace

TABLE 15.3 Comparison of Shifts in Teacher and Coach Education Programs

Teacher education advocating a move to programs with these characteristics	Implications for coach developers where coach education programs shift to ones with these characteristics
• Fully grounded in clinical (workplace/coaching) practice and interwoven with academic content and professional courses • Practice is at the center of teacher preparation and teachers have the opportunity to blend practitioner knowledge with academic knowledge as they learn by doing. • Subject-matter preparation, theory, and pedagogy is no longer taught in isolation but integrated into clinical (workplace) practice • Evidence-based knowledge (such as coach portfolios) is used rather than coursework to inform practice and address students' needs • Problem-based approaches adopted at Harvard Medical School are included, where case studies and simulations of problems in diagnosing patient conditions or working with families are used to construct an integrated spiral curriculum, thereby developing complex analytic and practical skills • Trained coaches and mentors are used to support trainee teachers in their workplace practice rather than providing ad hoc and variable experiences	• Grounded in workplace practice (actual coaching) with academic content (e.g., sport sciences) and professional aspects (e.g., coaching philosophy, coach–athlete relationships) woven in • Actual coaching practice (learning by doing) is central to coach preparation • Professional knowledge (e.g., of the sport, of coaching pedagogy), interpersonal knowledge (e.g., coach–athlete relationships), and interpersonal knowledge (e.g., self-reflection and awareness) are integrated into workplace practice • Practice is informed and assessed through evidence-based methods (e.g., coach portfolio) rather than coursework (e.g., knowledge tests) • Delivery strategies (such as problem-based learning methods) are used to develop the essential decision-making skills required in coaching • Coach developers are engaged not just in formal learning situations but work with coaches in the field

learning, which includes the creation of modern content that must support social learning and include a range of different learning opportunities with content that is flexible and informal and that can be drip fed to meet learners' unique needs and preferences (Hart 2015).

No evidence has been found to validate what constitutes expertise in someone who develops coaches; however, there is considerable literature on what is required to be an effective teacher or trainer. For example, following a consultation with teachers and staff from across all areas of education and training, The Education and Training Foundation–England launched a new set of professional standards in May 2014. This document defined teachers and trainers as "reflective and enquiring practitioners who think critically about their own educational assumptions, values and practice in the context of a changing contemporary and educational world. They draw on relevant research as part of evidence-based practice" (The Education and Training Foundation 2014, 1). The foundation goes on to explain that teachers and trainers are dual professionals with a subject specialism and an expertise in teaching and learning. They must therefore maintain and develop their skills and knowledge in each area to ensure the best outcome for their learners. Professional standards are described as having three equally important areas: professional values and attributes, professional knowledge and understanding, and professional skills. Having professional values and attributes means having developed a personal sense of judgment regarding what works and does not work for an individual as they teach and train others. Of equal value are the development of a deep and critically informed professional knowledge and understanding in theory and practice as well as the personal development of the expertise and skills to ensure the best outcomes for learners.

It is suggested that coach developers need to conform to the same set of professional standards and so be able to

- structure and apply knowledge about coaching and learning based on a significant, extensive, and rich experience of developing coaches;
- categorize coach behaviors and learning strategies to facilitate and accelerate problem solving and decision-making;
- interpret cues and recognize patterns quickly and accurately;
- design and adapt innovative learning and teaching strategies according to the person and context;
- demonstrate high emotional intelligence; and
- be an autonomous and continuous learner, demonstrating strong reflective skills and a desire for excellence.

Training Coach Developers

Coach developer training has sometimes been confused with programmer orientation; in other words, developer training has provided the content and delivery mechanism required to teach a specific program. Modern coach developer training provides a range of learning situations to enable people to acquire the complex skills required to accelerate coach learning and assess progress. Where this type of training has been offered, it has frequently mirrored the format of coach education with an emphasis on formal, mediated learning through face-to-face workshop time (often classroom-based) and, in better cases, with significant supported practice (mediated, nonformal) and assessment in the field training real coaches.

However, many of the criticisms that have been leveled at coach education might also be leveled at many coach developer training programs. For example Trudel, Gilbert, and Werthner state "the scientific evidence that does exist suggests that coach education training programs have no long-term significant impact on actual coaching practice" (2010, 135). The same could be leveled at coach developer training. They go on to say "there is no substantial body of evidence to support the wide-spread or long-term effectiveness of coach education training programs, even in highly controlled and small-scale quasi-experimental settings" (139). Their review of studies in coach education effectiveness in various settings concluded "that coach education programs typically play a marginal role in coach development in comparison to learning from experience" (Trudel, Gilbert, and Werthner 2010, 144). The authors add that this is hardly surprising because time spent on coach education programs is minimal compared with the number of hours accumulated actually coaching. As Jarvis (2010) has noted, learning occurs within the whole person, not in segmented boxes, and as such much of our learning is not recognized and is often discounted because it occurs across all our interactions and is hidden within daily living.

Similarly, many of the recommendations for coach education can also be applied to coach developer education. For example, Armour (2010) suggests that constructivist theories are appropriate for studying coaching and coach development. The same should surely be true of the way we train coach developers, and indeed this is an approach adopted by Sport New Zealand (unpublished report). The need to include episodes of unmediated, informal learning for coach developers is advocated by Knowles et al. (2005, 1713), "It appears that coaching expertise cannot be created within formal educational courses alone but requires coaches to engage mentally with their own practice to learn and develop." Nash (2014) also supports this view, stating "it is difficult if not impossible to teach learner autonomy through conventional didactic methods" and "it is also difficult to teach and learn the skills necessary to become a self-directed learner" (179).

Challenges in Coach Developer Training

There is no doubt that there are significant challenges in training coach developers to be able to provide a range of effective formal and nonformal coach education programs and to foster autonomous learners and reflective practitioners capable of developing their coaching expertise in a dynamic and changing environment. The way coach developers are trained in the future needs to reflect the broader range of roles they need to play in order to optimize mediated learning and promote unmediated and internal learning. Strategies need to be adopted to encourage deep rather than superficial learning, and a blend of learning opportunities is advocated. The South African coaching strategy, initially led by the ICCE (Vardhan and Duffy 2011), adopted the concept of coach developers and instigated a selection and training regimen that included e-learning modules, face-to-face workshops, and supported practice in the workplace. The supported practice was challenging to implement and occurred very effectively on the larger sport codes (e.g., netball, cricket, rugby).

Program Recommendations for Selecting and Training Coach Developers

Coach developers are critical to the health and effectiveness of any coaching system, so it is important to take great care in selecting potential coach developers. Assumptions are easily made about long-standing service, expertise, and coaching, but developing coaches demands a different mindset from coaching athletes; it requires different skills and expectations. "The best coach developers are experts in learning, they role-model best practice, portraying a growth mindset, critical reflective skills and a hunger for personal improvement. They are able to help coaches to become 'learning coaches' by teaching them how to learn and reflect" (ICCE 2014). To do this, they must have a certain mindset, a willingness to stay up to date in knowledge in the area they are teaching and in some core skills that enable them to create effective learning opportunities for coaches.

Programs may give in to a temptation to select and train too many coach developers at the onset of shifting the program. Usually this means that the trainees will have insufficient opportunities to practice and hone their skills with real coaches in the field. British Wrestling adopted an excellent strategy that limited the number of coach developers to four in the initial phase to ensure all could achieve excellent practice before training additional coach developers. The list below shows the British Wrestling Association's coach developer specification guidelines (2016) used to aid selection of those with the greatest potential to be effective posttraining. The specification should detail what the applicant must have and distinguish that from what would be nice to have. Remember here that while knowledge can be relatively easy to acquire and skills can be learned, attitudes and mindset are hard to change.

Mindset

- First and foremost, coach developers (CDs) need a growth mindset, a genuine belief that through commitment and purposeful practice, people can learn to do anything.

- A CD needs a passion for and a belief in the power of coaching and a desire to help coaches become the best they can be. This normally means significant and successful coaching experience in one or more coaching contexts.
- CDs need a willingness to engage in honest self-reflection and a hunger for personal growth and development; these attributes ensure that CDs stay up to date and role-model best practice.

Knowledge

A consistent characteristic of experts in any field is a wealth of relevant and up-to-date knowledge in their specialist area. For CDs, this would normally mean the following relevant knowledge:

- Professional knowledge
  - Learning, teaching, and competence-based assessment
  - Content area they will be teaching or assessing (e.g., the sport's rules, techniques, and tactics; coaching, coaches, and coaching methodology; sport science, sports medicine, talent development, coaching children, and disability sport)
- Interpersonal knowledge (e.g., relationships, the social context)
- Intrapersonal knowledge (about lifelong learning and their own philosophy)

Skills

CDs need to model best practice and, depending on what they will deliver or assess, would demonstrate the following abilities:

- Excellent how-to-coach skills (e.g., how to observe, provide feedback, build rapport)
- Good facilitation skills (e.g., questioning, listening, reviewing, and feedback skills)
- Sound planning, monitoring, and evaluation skills

In adopting a coach developer workforce approach, it is important to create a clear and detailed job description or specification for the coach developer work to be done. This document should include details such as these:

- What precisely the coach developer would be expected to do (e.g., deliver a Level 1 coach education program, deliver a coaching children program, deliver a strength and conditioning program for Level 2 coaches, assess coaches in simulated or actual coaching situations)
- How often the coach developer would be required to deliver (e.g., 6 days per year, 1 day a month); this is important as people only become expert at something if they do (and so practice) that thing sufficiently often to improve their skills

- The training required and qualifications to be gained (e.g., the number of days in training, any costs, specific dates if fixed, and assessment requirements)
- Any remuneration that would be made (e.g., following successful training when delivering or assessing)

Induction and Preparation of Coach Developers

To accelerate application and learning, it is advisable to prepare potential coach developers for the forthcoming face-to-face training. This might include reflective exercises; some core knowledge around learning; as well as information to cover expectations, resources, assessment requirements, and logistics.

The face-to-face training would need to cover all the areas in which competence for coach developers needs to be demonstrated; namely, facilitation skills, assessing skills, and personal development skills (see table 15.4). Additional areas would need to be covered at senior and master coach developer levels, such as mentoring, learning program design and evaluation, leadership, and change management.

Coach developer training should be delivered by master coach developers who model expert facilitation styles and demonstrate the following characteristics:

- Have done significant amounts of microtutoring in both classroom and practical situations where the trainee coach developer can practice facilitating learning with small groups of peers acting as coaches
- Are content to help apply adult learning theories and models to accelerate coaches' learning
- Are proficient in delivery strategies

TABLE 15.4 Key Skills of a Coach Developer

Skills	Coach developer requirements
Facilitation skills	• Communicate with individuals and groups • Accelerate the learning of coaches • Adopt a learner-centered approach to facilitation • Select and use a range of delivery strategies to optimize learning • Set, lead, and review microcoaching sessions • Plan and evaluate sessions to optimize learning • Develop questioning, listening, and reviewing skills
Assessing skills	• Conduct coach assessments
Personal development skills	• Assess and develop own practice • Identify responsibilities of a coach developer in your organization

Reprinted by permission from International Council for Coaching Excellence, Association of Summer Olympic International Federations, and Leeds Metropolitan University, *International Coach Developer Framework (Version 1.1)* (Leeds: Leeds Beckett University, 2014), 20.

- Possess good facilitation skills including questioning, listening, feedback, reflection, and reviewing
- Are experienced in climate setting and ways to engage learners
- Are experienced in planning and preparing to facilitate
- Have plenty of time for assimilation, reflection, and practice

The term master coach developer was coined by the ICCE coach developer working group (ICCE 2013) to describe the people responsible for the initial training and support of coach developers within their organization. They are typically highly experienced in helping coaches to learn and through this experience have identified the core knowledge, skills, and attitudes required to be an effective coach developer. Currently, as this is an emerging area of expertise within the sport coaching education and sport science discipline, master coach developers may or may not have formal educational backgrounds or qualifications. However, they have a wealth of practically acquired know-how about engaging and developing coaches through formal and nonformal routes, and indeed are skilled at nurturing the desire in coaches to pursue self-directed and nonformal learning. The term trainer is used to describe exceptional master coach developers and educationalists who provide leadership in coach developer initiatives either within a larger coaching organization or even across different sport organizations. More recently, a modified version of the original pathway has been offered in the light of applications and experiences in delivering coach developer training to academy delegates in Japan from a broad range of countries.

Application and Supported Practice of Coach Developers in Training

The importance of both clinical experience and real-world practice has been well documented, particularly in teacher and medical education programs. Similarly, support in the field (e.g., nursing) is essential for coach developers to gain the confidence and skills to deliver in the workplace on their own. Support is also important for quality assurance and consistency of the delivery of your program. Support in the field should be provided within six weeks of the training intervention. Supported practice can take many forms, but it should include

- induction to the program that will be delivered;
- mentored support from a senior or master coach developer;
- co-delivery with a respected, experienced, coach developer that would include leading small areas of the program while assisting with all group work and microcoaching, gradually leading more and more

until confidence and competence is gained in all areas of the learning program delivery, and

- planning, assisted reflection, and action planning.

Coach Developer Assessment

The time taken to reach the assessment phase will vary depending on the initial skills and experience of each coach developer and the amount and quality of the practice opportunities provided. Assessment should be undertaken wherever possible in the field with real coaches using the competence framework with underpinning criteria. Currently coach developers are expected to be able to demonstrate competence in the facilitation skills, assessing skills, and personal skills.

Initial coach developer training can be competence-based; in other words, focused on testing what coach developers can do with what they know. For this reason, there is often a strong emphasis on their ability to facilitate learning with a group of coaches and support coaches in the field (mentoring as well as coach review or assessment). An example of the ICCE assessment strategy for a coach developer is shown in table 15.5.

The ongoing training of coach developers then needs to be addressed so that they can continue to hone their skills and extend their knowledge and, if appropriate, move up the pathway to take on the responsibilities

TABLE 15.5 Overview of Assessment Strategy for ICCE Coach Developers

Facilitation skills	Assessing skills	Personal skills
• Observed formative delivery of a session at least 10–30 minutes long with peers acting as coaches • Observed summative delivery of a 20+ minute session with actual coaches out in the field (this could be submitted on video if face-to-face observed session impossible) • Creative knowledge test focused on all modules but particularly on learning principles and models, individual differences, and delivery styles/methods • Portfolio of evidence including logged delivery of coach education (formal or informal) to at least 3 coaches on at least 6 different occasions	• Observed formative simulated assessment of assessor skills • Observed final summative workplace assessment • Creative knowledge test on assessment principles and steps • Portfolio evidence including logged a minimum of 5 assessments of coaches in the workplace with associated assessment plan, transcripts, and reflections of all assessment steps	• Portfolio of evidence including role as coach developer in fulfilling organization's mission and personal reflection and action plans

and associated skill sets of more experienced coach developers. Once an initial baseline of coach developer competence has been met, the focus will shift from competence-based to an expertise model with the associated communities of practice and peer review and challenge.

Coach Development System Development

Coach education work should not exist in a vacuum; it needs to be an integral part of the organization's coaching system and a central tenet of its coaching strategy. A coaching system refers to "the structures and delivery mechanisms in any given sport or nation to support coaches and the development of coaching" (ICCE 2013, 53). The quality of coaching is dependent on the quality of the coaching system and strategy as well as the expertise of the coach developers.

For many years, the health care services have adopted a systems approach in many European countries. An example of this is a model adapted from Ferlie and Shortell (2001) that is divided into four nested levels (figure 15.5):

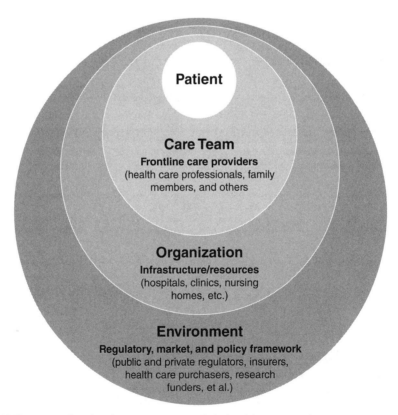

FIGURE 15.5   Four-level systems approach in health care services.

Adapted from E.W. Ferlie and S.M. Shortell, "Improving the Quality of Health Care in the United Kingdom and the United States: A Framework for Change," *Milbank Quarterly* 79, no. 2 (2001): 281-315.

1. The individual patient

2. The care team, which includes clinicians, pharmacists, the patient, and family members

3. The organization, infrastructure, and resources that would include the hospital, clinic, or nursing home that supports the development and work of care teams

4. The political and economic environment under which the care providers operate

Lara-Bercial (2016) identified seven key elements in a successful high performance sport system (figure 15.6). First, it is important to develop a very clear vision and plan for sport. Next, to ensure system alignment, all stakeholder organizations need to be aligned to the common vision. There is a need to put in place an appropriate but necessarily highly sophisticated infrastructure to support the system development. A performance model needs to be identified to show how athletes or players can progress through to the high-performance arena. Linked to this is the need for a long-term athlete development model to ensure that young people are enabled to develop sound fundamental movement skills and only develop their training skills as they specialize and

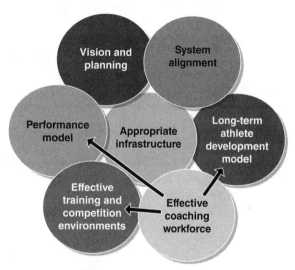

FIGURE 15.6 Key elements of a successful high-performance sport system.

Adapted from North et al. 2016.

progress through their chosen sport. An effective training and competition environment must be established. Of course, an effective coaching workforce is central to the long-term athlete development model, the performance model, and the training and competition environment. To be able to have an effective coaching workforce of course requires a highly successful coach developer system.

Coach developers need to be deployed within an effective sport and coaching system that supports their ongoing professional development alongside a framework that trains, sustains, and grows novice and experienced coaches. Coach developers are not yet common in every country, but coach developer training has been well-developed in some countries such as Australia, Canada, Finland, and the United Kingdom. A model has been developed by the ICCE working group to help countries audit and develop their systems (figure 15.7), identifying where their organization sits and where it wishes to be to provide the best coaching service. Not every organization needs a highly evolved system to meet its current needs. The smaller the number of active coaches, the less sophisticated the system required to service the coaches. However, this does not mean that the quality of the program or the leadership within the smaller programs should be any less informed or constructed according to current great practice recommendations.

The ICCE's System Development Continuum describes unstructured systems as organizations where guidance for novice coaches is provided in an episodic and haphazard way, largely on the job, by a more experienced coach or possibly a named coach acting as an untrained coach developer. The need for more and better coaches may make the system an emerging system. Emerging systems describe organizations that recognize the unique skills of coach developers and have a need to develop more coaches. They identify personnel to become dedicated coach developers who gain some sort of training to fulfil their role. More experienced coach developers are assigned the role of training and supporting new coach developers, which might be done through formal training or through an apprenticeship style of on-the-job training. Organizations with mature systems are those having dedicated, experienced coach developers working alongside coach developers and specialists who deliver coach developer training. Mature systems have a comprehensive system of initial and ongoing coach education for all levels of coaches in all contexts. A highly evolved system may have a three-tier system of coach developers and a coach developer trainer responsible

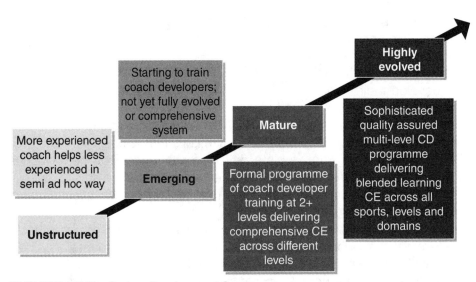

FIGURE 15.7 System Development Continuum.

Reprinted by permission from International Council for Coaching Excellence, Association of Summer Olympic International Federations, and Leeds Metropolitan University, *International Coach Developer Framework (Version 1.1)* (Leeds: Leeds Beckett University, 2014), 29.

for training coach developers; they have a very comprehensive system of formal and informal coach education at all levels across all contexts. However, this should be very context-specific and any model should be adapted to meet the cultural needs of the organization as well as the unique needs of the coaches within the coaching system.

Figure 15.8 outlines the ICCE's strategic plan for developing a coaching system that evolves from an initial audit (Step 1) and forecast of needs (Step 2). It might then include the identification, training, and support of new coach developers (Step 4) as well as strategies for growing existing coach developers and perhaps senior and master coach developers (Step 4). All this takes place within a continuous process of monitoring, evaluating, re-auditing, and re-forecasting (Step 5).

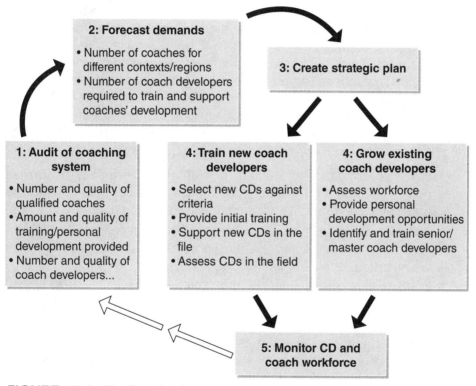

FIGURE 15.8 The Coaching System.

Adapted by permission from International Council for Coaching Excellence, Association of Summer Olympic International Federations, and Leeds Metropolitan University, *International Coach Developer Framework (Version 1.1)* (Leeds: Leeds Beckett University, 2014), 26.

Summary

The changing and increasingly demanding role of coaches necessitates a re-examination of the role coach developers play both in coach training and for the ongoing support role they can play in the continuing education of coaches. With appropriate knowledge and training, coach developers play an important role in the development and support of coaches, which will have a direct impact on the quality of the athlete experience. Alongside a long-term coach development pathway to nurture coaches as they develop their expertise should run a corresponding pathway to grow coach developers within the organization's coaching system.

Well-designed long-term research studies to address the limitations of current studies and to expand the knowledge within the sport setting are necessary to measure the impact of coach education and coach developer training needs. In addition, a more constructivist approach should be adopted, where "the focus of the coach education courses should be to provide opportunities for coaches to construct knowledge, not just receive it. . . . Coaches should be involved in constructing knowledge through direct experience of coaching practice" (Nash 2015, 182–3). Research has also shown that coaches, and probably coach developers, learn better from practical experience and interaction with other coaches (Carter and Bloom 2009). Therefore there is a need to design more practically based blended-learning programs that comprise all types of learning opportunities. In these programs, coach developers stimulate unmediated learning and thereby create learning coaches who take responsibility for additional self-directed learning.

If the work of the coach developer is to continue to evolve and improve, there is a growing need for research to

- construct longitudinal studies to examine the efficacy of formal, nonformal, and informal learning situations for coaches outside the university environment and operating in a range of different contexts;
- assess the impact of expert coach developers on coaches at different levels of experience and examine how experts foster autonomous learners and reflective practitioners;
- evaluate the effectiveness of the ICCE initial coach developer program and investigate the use of an expertise-based rather than a competence-based model; and
- explore the impact of additional methodologies (e.g., constructivist and social learning approaches) on coach developer and coach training.

PART IV

EVALUATING THE IMPACT OF COACH EDUCATION

Chapter 16

Reflection on Accreditation and Endorsement of Coach Education and Development Programs

Lori A. Gano-Overway

Coaching effectiveness has been defined as "the consistent application of integrated professional, interpersonal, and intrapersonal knowledge to improve athletes' competence, confidence, connection, and character in specific coaching contexts" (Côté and Gilbert 2009, 319). Throughout this text, much has been learned about how to improve a coach's effectiveness that could be implemented by coach education and development programs. However, opinion on whether programs include this content in ways that are effective for coach learning and result in positive learning outcomes and quality sport experiences for athletes is quite varied. To encourage a level of quality assurance among coach education and development programs, accreditation and endorsement agencies have emerged. This chapter will review accreditation and endorsement schemes, identify some of the issues and concerns surrounding accreditation and endorsement, and explore future considerations in the accreditation landscape.

Accreditation: What It Is and Why It Is Important

Prior to exploring accreditation, it is necessary to clarify the meaning of accreditation because it has been assigned different defining characteristics in the sport coaching literature. Within this chapter, accreditation is defined similarly to accreditation in higher education; that is, "a guided self-evaluation and self-improvement process" that undergoes peer review and encourages periodic evaluation of ongoing effectiveness of a program (Gelmon 1997, 54). In a similar vein, the National Committee for Accreditation of Coaching Education (NCACE) has defined accreditation as "the process of verifying that professional preparation is of sufficient quality to ensure that those completing such preparation will engage in safe and appropriate practice" (NCACE 2017a, 4). Therefore, accreditation relates to ensuring the quality of coach education and development programs rather than certifying individual coaches within a particular program. In the end, accreditation should hold coach educators and coach developers accountable for creating quality professional programs that help coaches achieve scientifically and practically relevant coaching knowledge and competence in an environment that maintains the best educational practices while still allowing flexibility in philosophies and approaches among programs (NCACE 2017a) [1].

As can easily be deduced from the definition of accreditation, there are some valuable reasons for promoting accreditation and seeking to accredit coach education and development programs. In reviewing the history of accreditation in higher education, Driscoll (2006) notes accreditation helps institutions to explore whether they are meeting their objectives and encourages organizations to assess their effectiveness in achieving their desired outcomes. Thus, it can encourage a level of accountability as well as provide a level of credibility. Furthermore, accreditation can also encourage program improvement as program developers reflect on whether they are incorporating best practices in coach education and development or incorporating the most current and scientifically supported coaching competencies. Using these standards and frameworks can also create consensus among all programs as to what coaches should know and be able to do. This information can be shared with the general public and employers so they know what to expect (i.e., knowledge, skills, and practices) from quality coaches. Therefore, accreditation benefits not only individual coaching programs but also the greater community.

Insight into Accreditation and Endorsements: What It Looks Like Now

Given the advantages of accreditation, it is worth looking at agencies that accredit as well as those that endorse coach education and development programs. Endorsement schemes are similar to accreditation in many ways; however, they tend to focus more on whether programs meet particular criteria outlined by an endorsing agency and may have more limited requirements for program structure and program evaluation. Therefore, it is beneficial to utilize them to obtain a broader understanding of how coach education and development programs validate the quality of their programs.

National Committee for Accreditation of Coaching Education

The National Committee for Accreditation of Coaching Education (NCACE) began accrediting coaching programs within the United States in 2000. According to NCACE's Guidelines for Accreditation of Coaching Education, "the goal of NCACE is to maximize the opportunities for providing qualified coaches at all levels of sport programs" by encouraging "continuous improvement in the professional knowledge and competence of sport coaches" and providing "consistent and scientifically based guidelines by which to assess (a) the content of programs for the education of coaches, (b) the qualifications of instructors who provide coaching education, and (c) the process by which coaching education is provided" through the accreditation process (NCACE 2017a, 1). Currently, 20 coach education and development programs have attained comprehensive accreditation, 12 of which are college and university programs (NCACE 2017a).

The NCACE accreditation process involves program coordinators developing a portfolio, which provides evidence that their program complies with 16 accreditation guidelines. The guidelines are organized around four main areas: (1) organizational overview, (2) personnel, (3) operational procedures, and (4) content. The organizational overview guidelines involve the program coordinator identifying the program's mission, goals, and objectives; who has systematic oversight of the program; and record-keeping procedures. The personnel guidelines focus on whether program instructors have expertise in the field, understand and practice effective pedagogy, and have knowledge of the National Standards for Sport Coaches (NASPE 2006). The operational procedures guidelines ask program coordinators to demonstrate how program content is in line with the stated mission, goals, and objectives; how practical experiences are integrated into program content; and how successful completion of the program is based on participants' achievement of program objectives through valid and reliable assessments. Additionally, program coordinators describe how the program content, requirements, evaluation, qualifications for certification, and fees for enrollment and materials are provided to participants and how the program demonstrates a commitment to diversity and inclusiveness. The operational procedures guidelines also expect program coordinators to provide documentation of periodic evaluation procedures for determining program effectiveness along with evidence of program effectiveness. The last area of focus is on content. Under content guidelines, program coordinators illustrate how the program curriculum is in line with the National Standards for Sport Coaches (NASPE 2006) and demonstrate that there is appropriate time available in the program for participants to master the standards. Once program coordinators submit their portfolios for review, expert readers trained by NCACE are assigned to determine whether the program has met the 16 guidelines, highlight program strengths and weaknesses, and provide constructive feedback to the submitter on ways the programs could improve. The review coordinator consolidates these reviews and forwards a decision to the NCACE committee for vote on accreditation status. Programs not receiving initial approval for accreditation are encouraged to submit a rejoinder within a year noting how the program complies with the accreditation guidelines or resubmit an accreditation portfolio at a later date.

There are many strengths affiliated with the NCACE accreditation program, including its allowance of flexibility in achieving the accreditation guidelines by a variety of programs (e.g., college/university programs, national governing bodies, youth sport programs), its emphasis on evaluating program effectiveness, and its incorporation of some level of practical experience. In addition to these strengths, NCACE also uses the National Standards for Sport Coaches (NSSC) as a foundation to guide curriculum development and appropriately identify what coaches should know and be able to do in their respective sport context. These 40 NSSC standards are organized around eight domains (i.e., philosophy and ethics, safety and injury prevention, physical conditioning, growth and development, teaching and communication, sports skills and tactics, organization and administration, and evaluation; NASPE 2006). Moreover, NASPE (now SHAPE America) broke each standard down into a series of benchmarks to be achieved depending on the type of athlete and context served in a program (i.e., beginning or intermediate athletes in recreational programs, intermediate athletes in structured programs, elite athletes in structured programs). Therefore, the national standards consider context-specific athlete development. A final strength worth mentioning is the improvement in the quality of a coach education or development program simply by going through the accreditation process. Having worked with NCACE over many years, I have spoken with a majority of the program coordinators who have achieved accreditation. Many of these program coordinators have noted that working through the process helped them align their program with the national standards and helped them identify areas of weakness they could improve in their program.

While there are many strengths, there are also a few weaknesses in the NCACE accreditation program. Gould (2013) noted that in preparing coaches, educational programs often focus on everything that is needed to know versus what is most important for a coach to know depending on their own stage of development and their athletes' developmental level. This is certainly true for NCACE because it advocates for programs to align their curriculum with the national standards, which include everything a coach needs to know. While some variation is provided in the benchmarks based on the type of athlete and sport context, considerations of what a beginning coach versus a master coach needs to know and do are not delineated. Another weakness for NCACE revolves around its desire to make the accreditation process as flexible as possible to meet the needs of a variety of program approaches. While the accreditation process has guaranteed a certain level of quality in coach education and development programs, a distinction needs to be made between accredited programs that have greater depth and breadth in content and more in-depth practical experiences in comparison to others. For example, NCACE's guideline for incorporating practical experiences allows for a great variation in the types of practical experiences that can be achieved by accredited programs ranging from in-class role-playing and case studies to in-depth supervised coaching experiences. While it can be argued that the inclusion of any practical experience is valuable to coach learning, incorporating more extensive mentored coaching experiences represents better quality practice for coaches in training and should be recognized. Another weakness worth noting is the need to incorporate some of our latest understanding of coach development from the literature (Côté and Gilbert 2009; Cushion and Nelson 2013; Gilbert and Trudel 2001; Trudel, Culver, and Werthner 2013), most notably, reflective practice. Currently, standards or guidelines for incorporating reflective practice are minimal and could be further augmented. A final weakness relates to the cumbersome nature of completing the accreditation materials. As Driscoll (2006) noted about higher education accreditation, "Accreditation has a history of being viewed as a burden, an expensive, and strenuous routine, a quality assurance process for the public, an external pressure by institutions of higher education" (8). However, Driscoll also noted that it could either be viewed as a chore or a way to help instructors do their best to achieve quality programming that will result in effectiveness. Yet, it is important to recognize that program coordinators spend a great deal of time writing, organizing, and gathering evidence to support the quality of their program for accreditation. While this may be unavoidable, it is worth considering whether a more streamlined approach with a reduced number of benchmarks is possible or whether a multitiered review process (i.e., folio submission and site visit with presentation and question and answer sessions) would be advantageous. After all, NCACE needs a system that can account for the myriad of programs seeking accreditation (e.g., college/university programs or youth sport organizations).

Overall, NCACE provides one framework for accrediting coach education and development programs. However, it is important to explore additional frameworks that could provide a richer description of the accreditation landscape and possibilities for moving forward.

Endorsement Scheme for Higher Education for Sports Coach Education

The Endorsement Scheme for Higher Education (HE) for Sports Coach Education, operated by SkillsActive, began in 2011 with the purpose of endorsing sports coach education programs in higher education in the United Kingdom. The scheme was meant to "play a part in the development of the coaching workforce" and "provide clarity to students, parents and employers on the relevance of HE courses that are most likely to enhance employability and result in employment within the sport and fitness industry" (Active Endorsement: Higher Education Endorsement Scheme for Sports Coach Education 2015, 4).

To become an endorsed program, programs were assessed on whether they meet the specific criteria for sport coach education. The most prominent component of achieving endorsement revolves around the knowledge, understanding, and capability students need to possess to become quality sport coaches. The criteria for the knowledge and understanding of coaching were based on the UK Coaching Framework, the National Occupational Standards for Sports Coaching, and particular subject-matter content. The subject-matter content included the following areas: (a) pedagogy of coaching practice; (b) professional practice; (c) physiological aspects of sport performance; (d) social psychological aspects of sport coaching and performance psychology, (e) analysis of sport performance, (f) biomechanical, movement analysis, and development of movement skills; (g) management and development of coaching; and (h) research skills. The capability of coaching, which involved "the ability to combine knowledge and understanding within the practice of sports coaching" (Active Endorsement: Higher Education Endorsement Scheme for Sports Coach Education 2015, 12), was developed and evaluated by program personnel during coaching practice with a minimum requirement of 150 hours of coaching practice required by students. Other components necessary for achieving endorsement included identifying how assessment strategies used within courses are developed and calibrated, informing students about the qualifications for admission, which must go beyond academic achievement to include an interview or coaching portfolio, having adequate facilities for appropriate instruction, and having qualified instructors and mentors. Specifically noteworthy is that qualified staff needed to possess expertise in their field of study as a physical education or sport coaching lecturer as well as be an approved coach educator within a governing body of sport and have an assessor award, which involved training in assessment practices specific to coaching practice. Program personnel seeking endorsement submitted an application outlining how their program met the endorsement criteria for sport coach education and underwent a site visit.

The Higher Education Endorsement Scheme for Sports Coach Education provided another framework to consider in the accreditation milieu and outlined the knowledge, understanding, and capabilities needed by students to enter the coaching workforce. Clearly, the strengths of the program included having high-quality staff and incorporating a significant practical experience, which allowed future coaches to apply their knowledge and understandings as well as reflect on this practice. Additionally, the specific inclusion of research skills helped future coaches to understand the importance of blending science with practice.

Endorsement of Sports Coach Education Programs by Governmental Agencies

Some countries, including Canada and the United Kingdom, have governmental agencies that endorse sport coach education and development programs usually created and implemented by a governing body of sport. Achievement of endorsement occurs if a programs' curricular content and assessment corresponds to the national standards and criteria set by the governmental agency based on the research and best practices in coaching practice. The number and depth of standards required may be dependent upon the coaching role (e.g., beginner coach [Level 1, trained coach] or master coach [Level 4/5]); type of coaching (e.g., instruction, community or participation, competitive); and type of athlete (e.g., introductory, development, or elite). While programs seeking endorsement do not present a program evaluation, agencies do conduct system-wide evaluations as well as provide assessments and quality assurance testing. Governmental agencies vary in whether endorsement is required and the level of assistance provided in helping to frame and create programs. However, agencies have adopted mechanisms to help train coach developers and provide resources for program development.

Conclusion

In concluding this section, it is clear that national organizations and governmental agencies are working toward improving the quality of coaching practice through endorsement procedures and accreditation processes. While procedures do vary across accreditation and endorsement programs, there are many things these programs have in common. First, there is a commitment to a set of standards that represent the knowledge and skills coaches need to be successful on the job as well as an assessment of the achievement of the standards. These standards are continually undergoing revision to keep up to date with the latest research in coach effectiveness and coach development. Additionally, there appears to be some level of practical experiences incorporated into criteria. Finally, all programs seem to value coaches being instructed by qualified coach developers. Overall, these efforts play an instrumental role in continuing to promote the professionalization of coaching and help the public realize the importance of professionally trained coaches as well as increasing the quality of sport experiences for all athletes.

Coach Learning and Development: Issues and Concerns for Accreditation and Endorsement Programs

While accreditation and endorsement programs have contributed to the landscape of coach development and learning, it is important to look at some of the inherent and practical limitations of the accreditation process. Prior to identifying these issues, it is beneficial to discuss how coaches learn. Given that this has been extensively reviewed in other chapters of this text (see chapters 1, 11, 12, and 15), this will only be discussed briefly.

One of the first studies to explore how elite-level coaches learned revealed that coaches had engaged in several formal educational experiences (e.g., coaching classes, clinics, and seminars) and informal learning (e.g., reading books and journals) (Gould et al. 1990). Additionally, while a majority of coaches indicated a willingness to attend coaching seminars or coaching science courses, coaches indicated that informal and experiential learning most influenced how they coached. More recently, Cushion, Armour, and Jones (2003) noted some of the first lessons coaches may have about coaching practice might be through their observations of their own coaches during their athletic years and informal apprenticeships as assistant coaches. While, Carter and Bloom (2009) stated coaches learned from their formal education as well as their own coaching experience and interacting with other coaches. Building on this and other research as well as exploring learning models, Trudel, Culver, and Werthner (2013) have identified that coach learning involves a combination of mediated learning organized by others, and unmediated learning, which is learning controlled by the coach. Both types of learning require the individual to make sense of information and make meaning by integrating it with current knowledge and expertise as well as cognitive elements of introspection and reflection. Similarly, Cushion and Nelson (2013) identified a coach learning process that incorporates both informal and formal learning experiences with informal learning occurring through personal self-direction, experience, and mentoring. The research and conceptualizations of coach learning is beginning to lay out a framework for how coaches learn. However, as Cushion and his colleagues (Cushion et al. 2010; Cushion and Nelson 2013) noted, there is still much to discover about how coaches learn to be effective coaches because there is limited research on formal learning across the scope of coaching levels and contexts as well as its effectiveness. Further evidence on mechanisms underlying coach learning such as reflection, mentoring, and the role of intentional and unintentional experiential learning has not been thoroughly vetted.

Review of this research provides insight into a couple of weaknesses facing accreditation and endorsement agencies. The first weakness is agencies may be accrediting and endorsing programs that may have limited utility in promoting coach learning or resulting in effective coaching. While some evidence does exist that coach education programs are effective (e.g., Malete and Feltz 2000; Smoll and Smith 2002), more research is needed to verify the effectiveness of formal coach education and development programs to increase the credibility of accreditation and endorsement. A second weakness is agencies accredit or endorse mediated learning experiences. However, it is clear that coaching education and development programs are encouraged to foster some level of unmediated or informal learning. For instance, some agencies have included significant experiential learning with reflective practice and mentoring (e.g., The UK's Endorsement Scheme for Higher Education for Sports Coach Education 150 hours of coaching practice). However, further encouragement of critical thinking, problem solving, and reflective practice is warranted to support later unmediated learning experiences. Gould (2013) noted that youth coach education and development programs should not only include more formal educational opportunities for youth sport coaches but also incorporate opportunities for reflective practice by building in "experiential activities and exercises" as well as "opportunities for coaches to discuss their experiences" (8). Trudel, Culver, and Werthner (2013) stated that coach education and development programs might be able to help foster unmediated learning by encouraging journaling and reflection as well as developing coach networks or communities of practice. As an example, Cassidy, Potrac, and McKenzie (2006) found that a coach education program was helpful for rugby coaches because, among other things, it introduced them to the process of reflecting on their coaching and provided the opportunity to discuss the process of coaching with other coaches in the sport. Therefore, while unmediated learning is outside the realm of formalized educational experiences, it is worth reflecting on how much accreditation and endorsement agencies can help coach education and development programs more fully help coaches learn to be effective beyond the formal educational and practical experiences currently incorporated into accreditation and endorsement guidelines.

Extending this critique of formal educational experiences, Nelson and Cushion (2006) describe the coaching context as filled with ambiguities and complexities that require that learning occur in a contextualized setting so as not to stifle creativity, complex problem solving, or critical thinking. Further, Cushion and Nelson (2013) as well as Mallet et al. (2009) contend that learning is not a linear process and it is not clear how formal and informal learning experiences should be sequenced for effective learning. Therefore, another weakness of accrediting and endorsing agencies might be that the standards or criteria required to achieve accreditation or endorsement are decoupled from practice, making it difficult for coaches to adequately apply them in practice. That is, they do not allow coaches to creatively solve coaching issues as they arise using evidenced-based knowledge in concert with their previous experience and current practice (Cushion, Armour, and Jones 2003). The question facing these agencies is, How can they account for the myriad ways coaches learn and blend the science and art of coaching?

A final critique regarding accreditation and endorsement schemes is the danger of creating conformity in coach education and development programming that could stifle creativity, limit particular philosophies or pedagogical approaches, or not meet the needs of particular sport organizations. While this certainly can be an issue, Demers, Woodburn, and Savard (2006) document how the National Coaching Certification Program (NCCP) learned through program evaluation the need to be more flexible to accommodate the needs of sport organizations and took steps to increase flexibility in their structure. Therefore, agencies are able to make adjustments; however, it is an important issue of which to be aware.

Sport Coaching Standards and Competencies: Issues and Concerns for Accreditation and Endorsement Programs

Accreditation and endorsement schemes rely on quality standards of practice or competences that identify what coaches should know and do to engage in effective coaching practice. While each agency has a different set of standards, they are based on scientific research and occupational duties of coaches, meaning there are many commonalities. For example, Canada's NCCP (Canadian Coaching Association 2013) has five core competences (i.e., valuing, interacting, leading, problem solving, and critical thinking). These core competences are fostered in seven outcome areas (i.e., make ethical decisions, provide support to athletes in training, plan a practice, support the competitive experience, analyze performance, design a sport program, and manage a sport program); often, sport organizations include sport-specific outcomes (NCCP, n.d.). The United States' NSSC, presented earlier in the chapter, demonstrates some definite crossover in areas such as ethical issues, managing programs, and teaching and training athletes. However, differences also emerge, such as the NCCP demarcating the outcomes and competencies by coaching context (i.e., instruction, community sport, and competition streams), type of athlete, and coaching role as well as incorporating overarching competency-based standards. Noting the differences across countries, the International Council for Coaching Excellence (ICCE), the Association of Summer Olympic Federations (ASOIF), and Leeds Metropolitan University (LMU) developed an International Sport Coaching Framework (ISCF) to create consistency in language and coaching principles while still allowing for adaptability across countries and sport organizations (ICCE, ASOIF, and LMU 2013). The ISCF provides functional competence and coaching knowledge built upon the work of Côté and Gilbert (2009) and based on other research and work on coaching competencies and qualifications. It outlines the need for coaches to acquire professional, interpersonal, and intrapersonal knowledge as well as develop mastery in primary coaching functions including (a) set vision and strategy, (b) shape the environment, (c) build relationships, (d) conduct practices and prepare for competitions, (e) read and react to the field, and (f) learn and reflect (ICCE, ASOIF, and LMU 2013, 31). These competencies are broken down to meet the needs of the coaching role (e.g., coaching assistant, coach, advanced coach, and master coach) and their coaching context (i.e., participation or performance coaching). While the ISCF may offer guidance for common language and competencies to frame country-specific standards, accrediting and endorsing agencies still face issues identifying the quality standards necessary for coach effectiveness such as developing physically literate athletes as well as nurturing athletes' social, emotional, and mental skills, allowing them to flourish in society.

One of the main issues is that there is still much to learn about what knowledge, understandings, and capabilities coaches need to be effective (for further discussion, see chapters 15 and 17). More research is needed to help identify which effective coaching practices promote physical literacy, encourage lifelong physical activity, promote life skills, and result in improved performance. Additionally, more complete job analyses and evaluative research may be needed to identify which coaching practices are needed for each coaching context and developmental level of the athlete. That is, a participation coach who may focus on developing physical literacy, encouraging lifelong physical activity, and promoting life skills may need a slightly different skill set than a performance coach working with elite-level athletes. While working models are available, efforts will need to be made to encourage this research to improve coaching practice, and accrediting and endorsing agencies will need to update schemes to meet the growing and changing landscape of coach education and development.

Another significant issue to address is the form of the standards, which influences the type of learning environment and assessments used to determine whether a coach has achieved a particular certification stage. The three types of learning that have formed the basis of standards adopted by agencies or have been noted in the literature are standards-based, competency-based, and expertise-based.

"In education, the term standards-based refers to systems of instruction, assessment, grading, and academic reporting that are based on students demonstrating understanding or mastery of the knowledge and skills they are expected to learn as they progress through their education" (Standards-based 2017, 1). In standards-based learning, standards are taught and assessed using a variety of instructional methods and the standard can be broad to fit all aspects of Bloom's taxonomy. Therefore, standards-based learning can encapsulate what a coach should know and be able to do in the coaching context.

In contrast, competency-based learning requires applying skills and knowledge in performance settings, and this performance is measured objectively against the competency. As Klein-Collins (2012) noted in the Council for Adult and Experiential Learning Report, "while learning outcomes typically include specific skills and knowledge, competencies are at a higher categorical level. Acquiring skills and knowledge is important, but a competency requires students to process that learning in a way that enables them to apply it in a variety of situations" (9). Therefore, competency-based learning requires the learner to engage in complex actions based on developing knowledge of and skills for a task that is in as an authentic environment as possible (Demers, Woodburn, and Savard 2006). The Coaching Association of Canada, which has adopted a set of five core competencies within their program, further clarifies competency as "a system of declarative knowledge (i.e., the what), conditional knowledge (i.e., the when and the why), and procedural knowledge (i.e., the how) that is organized into operational structures and which, in a given set of situations, makes it possible to identify problems and to resolve them effectively" (Coaching Association of Canada 2013, 49). Competency-based learning programs have been reported in the literature (Demers, Woodburn, and Savard 2006; van Klooster and Roemers 2011) providing insight into how they might be implemented in coach development programs. Key components have included defining competencies, structuring learning experiences that allow for the integration of knowledge and skills in coaching practice, providing opportunities for reflection and mentorship, and developing meaningful assessments that address the competencies.

More recently, Collins and colleagues (2015) have critiqued competency-based learning for neglecting the subtleties of decision-making necessary (i.e., understanding what to do rather than why it is done), simplifying the inherent complexity of the coaching profession, and not differentiating the importance of certain competencies over others. Therefore, the authors suggest an expertise-based model involving "scenario-based learning" and "formative testing of expertise" using a "four-part curriculum of judgment, elaboration, flexibility, and decision-making" (5). This model focuses on developing professional competence by seeking to blend "systematic analysis," intuition, critical thinking, and reflection (5). The expertise-based learning model provides a nice extension of competency-based learning by encouraging coach developers to attend to the cognitive complexity of coaching and develop evaluation processes that capture the intrapersonal and interpersonal knowledge and skills or "mental models of practice" (5).

The question facing accreditation and endorsing agencies is whether the standards adopted should be standards-based, competency-based, and/or expertise-based. Currently, there is a need for further research to determine how to construct learning environments and effective assessment tools as well as determine effectiveness in coach learning and practice under the varying learning models. However, there is certainly intuitive and conceptual appeal to competency-based and expertise-based models because each attends to some aspects of mediated and unmediated learning. They also provide coaches the opportunity to elaborate their understanding and practice of coaching. Another potential benefit of these models is the ability to recognize the coaches' unmediated learning experience by having coaches test out of competencies using appropriate assessments. Yet, as Demers, Woodburn, and Savard (2006) note, one of the biggest challenges of competency-based education is how demanding and time-consuming it can be for instructors to identify appropriate assessments for competencies as well as to assist prospective coaches in meeting those competencies. Additionally, in considering the varying types of learning, agencies will need to consider the level of coach development. For example, a widespread coach education program for entry-level youth sports coaches may necessitate a different type of learning that may be more appropriate given the time commitment and knowledge level of the volunteer first-year coach. The benefits and weaknesses will need to be considered seriously while agencies adopt or develop types of learning.

Future Considerations for Accreditation and Endorsement Schemes

Having expounded upon some of the issues and concerns facing accrediting and endorsing agencies, it is worth identifying actions that these agencies could take in the future to strengthen coaching practice. While this list is not exhaustive, it represents things that are within an agency's control and may be most impactful for improving quality coaching practice.

Incorporating Coaching Role, Coaching Context, and Stage of Athlete Development

As noted in the ISCF, it is important to consider context (i.e., participation or performance), the stage of athlete development (e.g., emerging, performance, high performance), and coaching role (i.e., assistant coach, coach, advanced coach, and master coach). While some agencies follow such a framework when developing and endorsing programs (e.g., NCCP), it is important for agencies to reflect on how best to incorporate these into accreditation and endorsement frameworks. For example, what knowledge and capabilities will an assistant performance coach of emerging athletes need, and how does this differ from a senior performance coach of performance athletes? More work is certainly needed to identify what coaches at each level need to know and be able to do.

Aligning Sport Coaching Standards and Competencies Internationally

Examination of standards and competencies adopted by accreditation or endorsing agencies reveal commonalities and differences. While some of these differences may be cultural or specific to a sport organization's needs, more could be done to streamline the qualifications for effective sport coaching. In fact, Roetert and Bales (2014) call for aligning the sport coaching standards internationally, which could provide consistency in coach education and development while still being flexible to accommodate needs of sport organizations and cultural differences. The framers of the ISCF (ICCE, ASOIF, and LMU 2013) also suggest that a common language and templates for coach qualifications provide some consistency across countries, which will not only benefit global recognition of coaching qualification but also promote the exchange of information that will continue to improve coaching effectiveness.

The current ISCF offers a viable starting point for aligning standards and competencies because the framework includes the most comprehensive definition of coaching effectiveness noted in the literature (i.e., Côté and Gilbert 2009); identifies broad knowledge and competencies that can be adapted by organizations; and considers the coaching context, athlete development, and coaching role. This framework also offers organizations flexibility to delineate the specific types of knowledge and competencies that work for their situation and allows the opportunity to pursue competency-based, expertise-based, or standards-based learning.

Using the ISCF, the ICCE has begun this process by developing the International Sport Coaching Bachelor Degree Standards (Lara-Bercial et al. 2016). Using the primary coaching functions as a starting point, these Standards outline competencies to be achieved by coaches participating in higher-education degree programs. The Standards also outline areas of knowledge development across professional, interpersonal, and intrapersonal knowledge categories. The authors acknowledge that the Standards are meant to be "a flexible, noncompulsory set of guidelines for the development of high quality, suitable curricula and delivery programmes to develop the next generation of coaches" (Lara-Bercial et al. 2016, 345). Further, they anticipate that the Standards will help to align education endeavors with the needs of coaches and their athletes, develop collaboration between coach education providers, support quality assurance processes in current coaching degree programs, and raise the professionalization of sport coaching.

Based on the recommendations and recent international advances in framing sport coaching, it is clear that agencies will need to contemplate how to approach alignment with international developments in coach education. Finally, as noted previously, there is still a need for a stronger knowledge base in regard to what coaches need to know and do. The ISCF and the International Sport Coaching Bachelor Degree Standards provide a good starting point and help drive additional research questions and exploration into best practices for coaching practice.

Encouraging Blended Learning Programs and Learner-Centered Approaches

As researchers have uncovered how coaches learn, it is clear accrediting and endorsing agencies need to account for the myriad ways by which coaches learn and encourage coach education and development programs to develop more blended learning programs (i.e., incorporating mediated and unmediated learning) that incorporate learner-centered approaches. While coach developers need flexibility to develop pedagogically sound programs that meet the needs of their coaches and organizations and fit their own philosophical and creative style, agencies can impress upon coach developers the need to incorporate opportunities for mediated and unmediated learning that strive to place the learner at the center.

For mediated learning opportunities, the designers of the International Coach Developer Framework (ICDF) encourage coach developers to utilize the full range of the delivery style continuum, which ranges from directive teaching styles to more facilitative and collaborative teaching styles depending upon the needs of the learner (ICCE, ASOIF, and LMU 2014). While coach developers may have a great deal of experience with more directive teaching styles (e.g., highly structured lecture), the facilitative and collaborative styles may need further elaboration. These styles of teaching represent learner-centered teaching, which Weimer (2013) identified as having five defining characteristics. These characteristics include involving the learners in the learning process (i.e., they practice learning); helping the learners develop critical thinking, problem solving, and reflective practice skills; asking the learners to reflect on what and how they learn; providing some choice in the learning process; and creating a community of learners in which participants learn from one another.

In fact, quite a few of the proposed practices for helping coaches learn seem to correspond to learner-centered teaching. Here are three examples. To start, the call for more contextualized learning in which instructors teach coaches what they need to know and what they can learn from theory in a contextualized setting that does not stifle creativity and recognizes the ambiguities and complexities of the context (Cushion, Armour, and Jones 2003; Cushion et al. 2010; Nelson and Cushion 2006) is a learner-centered approach. Therefore, coach developers could incorporate more contextualized learning or practical experiences by using scenarios, case studies, microcoaching, problem-based learning, coach observation, and field experiences in which the coach is encouraged to apply and practice content learned, think critically and make choices about how to solve particular problems, and try out strategies in practice and reflect upon their success.

Learner-centered teaching also meshes well with the call for more mentored field experiences where coaches are encouraged to practice their learning by applying content in the field, engage in problem solving as various issues arise, and reflect upon their experience, hopefully using reflective practice frameworks (e.g., Gilbert and Trudel 2001; Schön 1983, 1987). In fact, it would be advantageous if there were multiple mentored field experiences across a variety of contexts to help coaches develop a broader schema of coach practice (Cushion, Armour, and Jones 2003).

Finally, learner-centered teaching is apparent in communities of practice where coaches come together to discuss coaching issues and dilemmas, problem solve the issues with trained facilitators, implement agreed-upon solutions, and reflect on the strategies and outcomes (Gilbert, Gallimore, and Trudel 2009). Therefore, accrediting and endorsing agencies should encourage programs to include learning-centered approaches or, more ideally, ask programs to provide evidence of its incorporation into the curriculum.

While it may be challenging to "stimulate and trigger" unmediated learning (ICCE, ASOIF, and LMU 2014, 14), given the importance coaches place on these learning experiences it is important to encourage coach education and development programs to consider the integration of unmediated learning opportunities. Trudel, Culver, and Werthner (2013) suggested coach developers encourage coaches to create a reflective journal for their informal coaching experiences, develop learning networks, or model and implement communities of practice. Additionally, helping coaches become aware of resources they can use later (e.g., coaching journals, conferences, criteria for identifying quality coaches to include in their learning networks) and implementing strategies to develop a growth mindset so as to encourage lifelong learning also supports unmediated learning over time.

Overall, while it is important to be cognizant of the need for flexibility in program development and recognize that there are multiple ways to help coaches effectively learn, accreditation and endorsement schemes should promote blended learning along with incorporation of more learner-centered teaching.

Enhancing Assessment and Evaluation

A significant need within coach education and development programs is construction of effective assessment tools. As programs seek to blend mediated and unmediated learning, incorporate more experiential learning, and seek to evaluate standards and competencies on what coaches should be able to do in the coaching environment, authentic assessments are needed. For example, while the authors of the South African Long-Term Coach Development Model emphasized the need to "recognize and validate" all assessments, they also recognized the need to include authentic assessments such as reflective journals and peer observations to meet learning outcomes (South African Sports Confederation and Olympic Committee 2012, 87). Other authentic assessments could include reflections on scenarios or problem-based learning, video analysis, season and practice plan submissions, and mentor or supervisor observations and evaluations. However, imperative for any of these authentic assessments is intentionally creating them to correspond to competencies for where coaches are in their learning journey as well as creating valid and reliable assessment rubrics. Endorsing and accrediting agencies could advocate for the creation and testing of such tools as well as provide a clearinghouse for such assessments. It would also be advantageous for agencies to encourage coach developers to share pedagogical practices and corresponding assessment findings to help identify best practices in coach development, which would also further support quality assurance efforts.

Moreover, accrediting and endorsing agencies could be more proactive in facilitating broader program evaluation protocols by coach education and development programs. A useful framework is Kirkpatrick's Four Level Training Evaluation Model (Kirkpatrick and Kirkpatrick 2006). The four levels of the model include reaction, learning, behavior, and results. Therefore, coach education and development programs could look at the following: (a) how satisfied coaches were with the training and what experiences were most meaningful, (b) what learning outcomes were achieved throughout or by the end of the program and what learning experiences resulted in these outcomes, (c) how coaching behavior changed over the course of the program, and (d) what program outcomes occur that influence coach effectiveness. Concerning this last point, there are several possible frames by which to identify outcomes. For example, the four Cs (Competence, Confidence, Connection, and Character) of coaching effectiveness (Côté and Gilbert 2009); the ISCF Coaching Objectives (e.g., sport, personal and life course competencies, and lifelong lessons), physical literacy outcomes of ability, confidence, and desire (The Aspen Institute Sports and Society Program 2015); and/or increases in physical activity patterns could be used. Obviously, program evaluators will also look at how well a program was implemented and the effectiveness of the teaching practices of the coach educator. However, this information would prove to be very useful in improving program effectiveness and coach effectiveness as well as sharing with others as programs seek to develop quality programming.

Supporting Coach Developers

Critical to the effective implementation of coach education and development programs is having quality coach developers. Therefore, accrediting and endorsing agencies should work toward providing training and resources for their coach developers. Some agencies have already begun this process by providing coach developer training (e.g., NCCP Coach Developer Training). The International Coach Developer Framework (ICCE, ASOIF, and LMU 2014) provides useful information for agencies to help train coach developers, including clarifying coach developers' roles and capabilities, identifying effective learning approaches, and developing an educational system. Additionally, agencies could develop resource centers to provide coach developers with best practices in coach development, innovations occurring in coach development, and assessment and evaluation tools. These centers could also provide a forum for coach developers—i.e., a community of practice—where individuals could share what has worked for their programs or seek advice from other developers regarding program struggles. Finally, agencies should promote national and international conferences where coach developers can gather to learn and share.

Exploring Accreditation Tracks Within NCACE: A Roadmap

While endorsement schemes are targeted toward one particular group (e.g., a national sport organization or a higher-education coach development program), programs seeking accreditation through NCACE are quite diverse (e.g., single-sport youth organizations or multisport high school organizations, or college/university programs). As noted previously, there is a need to distinguish between programs that offer more breadth and depth in educational offerings as well as practical experiences. Therefore, it would be beneficial for NCACE to explore two distinct accreditation tracks.

The first accreditation track, possibly labeled the Initial Coach Education Track, would primarily be formal, mediated learning. This learning would incorporate the basic and necessary content identified by the NSSC, which helps coaches improve their professional, interpersonal, and intrapersonal knowledge as well as provide initial tools and skills needed to develop into competent coaches. As the NSSC does not fully incorporate reflective practice, this would also need to be added to curriculum content (however it is hoped that the NSSC will undergo revisions based on earlier considerations noted in this chapter). The Initial Coach Education Track would incorporate the full spectrum of the delivery style continuum as portrayed in the ICDF (ICCE, ASOIF, and LMU 2014). While it may be a bit more directive, it would still incorporate learner-centered teaching (e.g., focusing more on scenario-based learning and case studies rather than microcoaching or supervised coaching experiences). Following completion of the program, coaches would be encouraged to become part of a program-facilitated learning network to encourage coaches to continue their professional development by learning and contributing to best practices within their sport and interacting with other coaches.

The second accreditation track, possibly labeled the Coach Development Track, would be a blended learning approach incorporating significant experiential learning. The curricular content would still follow the NSSC, but with greater depth and breadth to help develop the knowledge and skills to be a competent or proficient sport coach. The delivery style would be varied, moving from directive and instructional to facilitative and collaborative; however, greater emphasis would be placed on facilitative and collaborative learning as well as reflective practice based upon practical learning experiences occurring within the program (e.g., role-playing, problem-based learning, microcoaching, coaching observations, supervised coaching experiences, communities of practice, etc.). Therefore, the Coach Development Track programs would be integrating knowledge and practice across their programs, which may mean more individualized and developmental learning, authentic assessments of coaching practices, and evaluations of coaching from supervised experiences. Finally, helping to foster unmediated learning experiences is another key component to this second track. As noted earlier, coach development programs could include making coaches aware of helpful resources, developing a growth mindset, encouraging reflective journaling of informal coaching experiences, helping coaches develop learning networks, and modeling how to implement communities of practice.

Summary

Throughout this chapter, a case has been made for how accreditation and endorsing agencies can play a role in improving the quality of coach education and development programs. While there are many hurdles and some inherent flaws that still face these agencies, they are well positioned to make positive change in coach effectiveness. This can be accomplished as accrediting and endorsing agencies become supporters, facilitators, evaluators, and promoters of coach education and development. Agencies are supporters as they provide coach developers with appropriate training, resources, tools, and frameworks based on best practices to develop high-quality coaching programs. This includes creating standards and competencies that are scientifically based and aligned with the ISCF. Through the accreditation or endorsement process, agencies can facilitate coach developers in determining whether their programs are meeting the standards of practice and best practices in coach learning as well as in evaluating their program against the set standards and guidelines of their organization. Accrediting and endorsing agencies can also engage in quality control by encouraging more rigorous and comprehensive program evaluations to ensure program effectiveness. Finally, agencies can become promoters of coach education and development by promoting the need for further research into coach learning and coach effectiveness, educating the public about quality coach practice, and advocating for the professionalization of sport coaching. If accrediting and endorsing agencies can continue to work toward these ends, despite some inherent flaws, they will help to improve coaching practice.

---

[1] Coaching education programs in the United States are reviewed and accredited by the NCACE under the apices of the United States Center of Coach Excellence (USCCE). The NCACE Registry (2017b) of the accredited program can be found on the USCCE website at www.USCoachExcellence.org.

Chapter 17

Standards for Coaching Effectiveness

Wade Gilbert

What does "good" coaching look like? Traditionally, the most common, and visible, standard for measuring good coaching has been athlete performance. Although coaches play the central role in guiding athletes, countless factors beyond a coach's control affect the outcome of a sporting contest. Relying on athlete performance as the sole or primary standard of coaching effectiveness greatly diminishes the complexity of the coaching process and the ever-changing dynamics of coach–athlete relationships.

Ultimately, coaches should be measured against their ability to develop their athletes and put them in a position to succeed, outcomes that often are not evident until many years after the coaching occurs. If a youth sport coach loses every game in a season but instills a love for the game in the players, and they all return to the sport the following season, is that coach not effective? If a high school coach helps athletes develop strong practice habits that carry over into other aspects of school and life but fails to make the playoffs, is that coach not effective? If an Olympic coach builds a program in which athletes feel supported in their pursuit of excellence and learn how to serve as model representatives for their country yet fails to win an Olympic championship, is that coach not effective?

Make no mistake, winning matters—to coaches and athletes alike—and will always be used as a standard of coaching effectiveness. However, a genuine appreciation and recognition of quality coaching requires a much broader perspective. The purpose of this chapter is to present an overview of the literature on standards for coaching effectiveness, along with examples of tools that can be used to measure coaching effectiveness. The goal of this exercise is to stimulate reflection and dialogue among coaches, coach educators, and athletic administrators about which standards should be used, and how they should be used, to define and measure good coaching.

The Journey from Coaching Legend to Scientific Frameworks for Quality Coaching: Learning From the "Coach of the Century"

The seminal 1976 study on John Wooden, the legendary coach of the 20th century, conducted by Tharp and Gallimore (1976) is widely regarded as the starting point in the ongoing quest to identify standards for coaching effectiveness (Gilbert and Trudel 2004). As young psychology professors at UCLA, Tharp and Gallimore decided it would be interesting to document the practice behaviors of the "Wizard of Westwood." Their motive was simply to capture a great coach in action before he hung up the whistle. The field of coaching science we know today did not yet exist—no sport coaching handbooks or peer-reviewed journals, and few formalized coach education programs. A logical place to begin, then, was to go out and observe a successful coach in action.

They caught coach Wooden just in time. He retired at the end of the season during which Tharp and Gallimore completed their observations (a season that culminated with coach Wooden's team winning a record 10th national championship). They watched coach Wooden for 30 hours (15 practices) and recorded his behaviors using a systematic observation system. They discovered that most of his time during practices was spent giving instruction (50.3%), followed by hustle (12.7%) and scold/reinstruction (8.0%). One of the most common patterns of behavior exhibited by coach Wooden was showing the correct way to perform a skill (positive modeling), demonstrating the incorrect way in which the athlete performed the skill (negative modeling), followed by once again showing the correct form (positive modeling). This sequence of coaching behaviors was deemed to be so critical to coach Wooden's success style that Tharp and Gallimore referred to it as a "Wooden."

Although their landmark study spawned several decades worth of research on coaching effectiveness, Tharp and Gallimore only conducted one additional coaching study together. In the early 2000s, they returned to interview coach Wooden about the behavioral data they collected nearly 30 years prior (Gallimore and Tharp 2004). Sharp as ever, even in his 90s, coach Wooden provided valuable insight on the rationale behind his behaviors. First, the quality of his teaching rested on the quality of his planning. He reported spending as much or more time every day planning the practices as he did running the practices. He also kept detailed notes on his practice and teaching behaviors. Second, coach Wooden seldom praised players, because in his mind giving players the informative learning cues was the most "positive" approach to coaching that would result in optimal development and game performance.

Results from the two research papers, and the coaching approach coach Wooden used to become the "coach of the century" were explored in much greater detail when Gallimore enlisted one of coach Wooden's former championship athletes, Swen Nater, to recount what it felt like to be coached by coach Wooden (Nater and Gallimore 2010). Wooden's coaching methodology was also then compared to the science of teaching and learning. They concluded that coach Wooden's standards of coaching effectiveness could be summarized in eight general principles. The principles are summarized below along with some of coach Wooden's favorite maxims (in parentheses) that succinctly capture his views on each principle (Nater and Gallimore 2010).

- Coach–athlete relationships are the foundation of effective coaching, and coaches must learn how to best connect with athletes depending on each athlete's unique needs and personalities. ("Equal treatment is not equitable treatment.")

- Athlete motivation to learn and perform is highest when the coach emphasizes improvement, skill mastery, and reaching your potential as opposed to winning and comparing one's performance against others. ("Success is peace of mind in knowing that you made the effort to become the best of which you are capable.")

- Coaching effectiveness requires a continuous improvement mindset and a commitment to ongoing learning and self-reflection ("It's what you learn after you know it all that counts the most.")

- The level of coaching effectiveness a coach will achieve is directly proportional to the depth of their knowledge of the game and how to teach it. ("You can't teach what you don't possess.")

- Detailed preparation and planning provide the foundation for quality coaching. ("Failure to prepare is preparing to fail.")

- Athlete learning is optimized when coaches follow basic laws of learning—explanation, demonstration, imitation, correction, and repetition. ("Create habits that provide the foundation for creativity and innovation.")

- The true measure of coaching effectiveness is athlete development. ("You haven't taught until they have learned.")

- Effective coaches model the attitudes and behaviors they want to see demonstrated by their athletes. ("It's what the teachers are themselves.")

Although coach Wooden is most recognized for his tenure as a high-performance coach with collegiate athletes, the seeds for his principles of coaching effectiveness were sown in the many years he spent coaching and teaching adolescents. Therefore, coach Wooden always believed that his principles of coaching effectiveness were applicable to any level of sport coaching. The transferability of coach Wooden's principles of coaching effectiveness to youth sport settings was confirmed in a longitudinal case study of a successful high school basketball coach who was mentored by coach Wooden (Gallimore, Gilbert, and Nater 2014). By implementing coach Wooden's principles, the high school coach (Hank) was able to dramatically transform both the quality of his coaching and the performance outcomes of his athletes, leading to unprecedented success for his high school basketball program.

Coach Hank attributed the dramatic improvement in coaching effectiveness and athlete outcomes to his realization that quality teaching is the key to coaching effectiveness: "When I look back on it now I did not understand that the job, more than anything, was the job of a teacher" (Gallimore, Gilbert, and Nater 2014, 4). Results of the study show that coach Hank's approach to teaching and practice design was drastically revised. Practices were meticulously planned down to the minute, and no practice activity would exceed eight minutes. Water breaks were eliminated because time was scheduled into the activities to allow players to get water as needed without disrupting the flow of the drill or the practice, and the sequence of activities was designed to minimize transition time between each activity.

For example, player groupings for each practice activity were posted in the locker room before practice and players were expected to remember their groupings and responsibilities to avoid wasting time moving from drill to drill. Also, detailed practice plans were distributed to all members of the coaching staff so equipment could be positioned as needed in advance of each drill. In terms of actual teaching behaviors, coach Hank learned to observe more and intervene less, keep corrections and feedback to a maximum of ten seconds, and use simple teaching cues instead of overly complicated explanations (e.g., "fast outlet pass" or "cut to the right").

This influential collection of research and personal observations on coach Wooden clearly highlights the fundamental importance of quality teaching as perhaps the single most valuable standard for measuring coaching effectiveness. For example, the teaching profile demonstrated by coach Wooden has also been found in studies with other championship coaches including Pat Summitt, the all-time winningest coach in collegiate basketball (Becker and Wrisberg 2008). Clearly, any discussion about standards for coaching effectiveness requires consideration of the coach's ability to teach.

In an attempt to succinctly capture and share the standards of coaching effectiveness that exemplify coach Wooden's emphasis on quality teaching, the Pyramid of Teaching Success in Sport (PoTSS) was created (Gilbert, Nater, Siwik, and Gallimore 2010). The PoTSS includes 15 athlete-centered coaching characteristics organized into five tiers (see figure 17.1). The foundational tier reinforces that an athlete-centered coaching philosophy starts with a deep concern for connecting to and building quality relationships with athletes. This first tier includes Love, Friendship, Loyalty, Cooperation, and Balance. Love and Balance were selected as the cornerstones of the PoTSS because they are considered timeless and universal principles of athlete-centered coaching. Love is defined as the selfless altruistic and unconditional dedication to athlete improvement and success. A coach exhibits balance when there is alignment between his or her actions and the athlete-centered coaching philosophy. A genuine concern (love) for your athletes means that perspective is needed to inform coach decision-making, ensuring that a balanced decision can be made.

The second tier includes Industriousness, Curiosity, Resourcefulness, and Self-Examination. Whereas the first tier focuses externally on connection to your athletes, the second tier focuses internally on self-awareness and self-growth. An athlete-centered coaching philosophy requires that you embrace continuous improvement to increase your ability to best help your athletes meet their learning needs. The third tier, considered the heart of the PoTSS, captures the essence of teaching: Pedagogical Knowledge, Subject Knowledge, and Condition. It is not enough to be knowledgeable about your particular sport (subject knowledge). Adoption of an athlete-centered coaching philosophy also requires teaching skill, the ability to translate what

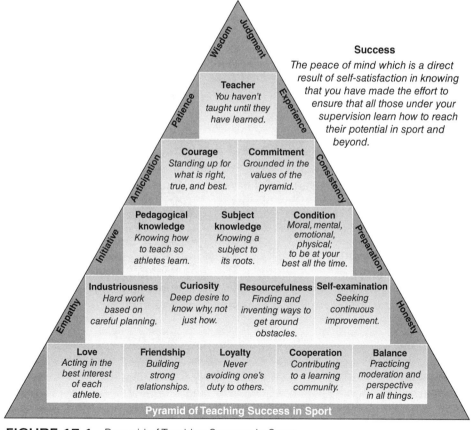

FIGURE 17.1 Pyramid of Teaching Success in Sport.

you know about your sport into meaningful learning experiences for your athletes (referred to as pedagogical knowledge, or knowledge of teaching).

Much like athletes require fortitude, coaches require physical, mental, and moral conditioning in order to model an athlete-centered coaching philosophy on a daily basis. Due to the public and interpersonal nature of coaching, coaches are faced with countless moral and ethical challenges (for more on this, see chapter 2). Courage and Commitment, the two characteristics represented in the fourth tier of the PoTSS (see figure 17.1), are needed to stay the course and ensure that coaching actions are consistent with an athlete-centered coaching philosophy. The apex of the PoTSS is Teacher. Great coaches think of themselves first and foremost as teachers—teachers of sport and teachers of life. Adoption of an athlete-centered coaching philosophy results in re-imagining how success is defined in sport. Contrary to the popular definition of success that is dependent on defeating others, in the PoTSS success is defined from a self-referenced perspective: "Peace of mind . . . is a direct result of self-satisfaction in knowing that you have made the effort to ensure that all those under your supervision learn how to reach their potential in sport and beyond."

Scientific Frameworks and Standards for Coaching Effectiveness

Although coach Wooden provides a compelling and thorough example of coaching effectiveness in action, thousands of coaching studies have been conducted since Tharp and Gallimore (1976) published their original account of coach Wooden. Every single one of these coaching studies contributes another small piece to the coaching effectiveness puzzle. Fortunately, several coaching scientists have combed this body of literature to provide the rest of us with summaries of what has been learned about coaching effectiveness.

Becker (2012) analyzed nearly 150 scientific articles related to quality coaching and identified seven common qualities. These qualities provide an evidenced-based guide for creating standards for coaching effectiveness (table 17.1). Collectively, these qualities reinforce the importance of people skills as the basis for coaching effectiveness, and lend credence to the popular saying, "people don't care how much you know until they know how much you care."

Whereas the Becker framework provides a snapshot of quality coaching behaviors, the model of coaching effectiveness created by Horn (2008) sheds light on the many factors that influence coaching behaviors, as well as the results of quality coaching. The Working Model of Coaching Effectiveness delineates three components of coaching effectiveness: antecedents, coach behaviors, and outcomes. The first component identifies some of

TABLE 17.1 Qualities of Effective Coaching

Quality	Description
Positive	Be instructive; focus on strengths rather than weaknesses; convey optimism and confidence; emphasize attitude, effort, and skill execution rather than performance outcomes
Supportive	Demonstrate caring, empathy and understanding; build trusting coach-athlete relationships through open and honest communication
Individualized	Tailor coaching behaviors to match athlete needs and unique personalities and learning styles
Fair	Invest comparable amount of time and energy in each athlete's development; do not treat each athlete the same; athlete privileges and consequences are earned depending on athlete behavior
Appropriate	Demonstrate the right behavior at the right time; properly align coaching behaviors to match the moment (athlete characteristics, the situation, and awareness of how the message will be perceived by the athlete)
Clear	Use straightforward and easy to understand language; provide explanations and rationale for coaching decisions
Consistent	Regularly model core values; act with genuine emotion; stay true to your personal coaching philosophy and unique personality

Adapted from Becker 2013.

the many variables that directly influence coaching behavior. Types of antecedents include the sociocultural context, the organizational climate, the coaches' personal characteristics, and coaching values and goals. Although not explicitly identified as such in Horn's Working Model, athletes' personal characteristics most definitely also influence a coach's behavior.

The second component of coaching effectiveness identified in the Model is coaching behavior. Horn stresses the importance of acknowledging that coaching behaviors are always filtered through athletes' perceptions, interpretations, and evaluations of the coach's behaviors. Furthermore, athletes' self-perceptions, beliefs, attitudes, and motivations will also mediate coach behavior and athlete response to the behavior. In this sense, when discussing standards for coaching effectiveness it is always important to remember that coaching effectiveness is ultimately dependent upon how well the coach can tailor the behaviors to the momentary and individualized needs of the athletes and the coaching context. The third and final component of coaching effectiveness is the result of the coaching; the performance and developmental outcomes effective coaches strive to help their athletes achieve.

Horn's (2008) summary is perhaps the most comprehensive and all-encompassing framework for coaching effectiveness, and should be required reading for anyone serious about understanding the science that underpins current views of coaching effectiveness. Horn concluded that five specific coaching styles or behaviors distinguished "good" coaching from "poor" coaching (table 17.2).

TABLE 17.2 Summary of Coaching Behaviors
That Facilitate or Deter Athlete Outcomes

Facilitative Coaching Styles or Behaviors	Detrimental Coaching Styles or Behaviors
High frequency of training and instructional behavior	Ignoring athletes' skill errors
High level of social support and positive feedback	High frequency of punishment-oriented feedback (especially feedback not accompanied by skill-relevant information)
Democratic or autonomy-supportive leadership style	Autocratic or controlling leadership style
Creation of a mastery-oriented (task-involving) motivational climate	Creation of a performance-oriented (ego-involving) motivational climate
Provision of positive, supportive, and informationally based feedback in response to athletes' performance successes and failures	Failure to recognize or respond to athletes' performance successes

Reprinted by permission from T.S. Horn, "Coaching Effectiveness in the Sport Domain," in *Advances in Sport Psychology*, 3rd ed., edited by T.S. Horn (Champaign, IL: Human Kinetics), 239-267.

Coincidentally, these five standards of coaching effectiveness are clearly evident in more recent reviews of coaching effectiveness. For example, Erickson and Gilbert (2013) and Vella and Gilbert (2014) found several common characteristics of effective youth sport coaches: (a) setting challenging learning and performance expectations while expressing confidence in athletes' ability to meet the challenges, (b) giving praise for desirable behaviors and encouragement and instruction after mistakes, (c) including athletes' perspectives when making coaching decisions, (d) focusing on athletes' self-referenced improvement, learning, and effort, and (e) promoting athletes' open discussion and questioning of coaching behaviors while regularly checking for athletes' understanding.

Meanwhile, Vella and Perlman (2014) reviewed three commonly recommended approaches to quality coaching—mastery, autonomy-supportive, and transformational. They concluded that two coaching behaviors in particular could be considered generic standards of coaching effectiveness: (a) positive reinforcement of desired athlete behaviors with an emphasis on shaping, versus controlling, athlete behavior, and (b) individualized attention for each athlete that acknowledges athlete feelings and opinions.

Clearly there are some well-documented *standards of* coaching effectiveness that are grounded both in the practice of great coaches and the coaching science. For example, the National Standards for Sport Coaches in the United States (NASPE 2006) represented a major milestone in the quest to understand and develop benchmarks for coaching effectiveness. The standards are described as the "basic knowledge required of coaches . . . as they progress from a novice to a highly skilled professional, master coach" (5). The National Standards are periodically revised to ensure alignment with the latest coaching science. However, coaching knowledge, and how it is translated into coaching behavior, is but one—albeit central—component of coaching effectiveness. Recall for example how the Working Model of

Coaching Effectiveness (Horn 2008) acknowledges both antecedents to and consequences of coaching behavior. Any discussion then of standards for coaching effectiveness demands inclusion not only of coaching knowledge and behaviors but also of contextual factors that influence coaching behavior and the result of effective coaching—namely, athlete outcomes.

An Integrative Definition of Coaching Effectiveness

In an attempt to recognize the fundamental components of coaching effectiveness, and build upon existing coaching science and standards frameworks, the Integrated Definition of Coaching Effectiveness was created (Côté and Gilbert 2009; Gilbert and Côté 2013). Based on a comprehensive review of the coaching and human development literature, the following definition for coaching effectiveness was proposed:

> The consistent application of integrated professional, interpersonal, and intrapersonal knowledge to improve athletes' competence, confidence, connection, and character in specific coaching contexts. (Côté and Gilbert 2009, 316)

The first component of the definition identifies the different types of coaching knowledge required to become an effective coach. For the purpose of the definition, knowledge is broadly defined both as what coaches should know (declarative knowledge) and how to use the knowledge (procedural knowledge). The three types of coaching knowledge are professional, interpersonal, and intrapersonal knowledge. Professional knowledge encompasses declarative knowledge in the sport sciences (i.e., ologies), sport-specific knowledge (i.e., techniques, tactics, rules, history), and pedagogical knowledge (i.e., how to teach what the coach knows). Due to the complex interactional nature of sport coaching, professional knowledge is most evident in the decisions coaches make. Effective decision-making, sometimes referred to as "strategic knowledge," requires the ability to successfully anticipate potential outcomes of multiple decision options. Professional knowledge would also encompass a coach's ability to operate a safe and organized sports program.

The second type of coaching knowledge comprises a coach's interpersonal skills. A coach's ability to build positive and trustworthy relationships with others is critical for becoming an effective coach. For example, connecting with athletes requires sensitivity to individual and changing athlete needs and profiles. Coaches who are skilled at communicating with and understanding others are sometimes described as having high emotional intelligence (Chan and Mallett 2011). Emotional intelligence is generally viewed as an ability to effectively identify, use, understand, and manage emotions (Gilbert and Côté 2013).

The third and final type of coaching knowledge is knowledge of self, also referred to as intrapersonal knowledge. Having a clear sense of purpose, core values, and coaching philosophy requires strong intrapersonal knowledge.

Self-knowledge requires introspection; a willingness to regularly subject coaching views and assumptions to scrutiny—both in the form of self-reflection and also with trusted peers in the form of collective inquiry. Expert coaches are renowned for using a wide range of self-monitoring strategies, such as building peer learning networks and constantly reading material across a wide range of sport and nonsport topics, to ensure their learning journey never ends (Schempp et al. 2007).

The second component of the integrated definition of coaching effectiveness is athlete outcomes. Athlete outcomes can be separated into four categories: competence, confidence, connection, and character. Athlete competence naturally refers to sport-specific technical and tactical skills. Athlete competence also includes the foundation skills upon which techniques and tactics rest, such as overall health and fitness and healthy training habits. Athlete confidence refers to an athlete's internal sense of overall positive self-worth, or feelings of self-efficacy. The third targeted outcome for athletes participating in sport is athlete connection. Athlete connection requires the ability to build positive bonds and social relationships with others. The fourth and final athlete outcome is athlete character, which is demonstrated through respect for the sport, responsible and moral behavior, and empathy for others.

In order to consistently achieve the desired athlete outcomes, coaches must adapt their coaching knowledge to the unique demands of the coaching context—the third component of the integrated definition of coaching effectiveness. For the purpose of the definition, coaching contexts are separated into two broad settings, participation coaching and performance coaching. In participation coaching contexts the primary goals are enjoyment and skill development in a low-intensity and minimally competitive environment. Conversely, performance coaching contexts place a much greater emphasis on competition and require more intensive training and commitment along with a high degree of specificity in the training program. Coaching contexts can further be delineated by the goal being pursued and the developmental level of the athlete, resulting in four distinct settings: (a) participation coaches for children, (b) participation coaches for adolescents and adults, (c) performance coaches for young adolescents, and (d) performance coaches for older adolescents and adults.

Quality Coaching Frameworks

The integrated definition of coaching effectiveness has been well received and is currently being used as a guide for designing coaching effectiveness frameworks around the world. The most vivid example of this is the International Sport Coaching Framework (ISCF; International Council for Coaching Excellence, Association of Summer Olympic International Federations, and Leeds Metropolitan University 2013). It is anticipated that the ISCF will serve as a multipurpose tool for (a) creating high-quality coach education programs, (b) evaluating and improving existing coach education programs,

(c) defining areas for coaching research and evaluation, (d) making informed political and legal decisions in sport, and (e) stimulating global exchange of sport coaching information.

At the heart of the ISCF, and coaching effectiveness, is functional coaching competence. Functional coaching competence, then, represents the latest step in the evolution of the global quest to identify and define standards of coaching effectiveness. Functional coaching competence is described broadly as an approach to guiding athlete improvement in unique social and organizational contexts (participation or performance coaching) while acknowledging that coaching is a complex and dynamic activity. Effective coaches use well-developed coaching knowledge (professional, interpersonal, intrapersonal) to set goals and perform six primary functions: (1) set vision and strategy, (2) shape the environment, (3) build relationships, (4) conduct practices and prepare for competitions, (5) read and react to the field, and (6) learn and reflect. These six functions, and the coaching knowledge required to effectively perform the functions in specific coaching contexts, represent the sum of the collective body of knowledge produced on coaching effectiveness (figure 17.2).

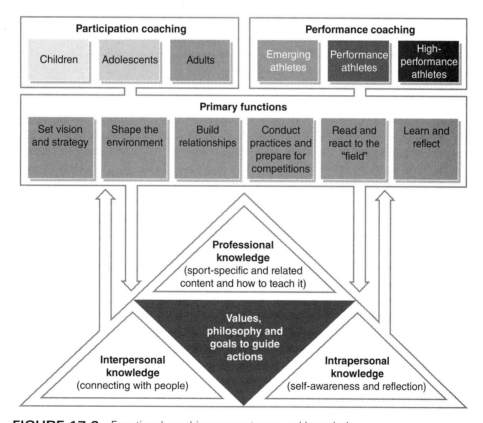

FIGURE 17.2 Functional coaching competence and knowledge.

Reprinted by permission from International Council for Coaching Excellence, Association of Summer Olympic International Federations, and Leeds Beckett University, *International Sport Coaching Framework (Version 1.2)* (Champaign, IL: Human Kinetics, 2013), 31.

The last function of a coach is a timeless hallmark of coaching effectiveness—ongoing learning. The surest way for a coach to lose their competitive edge is to stop refining their coaching knowledge. Championship field hockey coach Ric Charlesworth (2001), who coached teams to multiple Olympic gold medals, summed it up well when he stated that "The tendency to do what worked before is quite seductive. While one ought not discard proven methods lightly it is important to keep looking for improvement all the time" (192). The best coaches never stop learning because they always view their coaching knowledge as a work in progress, sometimes referred to as a growth mindset (Dweck 2006). Growth-mindset coaches immerse themselves in active and supportive coach learning networks to ensure their coaching strategies and philosophies remain current and effective.

The International Sport Coaching Framework, and the Integrated Definition of Coaching Effectiveness that underpins it, have served as the foundation for more recent coaching standards frameworks such as the European Sport Coaching Framework. The European Sport Coaching Framework identifies 31 task-related coaching competencies (Lara-Bercial et al. 2017). The task-related competencies represent the application of coaching knowledge that is needed to fulfill the six primary functions of a coach (table 17.3).

TABLE 17.3   Primary Coaching Functions and Task-Related Competences

Primary functions[a]	Task-related competences *The coach is able to*
Set the vision and strategy	• Understand the big picture and align methods with local, regional and national policy and objectives • Develop a suitable vision for the program relevant to the athletes in it and also to institutional priorities • Set up a relevant strategy that supports the fulfilment of the vision • Make effective and informed decisions relating to the planning, implementation, monitoring and evaluation of medium- to long-term programs of practice and competition based on institutional and athlete needs
Shape the environment	• Effectively identify and recruit athletes and staff • Identify, reflect on and challenge prevailing beliefs, values and assumptions within the coaching environment to establish a suitable culture • Identify and source the relevant resources (human and material) required to fulfil program and participant needs • Employ all reasonable measures to keep athletes and staff safe from harm
Build relationships	• Lead and influence the attitudes, behaviors and understanding of key stakeholders (e.g., parents, managers) through the meaningful presentation of ideas • Establish and maintain an ethical, effective, inclusive and empathetic relationship with athletes, staff and other stakeholders • Appreciate physical, mental and cultural diversity in participants and adapt practice accordingly • Adhere to established codes of conduct and legal requirements in coaching • Educate athletes, staff and other stakeholders to enhance their contribution to their own objectives, the program's objectives and their overall well-being

Primary functions[a]	Task-related competences *The coach is able to*
Conduct practices and prepare and manage competitions	• Conduct comprehensive needs analyses for individual athletes or teams in order to design and deliver tailored coaching programs, taking into account participant needs and capabilities in the context of wider programs, curricula, policies and targets • Select, design and justify appropriate pedagogy, coaching practice and communication methods to facilitate the short-term, medium-term and long-term learning needs of participants • Conduct a functional analysis of multiskill[b] activity or of their chosen sport (or sports) and identify the implications for coaching practice • Identify the core elements of their chosen sport (or sports) at the key stages of participant development • Devise, interpret and apply an appropriate curriculum for a multiskill environment or in their chosen sport (or sports) in line with participant needs and agreed-upon industry standards • Deliver a series of coaching sessions in the context of medium- and long-term planned programs of practice and competition using a wide range of appropriate learning modes for participants and coaching behaviors • Conduct risk assessments in order to deliver safe and ethical coaching • Identify, create and manage suitable competitive opportunities to contribute to ongoing athlete development • Develop appropriate competition strategies to maximize chances of learning and success • Maintain a professional attitude toward coaching practice, athletes and all stakeholders at all times
Read and react to the field	• Conduct an insightful analysis of coaching practice to make informed judgments relating to the efficacy of the learning environment established • Conduct an insightful analysis of athlete performance or team performance to make informed decisions regarding on-the-spot adjustments to enhance performance • Conduct an insightful analysis of the program to make informed judgments relating to the efficacy of the environment established • Make good in-action and post-action decisions to increase the chances of reaching objectives
Reflect and learn	• Identify and reflect on assumptions and methods as a coach and student, demonstrating the ability to conduct • Informed analysis and a willingness to apply the principle of continuous improvement to his or her own coaching • Identify his or her own learning needs and take responsibility for the development and application of strategies for further self-development as part of an ongoing process • Take an objective and critical approach to problem identification and solution, using evidence-based approaches and appropriate research methodologies • Develop an initial personal coaching philosophy and style, recognizing the need for further growth based on learning, evidence and experience

[a]The capacity to engage in meeting these primary functions requires a synoptic application of knowledge, skills and professional competences, the contribution of each being dependent of the specific context and demands.

[b]Multiskill activity refers to sport sessions aimed at the development of overall psychomotor skills, typically in children, sometimes referred to as fundamental movement skills. These types of activity can be done as part of a sport-specific session (e.g., multiple skills with a theme of tennis) or as outright multiskill sessions.

Reprinted by permission S. Lara-Bercial, J. North, K. Hämäläinen, K. Oltmanns, J. Minkhorst, and L. Petrovic, *European Sport Coaching Framework* (Champaign, IL: Human Kinetics, 2017), 29-31. Adapted by permission from the *ICCE Standards for Higher Education Sport Coaching Bachelor Degrees*, © 2016 International Council for Coaching Excellence.

Shortly after publication of the European Sport Coaching Framework, the United States Olympic Committee (2018) prepared its own Quality Coaching Framework (USOC QCF). Coaching effectiveness in the USOC QCF is directly aligned with the American Development Model, which organizes athlete development into five stages (USOC 2017). Although principles of coaching effectiveness remain the same across the five stages, the standards used to define and measure coaching effectiveness must be adapted to the unique development profiles and needs of athletes competing in each stage. Unlike other frameworks for coaching effectiveness, the USOC QCF does not focus on specific coaching competencies. Instead, the QCF identifies key areas that should be addressed when creating sport-specific standards of coaching effectiveness, such as essential coaching knowledge, an emphasis on an athlete-centered coaching approach, and the USOC ethics principles. Collectively, these standards characterize a recommended philosophy of coaching effectiveness (figure 17.3).

Measuring Standards of Coaching Effectiveness

Although measuring standards of quality coaching has long been regarded as a key to coach development, formal and systematic coach evaluation is still a rarity in most sport organizations (Gillham, Hansen, and Brady 2015). In order for the measurement of coaching effectiveness to become commonplace in sport, athletic directors and other sport leaders must learn to view

FIGURE 17.3   Recommended philosophy of coaching effectiveness.

Reprinted by permission from United States Olympic Committee, *USOC Quality Coaching Framework* (Champaign, IL: Human Kinetics, 2018), 34.

performance appraisals as fundamental to creating and sustaining cultures of continuous improvement. Measuring coaching effectiveness needs to be ongoing, multifaceted, and formative.

It is recommended that four steps be followed when preparing to evaluate standards of quality coaching (USOC 2018). Step one is determining what aspects of quality coaching to evaluate. A coach's primary function is to develop athletes. Therefore, all coach evaluation systems should include tools for measuring athlete development across the 4 C's: competence, confidence, connection, and character. A suggested athlete development toolkit that provides data across the 4 C's has been provided by Vierimaa et al. (2012). The recommended tools for measuring a coach's effectiveness at developing athletes across each of the 4 C's are listed in table 17.4. A condensed version of the 4 C's evaluation toolkit that has been successfully tested in high school coaching settings is also available (Gilbert 2017).

The second step is to decide who will be asked to provide coach evaluation feedback. Coach self-evaluations can prove valuable for stimulating personal reflection on standards of coaching effectiveness. However, to obtain a more objective and comprehensive assessment, coach self-evaluations should be supplemented with feedback from others. Sampling multiple sources of data to make informed evaluations of coaching effectiveness is more closely aligned with the multi-rater and ongoing approach to performance appraisals increasingly used in other fields, commonly referred to as a 360-degree feedback approach (O'Boyle 2014). Ideally, the evaluation process will at minimum include athletes, other members of the coaching staff, and administrators. This can be as simple as asking senior or departing athletes to complete a short evaluation questionnaire at the end of a season (Sabock and Sabock 2011).

In step three, the specific evaluation tools are selected and used to collect data. Any tool that is used must account for more than observable performance outcomes. That is, coaching effectiveness should not be solely

TABLE 17.4 Suggested Tools for Measuring Standards of Coaching Effectiveness Across the 4 C's of Athlete Development

Athlete Development Outcome	Measurement Tool
Competence	Sport competence inventory (Adapted from Causgrove et al. 2007)
Confidence	Self-confidence subscale of CSAI-2R (Cox, Martens, and Russell 2003)
Connection (coach–athlete)	Coach–athlete relationship questionnaire (Jowett and Ntoumanis 2004)
Connection (athlete–athlete)	Peer connection inventory (Adapted from Coie and Dodge 1983)
Character	Prosocial and antisocial behavior in sport scale (Kavussanu and Boardley 2009)

equated with winning. One such tool is the Coaching Behavior Scale for Sport (CBS-S), which has been used and validated in several studies with coaches from multiple countries (Koh, Kawabata, and Mallett 2014; Mallett and Côté 2006). The CBS-S is used to measure athlete perceptions of coaching effectiveness along seven dimensions. Athletes rate each coaching behavior on a 7-point scale. The seven coaching dimensions are: (1) Physical Training and Planning, (2) Goal Setting, (3) Mental Preparation, (4) Technical Skills, (5) Personal Rapport, (6) Negative Personal Rapport, and (7) Competition Strategies.

In a similar vein, the Coaching Success Questionnaire-2 (CSQ-2) was created through a rigorous three-step validation process (Gillham, Burton, and Gillham 2013). The CSQ-2 contains 40 questions organized into 10 coaching variables. The CSQ-2 asks athletes to rate their coach using a 6-point scale on the following variables:

1. Attitudes about Winning: the priority coaches place on winning over athlete development
2. Winning: how well coaches prepare athletes to win
3. Enjoyment: how well coaches instill and nurture athlete passion for the sport
4. Physical Development: how well coaches prepare athletes for physical demands of the sport
5. Wellness: how well coaches develop athlete general fitness
6. Skills and Strategies: how well coaches develop athlete sport competence
7. Self-Confidence: how well coaches enhance athlete beliefs about abilities and contributions
8. Emotion Management: how well coaches teach athletes emotional control and resiliency
9. Sportsmanship: how well coaches teach ethical and moral behavior
10. Teamwork: how well coaches promote team cohesion

Coach effectiveness measurement tools such as the CBS-S and the CSQ-2 have proven to be useful ways to obtain athlete feedback about their perceptions of coaching behaviors. However, when possible a multifaceted approach to measuring coaching effectiveness is advised. For example, for coaches who work in college settings, it has been suggested that coaching effectiveness be assessed across at least six coaching areas: (1) Athlete Outcomes, (2) Academic Outcomes, (3) Ethical Behavior, (4) Fiscal Responsibility, (5) Recruit Quality, and (6) Athlete Satisfaction (Cunningham and Dixon 2003). Possible metrics for assessing the different areas include graduation rate, post-season appearances, team grade point average, violations of organizational or league policies, and budget agreements.

The fourth and final step in evaluating standards of coaching effectiveness is determining how the results will be used. Regardless of whether coaching effectiveness is evaluated using an existing tool from the literature or one adapted to fit the values and standards of a particular coaching context, the purpose is to use the results to stimulate an informed discussion about quality coaching. Results from coach evaluations should not be used to make summative decisions about coaching effectiveness. Results are best viewed as supplementary information for coaches and administrators to use when meeting to review coaching strengths and coaching weaknesses.

A formal method for reporting evaluation results, such as writing an evaluation narrative or preparing an end-of-season statistical report with summary observations from selected feedback sources, is essential. Evaluation reports should be kept on file for formal debriefings and to spot trends across time. Evaluating standards of coaching effectiveness works best when it is done regularly and often, and when results are used to make constant incremental improvements.

Summary

Coaching effectiveness depends on the needs and objectives of the particular coach and his or her athletes, the complex and ever-changing dynamics of the coach–athlete relationship, and the context in which coaches are performing. The collective body of coaching science, then, simply illuminates thousands of microexamples of coaching effectiveness. Each study and every coaching biography is a single point of light in the constellation, providing a momentary glimpse of standards of coaching effectiveness in action.

The intent of this chapter was to provide a broad view of this constellation, showing both the evolution of and current recommendations for standards for coaching effectiveness. The journey started with a review of the coaching approach used by legendary coach John Wooden, followed by a summary of key research and coach effectiveness frameworks, concluding with a description of some recommended evaluation tools. The early study of coach Wooden's practice behaviors represents one of the first systematic glimpses of coaching effectiveness in action. Coach Wooden showed us that quality teaching is the principal standard of coaching effectiveness. More recent developments, such as the International Sport Coaching Framework, represent all-encompassing views of the recommended standards for coaching effectiveness. Standards for coaching effectiveness now extend well beyond quality teaching and include primary coaching functions such as setting vision and strategy, shaping the environment, and building quality relationships. Coaches and coach educators now have a range of evaluation tools to consider that collectively address standards for coaching effectiveness.

The four-decade journey from coach Wooden to the global coaching frameworks and a repository of coach evaluation tools is linked by momentary pauses in which influential coaching frameworks such as the Working Model of Coaching Effectiveness, the National Standards for Sport Coaches, and the Integrated Definition of Coaching Effectiveness were created. Each one of these frameworks represented the next best step in the journey, and surely more frameworks will be created as the journey continues. By taking an "evolution, not revolution" approach, each new step builds upon the preceding one. Like coach Wooden used to say, "it's what you learn after you know it all that matters most."

Chapter 18

Coach Behavior and Performance Analysis

Stephen Harvey, Edward Cope, and Luke Jones

This chapter will discuss information concerning the knowledge base for coach behavior and performance analysis. It examines research related to coaches' and players' behavior or performance within practice and competition settings. Research has been conducted on coach behavior since the early 1970s and was, in fact, one of the first arenas for sport coaching research, specifically with respect to the systematic observation of coach behavior. Concurrently, this notion of behavioral observation emerged in performance contexts with players through the utilization of notational methods in the mid- to late 1970s. Due to the methodologies and methods chosen for analysis, coach behavior and performance analysis was initially conducted under the positivistic tradition with a behavioristic/reductionist worldview. This is an approach that views human behavior as measurable, as predictable, and, consequently, as controllable (Smith 1989). In more recent times, coaching researchers have utilized theoretical perspectives from other disciplines to better understand the inherent complexities of coaching and athlete performance because coaching occurs within a variety of different domains and contexts. Thus, the limitations of this model were exposed because different athletes have different needs and different coaches have different prior experiences and knowledge to offer their athletes.

In contrast to a behavioristic/reductionist worldview, a social constructivist considers coaching to be messy, complex, unpredictable, and nonlinear (Potrac, Jones, and Armour 2002). Consequently, social constructivist theories have been employed to increase sociological and pedagogical theorizing in coaching to answer research questions related to the construction of the coach–athlete relationship and the factors that influence this (i.e., how coaches structure their learning environment and what this means for the learners, the pedagogies the coach utilizes and the athletes' perspective of these, how coaches reflect on their behavior and practice, etc.).

These changes in the conceptualization of coaching and coaching practice have been further enabled by the addition of new technologies, which have permitted a more in-depth and nuanced picture of coaching and athlete performance, again better depicting the realities of the contexts in which coaching and athletic performance take place. For example, the utilization of video to enable the development of a reflective conversation (Schön 1983) between coaches or between coaches and players pre- and postperformance and ongoing performance has opened up new avenues for research. The increasing body of knowledge in coach behavior and performance analysis that examines coaching from a wider range of theoretical perspectives provides some opportunity to influence coach education and training.

To cover material relative to both coach behavior and performance analysis, this chapter is organized into three main sections. In the first two sections, we provide a rationale for the study of coach behavior or performance analysis, followed by an overview of coach behavior or performance analysis research from a quantitative, qualitative, and mixed-method perspective. The third and final part of these two sections will offer implications for coach education and coaching practice. In the final part of the chapter, we draw together a number of common themes between coach behavior and performance analysis, one of which is the shift toward a social constructivist perspective within both disciplines of study. We begin, however, by discussing coach behavior.

Coaching Behavior

Coach behavior is of central importance to the coaching process because it affects, both directly and indirectly, athlete outcomes (Horn 2008). This includes psychosocial aspects such as motivation and confidence (Mageau and Vallerand 2003), as well as athlete performance outcomes such as skill acquisition (Ford, Yates, and Williams 2010) and cognitive activities, which include problem solving and decision-making (Smith and Cushion 2006). Moreover, coach behavior is influenced by coaches' values and beliefs, as well as situational context, organizational climate, and personal characteristics of the coach (Horn 2008). Because of the number of factors influencing coach behavior and the fact that coach behavior affects athletes' outcomes, it is our contention throughout this chapter that coach behavior is measurable and changeable through research and, most important, via interventions on practice (Cushion 2013; Cushion, Ford, and Williams 2012). Accordingly, a key determinant in effective coaching programs is the relationship between the coach and athlete. While we will argue in this chapter that there is no right way to coach and that athletes will learn regardless of the coach, coaches can (sometimes) help this process through their practice and behavior

(Denison and Mills 2014). Due to the inherent complexities of coaching, we will demonstrate in the sections that follow how research traditions have changed over time to recognize this shift in appreciation for the need to study behaviors in the context in which they occur. This is an alternative to making generalizations from one context to another, which have often been based upon on a snapshot of coaches' behavior and practice.

Systematic Observation Studies

In a review of coaching science research, Gilbert and Trudel (2004) found the study of coach behavior using quantitative methodologies to be a main focus. More specifically, the method of systematic observation has been widely employed in a number of sport coaching contexts (e.g., Bloom, Crumpton, and Anderson 1999; Cushion and Jones 2001; Segrave and Ciancio 1990) in an attempt to capture what coaches actually do in practice (Brewer and Jones 2002; Kahan 1999) and competition (Smith and Cushion 2006).

> Systematic observation permits a trained observer to use a set of guidelines and procedures to observe, record, and analyze observable events and behaviors, with the assumption that other observers using the same observation instrument, and viewing the same sequence of events, would agree with the recorded data. (Franks 1997, 179)

The rationale for the use of this method is founded on the premise that in order to advance knowledge about coaching effectiveness, it is important to identify the behavior of coaches (Côté et al. 1995). There are three ways in which systematic observation data can be recorded (van der Mars 1989). Interval recording is the means by which behaviors are recorded at predefined intervals. For example, behaviors are recorded for one-minute intervals with a thirty-second break between each interval where behaviors are not recorded. Time-sampled recording differs from interval recording in that it records behavior in chronological order during standard intervals of time for the entirety of the session. For example, behaviors would be recorded during thirty-second intervals in the order that they occurred during practice. Event-recording documents the total number of behaviors within a session, but does not take account of when the behaviors were used.

Studies of coach behavior using systematic observation were originally undertaken in physical education settings in the 1960s (Metzler 2000). However, given the scope, importance, and application, researchers began to carry out systematic observation of coaches during the 1970s. The first significant study was by Tharp and Gallimore (1976) who observed the behaviors of legendary university basketball coach, John Wooden. They devised a 10-behavior observational instrument to objectively measure the number of times coach Wooden would perform a defined behavior. Tharp and Gallimore (1976) constructed their observational instrument based on a series of informal observations that allowed them to validate the coach behaviors they believed coach Wooden used in practice. These included instruction, hustle, negative and positive modeling, praise, reproofs, nonverbal reward, nonverbal punishment, a "Wooden," other, and uncodable.

With few exceptions (Langsdorf 1979; Williams 1978), systematic observation studies of coach behavior were limited up until the middle of the 1980s based on a series of informal observations that allowed researchers to validate the coach behaviors they believed coach Wooden used in practice. These studies prompted the creation of the Arizona State University Observation Instrument (ASUOI) (Lacy and Darst 1984). Although built upon the work of Tharp and Gallimore (1976), this was the first systematic observation instrument that included a generic set of coach behaviors that could be applied across a range of sports. Consequently, studies using the ASUOI have been carried out in basketball (Becker and Wrisberg 2008; Bloom, Crumpton, and Anderson 1999), soccer (Cushion and Jones 2001; Ford, Yates, and Williams 2010; Miller 1992; Potrac et al. 2002), tennis (Claxton 1988), American football (Lacy and Darst 1985), and volleyball (Isabel et al. 2008), and across a range of contexts, which include professional, university or collegiate, developmental elite, and recreational (Kahan 1999). Another prominent systematic observation instrument created during this period was the Coach Behavior Assessment System (CBAS) (Smith, Smoll and Hunt 1977). CBAS was a 12-behavioral-category system that also originated from content analysis of coach behavior during practice and competition. However, CBAS differed from the ASUOI because it placed greater focus on the interpersonal behaviors coaches used as underpinned by psychological theory (Smith and Smoll 1990).

Despite the breadth of coach behavior research, there have been few findings to suggest that this differs as a consequence of context (Ford, Yates, and Williams 2010; Partington and Cushion 2013). For example, in many studies (e.g., Ford, Yates, and Williams 2010; Harvey et al. 2013; Isabel et al. 2008; Potrac, Jones, and Cushion 2007; Segrave and Ciancio 1990) instruction and general feedback/praise (note that this term changes dependent on the systematic observation instrument used) have consistently been found to be the most employed coach behaviors at the expense of specific feedback and questioning.

From a review of literature, it was found that nearly all studies that employed a systematic observation method were conducted in the United States or the United Kingdom. Kahan's (1999) review of systematic observation research showed that prior to the year 1997, the primary context studied was youth sports. Most of these studies up to the period of Kahan's review were undertaken in the United States. Since 1997, there has been an influx of studies carried out in the United Kingdom, most of which study the behavior of coaches who work in elite development contexts. Notably, there are few studies investigating coaches who operate in professional contexts. In fact, only two studies have been conducted in this context since the year

2000. Consequently, while studies using systematic observation in coaching have been a main research focus, knowledge of the behavior coaches use in some contexts is absent.

Additional criticisms can also be leveled at studies that have employed systematic observation. First, early observational research in sport settings was condemned for failing to invest time in undertaking longitudinal research (Lombardo and Cheffers 1983). This failure can be extended to many of the studies of coach behavior because researchers have often recorded only a small number of coaching sessions. For example, in the study by Isabel and colleagues (2008), 11 coaches were observed only once for a 45-minute duration. In studies by Lacy and Darst (1985) and Claxton (1988), the coaches who participated, although observed at various phases in the season, were still only observed on three occasions in totality. Ford, Yates, and Williams' (2010) analysis of elite, subelite, and nonelite football coaches working with children is an additional study where coaches were observed only once at different phases of the season, upon which generalizable conclusions were made about coaches' practice and behavior. It could be reasonably argued that these studies and others that have adopted a similar approach may only gain a "snapshot" of coaches' behavior, and therefore they fail to get an accurate representation of coach behavior, which, incidentally, is the purpose of the method.

Further problems with much of the systematic coach behavior research have centered on the procedures used to collect data. Issues with time-sampled and interval recording have been raised based on their failure to capture all single behaviors that happen in any one session (Cushion, Ford, and Williams 2012). However, event-recording has also received some criticism when sessions are coded live because the observer may miss some behaviors while noting down observations. In fact, live coding using hand notation has been criticized, regardless of the method used, due to its inaccuracy in reporting all behaviors (Cushion, Ford, and Williams 2012).

Developments in technology have seen the advent of more sophisticated systematic observation tools, which more closely track the complexities and nuances of coach behavior and deal with the limitations of hand notation tools (Cushion, Ford, and Williams 2012). The coach analysis intervention system (CAIS) is a 23-item systematic observation tool designed to record coach behavior (Cushion et al. 2012). Unlike any other systematic observation tool used in coaching, CAIS involves a multilevel, time-sampled event-recording protocol (Cushion, Ford, and Williams 2012). This means that both the total frequency of behaviors is recorded, as well as the chronological order in which they occur. The multilevel aspect of the instrument means that primary behaviors (i.e., instruction, questioning, and silence) have a series of secondary behaviors attached to them (i.e., recipient, timing, content).

This greater level of detail provides additional information that can have implications for learning beyond just knowing the primary behaviors that coaches employ. For example, it has been suggested that while providing feedback during a skill attempt improves immediate performance, it is detrimental to learning (Wulf and Shea 2004). Furthermore, providing feedback during or immediately after a performer's practice attempt means he or she doesn't need to retrieve previously learned information, which again is detrimental to learning (Wulf, Lee, and Schmidt 1994). Without capturing the timing of coach behavior, these conclusions cannot be drawn.

Qualitative Methods

Although systematic observation has been the predominant method to capture the behavior of coaches, some studies have employed qualitative methods in an attempt to better understand the cognitive process underpinning coach behavior. For example, Côté et al.'s (1995) study used a semistructured interview method to explore the knowledge expert coaches used in training and competition. Also in a study of expert coaches, Nash, Sproule, and Horton (2011) investigated the constructs that underpinned the coaches' practice. Data revealed coaches' perceptions of the behavior they think they employed, with supporting justification for the use of these behaviors.

While it is important to appreciate how coaches view their practice and behaviors, research has identified coaches lack self-awareness of these (Partington and Cushion 2013; Partington, Cushion, and Harvey 2014; Smith and Smoll 1990, 1997; Smith, Smoll, and Curtis 1979). Partington and Cushion (2013) call this the "epistemological gap," which is the distance between what coaches think they do and what they actually do. Subsequently, relying only on coaches' perceptions of their practice is not useful if the aim is to find out about the behaviors coaches employ.

Mixed Methods

While systematic observation has been suggested to be the most effective way to find out what it is coaches do (Brewer and Jones 2002), using this method in isolation fails to take account of what coaches are trying to achieve in their coaching practice as dictated by context (Cushion and Jones 2001; Potrac, Jones, and Armour 2002; Potrac, Jones, and Cushion 2007; Smith and Cushion 2006). Equally, studies that only use an interview framework to explore coaches' perceptions of behavior are limited given that coaches are very poor at being able to accurately report their behavior (Partington and Cushion 2013). Consequently, without some form of objective, observational data, inaccurate assumptions are likely to be made.

What we are advocating is a mixed-method approach, which leads to an accurate identification of coach behavior as well as an underpinning rationale that helps explain this behavior. It has also been acknowledged that coaches' prior socialization experiences significantly contribute toward coaches adopting certain behavioral strategies (Christensen 2009; Cushion, Armour, and Jones 2003; Stoszkowski and Collins 2014). As Evans (2004) asserts, action does not occur in isolation, but rather is the product of a person's biography. Potrac, Jones, and Armour (2002) further contend that coaching is a social endeavor and therefore the coaching environment must capture how the social context is responsible for shaping the behaviors of coaches.

The use of qualitative methods alongside quantitative methods has been argued for, as this provides an understanding of not only what coaches do but also why they coach in this way, and how the sociocultural coaching context influences their behavior (Becker and Wrisberg 2008; Cushion and Jones 2001). For example, the professional football coach in the study by Potrac, Jones, and Armour (2002) rationalized his high use of instruction as he felt he needed to be perceived as controlling the coaching environment to ensure job security. As this coach operated within a performance context, he believed that there was an expectation placed on him from the players to demonstrate his "knowledge of the game." Therefore, qualitative methods help explain how both individual agency and social structures affect coaches' behavior (Jenkins 2010; Larson and Silverman 2005; Rovegno 2003), and have provided much needed insight into how coaches think about their coaching (Cushion and Jones 2001; Smith and Cushion 2006).

While using qualitative data to supplement quantitative data provides information that goes beyond describing just what a coach does, there is also a need to consider the perceptions of athletes concerning the behavior of their coaches (Côté and Sedgwick 2003; Smith and Smoll 1997). Without appreciating athletes' learning needs and wants, coaches' behavior is likely to be ineffective (Côté et al. 1995). Unfortunately, research evidence in this area has not been forthcoming, which has led to suggestions that the athlete's voice has been marginalized (Cushion 2001; Dyson 1995; Pitchford et al. 2004; Thomson 2008). Of the research that has examined athletes' perceptions of coach behavior, findings indicate coaches who are supportive and encouraging and who limit their use of instruction, general feedback, and punishment are preferred by athletes (Coatsworth and Conroy 2009; Pelletier et al. 2001; Newton, Duda, and Yin 2000; Smith and Smoll 1990; Smith, Smoll, and Curtis 1979). However, research is limited and has mostly been conducted within the context of children's sports, thus limiting the generalizable nature of these findings.

Implications of Coach Behavior Research for Coaches and Coach Education

Notwithstanding some of the current limitations in the research cited earlier, there are a number of clear "take home messages" for coaches in terms of continuing to develop their coach behavior and practice. These are centered on notions of coaches using information about their behavior and practice to develop a reflective conversation (Schön 1983), which is underpinned by a social constructivist view of coaching. For example, through examination of their coach behavior and practice, reflection and the reflective conversation can be initiated through what Kuklick et al. (2015) call "a cycle of a problem setting (i.e., dilemma), strategy generation, experimentation, and evaluation" (12). We offer some recommendations of a behavioral profile that research has reported "good" coaches do:

- Reduce punitive behaviors because only a small number make a significant difference to athletes' perceptions (Smith and Smoll 1996);
- Plan patterns of behavior for coaching sessions that meet the aims of the coaching session and the athletes being coached in that particular context (Cushion, Ford, and Williams 2012). This avoids (1) "shooting from the hip" coaching, (2) the utilization of a blanket positive feedback approach that lacks quality information for the athletes/players being coached (e.g., "super," "great," "lovely," "I like that"), and (3) the utilization of the same coach behaviors irrespective of the athletes being coached.
- Combine behaviors that work well together (i.e., a positive sandwich: an interaction that begins with a positive feedback statement that is followed by corrective feedback and concludes with another positive feedback statement) (Erickson et al. 2011);
- Spend as much time with as many individual athletes as possible in the context of the coaching session (Erikson et al. 2011);
- Use more externally focused feedback (Wulf et al. 2002);
- Develop open questioning strategies. Research suggests coaches use questioning that is closed and merely as a way of reinforcing previous instructions rather than as a specific pedagogical strategy (Harvey et al. 2013); and
- Be comfortable with silent observation, and utilize this as a deliberate coaching strategy (Partington and Cushion 2013; Smith and Cushion 2006).

Although this list provides a good summary of what coaches should do and provides some ideas for what Kuklick and colleagues (2015) call "problem setting," a lot of these findings are not incredibly new, nor are all applicable for all coaches working in all coaching contexts. Moreover, as coaches' behavior and practice is situated in a wider political and cultural milieu than simply at the microlevel of the actual coaching session, operationalizing some of the above strategies is very challenging. An important fact of the reflective conversation framework of Kuklick and colleagues (2015) would therefore be to identify the specific problem but, moreover, also identify some solutions for each individual coach by generating strategies to help coaches overcome some of their coaching dilemmas related to their behavior and practice. Furthermore, it must be acknowledged that a key ingredient in this complex process of reviewing coach behavior is the relationship between the coach and the athlete and the mix of personalities that become part of this process.

One specific strategy for ensuring the experimentation for and evaluation of improving coach behavior and practice occurs in a robust manner is through the combination of quantitative (via systematic observation) and qualitative (via journals or video clips) reflection tools. The utilization of these two tools in combination provides the means by which coaches can begin to critically reflect on their practice and the actual behaviors they use, thus increasing levels of self-awareness (Carson 2008).

The utilization of systematic observation is required because relying on coaches' thoughts and perceptions alone does not provide accurate measurements of what coaches actually do in practice, and has instead led to the development of a culture of coaches relying on tried and tested methods based on the notion of "folk pedagogies" (Bruner 1999). For example, research shows that a low correlation exists between coaches' observed and self-reported behavior (Partington and Cushion 2013; Smith, Smoll, and Curtis 1979). The generation of systematic observation data therefore provides the "front porch" and drives the ongoing process linking the coaches' cognition, reflection, and development. These baseline data act as a basis for coach development. For example, More and Franks (1996) demonstrated that the modification of verbal coach behavior can be achieved through the use of ongoing behavioral feedback with collaboration (in this case a researcher).

In addition to generating hard data, however, the simultaneous generation of video footage provides assistance in bridging the gap between experience and formal coach education through informed reflection (Light et al. 2015). The coupling of these two mechanisms is therefore imperative in challenging coaches' previous held beliefs and assumptions about learning so that behavior and practice are informed less by tradition, uncritical inertia, or folk pedagogies (Bruner 1999) and becomes evidenced-based. It is our contention that a reliance on systematic observation itself without the video analysis and feedback associated with this utilization of video footage will be insufficient in this regard because this will not stimulate the changes in self-awareness required by coaches, especially for long-term change in coaching practice. Reviewing video footage permits coaches to reflect at a deeper level and one that appreciates the nuanced, intricate, and complex nature of coaching (Cushion, Ford, and Williams 2012; Jones and Wallace 2005). Moreover, qualitative descriptions can reveal coach mannerisms; athletes' attitude, effort, and behavior; and the impact of context. Qualitative descriptions also relate to how coaches structure practice and the behaviors they employ. However, bear in mind that without the initial systematic observation data, there is little context for the coaches' reflection.

The operationalization of this reflective style can be a somewhat problematic process, particularly for coaches insufficiently resourced in terms of video equipment and wireless microphones that enable the capture of high-quality video for subsequent analysis. Having said that, advancements in technology make having the resources to enable coaching sessions to be filmed no longer as problematic as it once was (O'Donoghue 2010). Still, reviewing sessions from both a quantitative and qualitative perspective is a lengthy and time-consuming process, which may affect the extent to which coaches are able to fully review sessions. However, below we provide some suggestions for coaches who would like to begin conducting some systematic observation in their practice:

- *Start small.* Choose one short segment of your coach behavior and practice in which to code initially, say 15 minutes. Situate your coding on one or two primary coach behaviors. We provide a list of sample primary and secondary behaviors in table 18.1 to help you get started, which have been adapted from the Coach Analysis Intervention System (Cushion, Ford, and Williams 2012) and the West Virginia Teaching Evaluation System (Hawkins and Wiegand 1989). This coding work can be completed by hand by generating a coding form or by using performance analysis software or iPad applications [1].

- *Increase complexity over time.* As you develop your confidence, code different behaviors or additional behaviors by considering the practice type (i.e., a "drill" versus a competition-related practice) or game context (i.e., first half/second half; winning/losing) within which these behaviors were coded. You can also begin to utilize some of the secondary behaviors seen in table 18.1, such as recipient or content.

- *Don't work alone.* Work with peers (i.e., other coaches) in a learning community (Kuklick et al. 2015) to code behavior from each other's sessions.

- *Link behaviors to video.* This will help contextualize the behaviors. Today's technology makes it possible to link a wireless microphone to a tablet so you can capture video and sound while observing coaching behavior. Wearable video/audio technologies such as a GoPro™ camera are also an option.

Coach educators can also utilize this same process. As a requirement of attendance at the formal coach education event, coaches will need to bring some video footage of their coaching. Then other coaches, working in small groups and using the definitions from table 18.1, will review the footage. The observer's/coder's role would be to assist the coaches who brought the video to make meaning of what they experienced and why. The role of the coach educator, as mentioned previously, becomes very much a facilitator whereby they promote further discussion and challenge coaches' thoughts and beliefs. It is strategies such as reflective conversations and reviewing of coaching sessions that Piggott (2015) talks about as being necessary for effective coach education. Piggott further discusses the need for coach education to remain flexible by offering coaches a range of education and development opportunities, which include mentoring and social networking.

In this section, we have provided some ways in which coach education could be re-positioned in order to deal with the rigid, one-size-fits-all approach it currently adopts (Piggott 2012) and to better support the inherent realities

TABLE 18.1 Sample Coach Behaviors

Primary Coaching Behaviors	
Behavior	**Definition**
Instruction	Coach gives information to players about how a desired action (i.e., skill, play, strategy) is to be executed. This can also include verbal cues, reminders, or prompts to instruct or direct skill or play related to player performance during its actual execution. Examples: "Talk," "Press," "Keep them there," "Mark up," "Go with the runner," "Move left," "Now run left," "Pass the ball," "Take a shot," "Get behind them," "Bend your elbow," "Point your toe to the ground"
Positive feedback	Coach gives general or specific verbal statements or nonverbal gestures that are positive or supportive (delivered after a skill attempt). Examples (General): "Well tried," "Well done," "Good job," "Much better," "That's lovely," "I like that" clapping Examples (Specific): "Good, you followed through well," "Good drag," "That was good defending," "I liked the way that you got nice and low in the tackle," "Good serve," "Excellent counter attack/fast break"
Negative feedback	Coach gives general or specific verbal statements or nonverbal gestures that are negative or unsupportive (delivered after a skill attempt). Examples (General): "Don't do that again," "Oh, guys, please," "That was rubbish," "You got that wrong," "Not from there," holding head in hands Examples (Specific): "Don't lose sight of the ball and your man," "Don't force the pass," "The attack is too slow," "You're swinging too early," "You've got to talk, guys," "You maybe got caught a bit too wide"
Corrective feedback	Coach gives corrective statements that contain information that specifically aim to improve player performance at the next skill attempt (can be delivered concurrently or after a skill attempt). Examples: "It would help if your stance was not a meter wide," "You probably do not want to be on the same side as your teammate initially," "Move your feet and not your stick," "Pass it earlier next time," "Force them away from the goal when they are attacking," "We need to increase the ball pace"
Convergent questioning	Coach asks a question about skill, strategy, procedure, or score; the status of a player's injury; about the welfare of a player; or to a match official; etc. with a limited number of correct answers or options (i.e., closed responses, often yes or no answer). For example, "Which is the best passing option from here, forward or back?"
Divergent questioning	Coach asks a question about skill, strategy, procedure or score; the status of a player's injury; about the welfare of a player; or to a match official; etc. with multiple responses or options (i.e., open responses with various possible replies). For example, "What options do you have available in that position?"
General observation	Coach is watching groups or individuals engaged in any category of behavior. Coach must not be engaged in any other category of behavior in order to record general observation. This must also last longer than five seconds to be considered "observation," e.g., watching the whole class as they do warm-up laps.

> continued

Table 18.1 > *continued*

Primary Coaching Behaviors	
Behavior	**Definition**
Specific observation	Coach is watching one student engaged in a subject-matter task for the purpose of providing feedback related to performance. Coach's position must be proximal to the learner position so that observation is clearly focused on a specific learner who is performing. This must also last longer than five seconds to be considered "observation," e.g., watching one player performing a chest pass in basketball, or watching five players execute a fast break.

Secondary Coaching Behaviors	
Recipient of coaching behavior	**Definition**
Individual	Coach talks or responds nonverbally to a single player (either one-to-one by pulling a player aside during practice, or, in a match/competition, by using a player's name, number, etc.).
Group	Coach talks or responds nonverbally to more than one player, up to half of the team of players.
Team	Coach talks or responds nonverbally to more than one half of the team of players.
Other	Coach talks or responds nonverbally to an assistant coach, referee, parent, spectator, etc.

Content	
Feedback focus	**Definition**
Technical	Coach addresses individual techniques such as passing, shooting, dribbling, etc.
Tactical	Coach addresses specific tactical areas such as patterns of play, formations (e.g., defensive shape), counter attacking, pressing, player movement and connections, etc.
Other	Coach addresses areas that do not fit any other behavior category.

Adapted from A.H. Hawkins and R.L. Wiegand, "West Virginia University Teaching Evaluation System and Feedback Taxonomy," in *Analyzing Physical Education and Sport Instruction*, 2nd ed., edited by P.W. Darst, R.B. Zakrajsek, and V.H. Mancini (Champaign, IL: Human Kinetics, 1989), 277-293.

and complexities of coaching practice. We now transition to considering performance analysis before offering a chapter summary.

A Rationale for Performance Analysis Practices in Coaching

What Hughes and Bartlett (2008) named "performance analysis" (PA) originated in the United States in the 1960s in the team sports of American football and basketball (Hughes and Franks 2004). It is an aspect of the coaching process that has attracted significant attention from an ever-diversifying range of research perspectives (for a comprehensive review of performance analysis in Association Football, see Mackenzie and Cushion 2013). The accuracy of the technologies adopted to trace the movement of athletic bodies has, over time, improved. Furthermore, developments in video and computer technology mean PA tools are now affordable and that the use of PA has become widespread across a multitude of sports (Carling, Williams, and Reilly 2005). This increased integration of PA runs parallel with the increasing involvement of modern technologies within elite sport. Indeed, Carter (2006) has revealed how the modern age and the rationalist ethos associated with this period has influenced all aspects of coaching and management in sport. One salient outcome of the modernization of sport is that practitioners have become increasingly acclimatized to the use of modern technology for the purposes of preparing, training, and monitoring athletes (Denison, Mills, and Jones 2013). This process of measurement and constant surveillance is achieved through a range of technologies designed to record the performance outputs of elite athletes in various contexts. Historically, the three most widely acknowledged methods for this process are notational analysis, time–motion analysis, and quantitative biomechanical analysis (Hughes and Bartlett 2008).

In order to assess the merits of performance analysis tools for the development of quality coaching, we briefly trace the important stages in the evolution of performance analysis research and development. Carling and colleagues (2014) have identified that today's practitioners are "using an ever-increasing range of technologies to quantitatively and qualitatively track and monitor performance" (6). It is our aim here to provide a short summary of the various performance tools these authors mention, and later, to link them to the applied coaching setting. To begin, we consider the merits of quantitative techniques derived from a rationalist/behaviorist mindset. We then move on to introduce several qualitative approaches that have emerged from a constructivist research perspective focused upon athlete learning. We also briefly introduce contemporary sociocultural research into the study of performance analysis in coaching settings. Finally, we discuss the implications for the coach and athlete of having performance analysis be a central tenet of the coaching process (Drust 2010).

Quantitative Methods (Athlete Output)

Mackenzie and Cushion (2013) noted that the questions performance analysis research has posed have been shaped by the methods and assumptions of the positivist paradigm, that behavior is observable and measurable and with this knowledge, controllable. Specifically, a reductionist, or simplification, approach has dominated. It is therefore unsurprising that quantitative methods have been predominantly promoted as appropriate to collect performance data in order to answer the question, How can we measure how athletes perform in order to better control their performance? This positivist status quo has inspired a whole host of efforts to develop PA tools capable of doing just this; below we discuss the most prominent of these.

Notational analysis has been defined as an "objective way of recording performance so that key elements of that performance can be quantified in a valid and consistent manner" (Hughes 2005, 1). This data can only be gathered if the four necessary components (player, position, action, and time) are considered and are represented through scatter diagrams, frequency tables, and sequential systems. Carling, Williams, and Reilly (2005) have identified that the benefits of notational analysis lie in its ability to collate statistical information relating to the execution of actions and the evaluation of tactical aspects of performance.

Time–motion analysis, as a technology of PA, has evolved from using a single camera, to using a multicamera approach, and more recently, to utilize Global Positioning Satellites (GPS) in order to track the movements of performing athletes. Time–motion analysis is centered upon the monitoring of athletes and fundamentally seeks to understand the physical component of sport performance (O'Donoghue 2010). It is important to note that there is no recognized gold standard for time–motion analysis because there are significant variations in data generated by different systems. However, a comparison study has found that despite contradictory data being generated, contemporary time–motion analysis techniques are now more capable of the reliable and comprehensive study of locomotion patterns in sport (Randers et al. 2010). As a result of the perceived applicability of PA tools in football, time–motion analysis has also been used to break down various aspects of the game, including how and when goals are scored (Garganta, Maia, and Basto 1997), patterns of player behavior during games (James, Mellalieu, and Hollely 2002), comparing the output of players in various leagues (Dellal et al. 2011), noting the sprinting output of elite players (Di Salvo et al. 2009), and also analyzing of major injuries that occur during play (Hewett, Torg, and Boden 2009). This range of purposes from just one of the major global team sports clearly shows that quantitative time–motion performance analysis tools are believed to provide coaches with a wealth of information that they in turn use to assist in their decision-making process.

While time–motion analysis is focused upon the larger motor patterns of moving athletes, quantitative biomechanical analysis is concerned with the finer features of sport technique (Hughes and Bartlett 2008). Using this means of analysis, numerous aspects of athletic movement can be recorded, analyzed, and better coordinated in an attempt to improve athletic output. This PA tool then provides coaches with an individually tailored biomechanical portfolio from which to adapt and improve the specifics of the practices they prescribe to their athletes.

While it is clear that the ways in which data are gathered are becoming increasingly efficient, several practical and theoretical problems exist with solely considering PA as an objective fact-finding mission. Methodological concerns related to sample sizes, a lack of operational definitions, and conflicting classifications (Mackenzie and Cushion 2013) lead to performance analysts drowning themselves and the coaches they assist in unfathomable data with a short shelf life (Carling et al. 2014). Furthermore, as a result of the lack of critical engagement with the context within which the data is generated, the applied value of the data gathered is questionable, or even conflicting, in its nature. To summarize, Cushion (2007) has suggested that existing PA research consistently reduces the complexity of performance by presenting it in a way that is overly descriptive, systematic, and unproblematic. This view mirrors much of the coach behavior research that currently exists, which we have discussed above (research that is for the most part rooted in the positivist paradigm).

Qualitative Methods (Athlete Learning)

Given the positivist origins of PA techniques mentioned, it is no surprise that quantitative tools have dominated the recording of athletic performance. However, in response to the dominance of objective PA tools and attitudes, Nelson and Groom (2012) have recognized the value of subjectively based qualitative analysis of athletic performance and the role it can play. Much in the same way as with coach behavior, a qualitative approach to PA can help to move beyond the aforementioned restrictions associated with the generation of large amounts of hard-to-use data. Specifically, qualitative PA techniques and tools can help the coach and athlete to experience a two-way, feedback-centered relationship, as opposed to the expert–novice framework dictated by the existing quantitative PA techniques mentioned previously. Many have questioned the accuracy of qualitative PA; however, as a result of its ability to capture the complex nature of sport performance (Nelson and Groom 2012), it has lent itself more to the applied coaching setting. For example, Groom, Cushion, and Nelson (2011) were among the first to consider how the coach uses a qualitative approach to PA to specifically enhance athlete learning and performance. Furthermore, James (2006) noted that almost all professional sport teams now use PA as a means of providing feedback to athletes. He also saw that PA is popular not only because it is considered to accelerate learning but also because it is considered to be a disciplinary tool that can be used to modify athlete behaviors (Court 2004), including athletes' technical output at important stages of development (Tursi et al. 2013).

Following the qualitative trend in PA, Nelson, Potrac, and Groom (2014) began to examine the use of video-based performance analysis from the players' perspective. These authors are among the first to consider how PA, as a pedagogical approach, affects how the athlete learns. They highlighted that, historically, coaches expose players to lengthy video analysis sessions as a form of punishment, to correct behavior or skills, and to reiterate repeated mistakes. In this paper, these authors reviewed existing PA techniques and identified that there are clear *potential* benefits of using PA for players and coaches alike. It is already understood that the social interactions that occur between coach and learner can have a significant impact upon athlete learning, and Nelson, Potrac, and Groom (2014) have identified that the stability of this relationship is key to the efficacy of any PA tools adopted. What is also clear is that the contextual element of athletic performance and the coach–athlete relationship is of extreme significance with regard to the efficacy of PA tools. Furthermore, it is impossible to capture the wide-ranging elements of a specific sport context using quantitative PA techniques in isolation. However, it is clear that coordinated performance analysis that is cognizant of the context within which an athlete is performing can be efficiently used as a feedback mechanism to improve athlete learning in a functional coach–athlete relationship (Groom and Nelson 2013). Carling and colleagues (2014, 7) suggested that in order to understand the complexities associated with the social context of using performance analysis in sport, scholars needed "to expand their disciplinary gaze to include sociological and pedagogical theorizing." In response to this call, several surveillance scholars have turned to poststructural theory to attempt to understand the social realities of the presence of performance analysis techniques in the coaching context (Manley, Palmer, and Roderick 2012; Taylor et al., forthcoming; Williams and Manley 2014).

To summarize, what was once a basic tool for monitoring the movement outcomes of performers (Church and Hughes 1987) has since evolved into a vehicle for the provision of a range of benefits for the accentuation of athletic life. The data gathered from performance analysis are now used in numerous ways. These include tactical strategizing, performance preparation, feedback mechanisms, and the formation of training interventions, as well as scouting and talent identification purposes (Carling et al. 2014). Clearly, the role of performance analysis is an ever-evolving phenomenon that should now be articulated as an integral part of the coaching process (Carling, Williams, and Reilly 2005) and as a commonplace coaching practice with a "high degree of salience for coaching practitioners" (Nelson and Groom 2012, 688). Like Nelson and Groom, as a result of reviewing both the quantitative and qualitative approaches to performance analysis in sport coaching contexts, we suggest a real need for coaching practitioners to better understand the benefits and implications of the increased usage of PA techniques. This is because if left unquestioned, PA in sport has been identified as a powerful process with very real potential ramifications for both the coach and the athlete (Taylor et al., forthcoming; Williams and Manley 2014). In the next section we tentatively outline what we see as the important implications surrounding the use of PA, for both coach educators and working coaches alike.

Implications for Sport Coaching Practice and Athlete Learning

To understand PA and its role in the coaching process it is essential to go beyond discussing the quality, validity, or applicability of data generated through the various mechanisms introduced previously. Groom, Cushion, and Nelson (2011) have quite correctly identified that one must place the use of these PA techniques within the ever-changing, messy, and complex context of sport coaching (Potrac, Jones, and Armour 2002). Therefore, what *is* important to consider are the consequences of the regular use of these PA technologies and how they relate to coaching pedagogy, behavior, and athlete learning.

The positives associated with using PA techniques to assist coaches in their quest for improving athletic performance have been widely established, as discussed previously. It is true that, if applied appropriately, the athletic body can be produced with greater efficiency and control with the assistance of PA. However, the coach or coach educator must proceed with caution. As Potrac and colleagues (2000) have noted, very little is known about how athletes experience, understand, and subsequently respond to their coaches' application of PA. Consequently, in regard to coaching effectiveness it is important to discuss (a) how to use these technologies in an appropriate manner in order to facilitate ethical athlete learning, and (b) that coaches be aware of the potentially problematic outcomes of the improper or unthinking adoption of these powerful coaching technologies.

We suggest that it is important that coaches take these concerns seriously because the misappropriation of PA technologies has been seen to have an adverse effect, not only on the performing athlete (Taylor et al., forthcoming), but also on the philosophy and practice of the working coach (Williams and Manley 2014). The negative effects on the athlete can stem from PA being used to sustain the overtly disciplinary coaching context of many elite sports, where deviation from expected norms leads to athlete punishment and isolation (Cushion and Jones 2006). With regard to the coach, Williams and Manley (2014) have identified how the coach's role has been changed by an overreliance on PA data, enforcing a reduction in the expert coach's engagement with the coaching process. This has contributed to the reduction of coaching to the constant analysis of data, rather than the provision of social and contextual guidance surrounding the specific sport concerned. As Carter (2006) warned, the modern trend is the biggest threat to the traditional notions of what it is to be a coach. With this in mind, we make a couple of tentative suggestions for the coach educator here. In order to reduce the potentially negative outcomes associated with overly stringent analysis of performance and to maximize the performance gains while safeguarding the athlete, coaches need to be counseled to engage in a couple of key behaviors. First, coaches must be educated to constantly review the context and the extent to which they apply monitoring techniques—does an athlete's every movement need to be recorded and analyzed? Optimal control over an athlete's performance may not automatically lead to better outcomes. Second, coaches must recognize the importance of a clear and consistent dialogue with any athlete who is under surveillance using PA technology. All those responsible for recording athlete movement must develop the skills necessary to liaise with the people whose performances they are so closely recording and dissecting.

To summarize, as an increasingly important tenet of coach behavior, the application of PA techniques is one area where a movement toward a more subjective, constructivist approach has facilitated a greater understanding of how to elevate the role of the working coach. And while video analysis prevails in performance assessment across sport, it might be worth making the point that evaluation should never become entirely technology driven. Relationship-building, professional and personal communication, and other things not seen on the camera are at least as important as any action a recording may capture. Through an appreciation that athletes need to be involved in their own learning practice (Nelson, Potrac, and Groom 2014), attitudes toward PA are beginning to broaden, leading to the adoption of a more rounded approach to this modern coaching tool (Nelson and Groom 2012). We are encouraged by this emerging trend, as we believe it enables the coach to avoid the aforementioned potential pitfalls that can and do arise from the improper application of the now ubiquitous PA tools found in the contexts of elite sport.

Summary

The purpose of this chapter was to provide an overview of research conducted in the disciplines of coach behavior and performance analysis. We have identified how research in both disciplines has shifted from a behavioristic/reductionist worldview toward a social constructivist focus. This shift has coincided with evolving thinking about coaching, from being linear and relatively simple to being considered complex and problematic. This emergence has required the employment of new or alternative methods of research in these disciplines. These new methods have revealed new knowledge with the aim of making coaches' practice more effective and, in turn, improving player outcomes. However, we strongly suggest exercising caution concerning what we actually know leads to effective coaching.

The breadth and depth of coach behavior research lacks consistency, with conclusions being drawn based on incomplete pictures of coaching practice. Consequently, coach behavior research can be summarized as fragmented, and providing only a snapshot of what it is coaches actually do. Similarly, PA research that reflects the realities of coaching practice is underdeveloped and currently insufficient to enable claims to be made as to how coaches should use this in their practice. Nonetheless, we believe research is moving in a direction that is developing the field's understandings of these disciplines. As a result of more recent findings and thinking about coaching, we have been able to offer some recommendations for practicing coaches and coaching researchers as a means to affect as well as advance the theory and practice of coaching.

---

[1] Generic performance analysis software that can be used to code coach behavior and link this to video are Dartfish, SportsCode, etc. Generic iPad applications such as behavior snap can also be used for coding. A specific iPad application that is available for sport coach behavior is Axis Coaching from www.axiscoachingtechnology.com.

APPENDIX A

The Role of the National Standards for Sport Coaches in Coach Learning

Coaching is an ever-evolving profession informed by the latest scientific research and best practices of effective coaches. Therefore, for a coach to achieve and maintain effectiveness and achieve sustainability requires staying up to date with the profession. When defining coaching effectiveness, Côtè and Gilbert (2009, 319) further document the importance of coach knowledge by noting that to be an effective coach requires "the consistent application of integrated professional, interpersonal, and intrapersonal knowledge." More recently, Rynne and Mallett (2014, 12) make the case that coaches, particularly high-performance coaches, must learn in order to achieve sustainability, which they view as being able to develop and maintain the "environments and behaviours that make efficient and ethical use of resources." Specifically, they contend, "Without engaging in continued and quality learning practices, coaches will condemn themselves to a future where they repeat past mistakes. They also risk opting for uninformed, short-term gains that jeopardize their own and their athletes' futures" (Rynne and Mallett 2014, 15). Thus, coaches face a call to action, that is, engage in the pursuit of lifelong learning. However, the questions facing coaches are

1. What do I need to learn to help myself and my athletes develop?
2. How do I go about learning it?

The purpose of this article is to discuss how the National Standards for Sport Coaches can contribute to answering these questions and support the coach learning process.

Appendix A reprinted by permission of the United States Olympic Committee from *Olympic Coach* 29, no. 2 (December 2018), accessed January 10, 2019, https://www.teamusa.org/-/media/TeamUSA/CoachingEd/Fall2018.pdf.

The National Standards for Sport Coaches

Recognizing the need to help sport coaches adequately prepare to work with athletes, the National Association for Sport and Physical Education (NASPE), a former association within the American Alliance for Health, Physical Education, Recreation and Dance (now SHAPE America) developed a task force to identify the knowledge and skills sport coaches should possess to provide a quality sport experience for amateur athletes. The result of this work was the creation of the National Standards for Sport Coaches (NSSC). While the NSSC originated in 1995, the last revision was completed in 2006. The current NSSC consists of 40 standards organized around eight domains (NASPE 2006; https://www.shapeamerica.org/standards/coaching). These domains include philosophy and ethics, safety and injury prevention, physical conditioning, growth and development, teaching and communication, sport skills and tactics, organization and administration, and evaluation.

In 2017, a new task force, representing coaches, coach educators, coach developers, sport administrators and national organizations involved in coaching[1], began a third revision of the standards to be released early next year. The task force sought to update standards to correspond to the latest scientific research and practical work in coaching as well as more closely align with the International Sport Coaching Framework (ISCF; ICCE, ASOIF, and Leeds Metropolitan University 2013). The intent of the revised NSSC is to document the core responsibilities coaches should possess along with supporting competences (i.e., standards) which encourage the application of knowledge and skills to support a quality amateur sport experience for athletes (SHAPE America, forthcoming).

The revised NSSC are organized into seven core responsibilities (see table 1). Like the primary coaching functions in the ISCF, the responsibilities represent core coaching functions that require the integration of professional, interpersonal and intrapersonal knowledge. Each core responsibility is associated with a set of standards that represent task-related competences coaches can develop. The standards identify the knowledge and skills coaches can acquire and apply to further enhance their coaching practice. For example, one core responsibility is to build relationships (see table 1). There are three underlying standards that correspond to this responsibility: a) acquire and utilize interpersonal and communication skills, b) develop competencies to work with diverse individuals, and c) demonstrate professionalism and leadership (SHAPE America, in preparation). As coaches develop these task-related competences, their ability to build relationships within their sport program should improve. While the seven core responsibilities reflect the fundamental actions administrators, athletes and the public can expect of sport coaches within their sport context, differences in depth and breadth of knowledge and skills can be expected based on the level of coach expertise (e.g., volunteer

TABLE 1: Core Responsibilities of the Third Revision of the National Standards for Sport Coaches

Core Responsibility	Brief Summary of Knowledge and Skills
Set Vision, Goals, and Standards for Sport Program	Sport coaches establish a clearly defined coaching philosophy and vision for their program. They develop, implement, and manage the goals for the program, in collaboration with sport program directors and aligned with the American Development Model. (5 Standards)
Engage in and Support Ethical Practices	Sport coaches understand the importance of ethical practices, engage in ethical behavior, abide by codes of conduct affiliated with their sport and coaching context, develop ethical decision-making tools, and model and teach ethical behavior in their sport program. (3 Standards)
Build Relationships	Sport coaches develop competencies (e.g., interpersonal, communication, and socio-cultural) to effectively communicate, collaborate, educate, and support all stakeholders associated with the sport program. They also demonstrate professionalism and leadership. (3 Standards)
Develop a Safe Sport Environment	Sport coaches create an emotionally and physically safe sport environment by following the practices outlined by sport organizations, coaching science, and state and federal laws. (9 Standards)
Create a Positive and Inclusive Sport Environment	Sport coaches develop practices to maximize positive outcomes for their athletes by building season plans that promote physical, psychological, and social benefits for their athletes and encourage participation in sport. Sport coaches implement strategies to promote participation of all athletes. (3 Standards)
Conduct Practices and Prepare for Competition	Sport coaches draw upon current coaching science, sport-specific knowledge, and best practices to conduct quality sport practices, prepare athletes for competition, and effectively manage contests. This practice is framed around how coaches plan, teach, assess, and adapt in practice and competition settings. (14 Standards)
Strive for Continuous Improvement	Sport coaches continually improve through self-reflection, mentorship, professional development, evaluation, and self-care. (5 Standards)

Reprinted by permission of the United States Olympic Committee from *Olympic Coach* 29, no. 2 (December 2018), accessed January 10, 2019, https://www.teamusa.org/-/media/TeamUSA/CoachingEd/Fall2018.pdf.

beginning coach versus high school coach) and the sport-coaching context (e.g., youth sport versus intercollegiate sport).

Connecting the National Standards to Coach Learning

To understand how the NSSC might assist with coach learning, it is important to recognize how coaches learn. One model for understanding how coaches learn was documented by Werthner and Trudel (2006). While Werthner and Trudel suggest that coach learning is unique for each coach, there are three specific learning situations, i.e., mediated, unmediated, and internal. These learning situations work best when integrated with and informed by coaches' own experiences in the field. Understanding of the NSSC, may inform how coaches approach each of these learning situations.

One learning situation is mediated learning which involves learning through formal experiences like coaching workshops, coaching conferences and coach education programs. Coaches, informed by the NSSC, can seek out mediated opportunities that correspond to the NSSC. In fact, the NSSC might be a good starting point for coaches entering the profession. As Jennifer King, collegiate basketball coach, states

> My best advice for young coaches is to be the best you can be which means investing in your craft through books, workshops and any other avenue you can use to gain experiences and knowledge that can make you a better person and coach. (Female Coaching Network, n.d.)

As the NSSC identify the knowledge and skills coaches can acquire to develop their coaching practice, new coaches can look for coaching education programs, workshops and books that will help them to develop the task-related competences associated with the NSSC. However, experienced coaches can also benefit from using the NSSC to identifying mediated learning experiences. For example, if more experienced coaches are interested in conducting better practices to enhance athlete performance they can turn to the standards corresponding to this core responsibility (i.e., conduct practices and prepare for competition). They could then seek out workshop or conference opportunities related to these standards (e.g., how to design appropriate progressions for improving sport-specific physiological systems; how to use effective teaching principles in practice to improve technique; how to use motivational techniques in practice; how to implement strategies to evaluate athlete training and performance; or learning rules of thumb for adjusting training plans based on athlete needs).

Another learning situation is unmediated learning experiences that are sought out by coaches to improve coach practice. Example situations may include searching the internet or print material for answers and/or having discussions with coaches or athletes. While these learning situations are often sought out by coaches because of a difficult coach situation prompting the need for more information, they could still be informed by the NSSC. As Werthner and Trudel (2006) note,

> the potential of these unmediated learning situations is limited by a number of significant aspects—the level of coaches' ability to learn by themselves, their openness and eagerness to create new learning opportunities, and the fact that coaches cannot look for information on a topic if they do not know it exists. (p. 204)

Their last point may be a place where the NSSC can offer assistance to coaches. As the standards are based on the latest research and coaching practice, it may help coaches identify the topic they need to pursue to improve their coaching. For example, if an athlete becomes injured a coach may reflect upon whether safe training practices were utilized. However, reviewing the core responsibility associated with creating a safe sport environment (see Table 1) the coach may realize it is important to reflect upon mitigating conditions that predispose this particular athlete to injury or how nutritional practices may have contributed to the injury. The NSSC may also assist in unmediated learning situations involving discussions between coaches (or communities of practice). That is, the NSSC could provide topics of discussion between coaches which can help them learn from one another.

A final learning situation is internal learning which entails the coach thinking about how to integrate their coaching experiences with other learning situations to inform practice and/or reflecting upon their practices to seek out ways to solve coaching problems. In fact, one of the core responsibilities in the NSSC is continuous self-improvement which encourages coaches to regularly engage in internal learning (e.g., practicing self-reflection, seeking opportunities to learn to integrate in practice) to support their development as a coach. Coaches might also use the NSSC to reflect upon their own development. For example, coaches can ask themselves how well are they achieving each of the seven core responsibilities and identify areas in need of further reflection and improvement.

Overall, the NSSC can help in each area of coach learning. While the standards only represent one piece of the coach learning process, they can be of assistance to coaches at any stage of their learning not just formal coach education courses.

Conclusion

The National Standards for Sport Coaches (NSSC) were created to identify the core responsibilities and corresponding knowledge and skills to assist coaches in providing quality sport experiences for their athletes. While these standards will be used by many coach educators and coach developers to drive coach education programming, it is clear the NSSC can also be used to assist coaches in identify meaningful learning experiences that meet them where they are in their learning process. Coaches are encouraged to seek out the standards as one way to improve their coach effectiveness.

Author's Note

Task force members include Lori Gano-Overway (chair), Bob Benham, Christine Bolger, Andy Driska, Melissa Long, Anthony Moreno, Dan Schuster, Melissa Thompson, Pete Van Mullem, Michelle Carter (SHAPE America Liaison), and Wendy Fagan (advisory)

APPENDIX B

Summary of National Standards for Sport Coaches

Founded in 1885, the Society of Health and Physical Educators—SHAPE America—is the nation's largest membership organization for health and physical education professionals. In an effort to promote and advance the professional practice of physical educators, SHAPE provides programs and resources to support the physical educators from preschool through university graduate programs.

In recognition of the considerable overlap in Physical Education and Sport Coaching, and as a means to support the development of sport coaches throughout the United States, SHAPE America created a task force to develop the first version of the National Standards for Sport Coaches in 1995, which were slightly revised in 2005. These standards were organized by primary domain and associated standards. In 2017, SHAPE organized a task force to revise the standards again. This task force was comprised of members of a variety of sport organizations and higher education institutions. The task force created an extensive list of the roles and responsibilities of sport coaches, organized those into 'primary roles', compiled research evidence to support the underlying discipline or knowledge-base for the role, and constructed standards that attempt to encompass each responsibility. The new version of the standards outline the requisite knowledge and skills sport coaches should possess in order to provide quality, safe athletic programing for individuals at all ages and ability levels. Within each of the seven primary functions of a sport coach, individual standards are identified (42 in total). Drafts of the revised standards were distributed widely to researchers and practitioners for feedback and edits on at least three occasions prior to the adoption of the final version.

For more information on the National Standards for Sport Coaches, visit: https://www.shapeamerica.org/standards/coaching/

APPENDIX C

Bachelor Degree Coaching Education Program Guidelines

The International Council for Coaching Excellence is a not-for-profit organization that seeks to lead and develop sport internationally by enhancing the quality of sport coaching at every level. With this goal in mind, the ICCE has developed an International Sport Coaching Framework (ISCF) and the International Coach Developer Framework (ICDF), which seek to provide a global consensus and understanding of the role of the coach as well as quality coach education and development. Further, the ICCE has released a set of standards for higher education (described below).

The ICCE recognizes that the mechanisms of coaching practice, education, and sport itself vary a great deal throughout the world. As such, the frameworks and standards should be viewed as a complementary piece to the local higher education institutions, sport governing bodies, and national and international sport federations. When taken as a suggestion for best practices, the frameworks and standards can serve as a guideline for the development and implementation of sport coaching education that will fit with the national and local context of the implementing organization.

Established in October of 2016, the ICCE Standards for Higher Education provide guidelines for the development and implementation of Sport Coaching Bachelor Degrees around the world. Through several iterations and consultation with expert members from around the globe, the International Sport Coaching Degree Standards Group released the first version of these standards. Considering national and local context, these recommendations will assist coach developers within university systems in advancing coach education. These standards were drafted with current best practices in mind; however, as research and sport continues to evolve, the needs of coach developers will continue to shift. Therefore, experts will continue to meet every four years beginning in 2020 after the conclusion of the Tokyo Olympic Games to review and update the standards.

For more information about the ICCE, please visit www.icce.ws.

References

Chapter 1

American Alliance for Health, Physical Education, Recreation and Dance. 2013. *Recommended Requisites for Sport Coaches* [Position statement]. Reston, VA: Author.

Aspen Institute. 2015. *Sport for All: Play for Life: A Playbook to Get Every Kid in the Game.* Washington, DC: Author.

Bowes, I., and R.L. Jones. 2006. "Working at the Edge of Chaos: Understanding Coaching as a Complex, Interpersonal System." *Sport Psychologist* 20 (2): 235.

Brenner, J.S. 2007. "Overuse Injuries, Overtraining, and Burnout in Child and Adolescent Athletes." *Pediatrics* 119 (6): 1242-45.

Caine, D., J. DiFiori, and N. Maffulli. 2006. "Physical Injuries in Children's and Youth Sports: Reasons for Concern?" *British Journal of Sports Medicine* 40 (9): 749-60.

Conroy, David E., and J. Douglas Coatsworth. 2006. "Coach Training as a Strategy for Promoting Youth Social Development." *The Sport Psychologist* 20 (2): 128-44.

Côté, J., and W. Gilbert. 2009. "An Integrative Definition of Coaching Effectiveness and Expertise." *International Journal of Sports Science & Coaching* 4 (3): 307-23.

Cushion, C. 2007. "Modelling the Complexity of the Coaching Process." *International Journal of Sports Science & Coaching* 2 (4): 395-401.

Davis, P. 2003. "Why Coaches Education?" *Olympic Coach* 15 (4): 16-17.

Dewar, A.M., and H.A. Lawson. 1984. "The Subjective Warrant and Recruitment into Physical Education." *Quest* 36 (1): 15-25.

Dieffenbach, K.D., and V. Wayda. 2010. "A Critical Review of American Academic Coaching Education Programs." *Journal of Coaching Education* 3 (2): 21-39.

DiFiori, J.P., H.J. Benjamin, J.S. Brenner, A. Gregory, N. Jayanthi, G.L. Landry, and A. Luke. 2014. "Overuse Injuries and Burnout in Youth Sports: A Position Statement from the American Medical Society for Sports Medicine." *British Journal of Sports Medicine* 48 (4): 287-88.

EuropeActive. 2016. *EuropeActive Standards.* Accessed July 17, 2017. www.ehfa-standards.eu/es-home.

Fasting, K. 2015. "Dangerous Liaisons: Harassment and Abuse in Coaching." In *Routledge Handbook of Sports Coaching*, edited by P. Potrac and W. Gilbert, 333-44. London, UK: Routledge.

Ferrar, P., L. Hosea, M. Henson, N. Dubina, G. Krueger, J. Staff, and W. Gilbert. 2018. "Building High Performance Coach-Athlete Relationships: The USOC's National Team Coach Leadership Education Program (NTCLEP)." *International Sport Coaching Journal* 5 (1): 60-70.

Fraser-Thomas, J.L., J. Côté, and J. Deakin. 2005. "Youth Sport Programs: An Avenue to Foster Positive Youth Development." *Physical Education & Sport Pedagogy* 10 (1): 19-40.

Guttmann, A. 2007. *Sports: The First Five Millennia.* Amherst, MA: University of Massachusetts Press.

Hedstrom, R., and D. Gould. 2004. *Research in Youth Sports: Critical Issues Status.* East Lansing: MI: Michigan State University.

Hill, M. 2007. "Achievement and Athletics: Issues and Concerns for State Boards of Education." *The State Education Standard* 8 (1): 22-31.

ICCE. 2013. *International Sport Coaching Framework*. Champaign, IL: Human Kinetics.

———. 2015. *International Sport Coach Developer Framework*. Leeds, UK: ICCE.

———. 2016. *ICCE Standards for Higher Education: Sport Coaching Bachelor Degree*. Leeds, UK: ICCE.

Jones, R. 2007. "Coaching Redefined: An Everyday Pedagogical Endeavour." *Sport, Education and Society* 12 (2): 159-73.

Kirby, S.L., L. Greaves, and O. Hankivsky. 2000. *The Dome of Silence: Sexual Harassment and Abuse in Sport*. Halifax, UK: Fernwood.

Klomhaus, S. 2015. "Are Premier League Teams Firing Managers Too Fast?" *The 18*. November 7. http://the18.com/news/are-premier-league-teams-firing-managers-too-fast.

Kuhn, G.D. 2008. *High-Impact Educational Practices: What They Are, Who Has Access to Them, and Why They Matter*. Washington, DC: Association of American Colleges and Universities.

Lara-Bercial, S., A. Abraham, C. Colmaire, K. Dieffenbach, O. Mokglate, S. Rynne. A. Jiménez, J. Bales, J, Curado, M. Ito, and L. Nordmann. 2016. "The International Sport Coaching Bachelor Degree Standards of the International Council for Coaching Excellence." *International Sport Coaching Journal* 3 (3): 344-8.

Lyle, J. 2005. *Sports Coaching Concepts: A Framework for Coaches' Behaviour*. London, UK: Routledge.

Mechlikoff, R. 2013. *A History and Philosophy of Sport and Physical Education: From Ancient Civilization to the Modern World*. 6th ed. New York, NY: McGraw-Hill.

Merriam-Webster. n.d. *Athlete*. Accessed August 1, 2016. www.merriam-webster.com/dictionary/athlete.

———. n.d. *Kinesiology*. Accessed August 1, 2016. www.merriam-webster.com/dictionary/kinesiology.

———. n.d. *Profession*. Accessed August 1, 2016. www.merriam-webster.com/dictionary/profession.

National Association of Sport and Physical Education. 2006. *National Standards for Sport Coaches*. 2nd ed. Washington, DC: AAHPERD.

Nelson, L.J., and C.J. Cushion. 2006. "Reflection in Coach Education: The Case of the National Governing Body Coaching Certificate." *The Sport Psychologist* 20: 174-83.

Nohria, N., and R. Khurana. 2010. *Handbook of Leadership Theory and Practice*. Cambridge, MA: Harvard Business Review.

Northouse, P. G. 2018. *Leadership: Theory and Practice*. Thousand Oaks, CA: Sage Publications.

Poliquin, B. 2014. "Do College Football's Head Coaches Get Fired Too Quickly and Too Easily? (Chat with Bud Poliquin)." *Syarcuse.com*, December 2. www.syracuse.com/poliquin/index.ssf/2014/12/do_college_footballs_head_coaches_get_fired_too_quickly_and_too_easily_chat_with.html.

Portch, J. 2018. "Can Former Athletes Be Taught How To Coach?" Accessed August 5, 2018. https://leadersinsport.com/performance/can-former-athletes-taught-coach.

Potrac, P., C. Brewer, R. Jones, K. Armour, and J. Hoff. 2000. "Toward an Holistic Understanding of the Coaching Process." *Quest* 52 (2): 186-99.

Potrac, P., W. Gilbert, and J. Dennison, eds. 2015. *Routledge Handbook of Sports Coaching*. London, UK: Routledge.

Reimer, A. 2016. "NFL Teams Are Firing Their Head Coaches Too Quickly." *SB Nation*, January 4. www.sbnation.com/nfl/2016/1/4/10691144/nfl-black-monday-coach-firing-rumors.

Respect in Sport. 2008. Types of Power Leaders Have Over Participants. Canada. http://respectgroupinc.com/respect-in-sport/.

Schempp, P., B. McCullick, and I. Mason. 2014. "The Development of Expert Coaching." In *The Sports Coach as Educator: Reconceptualising Sports Coaching,* edited by RL. Jones, 7-12. London, UK: Routledge.

Schoenstedt, L., B. Vickers, and D. Carr. 2016. "Perceptions of Coaching Education in 17 Physical Education Curriculums." *International Journal of Humanities and Social Science* 6 (2): 1-8.

Sheehy, T., K. Dieffenbach, and P. Reed. 2018. "Exploration of Coaching Research in the Journal of Applied Sport Psychology: A Review from 1989-2017." *Journal of Applied Sport Psychology*: 1-14.

Smith, R.E., F.L. Smoll, and S.P. Cumming. 2007. "Effects of a Motivational Climate Intervention for Coaches on Young Athletes' Sport Performance Anxiety." *Journal of Sport and Exercise Psychology* 29 (1): 39.

Smoll, F.L., and R.E. Smith. 2002. "Coaching Behavior Research and Intervention in Youth Sports." *Children and Youth in Sport: A Biopsychosocial Perspective* 2: 211-34.

Statistica. 2016. *Global Sports Market: Total Revenue from 2006-2015.* Accessed August 5, 2017. www.statista.com/statistics/194122/sporting-event-gate-revenue-worldwide-by-region-since-2004.

Stoddart, B. 2013. *Sport, Culture, and History.* London, UK: Routledge.

USA Volleyball. n.d. "CAP: Coaching Acceleration Program." Accessed August 5, 2017. www.teamusa.org/USA-Volleyball/Education/Coaching-Education-Programs/Indoor-Courses/CAP-I.

Strauss, R. 2016. "Assistant Coaches Join the Millionaire's Club." *New York Times,* February 12. www.nytimes.com/2016/02/14/your-money/assistant-coaches-join-the-millionaires-club.html?_r=0.

Young, D.S., and R.E. Baker. 2004. "Linking Classroom Theory to Professional Practice: The Internship as a Practical Learning Experience Worthy of Academic Credit." *Journal of Physical Education, Recreation & Dance* 75 (1): 22-24.

Chapter 2

Balaguer, I., J.L. Duda, and M. Crespo. 1999. "Motivational Climate and Goal Orientations as Predictors of Perceptions of Improvement, Satisfaction and Coach Ratings Among Tennis Players." *Scandinavian Journal of Medicine & Science in Sports* 9 (6): 381-8.

Bandura, A. 1997. *Self-Efficacy: The Exercise of Control.* New York: W. H. Freeman.

Barber, B. 1963. "Some Problems in the Sociology of Professions." *Daedalus* 92 (4): 669-88.

Bebeau, M.J. 1994a. "Can Ethics Be Taught? A Look at the Evidence: Revisited." *The New York State Dental Journal* 60: 51-7.

———. 1994b. "Influencing the Moral Dimension in Dental Practice." In *Moral Development in the Professions: Psychology and Applied Ethics,* edited by J. Rest and D. Narvaez, 121-46. Hillsdale, NJ: Lawrence Erlbaum Associates Inc.

Beller, J.M., and S.K. Stoll. 1992. "A Moral Reasoning Intervention Program for Division I Athletes." *Academic Athletic Journal* 5: 43-57.

———. 1995. "Moral Reasoning of High School Student Athletes and General Students: An Empirical Study versus Personal Testimony." *Pediatric Exercise Science* 7 (4): 352-63.

Bredemeier, B.J., and D.L. Shields. 1984. "Divergence in Children's Moral Reasoning about Sport and Everyday Life." *Sociology of Sport Journal* 1: 348-57.

———. 1986. "Game Reasoning and Interactional Morality." *The Journal of Genetic Psychology: Research and Theory on Human Development* 147: 257-75.

———. 1994. "Applied Ethics and Moral Reasoning in Sport." *Moral Development in the Professions: Psychology and Applied Ethics*: 173-87.

Bredemeier, B.J., M.R. Weiss, D.L. Shields, and B.A.B. Cooper 1987. "The Relationship Between Children's Legitimacy Judgements and Their Moral Reasoning, Aggression Tendencies, and Sport Involvement." *Sociology of Sport Journal* 4: 48-60.

Bredemeier, B.J., M.R. Weiss, D.L. Shields, and R.M. Shewchuk 1986. "Promoting Moral Growth in a Summer Sport Camp: The Implementation of Theoretically Grounded Instructional Strategies." *Journal of Moral Education* 15: 212-20.

Caswell, S.V., and T.E. Gould. 2008. "Individual Moral Philosophies and Ethical Decision Making of Undergraduate Athletic Training Students and Educators." *Journal of Athletic Training* 43 (2): 205-14.

Côté, J., and W. Gilbert. 2009. "An Integrative Definition of Coaching Effectiveness." *International Journal of Sports Science & Coaching* 4: 307-23.

Council for the Advancement of Standards in Higher Education. 2015. *Statement of Shared Ethical Principles*. Accessed December 30, 2015. www.cas.edu/ethics.

Cumming, S.P., F.L. Smoll, R.E. Smith, and J.R. Grossbard. 2007. "Is Winning Everything? The Relative Contributions of Motivational Climate and Won-Lost Percentage in Youth Sports." *Journal of Applied Sport Psychology* 19: 322-37.

Cushion, C.J., K.M. Armour, and R.L. Jones. 2003. "Coach Education and Continuing Professional Development: Experience and Learning to Coach. *Quest* 55: 215-30.

Duckett, L.J., and M.B. Ryden. 1994. "Education for Ethical Nursing Practice." In *Moral Development in the Professions: Psychology and Applied Ethics,* edited by JR. Rest and D. Narvaez, 51-70. Hillsdale, NJ: Lawrence Erlbaum Associates.

Duda, J.L. 1989. "Relationship Between Task and Ego Orientation and the Perceived Purpose of Sport Among High School Athletes." *Journal of Sport and Exercise Psychology* 11: 318-35.

———, and I. Balaguer. 2007. "Coach-Created Motivational Climate." In *Social Psychology in Sport,* edited by S. Jowett and D. Lavallee, 117-30. Champaign, IL: Human Kinetics.

Duda, J.L., L.K. Olson, and T.J. Templin. 1991. "The Relationship of Task and Ego Orientation to Sportsmanship Attitudes and the Perceived Legitimacy of Injurious Acts." *Research Quarterly for Exercise and Sport* 62 (1): 79-87.

Dunn, J.G.H., and J.C. Dunn. 1999. "Goal Orientations, Perceptions of Aggression, and Sportspersonship in Elite Male Youth Ice Hockey Players." *The Sport Psychologist* 13 (2): 183-200.

Federal Acquisition Regulation (FAR). 2015. *Contractor Code of Business Ethics*. Accessed December 30, 2015. www.acquisition.gov/?q=browse/far/3/10&searchTerms=code%20 of%20ethics.

Forsyth, D.R. 1980. "A Taxonomy of Ethical Ideologies." *Journal of Personality and Social Psychology* 39 (1): 175.

———, and R.E. Berger. 1982. "The Effects of Ethical Ideology on Moral Behavior." *The Journal of Social Psychology* 117: 53-6.

Forsyth, D.R., Nye, J.L., and K. Kelley. 1988. "Idealism, Relativism, and the Ethic of Caring." *Journal of Psychology* 122 (3): 243-49.

Forsyth, D.R., and W.R. Pope. 1984. "Ethical Ideology and Judgements of Social Psychological Research: Multidimensional Analysis." *Journal of Personality and Social Psychology* 46: 1365-75.

Fry, M.D., and L.A. Gano-Overway. 2010. "Exploring the Contribution of the Caring Climate to the Youth Sport Experience." *Journal of Applied Sport Psychology* 22: 294-305.

International Council for Coaching Excellence (ICCE). 2016. "Serial Winners: Why Some Coaches Get to the Top . . . and Stay There." Accessed July 7, 2016. www.icce.ws/news-and-newsletters/news/serial-winners-why-some-coaches-get-to-the-top-and-stay-there.html.

Jones, R.L., K.M. Armour, and P. Potrac. 2003. "Constructing Expert Knowledge: A Case Study of a Top-Level Professional Soccer Coach." *Sport, Education, and Society* 8: 213-29.

Kavussanu, M., and G.C. Roberts. 2001. "Moral Functioning in Sport: An Achievement Goal Perspective." *Journal of Sport and Exercise Psychology* 23 (1): 37-54.

Kavussanu, M., and N. Ntoumanis. 2003. "Participation in Sport and Moral Functioning: Does Ego Orientation Mediate Their Relationship?" *Journal of Sport and Exercise Psychology* 25: 501-18.

Kohlberg, L. 1973. "The Claim to Moral Adequacy of a Highest Stage of Moral Judgement." The *Journal of Philosophy* 70: 630-46.

———. 1976. "Moral Stages and Moralization: The Cognitive-Developmental Approach." In *Moral Development and Behavior: Theory, Research, and Social Issues*, edited by T. Lickona, 31-53. New York, NY: Holt, Rinehart, & Winston.

Krebs, D.L., and K. Denton. 2005. "Toward a More Pragmatic Approach to Morality: A Critical Evaluation of Kohlberg's Model." *Psychological Review* 112 (3): 629.

Krichbaum, K., M. Rowan, L. Duckett, M. Ryden, and K. Savik. 1994. "The Clinical Evaluation Tool: A Measure of the Quality of Clinical Performance of Baccalaureate Nursing Students." *The Journal of Nursing Education* 33: 395-404.

Mackenzie, B. 2001. *Code of Ethics and Conduct for Sports Coaches*. Accessed September 15, 2015. www.brianmac.co.uk/ethics.htm.

McHoskey, J.W. 1996. "Authoritarianism and Ethical Ideology." *The Journal of Social Psychology* 136 (6): 709-17.

National Alliance for Youth Sports (NAYS). 2015. *Code of Ethics*. www.nays.org/coaches/training/code-of-ethics.

National Association for Healthcare Quality (NAHQ). 2015. *Code of Ethics and Standards of Practice*. Accessed December 30, 2015. www.nahq.org/uploads/files/about/codestandards.pdf.

Nicholls, J.T. 1989. *The Competitive Ethos and Democratic Education*. Cambridge, MA: Harvard University Press.

Ntoumanis, N., and S.J.H. Biddle. 1999. "A Review of Motivational Climate in Physical Activity." *Journal of Sport Sciences* 17: 643-55.

Pensgaard, A.M., and G.C. Roberts. 2002. "Elite Athletes' Experiences of the Motivational Climate: The Coach Matters." *Scandinavian Journal of Medicine & Science in Sports* 12: 54-9.

Piaget, J. 1965 [1932]. *The Moral Judgement of the Child*. London, UK: Routledge & Kegan Paul.

Rest, J.R. 1983. "Morality." *Handbook of Child Psychology* 3: 556-629.

———, and D.M. Narvaez. 1994. *Moral Development in the Professions*. Hillsdale, NJ: Lawrence Erlbaum Associates.

———, S.J. Thoma, and M.J. Bebeau. 1999. *Postconventional Moral Thinking: A Neo-Kohlbergian Approach*. New York, NY: Psychology Press.

Rokeach, M. 1988. *Rokeach Value Survey*. Palo Alto, CA: Consulting Psychologists Press.

Romance, T.J., M.R. Weiss, and J. Bockoven. 1986. "A Program to Promote Moral Development Through Elementary Physical Education." *Journal of Teaching Physical Education* 5: 126-36.

Rudd, A., and S. Stoll. 2004. "Measuring Student's Characteristics in Secondary Education: The Development of the Principled Thinking Inventory." *Journal of Research in Character Education* 2 (2): 151.

Saury, J., and M. Durand, 1998. "Practical Knowledge in Expert Coaches: On-Site Study of Coaching in Sailing." *Research Quarterly for Exercise and Sport* 69: 254-66.

Sheehan, T.J., S.D.R. Husted, D. Candee, C.D. Cook, and M. Bergen. 1980. "Moral Judgement as a Predictor of Clinical Performance." *Evaluation and the Health Professions* 3 (4): 393-404.

Shields, D.L.L., and B.J.L. Bredemeier. 1995 *Character Development and Physical Activity.* Champaign, IL: Human Kinetics.

Simons, T. 2002. "Behavioral Integrity: The Perceived Alignment Between Managers' Words and Deeds as a Research Focus." *Organizational Science* 13: 18-35.

Stringer, D.M., and P.A. Cassiday. 2003. *52 Activities for Exploring Values Differences.* Yarmouth, ME: Intercultural Press.

Thompson, M., and K. Dieffenbach. 2016. "Measuring Professional Ethics in Coaching: Development of the PISC-Q." *Ethics & Behavior* 26 (6): 507-23.

Tucker, L.W., and J.B. Parks. 2001. "Effects of Gender and Sport Type on Intercollegiate Athletes' Perceptions of the Legitimacy of Aggressive Behaviors in Sport." *Sociology of Sport Journal* 18 (4): 403-13.

United States Olympic Committee 2016. *Coaching Ethics Code.* Accessed June 8, 2016. www.teamusa.org/About-the-USOC/Athlete-Development/Coaching-Education/Code-of-Ethics.

Vargas-Tonsing, T.M. 2007. "Coaches' Preferences for Continuing Coaching Education." *International Journal of Sports Science & Coaching* 2 (1): 25-35.

White, S.A., J.L. Duda, and M.R. Keller. 1998. "The Relationship Between Goal Orientation and Perceived Purposes of Sport Among Youth Sport Participants." *Journal of Sport Behavior* 21: 474.

Chapter 3

Abraham, A., and D. Collins. 2011. "Taking the Next Step: Ways Forward for Coaching Science." *Quest* 63: 366-84.

———, and R. Martindale 2006. "The Coaching Schematic: Validation Through Expert Coach Consensus." *Journal of Sports Sciences* 24: 549-64.

Anshel, M.H. 2003. *Sport Psychology: From Theory to Practice.* 4th ed. San Francisco, CA: Benjamin Cummings.

Bailey, R., C. Hillman, S. Arent, and A. Petitpas. 2013. "Physical Activity: An Underestimated Investment in Human Capital?" *Journal of Physical Activity and Health* 10: 289-308.

Bancroft, J.H. and W.D. Pulvermacher. 1917. *Handbook of Athletic Games.* New York: Macmillan.

Black, S.J., and M.R. Weiss. 1992. "The Relationship Among Perceived Coaching Behaviors, Perceptions of Ability, and Motivation in Competitive Age-Group Swimmers." *Journal of Sport & Exercise Psychology* 14: 309-25.

Burton, D., and T.D. Raedeke. 2008. *Sport Psychology for Coaches.* Champaign, IL: Human Kinetics.

Burton, L., and J.W. Peachey. 2013. "The Call for Servant Leadership in Intercollegiate Athletics." *Quest* 65: 354-71.

Cassidy, T. 2010a. "Holism in Sports Coaching: Beyond Humanistic Psychology." *International Journal of Sports Science & Coaching* 5: 439-43.

———. 2010b. "Holism in Sports Coaching: Beyond Humanistic Psychology: A Response to Commentaries." *International Journal of Sports Science & Coaching* 5: 497-501.

Coakley, J. 2015. *Sports in Society: Issues and Controversies.* 11th ed. New York, NY: McGraw Hill.

Ehrmann, J. 2011. *InSideOut Coaching: How Sports Can Transform Lives.* New York:, NY Simon & Schuster.

Frey, M. 2007. "College Coaches' Experiences With Stress: 'Problem Solvers' Have Problems, Too." *Sport Psychologist* 21: 38-57.

Gearity, B.T., and M.A. Murray. 2011. "Athletes' Experiences of the Psychological Effects of Poor Coaching." *Psychology of Sport and Exercise* 12: 213-21.

Goodger, K., T. Gorely, D. Lavallee, and C. Harwood. 2007. "Burnout in Sport: A Systematic Review." *The Sport Psychologist* 21: 127-51.

Gould, D. 1984. "Psychosocial Development and Children's Sport." In *Motor Development during Childhood and Adolescence*, edited by Jerry R. Thomas, 212-36. Minneapolis, MN: Burgess Pub. Co.

———. 1987. "Your Role as a Youth Sports Coach." *Handbook for Youth Sport Coaches*, edited by V. Seefeldt, 17-32. Reston, VA: American Alliance for Health, Physical Education, Recreation, and Dance.

Hamel, T., and W. Gilbert. 2010. "Holism in Sports Coaching: Beyond Humanistic Psychology: A Commentary." *International Journal of Sports Science & Coaching* 5: 485-8.

Hodge, K., and C. Lonsdale. 2011. "Prosocial and Antisocial Behavior in Sport: The Role of Coaching Style, Autonomous vs. Controlled Motivation, and Moral Disengagement." *Journal of Sport & Exercise Psychology* 33: 527-47.

Hollembeak, J., and A.J. Amorose. 2005. "Perceived Coaching Behaviors and College Athletes' Intrinsic Motivation." *Journal of Applied Sport Psychology* 17: 20-36.

Huber, J.J., 2013. *Applying Educational Psychology in Coaching Athletes*. Champaign, IL: Human Kinetics.

Huffman, L.T. 2014. "Examining Perceived Life Stress Factors among Intercollegiate Athletes: A Holistic Perspective." PhD diss. University of Tennessee. http://trace.tennessee.edu/utk_graddiss/2699.

International Council for Coaching Excellence and Association of Summer Olympic International Federations. 2012. *International Sport Coaching Framework*. Champaign, IL: Human Kinetics.

Irwin, J., exec. prod. 2015. *Coaching Bad* [Television Series]. New York, NY: Viacom Media Networks.

Jones, R.L., C. Edwards, and I.A. Viotto Filho. 2014. "Activity Theory, Complexity and Sports Coaching: An Epistemology for a Discipline." *Sport, Education, and Society*: 1-17.

Kamphoff, C.S. 2010. "Holism in Sports Coaching: Beyond Humanistic Psychology: A Commentary." *International Journal of Sports Science & Coaching* 5: 481-83.

Kavussanu, M., and N. Ntoumanis. 2003. "Participating in Sport and Moral Functioning: Does Ego Orientation Mediate Their Relationship?" *Journal of Sport & Exercise Psychology* 25: 501-18.

Kelley, B.C., and D.L. Gill. 1993. "An Examination of Personal/Situational Variables, Stress Appraisal, and Burnout in Collegiate Teacher-Coaches." *Research Quarterly for Exercise and Sport* 64 (1): 94-102.

Kidman, L. 2010. "Holism in Sports Coaching: Beyond Humanistic Psychology: A Commentary." *International Journal of Sports Science & Coaching* 5: 473-5.

Kingston, K.M., and L. Hardy. 1997. "Effects of Different Types of Goals on Processes That Support Performance." *The Sport Psychologist* 11 (3): 277-93.

Kretchmar, R.S. 2010. "Holism in Sports Coaching: Beyond Humanistic Psychology: A Commentary." *International Journal of Sports Science & Coaching* 5: 445-47.

Lombardo, B. 2010. "Holism in Sports Coaching: Beyond Humanistic Psychology: A Commentary." *International Journal of Sports Science & Coaching* 5: 477-8.

———. 1987. *The Humanistic Coach: From Theory to Practice*. Springfield, IL: Thomas.

Lyle, J. 2010. "Holism in Sports Coaching: Beyond Humanistic Psychology: A Commentary." *International Journal of Sports Science & Coaching* 5: 449-52.

Mallett, C. 2005. "Understanding Motivation to Enhance the Quality of Coaching." *Sports Coach: An Online Magazine for Coaches* 28 (3): 16-18.

———, and S.B. Rynne. 2010. "Holism in Sports Coaching: Beyond Humanistic Psychology: A Commentary." *International Journal of Sports Science & Coaching* 5: 453-57.

Maranz, M., exec. prod. 2014. *Friday Night Tykes* [Television Series]. New York, NY: National Broadcast Company Universal.

Martens, R. 2012. *Successful Coaching.* 4th ed. Champaign, IL: Human Kinetics.

Marx, J. 2003. *Season of Life: A Football Star, a Boy, a Journey to Manhood.* New York, NY: Simon & Schuster.

McGladrey, B.W., M.A. Murray, and J.C. Hannon. 2010. "Developing and Practicing an Athlete-Centered Coaching Philosophy." *Youthfirst: The Journal of Youth Sports* 5 (2): 4-8.

National Association for Sport and Physical Education. 2006. *Quality Coaches, Quality Sports: National Standards for Sport Coaches.* 2nd ed. Reston, VA: Author.

Nelson, L., P. Potrac, and P. Marshall. 2010. "Holism in Sports Coaching: Beyond Humanistic Psychology: A Commentary." *International Journal of Sports Science & Coaching* 5: 481-3.

Nichols, J.G. 1984. "Achievement Motivation: Conceptions of Ability, Subjective Experience, Task Choice, and Performance." *Psychological Review* 91: 328-46.

Olusoga, P., J. Butt, K. Hays, and I. Maynard. 2009. "Stress in Elite Sports Coaching: Identifying Stressors." *Journal of Applied Sport Psychology* 21: 442-59.

Pierce, B.E., and D. Burton. 1998. "Scoring the Perfect 10: Investigating the Impact of Goal-Setting Styles on a Goal-Setting Program for Female Gymnasts." *The Sport Psychologist* 12 (2): 156-68.

Richman, J.M. 1992. "Perceived Stress and Well-Being in Coaching: Impact of Hassles, Uplifts, Gender, and Sport." Unpublished doctoral dissertation. The Ohio State University.

Rieke, M., J. Hammermeister, and M. Chase. 2008. "Servant Leadership in Sport: A New Paradigm for Effective Coach Behavior." *International Journal of Sports Science & Coaching* 3: 227-39.

Roberts, Glyn C. 1984. "Achievement Motivation in Children's Sport." *Advances in Motivation and Achievement* 3: 251-81.

———. 1993. "Motivation in Sport: Understanding and Enhancing the Motivation and Achievement of Children." *Handbook of Research on Sport Psychology*: 405-20.

Rominger, R., and H. Friedman. 2013. "Transpersonal Sociology: Origins, Development, and Theory." *International Journal of Transpersonal Studies* 32 (2): 17-33.

Ryan, R.M., and E.L. Deci. 2000. "Self-Determination Theory and the Facilitation of Intrinsic Motivation, Social Development, and Well-Being." *American Psychologist* 55: 68-78.

Ryan, R. M., J. Kuhl, and E.L. Deci. 1997. "Nature and Autonomy: An Organizational View of Social and Neurobiological Aspects of Self-Regulation in Behavior and Development." *Development and Psychopathology* 9: 701-28.

Scanlan, T.K., P.J. Carpenter, G. W. Schmidt, J.P. Simons, and B. Keeler. 1993. "An Introduction to the Sport Commitment Model." *Journal of Sport & Exercise Psychology* 15: 1-15.

Smith, S.L., M.D. Fry, C.A. Ethington, and Y. Li. 2005. "The Effect of Female Athletes' Perceptions of Their Coaches' Behaviors on Their Perceptions of the Motivational Climate." *Journal of Applied Sport Psychology* 17: 170-77.

Smoll, F.L., R.E. Smith, N.P. Barnett, and J.J. Everett. 1993. "Enhancement of Children's Self-Esteem Through Social Support Training for Youth Sport Coaches." *Journal of Applied Psychology* 78: 602-10.

van Nieuwerburgh, C. 2010. "Holism in Sports Coaching: Beyond Humanistic Psychology: A Commentary." *International Journal of Sports Science & Coaching* 5: 463-4.

Vealey, R. S. 2005. *Coaching for the Inner Edge.* Morgantown, WV: Fitness Information Technology.

Vella, S., L. Oades, and T. Crowe. 2010. "Review: The Application of Coach Leadership Models to Coaching Practice: Current State and Future Directions." *International Journal of Sports Science and Coaching* 5: 425-34.

Visek, A.J., S.M. Achrati, H. Manning, K. McDonnell, B.S. Harris, and L. DiPietro. 2015. "The Fun Integration Theory: Towards Sustaining Children and Adolescents Sport Participation." *Journal of Physical Activity & Health* 12: 424-33.

Wang, J., and J. Ramsey. 1998. "The Relationships of School Type, Coaching Experience, Gender and Age to New Coaches' Challenges and Barriers at the Collegiate Level." *Applied Research in Coaching and Athletics Annual*: 1-22.

Weiss, M.R., A.J. Amorose, and A.M. Wilko. 2009. "Coaching Behaviors, Motivational Climate, and Psychosocial Outcomes Among Female Adolescent Athletes." *Pediatric Exercise Science* 21: 475-92.

Wilson, C.H. 2014. "Peace Under Pressure: Portraits of Christian Leadership in College Basketball Coaches," PhD diss. University of Tennessee. http://trace.tennessee.edu/utk_graddiss/2905.

Wooden, J. 2009. "John Wooden on the Difference Between Winning and Success." March 26, 2009. http://dotsub.com/view/14f5ba4c-c5a3-44b6-91b7- 4ea4bddf2b5e/viewTranscript/eng.

Chapter 4

Abbott, A., and D. Collins. 2004. "Eliminating the Dichotomy Between Theory and Practice in Talent Identification and Development: Considering the Role of Psychology." *Journal of Sports Sciences* 22 (5): 395-408.

———, K. Sowerby, and R. Martindale. 2007. "Developing the Potential of Young People in Sport: A Report for Sport Scotland." Edinburgh, UK: The University of Edinburgh, Sport Scotland.

Bailey, R., and D. Morley. 2006. "Towards a Model of Talent Development in Physical Education." *Sport, Education and Society* 11 (3): 211-30.

Bailey, R.P., D. Collins, P.A. Ford, A. MacNamara, G. Pearce, and M. Toms. 2010. *Participant Development in Sport: An Academic Literature Review*. Commissioned report for Sports Coach UK. Leeds, UK: Sports Coach UK.

Balyi, I., and A. Hamilton. 2004. *Long-Term Athlete Development: Trainability in Childhood and Adolescence. Windows of Opportunity, Optimal Trainability*; Victoria, Canada: National Coaching Institute British Columbia and Advanced Training and Performance.

Balyi, I., R. Way, and C. Higgs. 2013. *Long-Term Athlete Development*. Champaign, IL: Human Kinetics.

Bloom, B. 1985. *Developing Talent in Young People*. New York, NY: Ballantine Books.

Colvin, J. 2008. *Talent is Overrated: What Really Separates World-Class Performers from Everybody Else*. New York, NY: Penguin Publishing.

Côté, J. 1999. "The Influence of the Family in the Development of Talent in Sports." *The Sport Psychologist* 13: 395-417.

———, and J. Hay. 2002. "Children's Involvement in Sport: A Developmental Perspective. In *Psychological Foundations of Sport*, edited by J. Silva and D. Stevens, 484-502. Boston, MA: Allyn & Bacon.

Côté, J., and W. Gilbert. 2009 "An Integrative Definition of Coaching Effectiveness and Expertise." *International Journal of Sports Science & Coaching* 4 (3): 307-23.

De Bosscher, V., J. Bingham, S. Shibli, M. Von Bottenburg, and P. De Knop. 2008. *The Global Sporting Arms Race: An International Comparative Study on SPLISS*. New York, NY: Meyer & Meyer Sport.

Ericsson, K.A, R.T. Krampe, and C. Tesch-Romer. 1993. "The Role of Deliberate Practice in the Acquisition of Expert Performance." *Psychological Review* 100 (3): 363-406.

Ford, P., M. De Ste Croix, R. Lloyd, R. Meyers, M. Moosavi, J. Oliver, K. Till, and C. Williams. 2011. "The Long-Term Athlete Development Model: Physiological Evidence and Application." *Journal of Sports Sciences* 29 (4): 389-402.

Gilbert, W., and J. Côté. 2013. "Defining Coaching Effectiveness: A Focus on Coaches' Knowledge. In Routledge Handbook of Sports Coaching," edited by P. Potrac, W. Gilbert, and J. Denison, 147-59. London, UK: Routledge.

Gulbin, J., K. Oldenziel, J. Weissensteiner, and F. Gagné. 2010. "A Look Through the Rear View Mirror: Developmental Experiences and Insights of High Performance Athletes." *Talent Development & Excellence* 2 (2):149-64.

ICCE. 2013. *International Sport Coaching Framework*. Champaign, IL: Human Kinetics.

Kuper, S., and S. Szymanski. 2009. *Soccernomics: Why England Loses, Why Germany and Brazil Win and Why the U.S., Japan, Australia, Turkey and Even Iraq Are Destined to Become the Kings of the World's Most Popular Sport*. London, UK: Nation Books.

Lehrer, M., and B. Smith. 2015. "LTAD: What About the Coaches?" *Olympic Coach* 26 (1): 36-49.

Lloyd, R.S., L. Jon, and J.L. Oliver. 2012. "Youth Physical Development Model: A New Approach to Long-Term Athletic Development." *Strength and Conditioning Journal* 34 (3): 61-72.

Malina, R., 2014. "Top 10 Research Questions Related to Growth and Maturation of Relevance to Physical Activity, Performance, and Fitness." *Research Quarterly for Exercise and Sport* 85 (2): 157-73.

Robinson, M., A. Dorrance, T. DiCicco, and H. Steinbrecher. 2011. "Women Soccer Player Development: A Comparative Analysis of Top 10 Women's Soccer Countries." Commissioned study for United Stated Soccer Federation.

Simon, H.A., and W.G. Chase. 1973. "Skill in Chess." *American Scientist* 61: 394-403.

United States Olympic Committee. 2017. *Quality Coaching Framework*. Champaign, IL. Human Kinetics.

Vaeyens, R., M. Lenoir, A.M. Williams, and R. Philippaerts. 2008. "Talent Identification and Development Programmes in Sport: Current Models and Future Directions." *Sports Medicine* 38 (9): 703-14.

Vygotsky, L. S. 1978. *Mind in Society: The Development of Higher Psychological Processes*. Cambridge, MA: Harvard University Press.

Wood, D., J. Bruner, and G. Ross. 1976. "The Role of Tutoring in Problem Solving." *Journal of Child Psychology and Child Psychiatry* 17 (2): 89-100.

Chapter 5

Abernethy, B., J.P. Maxwell, R.S.W. Masters, J. Van der Kamp, and R.C. Jackson. 2007. "Attentional Processes in Skill Learning and Expert Performance." In *Handbook of Sport Psychology*, 3rd ed., edited by G. Tenenbaum and R. C. Eklund, 245-63. Hoboken, NJ: John Wiley & Sons, Inc.

Adams, J.A. 1971. "A Closed-Loop Theory of Motor Learning." *Journal of Motor Behavior* 3: 111-50.

———, E. T. Goetz, and P. H. Marshall. 1972. "Response Feedback and Motor Learning." *Journal of Experimental Psychology* 92: 391-7.

Anderson, D.I., R.A. Magill, and H. Sekiya. 1994. "A Reconsideration of the Trials-Delay of Knowledge of Results Paradigm in Motor Skill Learning." *Research Quarterly for Exercise and Sport* 65: 286-90.

———. 2001. "Motor Learning as a Function of KR Schedule and Characteristics of Task-Intrinsic Feedback." *Journal of Motor Behavior* 33: 59-66.

Bell, M. 1997. "The Development of Expertise." *Journal of Sport, Recreation and Dance* 68 (2): 34-8.

Berliner, D.C. 1994. "Expertise: The Wonder of Exemplary Performances." In *Creating Powerful Thinking in Coaches and Athletes: Diverse Perspectives,* edited by J. Mangieri and C. Block, 161-86. Fort Worth, TX: Harcourt Brace College.

Bloom, B. 1986. "The Hands and Feet of Genius: Automaticity." *Educational Leadership* 43 (5): 70-7.

Brisson, T.A., and C. Alain. 1996. "Should Common Optimal Movement Patterns Be Identified as the Criterion to Be Achieved?" *Journal of Motor Behavior* 28: 211-23.

Cauraugh, J.H., D. Chen, and S.J. Radio. 1993. "Effects of Traditional and Reversed Bandwidth Knowledge of Results on Motor Learning." *Research Quarterly for Exercise and Sport* 64 (4): 413-17.

Carter, K., D. Sabers, K. Cushing, P. Pinnegar, and D.C. Berliner. 1987. "Processing and Using Information About Students: A Study of Expert, Novice and Postulant Teachers." *Teaching and Teacher Education* 3: 147-57.

Chiviacowsky, S., and G. Wulf. 2002. "Self-Controlled Feedback: Does It Enhance Learning Because Performers Get Feedback When They Need It?" *Research Quarterly for Exercise and Sport* (4): 408-15.

Coker, C.A. 2009. *Motor Learning and Control for Practitioners.* 2nd ed. Scottsdale, AZ: Holcomb Hathaway Publishers.

DeGroot, A.D. 1966. "Perception and Memory Versus Thought: Some Old Ideas and Recent Findings." In *Problem Solving: Research, Method, and Theory*, edited by B. Keinmuntz, 19-50. New York, NY: Wiley.

DeMarco, G.M., and B.A. McCullick. 1997. "Developing Expertise in Coaching: Learning From the Legends." *Journal of Physical Education, Recreation, & Dance* 68 (3): 37-41.

Dreyfus, H.L., and S.E. Dreyfus. 1986. *Mind Over Machine.* New York, NY: Free Press.

Duda, J.L., and D.C. Treasure. 2006. "Motivational Processes and the Facilitation of Performance, Persistence, and Well-Being in Sport. *Applied Sport Psychology: Personal Growth to Peak Performance* 5: 57-81.

Ericsson, K.A. 2006. "An Introduction to the Cambridge Handbook of Expertise and Expert Performance: Its Development, Organization, and Content." In *The Cambridge Handbook of Expertise and Expert Performance,* edited by K. A. Ericsson, N. Charness, P. J. Feltovich, and R. R. Hoffman, 21-30. New York, NY: Cambridge University Press.

———. 1998. "The Scientific Study of Expert Levels of Performance: General Implications for Optimal Learning and Creativity." *High Ability Studies* 9 (1): 75-100.

———, and N. Charness. 1994. "Expert Performance: Its Structure and Acquisition." *American Science* 70: 725-47.

Ericsson, K.A., R.T. Krampe, and C. Tesch-Romer. 1993. "The Role of Deliberate Practice in the Acquisition of Expert Performance." *Psychological Review* 100: 363-06.

Ericsson, K.A., and A.C. Lehmann. 1996. "Expert and Exceptional Performance: Evidence of Maximal Adaptation to Task Constraints." *Annual Review of Psychology* 47: 273-305.

Ericsson, K.A., and J. Smith. 1991. *Toward a General Theory of Expertise: Prospects and Limits.* Cambridge, England: Cambridge University Press.

Feltovich, P.J., M.J. Prietula, and K.A. Ericsson. 2006. "Studies of Expertise from Psychological Perspectives." In *Cambridge Handbook of Expertise and Expert Performance*, edited by K.A. Ericsson, N. Charness, P.J. Feltovich, and R.R. Hoffman, 21-30. New York, NY: Cambridge University Press.

Fincher, M., and P. Schempp. 1994. "Teaching Physical Education: What Do We Need to Know and How Do We Find It?" *GAHPERD Journal* 28: 7-10.

Fishman, S., and C. Tobey. 1978. "Augmented Feedback: What's Going on in Gym? Descriptive Studies of Physical Education Classes." *Motor Skills: Theory into Practice, Monograph* 1: 51-62.

Fitts, P.M. 1965. "Factors in Complex Skill Training." *Training Research and Education*: 177-97.

———, and M.I. Posner. 1967. *Human Performance*. Belmont, CA: Brooks/Cole Publishing Company.

Gentile, A.M. 1972. "A Working Model of Skill Acquisition With Application to Teaching." *Quest* 17: 3-23.

———. 2001. "Skill Acquisition: Action, Movement, and Neuromotor Processes." In *Movement Science: Foundations for Physical Therapy in Rehabilitation*, 2nd ed., edited by J. Carr and R Sheperd, 111-87. Gaithersburg, MD: Aspen Publishers.

Glaser, R. 1965. *Training, Research, and Education*. New York, NY: Wiley and Sons, Inc.

———, and M.H.T. Chi. 1988. "Overview." In *The Nature of Expertise*, edited by M.H.T. Chi, R. Glaser, and M.J. Farr, XV-XXVIII. Hillsdale, NJ: Erlbaum.

Grant, M.A., and S. Dorgo. 2014. "Developing Expertise in Strength and Conditioning Coaching. *Strength & Conditioning* 36 (1): 9-15.

Hodges, N.J., and I.M. Franks. 2002. "Modelling Coaching Practices: The Role of Instruction and Demonstration." *Journal of Sports Sciences* 20: 793-811.

Housner, L.D., and D. Griffey. 1985. "Teacher Cognition: Differences in Planning and Interactive Decision Making Between Experienced and Inexperienced Teachers." *Research Quarterly for Exercise & Sport* 56: 44-53.

Huber, J.J. 2013. *Applying Educational Psychology in Coaching Athletes*. Champaign, IL: Human Kinetics.

ICCE. 2013. *International Sport Coaching Framework*. Champaign, IL: Human Kinetics.

Janelle, C.M., J. Kim, and R.N. Singer. 1995. "Subject-Controlled Performance Feedback and Learning of a Closed Motor Skill." *Perceptual and Motor Skills* 81: 627-34.

Johnson, B.J., G. Tenenbaum, and W.A. Edmonds. 2006. "Adaptation to Physically and Emotionally Demanding Conditions: The Role of Deliberate Practice." *High Abilities Studies* 17 (1): 117-36.

Lee, T.D., and R.A. Magill. 1983. "The Locus of Contextual Interference in Motor-Skill Acquisition." *Journal of Experimental Psychology: Learning, Memory, and Cognition* 9 (4): 730.

Lindor, R. 2004. "Developing Metacognition Behavior in Physical Education Classes: The Use of Task-Pertinent Learning Strategies." *Physical Education and Sport Pedagogy* 9 (1): 55-71.

Lui, J., and C.A. Wrisberg. 1997. "The Effect of Knowledge of Results Delay and the Subjective Estimation of Movement Form on the Acquisition and Retention of a Motor Skill." *Research Quarterly for Exercise and Sport* 68 (2): 145-51.

Magill, R.A. 2001. "Augmented Feedback in Motor Skill Acquisition. In *Handbook of Sport Psychology*, 2nd ed., edited by R.N. Singer, H.A. Hausenblas, and C.M. Janelle, 86-114. New York, NY: John Wiley & Sons.

———. 2010. *Motor Learning and Control: Concepts and Applications*. 9th ed. New York, NY: McGraw-Hill.

———, and D. I. Anderson. 2012. "The Roles and Uses of Augmented Feedback in Motor Skill Acquisition." In *Skill Acquisition in Sport: Research, Theory, and Practice*, edited by N.J. Hodges and A.M. Williams, 3-21. New York, NY: Routledge.

Magill, R.A., J.M. Porter, and W.F.W. Wu. 2005. "New Directions in the Study of the Contextual Inference Effect in Motor Learning. Abstract." Presented at the XIth Congress of ACAPS, Paris, France. In *Researches Actuelles En Sciences Du Sport*, edited by N. Benguigui, P. Fontayne, M. Desbordes, and B. Brady, 333-4. Paris, France: EDP Sciences.

Magill, R.A., and C. Wood. 1986. "Knowledge of Results Precision as a Learning Variable in Motor Skill Acquisition." *Research Quarterly for Exercise and Sport* 57: 170-3.

Martens, R. 2012. *Successful Coaching*, 4th ed. Champaign, IL: Human Kinetics.

Masters, R.S.W. 2000. "Theoretical Aspects of Implicit Learning in Sport." *International Journal of Sports Psychology* 31: 530-41.

McMorris, T. 2004. *Acquisition and Performance of Sports Skills.* New York, NY: John Wiley & Sons.

Miller, J. E. 2004. Lawrence Welk and John Wooden: Midwestern Small-Town Boys Who Never Left Home. *Journal of American Studies* 38 (1): 109-25.

Moe, V.F. 2004. "How to Understand Skill Acquisition in Sports." *Bulletin of Science, Technology & Society* 24 (3): 213-24.

Nater, S., and R. Gallimore. 2006. *You Haven't Taught Until They Have Learned.* Morgantown, WV: Fit Information Technology.

Newell, K.M. 1991." Motor Skill Acquisition." *Annual Review of Psychology* 42: 213-37.

Salmoni, A.W., R.A. Schmidt, and C.B. Walter. 1984. "Knowledge of Results and Motor Learning: A Review and Critical Reappraisal." *Psychological Bulletin* 95: 353-86.

Schempp, P.G. 1985. "Becoming a Better Teacher: An Analysis of the Student Teaching Experience." *Journal of Teaching in Physical Education* 4: 158-66.

———. 1997. "Developing Expertise in Teaching and Coaching." *Journal of Physical Education, Recreation, and Dance* 68: 29.

———. 2003. *Teaching Sport and Physical Activity: Insights on the Road to Excellence.* Champaign, IL: Human Kinetics.

———, D. Manross, S. Tan, and M. Fincher. 1998. "Subject Expertise and Teachers' Knowledge." *Journal of Teaching in Physical Education* 17: 342-56.

Schempp, P.G., B.A. McCullick, and M.A. Grant. 2012. "Teaching Coaching Expertise: How to Educate for Coaching Excellence." In *Current Issues and Controversies in Health, Sport, and Physical Education,* edited by J. O'Dea, 251-63. New York, NY: Nova Science Publishers.

Schempp, P., B.A. McCullick, and I. Mason. 2006. "The Development of Expert Coaching." In *The Sports Coach as Teacher: Reconceptualising Sports Coaching,* edited by R. Jones. 145-61. London, UK: Routledge.

Schmidt, R.A. 1982. *Motor Control and Learning.* Champaign, IL: Human Kinetics.

———. 1988. *Motor Control and Learning: A Behavioral Emphasis.* Champaign, IL: Human Kinetics.

———, and D.C. Shapiro. 1986. *Optimizing Feedback Utilization in Motor Skill Training* (Report No. 1/86). Alexandria, VA: US Army Research Institute (Basic Research).

Schmidt, R.A., and C.A. Wrisberg 2000. *Motor Learning and Performance.* Champaign, IL: Human Kinetics.

Schmidt, R.A. and D.E. Young. 1991. "Methodology for Motor Learning: A Paradigm for Kinematic Feedback." *Journal of Motor Behavior* 23: 13-24.

Shea, C.H., R. Kohl, and C. Indermill. 1990. "Contextual Inference: Contributions of Practice." *Acta Psychologica* 73: 145-57.

Siedentop, D., and E. Eldar. 1989. "Experience, Expertise and Effectiveness." *Journal of Teaching in Physical Education* 8 (3): 254-60.

Simon, H.A., and W.G. Chase. 1973a. "Perception in Chess". *Cognitive Psychology* 4 (1): 55-81.

———. 1973b. "Skill in Chess." *American Science* 61: 394-403.

Swinnen, S.P., R.A. Schmidt, D.E. Nicholson, and D.C. Shapiro. 1990. "Information Feedback for Skill Acquisition: Instantaneous Knowledge of Results Degrades Learning." *Journal of Experimental Psychology: Learning, Memory, and Cognition* 16: 706-16.

Tan, S. 1997. "The Elements of Expertise." *Journal of Physical Education, Recreation, and Dance* 68 (2): 30-33.

Trudel, P, and W. Gilbert 2006. "Coaching and Coach Education." In *Handbook of Physical Education*, edited by D. Kirk, D. Macdonald, and M. O'Sullivan, 516-39. Thousand Oaks, CA: Sage.

Wall, A.E. 1985. "A Knowledge-Based approach to Motor Skill Acquisition." In *Motor Development in Children: Aspects of Coordination and Control*, edited by M. G. Wade and H. T. A. Whiting, 33-49. Maastricht, Netherlands: Martinus Nijhoff Publishers.

Wallace, S.A., and R.W. Hagler. 1979. "Knowledge of Performance and the Learning of a Closed Motor Skill." *Research Quarterly. American Alliance for Health, Physical Education, Recreation and Dance* 50 (2): 265-71.

Weeks, D.L, and R.N. Kordus. 1998. "Relative Frequency of Knowledge of Performance and Motor Skill Learning." *Research Quarterly for Exercise and Sport* (3): 224-30.

Weeks, D.L., and D.E. Sherwood. 1994. "A Comparison of Knowledge of Results Scheduling Methods for Promoting Motor Skill Acquisition and Retention." *Research Quarterly for Exercise and Sport* 65: 136-42.

Winstein, C.J., P.S. Pohl, and R. Lewthwaite. 1994. "Effects of Physical Guidance and Knowledge of Results on Motor Learning: Support for the Guidance Hypothesis." *Research Quarterly for Exercise and Sport* 65 (4): 316-23.

Wright, D.L., V.L. Smith-Munyon, and B. Sidaway. 1997. "How Close Is Too Close for Precision Knowledge of Results?" *Research Quarterly for Exercise and Sport* 68 (2): 172-6.

Wu, W.F.W., and R.A. Magill. 2011. "Allowing Learners to Choose: Self-Controlled Practice Schedules for Learning Multiple Movement Patterns." *Research Quarterly for Exercise and Sport* 82 (3): 449-57.

Wulf, G., and T. Tool. 1999. "Physical Assistance Devices in Complex Motor Skill Learning: Benefits of a Self-Controlled Practice Schedule." *Research Quarterly for Exercise and Sport* 70: 265-72.

Young, D.E., and R.A. Schmidt. 1992. "Augmented Kinematic Feedback for Motor Learning." *Journal of Motor Behavior* 24 (3): 261-73.

Chapter 6

American Psychological Association Task Force on Psychological Intervention Guidelines. 1995. *Template for Developing Guidelines: Interventions for Mental Disorders and Psychological Aspects of Physical Disorders*. Washington, DC: American Psychological Association.

Ames, C. 1992a. "Classrooms: Goals, Structures, and Student Motivation." *Journal of Educational Psychology* 84: 261-71.

———. 1992b. "Achievement Goals and Adaptive Motivational Patterns: The Role of the Environment." In *Motivation in Sport and Exercise*, edited by G.C. Roberts, 161-76. Champaign, IL: Human Kinetics.

———, and J. Archer. 1988." Achievement Goals in the Classroom: Students' Learning Strategies and Motivation Processes." *Journal of Educational Psychology* 80: 260-7.

Baldwin, J.D., and J.I. Baldwin. 2001. *Behavior Principles in Everyday Life*. Upper Saddle River, NJ: Prentice-Hall.

Bandura, A. 1969. *Principles of Behavior Modification*. New York, NY: Holt, Rinehart, & Winston.

Barnett, N.P., F.L. Smoll, and R.E. Smith. 1992. "Effects of Enhancing Coach-Athlete Relationships on Youth Sport Attrition." *The Sport Psychologist* 6: 111-27.

Brown, J.D. 2007. *The Self*. New York, NY: Psychology Press.

Burton, D., and D. Tannehill. 1987, April. *Developing Better Youth Sport Coaches: An Evaluation of the American Coaching Effectiveness Program (ACEP) Level 1 Training*. Paper presented at the meeting of the American Alliance of Health, Physical Education, Recreation and Dance, Las Vegas, NV.

Carpenter, P.J., and K. Morgan. 1999. "Motivational Climate, Personal Goal Perspectives, and Cognitive and Affective Responses in Physical Education Classes." *European Journal of Physical Education* 4: 31-44.

Carroll, P., Y. Roth, and K.A. Garin. 2011. *Win Forever: Live, Work, and Play Like a Champion.* Knoxville, TN: Portfolio Hardcover Publishers.

Chambless, D.L., and S.D. Hollon. 1998. "Defining Empirically Supported Therapies." *Journal of Consulting and Clinical Psychology* 66: 7-18.

Chi, L. 2004. "Achievement Goal Theory." In *Sport Psychology: Theory, Applications, and Issues,* 2nd ed., edited by T. Morris and J. Summers, 152-74. Milton, Australia: Wiley.

Coatsworth, J.D., and D.E. Conroy. 2006. "Enhancing the Self-Esteem of Youth Swimmers Through Coach Training: Gender and Age Effects." *Psychology of Sport and Exercise* 7: 173-92.

Conroy, D.E., and J.D. Coatsworth. 2004. "The Effects of Coach Training on Fear of Failure in Youth Swimmers: A Latent Growth Curve Analysis From a Randomized, Controlled Trial." *Journal of Applied Developmental Psychology* 25: 193-214.

Crews, D.J., M.R. Lochbaum, and P. Karoly. 2001. Self-Regulation: Concepts, Methods and Strategies in Sport and Exercise." In *Handbook of Research on Sport Psychology,* 2nd ed., edited by R.N. Singer, H.A. Hausenblaus, and C.M. Janelle, 566-84. New York, NY: John Wiley & Sons.

Cruz, J., A. Mora, C. Sousa, and S. Alcaraz. 2016. "Effects of an Individualized Program on Coaches' Observed and Perceived Behavior." *Revista de Psicologia del Deporte* 25: 137-44.

Cumming, S.P., R.E. Smith, F.L. Smoll, M. Standage, and J.R. Grossbard. 2008. "Development and Validation of the Achievement Goal Scale for Youth Sports." *Psychology of Sport and Exercise* 9: 686-703.

Cumming, S.P., F.L. Smoll, R.E. Smith, and J.R. Grossbard. 2007. "Is Winning Everything? The Relative Contributions of Motivational Climate and Won-Lost Percentage in Youth Sports." *Journal of Applied Sport Psychology* 19: 322-36.

Curtis, B., R.E. Smith, and F.L. Smoll. 1979. "Scrutinizing the Skipper: A Study of Leadership Behaviors in the Dugout." *Journal of Applied Psychology* 64: 391-400.

De Knop, P., L-M. Engstrom, B. Skirstad, and M.R. Weiss. 1996. *Worldwide Trends in Youth Sport.* Champaign, IL: Human Kinetics.

Duda, J.L. 2013. "The Conceptual and Empirical Foundations of Empowering Coaches: Setting the Stage for the PAPA Project." *International Journal of Sport and Exercise Psychology* 11: 311-18.

———, and L. Balaguer. 2007. "Coach-Created Motivational Climate." In *Social Psychology in Sport*, edited by S. Jowett and D. Lavallee, 117-130. Champaign, IL: Human Kinetics.

Duda, J.L., and H. Hall. 2001. "Achievement Goal Theory in Sport: Recent Extensions and Future Directions." In *Handbook of Sport Psychology,* 2nd ed., edited by R.N. Singer, H.A. Hausenblas, and C.M. Janelle, 417-43. New York, NY: Wiley.

Duda, J.L., and N. Ntoumanis. 2005. "After-School Sport For Children: Implications Of Task-Involving Motivational Climate." In *Organized Activities as Contexts of Development: Extracurricular Activities, After School, and Community Programs*, edited by J.L. Mahoney, R.W. Larson, and J.S. Eccles, 311-30. Mahwah, NJ: Erlbaum.

Duda, J L., and J. Whitehead. 1998. "Measurement of Goal Perspectives in the Physical Domain." In *Advances in Sport and Exercise Psychology Measurement*, edited by J.L. Duda, 21-48. Morgantown, WV: Fitness Information Technology.

Duffy, P., M. Harrington, and S.L. Bercial., eds. 2013. *International Sport Coaching Framework (Version 1.2).* Champaign, IL: Human Kinetics.

Dweck, C. S. 1986. "Motivational Processes Affecting Learning." *American Psychologist* 41: 1040-8.

———. 1999. *Self-Theories and Goals: Their Role in Motivation, Personality, and Development.* Philadelphia, PA: Taylor & Francis.

Edelstein, B.A., and R.M. Eisler. 1976. "Effects of Modeling and Modeling With Instructions and Feedback on the Behavioral Components of Social Skills." *Behavior Therapy* 7: 382-9.

Epstein, J. 1988. "Effective Schools or Effective Students? Dealing With Diversity." In *Policies for America's Schools*, edited by R. Haskins and B. MacRae, 89-126. Norwood, NJ: Ablex.

———. 1989. "Family Structures and Student Motivation: A Developmental Perspective." In *Research on Motivation in Education: Vol. 3. Goals and Cognitions*, edited by C. Ames and R. Ames, 259-95. New York: Academic Press.

Goudas, M., S.J.H. Biddle, K. Fox, and M. Underwood. 1995. "It Ain't What You Do, It's the Way You Do It! Teaching Style Affects Children's Motivation in Track and Field Lessons." *Sport Psychologist* 9: 254-64.

Huberman, W.L., and R.M. O'Brien. 1999. "Improving Therapist and Patient Performance in Chronic Psychiatric Group Homes Through Goal-Setting, Feedback, and Positive Reinforcement." *Journal of Organizational Behavior Management* 19: 13-36.

Kanfer, F.H., and L. Gaelick-Buys. 1991. "Self-Management Methods." In *Helping People Change: A Textbook of Methods,* 4th ed., edited by F.H. Kanfer and A.P. Goldstein, 305-60. New York, NY: Pergamon.

Langan, E., C. Blake, and C. Lonsdale. 2013. "Systematic Review of the Effectiveness of Interpersonal Coach Education Interventions on Athlete Outcomes." *Psychology of Sport and Exercise* 14: 37-49.

Lewis, C J., R. Groom, and S.J. Roberts. 2014. "Exploring The Value of a Coach Intervention Process Within Women's Youth Soccer: A Case Study." *International Journal of Sport and Exercise Psychology* 12: 245-57.

Lipsey, M.W., and D.S. Cordray. 2000. "Evaluation Methods for Social Intervention." *Annual Review of Psychology* 51: 345-76.

McHugh, R.K., and D.H. Barlow. 2010. "The Dissemination and Implementation of Evidence-Based Psychological Treatments." *American Psychologist* 65: 73-84.

McLaren, C.D., M.A. Eys, and R.A. Murray. 2015. "A Coach-Initiated Motivational Climate Intervention and Athletes' Perceptions of Group Cohesion in Youth Sport." *Sport, Exercise, and Performance Psychology* 4: 113-26.

Midgley, C., M.L. Maehr, L.Z. Hruda, E. Anderman, L. Anderman, K.E. Freeman, M. Gheen, A. Kaplan, R. Kumar, M.J. Middleton, J. Nelson, R. Roeser, and T. Urdan. 2000. *Manual for the Patterns of Adaptive Learning Scales.* Ann Arbor, MI: University of Michigan School of Education. Accessed February 2, 2004. www.umich.edu/~pals/pals.

Mischel, W. 1973. "Toward a Cognitive Social Learning Reconceptualization of Personality." *Psychological Review* 80:252-83.

Nicholls, J.G. 1989. *The Competitive Ethos and Democratic Education.* Cambridge, MA: Harvard University Press.

Papaioannou, A., and O. Kouli. 1999. "The Effect of Task Structure, Perceived Motivational Climate and Goal Orientations on Students' Task Involvement and Anxiety." *Journal of Applied Sport Psychology* 11: 51-71.

Project PAPA. 2016. "Key Findings: Empowering Coaching Changes the Youth Sport Climate for the Better!" June 28. http://projectpapa.org.

Roberts, G.C., D.C. Treasure, and D.E. Conroy. 2007. "Understanding the Dynamics of Motivation in Sport and Physical Activity: An Achievement Goal Interpretation." In *Handbook of Sport Psychology,* 3rd ed., edited by G. Tenenbaum and R.C. Eklund, 3-30. New York, NY: Wiley.

Roberts, G.C., D.C. Treasure, and M. Kavussanu. 1997. "Motivation in Physical Activity Contexts: An Achievement Goal Perspective." In *Advances in Motivation and Achievement*, vol. 10, edited by M.L. Maehe and P.R. Pintrich, 413-47. Greenwich, CT: JAI Press.

Smith, R.E. 2015. "A Positive Approach to Coaching Effectiveness and Performance Enhancement." In *Applied Sport Psychology: Personal Growth To Peak Performance,* 7th ed., edited by J.M. Williams and V. Krane, 40-56. Boston, MA: McGraw-Hill.

———, S.P. Cumming, and F.L. Smoll. 2008. "Development and Validation of the Motivational Climate Scale for Youth Sports." *Journal of Applied Sport Psychology* 20: 116-36.

Smith, R.E., Y. Shoda, S.P. Cumming, and F.L. Smoll. 2009. "Behavioral Signatures at the Ballpark: Intraindividual Consistency of Adults' Situation-Behavior Patterns and Their Interpersonal Consequences." *Journal of Research in Personality* 43: 187-95.

Smith, R.E., and F.L. Smoll. 1990. "*Self-Esteem and Children's Reactions to Youth Sport Coaching Behaviors: A Field Study of Self-Enhancement Processes.*" *Developmental Psychology* 26: 987-93.

———. 2012. *Sport Psychology for Youth Coaches: Developing Champions in Sports and Life.* Lanham, MD: Rowman & Littlefield.

———, and N.P. Barnett. 1995. "Reduction of Children's Sport Performance Anxiety Through Social Support and Stress-Reduction Training for Coaches." *Journal of Applied Developmental Psychology* 16: 125-42.

Smith, R.E., F.L. Smoll, and D.S. Christensen. 1996. "Behavioral Assessment and Intervention in Youth Sports." *Behavior Modification* 20: 3-44.

Smith, R.E., F.L. Smoll, and S.P. Cumming. 2007. "Effects of a Motivational Climate Intervention for Coaches on Children's Sport Performance Anxiety." *Journal of Sport & Exercise Psychology* 29: 39-59.

Smith, R.E., F.L. Smoll, and B. Curtis. 1978. "Coaching Behaviors in Little League Baseball". In *Psychological Perspectives in Youth Sports*, edited by F.L. Smoll and R.E. Smith, 173-201. Washington, DC: Hemisphere.

———. 1979. "Coach Effectiveness Training: A Cognitive-Behavioral Approach to Enhancing Relationship Skills in Youth Sport Coaches." *Journal of Sport Psychology* 1: 59-75.

Smith, R.E., F.L. Smoll, and E.B. Hunt. 1977. "A System for the Behavioral Assessment of Athletic Coaches." *Research Quarterly* 48: 401-7.

Smith, R.E., F.L. Smoll, and M.W. Passer. 2002. "Sport Performance Anxiety In Young Athletes." In *Children and Youth in Sport: A Biopsychosocial Perspective,* 2nd ed., edited by F.L. Smoll and R.E. Smith, 501-36. Dubuque, IA: Kendall/Hunt.

Smith, R.E., N.W.S. Zane, F.L. Smoll, and D.B. Coppel. 1983. "Behavioral Assessment in Youth Sports: Coaching Behaviors and Children's Attitudes." *Medicine and Science in Sports* 15: 208-14.

Smoll, F.L., S.P. Cumming, and R.E. Smith. 2011. "Enhancing Coach-Parent Relationships in Youth Sports: Increasing Harmony and Minimizing Hassle." *International Journal of Sports Science and Coaching* 6: 13-26.

Smoll, F.L., and R.E. Smith. 1989. "Leadership Behaviors in Sport: A Theoretical Model and Research Paradigm." *Journal of Applied Social Psychology* 19: 1522-51.

———, eds. 2002. *Children and Youth in Sport: A Biopsychosocial Perspective.* 2nd ed. Dubuque, IA: Kendall/Hunt.

———. 2009a. *Mastery Approach to Coaching: A Leadership Guide for Youth Sports.* Seattle, WA: Youth Enrichment in Sports.

———, producers. 2009b. *Mastery Approach to Coaching: A Self-Instruction program* [Video]. Seattle, WA: Youth Enrichment in Sports.

———. 2012. *Parenting Young Athletes: Developing Champions in Sports and Life.* Lanham, MD: Rowman & Littlefield.

———. 2015. "Conducting Evidence Based Coach-Training Programs: A Social-Cognitive Approach." In *Applied Sport Psychology: Personal Growth to Peak Performance,* 7th ed., edited by J.M. Williams and V. Krane, 359-82. New York, NY: McGraw-Hill.

———, N.P. Barnett, and J.J. Everett. 1993. "Enhancement of Children's Self-Esteem Through Social Support Training for Youth Sport Coaches." *Journal of Applied Psychology* 78: 602-10.

Smoll, F.L., R.E. Smith, and S.P. Cumming. 2007. "Effects of a Psychoeducational Intervention for Coaches on Changes in Child Athletes' Achievement Goal Orientations." *Journal of Clinical Sport Psychology* 1: 23-46.

Smoll, F.L., R.E. Smith, B. Curtis, and E. Hunt. 1978. "Toward a Meditational Model of Coach-Player Relationships." *Research Quarterly* 49: 528-41.

Sousa, C., J. Cruz, M. Torregrosa, D. Vilches, and C. Viladrich. 2006. "Behavioral Assessment and Individual Counseling Programme for Coaches of Young Athletes." *Revista de Psicologia del Deporte* 15: 263-78.

Sousa, C., R.E. Smith, and J. Cruz. 2008. "An Individualized Behavioral Goal-Setting Program for Coaches: Impact on Observed, Athlete-Perceived, and Coach-Perceived Behaviors." *Journal of Clinical Sport Psychology* 2: 258-77.

Sports & Fitness Industry Association. 2015. *2015 U.S. Trends in Team Sports.* Silver Springs, MD: Author.

Swann, W.B. 1990. "To Be Known or to Be Adored? The Interplay of Self-Enhancement and Self-Verification." In *Handbook of Motivation and Cognition: Foundations of Social Behavior,* vol. 2, edited by R.M. Sorrentino and E.T. Higgins, 408-88. New York, NY: Guilford Press.

U.S. Census Bureau. 2013. *Current Population Survey* (Annual Social and Economic Supplement, 2012). Washington, DC: Author.

U.S. Institute of Medicine. 2001. *Crossing the Quality Chasm: A New Health System for the 21st Century.* Washington, DC: Author.

Walling, M.D., J.L. Duda, and L. Chi. 1993. "The Perceived Motivational Climate in Sport Questionnaire: Construct and Predictive Validity." *Journal of Sport & Exercise Psychology* 15: 172-83.

Wooden, J. 2003. *They Call Me Coach.* New York, NY: McGraw-Hill.

Chapter 7

Amorose, A.J., and D. Anderson-Butcher. 2007. "Autonomy-Supportive Coaching and Self-Determined Motivation in High School and College Athletes: A Test of Self-Determination Theory." *Psychology of Sport and Exercise* 8 (5): 654-70.

Coakley, J. 2011. "Youth Sports: What Counts as 'Positive Development?'" *Journal of Sport & Social Issues* 35: 306-24.

Côté, J., R. Lidor, and D. Hackfort. 2009. "ISSP Position Stand: To Sample or to Specialize? Seven Postulates About Youth Sport Activities That Lead to Continued Participation and Elite Performance." *International Journal of Sport and Exercise Psychology 9:* 7-17.

DiFiori, J.P., H.J. Benjamin, J.S. Brenner, A. Gregory, N. Jayanthi, G.L. Landry, and A. Luke. 2014. "Overuse Injuries and Burnout in Youth Sports: A Position Statement From The American Medical Society for Sports Medicine." *British Journal of Sports Medicine* 48 (4): 287-8.

Donnelly, P. 1993. "Problems Associated With Youth Involved in High-Performance Sport." In *Intensive Participation in Children's Sports*, edited by B.R. Cahill and A.J. Pearl, 95-126. Champaign, IL: Human Kinetics.

Eccles, J.S., and B.L. Barber. 1999. "Student Council, Volunteering, Basketball, or Marching Band: What Kind of Extracurricular Involvement Matters?" *Journal of Adolescent Research* 14: 3.

———, M. Stone, and J. Hunt. 2003. "Extracurricular Activities and Adolescent Development." *The Journal of Social Issues* 59: 865-89.

Eime, R.M., J.A. Young, J. Harvey, M.J. Charity, and W.R. Payne 2013. "A Systematic Review of the Psychological and Social Benefits of Participation in Sport for Children and Adolescents: Informing Development of a Conceptual Model of Health Through Sport." *International Journal of Behavioral Nutrition and Physical Activity* 10: 98.

Ewing, M.E., B. Laskey, and D. Munk. 2008, March. *Athletes', Coaches' and Parents' Views of the Pros and Cons of Participation in Multiple Sports Versus Specializing in One Sport.* Paper presented at the American Alliance of Heath, Physical Education, Recreation and Dance, Fort Worth, TX.

FIFA. 2007. "FIFA Big Count 2006: 270 Million People Active in Football." www.fifa.com/mm/document/fifafacts/bcoffsurv/bigcount.statspackage_7024.pdf.

Fredericks, J.A., and J.S. Eccles. 2005. "Family Socialization, Gender, and Sport Motivation and Involvement." *Journal of Sport and Exercise Psychology* 27: 3-31.

Fry, M.D. 2010. "Creating a Positive Climate for Young Athletes From Day 1." *Journal of Sport Psychology in Action* 1 (1): 33-41.

Gould, D. 2010. "Early Sports Specialization: A Psychological Perspective." *Journal of Physical Education, Recreation and Dance* 81: 33-7.

Gould, D., K. Collins, L. Lauer, and Y. Chung. 2007. "Coaching Life Skills Through Football: A Study of Award Winning High School Coaches." *Journal of Applied Sport Psychology* 19 (1): 16-37.

Gould, D., I. Cowburn, and S. Pierce. 2012. *Sport Parenting Research: Current Status, Future Directions and Practical Implications.* Boca Raton, FL: USTA Player Development.

Gould, D., I. Cowburn, and A. Shields. 2014. "'Sports for All'—Summary of the Evidence of Psychological and Social Outcomes of Participation." Elevate Health Series 15 (3). Rockville, MD: President's Council on Fitness, Sports & Nutrition Science Board.

Gould, D., M.R. Flett, and L. Lauer. 2012. "The Relationship Between Psychosocial Developmental and the Sports Climate Experienced By Underserved Youth." *Psychology of Sport & Exercise* 13 (1): 80-7.

Gould, D., and J. Nalepa. 2015. "Mental Development of the Young Player." In *The Young Tennis Player: Injury Prevention and Treatment*, edited by A. Colvin, A. and J. Gladstone, J. NY: Springer.

Hansen, D.M., and R. Larson. 2007. "Amplifiers of Developmental and Negative Experiences in Organized Activities: Dosage, Motivation, Lead Roles, and Adult-Youth Ratios." *Journal of Applied Developmental Psychology* 28: 360-74.

Haywood, K.M., and N. Getchell. 2014. *Life Span Motor Development.* 6th ed. Champaign, IL: Human Kinetics.

Hill, G.M., and J. Simons. 1989. "A Study of Sports Specialization on High School Athletes." *Journal of Sport & Social Issues* 13 (1): 1-13.

Holt, N.L., and C.J. Knight. 2014. *Parenting in Youth Sport: From Research to Practice.* New York, NY: Routledge.

Horn, T., M. Byrd, E. Martin, and C. Young. 2012. "Perceived Motivational Climate and Team Cohesion in Adolescent Athletes." *Sport Science Review* 21 (3-4): 25-48.

Jayanthi, N., C. Pinkham, L. Dugas, B. Patrick, and C. LaBella. 2013. "Sports Specialization in Young Athletes: Evidence-Based Recommendations." *Sports Health* 5 (3): 251-7.

Kendellen, K., and M. Camire. 2015. "Examining Former Athletes' Developmental Experiences in High School Sport." *Sage Open*, October-December: 1-10.

Kenny, W.L., J.H. Wilmore, and D.L. Costill. 2012. *Physiology of Sport and Exercise.* 5th ed. Champaign, IL: Human Kinetics.

LaPrade, R.F., J. Agel, J. Baker, R.S. Brenner, F.A. Cordasco, J. Cote, L Engebretsen, B.T. Feeley, D. Gould, B. Hainline, T. Hewett, N. Jayanthi, M.S. Kocher, G.D. Myer, C.W. Nissen, M.J. Philippon, and M.T. Provencher. 2016. "Early Sports Specialization Consensus Statement." *The Orthopaedic Journal of Sports Medicine* 4 (4).

Larson, R.W. 2012. "Positive Development in a Disorderly World." *Journal of Research on Adolescence* 21 (2): 317-34.

———, D.M. Hansen, and G. Moneta. 2006. "Differing Profiles of Developmental Experiences Across Types of Organized Youth Activities." *Developmental Psychology* 42 (5): 849-63.

Mahoney, J.L., R.W. Larson, J.S. Eccles, and H. Lord. 2005. "Organized Activities as Developmental Contexts for Children and Adolescents." In *Organized Activities as Contexts for Development: Extracurricular Activities, After-School and Community Programs*, edited by J.J. Mahoney, R.W. Larson, J.S. Eccles, 3-22. Mahwah, NJ: Lawrence Erlbaum.

Martens, R. 1978 *Joy and Sadness in Children's Sports*. Champaign, IL: Human Kinetics.

———. 2004. *Successful Coaching*. Champaign, IL: Human Kinetics.

National Federation of State High School Associations. 2015. "Participation Statistics." Accessed January 2015. www.nfhs.org/ParticipationStatistics/ParticipationStatistics.

Naughton, G., N.J. Farpour-Lambert, J. Carlson, M. Bradney, and E. Van Praagh. 2000. Physiological Issues Surrounding the Performance of Adolescent Athletes." *Sports Medicine* 30 (5): 309-25.

NCAA. 2016. "Estimated Probability of Competing in Professional Athletics." www.ncaa.org/about/resources/research/mens-basketball.

Pate, R.R., S.G. Trost, S. Levin, and M. Dowda. 2000. "Sports Participation and Health Related Behaviors Among US Youth." *Archives of Pediatrics & Adolescent Medicine* 154 (9): 904-11.

Powell, J.W., and K.D. Barber-Foss. 1999. "Injury Patterns in Selected High School Sports: A Review of the 1995-1997 Seasons." *Journal of Athletic Training* 34 (3): 277-84.

Rechel, J.A., E.E. Yard, and R.D. Comstock. 2008. "An Epidemiologic Comparison of High School Sports Injuries Sustained in Practice and Competition." *Journal of Athletic Training* 43 (2): 197-204.

Roberts, J. 2008. A sane Island surrounded. *Phi Delta Kappan* 89 (4): 278-82.

Smoll, F.L., and R.E. Smith. 2001. "Conducting Sport Psychology Training Programs for Coaches: Cognitive-Behavioral Principles and Techniques." In *Applied Sport Psychology: Personal Growth to Peak Performance,* 4th ed., edited by J.M. Williams, 378-400. Mountain View, CA: Mayfield.

Strachan, L., J. Cote, and J. Dekin. 2009. "'Specializers' Versus 'Samplers' in Youth Sport: Comparing Experiences and Outcomes." *The Sport Psychologist* 23: 73-92.

Strong, W.B., R.M. Malina, C.J. Blimkie, S.R. Daniels, R.K. Dishman, B. Gutin, A.C. Hergenroeder, A. Must, P.A. Nixon, J.M. Pivarnik, T. Rowland, S. Trost, and F. Trudeau. 2005. "Evidence Based Physical Activity for School-Age Youth." *The Journal of Pediatrics* 146 (6): 732-7.

Treasure, D.C., and G.C. Roberts. 1995. Applications of Achievement Goal Theory to Physical Education: Implications for Enhancing Motivation. *Quest* 47 (4): 475-89.

Vealey, R. S. 2005. *Coaching for the Inner Edge*. Morgantown, WV: Fitness Information Technology.

Vella, S.A., L.G. Oades, and T.P. Crowe. 2013. "The Relationship Between Coach Leadership, the Coach–Athlete Relationship, Team Success, and the Positive Developmental Experiences of Adolescent Soccer Players." *Physical Education and Sport Pedagogy* 18 (5): 549-61.

VonMeter, K. 2004. "Coaching Adolescent Athletes." *Strategies* 17 (6): 17-9.

Weiss, M.R., N.D. Bolter, and L.E. Kipp. 2016. "Evaluation of *The First Tee* in Promoting a Positive Youth Development Program: Group Comparisons and Longitudinal Trends." *Research Quarterly for Exercise and Sport* 85: 263-78.

Weiss, M.R., and S.D. Fretwell. 2005. "The Parent-Coach/Child-Athlete Relationship in Youth Sport: Cordial, Contentious, or Conundrum?" *Research Quarterly for Exercise and Sport* 76 (3): 286-305.

Whitmore, J. 2009. *Coaching for Performance.* 4th ed. Boston, MA: Nicholas Brealey.

Chapter 8

Belias, D., A. Koustelios, E. Zoutnatizi, M. Koutiva, L. Sdolias, and A.K. Barbiioanna. 2013. "Job Satisfaction and Job Burnout—A Review of International Literature." *International Journal of Human Resource Management and Research* 3 (3): 27-38.

Bloom, G.A., R. Crumpton, and J.E. Anderson. 1999. "A Systematic Observation Study of the Teaching Behaviors of an Expert Basketball Coach." *The Sport Psychologist* 13: 157-70.

Bloom, G.A., N. Durand-Bush, and J.H. Salmela. 1997. "Pre- and Post-Competition Routines of Expert Coaches of Team Sports." *The Sport Psychologist* 11 (2): 127-41.

Bompa, T., and M. Carrera. 2015. *Periodization Training for Sports.* 3rd ed. Champaign, IL: Human Kinetics.

Côté, J., and W. Gilbert. 2009. "An Integrative Definition of Coaching Effectiveness and Expertise." *International Journal of Sports Science & Coaching* 4 (3): 307-23.

Côté, J., and W.A. Sedgwick. 2003. "Effective Behaviors of Expert Rowing Coaches: A Qualitative Investigation of Canadian Athletes and Coaches." *International Sports Journal* 7 (1): 62-77.

Cushion, C. 2007. "Modelling the Complexity of the Coaching Process." *International Journal of Coaching and Sport Sciences* 2 (4): 395-401.

Duda, J.L. 1989. "Goal Perspectives, Participation and Persistence in Sport." *International Journal of Sport Psychology* 20 (1): 42-56.

Fletcher, D., and M. Scott. 2010. "Psychological Stress in Sports Coaches: A Review of Concepts, Research, and Practice. *Journal of Sport Sciences* 28 (2): 127-37.

Frey, M. 2007. "College Coaches' Experiences With Stress—'Problem Solvers' Have Problems, Too." *The Sport Psychologist* 21: 38-57.

Hersch, P.L. 2012. "Does the NCAA Coaching Carousel Hamper the Professional Prospects of College Football Recruits?" *Journal of Sports Economics* 13 (1): 20-33.

International Council for Coaching Excellence. 2013. *International Sport Coaching Framework (v1.2).* Human Kinetics: Champaign, IL.

Janssen, J. 2014. *How to Build and Sustain a Championship Culture: Your Ten-Step Blueprint to Build a Winning Culture of Commitment, Accountability, and Ownership.* Winning the Mental Game.

Jowett, S., and V. Chaundy. 2004. "An Investigation into the Impact of Coach Leadership and Coach-Athlete Relationship on Group Cohesion." *Groups Dynamics: Theory, Research and Practice* 8: 302-11.

Jowett, S., and G. Don Carolis. July, 2003. "*The Coach-Athlete Relationship and Perceived Satisfaction in Team Sports.* 11th World Congress of Sport Psychology. Copenhagen, Denmark.

Kamphoff, C., and D. Gill. 2008. "Collegiate Athletes' Perceptions of the Coaching Profession." *International Journal of Sports Science & Coaching* 3 (1): 55-72.

Ntoumanis, N., and S.J.H. Biddle. 1999. "A Review of Motivational Climate in Physical Activity." *Journal of Sport Sciences* 17: 643-65.

Penney, D. 2006. "Coaching as Teaching: New Acknowledgements in Practice." In *The Sports Coach as Educator*, edited by R.L. Jones, 25-36. London, UK: Routledge.

Smith, R.K. 2000. A Brief History of the National Collegiate Athletic Association's Role in Regulating Intercollegiate Athletics. *Marquette Sports Law Review* 11: 9.

Swigonski, N.L., B.A. Enneking, and K.S. Hendrix. 2014. "Bullying Behavior By Athletic Coaches." *Pediatrics* 133 (2): 273-75.

Vallee, C.N., and G.A. Bloom. 2005. "Building a Successful University Program: Key and Common Elements of Expert Coaches." *Journal of Applied Sport Psychology* 17 (3): 179-96.

Wankel, L.M., and J.M. Sefton. 1989. "A Season-Long Investigation of Fun in Youth Sports." *Journal of Sport and Exercise Psychology* 11 (4): 355-66.

Wolanin, A., E. Hong, D. Marks, K. Panchoo, and M. Gross. 2016. "Prevalence of Clinically Elevated Depressive Symptoms in College Athletes and Differences By Gender and Sport." *British Journal of Sports Medicine* 50 (3): 167-71.

Chapter 9

Abernethy, B. 1989. "Expert-Novice Differences in Perception: How Expert Does the Expert Have to Be? *Canadian Journal of Sport Sciences* 14: 27-30.

———. 1990. "Expertise, Visual Search, and Information Pick-Up in Squash." *Perception* 19 (1): 63-77.

———. 1991. "Visual Search Strategies and Decision-Making in Sport." *International Journal of Sport Psychology* 22 (3-4): 189-210.

Allen, S. 2007. "Expertise in Sport: A Cognitive-Developmental Approach." *Journal of Education* 187: 9-29.

Anderson, J.R. 1981. *Cognitive Skills and Their Acquisition.* Hillsdale, NJ: Erlbaum.

Arthur, M.B., and D.M. Rousseau. 1996. *The Boundaryless Career: A New Employment Principle for a New Organizational Era."* New York, NY: Oxford University Press.

Arthur, M.B., D. Inkson, and J. Pringle. 1999. *The New Careers: Individual Action and Economic Change.* London, UK: Sage.

Arthur, M.B., S.N. Khapova, and C.P.M. Wilderom. 2005. "Career Success in A Boundary-less Career World." *Journal of Organizational Behvior* 26 (2): 177-202.

Audas, R., J. Goddard, and G. Rowe. 2006. "Modelling Employment Durations of NHL Head Coaches: Turnover and Post-Succession Performance." *Managerial and Decision Economics* 27 (4): 293-306.

Baker, J., J. Cote, and B. Abernethy. 2003. "Sport-Specific Practice and the Development of Expert Decision-Making in Team Ball Sports." *Journal of Applied Sport Psychology* 15: 12-25.

Baker, J., S. Horton, J. Robertson-Wilson, and M. Wall. 2003. "Nurturing Sport Expertise: Factors Influencing the Development of Elite Athlete." *Journal of Sports Science & Medicine* 2: 1-9.

Bandura, A. 1977. "Self-Efficacy: Toward a Unifying Theory of Behavioral Change. *Psychological Review* 84 (2): 191.

———. 1986. "Fearful Expectations and Avoidant Actions as Coeffects of Perceived Self-Inefficacy." *American Psychologist* 41 (12): 1389-91.

———. 1990. "Perceived Self-Efficacy in the Exercise of Personal Agency." *Journal of Applied Sport Psychology* 2 (2): 128-63.

———, and S. Wessels. 1997. *Self-Efficacy.* New York, NY: W.H. Freeman & Company.

Baxter-Jones, A.D.G., P. Helms, N. Maffulli, J.C. Baines-Preece, M. Preece. 1995. "Growth and Development of Male Gymnasts, Swimmers, Soccer and Tennis Players: A Longitudinal Study." *Annals of Human Biology* 22 (5): 381-94.

Berliner, D.C. 1994. "Expertise: The Wonder of Exemplary Performances." In *Creating Powerful Thinking in Teachers and Students: Diverse Perspectives*, edited by J.M. Mangier and C.C. Block, 161-86. Fort Worth, TX: Holt, Rinehart & Winston.

Binet, A. 1894. *La psychologie des grands calculateurs*. Paris, France: Hachette.

Bloom, B.S. 1985. *Developing Talent in Young People*. New York, NY: Ballentine.

Bloom, G.A., and J.H. Salmela. 1998. "Personal Characteristics of Expert Team Sport Coaches." *Journal of Sport Pedagogy* 6 (2): 56-76.

Boucher, J.L., and B.T. Mutimer. 1994. "The Relative Age Phenomenon in Sport: A Replication and Extension with Ice-Hockey Players." *Research Quarterly for Exercise and Sport* 65 (4): 377-81.

Bowes, I., and R.L. Jones. 2006. "Working at the Edge of Chaos: Understanding Coaching as a Complex Interpersonal System." *The Sport Psychologist* 20 (2): 235-45.

Brewer, J., P. Balsom, J. Davis, and B. Ekblom. 1992. "The Influence of Birth Date and Physical Development on the Selection of a Male Junior International Soccer Squad." *Journal of Sport Sciences* 10: 561-2.

Bryan, W.L., and N. Harter. 1897. "Studies in the Physiology and Psychology of the Telegraphic Language." *Psychological Review* 4: 27-53.

———. 1899. "Studies on the Telegraphic Language: The Acquisition of a Hierarchy of Habits." *Psychological Review* 6: 345-75.

Charness, N., R.T. Krampe, and U. Mayr. 1996. "The Role of Practice and Coaching in Entrepreneurial Skill Domains: An International Comparison of Life-Span Chess Skill Acquisition. In *The Road to Excellence: The Acquisition of Expert Performance in the Arts and Sciences, Sports, and Games*, edited by K.A. Ericsson, 51-80. Mahwah, NJ: Erlbaum.

Chase, W.G. 1973. *Visual Information Process*. New York, NY: Academic Press.

———, and H.A. Simon. 1973. "Perception in Chess." *Cognitive Psychology* 4: 55-81.

Chi, M.T. 1978. "Knowledge Structures and Memory Development." *Children's Thinking: What Develops* 1: 75-96.

———, R. Glaser, and M.J. Farr, eds. 1988. *The Nature of Expertise*. Hillsdale, NJ: Erlbaum.

Christopher, M. 2008. *The Olympics: Unforgettable Moments of the Games*. New York, NY: Hachette Digital.

Clancey, W.J., and E.H. Shortliffe. 1984. *Readings in Medical Artificial Intelligence: The First Decade*. Boston, MA: Addison-Wesley Longman Publishing Co., Inc.

Claparède, E. 1917. "La psychologie de l'intelligence." *Scientia* 22: 353-68.

Collins, B.E., and B.H. Raven. 1969. "Group Structure: Attraction, Coalitions, Communication, and Power." *The Handbook of Social Psychology* 4: 102-204.

Cornford, I., and J. Athanasou. 1995. "Developing Expertise through Training." *Industrial and Commercial Training* 27 (2): 10-8.

Côté, J., and W.D. Gilbert. 2009. "An Integrative Definition of Coaching Effectiveness and Expertise." *International Journal of Sports Science & Coaching* 4 (3): 307-23.

Côté, J., J. Baker, and B. Abernethy. 2007. "Practice and Play in the Development of Sport Expertise." In *Handbook of Sport Psychology*, edited by R. C. Eklund and G. Tenenbaum, 184-202. Hoboken, NJ: Wiley.

Côté, J., J.H. Salmela, and S. Russell. 1995. "The Knowledge of High-Performance Gymnastic Coaches: Methodological Framework." *The Sport Psychologist* 9: 65-75.

Cushion, C.J., K.M. Armour, and R.L. Jones. 2006. "Locating the Coaching Process in Practice: Models 'for' and 'of' Coaching." *Physical Education & Sport Pedagogy* 11 (1): 83-99.

Dawson, P.M., and S.M. Dobson. 2002. "Managerial Efficiency and Human Capital: An Application to English Association Football." *Managerial and Decision Economics* 27: 471-86.

———, and B. Gerrard. 2000. "Estimating Coaching Efficiency in Professional Team Sports: Evidence From English Association Football." *Scottish Journal of Political Economy* 47: 399-421.

De Groot, A.D. 1946. "Het denken van den schaker, een experimenteel-psychologische studie." Unpublished doctoral dissertation. University of Amsterdam. Amsterdam.

———. 1965. *Thought and Choice in Chess*. The Hague, Netherlands: Mouton.

De Marco, G.M., and B.A. McCullick. 1997. "Developing Expertise in Coaching: Learning From Legends. *Journal of Physical Education Recreation & Dance* 68 (3): 37-41.

DeWeese, B.H. 2012. "Defining the Constructs of Expert Coaching: A Q-Methodological Study of Olympic Sport Coaches." Doctoral dissertation. North Carolina State University.

Djakow, I.N., N.W. Petrowski, and P.A. Rudik. 1927. *Psychologie des schachspiels*. Berlin, Germany: Walter de Gruyter.

Duncker, K., and L.S. Lees. 1945. "On Problem-Solving." *Psychological Monographs* 58 (5): 1-113.

Eby, L.T., M. Butts, and A. Lockwood. 2003. "Predictors of Success in the Era of the Boundaryless Career." *Journal of Organizational Behavior* 24 (6): 689-708.

Epstein, D. 2014. *The Sports Gene: Inside the Science of Extraordinary Athletic Performance*. New York, NY: Penguin.

Erickson, K., J. Côté, and J. Fraser-Thomas. 2007. "Sport Experiences, Milestones, and Educational Activities Associated with High-Performance Coaches' Development." *The Sport Psychologist* 21 (3): 302-16.

Ericsson, K.A., and R. Pool. 2016. *Peak: Secrets From the New Science of Expertise*. Boston, MA: Houghton Mifflin Harcourt.

———. 1996. *The Road to Excellence: The Acquisition of Expert Performance in the Arts and Sciences, Sport and Games*. Mahwah, NJ: Erlbaum.

———. 1996. "The Acquisition of Expert Performance: An Introduction to Some of the Issues." In *The Road to Excellence: The Acquisition of Expert Performance in the Arts and Sciences, Sports, and Games*, edited by K.A. Ericsson, 1-50. Mahwah, NJ: Erlbaum.

———. 2006. "The Influence of Experience and Deliberate Practice on the Development of Superior Expert Performance." *The Cambridge Handbook of Expertise and Expert Performance* 38: 685-705.

———, and A.C. Lehmann. 1996. "Expert and Exceptional Performance: Evidence of Maximal Adaptation to Task Constraints." *Annual Review of Psychology* 47: 273-305.

Ericsson, K.A., and J. Smith. 1991. "Prospects and Limits in the Empirical Study of Expertise: An Introduction." In *Toward a General Theory of Expertise: Prospects and Limits*, edited by K.A. Ericsson and J. Smith, 1-38. Cambridge, New York, NY: Cambridge University Press.

Ericsson, K.A., and N. Charness. 1994. "Expert Performance: Its Structure and Acquisition." *American Psychologist* 49 (8): 725-47.

Ericsson, K.A., R.T. Krampe, and C. Tesch-Rˆmer. 1993. "The Role of Deliberate Practice in the Acquisition of Expert Performance." *Psychological Review* 100 (3): 363.

Fabianic, D. 1993. "Managerial Selection and Organizational Effectiveness in Professional Baseball: The Eighties." *Journal of Sport Behavior* 16 (2): 111-21.

Feltovich, P.J., K.M. Ford, and R.R. Hoffman. 1997. *Expertise in Context: Human and Machine*. Cambridge, MA: MIT Press.

Feltz, D.L., and C.D. Lirgg. 1998. "Perceived Team and Player Efficacy in Hockey." *Journal of Applied Psychology* 83 (4): 557.

Findling, J.E., and K.D. Peele. 2004. *Historical Dictionary of the Modern Olympic Movement*. Westport, CT: Greenwood Press.

Fizel, J.L., and M. D'itri. 1996. "Estimating Managerial Efficiency: The Case of College Basketball Coaches." *Journal of Sport Management* (4): 435-45.

Flavell, J. 1979. "Metacognition Monitoring: A New Area of Cognitive-Developmental Inquiry." *American Psychologist* 34: 906-11.

French, J.R., B. Raven, and D. Cartwright. 1959. "The Bases of Social Power." *Classics of Organization Theory* 7: 311-20.

French, K.E., and J.R. Thomas. 1987. "The Relation of Knowledge Development to Children's Basketball Performance." *Journal of Sport Psychology* 9: 15-32.

Gallimore, R., W. Gilbert, and S. Nater. 2014. "Reflective Practice and Ongoing Learning: A Coach's 10-Year Journey." *Reflective Practice* 15 (2): 268-88.

Galton, F. 1869. *Hereditary Genius: An Inquiry into Its Laws and Consequences*. Vol. 27. London, UK: Macmillan.

Gamson, W.A., and N.A. Scotch. 1964. "Scapegoating in Baseball. *American Journal of Sociology* 70: 69-72.

Germain, M.L. 2011. "A Chronological Synopsis of the Dimensions of Expertise: Toward the Expert of the Future." *Performance Improvement* 50 (7): 38-46.

Giambatista, R.C. 2004. "Jumping Through Hoops: A Longitudinal Study of Leader Life Cycles in the NBA." *The Leadership Quarterly* 15 (5): 607-24.

Glaser, R. 1996. "Changing the Agency for Learning: Acquiring Expert Performance." In *The Road to Excellence: The Acquisition of Expert Performance in the Arts and Sciences, Sports, and Games*, edited by K. A. Ericsson, 303-11. Mahwah, NJ: Erlbaum.

———, and M.T.H. Chi. 1988. "Overview." In *The Nature of Expertise*, edited by M.T.H. Chi, R. Glaser and M.J. Farr, xv-xxviii. Hillsdale, NJ: Erlbaum

Gould, D., J. Giannini, V. Krane, and K. Hodge. 1990. "Educational Needs of Elite U.S. National Team, Pan American and Olympic Coaches." *Journal of Teaching in Physical Education* 9 (4): 332-44.

Gouldner, A.W. 1954. *Patterns of Industrial Bureaucracy*. Glencoe, IL: Green Press.

Green, E.L. 1918. "A Family of Athletes." *The Classical Journal* 13 (4): 267-71.

Green, M., and B. Houlihan. 2005. *Elite Sport Development: Policy Learning and Political Priorities*. London, UK: Routledge.

Grusky, O. 1963. "The Effects of Formal Structure on Managerial Recruitment: A Study of Baseball Organization." *Sociometry* 26 (3): 345-53.

Gunz, H., M. Evans, and M. Jalland. 2000. "Career Boundaries in the 'Boundaryless' World." In *Career Frontiers: New Conceptions of Working Lives*, edited by M. A. Peiperl, M. B. Arthur, R. Goffee, and T. Morris, 24-53. Oxford, UK: Oxford University Press.

Gustin, W.C. 1985. "The Development of Exceptional Research Mathematicians." In *Developing Talent in Young People*, edited by B. S. Bloom, 270-331. New York, NY: Ballantine Books.

Hadley, L., M. Poitras, J. Ruggiero, and S. Knowles. 2000. "Performance Evaluation of National Football League Teams." *Managerial and Decision Economics* 21 (2): 63-70.

Hayes J.R. 1981. *The Complete Problem Solver*. Philadelphia, PA: Franklin Institute Press.

Helsen, W.F., J.L. Starkes, and N.J. Hodges. 1998. "Team Sports and the Theory of Deliberate Practice." *Journal of Sport and Exercise Psychology* 20: 12-34.

Hodge, T., and J.M. Deakin. 1998. "Deliberate Practice and Expertise in the Martial Arts: The Role of Context in Motor Recall." *Journal of Sport & Exercise Psychology* 20 (3): 260-79.

Hodges, N.J., and J.L. Starkes. 1996. "Wrestling with the Nature of Expertise: A Sport Specific Test of Ericsson, Krampe, and Tesch-Römer's 1993, Theory of 'Deliberate Practice'." *International Journal of Sport Psychology* 27 (4): 400-24.

Hoffman, R.R., ed. 1992. *The Psychology of Expertise: Cognitive Research and Empirical AI*. New York, NY: Springer-Verlag.

Horton, S., and M.J. Deakin. 2008. "Expert Coaches in Action." In *Developing Sports Expertise: Researchers and Coaches Put Theory Into Practice*, edited by D. Farrow, J. Baker and C. MacMahon, 75-88. New York, NY: Routledge.

Howe, M.J.A., J.W. Davidson, and J.A. Sloboda. 1998. "Innate Talents: Reality or Myth?" *Behavioral and Brain Sciences* 21 (3): 399-442.

Johnson, M.B., and G. Tenenbaum. 2006. "The Roles of Nature and Nurture in Expertise in Sport." In *Essential Processes for Attaining Peak Performance*, edited by D. Hackfort and G. Tenenbaum, 26-43. Oxford, UK: Meyer & Meyer.

Jones, R.L., and M. Wallace. 2005. Another Bad Day at the Training Ground: Coping With Ambiguity in the Coaching Context." *Sport Education and Society* 10 (1): 119-34.

Jones, R.L., K.M. Armour, and P. Potrac. 2002. "Understanding the Coaching Process: Framework for Social Analysis." *Quest* 54 (1): 34-48.

———. 2003. "Constructing Expert Knowledge: A Case Study of a Top-Level Professional Soccer Coach." *Sport, Education & Society* 8 (2): 213-29.

Kahn, L. 1993. "Managerial Quality, Team Success, and Individual Player Performance in Major League Baseball." *Industrial & Labor Relations Review* 46: 531-47.

Kalinowski, A.G. 1985. "The Development of Olympic Swimmers." In Developing Talent in Young People, edited by B. S. Bloom, 139-92. New York, NY: Ballantine Books.

Kesner, F., and T. Sebora. 1994. "Executive Succession: Past, Present and Future." *Journal of Management* 20 (2): 327-72.

Klissouras, V. 2001. "The Nature and Nurture of Human Performance." *European Journal of Sport Science* 1 (2): 1-10.

Lyle, J. 2002. *Sports Coaching Concepts: A Framework for Coaches' Behaviour.* New York, NY: Routledge.

Mallett, C.J., and J. Côté. 2006. "Beyond Winning and Losing: Guidelines for Evaluation High Performance Coaches." *The Sport Psychologist* 20: 213-21.

Mamede, S., and H.G. Schmidt. 2004. "The Structure of Reflective Practice in Medicine. *Medical Education* 38 (12): 1302-8.

Mann, D.T., A.M. Williams, P. Ward, and C.M. Janelle. 2007. "Perceptual-Cognitive Expertise in Sport: A Meta-Analysis." *Journal of Sport and Exercise Psychology* 29 (4): 457-78.

Martens, R., R.S. Vealey, and D. Burton. 1990. *Competitive Anxiety in Sport.* Champaign, IL: Human Kinetics.

McPherson, S.L., and J.R. Thomas. 1989. "Relation of Knowledge and Performance in Boys' Tennis: Age and Expertise." *Journal of Experimental Child Psychology* 48 (2): 190-211.

Mendel, G. 1865. "Experiments in Plant Hybridization." *Verh Naturforsch Vereines Brunn* 4: 3-47.

Miller, G.A. 1956. "The Magical Number Seven, Plus or Minus Two: Some Limits on Our Capacity for Processing Information." *Psychological Review* 63 (2): 81.

———. 1994. "The Magical Number Seven, Plus or Minus Two: Some Limits on Our Capacity for Processing Information." *Psychological Review* 101 (2): 343.

Mondello, M., and J. Maxcy. 2009. "The Impact of Salary Dispersion and Performance Bonuses in NFL Organizations." *Management Decision* 47 (1): 110-23.

Monsaas, J.A. 1985. "Learning To Be a World-Class Tennis Player." In *Developing Talent in Young People*, edited by B. S. Bloom, 211-69. New York, NY: Ballantine Books.

Munsterberg, H. 1892. "The Problems of Experimental Psychology." *Proceedings of the American Psychological Association*: 10-11.

Nash, C.S., J. Sproule, and P. Horton. 2011. "Excellence in Coaching: The Art and Skill of Elite Practitioners." *Research Quarterly for Exercise and Sport* 82 (2): 229-38.

Ng, T.W.H., L.T. Eby, K.L. Sorensen, and D.C. Feldman. 2005. "Predictors of Objective and Subjective Career Success: A Meta-Analysis." *Personnel Psychology* 58: 367-409.

Partington, J.T. 1988. "Becoming a Complete Coach." *Science Periodical on Research and Technology in Sport* 8 (6): 1-7.

Picazo-Tadeo, A.J., and F. Gonzalez-Gomez. 2010. "Does Playing Several Competitions Influence a Team's League Performance? Evidence From Spanish Professional Football." *Central European Journal of Operations Research* 18 (3): 413-32.

Poczwardowski, A., J.E. Barott, and K.P. Henschen. 2002. "The Athlete and Coach: Their Relationship and Its Meaning: Results of an Interpretive Study." *International Journal of Sport Psychology* 33 (1): 116-40.

Porter, P., and G. Scully. 1982. "Measuring Managerial Efficiency: The Case of Baseball." *Southern Economic Journal* 48: 642-50.

Potrac, P., and R.L. Jones. 2009. "Power, Conflict and Cooperation: Toward a Micropolitics of Coaching. *Quest* 61: 223-36.

———, and K. Armour. 2002. "It's All About Getting Respect: The Coaching Behavior of an Expert English Soccer Coach." *Sport, Education & Society* 7 (2): 183-202.

Proctor, R.W., and A. Dutta. 1995. *Skill Acquisition and Human Performance*. Thousand Oaks, CA: Sage Publications, Inc.

Richman, H.B., F. Gobet, J.J. Staszewski, and H.A. Simon. 1996. "Perceptual and Memory Processes in the Acquisition of Expert Performance: The EPAM Model." *The Road to Excellence: The Acquisition of Expert Performance in the Arts and Sciences, Sports, and Games*, edited by K.A. Ericsson, 167-87. Hillsdale, NJ: Lawrence Erlbaum Associates, Inc.

Rowe, G., A. Cannella, D. Rankin, and D. Gorman. 2005. "Leader Succession and Organizational Performance: Integrating the Common-Sense, Ritual Scapegoating, and Vicious-Circle Succession Theories." *The Leadership Quarterly* 16 (2): 197-219.

Sari, I., and F. Soyer. 2010. "The Scope, Development and the Characteristics of Expertise in Sports Coaching Context." *International Journal of Human Sciences* 7 (2): 748-60.

Saury, J., and M. Durand. 1998. "Practical Knowledge in Expert Coaches: On-Site Study of Coaching in Sailing." *Research Quarterly for Exercise and Sport* 69 (3): 254-66.

Schempp, P.G., J.A. You, and B. Clark. 1999, December. "The Antecedents of Expertise in Golf Instruction." Paper presented at the World Scientific Congress of Golf, Leeds, UK.

Schinke, R.J., G.A. Bloom, and J.H. Salmela. 1995. "The Career Stages of Elite Canadian Basketball Coaches." *Avante* 1 (1): 48-62.

Sedgwick, W.A., Côté, J., and Dowd, J. 1997. "Confidence Building Strategies used by Canadian High-Level Rowing Coaches. *Avante* 3 (3): 80-92.

Seibert, S.E., J.M. Crant, and M.L. Kraimer. 1999. "Proactive Personality and Career Success." *Journal of Applied Psychology* 84 (3): 416-27.

Selinger, E.M., and R.P. Crease. 2003. "Dreyfus on Expertise: The Limits of Phenomenological Analysis." *Continental Philosophy Review* 35: 245-79.

Simon, H.A., and M. Barenfeld. 1969. "Information-Processing Analysis of Perceptual Processes in Problem Solving." *Psychological Review* 76 (5): 473.

Simonton, D.K. 1994. *Greatness: Who Makes History and Why*. New York, NY: Guildford Press.

Singell, L. 1993. "Managers, Specific Human Capital, and Firm Productivity in Major League Baseball." *Atlantic Economic Journal* 21: 47-59.

Singer, R.N., and C.M. Janelle. 1999. "Determining Sport Expertise: From Genes to Supremes." *International Journal of Sport Psychology* 30: 117-50.

Sloboda, J.A., J.W. Davidson, M.J.A. Howe, and D.G. Moore. 1996. "The Role of Practice in the Development of Performing Musicians." *British Journal of Psychology* 87: 287-309.

Smart, D., and R. Wolfe. 2003. "The Contribution of Leadership and Human Resources to Organizational Success: An Empirical Assessment of Performance in Major League Baseball." *European Sport Management Quarterly* 3: 165-88.

Smart, D., J. Winfree, and R. Wolfe. 2008. "Major League Baseball Managers: Do They Matter?" *Journal of Sport Management* 22 (3): 303-21.

Sosniak, L.A. 1985. "Learning to be a Concert Pianist." In *Developing Talent in Young People*, edited by B. S. Bloom, 19-67. New York, NY: Ballantine Books.

Starkes, J.L. 1987. "Skill in Field Hockey: The Nature of the Cognitive Advantage." *Journal of Sport Psychology* 9 (2): 146-60.

———. 2000. "The Road to Expertise: Is Practice the Only Determinant?" *International Journal of Sport Psychology* 31 (4): 431-51.

———, and K.A. Ericsson. 2003. *Expert Performance in Sports: Advances in Research on Sport Expertise*. Champaign, IL: Human Kinetics.

Starkes, J.L., J.M. Deakin, F. Allard, N.J. Hodges, and A. Hayes. 1996. "Deliberate Practice in Sports: What Is It Anyway?" *The Road to Excellence: The Acquisition of Expert Performance in the Arts and Sciences, Sports, and Games*, edited by K.A. Ericsson, 81-106. Mahwah, NJ: Erlbaum.

Starkes, J., and F. Allard, eds. 1993. *Cognitive Issues in Motor Expertise*. Vol. 102. Amsterdam, Netherlands: Elsevier.

Starkes, J., and W. Helsen. 1998. "Practice, Practice, Practice–Is That All It Takes?" *Behavioral and Brain Sciences* 21 (3): 425.

Stebbins, R.A. 1970. "Career: The Subjective Approach." *Sociological Quarterly* 11: 32-49.

Stogdill, R.M. 1950. "Leadership, Membership and Organization." *Psychological Bulletin* 47 (1): 1-14.

Taylor, F.W. 1911. *Scientific Management*. New York, NY: Harper and Brothers Publishers.

Tena, J.D., and D. Forrest. 2007. "Within-Season Dismissal of Football Coaches: Statistical Analysis of Causes and Consequences." *European Journal of Operational Research* 181 (1): 362-73.

Thomas, J.R., and K.T. Thomas. 1998. "Senior Women of Lower and Higher Golf Handicaps: How Psychological and Physiological Characteristics Influence Performance." In *Science and Golf III*, edited by M.R. Farrarlly and A.J. Cochran. Champaign, IL: Human Kinetics.

Thomas, K.T., and J.R. Thomas. 1994. "Developing Expertise in Sport: The Relation of Knowledge and Performance." *International Journal of Sport Psychology* 25 (3): 295-300.

Thorndike, E.L. 1921. *The Psychology of Learning*. New York, NY: Teachers College, Columbia University.

Tichomirov, O.K., and F.D. Poznyanskaza. 1966-1967. "An Investigation of Visual Search as Means of Analyzing Heuristics." *Soviet Psychology* 5: 2-15.

Trudel, P., and W.D. Gilbert. 2006. "Coaching and Coach Education." In *Handbook of Physical Education*, edited by D. Kirk, M. O'Sullivan, and D. McDonald, 516-39. London, UK: Sage.

Turner, R.J. 1960. "Sponsored and Contest Mobility and the School System." *American Sociological Review* 25: 855-67.

Van Lehn, K. 1996. "Conceptual and Meta Learning during Coached Problem Solving." Paper presented at the 3rd International Conference on Intelligent Tutoring Systems ITS, Berlin, Germany. June.

Walker, S. 2017. *The Captain Class: The Hidden Force That Creates the World's Greatest Teams*. New York, NY: Random House.

Wallingford, R. 1975. "Long Distance Running." In *The Scientific Aspects of Sports Training*, edited by A.W. Tayler and F. Landry, 118-30. Springfield, IL: Charles C Thomas

Wiman, M.L.. 2010. "The Development and Validation of an Expertise Development Model for Sport Coaches." Unpublished doctoral dissertation. The University of Western Ontario, London, Canada.

———. 2010. *The Development and Validation of an Expertise Development Model for Sport Coach.* Unpublished doctoral dissertation. London, Canada: The University of Western Ontario.

Woodman, L. 1993. "Coaching: A Science, an Art, an Emerging Profession." *Sport Science Review* 2 (2): 1-13.

Chapter 10

Abbott, M., C. Bourne, P. Eriksson, C. Higgs, G. Lagace, O. Sawiki, and A. Marion. 2005. *Coaching Athletes With a Disability.* Ottawa, Canada: Coaching Association of Canada.

Amorose, A., and T. Horn. 2000. Intrinsic Motivation: Relationships With Collegiate Athletes' Gender, Scholarship Status, and Perceptions of Their Coaches' Behavior." *Journal of Sport and Exercise Psychology:* 63-84.

Banack, H.R., C.M. Sabiston, and G.A. Bloom. 2011. "Coach Autonomy Support, Basic Need Satisfaction, and Intrinsic Motivation of Paralympic Athletes." *Research Quarterly for Exercise and Sport* 82: 722-30.

Berndt, T.J. 2002. "Friendship Quality and Social Development." *Current Directions in Psychological Science* 11: 7-10.

Biddle, S., and N. Mutrie. 2001. *Psychology of Physical Activity: Determinants, Well-Being and Interventions.* London, UK: Routledge.

Bloom, G.A. D.E. Stevens, and T.L. Wickwire. 2003. "Expert Coaches' Perceptions of Team Building." *Journal of Applied Sport Psychology* 15: 129-43.

Bloom, G.A., N. Durand-Bush, R.J. Schinke, and J.H. Salmela. 1998. "The Importance of Mentoring in the Development of Coaches and Athletes." *International Journal of Sport Psychology* 29: 267-81.

Bradbury, T. 1999. "Athletes Doing It for Themselves: Self-Coaching Guidelines for Elite Athletes." In *VISTA '99: The Outlook,* edited by R.D. Steadward et al., 81-89. Edmonton, AB: The University of Alberta Press.

Brault, M.W. 2011. *School-Aged Children with Disabilities in U.S. Metropolitan Statistical Areas: 2010.* U.S. Department of Commerce Economics and Statistics Administration U.S. Census Bureau. Retrieved from https://www.census.gov/prod/2011pubs/acsbr1012.pdf.

Caron, J.G., G.A. Bloom, T.M. Loughead, and M.D. Hoffmann. 2016. "Paralympic Athlete Leaders' Perceptions of Leadership and Cohesion." *Journal of Sport Behavior* 39 (3).

Carron, A.V., S.R. Bray, and M.A. Eys. 2002. "Team Cohesion and Team Success in Sport." *Journal of Sport Sciences* 20: 119-26.

Carter, A.D., and G.A. Bloom. 2009. "Coaching Knowledge and Success: Going Beyond Athletic Experiences." *Journal of Sport Behavior* 32: 419-37.

Carvalho, J., and A. Farkas. 2005. Rehabilitation Through Sport: Pilot Project With Amputees in Angola." *The Lancet* 366: S5-6.

Cassidy, T., R. Jones, and P. Potrac. 2009. *Understanding Sports Coaching: The Social, Cultural and Pedagogical Foundations of Coaching Practice,* 2nd ed. London, UK: Routledge.

Côté, J., and W. Gilbert. 2009. "An Integrative Definition of Coaching Effectiveness and Expertise." *International Journal of Sports Science & Coaching* 4: 307-23.

Cregan, K., G.A. Bloom, and G. Reid. 2007. "Career Evolution and Knowledge of Elite Coaches of Swimmers With a Physical Disability." *Research Quarterly for Exercise and Sport* 78: 339-50.

Cushion, C.J., K.M. Armour, and R.L. Jones. 2003. "Coach Education and Continuing Professional Development: Experience and Learning to Coach." *Quest* 55: 215-30.

DePauw, K., and S. Gavron. 2005. *Disability Sport.* Champaign, IL: Human Kinetics.

———. 1995. *Sport and Disability.* Champaign, IL: Human Kinetics.

Dieffenbach, K., and T. Statler. 2012. "More Similar Than Different: The Psychological Environment of Paralympic Sport." *Journal of Sport Psychology in Action* 3: 109-18.

Douglas, S., W.R. Falc„o, and G.A. Bloom. 2018. "Career Development and Learning Pathways of Paralympic Coaches with a Disability." *Adapted Physical Activity Quarterly* 35 (1): 93-110.

Duarte, T., and D. Culver. 2014. "Becoming a Coach in Developmental Adaptive Sailing: A Lifelong Learning Perspective." *Journal of Applied Sport Psychology* 26: 441-56.

Fairhurst, K.E., G.A. Bloom, and W.J. Harvey. 2017. "The Learning and Mentoring Experiences of Paralympic Coaches." Unpublished manuscript.

Falcão, W.R., G.A. Bloom, and T.M. Loughead. 2015. "Coaches' Perspectives of Building Cohesion in Paralympic Sports." *Adapted Physical Activity Quarterly* 32: 206-22.

Gilbert, W.D., J. Côté, and C. Mallett 2006. "Developmental Paths and Activities of Successful Sports Coaches." *International Journal of Sports Science & Coaching* 1: 69-76.

Goodwin, D. 2016. "Youth Sport and Dis/ability." In *Routledge Handbook of Youth Sport*, edited by K. Green and A. Smith, 308-20. New York, NY: Routledge.

———, K. Johnston, P. Gustafson, M. Elliot, R. Thurmeier, and H. Kuttai. 2009). "It's Ok to Be a Quad: Wheelchair Rugby Players Sense of Community." *Adapted Physical Activity Quarterly* 26: 102-17.

Goodwin, D.L., and S.G. Compton. 2004. "Physical Activity Experiences of Women Aging With Disabilities." *Adapted Physical Activity Quarterly* 21: 122-38.

Hanrahan, S.J. 2007. "Athletes With Disabilities." In *Handbook of Sport Psychology*, 3rd ed., edited by G. Tenenbaum and R.E. Eklund, 845-58. Hoboken, NJ: John Wiley.

Hollembeak, J., and A.J. Amorose. 2005. "Perceived Coaching Behaviors and College Athletes' Intrinsic Motivation: A Test of Self-Determination Theory." *Journal of Applied Sport Psychology* 17: 20-36.

Huntley, E., B. Cropley, D. Gilbourne, A. Sparkes, and Z. Knowles. 2014. "Reflecting Back and Forwards: An Evaluation of Peer-Reviewed Reflective Practice Research in Sport." *Reflective Practice: International and Multidisciplinary Perspectives* 15: 863-76.

International Paralympic Committee. 2007. "Paralympic Movement Info Sheets." Accessed December 1, 2007. www.paralympic.org/release/Main_Sections_Menu/Media/Infosheets.

Koh, K.T., G.A. Bloom, K.E. Fairhurst, D.M. Paiement, and Y.H. Kee. 2014. "An Investigation of a Formalized Mentoring Program for Novice Basketball Coaches." *International Journal of Sport Psychology* 45: 11-32.

Lee, J., and A. Porretta. 2013. "Document Analysis of Sports Literature for Individuals With Disabilities." *Perceptual & Motor Skills: Physical Development & Measurement* 116: 847-58.

Lefebvre, J.L., M.B. Evans, J. Turnnidge, H.L. Gainforth, and J. Côté. 2016. "Describing and Classifying Coach Development Programmes: A Synthesis of Empirical Research and Applied Practice." *International Journal of Sport Science & Coaching* 11: 887-99.

Liow, D.K., and W.G. Hopkins. 1996. "Training Practices of Athletes With Disabilities." *Adapted Physical Activity Quarterly* 13: 372-81.

MacDonald, D.J., K. Beck, K. Erickson, and J. Côté. 2016. "Understanding Sources of Knowledge for Coaches of Athletes with Intellectual Disabilities." *Journal of Applied Research in Intellectual Disabilities* 29: 242-9.

Mageau, G., and R. Vallerand 2003. "The Coach-Athlete Relationship: A Motivational Model." *Journal of Sport Sciences* 21: 883-904.

Mallett, C.J., P. Trudel, J. Lyle, and S.B. Rynne. 2009. "Formal vs. Informal Coach Education." *International Journal of Sports Science and Coaching* 4: 325-34.

Martin, L.J., A.V. Carron, and S.M. Burke. 2009. "Team Building Intervention in Sport: A Meta-Analysis." *Sport & Exercise Psychology Review* 5: 3-18.

McMaster, S., D. Culver, and P. Werthner. 2012. "Coaches of Athletes With a Physical Disability: A Look at Their Learning Experiences." *Qualitative Research in Sport, Exercise and Health* 4: 226-43.

Moffett, A., K. Dieffenbach, and T. Statler. 2009. "Exploring the Expectations and Experiences of U.S. Coaches and Athletes Participating in the Paralympic Games." Paper presented at the Association for Applied Sport Psychology Conference. Salt Lake City, UT, United States.

Nash, C., and J. Sproule. 2009. "Career Development of Expert Coaches." *International Journal of Sports Science and Coaching* 4: 121-38.

Reid, G., and A. Prupas. 1998. "A Documentary Analysis of Research Priorities in Disability Sport." *Adapted Physical Activity Quarterly* 15: 168-78.

Schinke, R.J., G.A. Bloom, and J.H. Salmela. 1995. "The Career Stages of Elite Canadian Basketball Coaches." *Avante* 1: 48-62.

Shapiro, D.R., and J.J. Martin. 2014. The Relationships Among Sport Self-Perceptions and Social Well-Being in Athletes With Physical Disabilities." *Disability and Health Journal* 7: 42-48.

Sport Canada. 2006. "Policy on Sport for Persons With a Disability." Publication No. CH24-14/2006. Ottawa, Canada: Canadian Heritage.

Steadward, R.D., and S.L. Foster. 2003. "History of Disability Sport." In *Adapted Physical Activity*, edited by R.D. Steadward, G.D. Wheeler, and E.J. Watkinson, 471-95. Alberta, Canada: The University of Alberta Press.

Tawse, H., G.A. Bloom, C.M. Sabiston, and G. Reid. 2012. "The Role of Coaches of Wheelchair Rugby in the Development of Athletes With a Spinal Cord Injury." *Qualitative Research in Sport, Exercise and Health* 4: 206-25.

Taylor, S.L., P. Werthner, and D. Culver. 2014. "A Case Study of a Parasport Coach and a Life of Learning." *International Sport Coaching Journal* 1: 127-38.

———, and B. Callary. 2015. "The Importance of Reflection for Coaches in Parasport. *Reflective Practice* 16: 269-84.

United Nations. 2016. *Youth with Disabilities*. Retrieved from http://www.un.org/esa/socdev/documents/youth/fact-sheets/youth-with-disabilities.pdf.

Vallée, C.N., and G.A. Bloom. 2005. "Building a Successful University Program: Key And Common Elements of Expert Coaches." *Journal of Applied Sport Psychology* 17 (3): 179-96.

Warburton, D., C. Nicol, and S. Bredin. 2006. "Health Benefits of Physical Activity: The Evidence." *Canadian Medical Association Journal* 174: 801-9.

Werthner, P., and P. Trudel. 2006. "Theoretical Perspective for Understanding How Coaches Coach. *The Sport Psychologist* 20: 198-212.

Chapter 11

Coombs, P.H., and M. Ahmed. 1974. "Attacking Rural Poverty: How Nonformal Education Can Help." A Research Report for the World Bank Prepared by the International Council for Educational Development.

ICCE. 2013. *International Sport Coaching Framework*. Champaign, IL: Human Kinetics.

———. 2015. *International Sport Coach Developer Framework*. Leeds, UK: ICCE.

National Coaching Foundation. 2012. UK Coaching Framework. North, J. 2009. *The UK Coaching Framework: The Coaching Workforce 2009-2016*. Leeds, UK: Sports Coach UK.

South African Sports Confederation and Olympic Committee. 2010. *The South African Coaching Framework*. Johannesburg, South Africa: SASCOC.

South African Sports Confederation and Olympic Committee: Coaches Commission. 2009. *National Coaches Education Framework Implementation Plan*. Johannesburg, South Africa: SASCOC.

Chapter 12

Duffy, P. 2010. "Foreword." In *Sport Coaching: Professionalization and Practice*, edited by J. Lyle and C. Cushion vii-x. London, UK: Elsevier.Duffy, P., and S. Lara-Bercial. 2012. *International Sport Coaching Framework v1.1*. Champaign, IL: Human Kinetics.

———, J. North, and J. Curado. 2013. *CoachNet: A Study to Identify the Current and Potential Future Voice of the Coach Within the European Union*. Report to the European Union Commission. Leeds, UK: Leeds Beckett University.

European Coaching Council. 2007. *Review of the EU 5-Level Structure for the Recognition of Coaching Qualifications*. K^ln, Germany: European Network of Sport Science, Education and Employment.

ICCE. 2015. *ICCE Strategy 2015-2020: Leading and Supporting the Development of Sport Coaching Globally*. Leeds, UK: ICCE.

———, ASOIF, and LBU. 2013. *The International Sport Coaching Framework,* version 1.2. Champaign, IL: Human Kinetics.

———. 2014. *The International Coach Developer Framework,* version 1.2. Leeds, UK: ICCE.

International Olympic Committee. n.d. "Athletes' Entourage." www.olympic.org/entourage#entourage.

———. 2006. *Olympic Solidarity: Creation and Development*. Lausanne, Switzerland: IOC.

———. 2011. *Guidelines for the Conduct of the Athletes' Entourage*. Lausanne, Switzerland: IOC.

———. 2013. *Olympic Solidarity: A Direct Line! 2013-2016 Quadrennial*. Lausanne, Switzerland: IOC.

International Sailing Federation (ISAF). 2013. *The ISAF Coaching Framework*. www.sailing.org/tools/documents/cf12onlineversion-[15983].pdf.

Lara-Bercial, S., L.C. Dohme, A.J. Rankin-Wright, J. North, and S. Ripoll. 2016. *Evaluation and Review of the Philippines Academy of Sport Coach Advancement Program – Report to Department for Education*. Leeds, UK: Leeds Beckett University

Lara-Bercial, S., J. North, L. Petrovic, K. Oltmanns, J. Minkhorst, and K. Hämälänien. 2017. *Understanding, Planning and Developing a Coaching System. Project CoachLearn Development & Implementation Tool Series: Tool #1*. CoachLearn Project, Leeds, UK: Leeds Beckett University

Lyle, J. 2002. *Sport Coaching Concepts: A Framework for Coaches' Behaviour*. London, UK: Routledge.

North, J. 2009. *The UK Coaching Workforce*. Leeds, UK: Sports Coach UK.

———, K. Hämälänien, K. Oltmanns, L. Petrovic, J. Minkhorst, S. Lara-Bercial, and J. McIlroy. 2016. *The Context and Motivation for the Collection and Application of Sport Coaching Workforce Data in Five European Countries*. Report #3, CoachLearn Project, Leeds, UK: Leeds Beckett University

Parlebas, P. 2011. *Jeux, Sports et Sociétés. Lexique de Praxeologie Motrice (Games, Sports and Societies: Lexicon of Motor Praxeology)*. Paris, France: INSEP.

Patterson, L., S. Backhouse, and S. Lara-Bercial. 2017. *Provision of Guidance for the Development of a Sustainable, Cooperative and International Anti-Doping Training Program for High Performance Coaches*. Montreal, Canada: WADA

Patterson, L., P. Duffy, and S. Backhouse. 2014. "Are Coaches Anti-Doping? Exploring Issues of Engagement With Education and Research." *Substance Use & Misuse* 49 (9): 1182-5.

South African Sport Confederation and Olympic Committee. 2011. *The South African Coaching Framework*. Johannesburg, South Africa: SASCOC.

Sports Coach UK. 2008. *The UK Coaching Framework*. Leeds, UK: Sports Coach UK.

World Anti-Doping Agency. 2009. *Play True*. Montreal, Canada: WADA.

————. 2015. *The WADA Code 2015.* Montreal, Canada: WADA.

Weiss, M.R., and D.M. Wiese-Bjornstal. 2009. "Positive Youth Development Through Physical Activity." *Research Digest.* Washington, DC: President's Council on Physical Fitness and Sports.

Chapter 13

Bauer, J., and R.H. Mulder. 2007. "Modelling Learning from Errors in Daily Work." *Learning in Health and Social Care* 6 (3): 121-33.

Bloom, B. 1985 *Developing Talent in Young People.* New York, NY: Ballantine Books.

Boshuizen, H.P.A., R. Bromme, and H. Gruber. 2004. *Professional Learning: Gaps and Transitions on the Way From Novice To Expert.* Berlin, Germany**:** Springer.

Cambridge Dictionary. n.d. *s.v.* "Expertise." https://dictionary.cambridge.org/dictionary/english/expertise.

Cassidy, T. 2008. "Coach Education or Coach Development: A Paradigm Shift or More of the Same?" Presented at the Korean Coaching Development Center 10th Anniversary Global Conference and International Council for Coach Education. *Asian Regional Coach Conference,* 69-72. Asan, South Korea: Hoseo University

Côté, J., and W. Gilbert. 2009. "An Integrative Definition of Coaching Effectiveness and Expertise." *International Journal of Sports Science & Coaching* 4 (3): 307-23.

Dawson, A., and P. Phillips. 2013. "Coach Career Development: Who Is Responsible?" *Sport Management Review* 16 (4): 477-87.

Durand-Bush, N., and J. H. Salmela. 2002. "The Development and Maintenance of Expert Athletic Performance: Perceptions of World and Olympic Champions." *Journal of Applied Sport Psychology* 14 (3): 154-71.

Ericsson, K.A. 1998. "The Scientific Study of Expert Levels of Performance: General Implications for Optimal Learning and Creativity." *High Ability Studies* 9 (1): 75-100.

————, R.T. Krampe, and C. Tesch-Römer. 1993. "The Role of Deliberate Practice in the Development of Expertise. *Psychology Review* 100: 363-406.

Friedman, A., and M. Phillips. 2001. "Leaping the CPD Hurdle: A Study of the Barriers and Drivers to Participation in Continuing Professional Development." Paper presented to the British Educational Research Association Annual Conference, University of Leeds, 13-15 September 2001. Accessed June 1, 2015. www.leeds.ac.uk/educol/documents/00001892.htm.

Giblin, G., D. Farrow, M. Reid, K. Ball, and B. Abernethy. 2013. "Keep Your Eye off the Ball: Expertise Differences in Visual Search Behavior of Tennis Coaches." *Journal of Sport & Exercise Psychology* 35: S29.

Gilbert, W., J. Côté, and C. Mallett. 2006. "Developmental Paths and Activities of Successful Sport Coaches." *International Journal of Sports Science & Coaching* 1: 69-76.

Gilbert, W., and P. Trudel. 2004. "Analysis of Coaching Science Research Published From 1970-2001." *Research Quarterly for Exercise & Sport* 75: 388-99.

Henriksen, K., N. Stambulova, and K. Roessler. 2010. "Holistic Approach to Athletic Talent Development Environments: A Successful Sailing Milieu." *Psychology of Sport & Exercise* 11 (3): 212-22.

Hoffman, R.R., P. Ward, P.J. Feltovich, L. DiBello, S.M. Fiore, and D.H. Andrews. 2014 *Accelerated Expertise: Training for High Proficiency in a Complex World.* New York, NY: Psychology Press.

ICCE. 2013. *International Sport Coaching Framework.* Champaign, IL: Human Kinetics.

Kandu, F. 2013 "Malawi FA Reveals Plan To Fast-Track Local Coaches." Accessed June 1, 2015. www.bbc.co.uk/sport/0/football/21699874.

Kerr, G., and A. Dacyshyn. 2000. "The Retirement Experiences of Elite, Female Gymnasts." *Journal of Applied Sport Psychology* 12 (2): 115-33.

Knowles, Z., G. Tyler, D. Gilbourne, and M. Eubank. 2006. "Reflecting on Reflection: Exploring the Practice of Sports Coaching Graduates. *Reflective Practice* 7 (2): 163-79.

Koon Teck, K., C. Mallett, and C.J. Wang. 2009. "Examining the Ecological Validity of the Coaching Behavior Scale (Sports) for Basketball." *International Journal of Sports Science & Coaching* 4 (2): 261-72.

Lajoie, S.J. 2003 "Transitions And Trajectories for Studies of Expertise." *Educational Researcher* 32 (8): 21-25.

Lavallee, D., J. Kremer, A. Moran, and M. Williams. 2012. *Sport Psychology: Contemporary Themes*. New York, NY: Macmillan International Higher Education.

Moon, J.A. 2004. *A Handbook of Reflective and Experiential Learning. Theory and Practice*. London, UK: Routledge-Falmer.

Nash, C. 2014. "How Coaches Learn and Develop." In *Practical Sports Coaching*, edited by C. Nash, 177-189. London, UK: Routledge/Taylor & Francis Group.

———, and D. Collins. 2006. "Tacit Knowledge in Expert Coaching: Science or Art?" *Quest* 58 (4): 465-77.

Nash, C., R. Martindale, D. Collins, and A. Martindale. 2012. "Parameterising Expertise in Coaching: Past, Present and Future." *Journal of Sports Sciences* 30 (10): 985-94.

Nash, C.S., and J. Sproule. 2009. "Career Development of Expert Coaches." *International Journal of Sports Science & Coaching* 4 (1): 121-38.

———. 2011." Insights Into Experiences: Reflections of an Expert and Novice Coach." *International Journal of Sports Science & Coaching* 6 (1): 149-62.

———. 2012. "Coaches Perceptions of Their Coach Education Experiences." *International Journal of Sport Psychology* 43 (1): 33-52.

———, M. Callan, K. McDonald, and T. Cassidy. 2009. "Career Development of Expert Coaches." *International Journal of Sports Science & Coaching* 4 (1): 121-38.

Nash, C., J. Sproule, E. Hall, and C. English. 2013. *Coaches Outside the System*. Research report for sport coach UK. Leeds, England: Sport Coach UK.

Nash, C.S., J. Sproule, and P. Horton. 2011. "Excellence in Coaching: The Art and Skill of Elite Practitioners." *Research Quarterly for Exercise and Sport* 82 (2): 229-38.

Nelson, L., C. Cushion, and P. Potrac. 2013. "Enhancing the Provision of Coach Education: The Recommendations of UK Coaching Practitioners." *Physical Education and Sport Pedagogy* 18 (2): 204-18.

Occhino, J.L., C.J. Mallett, S.B. Rynne, and K.N. Carlisle. 2014. "Autonomy-Supportive Pedagogical Approach to Sports Coaching: Research, Challenges and Opportunities." *International Journal of Sports Science & Coaching* 9 (2): 401-16.

Pakistan Press International. 2011. "Cricket: PCB Organizes Two Fast Track Coaching Programs." June 22.

Petty, N.J., J. Scholes, and L. Ellis. 2011. "Master's Level Study: Learning Transitions Towards Clinical Expertise in Physiotherapy." *Physiotherapy* 97 (3): 218-25.

Rynne, S. 2014. "'Fast Track' and 'Traditional Path' Coaches: Affordances, Agency and Social Capital. *Sport, Education & Society* 19 (3): 299-313.

———, C.J. Mallett, and K. Tinning. 2009. "A Review of Published Coach Education Research 2007-2008." *International Journal of Physical Education* 46 (1): 9-16.

Schempp, P., B. McCullick, and I. Mason. 2006. "The development of Expert Coaching." in *The Sports Coach as Educator: Reconceptualising Sports Coaching*, edited by R.L. Jones, 145-61. London, UK: Routledge.

Schoening, A.M. 2013. "From Bedside To Classroom: The Nurse Educator Transition Model." *Nursing Education Perspectives* 34 (3): 167-72

Scholes J. 2006. *Developing Expertise in Critical Care Nursing*. Oxford, UK: Blackwell.

Spiro, R.J., B.P. Collins, J. Thota, and P.J. Feltovich.2003. "Cognitive Flexibility Theory: Hypermedia for Complex Learning, Adaptive Knowledge Application, and Experience Acceleration." *Educational Technology* 43 (5): 5-10.

Smoll, F.L., and R.E. Smith. 2010. "Conducting Psychologically Oriented Coach-Training Programs: A Social-Cognitive Approach." *Applied Sport Psychology: Personal Growth to Peak Performance*: 392-416.

Sports Coach UK. 2007. *The UK Coaching Framework.* Leeds, UK: National Coaching Foundation.

Storm, L.K., K. Henriksen, C.H. Larsen, and M.K. Christensen. 2014. "Influential Relationships as Contexts of Learning and Becoming Elite: Athletes' Retrospective Interpretations." *International Journal of Sports Science & Coaching* 9 (6): 1341-56.

Turner, D. 2008. "The Usual Suspects: Critical Consideration of the Fast-Tracking of Ex-Elite Athletes Into High-Profile Coaching Roles." *Coaching Edge* 13: 18-19.

UK Sport. 2001. *The UK Vision for Coaching.* London, UK: UK Sport.

Zeng, H.Z., R.W. Leung, B. Wei, and L. Wenhao. 2009. "The Differences in Coaching Behaviors Between Individual and Team Sports at College Varsity Level." *Asian Journal of Physical Education & Recreation* 15 (2): 35-43.

Chapter 14

Abraham, A., and D. Collins. 1998. "Examining and Extending Research in Coach Development." *Quest* 50: 59-79.

———, and R. Martindale. 2006. "The Coaching Schematic: Validation Through Expert Coach Consensus." *Journal of Sports Sciences* 24 (6): 549-64.

Allen, T.D., L.T. Eby, and E. Lentz. 2006. "The Relationship Between Formal Mentoring Program Characteristics and Perceived Program Effectiveness." *Personnel Psychology* 59 (1): 125-53.

Balyi, I., R. Way, and C. Higgs. 2013. *Long-Term Athlete Development.* Champaign, IL: Human Kinetics.

Barnett, N.P., F.L. Smoll, and R.E. Smith. 1992. "Effects Of Enhancing Coach-Athlete Relationships On Youth Sport Attrition." *Sport Psychologist* 6 (2): 111-27.

Bloom, G.A., N. Durand-Bush, R.J. Schinke, and J.H. Salmela. 1998. "The Importance of Mentoring in the Development of Coaches and Athletes. / Importance du "Mentoring" Dans le Developpement des Entraineurs et des Athletes." *International Journal of Sport Psychology* 29 (3): 267-81.

Bowes, I., and R. Jones. 2006. "Working at the Edge of Chaos: Understanding Coaching as a Complex Interpersonal System." *The Sport Psychologist* 20: 235-45.

Brooks, D.D., D. Ziatz, B. Johnson, and D. Hollander. 2000. "Leadership Behavior and Job Responsibilities of NCAA Division 1A Strength and Conditioning Coaches. / Comportement de Leader et Responsabilite Professionelle d'Entraineurs et Preparateurs Physiques Dans le Haut Niveau." *Journal of Strength & Conditioning Research* 14 (4): 483-92.

Campbell, T., and P. Sullivan. 2005. "The Effect of a Standardized Coaching Education Program on the Efficacy of Novice Coaches." *AVANTE* 11 (1): 38-45.

Cassidy, T., R.L. Jones, and P. Potrac. 2009. *Understanding Sports Coaching: The Social, Cultural and Pedagogical Foundations of Coaching Practice.* 2nd ed. London, UK: Routledge.

Cassidy, T., P. Potrac, and A. McKenzie. 2006. "Evaluating and Reflecting Upon a Coach Education Initiative: The CoDe of Rugby." *Sport Psychologis,* 20 (2): 145.

Coakley, J. 1992. "Burnout Among Adolescent Athletes: A Personal Failure or Social Problem." *Sociology of Sport Journal* 9 (3): 271-85.

Conroy, D.E., and J.D. Coatsworth. 2006. "Coach Training as a Strategy for Promoting Youth Social Development." *Sport Psychologist* 20 (2): 128-44.

Côté, J., J. Baker, and B. Abernethy. 2003. "From Play to Practice: A Developmental Framework for the Acquisition of Expertise." In *Expert Performance in Sports: Advances in Research on Sport Expertise*, edited by J.L. Starkes and K.A. Ericsson, 89-113. Champaign, IL: Human Kinetics.

Côté, J., M. Bruner, K. Erickson, L. Strachan, and J. Fraser-Thomas. 2010. "Athlete Development and Coaching." *Sports Coaching: Professionalisation and Practice*: 63-84.

Côté, J., and W. Gilbert. 2009. "An Integrative Definition of Coaching Effectiveness and Expertise." *International Journal of Sport Science and Coaching* 4 (3): 307-23.

Côté, J., and M. Vierimaa. 2014. "The Developmental Model of Sport Participation: 15 Years After Its First Conceptualization." *Science & Sports* 29: S63-S69.

Côté, J., B. Young, P. Duffy, and J. North. 2007. "Towards a Definition of Excellence in Sport Coaching." *International Journal of Coaching Science* 1 (1): 3-17.

Culver, D.M. 2004. "Enriching Knowledge: A Collaborative Approach Between Sport Coaches and Consultant/Facilitator." PhD diss. University of Ottawa, Canada.

———, and P. Trudel. 2006. "Cultivating Coaches' Communities of Practice: Developing the Potential for Learning Through Interations." In *The Sports Coach as Educator: Re-Conceptualising Sports Coaching*, edited by R.L. Jones, 97-112. New York, NY: Routledge.

———, and P. Werthner. 2009. "A Sport Leader's Attempt to Foster a Coaches' Community of Practice." *International Journal of Sport Science and Coaching* 4 (3): 365-83.

Cushion, C. 2015. "Mentoring for Success in Sport Coaching." In *Mentoring in Physical Education and Sports Coaching*, edited by F.C. Chambers, 155-62. New York, NY: Routledge.

———, and L. Nelson. 2013. "Coaching Education and Learning: Developing the Field." In *Routledge Handbook of Sports Coaching*, edited by P. Potrac, W. Gilbert, and J. Denison, 359-74. New York, NY: Routledge.

———, K. Armour, J. Lyle, R. Jones, R. Sandford, and C. O'Callaghan. 2010. *Coach Learning and Development: A Review of Literature*. London, UK: Sports Coach UK.

Cushion, C.J., K.M Armour, and R.L. Jones. 2006. "Locating the Coaching Process in Practice: Models 'for' and 'of' Coaching." *Physical Education & Sport Pedagogy* 11: 83-99.

———. 2003. "Coach Education and Continuing Professional Development: Experience and Learning to Coach." *Quest* 55 (3): 215-30.

Cushion, C.J., and R.L. Jones. 2001. "A Systematic Observation of Professional Top-Level Youth Soccer Coaches." *Journal of Sport Behavior* 24 (4): 354-76.

Dorgo, S. 2009. "Unfolding the Practical Knowledge of an Expert Strength and Conditioning Coach." *International Journal of Sport Science and Coaching* 4 (1): 17-30.

Dubois, P.E. 1986. "The Effect of Participation in Sport on the Value Orientations of Young Athletes." *Sociology of Sport Journal* 3 (1): 29-42.

Durand-Bush, N., and J.H. Salmela. 2002. "The Development and Maintenance of Expert Athletic Performance: Perceptions of World and Olympic Champions." *Journal of Applied Sport Psychology* 14 (3): 154-71.

Dweck, C.S. 2008. *Mindset: The New Psychology of Success*. New York, NY: Random House Digital, Inc.

Ehrich, L., B. Hansford, and L. Tennent. 2004. "Formal Mentoring Programs in Education and Other Professions: A Review of Literature." *Educational Administration Quarterly* 40 (4): 518-40.

Erickson, K., M.W. Bruner, D.J. MacDonald, and J. Côté. 2008. "Gaining Insight Into Actual and Preferred Sources of Coaching Knowledge." *International Journal of Sports Science & Coaching* 3 (4): 527-38.

Erickson, K., J. Côté, and J. Fraser-Thomas. 2007. "Sport Experiences, Milestones, and Educational Activities Associated With High-Performance Coaches' Development." *Sport Psychologist* 21 (3): 302-16.

Farrell, P., and M. Van de Braam. 2014. "Mentoring Programmes: A Case Study With Tennis Coach Ireland." *Coaching & Sport Science Review* (63): 13-4.

Field, M., M.W. Collins, M.R. Lovell, and J. Maroon. 2003. "Does Age Play a Role in Recovery From Sports-Related Concussion? A Comparison of High School and Collegiate Athletes." *Journal of Pediatrics* 142 (5): 546-53.

Ford, P., E. Coughlan, and M. Williams. 2009. "The Expert-Performance Approach as a Framework for Understanding and Enhancing Coaching Performance, Expertise and Learning." *International Journal of Sports Science & Coaching* 4 (3): 451-63.

Gallimore, R., W. Gilbert, and S. Nater. 2014. "ReflLective Practice and Ongoing Learning: A Coach's 10-Year Journey." *Reflective Practice* 15 (2): 268-88.

Gearity, B.T., B. Callary, and P. Fulmer. 2013. "Learning To Coach: A Qualitative Case Study Of Phillip Fulmer." *Journal of Coaching Education* 6 (2): 65-86.

Gilbert, W., J. Côté, and C. Mallett. 2010. "Developmental Paths and Activities of Successful Sport Coaches." *Soccer Journal* 55 (3): 10-12.

Gilbert, W., R. Gallimore, and P. Trudel. 2009. "A Learning Community Approach to Coach Development in Youth Sport." *Journal of Coaching Education* 2 (2): 1-21.

Gilbert, W., L. Lichtenwaldt, J. Gilbert, L. Zelezny, and J. Côté. 2009. "Developmental Profiles of Successful High School Coaches." *International Journal of Sports Science & Coaching* 4 (3): 415-31.

Gilbert, W.D., and P. Trudel. 2001. "Learning to Coach Through Experience: Reflection in Model Youth Sport Coaches / Apprentissage du Metier d'Entraineur a Partir d'Experiences: Reflexions Dans le Milieu des Entraineurs de Jeunes." *Journal of Teaching in Physical Education* 21 (1): 16-34.

Gould, D., V. Krane, J. Giannini, and K. Hodge. 1990. "Educational Needs of Elite U.S. National Team, Pan American, and Olympic Coaches." *Journal of Teaching in Physical Education* 9 (4): 332-44.

Griffiths, M. 2015. "Training Coaches as Mentors." In *Mentoring in Physical Education and Sports Coaching*, edited by F.C. Chambers, 163-71. New York, NY: Routledge

———, and K. Armour. 2012. "Mentoring as a Formalized Learning Strategy With Community Sports Volunteers." *Mentoring & Tutoring: Partnership in Learning* 20 (1): 151-73.

Guskiewicz, K.M., and J.P. Mihalik. 2011. "Biomechanics of Sport Concussion: Quest for the Elusive Injury Threshold." *Exercise & Sport Sciences Reviews* 39 (1): 4-11.

Hammond, J., and J. Perry. 2005. "A Multi-Dimensional Assessment of Soccer Coaching Course Effectiveness." *Ergonomics* 48 (11-14): 1698-1710.

Handcock, P., and T. Cassidy. 2014. "Reflective Practice for Rugby Union Strength and Conditioning Coaches." *Strength & Conditioning Journal* 36 (1): 41-45.

Harwood, C. 2008. "Developmental Consulting in a Professional Football Academy: The 5Cs Coaching Efficacy Program." *Sport Psychologist* 22 (1): 109-33.

Hesse, D., and D. Lavallee. 2010. "Career Transitions In Professional Football Coaches." *Athletic Insight: The Online Journal of Sport Psychology* 12 (2).

International Council for Coaching Excellence [ICCE], Association of Summer Olympic International Federations [ASOIF], and Leeds Metropolitan University [LMU]. 2014. *International Coach Developer Framework* (Version 1.1). Leeds, UK: England

———. 2013. *International Sport Coaching Framework* (Version 1.2). Champaign, IL: Human Kinetics.

Irwin, G., S. Hanton, and D.G. Kerwin. 2004. "Reflective Practice and the Origins of Elite Coaching Knowledge." *Reflective Practice* 5 (3): 425-42.

Jones, R., and M. Wallace. 2006. "The Coach as 'Orchestrator': More Realistically Managing the Complex Coaching Context." In *The Sports Coach as Educator: Re-Conceptualising Sports Coaching*, edited by R. Jones, 51-64. Abingdon, UK: Routledge.

Jones, R.L., K.M. Armour, and P. Potrac. 2003. "Constructing Expert Knowledge: A Case Study of a Top-Level Professional Soccer Coach." *Sport, Education & Society* 8 (2): 213-29.

Jones, R.L., R. Harris, and A. Miles. 2009. "Mentoring in Sports Coaching: A Review of the Literature." *Physical Education & Sport Pedagogy* 14 (3): 267-84.

Jones, R.L., and P. Turner. 2006. "Teaching Coaches to Coach Holistically: Can Problem-Based Learning (PBL) Help?" *Physical Education & Sport Pedagogy* 11 (2): 181-202.

Knowles, Z., A. Borrie, and H. Telfer. 2005. "Towards The Reflective Sports Coach: Issues Of Context, Education And Application." *Ergonomics* 48: 1711-20.

Knowles, Z., D. Gilbourne, A. Borrie, and A. Nevill. 2001. "Developing the Reflective Sports Coach: A Study Exploring the Processes of Reflective Practice Within a Higher Education Coaching Programme." *Reflective Practice* 2 (2): 185-207.

Knowles, Z., G. Tyler, D. Gilbourne, and M. Eubank. 2006. "Reflecting on Reflection: Exploring the Practice of Sports Coaching Graduates." *Reflective Practice* 7 (2):163-79.

Kuklick, C.R., B.T. Gearity, and M. Thompson. 2015. "Reflective Practice in a University-Based Coach Education Program." *International Sport Coaching Journal* 2 (3): 248-60.

———, and L. Neelis. 2015. "A Case Study of One High Performance Baseball Coach's Experiences Within a Learning Community." *Qualitative Research in Sport, Exercise and Health* 8 (1): 61-78.

Lemyre, F., P. Trudel, and N. Durand-Bush. 2007. "How Youth-Sport Coaches Learn to Coach." *Sport Psychologist* 21 (2): 191-209.

Lyle, J. 2002. *Sports Coaching Concepts: A Framework for Coaches' Behaviour*. New York, NY: Routledge.

Magnusen, M.J., and J. Petersen. 2012. "Apprenticeship and Mentoring Relationships in Strength and Conditioning: The Importance of Physical and Cognitive Skill Development." *Strength & Conditioning Journal* 34 (4): 67-72.

Malete, L., and D.L. Feltz. 2000. "The Effect of a Coaching Education Program on Coaching Efficacy." *Sport Psychologist* 14 (4): 410-17.

Lave, J., E. Wenger, and E. Wenger. 1991. *Situated Learning: Legitimate Peripheral Participation*. Cambridge, UK: Cambridge University Press.

Nash, C., and D. Collins. 2006. "Tacit Knowledge in Expert Coaching: Science or Art?" *Quest 2006* 58 (4): 465-77.

Nash, C., and J. Sproule. 2009. "Career Development of Expert Coaches." *International Journal of Sports Science & Coaching* 4 (1): 121-38.

———. 2011. "Insights Into Experiences: Reflections of an Expert and Novice Coach." *International Journal of Sports Science & Coaching* 6 (1): 149-62.

———, M. Callan, K. McDonald, and T. Cassidy. 2009. "Career Development Of Expert Coaches." *International Journal of Sports Science & Coaching* 4 (1): 121-38.

National Association for Sport and Physical Education [NASPE]. 2008. *National Coaching Report*. Reston, VA: NASPE Publications.

Nelson, L.J., and C. Cushion. 2006. "Reflection in Coach Education: The Case of the National Governing Body Coaching Certificate." *The Sport Psychologist* 20: 174-83.

———, and P. Potrac. 2006. "Formal, Nonformal and Informal Coach Learning: A Holistic Conceptualisation." *Coach* 35: 59-69.

North, J. 2009. *Coaching Workforce 2009-2016*. Leeds, UK: Sports Coach UK.

———. 2010. "Using 'Coach Developers' to Facilitate Coach Learning and Development: Qualitative Evidence From the UK." *International Journal of Sports Science & Coaching* 5 (2): 239-56.

Occhino, J., C. Mallett, and S. Rynne. 2013. "Dynamic Social Networks in High Performance Football Coaching." *Physical Education and Sport Pedagogy* 18 (1): 90-102.

Roberts, R., and J.S. Olson. 1991. *Winning Is the Only Thing: Sports in America Since 1945*. Baltimore, MD: JHU Press.

Saury, J., and M. Durand. 1998. "Practical Knowledge in Expert Coaches: On-Site Study of Coaching in Sailing." *Research Quarterly for Exercise & Sport* 69 (3): 254-66.

Schempp, P.G., B. McCullick, and I.S. Mason. 2006. "The Development of Expert Coaching." In *The Sports Coach as Educator: Re-Conceptualising Sports Coaching*, edited by R.L. Jones, 145-61 New York, NY: Routledge.

Smith, R.E., F.L. Smoll, and N.P. Barnett. 1995. "Reduction of Children's Sport Performance Anxiety Through Social Support and Stress-Reduction Training for Coaches." *Journal of Applied Developmental Psychology* 16: 125-42.

Smith, R.E., F.L. Smoll, and B. Curtis. 1979. "Coach Effectiveness Training: A Cognitive-Behavioral Approach to Enhancing Relationship Skills in Youth Sport Coaches." *Journal of Sport Psychology* 1: 59-75.

Stoszkowski, J., and D. Collins. 2014. "Blogs: A Tool to Facilitate Reflection and Community of Practice in Sports Coaching?" *International Sport Coaching Journal* 1 (3): 139-51.

Sullivan, G.S. 2009. "Coaching Education: Staff Development Strategies for the Adult Learner." *International Journal of Sport Management & Marketing* 5 (3): 2.

Trudel, P., and W.D. Gilbert. 2006. "Coaching and Coach Education." In *Handbook of Physical Education*, edited by D. Kirk, M. O'Sullivan, and D. McDonald, 516-39. London, UK: Sage.

Vargas-Tonsing, T.M. 2007. "Coaches' Preferences for Continuing Coaching Education." *International Journal of Sports Science & Coaching* 2 (1): 25-35.

Visek, A.J., S.M. Achrati, H.M. Mannix, K. McDonnell, B.S. Harris, and L. DiPietro, L. 2015. "The Fun Integration Theory: Toward Sustaining Children and Adolescents Sport Participation." *Journal of Physical Activity & Health* 12 (3): 424-33.

Wenger, E. 1998. "Communities of Practice: Learning as a Social System." *Systems Thinker* 9 (5): 2-3.

Werthner, P., and P. Trudel. 2006. "A New Theoretical Perspective for Understanding How Coaches Learn to Coach." *Sport Psychologist* 20 (2): 198-212.

Wright, T., P. Trudel, and D. Culver. 2007. "Learning How to Coach: The Different Learning Situations Reported By Youth Ice Hockey Coaches." *Physical Education and Sport Pedagogy* 12 (2): 127-44.

Zehntner, C., and J.A. McMahon. 2014. "Mentoring in Coaching: The Means of Correct Training? An Autoethnographic Exploration of One Australian Swimming Coach's Experiences." *Qualitative Research in Sport, Exercise & Health* 6 (4): 596-616.

Chapter 15

"Approaches to Teaching, Learning and Assessment and the Subject Area Competences." n.d. PDF File. Available at http://www.unideusto.org/tuningeu/images/stories/teaching/TLA___NURSING.pdf.

Armour, K.M. 2010. "The Learning Coach . . . The Learning Approach: Professional Development for Sports Coach Professionals." In *Sports Coaching: Professionalisation and Practice*, edited by J. Lyle and C. Cushion, 153-64. Edinburgh, UK: Elsevier.

Benner, P. 1984. *From Novice to Expert*. Menlo Park, CA: Addison-Wesley.

British Wrestling Association. 2016. Coach Developer Specification. www.britishwrestling.org/page.asp?section=210&sectionTitle=Coach+Development.

Carter, A.D., and G.A. Bloom. 2009. "Coaching Knowledge And Success: Going Beyond Athletic Experiences." *Journal of Sport Behavior* 32 (4): 419.

Coombs, P.H., and M. Ahmed. 1974. "Attacking Rural Poverty: How Nonformal Education Can Help." A Research Report for the World Bank Prepared by the International Council for Educational Development.

Collins, D., V. Burke, A. Martindale, and A. Cruickshank. 2015. "The Illusion of Competency Versus the Desirability of Expertise: Seeking a Common Standard for Support Professions in Sport." *Sports Medicine* 45: 1-7.

Côté, J., and W. Gilbert. 2009. "An Integrative Definition of Coaching Effectiveness and Expertise." *International Journal of Sports Science and Coaching* 4 (3): 307-23.

Crisfield, P., and K. Brook. 2012. "The Importance of Coach Developers Within the Global Coaching Framework: A Position Statement." Unpublished paper.

Cushion, C.J., K.M. Armour, and R.L. Jones. 2003. "Coach Education and Continuing Professional Development: Experience and Learning to Coach." *Quest* 55: 215-30.

Cushion, C., L. Nelson, K. Armour, J. Lyle, R. Jones, R. Sandford, and C. O'Callaghan. 2010. *Coach Learning and Development: A Review of Literature.* Leeds, UK: Sports Coach UK.

Ericsson, A., and R. Pool. 2016. *Peak: Secrets from the New Science of Expertise.* Boston, MA: Houghton Mifflin Harcourt.

Ericsson, K.A., M.J. Prietula, and E.T. Cokely. 2007. "The Making of an Expert." *Harvard Business Review* 85 (7/8): 114.

Ferlie, E.B., and S.M. Shortell. 2001. "Improving the Quality of Health Care in the United Kingdom and the United States: A Framework for Change." *Milbank Quarterly* 79 (2): 281-315.

Fordham, A.J. 2005. "Using a Competency Based Approach in Nurse Education." *Nursing Standard* 19 (31): 41-48.

Gilbert, W. and P. Trudel. 2001. "Learning to Coach Through Experience: Reflection in Model Youth Sport Coaches." *Journal of Teaching in Physical Education* 21: 16-34.

Hart, J. 2015. *Modern Workplace Learning: A Resource Book for L & D.* Center for Learning and Performance Technologies. Available at https://www.modernworkplacelearning.com/cild/

Hensley, A. n.d. "Approaches to Teaching, Learning and Assessment and the Subject Area Competences Nursing." Accessed December 5, 2018. http://docplayer.net/1801927-Approaches-to-teaching-learning-and-assessment-and-the-subject-area-competences.html.

Hodkinson, P., and H. Hodkinson. 2005. "Improving Schoolteachers' Workplace Learning." *Research Papers in Education* 20: 190-231.

International Council for Coaching Excellence. 2013. *International Sport Coaching Framework.* Champaign, IL: Human Kinetics.

ICCE. 2015. *International Sport Coach Developer Framework.* Leeds, UK: ICCE.

Jarvis, P. 2010. *Adult Education and Lifelong Learning: Theory and Practice.* 4th ed. London, UK: Routledge.

Jennings, C. 2016. "From Courses to Campaigns: Using the 70:20:10 Approach." Accessed January 3, 2016. http://charles-jennings.blogspot.co.uk/Sunday.

Jones, R.L., and M. Wallace. 2005. "Another Bad Day at the Training Ground: Coping With Ambiguity in the Coaching Context." *Sport, Education and Society* 10 (1): 119-34.

Lara-Bercial, S. 2016. Presentation. April. India

Lyle, J., and C. Cushion. 2010. *Sports Coaching E-Book: Professionalisation and Practice.* Elsevier Health Sciences.

Kirkpatrick, D. 1994. *Evaluating Training Programs: The Four Levels.* San Franscisco, CA: Berrett-Koehler.

Knowles, Z., A. Borrie, and H. Telfer. 2005. "Towards the Reflective Sports Coach: Issues of Context, Education and Application." *Ergonomics* 48 (11-14): 1711-20.

Mallett, C.J., P. Trudel, J. Lyle, and S.B. Rynne. 2009. "Formal vs. Informal Coach Education." *International Journal of Sports Science & Coaching* 4 (3): 325-64.

Moon, J.A. 2004. *A Handbook of Reflective and Experiential Learning. Theory and Practice.* London, UK: Routledge-Falmer.

Nash, C. 2014. *Practical Sports Coaching*. London, UK: Routledge.

———, and D. Collins. 2006. "Tacit Knowledge in Expert Coaching: Science or Art?" *Quest* 58 (4): 465-77.

Nash, C., R. Martindale, D. Collins, and A. Martindale. 2012. "Parameterising Expertise in Coaching: Past, Present And Future." *Journal of Sports Sciences* 30 (10): 985-94.

NCATE. 2010. *Transforming Teacher Education Through Clinical Practice: A National Strategy to Prepare Effective Teachers."* Report of the Blue Ribbon Panel on Clinical Preparation and Partnerships for Improved Student Learning. www.ncate.org/LinkClick.aspx?filetick et=zzeiB1OoqPk%3D&tabid=7.

Nelson, L.J., C.J. Cushion, and P. Potrac. 2006. "Formal, Nonformal and Informal Coach Learning: A Holistic Conceptualisation." *International Journal of Sports Science and Coaching* 1: 247-53.

North, J., S. Lara-Bercial, A.J., Rankin-Wright, M. Ashford, M., and L. Whitaker. 2016. *Player Development Systems in the Performance Pathway in Four World-Leading Badminton Nations: A Literature Review and Interviews With Experts From Indonesia, Korea, Denmark And Spain* Leeds, UK: Leeds Beckett University.

Peskin, J. 2011. "It's Not Magic! Research on Developing Expertise." *Education Canada* 51 (4): 4.

Professional Standards Council of Australia. 2016. www.psc.gov.au.

Schempp, P.G., B. McCullick, and I.S. Mason. 2006. "The Development of Expert Coaching." In *The Sports Coach as Educator: Re-conceptualizing Sports Coaching*, 145-161. London, UK: Routledge.

The Education & Training Foundation. 2014. *Initial Guidance for Users of the Professional Standards for Teachers and Trainers in Education and Training: England.* www.et-foundation. co.uk/wp-content/uploads/2014/05/ETF-Prof-Standards-Guidance-v2-2.pdf.

Trudel, P., and W.D. Gilbert. 2006. "Coaching and Coach Education." In *Handbook of Physical Education*, edited by D. Kirk, M. O'Sullivan, and D. McDonald, 516-39. London, UK: Sage.

Trudel, P., D. Culver, and P. Werthner, P. 2013. "Considerations for Coach Development Administrators." In *Routledge Handbook of Sports Coaching*, 375. London, UK: Routledge.

Trudel, P., W. Gilbert, and P. Werthner. 2010. "Coach Education Effectiveness." In *Sport Coaching: Professionalisation and Practice*, edited by J. Lyle and C. Cushion, 135-52. Elsevier.

Vardhan, D., and P. Duffy. 2011. *The South African Coaching Framework*. www.srsa.gov. za/MediaLib/Downloads/Home/Miscellaneous/CurrentEvents/South-African-Coaching-Framework-Consultation-Doc%2021%20July%202011.pdf.

Wade, G., and Trudel, P. 1999. "An Evaluation Strategy for Coach Education Programs." *Journal of Sport Behavior* 22 (2): 234.

Werthner, P., and P. Trudel. 2006. "A New Theoretical Perspective for Understanding How Coaches Learn to Coach." *The Sport Psychologist* 20: 198-212.

Chapter 16

"Active Endorsement: Higher Education Endorsement Scheme for Sports Coach Education." 2015, June 26. www.skillsactive.com/PDF/endorsement/HE_Endorsement_Sports_ Coach_Education_Submission_Document.pdf.

Aspen Institute Sports & Society Program. 2015. *Sport for All, Play for Life: A Playbook to Get Every Kid in the Game*. Washington, DC: The Aspen Institute.

Carter, A.D., and G.A. Bloom. 2009. "Coaching Knowledge and Success: Going Beyond Athletic Experiences." *Journal of Sport Behavior* 32 (4): 419-37.

Cassidy, T., P. Potrac, and A. McKenzie. 2006. "Evaluating and Reflecting Upon a Coach Education Initiative: The CoDe of Rugby." *The Sport Psychologist* 20: 145-61.

Coaching Association of Canada. 2013. "NCCP Policy and Implementation Standards." www.coach.ca/files/NCCP_Policies_ImplementationStandards_Jan2013.pdf.

Collins, D., V. Burke, A. Martindale, and A. Cruickshank. 2015. "The Illusion of Competency Versus the Desirability of Expertise: Seeking a Common Standard for Support Professions in Sport." *Sports Medicine* 45: 1-7.

Côté, J., and W. Gilbert. 2009. "An Integrative Definition of Coaching Effectiveness and Expertise." *International Journal of Sports Science & Coaching* 4 (3): 307-23.

Cushion, C., L. Nelson, K. Armour, J. Lyle, R. Jones, R. Sandford, and C. O'Callaghan. 2010. *Coach Learning and Development: A Review of Literature*. Sports Coach UK. https://www.researchgate.net/publication/265566741_Coach_Learning_and_Development_A_Review_of_Literature.

Cushion, C.J., K.M. Armour, and R.L. Jones. 2003. "Coach Education and Continuing Professional Development: Experience and Learning to Coach." *Quest* 55: 215-30.

Cushion, C.J., and L. Nelson. 2013. "Coach Education and Learning: Developing the Field." In *Routledge Handbook of Sports Coaching*, edited by P. Potrac, W. Gilbert, and J. Denison, 359-74. London, UK: Routledge Taylor & Francis Group.

Demers, G., A.J. Woodburn, and C. Savard. 2006. "The Development of an Undergraduate Competency-Based Coach Education Program." *The Sport Psychologist* 20: 162-73.

Driscoll, A. 2006. "Assessment and Accreditation: Positive Partnership." In *Taking Ownership of Accreditation: Assessment Processes That Promote Institutional Improvement and Faculty Engagement*, edited by A. Driscoll and D. Cordero de Noriega, 1-18. Sterling, VA: Stylus.

Gelmon, S.B. 1997. "Accreditation, Core Curriculum and Allied Health Education: Barriers and Opportunities." *Journal of Allied Health* 26 (3): 119-25.

Gilbert, W., R. Gallimore, and P. Trudel. 2009. "A Learning Community Approach to Coach Development in Youth Sport." *Journal of Coaching Education* 2 (2): 1-21.

Gilbert, W.D., and P. Trudel. 2001. "Learning to Coach Through Experience: Reflection in Model Youth Sport Coaches." *Journal of Teaching in Physical Education* 21: 16-34.

Gould, D. 2013. "Effective Education and Development of Youth Sport Coaches." *President's Council on Fitness, Sports & Recreation Research Digest* 14 (4): 1-10.

———, J. Giannini, V. Krane, and K. Hodges. 1990. "Educational Needs of Elite U.S. National Team, Pan American, and Olympic Coaches." *Journal of Teaching in Physical Education* 9: 332-44.

"Standards-based." 2017. *The Glossary of Education Reform*. Accessed 7 November 2017. https://www.edglossary.org/standards-based/.

International Council for Coaching Excellence (ICCE), the Association of Summer Olympic Federations (ASOIF) and Leeds Metropolitan University. 2013. *International Sport Coaching Framework*. Champaign, IL: Human Kinetics.

———. 2014. *International Coach Developer Framework*. www.icce.ws/_assets/files/documents/PC_ICDF_Booklet_Amended%20Sept%2014.pdf.

Kirkpatrick, D.L., and J.D. Kirkpatrick. 2006. "Prepare for Evaluation." *Leadership Excellence Essentials* 23 (11): 13-5.

Klein-Collins, R. 2012. "Competency-Based Degree Programs in the U.S. Postsecondary Credentials for Measurable Student Learning and Performance." www.cael.org/pdfs/2012_competencybasedprograms.

Lara-Bercial, S., A. Jimènez, A. Abraham, J. Bales, P. Colmaire, J. Curado, S. Rynne. 2016. "The International Sport Coaching Bachelor Degree Standards of the International Council for Coaching Excellence." *International Sport Coaching Journal* 3: 344-48.

Malete, L., and D.L. Feltz. 2000. "The Effect of a Coaching Education Program on Coaching Efficacy." *The Sport Psychologist* 14: 410-17.

Mallet, C.J., P. Trudel, L. Lyle, and S.B. Rynne. 2009. "Formal vs. Informal Coach Education." *International Journal of Sports Science & Coaching* 4 (3): 325-34.

National Association for Sport and Physical Education (NASPE). 2006. *Quality Coaches, Quality Sports: National Standards for Sport Coaches.* 2nd ed. Reston, VA: Author.

National Coaching Certification Program (NCCP). n.d. "National Coaching Certification Program Model." www.coach.ca/files/NewNCCPmodel_diagram_Eng.pdf.

———. 2015. "NCCP Coach Developer Training." http://coach.ca/coach-developer-training-s16933.

National Committee for the Accreditation of Coaching Education (NCACE). 2017a. "Guidelines for the Accreditation of Coaching Education and Instructions for the Preparation of Folios." www.qualitycoachingeducation.org/wp-content/uploads/2017/07/NCACE_Guidelines_Accreditation_2017_Manual.pdf.

———. 2017b. "Registry of Accredited Programs." www.qualitycoachingeducation.org/accredited-programs.

Nelson, L.J., and D.J. Cushion. 2006. "Reflection in Coach Education: The Case of The National Governing Body Coaching Certificate." *The Sport Psychologist* 20: 174-83.

Roetert, E.P., and J. Bales. 2014. "A Global Approach to Advancing the Profession of Coaching." *International Sport Coaching Journal* 1: 2-4.

Schön, D.A. 1983. *The Reflective Practitioner: How Professionals Think in Action.* New York, NY: Basic Books.

———. 1987. *Educating the Reflective Practitioner.* San Francisco, CA: Jossey-Bass.

Smoll, F.L., and R.E. Smith. 2002. "Coaching Behavior Research and Intervention in Youth Sports." In *Children and Youth in Sport: A Biopsychosocial Perspective*, edited by F.L. Smoll and R.E. Smith, 211-33. Dubuque, IA: Kendall Hunt Publishing.

South African Sports Confederation and Olympic Committee. 2012. *South African Model for Long-Term Coach Development.* Johannesburg, South Africa: Author.

Trudel, P., D. Culver, and P. Werthner. 2013. "Looking at Coach Development From the Coach-Learner's Perspective." In *Routledge Handbook of Sports Coaching*, edited by P. Potrac, W. Gilbert, and J. Denison, 375-87. London, UK: Routledge Taylor & Francis Group.

van Klooster, T., and J. Roemers. 2011. "A Competency-Based Coach Education in the Netherlands. *International Journal of Coaching Science* 5 (1): 71-81.

Weimer, M. 2013. *Learner-Centered Teaching: Five Key Changes to Practice.* 2nd ed. San Francisco, CA: Jossey-Bass.

Chapter 17

Becker, A.J. 2012. "Quality Coaching Behaviors." In *Routledge Handbook of Sports Coaching*, edited by P. Potrac, W. Gilbert, and J. Denison, 184-95. London, UK: Routledge.

———, and C.A. Wrisberg. 2008. "Effective Coaching in Action: Observations of Legendary Collegiate Basketball Coach Pat Summitt." *The Sport Psychologist* 22: 197-211.

Causgrove Dunn, J., J.G.H. Dunn, and A. Bayduza. 2007. "Perceived Athletic Competence, Sociometric Status, and Loneliness in Elementary School Children," *Journal of Sport Behavior* 30 (3): 249-69.

Chan, J.T., and C. Mallett. 2011. "The Value of Emotional Intelligence for High Performance Coaching." *International Journal of Sports Science & Coaching* 6: 315-28.

Charlesworth, R. 2001. *The Coach: Managing for Success.* Sydney, Australia: Macmillan.

Coie, J.D., and K.A. Dodge. 1983. "Continuities and Changes in Children's Social Status: A Five-Year Longitudinal Study." *Merrill-Palmer Quarterly* 29: 261-82.

Côté, J., and W.D. Gilbert. 2009. "An Integrative Definition of Coaching Effectiveness and Expertise." *International Journal of Sports Science & Coaching* 4: 307-23.

Cox, R.H., M.P. Martens, and W.D. Russell. 2003. "Measuring Anxiety in Athletics: The Revised Competitive State Anxiety Inventory-2," *Journal of Sport and Exercise Psychology* 25: 519-33.

Cunningham, G., and M. Dixon. 2003. "New Perspectives Concerning Performance Appraisals of Intercollegiate Coaches." *Quest* 55: 177-92.

Dweck, C. 2006. *Mindset: The New Psychology of Success*. New York: Ballantine.

Erickson, K., and W. Gilbert. 2013. "Coach-Athlete Interactions in Children's Sport." In *Conditions of Children's Talent Development in Sport*, edited by J. Côté and R. Lidor, 139-56. Morgantown, WV: Fitness Information Technology.

Gallimore, R., W. Gilbert, and S. Nater. 2014. "Reflective Practice and Ongoing Learning: A Coach's Ten Year Journey." *Reflective Practice* 15 (2): 268-88.

Gallimore, R., and R. Tharp. 2004. "What a Coach Can Teach a Teacher, 1975-2004: Reflections and Reanalysis of John Wooden's Teaching Practices." *The Sport Psychologist* 18: 119-37.

Gilbert, W. 2017. *Coaching Better Every Season: A Year-Round System for Athlete Development and Program Success*. Champaign, IL: Human Kinetics.

———, S. Nater, M. Siwik, and R. Gallimore. 2010. "The Pyramid Of Teaching Success In Sport: Lessons Learned From Applied Science And Effective Coaches." *Journal of Sport Psychology in Action* 1: 86-94.

Gilbert, W.D., and J. Côté. 2013. "Defining Coaching Effectiveness: A Focus on Coaches' Knowledge." In *Routledge Handbook of Sports Coaching*, edited by P. Potrac, W. Gilbert, and J. Denison, 147-59. London, UK: Routledge.

Gilbert, W.D., and P. Trudel. 2004. "Analysis of Coaching Science Research Published From 1970-2001." *Research Quarterly for Exercise and Sport* 75: 388-99.

Gillham, A., D. Burton, and E. Gillham. 2013. "Going Beyond Won-Loss Record to Identify Successful Coaches: Development of the Coaching Success Questionnaire-2." *International Journal of Sports Science & Coaching* 8 (1): 115-38.

Gillham, A., K. Hansen, and C. Brady. 2015. "Coach Evaluation From Three Perspectives: An Athletic Director, a Coach and a Consultant." *International Sport Coaching Journal* 2: 192-200.

Horn, T. 2008. "Coaching Effectiveness in the Sport Domain." In *Advances in Sport Psychology*, 3rd ed., edited by T.S. Horn, 239-67. Champaign, IL: Human Kinetics.

International Council for Coaching Excellence, Association of Summer Olympic International Federations, and Leeds Metropolitan University. 2013. *International Sport Coaching Framework, Version 1.2*. Champaign, IL: Human Kinetics.

Jowett, S., and N. Ntoumanis. 2004. "The Coach-Athlete Relationship Questionnaire (CART-Q): Development and Initial Validation." *Scandinavian Journal of Medicine and Science in Sports* 14: 245-57.

Kavussanu, M., and I.D. Boardley. 2009. "The Prosocial and Antisocial Behavior in Sport Scale." *Journal of Sport and Exercise Psychology* 31: 97-117.

Koh, K.T., M. Kawabata, and C.J. Mallett. 2014. "The Coaching Behavior Scale for Sport: Factor Structure Examination of Singaporean Youth Athletes." *International Journal of Sports Science & Coaching* 9 (6): 1311-24.

Lara-Bercial, S., J. North, K. Hämäläinen, K. Oltmanns, J. Minkhorst, and L. Petrovic. 2017. *European Sport Coaching Framework*. Champaign, IL: Human Kinetics.

Mallett, C., and J. Côté. 2006. "Beyond Winning and Losing: Guidelines for Evaluating High Performance Coaches." *The Sport Psychologist* 20: 213-21.

Nater, S., and R. Gallimore. 2010. *You Haven't Taught Until They Have Learned: John Wooden's Teaching Principles and Practices*. Morgantown, WV: Fitness International Technology.

National Association for Sport and Physical Activity. 2006. *National Standards for Sport Coaches: Quality Coaches, Quality Sports."* 2nd ed. Reston, VA: Author.

O'Boyle, I. 2014. "Determining Best Practice in Performance Monitoring and Evaluation of Sport Coaches: Lessons From the Traditional Business Environment." *International Journal of Sports Science & Coaching* 9 (1): 233-46.

Sabock, M.D., and R.J. Sabock. 2011. *Coaching: A Realistic Perspective.* 10th ed. Lanham, MD: Rowman & Littlefield.

Schempp, P.G., C. Webster, B.A. McCullick, C. Busch, and I.S. Mason. 2007. "How the Best Get Better: An Analysis of the Self-Monitoring Strategies Used By Expert Golf Instructors." *Sport, Education and Society* 12 (2): 175-92.

Tharp, R.G., and R. Gallimore. 1976. "What a Coach Can Teach a Teacher." *Psychology Today* 9 (8): 75-78.

United States Olympic Committee. 2017. "The American Development Model." www.teamusa.org/About-the-USOC/Athlete-Development/American-Development-Model.

———. 2018. *Quality Coaching Framework.* Champaign, IL: Human Kinetics.

Vella, S., and W. Gilbert. 2014. "Coaching Young Athletes to Positive Development: Implications for Coach Training." In *Positive Human Functioning From a Multidimensional Perspective: Promoting High Performance* (vol. 3), edited by R. Gomes, R. Resende, and A. Albuquerque, 83-105. Hauppauge, NY: Nova.

Vella, S.A., and D.J. Perlman. 2014. "Mastery, Autonomy and Transformational Approaches to Coaching: Common Features and Applications." *International Sport Coaching Journal* 1: 173-79.

Vierimaa, M., K. Erickson, J. Côté, and W. Gilbert. 2012. "Positive Youth Development: A Measurement Framework for Sport." *International Journal of Sports Science & Coaching* 7: 603-16.

Chapter 18

Becker, A.J., and C.A. Wrisberg. 2008. "Effective Coaching in Action: Observations of Legendary Collegiate Basketball Coach Pat Summitt." *Sport Psychologist* 22 (2): 197-211.

Bloom, G.A., R. Crumpton, and J.E. Anderson. 1999. "A Systematic Observation Study of the Teaching Behaviors of an Expert Basketball Coach." *Sport Psychologist* 13: 157-70.

Brewer, C.J., and R.L. Jones. 2002. "A Five-Stage Process for Establishing Contextually Valid Systematic Observation Instruments: The Case of Rugby Union." *Sport Psychologist* 16 (2): 138-59.

Bruner, J. 1999. "Folk Pedagogies". In *Learners and Pedagogy*, edited by J. Leach and B. Moon, 4 – 20). London, UK: Paul Chapman.

Carling, C., A. Williams, and T. Reilly. 2005. *Handbook of Soccer Match Analysis: A Systematic Approach to Improving Performance.* London, UK: Routledge.

Carling, C., C. Wright, L.J. Nelson, and P.S. Bradley. 2014. "Comment on 'Performance Analysis in Football: A Critical Review and Implications for Future Research'." *Journal of Sports Sciences* 32 (1): 2-7.

Carson, F. 2008. "Utilizing Video to Facilitate Reflective Practice: Developing Sports Coaches." *International Journal of Sports Science and Coaching* 3: 381-90.

Carter, N. 2006. *The Football Manager.* London, UK: Routledge.

Christensen, M.K. 2009. "An Eye for Talent: Talent Identification and Practical Sense of Top-Level Soccer Coaches." *Sociology of Sport Journal* 26: 365-82.

Church, S., and M. Hughes. 1987. "Patterns of Play in Association Football: A Computerised Analysis."Communication to the First World Congress of Science and Football, Liverpool, UK, 13-17. April.

Claxton, D.B. 1988. "A Systematic Observation of More and Less Successful High School Tennis Coaches." *Journal of Teaching in Physical Education* 7 (4): 302-10.

Coatsworth, J.D., and D.E. Conroy. 2009. "The Effects of Autonomy-Supportive Coaching, Need Satisfaction, and Self-Perceptions on Initiative and Identity in Youth Swimmers." *Developmental Psychology* 45 (2): 320.

Côté, J., J. Salmela, P. Trudel, A. Baria, and S. Russell. 1995. "The Coaching Model: A Grounded Assessment of Expert Gymnastic Coaches' Knowledge." *Journal of Sport and Exercise Psychology* 17 (1): 1-17.

Côté, J., and W. Sedgwick. 2003. "Effective Behaviors of Expert Rowing Coaches: A Qualitative Investigation of Canadian Athletes and Coaches." *International Sports Journal* 7 (1): 62-77.

Court, M. 2004. "Perceptions of Performance Analysis." *Insight,* Winter, 8-11.

Cushion, C. 2001. *The coaching process in professional youth football: An ethnography of practice.* Doctoral dissertation, Brunel University.

———. 2007. "Modelling the Complexity of the Coaching Process." *International Journal of Sports Science and Coaching*: 395-401.

———, P.R. Ford, and A.M. Williams. 2012. "Coach Behaviours and Practice Structures in Youth Soccer: Implications for Talent Development." *Journal of Sports Sciences* 30 (15): 1631-41.

Cushion, C., S. Harvey, B. Muir, and L. Nelson. 2012. "Developing the Coach Analysis and Intervention System (CAIS): Establishing Validity and Reliability of a Computerised Systematic Observation Instrument." *Journal of Sports Sciences* 30 (2): 201-16.

Cushion, C., and R.L. Jones. (2006). "Power, Discourse, and Symbolic Violence in Professional Youth Soccer: The Case of Albion Football Club." *Sociology of Sport Journal* 23 (2): 142.

Cushion, C.J. 2013. Applying Game Centered Approaches in Coaching: A Critical Analysis of the 'Dilemmas of Practice' Impacting Change." *Sports Coaching Review* 2 (1): 61-76.

———, K.M. Armour, and R.L. Jones. 2003. "Coach Education and Continuing Professional Development: Experience and Learning to Coach." *Quest* 55 (3): 215-30.

Cushion, C.J., and R.L. Jones. 2001. "A Systematic Observation of Professional Top-Level Youth Soccer Coaches." *Journal of Sport Behavior* 24 (4): 354-76.

Dellal, A., K. Chamari, D. Wong, S. Ahmaidi, D. Keller, R. Barros, G. Bisciotti, and C. Carling. 2011. "Comparison of Physical and Technical Performance in European Soccer Match Play: FA Premier League and La Liga". *European Journal of Sport Science* 11 (1): 51-59.

Denison, J., and J.P. Mills. 2014. "Planning for Distance Running: Coaching With Foucault." *Sports Coaching Review* 3 (1): 1-16.

———, and L. Jones. 2013. "Effective Coaching as a Modernist Formation: A Foucauldian Critique." In *Routledge Handbook of Sports Coaching*, edited by P. Potrac, W. Gilbert, and J. Denison. 388-99. London, UK: Routledge.

Di Salvo, V., W. Gregson, G. Atkinson, B. P. Tordoff, B. Drust. 2009. "Analysis of High Intensity Activity in the Premier League." *International Journal of Sports Medicine* 30: 205-12.

Drust, B. 2010. "Performance Analysis Research: Meeting the Challenge." *Journal of Sports Sciences* 28: 921-22.

Dyson, B.P. 1995. "Students' Voices in Two Alternative Elementary Physical Education Programs." *Journal of Teaching in Physical Education* 14: 394.

Erickson, K., J. Côté, T. Hollenstein, and J. Deakin. 2011. "Examining Coach–Athlete Interactions Using State Space Grids: An Observational Analysis in Competitive Youth Sport." *Psychology of Sport and Exercise* 12 (6): 645-54.

Evans, J. 2004. "Making a Difference? Education and 'Ability' in Physical Education," *European Physical Education Review* 10 (1): 95-109.

Franks, I.M. 1997. Analysis of Coaching Behavior – A Review. In *Notational Analysis of Sport*, edited by M. Hughes and I.M Franks, 177-94. London, UK: E & FN Spon.

Ford, P.R., I. Yates, and A.M. Williams. 2010. "An Analysis of Practice Activities and Instructional Behaviours Used By Youth Soccer Coaches During Practice: Exploring the Link Between Science and Application." *Journal of Sports Sciences* 28 (5): 483-95.

Garganta, J., J. Maia, and F. Basto. 1997. "Analysis of Goal-Scoring Patterns in European Top Level Soccer Teams." In *Science and Football III*, edited by T. Reilly, J. Bangsbo, and M. Hughes, 246-50. London, UK: E & F.N. Spon.

Gilbert, W.D., and P. Trudel. 2004. "Analysis of Coaching Science Research Published From 1970-2001." *Research Quarterly for Exercise and Sport* 75 (4): 388-99.

Groom, R., C. Cushion, and L. Nelson. 2011. "The Delivery of Video-Based Performance Analysis by England Youth Soccer Coaches: Towards a Grounded Theory." *Journal of Applied Sport Psychology* 23 (1): 16-32.

Groom, R., and L.J. Nelson. 2013. "The Application of Video-Based Performance Analysis in the Coaching Process: The Coach Supporting Athlete Learning." In *The Routledge Handbook of Sports Coaching*, edited by P. Potrac, W. Gilbert, J. Denison, 96-107. London, UK: Routledge.

Harvey, S., C.J. Cushion, E. Cope, and B. Muir. 2013. "A Season Long Investigation Into Coaching Behaviours as a Function of Practice State: The Case of Three Collegiate Coaches." *Sports Coaching Review* 2 (1): 13-32.

Hawkins, A., and R. Wiegand. 1989. "West Virginia University Teaching Evaluation System and Feedback Taxonomy." In *Analyzing Physical Education and Sport Instruction,* 2nd ed., edited by P. Darst, R. Zakrajsek, and V. Mancini, 277-93. Champaign, IL: Human Kinetics.

Hewett, T., S. Torg, and B. Boden. 2009. "Video Analysis of Trunk and Knee Motion During Non-Contact Anterior Cruciate Ligament Injury in Female Athletes: Lateral Trunk and Knee Abduction Motion Are Combined Components of the Injury Mechanism." *British Journal of Sports Medicine* 43 (6): 417-22.

Horn, T.S., ed. 2008. *Advances in Sport Psychology.* Champaign, IL: Human Kinetics.

Hughes, M. 2005. "Notational Analysis." In *Encyclopaedia of International Sports Studies*, edited by R. Bartlett, C. Gratton, and C. Rolf, 1-7. London, UK: Routledge.

———, and B. Bartlett. 2008. *"What Is Performance Analysis?"* In *The Essentials of Performance Analysis: An Introduction*, edited by M. Hughes and I. Franks, 98-110. London, UK: Routledge.

Hughes, M., and I. Franks. 2004. *Notational Analysis of Sport, Second Edition: A Perspective on Improving Coaching.* London, UK: F.N. Spon.

Isabel, M., S. Antonio, R. Antonio, P. Felismina, F. Rosado, and M. Michel. 2008. "A Systematic Observation of Youth Amateur Volleyball Coaches Behavior." *International Journal of Applied Sports Science* 10 (2): 37-59.

James, N. 2006. "Notational Analysis in Soccer: Past, Present and Future." *International Journal of Performance Analysis of Sport* 6 (2): 67-81.

———, S. Mellalieu, and C. Hollely. 2002. "Analysis of Strategies in Soccer as a Function of European and Domestic Competition." *International Journal of Performance Analysis in Sport* 2 (1): 85-103.

Jenkins, R. 2010. "Pierre Bourdieu: From the Model of Reality to the Reality of the Model." In *Human Agents and Social Structures*, edited by P.J. Martin and A. Dennis, 86-99. Manchester, UK: Manchester University Press.

Jones, R.L., and M. Wallace. 2005. "Another Bad Day at the Training Ground: Coping With Ambiguity in the Coaching Context." *Sport, Education and Society* 10 (1): 119-34.

Kahan, D. 1999. "Coach behavior: A Review of the Systematic Observation Research Literature." *Applied Research in Coaching and Athletics Annual* 14: 17-58.

Kuklick, C.R., B.T. Gearity, M. Thompson, and L. Neelis. 2015. "A Case Study of One High Performance Baseball Coach's Experiences Within a Learning Community." *Qualitative Research in Sport, Exercise and Health* 8 (1): 1-18.

Lacy, A.C., and P.W. Darst. 1984. "Evolution of a Systematic Observation System: The ASU Coaching Observation Instrument." *Journal of Teaching in Physical Education* 3 (3): 59-66.

———. 1985. "Systematic Observation of Behaviors of Winning High School Head Football Coaches." *Journal of Teaching in Physical Education* 4 (4): 256-70.

Langsdorf, E.V. 1979. "A Systematic Observation of Football Coach behavior in a Major University Environment." Unpublished doctoral dissertation, Arizona State University.

Larson, A., and S.J. Silverman. 2005. "Rationales and Practices Used by Caring Physical Education Teachers." *Sport, Education, and Society* 10 (2): 175-93.

Light, R., J.R. Evans, S. Harvey, and R. Hassanin. 2015. *Advances in Rugby Coaching: An Holistic Approach.* London, UK: Routledge.

Lombardo, B.J., and J.T. Cheffers. 1983. "Variability in Teaching Behavior and Interaction in the Gymnasium." *Journal of Teaching in Physical Education* 2 (2): 33-48.

Mackenzie, R., and C. Cushion. 2013. "Performance Analysis in Football: A Critical Review and Implications for Future Research." *Journal of Sports Sciences* 31 (6): 639-76.

Mageau, G.A., and R.J. Vallerand. 2003. "The Coach–Athlete Relationship: A Motivational Model." *Journal of Sports Science* 21 (11): 883-904.

Manley, A., C. Palmer, and M. Roderick. 2012. "Disciplinary Power, The Oligopticon And Rhizomatic Surveillance In Elite Sports Academies." *Surveillance in Society* 10 (3/4): 303-19.

Metzler, M. 2000. *Instructional Models for Physical Education.* Needham Heights, MA: Allyn & Bacon.

Miller, A.W. 1992. "Systematic Observation Behavior Similarities of Various Youth Sport Soccer Coaches." *The Physical Educator* 49 (3): 136-43.

More, K.G., and L.M. Franks. 1996. "Analysis and Modification of Verbal Coaching Behaviour: The Usefulness of a Data-Driven Intervention Strategy". *Journal of Sports Sciences* 14 (6): 523-43.

Nash, C. S., J. Sproule, and P. Horton. 2011. "Excellence in Coaching: The Art and Skill of Elite Practitioners." *Research Quarterly for Exercise and Sport* 82 (2): 229-38.

Nelson, L., and R. Groom. 2012. "The Analysis of Athletic Performance: Some Practical and Philosophical Considerations." *Sport, Education and Society* 17 (5): 687-701.

Nelson, L., P. Potrac, and R. Groom. 2014. "Receiving Video-Based Feedback in Elite Ice-Hockey: A Players Perspective." *Sport, Education and Society* 19 (1): 19-40.

Newton, M., J.L. Duda, and Z. Yin. 2000. "Examination of the Psychometric Properties of the Perceived Motivational Climate in Sport Questionnaire-2 in a Sample of Female Athletes." *Journal of Sports Sciences* 18 (4): 275-90.

O'Donoghue, P. 2010. *Research Methods for Sports Performance Analysis.* London, UK: Routledge.

Partington, M., and C. Cushion. (2013). "An Investigation of the Practice Activities and Coach behaviors of Professional Top-Level Youth Soccer Coaches." *Scandinavian Journal of Medicine & Science in Sports* 23 (3): 374-82.

———, and S. Harvey. 2014. "An Investigation of the Effect of Athletes' Age on the Coaching Behaviours of Professional Top-Level Youth Soccer Coaches." *Journal of Sports Sciences* 32 (5): 403-14.

Pelletier, L.G., M.S. Fortier, R.J. Vallerand, and N.M. Briere. 2001. "Associations Among Perceived Autonomy Support, Forms of Self-Regulation, and Persistence: A Prospective Study." *Motivation and Emotion* 25 (4): 279-306.

Piggott, D. 2012. "Coaches' Experiences of Formal Coach Education: A Critical Sociological Investigation." *Sport, Education and Society* 17 (4): 535-54.

———. 2015. "The Open Society and Coach Education: A Philosophical Agenda for Policy Reform and Future Sociological Research." *Physical Education and Sport Pedagogy* 20 (3): 283-98.

Pitchford, A., C. Brackenridge, J.D. Bringer, C. Cockburn, G. Nutt, Z. Pawlaczek, and K. Russell. 2004. "Children in Football: Seen But Not Heard." *Soccer & Society* 5 (1): 43-60.

Potrac, P., C. Brewer, R. Jones, K. Armour, and J. Hoff. 2000. "Towards a Holistic Understanding of the Coaching Process." *Quest* 52 (2): 186-99.

———. 2002. "'It's All About Getting Respect': The Coach behaviors of an Expert English Soccer Coach." *Sport, Education and Society* 7 (2): 183-202.

Potrac, P., R. Jones, and C. Cushion. 2007. "Understanding Power and the Coach's Role in Professional English Soccer: A Preliminary Investigation of Coach Behaviour." *Soccer and Society* 8 (1): 33-49.

Randers, M., I. Mujika, A. Hewitt, J. Santisteban, R. Bischoff, R. Solano, A. Zubillaga, E. Peltola, P. Krustrup, and M. Mohr. 2010. "Application of Four Different Football Match Analysis Systems: A Comparative Study." *Journal of Sports Sciences* (2): 171-82.

Rovegno, I. 2003. "Teacher's Knowledge Construction." In *Student Learning in Physical Education: Applying Research to Enhance Instruction.* 2nd ed., edited by J.J. Silverman and C.D. Ennis, 295-310. Champaign, IL: Human Kinetics.

Schon, D. 1983. *The Reflective Practitioner: How Professionals Think in Action.* London, UK: Temple Smith.

Segrave, J.O., and C.A. Ciancio. 1990. "An Observational Study of a Successful Pop Warner Football Coach." *Journal of Teaching in Physical Education* 9 (4): 294-306.

Smith, J. 1989. *The Nature of Social and Educational Inquiry: Empiricism Versus Interpretation.* Norwood, NJ: Ablex.

Smith, M., and Cushion, C.J. 2006. "An Investigation of the In-Game Behaviours of Professional, Top-Level Youth Soccer Coaches." *Journal of Sports Sciences* 24 (4): 355-66.

Smith, R.E., and F.L. Smoll. 1990. "Self-Esteem and Children's Reactions to Youth Sport Coach behaviors: A Field Study of Self-Enhancement Processes." *Developmental Psychology* 26 (6): 987.

———. 1996. "The Coach as a Focus of Research and Intervention in Youth Sports." In *Children and Youth in Sport. A Biopsychosocial Perspective*, edited by F.L. Smoll and R.E. Smith, 125-41. Dubuque, IA: Brown & Benchmark.

———. 1997. "Coaching the Coaches: Youth Sports as a Scientific and Applied Behavioral Setting." *Current Directions in Psychological Science* 6 (1): 16-21.

———, and B. Curtis. 1979. "Coach Effectiveness Training: A Cognitive-Behavioral Approach to Enhancing Relationship Skills in Youth Sport Coaches." *Journal of Sport Psychology* 1 (1): 59-75.

Smith, R.E., F.L. Smoll, and E. Hunt. 1977. "A System for the Behavioral Assessment of Athletic Coaches." *Research Quarterly. American Alliance for Health, Physical Education and Recreation* 48 (2): 401-7.

Stoszkowski, J., and D. Collins. 2014. "Communities of Practice, Social Learning and Networks: Exploiting the Social Side of Coach Development." *Sport, Education and Society* 19 (6): 773-88.

Taylor, W., P. Potrac, L. Nelson, L. Jones, and R. Groom. Forthcoming. "An Elite Hockey Player's Experiences of Video Based Coaching: A Poststructuralist Reading." *International Review for the Sociology of Sport.*

Tharp, R.G., and R. Gallimore. 1976. "What a Coach Can Teach a Teacher." *Psychology Today* 9 (8): 75-78.

Thomson, P. 2008. "Children and Young People." In *Doing Visual Research With Children and Young People*, edited by P. Thomson, 1-20. London, UK: Routledge.

Tursi, D., A. Napolitano, L. Polidoro, and G. Raiola. 2013. "Video Analysis as an Instrument in Juvenile Soccer Training." *Journal of Human Sport and Exercise* 8: 688-93.

van der Mars, H. 1989. "Systematic Observation: An Introduction. In *Analyzing Physical Education and Sport Instruction*, edited by P.W. Darst, D.B. Zakrajsek, and V.H. Mancini, 3-19. Champaign, IL: Human Kinetics.

Williams, J.K. 1978. "A Behavioral Analysis of a Successful High School Basketball Coach." Unpublished master's thesis, Arizona State University.

Williams, S., and A. Manley. 2014. "Elite Coaching and the Technocratic Engineer: Thanking the Boys at Microsoft!" *Sport, Education and Society* 21 (6): 828-50.

Wulf, G., T.D. Lee, and R.A. Schmidt. 1994. "Reducing Knowledge of Results About Relative Versus Absolute Timing: Differential Effects on Learning." *Journal of Motor Behavior* 26 (4): 362-69.

Wulf, G., N. McConnel, M. Gartner, and A. Schwarz. 2002. "Enhancing the Learning of Sport Skills Through an External Focus of Attention." *Journal of Motor Behavior* 34 (2):171–82.

Wulf, G., and C.H. Shea. 2004. "Understanding the Role of Augmented Feedback: The Good, the Bad and the Ugly." In *Skill Acquisition in Sport: Research, Theory and Practice*, edited by M.A. Williams and N.J. Hodges, 121-44. London, UK: Routledge.

Appendix A

Female Coaching Network. n.d. Coaching tips. https://femalecoachingnetwork.com/coaches-corner/coach-quotes/

International Council for Coaching Excellence (ICCE), the Association of Summer Olympic Federations (ASOIF) and Leeds Metropolitan University. 2013. *International Sport Coaching Framework*. Champaign, IL: Human Kinetics.

National Association for Sport and Physical Education (NASPE). 2006. *Quality Coaches, Quality Sports: National Standards for Sport Coaches*. 2nd ed. Reston, VA: Author.

Rynne, S.B., and C.J. Mallett. 2014. "Coaches' Learning and Sustainability in High Performance Sport." *Reflective Practice* 15 (1): 12-26.

SHAPE America. (forthcoming). *Quality Coaches, Quality Sports: National Standards for Sport Coaches*. 3rd ed.

Werthner, P., and P. Trudel. 2006. "A New Theoretical Perspective for Understanding How Coaches Learn to Coach." *The Sport Psychologist* 20: 198-212.

Index

Note: The italicized *f* and *t* following page numbers refer to figures and tables, respectively.

About the Editors

Kristen Dieffenbach is an associate professor of athletic coaching education at West Virginia University and an Association of Applied Sport Psychology Certified Mental Performance Consultant. Kristen is currently the president of the United States Center for Coaching Excellence (USCCE) and the director of the CPASS Center for Applied Coaching and Sport Sciences at WVU. Her research interests focus on professionalism in coaching, ethics, and moral decision-making in coaching and long-term athletic talent development. A former division I NCAA athlete, she is also a professional coach with an elite USA Cycling license and a Level II endurance specialization from USA Track and Field.

Melissa Thompson is an associate professor in the School of Kinesiology and Nutrition at the University of Southern Mississippi. Melissa's research agenda focuses on coach development, specifically the development of coaching ethics and the impact of the internship process. She is credentialed as an Association of Applied Sport Psychology Certified Mental Performance Consultant as well as a Certified Strength and Conditioning Specialist. Melissa is currently serving as an inaugural board member for the United States Center for Coaching Excellence (USCCE) and is heavily involved in the discipline as an editorial board member and journal reviewer.

About the Contributors

Hal Wilson is a devoted husband and father of three who currently serves as an assistant professor of coaching education at Georgia Southern University. This is one of only two institutions in the United States to feature NCACE-accredited coaching education programs at both the graduate and undergraduate levels. A coach of multiple sports at the intercollegiate, scholastic, and youth levels for more than two decades, Wilson has worked sport camps and clinics in eleven different states. Since moving into higher education in 2012, Wilson has nearly 100 peer-reviewed publications and presentations across the globe. Wilson has also been an invited speaker by groups such as USA Basketball, the US Soccer Foundation, and the National Forum on Character. Wilson is also an affiliated scholar of the Center for the Study of Sport and Religion at the University of Tennessee. In addition to his scholarship into coaching, Wilson was recognized at the university level for both his teaching and his service. Wilson serves on the editorial boards of the *International Journal of Kinesiology in Higher Education* and the *Journal of Athlete Development and Experience*, the appeals panel of USA Basketball, and as a Court Appointed Special Advocate (CASA) for foster children in the Ogeechee Judicial Circuit. Wilson is passionate about the positive potential of sports and seeks to encourage, develop, and empower coaches to positively impact their players through holistic, athlete-centered coaching and their local communities through service and engagement.

Trey Burdette was an assistant professor of coaching education in the School of Health and Kinesiology at Georgia Southern University. He earned his EdD in Educational Leadership from Georgia Southern University, studying coaching behavior and leadership. He also received his MS in Health and Kinesiology from GSU in 2003, specializing in coaching behavior.

Matthew J. Robinson is a full professor and the area head of the Sport Management Program in the Lerner College of Business and Economics at the University of Delaware. Robinson serves as director of the International Coaching Enrichment Certificate Program (ICECP) and the International Coaching Apprenticeship in Basketball (ICAB). Dr. Robinson served as interim director of athletics and recreation for the University of Delaware during the 2016 spring semester and serves as chairman of the Delaware Sports Commission and the nationally acclaimed Slam Dunk to the Beach High School Basketball Tournament. Dr. Robinson is the author of the highly successful sport management texts *Profiles of Sport Industry Professionals: The People Who Make the Games Happen* and *Sport Club Management* and has authored over 25 articles and has made over 100 national and international scholarly and professional presentations.

Matthew Grant is an associate professor of kinesiology and physical education in the Dewar College of Education and Human Services at Valdosta State University and the graduate coordinator for the EdS in sport coaching and M.A.T. and M.Ed in health and physical education programs. He continues to research within sport coaching and physical education contexts, assists state and national organizations in writing and assessing physical education standards, and teaches future physical educators and coaches. This work includes researching sport coaching pedagogy and mentoring, helping to write the physical education standards for the state of Georgia, reviewing edTPA standards for SCALE, and presenting research and workshops on various topics within physical education and sport.

Frank L. Smoll is a professor of psychology at the University of Washington. He received his PhD from the University of Wisconsin. Dr. Smoll's research focuses on coaching behaviors in youth sports and on the psychological effects of competition on children and adolescents. He has published more than 145 scientific articles and book chapters, and he is coauthor of 22 books and manuals on children's athletics. Professor Smoll is a fellow of the American Psychological Association, the National Academy of Kinesiology, and the Association for Applied Sport Psychology (AASP). In 2002, he was the recipient of the AASP's Distinguished Professional Practice Award. Dr. Smoll has extensive experience in conducting psychologically oriented coaching clinics and workshops for parents of young athletes.

Ronald E. Smith is a professor of psychology and director of the Clinical Psychology Training Program at the University of Washington. He received his PhD in clinical psychology from Southern Illinois University. Professor Smith's interests include research methods in clinical psychology, personality assessment and research, stress and coping, and sport psychology research and intervention. He has published more than 200 scientific articles and book chapters, and he has authored or coauthored 34 books and manuals. Dr. Smith is a fellow of the American Psychological Association, a past president of the Association for Applied Sport Psychology, and the recipient of a Distinguished Alumnus Award from the UCLA Neuropsychiatric Institute. He has directed performance-enhancement programs for several professional baseball organizations, and his research team has developed widely used sport psychology measurement tools.

Dan Gould is the director of the Institute for the Study of Youth Sports and professor in the Department of Kinesiology at the Michigan State University. Dan's current research focuses on how coaches teach life skills to young athletes, the psychology of coaching, and developing youth leaders through the sport captaincy experience. In addition to his research interests, Dan has dedicated much of his career to applied sport psychology efforts as a mental skills training consultant, coaching educator, and author. Dan has given over 1000 coaching education clinic presentations and developed numerous coaching and coaching education programs aimed at coaches ranging from the youth to Olympic levels. He has written a number of books, including *the USTA Mental Skills and Drills Handbook*, *Sport Psychology for Young Athletes*, and *Foundations of Sport and Exercise Psychology*, the most widely used text in the field.

Jennifer Nalepa is an assistant professor at Michigan State University in the Department of Kinesiology. She teaches in the online Sport Coaching and Leadership Graduate Programs and conducts research examining modified sport, coaching education, and personal development of athletes. She also works with the USTA on the creation of a coach mentoring program and is developing an online training program for coach mentors.

Cecile Reynaud was the head women's volleyball coach at Florida State University for 26 years and a faculty member in sport management for 14 years. She has served in various national and international coaching and administrative positions with USA Volleyball. She has coaching experience at the World University Games, as a Junior National Team Coach, in the USA Volleyball High Performance Championships, and in the FIVB World Grand Prix. She was the deputy competition manager for Volleyball at the 1996 Olympic Games in Atlanta and served as the Head of Delegation for the USA Volleyball Women's Sitting Team at the 2012 Paralympic Games and the USA Volleyball Junior Boys Team at the 2015 World Championship. She was honored in 2016 with the "Friar Award," USA Volleyball's highest award. She has served as president of the American Volleyball Coaches Association (AVCA) and was inducted into the AVCA Hall of Fame in 2017. She has published several books, including *The Volleyball Coaching Bible Volumes I & II*, *Coaching Volleyball: Technical and Tactical Skills*, *She Can Coach*, and numerous volleyball DVDs.

Cam Kiosoglous has coached on the US Rowing national teams since 2002 and is a four-time US Olympic coach at the 2004, 2008, 2012, and 2016 Olympic Games. Cam began his coaching in Canberra, Australia, in 1991 and moved to the United States in 2000. He completed his PhD in adult education at Virginia Tech with a focus on sports coaching development in 2013. He has been published and presented at a variety of national international conferences and journals in the area of sports coaching development and performance improvement. Currently, Cam is an adjunct professor at Drexel University in the School of Education.

Gordon Bloom is a professor and director of the Sport Psychology Research Laboratory (http://sportpsych.mcgill.ca) in the Department of Kinesiology & Physical Education at McGill University. Dr. Bloom has developed an internationally recognized coaching research program related to the knowledge, strategies, and behaviors employed by coaches in terms of leadership practices, mentoring, and team building that are designed to create a culture of excellence that includes the development of successful and well-balanced athletes. Dr. Bloom has incorporated the findings of his research in his role as a sport psychology consultant with amateur, professional, Olympic, and Paralympic athletes and teams.

Sarah McQuade is the owner and director of e.t.c coaching consultants, a US-based performance coach development consultancy practice to create strategic, coherent, applied, and practical approaches to long-term coaching development. Sarah has spent 20 years working within education, sports, and sport coach education. She led the technical development of the UK Coaching Certificate (a professional qualifications framework) with sports coach UK, the UK government's lead agency for coaching. She spent ten years consulting with sports organizations in the United Kingdom to support the training and ongoing professional development of coaches and coach developers.

Sergio Lara-Bercial is a reader in sport coaching at Leeds Beckett University in England and the manager for strategy and development for the International Council for Coaching Excellence. His areas of interest span from coaching policy and systems and coach development to high performance coaching and positive youth development through sport. Sergio has co-authored the International and European Sport Coaching Frameworks, the International Coaching Degree Standards, and the European Coaching Children Curriculum. He also co-directed the Serial Winning Coaches study and is the founder and director of iCoachKids, a not-for-profit global movement developing high-quality online learning for coaches of children. Sergio has delivered keynotes, lectures, and workshops across five continents and consulted for organisations such as UEFA, FIBA, IOC, WADA, the Japanese Sport Council, and the USOC.

John Bales is president of the International Council for Coaching Excellence (ICCE), the not-for-profit, international organization with the mission of promoting coaching as a profession and enhancing the quality of coaching at every level of sport. The ICCE works with national coaching organizations, international sport federations, and educational institutions to develop coaches and enhance the voice of the coach in decision-making. A member of the ICCE founding board in 1997, John served as treasurer and secretary general before being elected president in 2005. He was chief executive officer of the Coaching Association of Canada (CAC) from 1996 to 2013, the founding director of the National Coaching Institute–Calgary, and worked as a senior consultant at Sport Canada, the federal government agency responsible for sport. A former national and Olympic coach in sprint canoe, John has an MBA from the Institut Européen d'Administration des Affaires (INSEAD) in Fontainebleau, France, and undergraduate degrees in physical education and mathematics from McMaster University in Hamilton, Ontario.

Christine Nash is currently head of the Institute for Sport, Physical Education and Health Sciences at the University of Edinburgh in Scotland, an honorary professor at the Institute for Advanced Study at the Technical University of Munich in Germany, and a program director for our online MSc in sport coaching and performance. Christine was a national swimming coach in the United Kingdom and coached in the United States. She is currently involved in supporting coach education with a variety of sports. She was a member of the Coaching Standards Group, the committee that endorses coach education courses in the United Kingdom. She also sits on the research committee of the International Council for Coaching Excellence.

Clayton Kuklick, CSCS, is a clinical assistant professor in the master of arts in the sport coaching program at the University of Denver, USA, where he teaches a variety of courses spanning motor learning and pedagogy, biomechanics, sports technology, exercise physiology, and kinesiology. His research interests center on coach learning and enhancing athlete performance. Kuklick acquired a master's degree in kinesiology, a PhD in human performance and recreation: administration and teaching, and has served as a high school and collegiate coach.

Brian Gearity is the director of the master of arts in the sport coaching program at the University of Denver, USA. His research interests include coaches' knowledge development, sociological theory, and quality coaching. Dr. Gearity serves as the editor in chief for the *NSCA Coach* journal. He has been an sports and conditioning (S&C) coach with the University of Tennessee, Cleveland Indians Baseball Club, and John Carroll University, and he has served as a football/S&C coach with a 4-A high school in Mississippi.

Penny Crisfield, following years in sport, education, and UK coaching, set up her own consultancy, Apollinaire, in 1999. Since then, she has built an international reputation and become a market leader in coaching development in sport. Over the years, she has worked with most sports organisations in the United Kingdom and many businesses that use coaching to develop their personnel. She now works particularly closely with the International Council for Coaching Excellence where she is the master trainer and chair of the Coach Developer work. Her reputation is founded on innovation, excellence, and a desire to customise her services to the unique needs and circumstances of her partner clients.

Lori Gano-Overway is an associate professor and coaching program coordinator at Bridgewater College. She has been involved in coaching education for over 20 years and conducts research on how the social psychological climate can be structured to provide positive experiences for young people and foster positive youth development. As an AASP-certified mental performance consultant, she collaborates with coaches on creating environments that foster positive experiences and performance enhancement outcomes for athletes. Lori serves on the editorial board of the *Journal of Sport, Exercise, and Performance Psychology*, the *Journal of Sport Psychology in Action*, the *International Sport Coaching Journal*, and is the editor for the *Women in Sport and Physical Activity Journal*. Lori serves as the accreditation chair for the United States Center for Coaching Excellence. She also serves on the Virginia High School League coaching education committee and the National Advisory Board for the Positive Coaching Alliance.

Wade Gilbert is an award-winning professor at California State University, Fresno. He has 25 years of experience conducting applied research with coaches around the world spanning all competitive levels, from youth leagues to the FIFA World Cup and the Olympic Games. In addition to authoring the acclaimed book *Coaching Better Every Season*, he was the lead author for the *USOC Quality Coaching Framework* and also serves as editor in chief of the *International Sport Coaching Journal*.

Stephen Harvey, PhD, is an associate professor of recreation and sports pedagogy at Ohio University. His research is focused on game-based approaches (GBAs) to teaching and coaching, and coaching behaviors utilized by coaches, and how they impact player learning. Stephen has published numerous peer-reviewed journal articles and book sections on both these topics. He has also co-authored one book and edited one volume on GBAs. Stephen is a former collegiate soccer and badminton coach, an international field hockey coach, and currently works with USA Field Hockey in coach developer capacity. He is a 2017 graduate of the Nippon Sport Science University Coach Developer Academy.

Ed Cope is the learning design and development manager at the Football Association and visiting lecturer at the University of Hull. Ed's research interests and expertise lie in coaching pedagogy and practice, including curriculum design, coaching behavior, and children's motivations and interests for taking part in sport and physical activity.

Luke Jones is a lecturer in sports coaching at the University of Hull in the United Kingdom. He completed his PhD in the philosophy of sport from the University of Alberta in Edmonton, Canada, where he was also assistant coach with the Pandas women's soccer program. His main area of expertise involves using the disciplinary analysis of Michel Foucault to reconsider entrenched coaching knowledge and practices, and, in particular, the excessively disciplinary practices and relationships common across elite sport.